Blurred Visionary

The Cuthbert Huntsman Trilogy

How Not To Live Your Life

Cop Lives Probably Matter

Trigger Warning

Rich Nash

First published in paperback in 2024 by Rich Nash

Copyright © Rich Nash 2024

The right of Rich Nash to be identified as the Author of the Work has been asserted by him in accordance with the Copyright, Designs and Patents Act 1988.

All rights reserved. No part of this publication may be reproduced, stored in a retrieval system, or transmitted in any form or by any means without the prior written permission of the publisher, nor otherwise be circulated in any form of binding or cover other than that in which it is published and without a similar condition being imposed on the subsequent purchaser.

All characters in this publication are fictitious and any resemblance to real persons, living or dead, is purely coincidental.

Artwork by 100 Covers.

The book reflects the language, standards, and attitudes of Cuthbert Huntsman, a gratuitously offensive and misguided individual.

An insensitivity reader was employed to ensure that everything is as triggering as possible. If you are affected by any of the issues raised, there is no helpline - just pull yourself together.

Do not under any circumstances follow Cuthbert's advice, unless under the direct supervision of a psychiatrist and an ambulance crew. There is a reason he is an unemployed life coach.

- www.cuthberthuntsman.com

For Lisa, Nia, Ivor & Archie

THE BOOKS

This volume comprises the first three novels in the comedy series *The Legend of Cuthbert Huntsman* by Rich Nash. They can be read in any order:

HOW NOT TO LIVE YOUR LIFE

The world's worst life coach discovers the rules of failure through hilarious encounters with eccentric losers. Meet Cuthbert Huntsman, a bankrupt barfly with eight broken marriages who thinks he's wiser than Jordan Peterson and Deepak Chopra combined, but clearly isn't. Learn how not to live your life from The Hans Christian Andersen of Incompetence - and have a good laugh along the way.

COP LIVES PROBABLY MATTER

When the world's worst life coach is jailed for breaking into his own home, he takes revenge by penning the most insultingly anti-cop crime novel in history - but the prison's creative writing tutor just wants him to arrange a hit on her husband. Cuthbert's story of a dishonest, cross-dressing detective hunting the deranged killer of Lonond's most corrupt cops takes no prisoners, and it unfolds in parallel with his inept attempts to avoid becoming a murderer himself.

TRIGGER WARNING

The fate of a disgraced SAS hero lies in the hands of the world's worst life coach in a hilarious, edge-of-the-pants thriller stuffed with survivalist advice, grit, guts, and bloodcurdling silliness. This laugh-out-loud parody takes the SAS blockbusters of Andy McNab and Chris Ryan and plonks a hopeless pillock at the centre of the action. When death is in your DNA, always give more than a four-figure percentage and never forget that the enemy of your enemy's enemy is also your enemy.

Contents

How Not To Live Your Life

Contents   3

1. RULE 1 - Face Your Fears And Run   5
2. RULE 2 - Set Yourself Goals And Miss Them   7
3. RULE 3 - Violence Is Golden   12
4. RULE 4 - Life Is Like A Box Of Frogs   21
5. RULE 5 - Gravity Is A Force To Be Reckoned With   31
6. RULE 6 - Eternity Goes On A Bit   43
7. RULE 7 - Time Travel Broadens The Mind   60
8. RULE 8 - Wait Until You're Dead To Get Found Out   66
9. RULE 9 - Love Is Blind Drunk   78
10. RULE 10 - Work Hard, Die Hard   93
11. RULE 11 - The Law Has Long Arms And Hairy Legs   106
12. RULE 12 - Spiritualism Is Best Kept In Bottles   130
13. RULE 13 - Revenge Is A Dish Best Served By A Voodoo Priestess   136
14. RULE 14 - Reality Is Overrated   147
15. RULE 15 - What Goes Around Comes Around, But Some People Duck   154

16.	RULE 16 - Cancel Gen Z	179
17.	CONCLUSION - How Not To Live Your Life	185
	MAKE CUTHBERT HAPPY	188

Cop Lives Probably Matter

Contents   191

1.	PRISON DIARY – ENTRY 1	194
2.	COPPING OFF	195
3.	PRISON DIARY – ENTRY 2	205
4.	ARRESTED DEVELOPMENT	209
5.	PRISON DIARY – ENTRY 3	218
6.	FELINE OF DUTY	221
7.	JUSTICE IS BLIND DRUNK	224
8.	PRISON DIARY – ENTRY 4	234
9.	ROLL OUT THE BARREL	237
10.	PRISON DIARY - ENTRY 5	245
11.	DEBRIEFING	248
12.	PRISON DIARY – ENTRY 6	257
13.	DEATH: THE SEQUEL	261
14.	PRISON DIARY – ENTRY 7	266
15.	A TOTAL CAR CRASH	269
16.	PRISON DIARY – ENTRY 8	278
17.	AGENT PROVOCATEUR	282
18.	PRISON DIARY – ENTRY 9	293
19.	POTHOLING	296
20.	PRISON DIARY – ENTRY 10	305
21.	INSERTION	307
22.	DEFUND THE POLICE	316
23.	PRISON DIARY – ENTRY 11	323

24.	SORRY	326
25.	PRISON DIARY – ENTRY 12	330
26.	TRIPLE BENDING	333
27.	PRISON DIARY – ENTRY 13	339
28.	PROUDCOCK	341
29.	BRITNEY MORIARTY	347
30.	PRISON DIARY – ENTRY 14	353
31.	GOODBYE DOLLY	355
32.	PRISON DIARY – ENTRY 15	364
33.	COCKY'S CORPSE	366
34.	PRISON DIARY – ENTRY 16	369
35.	SUSPENDERED	372
36.	PRISON DIARY – ENTRY 17	376
37.	MELONS	378
38.	PRISON DIARY – ENTRY 18	390
39.	DOGGING	392
40.	PRISON DIARY – ENTRY 19	408
41.	BONSAI-AND-I	410
42.	PRISON DIARY – ENTRY 20	416
43.	THE FOUR BRITNEYS OF THE APOCALYPSE	419
44.	PRISON DIARY – ENTRY 21	433
45.	THE TRUTH HURTS	436
46.	PRISON DIARY – FINAL ENTRY	439
	GO AHEAD, MAKE CUTHBERT'S DAY	442

Trigger Warning

Contents 445

1.	CHAPTER 1	447
2.	CHAPTER 2	451

3. CHAPTER 3 — 459
4. CHAPTER 4 — 479
5. CHAPTER 5 — 494
6. CHAPTER 6 — 505
7. CHAPTER 7 — 523
8. CHAPTER 8 — 534
9. CHAPTER 9 — 542
10. CHAPTER 10 — 552
11. CHAPTER 11 — 561
12. CHAPTER 12 — 565
13. CHAPTER 13 — 570
14. CHAPTER 14 — 578
15. CHAPTER 15 — 587
16. CHAPTER 16 — 610
17. CHAPTER 17 — 625
18. CHAPTER 18 — 634
19. CHAPTER 19 — 642
20. CHAPTER 20 — 646
21. CHAPTER 21 — 654
22. CHAPTER 22 — 662
23. CHAPTER 23 — 679
24. CHAPTER 24 — 686
25. CHAPTER 25 — 692
26. CHAPTER 26 — 713

HELP CUTHBERT - HE NEEDS IT — 716
FREE BOOK — 717
FOLLOW CUTHBERT — 718
SAS FLOWER ARRANGING - GLOSSARY — 719

ABOUT THE AUTHOR	720
ALSO BY RICH NASH	722
FILM ADAPTATIONS & OPTIONS	723

How Not To Live Your Life

Rich Nash

Contents

1. RULE 1 - Face Your Fears And Run — 5
2. RULE 2 - Set Yourself Goals And Miss Them — 7
3. RULE 3 - Violence Is Golden — 12
4. RULE 4 - Life Is Like A Box Of Frogs — 21
5. RULE 5 - Gravity Is A Force To Be Reckoned With — 31
6. RULE 6 - Eternity Goes On A Bit — 43
7. RULE 7 - Time Travel Broadens The Mind — 60
8. RULE 8 - Wait Until You're Dead To Get Found Out — 66
9. RULE 9 - Love Is Blind Drunk — 78
10. RULE 10 - Work Hard, Die Hard — 93
11. RULE 11 - The Law Has Long Arms And Hairy Legs — 106
12. RULE 12 - Spiritualism Is Best Kept In Bottles — 130
13. RULE 13 - Revenge Is A Dish Best Served By A Voodoo Priestess — 136
14. RULE 14 - Reality Is Overrated — 147
15. RULE 15 - What Goes Around Comes Around, But Some People Duck — 154
16. RULE 16 - Cancel Gen Z — 179
17. CONCLUSION - How Not To Live Your Life — 185

RULE 1 - FACE YOUR FEARS AND RUN

As an unemployed life coach, people often ask me, "Why the hell should I take advice from a homeless, bankrupt, alcoholic junkie with eight failed marriages, seventeen restraining orders and a kidnap conviction for holding his social worker hostage in a wheelie bin?"

This book is my answer: a comprehensive guide for anyone wishing to know how not to live their life. It chronicles my encounters with blurred visionaries and misguided muppets and draws step-by-step conclusions about their catastrophic errors. The Brothers Grimm and Hans Christian Andersen may have collected folk tales from illiterate peasants, but I have harvested textbook cockups from inebriated numpties and assorted weirdoes across the world and distilled their essence into pathetic parables and ridiculous rules. Together, they provide a foolproof guide for anyone wishing to know what not to do.

Before we begin, let's try one of my least popular life coaching techniques - negative visualisation:

Tense up, grit your teeth, and try to ignore your breathing. Remember, it's only air. Think of your happiest memory; then say goodbye to it. Walk up to a mirror and hug your reflection. Hard, isn't it? Blow a love bubble around your family. Prick it and watch them get covered in wet soap. Consider the gibbon. Contemplate its tree-swinging skills, poor hygiene, and dodgy table manners. Then forget it again. Who the hell needs gibbons? Beware Confusion, the cross-eyed monster. Remember, failure's all part of life's rich bicycle, wheels of misfortune turning on cogs of nonsense, moving along The Great Chain of Doubt. Face your fears and run. Set yourself goals and boot the ball as wide as the corner flag. Remember, every silver lining has a cloud. If God hands out lemons, make bitter lemon. Feeling better?

I'm Cuthbert Huntsman (I know, my parents hated me) and these are my rules.

RULE 2 - SET YOURSELF GOALS AND MISS THEM

Sport is a pantomime, with its heroes, villains, and clowns. A last-minute winner can make you a legend, but an own goal, a missed penalty or a defensive howler can consign you to the circus of history. Children may be taught that it's the taking part that matters, but I've long known that not taking part matters more. That doesn't mean I'm not fascinated by failure, particularly failure of the heroic kind. After all, knowing that you are inept and persisting regardless is what makes Britain what it is: a mess.

One Saturday at the grim end of February, I decided to investigate this phenomenon at a ninth-tier football match on the outskirts of an unpopular West Midlands town. The ground was sandwiched between a prison and a donkey sanctuary, and entrance was one-pound-fifty. I joined the other two spectators in a stand the size of a bus stop. The teams stumbled out to an elderly disco ditty farted out on a broken speaker. One linesman was a child, the other was in his seventies, and the ref walked with a limp. The pitch was doubly askew, sloping from goal to goal and from touchline to touchline, and there was a single advertising hoarding for haemorrhoid cream.

South-West Birmingham Athletic played in blue and were sponsored by a beautician. North-East Ladywood Academicals played in red and were sponsored by a crematorium. Athletic liked passing it out from the back, but always lost possession before the third touch. Academicals attempted route-one football, but always lobbed their own striker. Neither side could defend, shunning both zonal marking and man-marking in favour of menacing stares and violence. Short corners went to the opposition, long corners went out of play and set pieces either hit the wall or the horizon.

There wasn't a lot to see on the pitch, so I watched the other spectators instead. They were a pair of amateur footballers' wives, and no one could accuse them of being underdressed.

A small blonde lady with dappled spray-tan said, "Ace being an AWAG, irrenit, Jen?"

"Bostin, Shel," replied a taller brunette, who dripped junk jewellery, carried a cavernous handbag, and sported an unwieldy pair of sunglasses on her pointy nose.

"Double page spread in The Tamworth Tatler," Shel said.

"And free cider at Nuneaton's second most popular nightspot," Jen said.

A blundering tackle sent a heavy-bellied midfielder crashing into a crater. The ref blew his whistle and limped over. There were no physios, so the player's manager, who looked like an old school bank robber, shouted, "Pull yourself together yer big girl's blouse!" by way of treatment.

Jen and Shel started talking again. I liked them both, though not necessarily in the trouser department. They certainly seemed more entertaining than the match.

"Bostin handbag, Jen."

"Ta, Shel."

"I never knew you spelt *Gucci* with three *c's*."

"It's a genuine fake. Gary bought it off a Thai transsexual at a Patpong ping-pong show."

"It's dead roomy, Jen."

"It's gotta be, Shel. How else am I going to carry Tinkerbell around?"

"Yer pit bull?"

"He's a lovely dog." Jen opened her handbag, revealing a snarling, shark-jawed beast with a skull the size of a cannon ball.

"Yer dog's a bloke?"

"Course, Shel."

"And you call him Tinkerbell?"

"I've always liked Disney."

We all watched the match for a bit. What it lacked in quality, it made up for in incident. A defender nutmegged his own goalkeeper, a striker headed the post with his skull, a midfielder backheeled into his own net, two opposing players missed a drop ball and kicked the ref in both sets of ribs, a goal kick banana-ed backwards for a corner and a winger groined himself on the corner flag. It could have been the final of the

Incompetence World Cup. Eventually, my fellow spectators' attention was drawn to a miserable footballer adjusting his shin pad.

"Oh dear, Shel. Your Steve's looking as cheery as a freshly buggered bum hole."

"We had a bit of a tiff, Jen."

"He's never being stingy about your spending again?"

"Too right he is, Jen. Steve just doesn't realise how much it costs to be beautiful."

"What are you gonna get seen to this time?"

"Bloke down the Bull Ring's offered to Botox my G-spot."

"Pricey?"

"Bargain basement, Jen. The syringes are all second-hand, but he's happy to soak mine in creosote first."

"Better safe than sorry, Shel."

A free kick landed in the donkey sanctuary, triggering braying from the asses, and cheering from the players. The budget didn't stretch to a spare ball, so the bloke who had misplaced the free kick had to clamber over the fence and take his chances with the animals. He didn't seem happy about it and nor did the donkeys, judging by all the stomping and snorting.

"How's the wedding coming along, Jen?"

"Not so good, Shel. I wanted performing swans, a hot air balloon and six months in the Seychelles."

"Bostin, Jen. What happened?"

"I've got a male stripper, a second-hand bike and six days in Stafford."

"Oh, Jen. What went wrong?"

"Couldn't afford it. Gary's plumbing's up the spout."

"If the club paid our blokes more, Gary wouldn't need to spend half the week with his arms up people's u-bends."

"It's not like we haven't asked, Shel."

"What was their excuse last time?"

"Single-figure attendances."

"Pathetic."

"Their very word, Shel."

"I was so angry, Jen, I fell out of a minicab."

"I saw the pics in the East Bromwich Advertiser. Local paparazzi are a disgrace."

"There's only the one, Jen."

"Stu?"

"Got me to flash me minge. He told me it was for the final module of his media studies degree."

"Ooh, classy, Shel."

"Still, Jen. It's dead great you and Gary are gonna get hitched. He's a bostin bloke."

"He's got such a lovely speaking voice, Shel. I'll never forget the first words he said to me."

"What were they, Jen?"

"Show us your kidneys."

"Show us your kidneys?"

"I nearly fell off my pole."

"What were you doing up a pole, Jen?"

"Dancing."

"Dancing?"

"Upside down in a see-through thong."

"Jen! You never worked at *Spearmint Monkey*?"

"The tips were big and it's in a dead glam bit of Coventry."

"It's not a very romantic start to a relationship, is it Jen?"

"How do you mean, Shel?"

"You being arse-upwards on a pole and him shouting out, *Show us your kidneys!*"

"It wasn't what he said, Shel. It was how he said it. Beautiful speaking voice."

The AWAGs contemplated Gary's vocal attractions in silence, so my attention turned to the action unfolding on the pitch. A defender played a dummy to the opposing wing-back, who struck the ball with the outside of his boot and curved it back over the halfway line. A sliding tackle missed both the ball and the player in possession but created a trench deep enough for the Somme. The heftiest player tripped over the trench and went head-first into a puddle. He flailed about like he had been shot, until even his own players began to boo his theatrics. After an age, he got to his feet and swore at everyone, including the ref, who showed him a red card. He went ballistic and both teams joined forces to bundle him off the pitch.

Jen showed Shel her engagement ring.

"Is that diamond a real copy, Jen?"

"Genuine cubic zirconia, Shel."

"Must have cost a bomb."

"He nicked it."

"Bit of a cheapskate."

"Not really, no. He's on a suspended sentence, so he was putting his freedom on the line for me. I think it's dead romantic."

An Academicals player took possession and dribbled past two Athletic players before being scythed to the ground.

"Your Gary's just got a penalty, Jen."

"Hope he doesn't cock it up again, Shel. That South-West Birmingham Athletic goalie's a big fella."

"What's the score again?"

"7-4. All own goals."

"Gary got a hat-trick, didn't he?"

"Back-passing never was his strength."

The referee blew his whistle.

"Look out, Jen. Gary's running up to the spot."

"Come on, Gary, yer twat!"

"Boot it in their bloody net for a change!"

"Score and I'll shag yer!"

The ball thunked Jen in the face. She screamed and invaded the pitch.

Shel turned to me for the first time and said, "That's his best penalty this season."

We looked on as Jen headbutted Gary, triggering a mass brawl. I couldn't help feeling that they were all much better at fighting than football, and, as I watched the players, the officials and Jen flail around in the mud, inflicting injuries of varying degrees of severity on teammates and opponents alike, my heart swelled with pride. This is what it meant to be English. Twenty-two men had showcased their lack of talent with dogged determination for almost ninety minutes. Now, they were knocking seventeen shades of shit out of each other with a passion rarely seen outside of the honeymoon suite. There was such joyful abandon to the violence, and a real sense of togetherness. Everyone knew they were rubbish at football, and now they had switched to an older, less regimented sport. I felt so inspired by the unarmed skirmishing that I decided to join in: sometimes it's the taking part that's important.

RULE 3 - VIOLENCE IS GOLDEN

Live fast and, before you know it, you've run out of time. Live in the moment and, at my age, all you've got to savour is rheumatism. But live in the past, and it gets longer by the day. Sometimes, I relive my regrets, revisit my blunders and rage at the eternal *if only*. At other times, I go easy on myself and reflect on friends made, fun had, and kindnesses shown. But what if you've invested all your energy into doing the wrong thing? Would nostalgia still work if you had spent your life breaking every moral code known to Man?

Finding someone who had done exactly that took many nights of meticulous mingling with the worst customers East London's hostelries had to offer, but eventually I hit the jackpot and fixed up a drink with the villain of my dreams. Everyone called him Carroll. I'm guessing it was his surname, but one thing was for sure: this was a man who knew where all the bodies were buried, largely because he had buried them.

I made my way to a London postcode that Trip Advisor described as "London's answer to Chernobyl". That might have scared off some, but I'm no tourist and people don't generally bother to mug a man who looks like he has nothing to steal.

Some pubs want to be found. Others prefer to lie low. *The Goodwill* skulked at the end of an alley specifically designed for murder and vertical assignations. Its sign – a Stanley knife and knuckleduster - swung in the wind like a gibbet, and dangling off the doorknob, a worm-eaten notice read, *No Guide Dogs*. The place smelt like an old offenders' institution, largely due the prevalence of old offenders. The décor wasn't all that: keys grimaced through a piano's shattered lid, a bald Christmas tree rotted in the corner and the pool table had been slashed with a knife, much like many of the customers.

The young barman was menacingly smart: clean-cut, pristine shirt, boxer's build. I ordered a Snakebite, Pernod and Black and "Whatever Carroll's having."

At that, the room went silent, like a gunslingers' saloon bar after someone's called Clint Eastwood's cowboy a prancing fairy.

Thirty-odd pairs of eyes watched the barman pour my lager, cider, aniseed, and blackcurrant combo and trace a skull on the head of Carroll's Guinness. As I'd suspected, they only took cash.

Even among The Goodwill's line-up of ageing borstal-botherers, Carroll was not exactly tough to spot. He had more scars than hair and sported the reassuring demeanour of a Chechen warlord; features hacked out of granite, bone-breaking fists, and a suit specially tailored for making threats in.

Carroll had two tables to himself and there was no one within twenty feet of him, as if his body generated a hermetic circle of fear.

He accepted the skull-topped stout but declined my offer of a handshake.

I took the seat directly opposite him, and said, "Thanks for agreeing to ..."

"Let's get this done," he interrupted in a voice as melodic as a laryngitic bullfrog's.

He wasn't here to listen. That was my job. Luckily, that's just how I like it. I supped my Snakebite and let him unburden himself.

"I started off in the early fifties as a bookie's runner for Guy Ritchie," Carroll began. "Golden years, they was - Soho was just a village. Violent, mind you, but friendly; full of villains and well-known faces, not Jack-the-Lads and plastic gangsters like it is now. These days, there's no respect, just no-value nonce cases, toe rags and pansified druggies - phonies and frauds who've never done any proper bird and who'd rather get a kick in the assets than slip an old lady a few quid for a new coat. But back in the day, there was Ronnie "The Hat" McVitie, "Mad" Reggie Frazer, and the Kray Triplets - the true Wellingtons of Crime."

As Carroll paused to sup the skull off his Guinness, I took a moment to marvel silently at the prodigious inaccuracy of his memory. Don't get me wrong, I hadn't expected watertight testimony from a bloke who had bent the letter of the law for decades. But this was *Absolute Bullshit* – a point modern science has identified as beyond plausible. Had his memories turned against him? Was he beset by a cruel, brain-mangling medical condition? Or was he just having a laugh? He didn't strike me as the humorous type, but the jury was still out - and this was a man who knew a lot about juries. I let him continue.

"I did my first job with Crippled Jim the all-in wrestler, a bit of after-hours window-shopping. We bought a crooked van rung with false plates in a slaughter down the Borough. Earned a chunk of money - fifty large in the bin. Broadmoor Danny was the brains behind the whole operation. You know the fella; he planned The Great Tube Robbery, which would have gone down as a bigger job than Brinks Mat if the escalators hadn't been out of order at Mornington Crescent."

Carroll made a sound that could have been a laugh, but I wasn't sure. I did my best to echo it. He narrowed his eyes, as if he were taking aim at my temple through the sights of a Kalashnikov. It wasn't a relaxing moment, but I'd not come here to relax. I was here to unravel the secrets of another man's life. I wasn't entirely sure that that's what I was getting, but I wasn't about to argue.

Carroll narrowed the intensity of his gaze by a nano-smidgeon and continued, "When Broadmoor Danny done a runner with Norman No Legs, I teamed up with a gang of Hassidic Yardies and ran guns for Hummus, FETA and the RNLI."

I spluttered on my Snakebite. Carroll cracked his knuckles. I tried not to notice that his fists were tattooed with the words *Late* and *Hove*, but I couldn't help noticing that he had noticed my efforts not to be noticed.

"What are you looking at?" Carroll raged. "The tattooist was dyslexic!"

I raised a palm in apology.

"That's better," Carroll continued. "You wouldn't want to get on the wrong side of me. I ate my social worker! You should be pissing your pants with sheer respect." He gripped his Guinness like a Molotov cocktail. "Listen, I'm the kind of man who wouldn't say his glass is half empty and I wouldn't say it's half full neither, but if you keep looking at me in that tone of voice, I'll grind the glass into your throat."

At that, Carroll cackled like a cockney witch and leant in. "You know that robbery on *Crimewatch* last week. Everyone thinks it's me and they're dead right, it was. I'm dead proud of my reputation. I don't like other villains nicking all the attention, see. I stabbed one bloke's biographer to death with his own biro. Ghost writers, eh?"

He had another laugh. It was fit to scare the pants off a Norse berserker.

I couldn't copy the noise, and I had no clue how to respond, so I tried to head him off with a pun: "Violence is Golden."

It didn't work. "Are you taking the piss?" His forehead furrowed like a sheet of corrugated iron.

"Never," I replied. If I could have surrendered, I would have – but this wasn't a war, it just felt like it.

"You better not be," Carroll snarled. "I'm a man of considerable bollocks, I'll have you know. There can't have been a decent villain in Britain who hasn't asked me to plunge a mug for them. Fast Brian also known as Quick Eric also known as Puffing Patrick is a good for instance. He'd been marked down for being murdered. Now, this character, he was not pansified, or soft. He was a good class arsonist, but he was also a grass, so I paid him a visit. This no-value leery git was shitless – he lost two stone in sweat the moment he set eyes on me. I tried to calm things down by talking to him, but when I said, "I don't know whether to bite lumps out of you or tear your face off, but I'll be lenient. I'm going to rip off your head and shit down your neck," he got right saucy, so I plunged him with a corkscrew, banged his head on half-a-dozen steps, burned him with cigarettes, put him in a cold bath and tried to take his teeth out with pliers, but I needn't have bothered, he'd already died of fear."

"Poor guy," I observed, hoping this fate didn't lie in store for me.

"Poor? Poor!! Why are you taking his side?"

I had no answer, so I tried shifting my sympathy from the victim to the perpetrator. "Must have been tiring."

"What, dying?"

"No," I said. "All that murder. Arduous. For you."

He harrumphed. Not a conventional old man harrumph into his chin, but a death-metal throat-roar of a harrumph.

"I don't mind a bit of exercise," Carroll continued. "Keeps my ticker going. But someone grassed and I got done. Now, my lawyer's so bent, he could knobble a Jehovah's Witness and he got the charge reduced to manslaughter. The trial was still tricky, even though I do have a good knowledge of law through my way of living. We objected to seventy-three jurors in total, but after that the judge objected to us. Bearing in mind my previous, eighteen years was a result, but I can't say I was celebrating."

Carroll glared vindictively into his Guinness. It was nice to take a break from his malevolence and have the stout take up the slack for a bit, but I hadn't come here to sit in silence.

"Must have been tough," I said. Sympathy was worth another shot. Sometimes, even violent psychopaths just need someone to understand their suffering.

But not Carroll. He gave me a "Bollocks to that," then continued. "When you're doing serious bird, you've got to stand your ground. One time, this Geordie screw gave me a few verbal words, so I knocked him down. He got the raving hump, called for help and three of them bundled in. I did the lot of them with a big lump of lead I found in the yard. The Deputy Governor comes up and gives me some old fanny, so I chinned him and down he went like a sack of shit. He kicked up murders; twenty-eight riot police stormed in, and it was a right tear-up, but I creamed the lot of them. That's when they sent in the Marines. Thought I'd give them the benefit of the doubt."

The Marines, right. What is a man to do when faced by ever-escalating fibs? I dithered for a moment between questioning his recollection and drinking more Snakebite, Pernod and Black. I went with option two and let him carry on.

"I was taken in front of the Visiting Magistrates in a body-belt, but I fucked them off, dived under the table and bit their ankles. The Governor came in with a gun and started making threats, so I said "Listen, you mug, I've got to pull the plug on you there." I chewed through the strait jacket, took the shooter off him, knuckled him in the kidney, found an iron bar and really done him with it. I felt much better then, even though they gave me three years in solitary without a mattress surviving on Number One Diet."

I doubted Number One Diet would win many Michelin stars, and three years in solitary was unlikely to help hone a man's social skills. I would have felt sorry for him, had it not been for the heartless violence he had dispensed and described in detail.

"I served my stretch in full," Carroll continued. "Bollocks to good behaviour. As soon as I got out, I fled the country for a bit and joined the Happy Valley Super-Duper Troopers, the Kenyan equivalent of the SAS. Best years of my life, until I got court marshalled for flogging counterfeit bravery drugs to NATO."

While Carroll took a breather to sip his Guinness, I took the opportunity to stretch out my legs. They had gone numb during the bit about the prison governor assault and cramp had set in, but I knew this was a delicate procedure that shouldn't be rushed. To avoid kicking Carroll's shins, I rotated my arse around thirty degrees in my seat and stretched my legs out to the side. They hit something human, but Carroll didn't react. I looked down. An unconscious man lay under the table.

"Don't worry about him." Carroll said. "He's a hitman. I should know, I hit him." He threw back his head and opened his raptorial jaw, cackling like a power drill and displaying a set of teeth that would have embarrassed a self-respecting badger.

Fortunately, I didn't have to look at the inside of his jaw for long because he was soon talking again. "I've been off the villainy for a bit, renewing my acquaintance with the upper world, so to speak. I've got a tech idea - second class email. Second class email saves a packet on data but takes three days to arrive. It's important for messages that don't really matter. I got a little import-export business too and a share in an English pub in Spain. And I'm getting a new venture off the ground - shoplifting over the internet. The customer e-mails me a list. I nick the items, then deliver them to their door in a stolen van. It's the future. Interested?"

There didn't seem any point pretending that I was, so I just gave him a "No, but thanks." Why was I thanking him? Fear. What insights had I gained from our encounter? Nothing reliable. I felt like I had binge-watched Netflix's entire Untrue Crime selection. But there was one tangible thing I could lay my hand - or foot - on, and it was lying under the table. Maybe this undeniably solid chunk of reality could help unlock something truthful.

"Can I just ask you one last thing?" I asked.

"If you must," Carroll replied.

"It's about the bloke under the table."

"What about him?"

"Is he dead?"

"Who's asking?"

"No one."

"Good."

"Who is he?"

"You wouldn't believe me if I told you."

"Try me."

"Why should I?"

"I'll get you another drink."

"Fair enough," Carroll said.

Once again, the bar went quiet as all the customers watched the barman pour my Snakebite, Pernod and Black, and trace a skull on Carroll's stout.

I returned to the table and put down our drinks. As I took my seat, my foot knocked against the recumbent man on the carpet. If he wasn't dead, he was doing a passing impression of it.

I took a sip of Snakebite, and prepared to hear something truthful, something I could verify.

"You want to know who's under the table?" Carroll asked.

"Yes," I confirmed.

"Right."

"Go on."

"You really won't believe me."

"I don't mind. Just tell me."

"You're sure you want to know?"

"Yes."

"Information's not always a healthy thing to have."

"Do I look like I care about my health?"

"Curiosity killed the cat, and all that bollocks."

"Just tell me. Please."

"Okay."

"Who is he?"

"Vladimir Putin."

I spluttered on my Snakebite.

"He's not as tough as he reckons," Carroll continued. "All that bear wrestling, judo throwing, and bareback riding. It's a load of old fanny."

I had sat here and listen to Carroll tell me about the Great Tube Robbery, the Kray Triplets, and his time as a bookie's runner for Guy Ritchie, and now he was telling me that Vladimir Putin was lying under the table. Somehow, the President of Russia, and former lieutenant colonel of the KGB, had sauntered over to the worst pub in East London and got himself knocked out on the carpet. Rather than relying on his million-strong standing army or the world's largest stockpile of nuclear weapons, the terrifying trillionaire had opted for a fist fight with Carroll and lost.

"That's not true, is it?" I asked.

"Go ahead," he replied. "Take a look."

I crawled under the table. The lighting left a lot to be desired, but I eventually found the man's head. I switched on my phone's flashlight and examined him. He had thinning hair and a moon-shaped face with pronounced eyebrows and piggy eyes. So far, so Putin.

When I resurfaced, Carroll, just said, "Told you."

"It does look a bit like him," I replied.

"It is him."

"But what's he doing here?"

"He kept banging on about some geezer called Peter The Great. Apparently, he was the Russian boss some time ago, and he'd come to London to nick all our ideas about shipbuilding, and Vladmir, he wanted to do a similar thing, only about crime."

"He wanted to nick our ideas about crime?"

"That's what he said."

"But isn't Russia quite good at crime?"

"Not good enough for Vladimir. He reckons his boys are slacking, thinks they could learn from some old school London villains."

"So, he dropped in at the pub."

"Just after lunchtime."

"Today?"

"About two thirty."

"Right." Maybe it was Vladmir Putin, or perhaps it was a wind-up merchant who happened to look like him, I would never know.

"Now I've let you in on this, you're gonna to have to help me out."

"Another drink?"

Carroll indicated his untouched pint and shook his head. I knew what was coming, but that didn't make me any more able to avoid it.

"You're going to have to help me shift him," Carroll said.

"Can't he shift himself?"

"What do you think?"

So, he was dead. Now, don't get me wrong. I'm no shirker and I've had my share of criminal convictions, but accessory to murder was a new one on me.

"What about the other customers?" I asked.

"They won't say anything."

"The barman?"

Carroll laughed. "His dad's a lifer. I trained him."

"Okay, so we're just going to carry him out of here?"

"There's an industrial mincer in the kitchen."

"We're going to mince Vladimir Putin?"

"I'll do the honours. Just be a good bloke and help me shift him."

Put like that, it seemed rude to refuse. The corpse wasn't particularly heavy and none of the customers raised an eyebrow.

Once we had safely deposited the corpse at the back of the kitchen, Carroll just said,

"Be lucky," and I took that as my cue to leave.

On my way out, I noticed that something had dropped off the corpse. It was a gold star attached to a white, blue, and red band, a medal I now know to denote an elite "Hero of Russia."

As I made my way westwards to safer postcodes, I reflected on my two-pint encounter with Carroll. A man's memories are his own, and what version of them he chooses to share with the rest of the world, well, that's up to him. But when it comes to events in the here-and-now, the truth has a way of outing itself, and that truth can be stranger than the wildest imaginings of anyone on this sorry globule.

RULE 4 - LIFE IS LIKE A BOX OF FROGS

Four hours after gate-crashing the rugby club beer festival, I lost an arm-wrestle to a fly half. I bought him a pint and in return, he told me a secret: "When you die, you get to make one final phone call."

He spoke with the assurance of the expensively educated, but I thought it best to seek clarification. "You mean, if you're on a plane that's about to crash or you're on your deathbed?"

"I mean, after you die."

"Right." I didn't want to seem ungrateful for the information, but I did harbour a few doubts. "How do you know?"

He looked affronted. "How do I know?"

"You look ... alive."

"Thanks."

I thought about all my dearly departed relatives and acquaintances and wondered why none of them had bothered to give me a bell. Maybe I hadn't topped their phone-a-friend lists. I asked the rugger-bugger to explain himself and, after I agreed to sponsor the team's pub crawl, he was delighted oblige:

***

"It all happened after my stag do," the fly half explained. "Everyone got monumentally bladdered, and by the time we were thrown out, only three of us were still standing. We didn't want the night to end, but the only bars still open made us feel about as welcome as a dose of Monkey Pox. Then my mate Tommo had a brilliant idea: why not break in to one of those tree-swingers clubs and prat about on the zip wires? Now, I don't normally go in for all that team bonding malarkey, but it was my stag do, so why not?

I'd known Jonty and Tommo since school; both top blokes with everything to live for. Jonty had just launched a yacht-delivery app and Tommo's Insta was going Interstellar. Life was good, but that didn't mean we couldn't indulge in stupid stunts every now and again.

We shinned up to the tree canopy by the light of the moon. There wasn't a soul in sight and the night-time silence was only disturbed by the occasional rutting owl. The view wasn't great, due to the darkness, but we did manage to find a basket and a zip wire. I was the one getting married, so I had first dibs.

Jonty and Tommo cheered me on as I clambered into the basket and zoomed off. It didn't half shift! I was the fastest thing in the forest - completely in the moment, not a care in the world. I whooped my tits off; I'll tell you that for nothing. I'd never felt so alive, but a thunking great tree trunk had other ideas.

I had no clue how long I'd been out for the count, but when my brain got itself back into gear, I found myself in a wooden cabin decked out like it was about 1956. There was a juke box, a pinball machine, a dial telephone, and a dog-eared local directory. There was a gnarled oak door at one end and, at the other, an elderly chap drinking whisky and playing chess with himself.

I could only assume that the concussion was playing silly buggers with my brain. I blinked hard and often, but the cabin remained resolutely there. I checked my pockets – no wallet, no mobile, no keys. Maybe I was a victim of a mid-air mugging. It seemed unlikely.

When the chess player noticed I was stirring, he abandoned his pawns but not his spirit glass, and ambled over to my recumbent body. He had a bald patch across the centre of his skull and curly grey-black side-curtains over his ears. His bulging eyes were livelier than anyone's I had ever seen, but his expression was terminally unimpressed. His once expensive suit was worn to ruin, and his silk shirt was missing half its buttons. He took a few seconds to look me up and down, analysing me as if I were an inferior variation of the Sicilian Dragon.

"You are doubtless *wery* perplexed." The chess player's English was almost perfect, but the *w* was a giveaway.

"Are you Russian?" I asked.

"Russian?" He looked offended. "Your head must be *wery vobbly*. I am from *Latwia*."

I was in no mood to discuss the niceties of East European nationalism. "Where am I?"

Instead of answering, he took out a cigarette and attempted to light it. His hands shook so much, it was painful to watch. I've never smoked - couldn't see the point in curtailing my life for a lungful of ash – and looking at this chap, I was jolly glad I hadn't.

While he sparked up, I yanked myself backwards and hitched my torso up against the timber wall. The cabin felt too solid for a concussion-dream, but the fifties décor was unreal: "Am I back in Time?"

"Outside," he replied, his cigarette now ignited. "You're outside Time."

"Am I dead?"

The man nodded. That was annoying. I had my own wedding to attend. On the plus side, I still felt alive. When I pinched myself, it hurt, and my limbs all seemed to work. I performed a series of basic experiments on myself: I could cough, stretch, stand-up, itch my scalp.

The chess player smoked and drank his way through my life-affirming mimes, but he didn't seem to be enjoying them. After a few minutes of my poncing about, he said, "Finished?"

I performed a series of star-jumps to irritate him.

He took a gargantuan puff, coughed his lungs out, then took another drag.

"Don't you worry about your health?" I asked.

"My health?" He inhaled the remainder of his latest cigarette. "It's too late for health. I've already had most of my organs removed – a kidney, spleen, tonsils, a lung, a hip, a knee. Soon, there will be nothing left."

In the circumstances, I didn't find his final words particularly comforting. "Where am I?"

"A deep dark forest where two plus two equals five and the path leading out is only wide enough for one."

"Is it in Hertfordshire?"

"You won't find this forest on any maps."

"Are we still in the physical world?"

"Limbo. The in-between." The chess player indicated the gnarled door at the far end of the hut. "When I take you through there, that's it."

I stumbled across to check.

"No!" His gruff shout stopped me in my tracks. "Touch that door and that's it – oblivion."

"What are we waiting for?"

"You have one phone call."

"A call?"

He waved his scotch at the dial phone.

I had never used one. The oldest phone I'd ever owned was a Nokia 5110. "Who do I call?"

"Up to you. You get a minute on the line. Try explaining where you are, and the call is cut off, along with your soul." The chess player grinned at my discomfort. "Just choose your call well – and keep it general."

General? How the hell could I keep it general? I'd just died. That was a highly specific and deeply regrettable detail. I thought about ringing my fiancé, but I just couldn't face it. She already knew I loved her, so all I'd be doing would be breaking her heart. Anyway, weren't the police much better at that sort of thing? They had all passed exams in breaking bad news. It occurred to me that I could do something useful – I could warn my friends not to use the zip wire. The only problem was, I didn't know their numbers.

I went old school and looked in the dog-eared directory. Personal mobiles weren't listed. I was stuffed – who the hell remembers people's numbers?

"You look perplexed, my young friend," the chess player said. "You *vant* to ring who?"

"Tommo."

The chess player didn't hesitate before giving me a series of eleven digits.

"And that's Tommo's number?"

"Try for yourself." He waved his scotch at the dial phone.

The chess player repeated the numbers as I turned the dial. Was he winding me up? Would I get through to some celestial prank line?

But after a couple of rings, a familiar voice exclaimed, "Hugo!"

"Tommo!" I replied. God, it was good to hear a friendly voice.

"Where the devil are you?" Tommo asked.

"I haven't got long," I said.

"What do you mean?"

"You're a top bloke, I value your friendship, but there's something important I've got to tell you."

"This is all a bit odd, old chap. Are you quite alright?"

"Where are you?"

"That's what I asked you."

"I can't tell you."

"Don't be a doughnut."

"It's the rules."

"You're drunk."

"So are you."

"Get off the phone, stop fannying about and get back up here."

"I'm not fannying about. This is serious."

"Serious? It's a stag-do after-party."

"Listen."

"See you at the bottom."

"You're already on the zip wire?"

"Wheeeee!"

"But there's a tr..."

"Aaaagh!"

The line died. I swore. The chess player offered me a drink.

"A drink? I thought I was dead."

"Doesn't mean you can't enjoy yourself." He handed me a double scotch. I hadn't seen him pour it. He must have had it ready.

I hadn't got a lot to lose, so I downed it. My last liquid supper - a nice, smoky malt. That taste was the last thing I remembered before waking up on the floor again.

A familiar voice said, "Hugo?"

"Tommo?" He was bang next to me, similarly prone. Across the room, the chess player was at his board, fondling a bishop.

"Bloody tree trunk. Stepped right out in front of my head." Tommo wasn't making a lot of sense, but I knew exactly what he meant.

"I tried to warn you."

"That ridiculous phone call? Thought that was some kind of wind-up."

"It was life-or-death."

"Don't exaggerate, old man."

"We're dead."

"Really?" Tommo looked sceptically around the cabin, taking in the décor and the chess player. "Who's he?"

"He's Latvian."

"Oh."

Tommo and I dragged ourselves up. I felt even woozier than when I'd arrived. Maybe there was something in the whisky besides alcohol.

"Hugo, old chap," Tommo said in a matter-of-fact tone. "I don't suppose you've got a clue where we are?"

"Limbo."

"Isn't that a weird Caribbean sport people do when they're pissed?"

"Yes, but it's also where we are."

"Oh. Bloody hell. A purgatorial cabin?"

"That's the badger."

"I see. Is that a juke box?"

Tommo wandered across the room and started examining the selection of tracks on offer. "Cliff Richard, Perry Como, Pat Boone..."

"My apologies." The Latvian looked up from his pieces. "The *dewil* has all the best tunes."

"The *dewil*?" Tommo mocked. "Who the *dewil* are you?"

"That's immaterial." The chess player made a move that put his imaginary opponent in zugzwang, a terminal situation in which every move loses.

"Who's in charge?" Tommo asked.

The chess player turned his bulbous eyeballs heavenwards.

"Right," Tommo said in a business-like tone. "Enough of this nonsense. Are we dead or not?"

"Dead," the chess player replied.

Tommo jiggled his arms. "Then why on Earth are we intact?"

"Look, it's like this." The chess player sighed. "You go to The Beyond in one piece. The *vay* some people die – how *vould* I have a conversation with them? *Vhat* if a guy falls into an industrial mixer – I couldn't *wery* well talk to a heap of mince."

"No. Quite." Tommo slumped against the wall. "Is this the end?"

"The endgame." The chess player smiled.

"Can't we challenge you to a match?" I asked.

"Chess just keeps me occupied between jobs," he replied. "It is of no consequence."

"We can't play to save our lives?" Tommo asked.

"If you can't play to save your lives, you *vill* have *wery* little chance," the chess player joked.

Tommo swore under his breath. He didn't seem to be buying this situation at all. "So, all dead people come to this cabin?"

"This is just the local branch," the chess player replied.

"But you're from Latvia," Tommo objected.

"I live down the road," the chess player said.

"So, it's like a franchise?" Tommo said.

"There's no money in it," the chess player said.

Tommo glared at the chess player for an uncomfortably long time, realised it was not a wind up and slumped into a defeated hunch, muttering, "Some bloody stag night."

"It's not much consolation," I said. "But you get one phone call." I pointed at the dial-up antique.

"Who on Earth do I call?" Tommo asked.

"Jonty?" I suggested.

"But what about my family? My yacht app?"

"Just warn Jonty about the tree trunk."

"Oh, of course. Bloody hell, where's my phone?"

"Mine's gone too."

"Oi! What have you done with our phones?"

"They are not necessary," the chess player said.

"They jolly well are," Tommo said. "All my contacts are there."

"Your Earthly contacts," the chess player corrected. "You only need one."

"Well, I can't remember any," Tommo said.

The chess player recited an eleven-digit number without looking up from his board.

"How the hell do you know?" Tommo asked.

"He just does," I said. "It's probably some kind of death thing."

"A death thing?" Tommo said.

I shrugged, "Just dial."

As Tommo inserted his index finger and rotated the dial, the chess player repeated the digits.

"Jonty?" Tommo said into the dial phone.

"Tommo!" Jonty's voice was so loud, he could have been in the cabin. "What's happening?"

"No idea," Tommo replied.

"That's helpful," Jonty said.

"It's not, is it?" Tommo said.

"No, not particularly," Jonty said.

"Sorry, old chap," Tommo said.

"No problem."

There was a slight pause. I would have interrupted, but I didn't want to break any of the chess player's rules and have him cut off Tommo's call and soul.

Eventually, Tommo came up with the less than urgent, "How's Trix?"

"Bonza," Jonty replied.

"Jolly good," Tommo said.

"Well, I'm about to swing down now."

"No!"

"See you in a sec."

"Wait!"

"Aaaaaaagh!"

"Oh."

"You didn't warn him," I said.

"I was about to," Tommo said.

The chess player offered us both a drink. Tommo downed his. I knew what to expect, but I needed a scotch and I'd given up caring.

When we came to, Jonty had joined us on the floor. I had no idea how much later this was; all I knew was that I had a worse headache than on my previous two awakenings.

We went through the same rigmarole with Jonty: *Where are we? Dead. Where's my phone? Gone. Who's the weird dude? No idea.* Then we proceeded to the phone call. But there was no one left to warn about tree trunks. Who could Jonty inform about our hat-trick of fatalities? A girlfriend? A parent? A sibling? He didn't fancy any of them.

Jonty looked at the dial phone in disgust. "How about FaceTime, Zoom or Teams?"

"No," the chess player replied. "Voice only. That's the rule."

"Why?" Jonty asked.

"Look," the chess player replied. "You're *wery* lucky to get this – you are among the first people in human history to have this opportunity. Before you, the grave has been silent."

"Oh," I said, "Just how long has this phone call thing been going on?"

The chess player gave us a full-body shrug. "*Veeks.*"

"*Veeks?*" Jonty queried.

"He means weeks," I explained.

"He's Latvian," Tommo elaborated.

"A trial period," the chess player explained. "*Ve vant* to see how it goes."

"We're guinea pigs?" Jonty said, disbelievingly.

"Looks like it," I said.

Jonty picked up the local directory and perused it. After a while, he smirked. "They've got sex lines."

"No *vanking*!" the chess player shouted. "This is purgatory. Have some respect!"

The chess player may have been a spoil sport, but I couldn't help agreeing that a sex line was an underwhelming choice for a man's one posthumous call.

After he had leafed through the directory for some minutes, Jonty said, "I'm going to give this one a go."

"What is it?"

"Helpline."

"Bit late for the Samaritans," Tommo said, despondently.

"Forest zip-wire company. Out-of-hours emergencies."

"What if it goes to voicemail?"

"Just leave a message," the chess player replied, impatiently.

"Does a message count as your final call?" Jonty asked.

"Yes," the chess player snapped.

"Wow, my final contact with the world could be with a measly machine," Jonty grumbled, before dialling the number.

The phone rang. We waited. The phone rang again. The chess player reached into his pocket, took out a mobile and answered, "Night Caretaker. How can I help you?"

Jonty dropped the dial phone.

"Your property." The chess player took our phones, wallets, and keys out of his desk.

"We're not..." I began.

"No."

"Why?"

"I hate people breaking in," the Night Caretaker explained, and showed us to the gnarled door. It didn't lead to oblivion.

***

The fly-half looked at my expression and laughed. "Got you!"

He had. There was no use hiding it.

"Fifth one this evening."

"But I guess he got you too."

"Who?"

"The Latvian."

"What Latvian?" He paused. "You don't mean you believed it?"

Gullibility is an undervalued virtue, and I have been blessed with enough to get a medium-sized nation through the winter. Surprising really, as believing a load of gubbins suggests a character well-disposed towards humanity, an optimist full of hope and positivity. I am not that man, and yet I swallowed the story hook, line, and sinker. Still, truth is stranger than fiction and I'm stranger than most. Maybe the best conclusion to draw is that events, true or otherwise, can be mighty odd.

RULE 5 - Gravity Is A Force To Be Reckoned With

G ravity will take your loftiest ambitions and yank them out of the sky. And when gravity teams up with Time, you've got no chance, as one of the bravest men in Middlesbrough found when he turned thirty in mid-air.

I met the unfortunate bloke in one of those flat-roofed pubs with violence on tap and botulism on the menu. A sign read, *Pensioners Two Pounds A Pint*, which seemed a cruel under-evaluation of human life.

Establishments like this tend to welcome outsiders with clenched fists, but no one bothered me for the first hour or so. People often think that my face is already so beaten-up that there's no point making me any uglier by hitting it, and I can't disagree.

It wasn't until I'd sunk my third Snakebite, Pernod and Black that I heard the immortal question, a query that has resounded down the generations: "What are you looking at?" It was spoken with a Teesside twang, something akin to a Geordie-Yorkshire mélange.

"I don't know," I replied. "What *am* I looking at?" I knew from long experience that this exchange could play out in one of two ways: fight or friendship. It didn't much bother me which; the lad was as toned as a marshmallow.

He played for time with a classic, "You what?"

"What *am* I looking at?" I repeated. It wasn't a threat, just a question. Who did he reckon he was?

He waddled up to me and tested the resilience of the neighbouring bar stool with his humungous arse. "You want to know what I am?"

"I want to be able to answer your question and tell you what I was looking at."

"I'm the former parkour champion of Teesside."

"And what's parkour when it's at home?"

"Free running."

"Cross-country?"

"I run up buildings and jump across them."

"Any particular reason?"

"Because they're there."

This was the spirit that had conquered Everest, and I couldn't help but admire it. Personally, I have always felt more at home on the ground, and I am as likely to take up parkour as long-distance knitting, so I was happy to pay him a compliment. "Jumping up buildings must take balls the size of watermelons."

"They'd only get in the ruddy way," he smirked.

I was starting to break the ice, but now came the tricky bit. "I'm just wondering how you can dash up buildings when..." I fortified my resolve with a sip of Snakebite. "...you're built like a bouncy castle."

He slammed his fist on the table and regretted it instantly. It's hard to win a fight with an inanimate object. After he had sworn extensively and nursed his bleeding knuckles, he said, "I retired."

"Aren't you a bit young?"

"Thirty-one."

"All your life ahead of you."

"Not exactly."

"Just give it a few years and you'll see how young you were."

He took a long, hard glug of bitter and uttered one of the most morose statements I have ever heard: "It's my birthday." He sounded so miserable, he could have been saying *I've got cancer,* or *I just killed a man.*

"Happy birthday!" I exclaimed merrily. "If I get you another drink, will you tell me what happened?"

The ghost of a smile haunted his flabby face.

After I'd plonked a bitter in front of him, he clinked my Snakebite and began talking with the energy of a man half his weight:

***

"It was a year ago today. I'll never forget it. Everything changed at once. One moment I was one bloke. The next I was another bloke entirely. It was dead weird.

I'd been doing parkour since I was at school. I was no good at sport, not interested in lessons. I needed something to get up for and parkour did it for me. You see, life hereabouts is completely non-existent. Nowt happens all the time and most blokes need … an outlet. You see, in Middlesbrough, no one can hear you scream. Risking death seemed like the best way of getting a life and for years it worked a treat.

I was as thin as a whippet and I'd run up housing estates, shopping centres, you name it. After a while, just one final frontier remained – the power station. I'd gazed at it for years, planning when to break in, and how to approach it. No bugger had scaled the bastard. I suppose it was the threat of death that put people off, what with the volts and the drops. Understandable, now I come to think of it, but back then, I didn't bother much with fear.

On the night, it was everything I was looking for. Smoke-shrouded towers spewed flames, industrial waterfalls roared, transformers buzzed with electricity. The whole place was alive - like a giant electric dragon - and I was Saint-ruddy-George going into battle. I'd lived in the bastard building's shadow for almost thirty years, and it was high time I conquered it.

As I free-ran up the floodlit concrete, I was shadowed by my mates. Rob's twenty-two and a half-decent free runner. I never had to worry about him screwing up, I just had to watch my back – he was a glory-hunter, ready to fill my shoes if I ever slipped. Liam was seventeen and a total liability. Keen as mustard, but next to useless. He put his heart into it, but he just didn't have the legs.

I used a *Danger of Death* sign as a springboard to vault over a barbed wire fence. I landed, did a standing flip, and launched myself at a concrete wall. That gave me the momentum to sprint along its side, with my body practically parallel to the ground. I was a street acrobat, see. I laughed in the face of gravity, took its ruddy pants down and booted it up the bum! I grabbed a gas pipe and swung myself up to the next level. I never thought of falling; I just thought of flying.

Rob followed me up with an identical swing, but Liam didn't make it. We were going to have to rescue him again, and these things are never easy.

I jumped back down, crouched, and Liam stepped onto my shoulders. I held his feet and stood up, then Liam stood up on me, like a pair of circus acrobats. Rob reached down from the gas pipe and grabbed Liam's arms. I then pushed Liam's feet up until he tumbled onto Rob, landing in a pile and tearing his trousers on a steel spike.

"Liability Liam," Rob growled, as he untangled himself from the youngster.

I didn't like Rob's attitude, but we had a building to climb, and I couldn't be bothered to argue. I repeated my wall-dash and swung myself up to their level.

Now, when you're running up buildings, gravity's not your only problem. You've also got to worry about surveillance. We all had form, and another breaking-and-entering conviction would have done none of us any good. I picked up a rock and chucked it at a CCTV camera. It totalled the lens. There was glass all over the ruddy shop, mind you, but I'd got the job done.

I hurdled a bunch of razor-wire fences, climbed up the turbine hall roof and banister-bounced up a fire escape. Rob followed, practically breathing down my ruddy neck. Liam limped behind us, his trouser leg a-flap.

I stopped to look up. Two industrial towers speared the sky like an insult. I was determined to take them down a peg or two. You couldn't hold me in - barriers were my pathways, obstacles were my launch pads, chasms were my bridges - and in no sodding time at all I'd led us up to the roof of the nearest tower.

Climbing a tower is one thing, but jumping between two towers is quite another – particularly when the gap is wider than the River Tees - and that was what I was about to do. I was so buzzing, I made Liam take out his phone and record a video, not just of the leap, but of the build-up.

As I spoke, Rob stood at my side, jostling for equal frame-space.

"The world's my playground," I boasted into the phone screen. "Why walk when you can leap? Danger's a friend – it reminds me I'm alive."

Rob barged in, ranting, "He might be old, but our veteran leader is about to do a monkey-vault, a cat-leap and a four-metre gap jump seventy-five ruddy metres above ground!"

At that, Liam flipped his phone into selfie-mode and said, "And it's his birthday in a few seconds."

Once Liam had flipped it back, I added, "Age means nothing when you're free!"

I fixed my face with determination, monkey-vaulted across a spiky grid, cat-leapt onto some flimsy guttering, then flung myself into the void. As I hit mid-air, my watch struck midnight. The second hand stopped and so did I, frozen in the sky. I looked down at the distant concrete, felt myself drop like a rock and, in my mind's eye, my life rewound.

First, my girlfriend reversed across our bedroom, covering her underwear, and speaking backwards: "Yadhtrib Yppah!".

I felt my fall continue, conjuring another reverse memory. I was small and standing next to my mum, leaning over my birthday cake. I inhaled four times and the candles lit up one-by-one as mum reverse-shouted, "Snruter Yppah Ynam!".

As I dropped, I recalled a midwife un-smacking my arse, and lowering me by my tiny feet, as she exclaimed, "Yob a Sti!".

My fall ended just before I reached the ground. No idea how, but I looked down at the concrete a metre below me, then seventy-four metres up to the point where my fall had begun. It was ruddy odd dangling just above the ground, but before I could figure out what was going on, I was bouncing back up, only this time, my memories played forwards.

The midwife smacked my arse and lifted me up, shouting "It's a boy!".

As I rose higher, I blew out the candles on my fourth birthday cake as my mum shouted, "Many happy returns!"

Then, as I got to around sixty metres, my girlfriend walked forwards across our bedroom, removing her clothes with a "Happy Birthday!".

Once I'd reached the top, my body froze again. I was in mid-air, my feet level with the second tower's ledge two metres ahead. Something made me look at my watch. The second hand unfroze from midnight and made a single tick. The tick was so loud it could have been Big ruddy Ben and the force of the sound seemed to chuck me forward until my feet touched stone. My body swayed, then I flopped forward onto the roof.

The tick morphed into a cheer as Rob and Liam celebrated from the tower behind me. Luckily, I didn't appear to be dead. I counted my limbs. They were still there, and so was reality. A different kind of reality, a reality with fear in it. And tiredness. God, I was knackered. All the adrenalin had seeped out of me. I clambered to my feet and turned back to Rob and Liam on the tower roof I'd leapt from. They looked like I'd just scored a Championship League-winning goal for Middlesbrough.

Liam waved his arms. "Legend!"

Rob punched the air. "That was the biggest leap in the North-East!"

He was right, but it no longer meant 'owt to me. "It was the biggest mistake of my twenties," I said.

"Your twenties?" Rob shouted in total disbelief. "They were less than a ruddy minute ago. Happy birthday! You've just made history."

"Can't I rewrite it?" I asked.

"Rewrite it?" Rob scoffed. "Just jump back."

"I don't do that kind of thing anymore," I told them. "It's too risky."

Liam had gone quiet. He's a nice enough lad, but he's about as sharp as a dollop of custard. He turned to Rob, and I heard him ask, "What's happened to him?"

"Bastard's only gone and turned thirty in mid-air," Rob replied.

Rob was right. I was a changed man.

"I've decided to retire," I explained.

"But you're stuck on top of an industrial chimney!" Rob booted the air in frustration.

My so-called mates simply didn't get it. I gazed at the gap I had just leapt across and shuddered. "I could have died."

"Never think about death," Liam warned. "That's fatal."

Rob slapped him on the forehead, but I knew what Liam meant. A split-second of fear can kill any free runner - that was all it took. And that was why I knew it was no longer for me.

"I want to be a living legend, not a dead one," I said. "I want to live life with a safety net - take up gardening, open an ISA, commute, learn the trombone, get to know the neighbours, maybe join a library."

Rob couldn't have looked any fuller of contempt if I'd told him I'd stopped following Middlesbrough and started supporting Newcastle. "You've lost your bottle, mate".

I wasn't looking for my bottle. I was happy for it to stay lost, but I didn't expect Rob to understand that.

I looked out over the Middlesbrough skyline and pondered the constellations. Maybe I'd take up astronomy. It felt like a safe hobby.

The only sounds were a distant buzz of electricity and Robert and Liam moaning about me. It's amazing how sound carries when there's nothing between you but air:

"What are we going to do about Duncan, Rob?"

"I don't know, Liam. Point, laugh, sod off down the pub? What do you reckon?"

"We can't just leave him there," Liam said. "I mean, he changed my life."

"You mean he weaned you off roller-skating," Rob said, witheringly.

"You called him a *parkour superhero* on Insta."

"Course he is, Liam. Spiderman climbs buildings, Superman flies up buildings and

Duncan sits on top of buildings whingeing about his age. Face it, if he's a superhero, his cape's faded."

I didn't care what they ruddy thought of me. I just wanted to go to bed, so I shouted, "Can't you call the Fire Brigade or Mountain Rescue or someone?"

Rob shook his head. "There's no way I'm going to watch you being winched down by the emergency services."

"I've got responsibilities," I pleaded. "Pets."

Liam looked like he was about to burst into ruddy great tears. "I modelled myself on you."

"Then you're a moron," I explained.

"You've let us down," Rob complained.

"Then get me down!" I demanded.

We moped about in silence for a bit before Rob asked, "How?"

"Call my mum," I said.

"Look, Duncan," Rob said with brittle patience. "You've broken into a power station, scaled a turbine tower and performed a record-breaking parkour combo. Do you really want us to call your mum?"

"Yes!" I didn't hesitate. "Please."

Rob took out his phone and made a show of checking the screen. "Would you look at that? No service."

I wasn't convinced. "Liam?"

Liam checked his phone. His face brightened briefly before Rob elbowed him in the ribs. "No service," he said, without looking me in the eye.

"Must be the altitude," Rob lied.

I never took my phone running. I used to think it slowed me down. Now, I'd come to a complete stop, and it was looking terminal. No one was going to rescue me, and I wasn't going to jump.

I turned away from my friends and explored the roof of my tower. It was basically a concrete patio surrounded by sheer drops. Its only feature was a poxy brick structure with a door-shaped hole. Given that I was marooned, I decided to investigate.

"Anything in there?" Rob shouted.

"Nowt," I replied as I stepped through the doorway. My foot trod on air. I fell forward into darkness, grabbed the doorframe, and dangled into oblivion. My life was in my hands - let go now and my thirties would total about five ruddy minutes. Fear weighed on my fingers, loosening my grip. I screamed out in fury at my lost retirement, using the rage to drag my body back from the brink, and I flopped onto the roof in a reverse bellyflop.

"Think he's all right?" I heard Liam ask.

"Champion," Rob replied, wearily.

Once I'd recovered myself, I clambered to my feet and wandered back towards my mates. They just stood there, gawping at me, a traitor to my former heroism.

I couldn't face looking at them for long, so I gazed into the middle distance at rows of streetlights, minor roads, and interchangeable houses. After a while, I found myself asking, "Is this all there is?"

"What, Middlesbrough?" Liam asked.

"No," I replied. "Life."

"Life's got nowt to offer us," Rob said. "That's why we're doing this."

"But life's all I've got," I said. "And I don't want it to stop. Not yet."

Rob turned away in disgust. "You've picked a great time for a ruddy mid-life crisis."

"It could be an end-life crisis," I said, the reality of my predicament having just struck me like a ruddy baseball bat. "I'm going to have to jump back, aren't I?"

They didn't have to answer.

Before I leapt, I decided to recall the final moments I had spent with my nearest and dearest. First off, there was my girlfriend. Earlier that evening, we had been having a row in the kitchen, and she was cooking with violence. She'd plonked a saucepan onto a hob and hacked her way into a tin.

"Listen, love," I'd explained. "I'm not seeing someone else; I'm just running up a building."

She'd emptied the tin's bright red contents into the saucepan and stormed out, shouting "Selfish wanker!" for good measure.

After she'd slammed the door, I'd heated up the tomato soup, poured it into a bowl and sat down on the sofa to eat it. I'd scooped up my first spoon when my phone buzzed on the coffee table. It was my mum. I'd said hello then swallowed the first spoonful. My face flushed, sweat poured from my pores, and it seemed possible that I might explode. I looked across at the empty tin, read the label and shouted, "Chilli? Bollocks!" into the phone. This was clearly my girlfriend's idea of vengeance – a soup-sauce switcheroo.

I plonked down the bowl, killed the call, and poured myself a glass of water. I drained it in one, filled it up again, and slumped back onto the sofa, just in time to see my dog lap up the sauce. He'll eat anything, him – vindaloo, tom yum soup, jerk chicken – no matter how hot. I reckon he must have a steel gob. Anyway, he loved the chilli sauce so much, he polished it all off, leapt onto my lap and licked me in gratitude, practically force his tongue into my mouth.

So, that was it, my girlfriend's final words to me were, "Selfish wanker!", my last words to my parents were, "Chilli? Bollocks!", and my last ever kiss was from a Golden Retriever.

I shouted at the Middlesbrough skies in despair. "It can't end like this!"

The skies didn't reply, and nor did my mates, so I just stood there like a plonker.

After a bit, I realised that I was dead hungry. "My stomach thinks my throat's been cut."

"Want us to nip down the chippie for you?" Rob asked, sarcastically.

Frankly, I wanted us all to nip down the chippie together. But I wanted to get there by bus, not by leaping across a van-sized chasm between two industrial chimneys.

Liam delved into his coat pocket and said, "I've got an old pie. It's a bit flat. I fell on it."

"Flat's fine, Liam," I said. "You're a lifesaver." Ageing pastry would make a better final meal than chilli sauce. Maybe the kid had something going for him after all.

Liam lobbed the pie. It was a decent chuck. He really put some welly into it, but it fell short. I watched the pastry's seventy-five metre descent with dismay. Even from this height, there was something moving about its final moments - a pie becoming an ex-pie - and it seemed likely that I would soon be following the pastry to oblivion. "Bit of a lonely death," I observed.

"You've got us," Liam said.

I looked across at the sorry pair. It wasn't a world-beating consolation, but I knew I'd probably be best off getting it over with and leaping back.

"Come on, Duncan," Rob said, "Leap! It's self-preservation."

"Or self-destruction," I replied, still not convinced.

"You used to love the feel of air beneath your feet," Rob said.

"I don't trust air anymore," I said. "I trust ground."

"Stop thinking about it," Rob said, "And just live in the moment."

"I'm not a ruddy goldfish." I was starting to panic. An inch or two out and I'd be bungee jumping without elastic.

"Want me to film it?" Liam asked. "You know, for safety?".

"In case the first leap didn't come out the way you expected?" I asked.

"As a fall-back." Liam held up his phone.

I muttered the kind of prayer people make up at penalty shoot-outs and took a run at the chasm. I got as far as the edge, teetered, and stepped back. "Nah. Can't do it."

"That's a relief," Liam said.

Rob looked furious. "Why?"

"I forgot to press record." Liam said.

It was hard to tell which one of us Rob was most angry with, but I'm pretty sure it was still me.

"Hang on!" Liam fumbled about in his trousers. "I've got a Curly Wurly!"

This was good news, but I tried not to get over-excited. "This time," I said, "Take a run up."

Liam turned his concentration up to eleven, backed up and sprinted across the roof of his tower, spin-bowling the Curly Wurly into the air. All eyeballs were on the confectionary's trajectory, like a cricket ball headed for the boundary.

I fielded it perfectly and punched the air. Liam whooped with delight. Rob shook his head in embarrassment. And I held the Curly Wurly like a priceless artefact from an Inca tomb.

"A condemned man is entitled to a last meal," I said.

"It's a ruddy Curly Wurly," Rob said.

"And some final words," I continued.

Liam raised his phone and remembered to press *Record*.

I'd not prepared anything to say, but the Curly Wurly inspired me. "Living life on the edge is fine. But if you look down, you might fall off, and I never wanted to die the dream."

While I munched the Curly Wurly, I noticed that Rob and Liam were making strange gestures. Nothing particularly insulting, but I was puzzled. Maybe my words were moving them emotionally, or perhaps they just wanted me to stop talking. If so, I wasn't ready to oblige – I still had plenty to get off my chest.

"I had a mid-life crisis in mid-air. It's not the best place to realise you're mortal." I savoured the next bite. "Now, all I want is a little more conversation and a little less action." I was mid-way through the bar. It was like a contorted chocolate hourglass measuring my remaining time on Earth. I took another munch. "I want to live slow, die old, but it doesn't look like I've got a choice." I was almost out of Curly Wurly, so

I prepared myself for a last jump. "Running up this power station was on my list of things to do before I reached thirty. I've got a different list now and there's only one thing on it: death – eternal solitary." I took my final bite.

By now, Rob was waving like a drowning man, and Liam had stopped filming and joined in. What a pair of plonkers! I was about to risk my life for the second time, and they couldn't even watch properly. I shrugged, shoulders up, palms up, a full-on display of bewilderment. They pointed furiously, prodding the air like finger-boxers.

Something was clearly up. I turned around. The brick structure's doorway was no longer the void I had stepped into. Instead, it contained a hefty security guard and an Alsatian, both perched on an elevator platform – you know, one of those "dumb waiter" contraptions. The guard was a local bloke, probably an ex-squaddie, and he looked more bored than angry as he said, "Go ahead, lad. We're not jumping after you."

I looked back across the gap at Rob and Liam. They were cheering me on, just like they had when I'd jumped the other way. This was it. In a few seconds, I could be free running back down to solid ground.

"You won't have any trouble getting away, lad," the guard said. "There's only my mate Derek at the bottom and he's got his face in a Wordle."

Ahead, lay freedom. With one jump, I could avoid arrest, regain most of my mates' respect and be home before sunrise. Behind, lay a night in a cold cell and a couple of months in prison. It was a no-brainer: the guard had a lift. We descended together and I struck up a nice rapport with his dog.

Rob and Liam don't speak to me much these days, but I don't think we'd have a lot in common. They're still risking their lives, whilst I'm busy living mine. I'd never realised just how much good stuff was on the telly. After all those nights running up buildings, I had so much to catch up on – the soaps, local news, women's football. Food is great too. Even dead cheap stuff, like crisps. I wish I'd taken the time to appreciate it all when I was in my twenties, but you can't teach young people anything, can you?"

**

The retired parkour star finished the last of his bitter and eyed my empty glass. "Get you another?"

Three Snakebites was enough for most men, but I really like Snakebite, so I took up my high-flying friend's offer. We stayed until closing time, discussing his new hobbies

- stamp collecting was probably the most dangerous.

Heroism is a tough act to maintain, and we agreed that if you wanted a long, comfortable life, you were probably better off watching other people do the interesting stuff. He would not have struck a stranger as anything special, but if you judge man by what he is, it's easy to miss what he once was.

RULE 6 - Eternity Goes On A Bit

I once met a man who told me he was Satan's little brother. It was during a lock-in at a Somerset cider house and we'd both been drinking for a shade under eight hours.

Gerald had a weathered look, a local accent, and a modest farm near Frome. It had been a tough day: a dawn encounter with a Tamworth porker had left him face-down in a piggery and his subsequent dealings with The Dark Lord had brought Gerald's long existence into question. He had always felt overshadowed by his brother, and he couldn't help thinking that eternity was passing him by.

In retrospect, Gerald explained over our twelfth pint, joining the rebellion against God had been a bit of a mistake. He had only been a junior angel at the time and his big brother had led him astray. God had been quite lenient, all things considered, and instead of casting Gerald into oblivion and tormenting him with eternal flames, he'd dumped him in what was later to become rural Somerset and told him to keep his head down, stay out of trouble and evolve inconspicuously.

Life as an amoeba had been relatively uncomplicated, but he'd have given his amphibious years a miss – he'd felt as soggy as a used teabag. Primate life had its plusses - body hair was a boon and feeling his spine straighten over the millennia had been intriguing, but he'd hated the forest politics - apes could be very bitchy. Homo sapiens had their good points, but he'd preferred the Neanderthals - much less pretentious. The Ice Age had been quite bracing and one of Gerald's best mates, Tim, a decent spear-thrower despite his squint, had got himself refrigerated in a nearby cave. These days, people called him *Cheddar Man* and queued to see him. It would probably have pleased Tim, who had always been a bit of an exhibitionist.

After the planet warmed up, Gerald spent thousands of years as a hunter-gatherer in Selwood Forest, which had been ruddy knackering, particularly after he'd done his back in building Stonehenge. The invention of agriculture had certainly helped - it hadn't been his idea and he'd been a little slow to cotton on, but it had kept him busy for a few millennia. Gerald couldn't claim that farming had been in his family for generations as there had only ever been one generation, albeit a very long one.

Frome was far from fertile. Would-be crops floundered on a vast, unhelpful bed of clay, so he'd moved into livestock. Cattle had always struck Gerald as a little on the slow side and sheep were, in his eyes, no more than woolly maggots, so pigs, cleverer than most dogs and older than humanity, held great allure.

Gerald knew pigs and he liked to think that pigs knew him. In fact, he had a lot in common with his Tamworths. They were one of the most ancient breeds on Earth and had changed very little over the past few thousand years. Also, like Gerald, they had long snouts, pointy ears and looked a bit flushed.

Even though Gerald was millions of years old, his apparent age averaged out at about fifty-five. It moved in long cycles, dipping slowly to around thirty-eight and rising back to seventy-two, before slowly retreating again. Each year of ageing took several human years, so it gave other people the general impression that he was almost as susceptible to Time as they were, but no one lived long enough to notice the cheating.

Technically speaking, Gerald was a serial monogamist: he'd always wait for his wives to die of old age before starting new relationships. His current spouse, Claire, was just under halfway through an average human lifespan, so, with any luck, he'd have several decades to go before he needed to start looking for another. He wasn't looking forward to this - Claire was a cracker.

Gerald had sired over six hundred and fifty children – surprisingly few for a man of his vintage. His latest, Stephen, was a handful and today had been his second birthday. It was that fateful event that had brought Gerald face-to-face with his diabolical big brother for the first time in over three hundred years.

After his dawn-decking by the pig, Gerald had breakfasted on one of its relatives, swapped his farm clothes for something equally unfashionable, and set off for the bright lights of Frome Town Centre. His tractor was past its peak, and it was pockmarked by numerous unplanned encounters with pheasants, badgers, and fallow deer. The licence plate had fallen off and Gerald had scrawled the registration number on the chassis in mud.

After driving past a field sprouting stuffed bin liners, rusting machinery, and balding tires, Gerald joined the lane separating the hamlets of Inner and Outer Wallop. An ancient feud divided the two communities and Gerald was the only man alive who could remember who had caused it, partly because everyone else was dead but mostly because it had been him.

The warring hamlets had two pubs. *The Fat Man* at Inner Wallop and *The Thin Man* at Outer Wallop, so they called each other *Fatties* and *Skinnies* respectively, if not respectfully. There wasn't much to choose between the pubs. Neither had changed since World War One and both refused to provide food under any circumstances. Each pub barred the residents of the other hamlet, and when they were drawn against each other in skittles tournaments, they would do battle at a neutral venue eighteen miles away. Both landlords were teetotallers called Brian who despised each other and hadn't spoken for over forty years.

For budgetary reasons, the two hamlets shared a village hall, which was partitioned down the middle and had separate entrances. Entirely segregated pensioner luncheons, bingo evenings and slide shows were held there, and the two rival Neighbourhood Watch Clubs watched each other with considerable suspicion.

People were called *incomers* if their families had been in their respective hamlet for under four hundred years and, even though the area was virtually denuded of youth, the handful of teenagers maintained the segregation. They would sit on separate benches, buy cannabis from different dealers, and shoplift from the other hamlet's newsagent. After dark, they would travel to Frome or Warminster to steal cars and joyride against each other, making the rural night sound like a low-budget Monaco Grand Prix.

There were no streetlights in either hamlet, so the night skies had a remarkable clarity never seen in towns. This was magnificent for passing astronomers, but it meant that the inhabitants of each Wallop were always falling into ditches, stepping in knee-high puddles, and treading in cowpats.

Each hamlet boasted matching eccentrics. Outer Wallop had a Mrs Cozpissle, who ran beekeeping classes, and a Mr Cozpissle, who restored steam-powered tractors. Inner Wallop had a Mr Twirleigh, who kept owls and a Mrs Twirleigh, who housed thirty-seven homing pigeons in the loft.

There were minor differences. The owner of Outer Wallop's post office, general store and off-licence chain-smoked, whereas the owner of Inner Wallop's post office, general store and off-licence always served his customers with an unlit fag dangling from his mouth after being forced to give up smoking on medical advice. A visiting doctor held his fortnightly Outer Wallop surgeries in *The Fat Man's* snug but held his Inner Wallop surgeries under *The Thin Man's* dart board. Only Inner Wallop had an osteopath, a gentle soul who had considerably boosted his patient list by establishing an equestrian club to encourage back injuries. Only Outer Wallop had a water diviner, whose encroaching incontinence was threatening to curtail his career.

It was the day of the annual Wallop-on-Wallop Games, a series of rustic sports contested by the warring hamlets. The event featured cowpat bingo, shin-kicking, welly-chucking, ferret roulette, and bog-snorkelling. Gerald used to take part, but the skills he had honed over the centuries meant he won every time, boring himself and frustrating the other competitors.

Time passes more swiftly as you get older and when you're almost as old as the Earth, that can be pretty zippy. Some of the duller centuries had passed like seasons, but the last couple had dragged a bit, what with their industrial revolutions, world wars, and TV talent shows. It hadn't all been downhill, though. As he turned off Friggle Street and onto the Frome Road, Gerald couldn't help noticing that the town's streets were in much better condition since the 1757 Turnpike Act.

Gerald chugged past the sites of several Iron Age forts and the turning for Frome Market. He had been visiting the market every Saturday and Wednesday since 1086 in search of a bargain and was still looking.

Frome was the biggest, oldest town in the locality and there was something about its idiosyncratic streets and historical insignificance that appealed to Gerald. He passed the box-church plonked there by the Methodists the other century. Gerald hadn't liked them one bit. They'd turned up from nowhere and whinged about his hobbies. There was nothing wrong with bull baiting, cock fighting, and cudgel playing: much healthier than Space Invaders and Angry Bird.

Gerald parked his tractor behind the square where several of Monmouth's Protestant rebels had been hung, drawn and quartered a few hundred years earlier for annoying James II. The parking spaces were a little small for agricultural vehicles, so he'd bought two tickets to be on the safe side. Gerald had been cautious ever since his horse got clamped in 1871.

Frome had once been mildly famous for its stale beer and innovative use of human urine in the textile trade. But, although the town had more listed buildings than almost any other town in Britain, history had pretty much passed it by. Gerald knew how it felt.

The town clung precariously to the slopes of two hills and the streets were so narrow, vehicles practically had to breathe in to pass through. Their names - Hunger Lane, Apple Alley, and Leg of Mutton Lane - were not all that much younger than Gerald, and their cobbles took their toll on his superannuated legs. Even for a multi-million-year-old man, he wasn't in ruddy good health. Ever since he'd dropped out of the clouds, Gerald had been tormented by a variety of minor ailments: piles, eczema, migraines, kidney stones, asthma, diabetes, arthritis, and flatulence. Sometimes, he almost envied his brother – Satan only had to worry about the heat.

But Gerald had no time to complain; he was a man on a mission. He walked up Anchor Barton, for centuries a stinking accumulation of dunghills, slaughterhouses, and tallow melting sheds. Now, it sported shops selling pipes, cheese, and tourism, and a pub offering pensioner roasts. Whenever the staff doubted Gerald was old enough to qualify, he'd regale them with detailed reminiscences of the Crimean War, and they'd relent after the third or fourth anecdote.

Gerald found the toy shop he'd been looking for and bought his son a dinosaur mobile. He had found actual dinosaurs a grumpy lot on the whole, but these were all made of plastic, so it would probably be all right.

His task accomplished, Gerald walked past the pub in which he had inadvertently started the Frome Riot of 1832 and hopped back on board his tractor.

Gerald decided to drive back through Selwood Forest. He couldn't talk to its avian inhabitants, but he could read them. If rooks fed near their nests, rain was on its way; if they fed further afield, it would be sunny. If a raven perched on your house, you'd be rich; if it circled without landing, Death was on his way. But right now, a birthday was on the agenda, so Gerald stepped on the accelerator and took his tractor up to its maximum speed, twelve miles per hour.

Claire and Stephen were waiting for his return, and as soon as Gerald stepped off his tractor, Stephen ran up to Gerald, shouting "Upside down, daddy!" Gerald happily obliged and, while his inverted son dangled and giggled, he wondered what it must be like to be so impossibly young, to have a life spanning two years rather than a number adjacent to infinity.

But Claire brought his wool-gatherings to a close with the ominous words, "I think you'd better have a look at the back field."

"What's wrong, my love? Have them drains burst again?"

Her expression said it was more than a plumbing issue.

Gerald span Stephen upright and carried him round the back of the farmhouse on his shoulders.

"Daddy, look!" Stephen pointed across the field.

Gerald had seen crop circles before, but never on his own land, and where he was concerned, *never* was a very long time indeed. Gerald carried Stephen over to the mystery pattern and took a closer look. It was a fractal formation with a standing centre and a series of intricate grapeshot rings around its perimeter. The lay of the crop was also unusual, running from one side to the other, not spiralling like most other formations. The indentations were springy to the step, suggesting it was all freshly laid. Gerald had to admire the handiwork: everything was crafted with mathematical precision, every stalk was in place, there were no visible construction lines and the ground lay was superb.

A high-pitched "Dad!" snapped Gerald back to reality. He had got so wrapped up in the design's fiendish detail, he'd almost dropped his toddler.

Gerald steadied Stephen and gave the crop circle a final appraisal. To the uninitiated, it was an abstract pattern, but to Gerald, it was a message in a language popular before the Ice Age. It read: *Wotcha Lardy! Get in touch, Big Bruv x.*

Gerald groaned. He was going to have to summon Satan. It was a right pain in the rectum. He would have to dance naked in the woods, and Gerald had always been a touch sensitive about his weight and his dancing skills.

Once he had deposited his son with Claire, Gerald changed into a knee-length tunic and white hooded cloak. Gerald had never had time for druids, with their fashion crimes and drug abuse. But if he was going to get in touch with his big brother, he would have to go through the motions. Walking barefoot across Black Dog Hill in his pagan get-up, he felt a little foolish, but feelings can be deceptive - he looked extremely foolish.

Gerald couldn't help noticing that the ley lines were particularly pronounced that morning. Their orange glow stretched out across the landscape, and he could hear their buzz louder than a dawn chorus. Electricity pylons and mobile phone masts were mildly annoying, but they didn't make a tenth as much racket as these infernal ley lines, inaudible and invisible to all mortals but shriller than sirens to Gerald.

He found a secluded carpet of bramble with a thick oak canopy and began chanting a Latin incantation. He didn't know why Satan always insisted on Latin. Perhaps it was because he knew Gerald was the last remaining person to have spoken the language to

Ancient Romans. Even so, chanting Latin made it near-impossible for him to keep in step whilst he performed the requisite ritual jigging.

After stripping naked, waggling his beer belly, and gyrating his arthritic hips for far longer than seemed feasible, smoke billowed and a weedy voice remarked, "Fab-u-lous!" It was Beelzebub, the fussy little twerp. Satan hadn't even bothered to turn up in person.

"Oh, Christ," Gerald moaned.

Beelzebub winced. "Don't mention him."

"Then go easy on my dancing."

"I deeply respect your dancing."

"Thanks."

"It's like watching a walrus fitting."

"Watch it."

"Satan sends his apologies. He's a little tied up right now, but he'd appreciate it if you could you meet up for some nibbles."

"Nibbles? What's wrong with a quick pint at *The Fat Man*?"

"This is Satan we're talking about." Beelzebub had a point. He went on to explain that Satan had booked a table at the poshest restaurant in the area and had done so in Gerald's name so as not to alarm the waiting staff. Gerald always thought his brother a right prissy ponce and this was par for the course. Why Satan would spurn scrumpy and pies in favour of wine and morsels Gerald never could divine.

"I don't think he's decided precisely how he'll be manifesting himself yet," Beelzebub continued. "But the staff are awfully good and I'm sure everything will go swimmingly."

"What's it all about, Beelzebub? Did he tell you?"

"I wouldn't presume to understand your brother, but, if you ask me, he's feeling a bit broody."

"Broody?"

"You know, kids."

At that, an entrance to the underworld swallowed up Beelzebub and Gerald was once again alone with the trees, his belly, and his bare arse.

Gerald trudged home in his druid clobber, flung on his smartest clothes (a battered Barbour, worn cords, and an old cardigan) and took his tractor off down the Vobster Road. He wondered what Satan would turn up looking like this time. He tended not to visit Earth as a fallen angel, as people often found the broken wings off-putting, so he could be dining with anyone from a traffic warden to a bare-knuckle boxer.

The restaurant was as poncy as Gerald had feared. The building was Georgian, which felt almost contemporary to a man of his vintage, but it was decorated in expensively "rustic" style. In general, Gerald knew where he was with rustic. You didn't get much more rustic than him. He'd been living in Somerset for millions of years, after all.

The waiter led Gerald to an expansive, comfortable room with a real fire, a hand-knotted rug and a stone-flagged floor. It was the sort of place enjoyed by precisely no peasants whatsoever in rustic history, and the other diners all looked decidedly urban to him.

Before Gerald had a chance to decipher the menu, an elegant young woman approached the table and asked, "Can I tempt you with anything?"

"Do they do pie?" Gerald enquired.

The young woman laughed alluringly and sat down opposite him. Satan was a twisted git. For the first time in Gerald's eternal life, he'd got a posh dining date with a glamorous young woman, and it was his big sodding brother.

Satan gave him a seductive smile and asked, "How are the pigs?"

"Fine," Gerald replied. "How are everlasting fire, darkness, and ignominy?"

"Mustn't grumble."

"Beelzebub is still a twat."

"I know. I only sent him to give Hell a bit of a break."

The waiter came to take their order. This was bound to be tricky. It wasn't so much that Gerald was flummoxed by the menu's sophistication, it was more that Satan and the truth didn't really get on. As a fellow immortal, Satan could speak candidly to Gerald, but he was only ever able to lie to standard-issue humans. His compulsion to fib helped him stock up his stack of souls, but it hindered lunch. Satan could only answer the question, "What would you like, madam?" by ordering dishes his manifestation didn't like, meaning that there was a high risk of beetroot-and-turnip vol-au-vents all round.

Gerald wasn't governed by the same obligation to lie, so he silenced Satan and ordered the most expensive items on the menu: a half-cracked lobster, a char-grilled swordfish Niçoise and a bottle of Christal Roederer Champagne. When dining with the devil, you might as well push the boat out.

Once the waiter had retreated with the requisite obsequiousness, Gerald turned back to Satan. God, she was looking beautiful. "Any good sinners recently?"

"Nothing original." Satan fluttered her eyelashes. "It's soul destroying."

Gerald and Satan discussed eternity for what seemed like ages.

When the food eventually arrived, Satan scoffed everything in sight whilst making porcine noises that would have put a Tamworth runt to shame. There was laughter and pointing for a bit, then the fellow diners and waiting staff froze. Not in revulsion: they just froze.

Satan's eyes burned, literally, and her voice dropped numerous octaves. "Thank you for keeping our appointment, little bro."

"No probs."

"Sorry about the manners, but as they say, "When in Frome, do as the Fromans"."

"That's not how you pronounce Frome. It has a hidden o, like room."

"But that wouldn't rhyme," Satan protested. "And there's no such thing as a *Rooman*."

"Not that I recall, no." Gerald remembered the Romans well. They were a pernickety bunch, and wouldn't have taken kindly to a stray o.

"Tell me, Gerald, have you ever counted your children?"

"If I did, it wouldn't take me long. Right now, I've just got the one. It's his birthday."

"I know. I've bought young Stephen a present. What I meant was, have you ever counted the total number of children that have sprung from your loins, if I can use an unpleasantly biblical word?"

"About six hundred or so."

"Six-hundred and sixty-six, to be precise."

Gerald's lobster fell from his lips. He'd read Revelations when it first came out and Satan didn't have to remind him of the number's significance.

"Look, Satan," Gerald said. "Just because Stephen happens to be my six hundred and sixty-sixth child does not give you the right to poke your cloven hooves into his life."

Satan kicked Gerald with her stilettos.

"There's no need to be like that," Gerald said. "I'm just speaking my mind."

"But is your mind worth hearing?" Satan enquired.

If Gerald had one principle in life it was that he always spoke his mind, so he repeated the statement, rather unimaginatively: "I always speak my mind."

"How very tactless of you." Satan sipped her champagne and sneered.

Gerald knew better than to get angry with his brother. It was what he wanted.

"Stephen is two years old tomorrow," Satan said, "And he is your six hundred and sixty-sixth child, so I'm afraid, old chap, I've come to claim him."

"Bugger off. You can be his godfather, but that's your lot."

"Godfather? Not a role to which I'm ideally suited, given that I rebelled against God and became his everlasting opponent."

"Uncle then."

"Not good enough. Running Hell is getting tiresome. I want to hand it over to someone new one day - someone young with enthusiasm and ideas. It could be a great opportunity for Stephen."

At this, Satan handed him Stephen's birthday present. The wrapping paper was patterned with snakes and apples.

"Thanks," Gerald gently shook the gift. It jangled. "What is it?"

"The keys to Hell."

"He's two."

"It could be his home."

"Much appreciated, but there's no chance," Gerald said. "He is my son. I love him."

"I'll play you at poker for him," Satan suggested with a devilish look.

"You've beaten me over eight million, four hundred thousand times."

"Fiddle?"

"Six million, nine hundred thousand and seven – nil."

"So, you don't fancy your chances then?"

"Go to Hell."

"Not yet," Satan said. "And when I do, I'll take Stephen with me."

"No, you won't," Gerald said will all the determination of a multi-million-year-old man, "I've thought of something."

"Golf?"

"The Wallop-on-Wallop Games."

"You're on."

Champagne, lobster, and swordfish were not on many pre-match menus, but this was the first ever metaphysical battle to be conducted at the Wallop-on-Wallop Games, and both immortal brothers were buzzing.

The contest had to be waged on physically equivalent terms, so Satan dodged into the Ladies and re-emerged magically from the Gents as an ageing farmer of Gerald's ilk. They could almost have been identical twins had Satan not made himself slimmer and slightly better looking.

The tractor ride was fraught, as Satan ruthlessly mocked Gerald's meek adherence to the Highway Code. Gerald pointed out that it was rule-breaking that had seen them dumped in Somerset and Hell, prompting Satan to call him a "girly swot".

The Games committee were happy to accept late entries, due to the dearth of early entries. The six other participants were all in their late teens and early twenties, but Gerald didn't fancy their chances. They may have had youth on their side, but you'd be hard pushed to find a more experienced or cunning pair than the immortal siblings.

Gerald was made an honorary Fatty due to his weight, and Satan was made a Skinny to balance the numbers.

The crowd was segregated on hamlet grounds. Brian, landlord of *The Fat Man* at Inner Wallop, led the Fatty contingent, comprising the owl whisperer, the pigeon fancier, the non-smoking shopkeeper, and the incontinent water diviner. Brian, landlord of *The Thin Man* at Outer Wallop led the Skinny contingent, comprising the beekeeper, the tractor lover, the osteopath, and the chain-smoking shopkeeper. But to Gerald, the inter-Wallop rivalry was irrelevant; the battle for his six hundred and sixty-sixth son was an individual contest. Whether they bagged the medal positions or brought up the rear, the highest-placed brother would win custody of Stephen, and that was all that mattered.

The opening ceremony featured a Morris dance and a folk song about incest, then the first event was unveiled: a gentle round of cowpat bingo. A field was squared into sixty-four and participants placed personalized draughts on a corresponding board. Whoever correctly predicted the deposition of the heifer's dung would emerge triumphant. It was a game of bovine-bowel chequers, and the atmosphere was intense, even if the action wasn't.

Gerald thought of Stephen's first smile, his first words, his first steps, and tried to will the cow into dropping its load on one of his squares. But the animal appeared constipated.

Inter-Wallop excitement built to fever pitch as the cow hovered over a square owned by a young Skinny, but the beast just stopped to moo. This was shaping up to be an endurance event for the audience: pulses raced, hearts pounded, and the pigeon fancier was close to fainting. For Gerald, it was torture, and when the cow's rectum hovered above the epicentre of one of Satan's squares, he could have wept. But to his relief, the beast just mooed, paused for dramatic effect, and mooed once again. Satan mooed back. It wasn't much of a moo, particularly for the immortal personification of Evil, but it caught the cow's attention. The animal's head turned towards the Dark Lord, and Gerald realised just too late what his brother was playing at. Satan's eyes flared with flame and the cow emptied its bowels in terror. It wasn't just a cowpat; it was a cow mountain. Satan gave the air an upper cut. The Skinnies went wild. It was one-nil to Evil Incarnate.

Luckily, the next event was one of Gerald's favourites. If there was one thing he was good at, it was shin-kicking. His technique was like a violent river-dance, and he had all the rhythm of a seasoned Kilkenny prancer. Once he'd booted three Skinny opponents off their balance he stood shin-to-shin with Satan. It was as epic as Foreman-Ali, but without the fisting: perhaps Arsenal-Spurs would be a better comparison.

Satan mirrored Gerald's moves with uncanny accuracy. That was the thing about him: he did very good uncanny.

The mirroring accelerated, rival legs okey-cokey-ing like pistons on a speeding steam train. Spectators from the warring Wallops were hypnotized by the immortal shin jiggery, which could have gone on until the end of Time, had Gerald not brought his river-prancing to an abrupt halt. Almost instantaneously, Satan did the same. This offered Gerald the chance to throw a punch. Satan dodged it, as Gerald knew he would, but the distraction allowed Gerald to boot Satan's legs away from under him and The Dark Lord landed on his arse.

The Skinnies booed, and their beekeeper protested that punching wasn't allowed. Gerald was fully aware of that, but the punch hadn't connected so it didn't count. Satan 1 – Gerald 1.

Welly-chucking was not a classic field sport: take the precision of the javelin, the elegance of the discus and the rotational technique of shot-put and bin the lot of them. It was all about heft and heft was Gerald's middle name. He employed the centrifugal force of his gut to dispense with the best Skinny tossers, then went welly-to-welly with Satan.

The Dark Lord's svelte incarnation lacked Gerald's girth, but his elevated wellies remained airborne for far longer than seemed natural. They were like rubber gliders coasting on thermals. Gerald could see that Satan was muttering an infernal incantation, but he knew he could never persuade the judges that the wellies were possessed. Satan 2 – Gerald 1.

Gerald was worried about round four: ferret roulette. The pocket scores - nought to thirty-six - added up to 666, which was Satan's kind of number. The Wallopers arranged thirty-six drainpipes across the grass like spokes on a horizontal wheel and placed a traffic cone at the hub. The cone contained a ferret, and its choice of drainpipe would determine the winner.

The eight contestants chose four pipes each, with the remaining four pipes reverting to the House. Gerald had honed his ferret-fancying skills over the course of many millennia and opted for pipes that were almost as weathered and pungent as he was. Satan favoured the most straight and true ones, which surprised Gerald, as it seemed completely out of character.

The spectators went silent as the traffic cone was removed and the ferret contemplated its fateful decision. Gerald could barely believe that Stephen's future rested on a polecat and a drainpipe, but God moved in mysterious ways - and so did Satan. The Dark Lord crouched at the aperture of one of his four pipes and, moments later, the ferret disappeared down it. Gerald's heart sank. If the ferret emerged, it would be 3-1: an unassailable satanic lead.

Satan was making ferreting noises, rubbing his hands together and beckoning the animal. A furry nose appeared, but that wasn't enough: Satan needed the full head. The Dark Lord crouched down to greet it, and the nose disappeared. Gerald could barely believe it. This was the greatest reverse-ferret in history. Satan's stare was perfect for inducing cowpats, but hopeless at enticing ferrets.

As it re-emerged at the hub, all eyes fell on the ferret. Gerald felt like a defendant awaiting the jury's verdict, and this was made infinitely worse by the certain knowledge that the sentence would fall on his son.

The ferret sniffed the air, lowered its tail, and bolted down Gerald's smelliest drainpipe. He didn't make Satan's mistake and kept well clear. The ferret de-piped fully at his feet and relieved itself on his trousers. Result! Gerald 2 – Satan 2.

There could only be one suitable climax to such an Olympian contest: bog-snorkelling. The tiny crowds were going wild.

Come on You Fatties!

Come on You Skinnies!

Who Are Ya! Who Are Ya!

Fat! Fat! Fat!

Thin! Thin! Thin!

The water diviner was practically wetting himself. The beekeeper was buzzing. The osteopath leapt up and did his back in.

Each Wallop nominated an immortal brother as their champion. Satan donned his snorkel and flippers. Gerald donned his snorkel and flippers. They both looked ludicrous. Neither cared. This was war.

The organisers had pre-dug a fifty-five-metre trench through their rankest peat bog and filled it with muddy water from the nearest duck pond. The quickest contestant over two circuits would be declared the winner. Rarely had so much ridden on a bog snorkel.

Gerald won the toss, which surprised him – he had expected Satan to interfere with the tosser. A whistle blew, a timer started, and Gerald dived into the bog. It was a dank, cold soul-destroying battle through murk. Conventional swimming was forbidden, so it was all in the flippers. Gerald employed a technique he had honed during his amphibian years. Satan had never had that opportunity; he had been busy burning in Hell.

At one minute, fifty-three seconds, Gerald's time was a personal best, but as he flopped out, he felt anything but exultant. His son's fate now lay in Satan's legs.

Gerald looked on as The Dark Lord plummeted into the bog. The flippers of The Beast were visible, but the rest of him was submerged, and the water was so impenetrable, he could have been deploying any kind of sub-aquatic tactic unobserved. Whatever he was up to, Satan was bombing along like Moby Dick in Speedos.

The Dark Lord emerged. Gerald held his breath. The judge announced the time: one minute, forty-eight seconds. The Skinnies went bananas. All was lost. Little Stephen would spend eternity in Hell.

Gerald threw his hands up to Heaven. There was no thunderbolt, but there was a complaint. *The Fat Man*'s Brian bellowed "That Skinny boy's a rascal. He was swimming!"

It was a serious allegation. Bog-snorkelling was all in the flippers. Swimming was verboten. The judge summoned Gerald and Satan. All eyes were on the secretly immortal adversaries.

The judge began by turning to Gerald, and asking, "On your honour as a Walloper, did you use anything other than your flippers?"

"No, that I did not."

The judge turned to Satan. "I'll ask the same of you. Answer on your honour as a Walloper, did you use anything other than your flippers?"

"No," Satan replied.

"So, there we have it," the judge said, "A fair result."

Gerald couldn't hold back. "He'll lie about anything."

"I will not," Satan lied.

The judge told Gerald that he had made a grave accusation and would have to prove it.

"Very well," Gerald said, "I will. Anyone got pen and paper?"

The chain-smoking shopkeeper ambled over handed him a notepad and biro. "I may be a Skinny," he said, "But let's make sure this is all dealt with fair and square. I don't want anyone querying my right to crow."

Gerald wrote a series of questions and gave it back to the chain-smoking shopkeeper. Once he had taken a long draw on his umpteenth cigarette of the day, he said, "Fair enough. Question one. Is the Pope a Catholic?"

As the shopkeeper was a human, Satan had no choice but to reply, "No."

"The shopkeeper gave him an old-fashioned look. I think you'll find he is. Question two. Do bears shit in the woods?"

"No," Satan had to reply.

The shopkeeper raised an eyebrow. "I think you'll find that they do. Question three. Are you a monkey's uncle?"

"Yes," Satan lied.

The crowd gasped. A flicker of hope hovered.

"Three lies out of three," Gerald said.

The judge turned to Satan and asked, "Are you a compulsive liar?"

"No," Satan replied.

"Well, he would say that, wouldn't he?" Gerald protested.

Things seemed to have reached an impasse, so Gerald said, "Right you are then, more questions."

After he had filled another page, he handed the next set of questions to Mr Twirleigh the owl-whisperer, who perused the list and said simply, "Golly."

"He's biased!" the Skinnies protested. "He's a Fatty!"

"It's all about the answers," Gerald said. "Not who reads the questions."

"Is this really necessary?" Satan protested.

"Yes," Gerald replied. "You've already lied three times," Gerald said. "That's got to be grounds for doubt."

"Very well," the judge said. "Go ahead."

The owl whisperer cleared his throat and asked Satan Gerald's list of questions:

"Is Donald Trump a Las Vegas go-go girl with more nipples than teeth?"

"Yes."

"Was Adolf Hitler a lesbian?"

"Yes."

"Did Kim Kardashian invent quantum mechanics?"

"Yes."

"Is Dwayne *The Rock* Johnson a weakling who would rather hide in a Wendy house than have a fight?"

"Yes."

"Is Elon Musk on benefits?"

"Yes."

"Are Frome Town Under Elevens a better football team than Barcelona?"

"Yes."

The judge blew his whistle and announced The Dark Lord's disqualification. Gerald had defeated humanity's nemesis 3-2.

After Satan had taken Gerald aside, given him a grudging handshake, and dematerialised in a grump, Gerald headed home to his wife and six hundred-and-sixty-sixth son. He watched little Stephen play with his presents, tucked him up and told him a bedtime story from the Bronze Age. Never had immortal man been happier, until he had a set-to with Claire about the dollops of peat bog he had trodden all over the shagpile. He'd tried explaining what had happened, but she hadn't believe him for a moment, and he'd decided to sod off down the pub.

***

Gerald's everyday tale of bog-snorkelling, cowpat bingo and Satan had climaxed, and we spent another merry hour or two sinking even more scrumpy. I didn't have any anecdotes of matching metaphysical magnitude, so we stuck to football and women.

Time is definitely a thing. I have no idea what it looks like, but its effects are rarely pretty. Gerald had more of it than he knew what to do with, and many of us don't have nearly enough. But whether it's long and wasted, or short and wisely spent, Time still happens.

And as for siblings, don't get me going. "Brother", "Bro" and Bruv" may pass for friendly greetings, but sometimes these can be the gravest insults known to the Brotherhood of Man. Just because you shared a mother or rebelled against the same god doesn't make you mates. For every happy Wright or Marx brother, there's a Cain and Abel. Blood's thicker than water and I'm thicker than most, but if you ask me, fraternal love is best left to the freemasons.

RULE 7 - TIME TRAVEL BROADENS THE MIND

I had been in one of Amsterdam's oldest cannabis cafés for a little under four hours when I got talking to a time-traveller.

"I'm from eighteen minutes time," the man explained through a cloud of Laughing Buddha smoke.

"Is the technology incredibly advanced?"

"A bit."

I checked my watch: it was three minutes past six. He was claiming to be from six twenty-one. It was not a particularly impressive claim, but I was intrigued.

Gentle questioning revealed that he was a Dutch postman named Ruud Moos. He spent his mornings lugging snail mail around the soggy flatlands of Edam, rimming its dykes on his cherry-red bicycle, and emptying his sack at assorted windmills and cheese farms. He was a practical sort of bloke and he liked to relax after his rounds by fiddling about with old motorbike engines, vintage televisions and odds-and-ends from car boot sales. One day, he was tinkering with a first-generation mobile phone he had bought from a gypsy and discovered that he had accidentally turned his shed into a time machine.

I couldn't understand why he looked so miserable about it. Wasn't this an opportunity to witness the most glorious moments in history: the heights of Ancient Greek civilisation, the wonders of the Renaissance, the scientific breakthroughs of the Enlightenment? Surely, he could observe legendary acts of heroism, feast his eyes on immortal beauties and gain inspiration from stirring displays of character in adversity.

He could even solve the mysteries of the Ages – the construction of Stonehenge, the secrets of the pyramids, the assassination of Kennedy. And what about the future? Where would Artificial Intelligence take us all? How about inter-planetary travel? Nanotechnology? My excitement vied with my envy until I felt so conflicted, I was forced to roll another spliff.

Once I'd lit up a Lemon Haze doobie, Moos explained his predicament in a tone of utter dejection: "Every so often there is a Chosen Bloke and this generation, it's me. I'm destined to travel pathetically short distances in Time at inconvenient moments, crossing the space-time continuum in a quantum shed, powered by 1980s technology. I am the last of the Time Peasants. I am – The Lowlander."

Moos paused to pick something out of his hair. It appeared to be a small eel. I tried not to dwell on it, as I had a far greater interest in time travel than seafood.

"I mean well," Moos lamented. "But I stumble through Time, committing causality violations, creating predestination paradoxes, and triggering catastrophic butterfly effects. I helped a pensioner avoid a car clamp and that led the planet to the brink of World War Three. I prevented a football injury and that unleashed a plague of locusts across the Western Hemisphere. I resolved a teenage lovers' tiff and that reversed Evolution. I may be The Chosen Bloke, but I often wish they'd chosen somebody else."

I didn't want to cast doubt on any of this, but I do take an interest in current affairs and there hadn't been any locust plagues, global wars, or evolutionary reversals, as far as I was aware. When I politely pointed this out, Ruud explained that he had managed to avert these disasters before anyone had noticed.

"When did you first realise?" I asked.

"That I was The Chosen Bloke?" Ruud asked.

"Yes," I replied.

"It all happened in my shed. I'd owned it for maybe twenty years before I realised its time-travelling potential. Everything changed when I put this on my workbench." He reached into his postbag and showed me a breezeblock-sized mobile with massive keys and a tiny screen. I hadn't seen a phone that clunky in over thirty years. It was more like an item of furniture or a primitive weapon. "It might not have Bluetooth," Ruud continued. "But it's got built-in time-travel capability, the SIM card is made of Dark Matter and the battery is powered by an invisible web of cosmic strings."

I congratulated him on a seriously impressive piece of kit and asked him to talk me through what had happened.

"It was a Tuesday in early autumn," Ruud said. "I'd had a smoke and a pancake, then watched a documentary about Dutch mountains."

"Aren't the Netherlands flat?" I asked.

"It was a very short documentary," Ruud replied.

I was already finding his account unconvincing, and he hadn't even reached the time travel bit, but I didn't want to be unfriendly, so I said, "Do go on."

"I left my wife watching a soap and headed for the shed. It's crammed with vintage televisions, pre-war wirelesses, and early video recorders. I plonked the old mobile on a workbench and pressed a couple of buttons. The shed lurched and strange footage played backwards on the screens of my vintage televisions: mobility scooters reversed, burnt toast reverted to cold bread, plastic cuckoos withdrew into their clock-flaps.

I needed a dose of reality, so I opened the shed door and was about to step out when I realised that the shed was no longer in my garden, but in the infinite paisley wastelands of the space-time continuum. I turned back and slammed the door behind me."

I took a drag on my spliff. "The space-time continuum is paisley?"

"Surprised me too," Ruud said. "I'd expected something more …"

"Inter-galactic?"

"Exactly. This was more like …"

"A charity shop shirt?"

"But infinite." Ruud blew smoke out of his nostrils. "Where was I?"

"The infinite paisley wastelands of the space-time continuum."

"Of course," Ruud continued. "So, not long after I'd shut the shed door, my ancient gypsy mobile began to bleep. There was a message: *Contact Your Service Provider*. I pressed hash to see if anything would happen and a Call Centre Worker materialised beside me."

"A call centre worker?"

Ruud nodded.

"Literally materialised beside you?"

"In a sari."

As scenarios went, it wasn't the most convincing, but I hadn't come to a Dutch cannabis café for realism. "So, this call centre worker, what did she do?"

"Nothing," Ruud replied. "She just told me that she was my service provider."

"Your service provider?"

"Yes. Want to know what happened?"

I sensed that Ruud was tiring of my interruptions, so I decided to shut up for a bit and focus on smoking my spliff.

"So," Ruud began, "I'm in my shed, somewhere in the infinite paisley wastelands of the space-time continuum, and this woman has just shown up claiming to be my service provider, and I don't really know where to start, so I just ask her, "Travelled far?"

"Our HQ is in Mumbai," she replied. "But we've all been outsourced to the space-time continuum. Part of a cost-cutting exercise. Universalization, eh?"

"Not globalization?"

"If only it was."

"This is no ordinary shed, is it?"

"It's a faster-than-light flatpack."

"Wish I'd kept the receipt."

"It's not our fault that Edam's full of holes."

"That's Emmental."

"Wormholes. Edam's full of wormholes."

"Doesn't sound very hygienic."

"Hygiene's not the problem. It's the time-fidgets."

"What's a time-fidget?"

"A micro-jump to the Near-Future or the Just-Gone. Inconvenient if you're The Chosen Bloke."

"The chosen what?"

"The Chosen Bloke. It's you. Get used to it."

"What idiot chose me?"

"It's like cosmic jury service. Your name just came up."

"Look, I'm not from Sunnydale or Gallifrey, I'm from Edam. I can't slay demons or confuse Cybermen, I just deliver the post."

"Perfect. We don't need an Einstein we just need a Gump - someone who'll keep things simple and not try to change anything important."

She bunged me a weighty manual. The cover read, *The Panicker's Guide to Time-Hitches*. The space-time continuum is rather draughty, so I used it as a door-wedge.

She threw her arms up in despair. "Aren't you going to read it?"

"Can't you just give me the basics?"

"The basics are quite advanced."

"Well, I'm not."

"Okay, I'll get seriously remedial - the shed is for space travel."

"I can travel in space?"

"You can just about cross the North Sea."

"So not exactly Star Wars then. How about Time?"

"The Time bit is down to you. Sometimes, it's a random three-minute fidget, a surprise opportunity to re-boil a kettle. Other times, you can take a slightly longer trip and control it with your mobile."

"This antique?"

"It's an inter-dimensional space-brick."

"Couldn't be simpler."

"Nor could you."

"Thanks. What if I meet myself?"

"Just strike up a conversation. You'll get along fine."

"What if something goes wrong?"

"There's a Help Desk, but I wouldn't bother. They keep everyone on hold until they give up."

"Is there an app?"

"Your phone doesn't even do text messages."

She fiddled with my televisions, linking them up to an obsolete computer I'd bought at another gypsy funfair.

When I asked her what she was doing, she explained that she was building a chronological observatory. This would allow us to observe Time in the same way as an astronomer observes Space.

When she had stopped fiddling, there was a loud ping, and the computer's monitor filled with a map. Laser lines pulsed between the world's major cities.

"You're familiar with lines of Longitude and Latitude?" she enquired.

"I've done a bit of canoeing."

"Well, these are Lines of Attitude, supremely accurate pulses of Bohemian energy emitted by the world's most effete places: Paris's Left Bank, Tokyo's Fashion District, and – most reliable of all – Manhattan's Greenwich Village: it's got a seriously regular throb."

"Very rhythmic."

"I've got a precise fix on the Village's most Bohemian coordinates - a gay mime collective, a conceptual sculpture workshop and a nude poetry jam. This gives us Greenwich Village Mean Time – makes clockwork look irregular."

We worked together for ages, travelling a few minutes forward, a few back, always precisely measured by her Lines of Attitude and Bohemian Energy. It gave my life a completely new dimension. The trouble was, every time we would stream ourselves down one of Edam's faster-than-light wormholes, I'd get progressively more serious time travel sickness. Eventually, I had to stop, so I streamed myself back to when I had started, headed indoors, and watched the rest of the soap with my wife.

I looked at Ruud through my spliff smoke. How bored must a postman be to invent such a tissue of bollocks?

Then it happened. The front wall of the cannabis café collapsed, and a van swerved in. Its doors flew open, and its cargo of seafood flew across the room, showering us all.

As I picked eels out of my hair, I checked my watch: we'd been talking for exactly eighteen minutes.

In a sense, we are all time travellers, only most of it do it forwards in a straight line. The Lowlander was different, a zigzag merchant with a shed, an outdated phone, and issues.

I can't say I envied him. It wasn't as if I had any shortage of poor decisions to go back and correct, marriages to unbreak, crimes to uncommit, bottles to undrink, bets to unplace, or drugs to untake. But frankly, that does feel like a lot of work. My life is a linear catastrophe, and I wouldn't have it any other way.

RULE 8 - Wait Until You're Dead To Get Found Out

I once met a bloke who had seen Bigfoot. He was a down-to-Earth mountaineering type of around fifty, and I had no reason to doubt him.

I was lost in America. My fourth wife was wealthy and wanted to get divorced in Las Vegas. After an Elvis-themed separation ceremony, I had stolen her Cadillac and gone looking for aliens in Nevada. It seemed the kind of trip best enjoyed stoned, so I had bought some skunk off a Hell's Angel. It was excellent stuff, so powerful in fact that I had missed the turning for Area 51 and ended up in Washington State's Snohomish County. No, I had never heard of it either.

I had stopped off at a diner and got talking to the guy in question. His name was Tom, and his story began almost thirty years earlier in his hometown. The place was tiny, remote, and surrounded by dense forest and misty mountains. It had a fraternity lodge, a grappling hook emporium, a timber yard, a church, and a Sasquatch-themed bar owned by Tom's father, Jake, a former baseball pro.

Jake was a handsome, roguish charmer, as barrel chested as Tom was whip thin. They were the same height and could have been the same person a quarter of a century apart. The men were as close as father and son could be, and when Tom turned twenty-one, Jake threw him a yard party.

Most of the town showed up and Jake was bossing the barbeque. He asked Jake what he wanted, and Jake replied, "A Sasquatch sausage."

"With hair or without?" Jake asked.

They had repeated this exchange at every family barbeque for the past decade, and

Tom wondered whether they would keep it going for the next one. For as long as Tom could remember, Jake had been hunting Bigfoot. He would go off into the forest, follow tracks, lurk in his hide, and return many hours later – sometimes the next morning. When Tom was small, he had begged Jake to take him along, but he would just fob him off with wild stories about foul-smelling, fifteen-foot-high ape-men who liked to screech, yodel, and throw conkers. As Jake grew older, scepticism had set in, then embarrassment, and finally amusement. It was just one of those things that made his dad his dad.

Tom took his hot dog and mixed with the crowd. His dad's friends – the local cop, the pastor, a couple of loggers, and the grappling hook guy – all wished him luck on his big new ranger job at Seattle's Mount Rainier National Park and made familiar Sasquatch jokes.

Most of Tom's own friends had made it along to what was, for them, a bitter-sweet occasion, being both a birthday and a moment marking Tom's imminent move away from their shared nights of *Doom*, rooftop beers, and pointless dares. Tom's girlfriend was busy, but she'd promised to make it up to him later.

Tom heard his name called. It was his mother, Lauren, and she was gesturing frantically in the direction of his eight-year-old sister, Kitty. Kitty and her little friends were playing a tag game dangerously close to the shed where Jake stored his Sasquatch-hunting equipment. No one was allowed near it, so Tom scared the kids off with one of his trademark Bigfoot impersonations and they ran off squealing in terrified delight.

Jake knocked a couple of pans together. He was always going to make a speech, however much Tom wished he wouldn't.

"Not so long ago," Jake began. "Tom was falling off his tricycle, running about in a Batman outfit, and getting stuck up trees. But enough about his first beer."

Everyone laughed. Not so much at the joke, they just liked Jake.

"Now," he continued. "He's officially a man. Full of ... opinions."

More laughter.

"And maybe a little serious. But hey, he's as honest as the day is long and he sure has ambition. Now, ambition can be a great thing, but unfortunately, it's ambition that's taking him away from the greatest town in America. But you know what, he'll never forget where his home is. I can say that for sure. I give you my son, Tom!" He raised a can. "Please – take him!" After more laughter, Jake took a swig of beer and keeled over, sending a dozen Sasquatch sausages flying. A couple of people laughed, mistaking the fall for one of his pranks, but Lauren's screams drowned them out. Tom raced over, and helped the local cop try CPR, but Jake was gone.

Tom wanted space to mourn Jake in his own way and he wished the funeral had just been a family thing. But everyone loved Jake and his friends had brought along their friends, his neighbours had brought their neighbours, and there was an impressive line-up of retired baseball players.

Tom, the cop and two of Jake's former teammates, carried the coffin to the front of the church, then Lauren ran up and hugged it. Tom held her tight for a few seconds, then struggled to hold himself together. What should have stayed private was now public, and there was nothing he could do to stay detached. He attempted to prise Lauren off as gently as he could, but she just wouldn't let go of the coffin. It was painfully embarrassing. She couldn't just stay there all day, and he couldn't very well wrestle her off. As he was about to despair, Kitty scampered up, and hugged her mum's legs. Lauren loosened her grip on the coffin, and Tom led her and Kitty back to the pews.

The pastor's tribute was touching – Jake was a fine husband and father, and if the town had been big enough to have a mayor, he would have been our man. Jake was an excellent sportsman, a true friend to the community, and an enemy to Sasquatches. Come on, Jake would never forgive him if he didn't at least mention his hobby! Some guys take up golf or play bridge - but Jake was a true original. Sure, some of us may have laughed at his Sasquatch-hunting, but everyone's allowed a little madness, aren't they? And the world's a richer place for it.

The mourners retreated to Jake's bar. It was a strange place for a wake. Giant, inflatable Sasquatches stood watch from the corners. Bigfoot-baiting nets drooped from the ceiling. A variety of yeti portraits in impressionist, pre-Raphaelite and neo-realist styles lined the walls, and above the restrooms, there was a framed footprint the size of a truck wheel.

Everyone wanted to speak to Tom. Now the town's main man had passed, he was the focus of attention. Mourners expressed shock that such a lively, happy guy could pass before he'd even turned fifty. It didn't make any sense and there wasn't much else to say, so people made lame jokes about Sasquatches, with eighteen separate guys expressing their surprise that a Sasquatch hadn't shown up at the funeral. Other people wanted to know about the bar – was Tom going to stay and run it? Surely, after what had happened, he couldn't leave town.

There were lots of women Tom had never seen before. Plenty of them gazed at him. A few came up and remarked how much he looked like his dad.

Tom's girlfriend was chatting to a retired baseball player he half-recognised. The guy took Jake's Bigfoot fixation in his stride but was surprised to hear that Jake had settled down – he'd never seemed the marrying type.

People said they were concerned for Lauren, but almost no one wanted to speak to her. It was just too difficult to find the right words. She looked on the verge of tears, so Tom left a generous tab behind the bar and persuaded the local cop to lock up once it was spent.

There wasn't much Tom could say to his mum. They just sat on the sofa together and spent the evening watching game shows.

The next morning, Lauren woke early and seemed possessed by a surge of newfound energy, announcing that they were going to clear the Sasquatch shed. It didn't strike Tom as their highest priority, but maybe going through Jake's stuff would prove a comfort.

The shed walls were papered with forest maps festooned with coloured pins marking Sasquatch locations. There was a desk with a computer, a printer, and a fax machine, and beside it, a table covered with teetering towers of floppy discs, and piles of walkie-talkies, camera lenses and headphones. Over-stuffed cardboard boxes carpeted half the floor.

Lauren examined one of the boxes, then asked if she could have a few minutes alone. Her voice was so soft, and her smile was so brittle, it almost broke Tom's heart. He put a reassuring hand on her shoulder and headed out to fix the barbeque. Jake's fall had dented the grill and he wanted to straighten it out before packing it away.

It was a quick job, but he didn't get to finish it. Unholy, unformed words of anguish issued from the Sasquatch shed. Tom raced inside. Lauren was no longer the grieving widow, she was transfigured by anger. "Burn all this crap! Don't look at anything - just do it."

Tom waited for Lauren to storm across to the house, then turned to the boxes. If he did as Lauren said and burned everything, there would be no going back – the truth about his dad would be lost forever. He simply had to look in the boxes – he owed Jake that much.

Tom did not have to delve deep to discover that the largest box contained enough love letters and intimate Polaroids to seal a couple of hundred divorces. He gave the house one glance, then carried the box across to the trunk of his SUV. He returned to the shed and discovered that the other boxes contained nothing more than a chaotic library of Sasquatch sightings. These, he could burn. He stoked up the grill and began a cryptozoology barbeque.

A few minutes later, the kitchen door opened. The flames were leaping high, but it was still pretty evident that it was the Sasquatch articles rather than the letters and photographs. Luckily, it was only Kitty.

"Mommy's locked herself in her room," Kitty said. "Are we having a barbeque?"

"Not today," Tom replied. "Shall we go for a drive, give mom a bit of time to herself."

"Can we visit Bigfoot?"

"He might eat you."

"I don't mind."

"Okay, then. As soon as I've finished this."

While the newspapers burned, Tom and Kitty sang a silly song about Sasquatch sausages that made Kitty giggle. As soon as it was no longer possible to tell what had been barbequed, Tom damped down the embers and chased Kitty to his SUV.

This had to feel like an adventure, so Tom took them properly off-road. The car was up to it, but that didn't mean it was going to be a smooth ride. Kitty laughed as she bounced up and down in her seat. Tom smiled for the first time since Jake had died. They had to get away from Lauren's fury, and hitting the woods would do them both good.

Tom always loved the way light filtered through the treeline. It felt like the rays were alive, dancing on the windows. You never got the same effect driving through a solidly built city. He was about to put on some music when he sensed a movement ahead in his peripheral vision. He swerved as much as he could, then hit the brakes. There was a jolt. Kitty shrieked. Tom turned to look at her. She was sat bolt upright, staring at the shadows ahead. There were no grizzlies in this part of Washington state, so it was probably a black bear, and they tended to run away rather than attack.

"Don't be afraid." Tom put his hand on Kitty's shoulder. "Stay calm. Everything will be fine."

"Sas...qua...tch," Kitty mouthed in wonder.

Tom examined the most ominous shadow more closely. It might have had eyes, but that was about all he could say for sure. If it was a Sasquatch, it was a bit of a shortarse.

Littlefoot, perhaps."

But whether it was Littlefoot or a little black bear, it was best left alone. Tom eased the SUV away.

"Sasquatch!" Kitty giggled. "I want one!"

"I told you I'd show you one," Tom said, gamely. "But I don't think it'll fit in the trunk."

The purpose of their drive supposedly fulfilled; Tom circled back home.

As soon as they pulled up, Kitty ran towards the house singing, "We saw a Sasquatch! We saw a Sasquatch!"

In any other circumstances, this would have been cute, but Lauren looked ready to cry. Sasquatches were a sore subject.

Tom took Kitty to bed and invented a story about a Sasquatch who went to school and became a cheerleader. It wasn't going to win a Pulitzer Prize, but it sent her to sleep.

Downstairs, Lauren lowered her voice. "Did you burn them all?"

Tom nodded.

"You didn't look at anything?"

"No. Don't worry."

The evening passed slowly. Lauren watched an old movie they had seen countless times before. Tom sat with her, until she fell asleep on the sofa, then covered her with a blanket. He made one final check on Kitty, then headed out for a drive. This time, he went through town, past the bar, and out to an overlook.

Tom watched the sun set over the Skykomish River, the jagged peaks of the Cascade Mountains and the distant city of Sultan. Jake used to drive him to this spot when he was small, and he had made a habit of returning whenever he needed space to think.

It struck Tom that there were months when nothing much changed. The weekday routines, the weekend rituals, the same challenges, the same comforts. But other times, there were days that life took you by surprise and flipped everything on its head. And when that happened, a man needed time to think. Could he still go to Seattle? Would Lauren and Kitty cope alone? How about his girlfriend? Did she really want to follow him out there, or was this the end of the road? And how about his friends? Sure, there were rivalries, resentments and flashes of envy, but he was the one that held them all together.

It was too soon to reach any conclusions, so Tom shifted his attention to the matter in hand. He took the box out of the trunk and carried it to the front passenger seat.

There were hundreds of letters, and enough photographs for a dozen albums. It looked like Jake was seeing half the female population of Washington State. He clearly hadn't expected to die, so hadn't bothered keeping his affairs in order.

Jake really was the family man he seemed to be, but only in part. The rest of him was scattered between the other women. Tom couldn't figure out how Jake had found the time for them all. What with the town, the bar, the family, and all his Sasquatch-hunting commitments, there weren't too many hours left in the day. In one sense, Jake had been lucky. He would never have to explain himself to Lauren, at least not on this Earth.

As Tom drove back, it struck him that the town's lights were glowing brighter than usual. It suited the place, lent it a degree of warmth. It wasn't until Tom was a block away that he identified the true source of the light. He hit the gas, screeched to a halt, and threw open the doors. The Sasquatch shed was on fire.

Tom tore into the yard shouting, "Mom! Kitty!" No answer. There was no time to put the fire out; he would have to brave the flames. He wrapped his jacket around his head and prepared to charge in.

"Wait!" A female voice implored.

Tom turned. It was Lauren, just stood there, watching the Sasquatch shed burn.

"Kitty!?" Tom shouted.

"Bed," Lauren replied.

"Thank God!" Tom scrambled around for a hose and began to douse the flames. "What the hell happened?"

Lauren didn't answer. She just stared into the conflagration, transfixed.

"Did someone do this?"

Lauren simply smiled.

"What were you thinking of?"

"Your dad."

Jake had to pretend he didn't know why she was angry, so he said, "Dad wouldn't have wanted this."

"I know," Lauren replied. "I let Kitty have the Sasquatch map – she seems to like it."

Once Tom had drowned the last of the flames, he led Lauren inside and went upstairs to check on Kitty. She was on the carpet, facing away from the door and poring over Jake's map. Coloured pins marked a "Sasquatch Hide" and a multitude of "Bigfoot Hangouts". She hadn't noticed him, and there was only one way for a self-respecting big brother to announce his presence. Tom did the mother of all Bigfoot impersonations, a bloodcurdling gorilla-roar.

Kitty span around with a shrieking giggle. Tom swept her up, carried her to bed and told her stories about Jake's Sasquatch hunting. Tom had never gone with him, but Jake had talked in detail about Bigfoot fieldcraft and yeti-hunting gadgets. What Tom didn't remember, he made up, which was most of it.

Kitty was wonderstruck and, when Tom had finished, asked, "Can we see another Sasquatch tomorrow?"

"If you promise to go to sleep."

Tom didn't want to spend rest of the evening lying to Lauren about the letters, but he did want to keep an eye on her, so he sat in the lounge pretending to read "Touching The Void" while she half-watched a western.

The next morning, Tom was woken by a light but insistent knocking. Kitty was standing at the door, dressed for a Sasquatch hunt, and clutching Jake's inexpertly folded map.

It was ridiculously early, but Kitty was way too excited to go back to sleep, so Tom knocked together a substantial breakfast, and made up another Sasquatch story. As soon as the sun had risen, they drove off to Jake's main "Sasquatch Hide".

After twenty minutes spent singing about Sasquatch sausages, Tom and Kitty reached a fork in the road. One path read, "Rangers Only", the other led to Sultan City.

Jake had never been a ranger, but he was clearly no stickler for rules, and judging by the map, this was the correct route. They drove into the depths of the forest: branches knotted; roots curled out like tendrils. Kitty said it was spooky and Tom could only agree. Maybe there was something ancient lurking in the trees.

Tom tried to take Kitty's mind off the increasingly eerie journey. "What do you think the Hide will be like?"

"Hidden." Kitty giggled.

"You don't think we'll be able to find it?" Tom asked.

"It might be under something," Kitty said.

"The ground?" Tom asked.

"Maybe," Kitty said. "Or behind a big tree."

"It would have to be one wide tree," Tom said. "Should be easy to spot."

"I'll find it first," Kitty said.

Tom laughed. He was normally up for a game, but this was unfamiliar territory.

"We should stick together," Tom said.

The path came to an end around fifty-foot shy of the Sasquatch Hide's coordinates. Tom pulled up, grinned at Kitty and they hopped out into whatever adventure lay ahead.

Tom took Kitty's hand and, as they walked through the dense foliage, their shoes crunched on the forest floor.

"See any big footprints?" Tom whispered.

"Sasquatches!" Kitty squealed.

"Quiet!" Tom hushed her. "You'll scare them all off."

Kitty giggled.

The trees parted, revealing what could only be the Sasquatch Hide. It was a luxury log cabin, and about as discreet as a cartel boss's hacienda. There was even a barbeque under the porch; an identical make to the fateful one back home. Even the dimmest Sasquatch would know that humans were afoot.

"Found it!" Kitty shouted.

"You win," Tom conceded absent-mindedly, as they walked up to their dad's so-called Hide. Kitty knocked at the door. She seemed to think that a Sasquatch Hide was where Sasquatches hid rather than a place Jake had hidden to observe Sasquatches.

Tom decided to play along. "Do you think Mr Sasquatch will open it?"

Kitty nodded.

After waiting a few seconds, Tom checked the door. It was locked, but only on a latch, which was easily defeated by a bank card.

Kitty skipped inside. Tom followed. It was a perfect romantic hideaway: the lounge had an open fire, a fluffy rug, and a mink velvet sofa. The bedroom had a king size and a ceiling mirror. It was blatantly obvious that Jake wasn't hiding from Sasquatches, he was hiding his mistresses. Tom almost admired him. An average guy excused himself by working late, attending fictional conferences, going on business trips or maybe taking a boys' trip out of town for weekend's fishing or golf. Jake had disguised his affairs by hunting Sasquatch.

Kitty was amusing herself by jumping on the sofa, and Tom had seen enough, so he suggested they check out one of Jake's "Bigfoot Hangouts".

They drove for so long they ran out of forest. The location marked on the map was a suburban house, which didn't seem a likely spot for a Sasquatch to hang out.

Tom had his suspicions, so he told Kitty to wait in the car. She wasn't happy, but after he gave her some paper and pens, she agreed on condition that she could draw a

Sasquatch.

Tom walked up the well-tended path and knocked at the door. No one answered, but there were voices within: one male, one female, both laced with urgency. After well over a minute, the door was opened by a woman in hastily arranged clothing. She looked at Tom, froze, then screamed. Tom didn't normally have this effect on people. He was the kind of wholesome young guy people turned to for directions or assistance with luggage.

While he was figuring out what to do, a sneaker fell out of the sky, missing his head by a couple of feet. Tom looked up: a middle-aged man was dangling out of a first-floor window. This was not what he had expected from a Bigfoot hangout, but as an expert climber, Tom always had health and safety in mind. He tried to persuade the man to climb back in, then talked him through the safest way to drop. The man fell awkwardly, but Tom's guidance prevented any breaks. Not that he was grateful; the instant he was upright, he scarpered.

Utterly bewildered, Tom turned his attention to the woman, who had stopped screaming, but had continued staring at him whilst repeatedly muttering the word, "Impossible."

Tom just said, "Hello."

"You're dead."

"I don't think so."

"You look just like he did."

"My dad?"

"Jake."

"Maybe once, Tom said.

The woman broke her stare and seemed to snap out of whatever delusion she'd been harbouring. "I guess it has been a long time."

"I'm Tom. Can I come in for a minute?"

The woman took a moment to recover herself, then led Tom through the hall. "Sorry about … my friend."

"The friend in the window."

"He just dropped by."

"He certainly did."

They both laughed.

"We thought you were my husband," the woman explained.

"Sorry to disappoint you," Jake said.

"Disappoint?" she smiled. "You couldn't be better."

The woman made coffee and told Tom everything that was wrong with her marriage. Her husband was a workaholic gambler: whatever he earned, he lost. It was like being married to a zero sum. He was doing more and more overtime so he could become an even bigger loser. He was barely home, and she was lonely.

When the woman finally drew breath from the rant, she said, "You do look very like your dad," and "I do miss him," before putting her hand on Tom's knee.

Tom made his excuses and headed back to his vehicle. There was no need to visit the other Bigfoot hangouts: they were never going to be overburdened with cryptozoological primates. As he turned the ignition, he wondered whether marriage always had to be about deception and unhappiness. Did he really know his girlfriend? Did she really know him? He gazed out the windscreen. Maybe all love was doomed? He sighed, indicated, then noticed that Kitty wasn't there.

Tom leapt out of the car, scanned the street, and ran into the trees. How long had he been gone? Maybe twenty minutes. How far could Kitty have walked? A mile, at most. Why the hell hadn't he locked her in? Kitty was a good kid, always did what she was told - why would she just wander off? Had she been abducted? Jake's stupid Sasquatch lies had brought this about. But this was no time for recriminations. He had to be systematic. He would cover a square mile and if he hadn't found her, he would return to the car and raise a search party.

The fields beyond the street were flat and featureless, so Tom headed back into the forest, maintaining a steady pace and shouting "Kitty!" every fifteen seconds. Speed mattered, but he had to take care not to turn his ankle on the roots – her fate rested on him. Panic now and he'd be the one in need of rescue. He simply could not allow that to happen.

Tom thought about Lauren, and how Jake's betrayal had made her a brittle, bitter shell. If something had happened to Kitty, there would be nothing left of her.

Tom did not have to search far before he found Kitty sat in a clearing. Relief flooded through Tom's body, then flooded out again. She was sat cross-legged on the forest floor with an eight-hundred-pound hominid.

Tom wasn't armed and he had no means of overpowering the nine-foot beast. All he could do was follow the advice he'd given Kitty with the black bear and remain calm, which was easier said than done.

Tom watched aghast as Katie handed the Sasquatch her drawing. The hairy great stink-beast perused it with care. Would he be offended? Amused? Would he even recognise his own image rendered by an eight-year-old?

The giant man-thing leapt to its feet and thrust the picture aloft, like a World Series trophy. It issued a growl louder than a pride of lions and performed what could only be described as a celebratory caper.

Kitty giggled and waved goodbye to the Sasquatch, skipping back to Tom. He hugged her and led her gently away.

Kitty grinned. "Sasquatches are nice. He really liked my drawing."

Tom never spoke a word about the encounter and Kitty's account was treated as a child's fantasy. But he never took the job in Seattle and devoted his days to running Jake's Sasquatch themed bar.

***

Tom had finished his story, and his steak. I couldn't help but wonder whether he had inherited his father's predilection for untruth. There was no sure-fire way of knowing, but Tom simply didn't strike me as the imaginative type. If you wanted a tree chopped, a cabin built, or a mountain scaled, he was your man. If you wanted an elaborate cryptozoological fib invented, you'd be better off asking someone who had done considerably more drugs.

Tom and his little sister had met a Sasquatch at their first attempt, but, for all his hunts, hides and hangouts, Tom's father may never have clapped eyes on one in well over twenty years. I wondered whether this was testament to the Sasquatch's finely honed sense of irony. Perhaps the humorous hominids had spent two decades dodging out of adulterous Jake's path and waited for his demise before making themselves known to his descendants. If so, I take my hat off to them.

Say what you like about Americans, but they live in one hell of a country.

RULE 9 - LOVE IS BLIND DRUNK

Long after my seventh ex-wife's wedding had degenerated into fights and fumbles, I got talking to the pianist. He was a fine-looking fellow, and no more than thirty, but his world-beaten expression suggested he had lived more than was good for him.

The piano's rack didn't hold a score, it supported a sketch pad, and he would consult this at frequent intervals. I wondered whether it contained some advanced form of musical notation, but closer inspection revealed it to be one of the most childishly inept drawings I had encountered outside a kindergarten: a shoal of bemused mermaids watched a herd of embarrassed elephants bathe in a moonlit lagoon whilst nude women queued to use a beach-side diving board. It was a work of art so poor in both conception and execution, it would have shamed a chimp.

"Nice pic," I observed, by way of breaking the ice.

"It might not look like much," the pianist explained. "But it sounds great."

I couldn't disagree. His tunes had been the wedding's only highlight. I congratulated him on his virtuosity and asked his permission to peruse the pad. It didn't disappoint: a poodle played Russian Roulette with a water pistol, bearded cherubs drank pints, pixies Morris danced to an audience of cross-eyed woodland creatures. The collection could have been composed by a committee of the ungifted after they had got drunk on meths and hit the crayons.

I returned his pad to the rack. "Well, you've certainly got something."

"Really?" His eyes lit up.

"Maybe a disease."

The pianist laughed. I poured him a scotch from an unattended bottle, and we chinked a toast to his sketch.

"It's just a thing." He shrugged. "I see sound."

People tell me a lot of things, but this was a first. "What does it look like?"

"This." He indicated the lagoon sketch, smiled ruefully, and told me that he had once drawn a Platinum-selling album. It was quite a claim for a guy headlining weddings, so I asked him to elaborate.

"I didn't make a penny from the songs I drew," he explained. "But I did date the lead singer for a few years."

The singer in question was an Irish rock diva named Donna, mostly memorable for her leather catsuit, fragile voice and even more fragile ego. Her apoplectic fury at a novelty cover version of her hit, *Little Man*, had made headlines. I didn't entirely blame her: it had been performed by puppet leprechauns in Santa Claus outfits.

"Quite a lady," I recalled, tactfully.

"I thought she was the love of my life."

"I've had a few of those."

"I gave her all I had." The pianist sank his scotch. "My time, my talent - I even gave her regular surprises."

"How regular?"

"Every other week. Tuesdays mostly."

I poured him another scotch. The wedding guests didn't seem to care that he had stopped playing; their attentions were focused on the mass brawl, currently tumbling out to the car park.

"So, how come you didn't make any money from the platinum album?"

"Song-drawers aren't songwriters – we can't claim royalties."

"And you've been playing weddings ever since?"

"Only recently. I used to have a career as a vocal coach, teaching women to sing. Younger ones, mostly."

"A singing teacher? Is there much call for that?"

"Among certain women, yes. I was good and they were grateful – often, too grateful - but I never betrayed Donna. I'd tell them I'd been with her for years and that would only make it worse. They'd say things like: *You're so stable. I'd like to push you 'til you wobble* and *Just because you've already ordered doesn't mean you can't look at the menu.* Women seemed to find my fidelity a turn-on."

Life is nothing if not paradoxical. The bride and groom were on the dance floor, wrestling. She had him in a neck-lock and he was close to submission. I thought about the vows I had seen them exchange earlier in the day: *To have and to hold*. Well, she certainly seemed to have him in a hold.

I turned back to the pianist and asked him how things had played out with the catsuit sporting Irishwoman.

"I felt completely secure in my relationship with Donna," he said. "Right up until the moment she dumped me over a pair of *Screaming Orgasms*."

I knew the cocktail. It wasn't my favourite. I encouraged him to flesh out the scene.

He agreed and began his sorry story:

"We were drinking these Baileys, vodka, and amaretto concoctions in some bar, when Donna told me it was over. She wanted to tour Norway with a band, and I wasn't welcome to tag along."

I started whingeing, "But I'm loyal, I'm devoted..."

"You're dumped," Donna interrupted. "Why can't you behave like a real musician?"

"I will if you want me to."

"You're obedient too!" She was practically screaming. "I despise conformists."

She left and I got drunk – not on Screaming Orgasms, I was feeling anti-climactic. After my ninth bitter, a customer took pity on me, lodged a cigarette in my mouth and lit it. I coughed uncontrollably, as I didn't smoke, but it was a thoughtful gesture.

For days, I moped about in my pants, sporting a never-ending stare. One time, I lifted a coffee and missed my face. Another, I put my back out lifting a croissant. When I returned to work, I told the women who had propositioned me that I was available, but they'd just say things like *Where's the challenge in seducing a desperate single guy? If I ever need a puppy, I'll go to the pet shop*, and *Get lost - you're too bloody attainable*.

Eventually, I got over myself and tried to draw some more songs. I crayoned with intense fury. Bins filled with torn pictures until I finally had what I was looking for: sunset over a crazy golf course as a one-legged angel putted against Elvis Presley. This was it! I took it to the piano, placed it in the rack and played the best tune of my life. Donna was history and I had a new song. Things were looking up.

I went off to see a mate in the music biz. Jez uses a wheelchair, but he's a mean drummer and an even meaner fighter. He was rehearsing with a bored session guitarist, and that perma-wasted vocalist who used to be in *Vague Alien*.

They were halfway through a track called *The Skeletons Are Confused* when the vocalist stopped singing, burst into tears, and dropped to the carpet. Jez wheeled over to console him.

The vocalist was in bits. "Do you think my car's lonely?"

"Where's it parked?" Jez asked.

"The supermarket," the vocalist replied.

"It'll be fine there," Jez said. "The vehicles are very friendly."

The vocalist stopped crying.

The guitarist jabbed a finger at the wall clock. "Ready to get on with it?"

The vocalist wasn't. "I need a bit of time to … you know … think about who I am."

I'd seen Jez lose his patience and set about people with heavy objects, but this time, he was a model of restraint. "Sure," he said. "You get your head together."

"That could take decades," the guitarist protested. "I can't go past six. Hospital appointment."

"Lobotomist missed a bit, did he?" This was the Jez I knew and loved.

The guitarist looked monumentally affronted. "It's for my son."

The band abandoned the session, and I took Jez to the pub.

"What a twat!" he began.

"The vocalist?" I asked.

"The guitarist," he replied.

"You can't blame him for going to hospital with his son," I reasoned.

"I can," Jez replied. "He doesn't have any children. He's just a lazy, lying bastard."

Jez was pleased to hear about the new song, but when I explained my personal situation, he looked totally bemused. "Let me get this right, you're asking a drummer for advice?"

"It's fair to say I'm desperate."

"I've got enough problems of my own right now. The neighbour's started monitoring my drumming with a seismograph. I mean, get a life! I never practice after eleven in the morning."

"But you do start at midnight."

Jez knew I was right, but that didn't stop him glaring at me for five seconds flat before he said, "Where were we? Ah, yes, you were asking a divorced drummer for advice about women."

"I was, wasn't I? Well, when I was going out with Donna, women were throwing themselves at me. Now I'm single, they're not interested."

"You're a free man. Don't go looking for another cage."

We sat in silence for a couple of minutes. I was beginning to regret asking Jez for advice when he had a eureka moment. He slapped the table with his palm and said, "If that lazy guitarist has an imaginary child, why shouldn't you have an imaginary wife?"

"And have imaginary sex with her?"

"Or have real sex with the kinds of women who fancied you when you were with Donna."

"Real sex, imaginary adultery?"

"Exactly!"

The first step was to learn how to be a husband. Jez took me for a training session in Muswell Hill and showed me an array of soul-sapped men in tow to wives and children.

"Look and learn," Jez instructed. "For them, life's adventure's over, fashion's a memory, weekends are for jobs around the house. You've got to get the psychology right - think garden centres, DIY, and superstores."

Once I had mastered that mind-set, Jez took me to a jeweller, explaining that "Even an imaginary wife wouldn't let her husband go around ringless."

The jeweller said we made a lovely couple. I bought the cheapest ring and left.

We headed for the nearest greasy spoon and set about designing my imaginary wife. It seemed best if she were a workaholic with numerous hobbies, leaving me at a loose end most weekday evenings.

As Jez riffed on my imaginary wife's personal attributes; I started to sketch her. "She's not who you thought she was," Jez explained. "She's become cold, distant, and however hard you try you just can't get her to understand you. It makes you sad – you are a romantic type, and you did once carry a torch for her, but now it's just really, really sad."

I showed Jez my sketch. My imaginary spouse had the right number of limbs, but that was probably the best that could be said for her.

"No one looks like that," Jez observed, accurately.

"That's just what she sounds like," I explained.

Once we had sunk a couple of bacon butties, we ran through the lies a few more times, until Jez said, "Okay, enough preparation. Convince me."

"I've been married for seven years," I began, uncertainly. "I am incomprehensible to my missus and in urgent need of several intensive sessions of understanding."

"Sounds like you're reading an autocue! You're going to have to learn to improvise. Bullshit is like jazz."

"I always though jazz was bullshit."

"Same difference."

I gave it a go. "We met on the internet...It was love at first sight... It's been a whirlwind romance ever since school."

Jez despaired and wished me luck.

The next day, I put out a few ads for new clients. *Singing lessons - 1-on-1 tuition*; *Find your voice - intimate instruction*, and even *Music is the food of love – come and have a nibble*.

It worked a treat, and my diary was soon clogged with clients. The first was a young Kiwi woman called Kerry, who trudged listlessly through her lesson, but came to life as soon as she clocked my wedding ring. "When did you decide to tie the noose?"

After I'd lied about my non-existent wife and whinged about our failing marriage, she said, "I'll bet you're rampantly monogamous."

I told her that there was only one way to find out – and we did.

Another client was a hyperactive Anglo-Indian called Meena. She raced through all her arpeggios so quickly we had time to sit on the sofa and chat. I put the kettle on and lied in detail about my marriage.

When I'd finished reeling off all the nonsense I'd prepared with Jez, she said, "Your life's probably quite dull, isn't it?" and traced a well-manicured finger over my palm.

"Horribly predictable," I concurred.

"That's so hot!" She kicked off her shoes and rubbed her feet against my legs.

"You just fall into a routine," I continued. "Sharing the ironing, writing shopping lists, updating the direct debits on the joint account."

"Say that again!" Meena rubbed her toes against my groin. "Please!"

I had only got as far as *shopping lists* when she straddled my kneecap and started rocking backwards and forwards.

"Now," she panted. "Tell me what you did this weekend and make it boring."

"I took the in-laws to a garden centre."

Her breathing accelerated audibly.

"Borrowed a spirit level off the bloke next-door."

She began to gasp.

"And erected a bookcase."

We made love for a few seconds at a time in six different positions and she climaxed in time with the kettle.

"You're new to this, aren't you?" Meena asked, on her way out.

"I'm a virgin ...at adultery."

"Good. Pleasure deflowering you. There's nothing more desirable than someone else's faithful husband." She winked and shut the door behind her.

Now, don't get me wrong, this didn't work every time, but it did work a lot more often than I had expected.

Debbie was a rather melodramatic Mancunian who sang all her songs as if she were performing a death scene at the opera.

At the end of her third lesson, we got talking and I told her I was married. She said I looked like I needed cheering up.

I agreed that I did.

She nibbled my neck. "You don't taste married."

I kissed her. "Nor do you."

"I should. My husband betrayed us both by marrying me when he didn't mean it. I might be unfaithful, but he's faithless."

"Sorry. I didn't realise you were married too."

"Don't add guilt into the mix," she said. "I like my adultery unadulterated."

"When would you like it?"

"Thursday."

My imaginary marriage was going through a honeymoon period – sex on tap, no strings, no drama. But everything changed when I met Alicia. She was an adorable Afro-American with a Gospel voice so powerful, it filled the street, as she danced, clapped, and whooped her way through my songs.

I worked with her intensely, getting her to whisper the words, close her eyes and give an intimate delivery. I had never taught this well before. The effect was incredible. Musically, she couldn't have been more responsive, but nothing else happened.

One day, I decided to teach her my new song. Her rendition was fragile, honest, and entrancing. My song had found its natural singer.

I decided to move in for the kill. "I'm married, you know."

She congratulated me politely.

I explained that it wasn't really anything to be congratulated about, as my wife didn't understand me.

Alicia gave me a hug. I punched the air, inwardly.

"I'm really pleased you told me that." She let me go and looked straight into my eyes.

Alicia really was one of the most beautiful women I had ever seen in my life. I couldn't believe my luck, until she said, "I can help. I'm a marriage guidance counsellor."

"Oh God...good." I felt like fainting.

"I've got plenty of time," she said, kindly. "Tell me all about it. Please."

We sat on the sofa while I improvised about my non-existent marriage. "It's a question of irreconcilable similarities," I lied. "We're totally compatible – it's a nightmare. We've got the same taste in music, we've travelled to the same places, read the same books – we've got nothing new to tell each other. I know what she's about to say before she says it and it's the same for her, so we've stopped talking – there's no point."

She reached into her jacket and offered me a handkerchief. I took it and dabbed away imaginary tears.

Alicia asked me tactfully about my sex life. I told her that my wife and I had rampant sleep seven times a week and this morning I had made mad, passionate love to my wrist.

She listened sympathetically. "It's all about communication."

"We have an unspoken understanding – we're not speaking."

"Communication is like dancing."

"Is it?" She had a highly encirclable waist, so I couldn't help saying, "Show me."

She did. It wasn't as good as a date, but I enjoyed myself. I told her she had some great moves. She said I danced, "Like prose in motion". I asked her out to a salsa club, but she advised against me ever dancing in public.

We laughed about my sense of rhythm until it was time for her to go. On the way out, she said, "You and your wife just need quality time together. We'll talk about it at the next counselling session."

"You mean, the next singing lesson."

"Of course. My mistake. Now, spend some time with your wife."

I was in love, but that didn't stop me dating my other clients. Kerry the Kiwi took me to a one-man performance of *Finnegan's Wake* and back at her place we shared a soggy expanse of cold, Ethiopian flatbread and vegan dips. She detailed her PhD on "The build-up of volcanic activity over geological timescales," then took all night to orgasm. Afterwards, she said "That was the fastest climax I've had in years. I can't believe your wife lets you out of the bedroom."

"My wife?" I scoffed. "She just crosses her legs and thinks of Iceland."

Thursday came around and it was time to date Debbie the melodramatic

Mancunian. Beforehand, she explained that we would have to be careful because her husband had married her for money and if we ever got caught, she would lose half her anti-surveillance business.

After Debbie had outlined her security protocols and exit strategies, I complained that the date was turning into a spy film, but she just said, "I thought you fancied a bit of undercover activity.".

We arrived at the hotel separately and signed in under aliases. She frisked the room for bugs, then I frisked her for fun. I snogged her for a bit, but she broke away and whispered, "Stop! Footsteps!" and put a finger to my lips. After what seemed like a decade, she withdrew her digit and said, "It's okay, you can carry on now."

We snogged for another few seconds before she broke off again with a "Wait! I'm sure I heard a key turn." After another lengthy hiatus, she said, "Must have imagined it. Carry on."

A little later, Debbie climaxed in characteristically operatic style, bursting into tears of joy. At this, someone knocked on the wall. I couldn't really blame them, but it was the end of the world for Debbie. "I've broken our cover! Hide!" She threw herself under the bed and dragged me down with her.

After we had lain on the carpet for several minutes, she handed me a card. "Here's my address."

"Doesn't your husband live there too?"

"It's a dead letterbox."

There was a knock at the door. That really did it for Debbie.

"We'll have to evacuate!" Debbie raced for the fire door. I tried to follow, but she turned and held her hand to my chest. "We can't risk being seen using the same fire escape."

"There's only one."

"Don't worry." Debbie pointed at the window. "The place is covered in scaffolding."

I climbed out.

"I'll make sure you're not followed," Debbie said as she locked the window behind me.

I found myself outside the ninth floor of the hotel stood on what I had thought was scaffolding but was in fact a window-cleaning platform. This came as a bit of a shock and, in my initial panic, I dislodged a bucket and watched it drop onto the road one-hundred-and-fifty feet below. As it impacted, I was so overwhelmed by vertigo that my legs gave way, and I passed out on the platform.

I woke up on the pavement several hours later. I must have been winched down by the window cleaners. One of them had plonked a mop on my head.

I wasn't at my best, but I made sure I arrived home in time for Alicia's lesson.

"You look upset," she observed.

"It's nothing," I replied.

"I can tell," she said. "I'm trained."

It was awkward. I couldn't tell her about my window-cleaning trauma, so I looked out of the window for inspiration, and said, "My wife's been having an affair."

"You poor thing." Alicia hugged me.

"I've only just found out," I said.

This didn't accelerate the comforting process in the way I'd wished. She just said, "Don't blame her. It's the fault of the marriage. You just need to understand why it happened."

"Things hadn't been right for a while," I admitted with as much regret as I could muster.

"I know this must be painful for you," she said. "But you need to rebuild trust."

"I can't look at her. I don't have anything to say."

"Arguments are like onions."

"Tear-jerking?"

"Layered."

"Oh."

"Let's try a role play," she suggested.

This was more like it. "Shall we dress up?"

"No," Alicia replied. "Just imagine I'm your wife and you are having a calm, honest conversation."

I took a moment to manoeuvre my mind into a place where I could role play my made-up marriage.

"You ready?"

"Yes."

"Okay, let's begin." Alicia straightened her stance and her expression.

What would I say to my unfaithful wife if she existed? I opted for route one: "Was he better in bed than me?"

Alicia, gently annoyed, broke out of character. "Don't demand intimate details of the affair. You'll only hurt yourself."

"Okay. Sorry." I looked at Alicia, sat there all gorgeous and attentive, and I heard myself say, "Why don't we have sex?" before I remembered it was meant to be a role play and added, "... anymore?"

Alicia remained focused on her role. "I've been under a lot of stress at work recently."

"I know, dear."

"Let's try to find more time for each other," she continued. "Take more interest in each other's lives and feelings and try to sort out our sexual problems."

"Agreed."

"Let's commit to a new future together."

I liked the sound of that so much, I tried to kiss her.

She wasn't interested, but luckily, she just laughed it off.

Life became a carnival of dodgy dates. Manic Meena took me on an oxygen bar crawl. After I'd got her going by cataloguing my imaginary wife's tedious hobbies, we had sex on the London Eye. Kerry the Kiwi took me to an epic poetry evening in a community centre and she proposed a threesome with me and my wife, but after I told her that my wife was too much of a prude, we made do with a twosome. Melodramatic Debbie insisted we met at a goth bonk-bar, claiming that the black leather bondage outfits provided ideal cover. We had a heart-to-heart and she told me how romantic it was to meet someone else who understood what it meant to be unhappily married. After we'd retired to a dungeon-themed shag-room, she quipped, "If you're mad enough to believe in marriage, you deserve to be committed for life to an institution."

I almost lost count of the wife-related porkies I told along the way:

She laughs like a Kalashnikov, snores like a blue whale and farts like a Harley.

The sex is athletic but meaningless – I need it to mean more.

She never goes out. Her idea of an evening on the town is walking the recycling bin up the path.

It was cruel, but given that she didn't exist, I wasn't slandering anyone.

My next lesson with Alicia was exquisite. She performed my new song like an angel, finding nuances that I had never imagined. Afterwards, I praised her to the skies and laid into my wife so much, it backfired.

"You're spouting industrial quantities of nonsense," Alicia protested. "You're lying to yourself. You've no self-esteem and you don't value your partner. Maybe that's why your marriage is shipwrecked. You need a win-win style of arguing. Share a walk in the park, a drink in the pub or a coffee in the shops – value each other. Accept your life stage."

"Is *washed-up* a life stage?" I enquired.

"You're only washed up if you admit defeat," she replied.

"That's so true. Will you go out with me?"

"I don't date married men."

"What if I left her?"

She laughed briefly, realised I was serious, then burst into tears. It turned out that she cared

I thought it was probably time to ditch the imaginary wife. The question was, how? I decided to visit Jez. It was the middle of the night, but that was usually the best time to catch him in.

Jez's house was never hard to find. His entire terrace vibrated to the sound of drumming. I noticed that most neighbouring buildings were subsiding and had been covered in supportive scaffolding. I leant on the buzzer. There was no response, so I climbed through the open window and fell awkwardly onto his floor.

If Jez had thought I was a burglar, I would have been dead. Instead, he just looked down on me, said "Thanks for dropping in," and played one of those rimshot and cymbal crash combos once popular in cabaret clubs.

"Jez, this is serious."

"Looks like you've had a humour bypass."

"I have. And no one was around to give me an anaesthetic. My life's a mess. I wish I'd never invented a wife."

"Look, mate." Jez wheeled himself closer. "What else did you expect asking a drummer for advice?"

I laughed, he laughed, and not for the first time, we decided to exchange drummer jokes:

"What do you call a drummer with half a brain?"

"Gifted."

"How can you tell if the stage is level?"

"The drummer drools from both sides of his mouth."

"What do you call a drummer who splits up from his girlfriend?"

"Homeless."

There were no jokes about vocal coaches, but that didn't stop me thinking that my entire life was nothing more than as a joke.

"What's the best way to finish all these affairs?" I asked Jez.

"Tell them she's dying, pregnant or suspicious," he replied.

"Who?"

"The imaginary wife, of course." Jez wheeled back behind his kit and resumed his drumming.

He didn't have to say any more. I left via the window and fell headfirst into a bin.

Over the next fortnight, I ended my affair with Meena by telling her that my wife had died and my affair with Kerry by telling her that my wife was pregnant. There were tears and insults, but what else did I expect?

I feared that dumping Debbie would prove more complex, particularly as I was going to have to do it at the School Disco-themed evening she'd insisted we attend as cover.

On the fateful evening, I stood in a draughty hall looking a prize plonker in my cap, tie, and shorts. Debbie arrived a little late, carrying off her pencil skirt and ponytail with panache.

"Feeling nostalgic?" I asked.

"Takes me right back behind the bike shed." She pinched my bum.

I took her hand. "It's been amazing."

"It *is* amazing," she corrected.

"It was," I said.

"Was?"

"Sorry about the tense."

"I like tense," Debbie said. "It's calm I don't do."

"I can't go on like this," I said. "The guilt, the subterfuge…"

"Yes, isn't it great?"

"Breaking up is hard to do," I said.

Debbie saw that I was serious and went nuclear. "A failed mistress! I can't make my marriage work and I can't break yours up. I can't even make a go of my affair!" She burst into tears.

I heard sobbing from across the room. Another adult schoolgirl was also in tears. It was Alicia.

I strode over, trying to intercept her approach. "What are you doing here?"

"I wanted to catch a glimpse of the wife whose marriage I'd persuaded you to end," Alicia said.

"How did you know I was here?" I asked.

"Never mind that," Alicia said. "I've got to say something. I feel terrible."

Before I knew it, Alicia was speaking to Debbie. "You must be…"

"The other woman." Debbie said, bitterly.

"But that's me," Alicia replied.

"No," Debbie said. "You're the wife."

"That's you," Alicia said.

"Is it?" Debbie asked.

I weighed in with a "Sorry."

"Who are you apologising to?" they enquired in unison.

"Both of you," I said. "And my wife. All three of you, in fact. Oh, listen to that. The DJ's playing Madness." I skank-danced to the ska, but they didn't join in, so I decided that my only option was to come clean. "I've been lying to you both. I don't really have a wife."

Debbie howled with anger, hit me, and left.

Alicia just said, "I like comedians, but I don't want to date one. You wrote such an emotional song, but you have no emotion in your life – just games. I love you just the way you aren't."

"I've lost you, haven't I?"

"You never had me."

After sulking solo to *Don't You Want Me Baby?* I left the disco, pulled off my wedding ring, and booted it into the wasteland.

When I got home, Donna was in the kitchen with a pair of *Screaming Orgasms*. For a minute, I thought I was hallucinating; it had been months since the break-up.

"I'm so sorry," she said. "The tour gave me time to think, and I've realised what I need. I want someone monogamous and dependable like you. Will you give me another chance?"

I had no imaginary wife and no real girlfriends, so I caved in.

Later that evening, I told her all about my new song, and she tried it out while I accompanied her on the piano.

Her performance had none of the fragility of Alicia's rendition, but it was still beautiful. My drawing danced before my eyes: Elvis Presley, the one-legged angel, and the crazy golf course. It was magical.

When she had reached the end, Donna hugged me. "You're a genius! Leaving you was the biggest mistake of my life. I want to rebuild our relationship."

We lived together for many happy weeks before she stole my song and left me for the boss of a record label. My song is on her solo album, *Sensitive Resentment*, along with her hits, *Brittle Anger*, *Bishop, I Defy You* and *So Cross with Your Cross*. I decided to give up song-drawing and women. Now, I just play at weddings.

***

I placed a consoling hand on the pianist's shoulder. "Can you play your song?"

"I can do an instrumental."

"I hate instrumentals."

He gave me a wicked grin and belted out a song with exquisite piano accompaniment and a voice so grotesque it sounded like a vixen birthing triplets. Sometimes, sound is better seen and not heard.

As I endured his caterwauling, I thought about my eight failed marriages and wondered why any man would want to invent a wife. If I kept going at my current pace, I would soon have enough real ex-wives to field a football team. What would I call them? Vindictive United, perhaps.

Relationships are all about delusion. We fall in love with our own idea of someone else and we're surprised when they don't live up to it. Why do we do this to ourselves? Wouldn't it just be easier to watch pornography? Once the song was over, I decided to head home and do exactly that.

RULE 10 - WORK HARD, DIE HARD

I once met a man who had survived a daytime television show about Christmas decorations. It was a twenty-eight-part series for The Living Room Channel, and there was more than one fatality.

I had just broken up with my fifth wife and she had marked the occasion by emptying a pint of bitter over my head. I managed to get the worst of it off with a bar towel and, even back then, I didn't have enough hair to ruin.

Still, I wasn't at my happiest, so I scanned the room for a potential drinking partner. Most people were coupled up, or in groups. There was only one other loner, and he was hard to miss. The bloke wore an Argentina football shirt with Diego Maradona's name on the back. It was the kind of fashion choice that could get an Englishmen hospitalized, had he not been north of six-foot-six.

I've always liked contrarians, so I made a lame quip about the deceased South American footballing cheat and joined him for a lager. After we had shared moans about the government, social media, and the weather, we got talking about the worst jobs we'd ever had. I told him how I had once trained as an acupuncturist and hit an artery, and in return he revealed his involvement in the doomed festive filming. He was quick to point out that although he had been the boom operator, he was not personally responsible for the catastrophic *boom* that had obliterated the director, the producer, and the location. I had the feeling this wasn't the first time he had made play with his boom pun, but I humoured him with a chuckle, eager to learn more about the tinsel-themed tragedy.

"It all kicked off in the London Borough of Ealing," he began in a deep deadpan.

"We were in a detached house in a leafy crescent. Outside, it was a blazing day at the dog-end of August. Inside, it was Christmas. The lounge was stuffed with seven or eight Norwegian spruces, bauble mountains, colossal brandy bottle towers and mince pie pyramids. There was a coal-effect gas fire, and, on the table, trays of sloppily iced biscuits had been hacked into the shape of abominable snow men. What with all the camera lights and the heatwave, it was a bit like celebrating Christmas on an Australian beach, except indoors.

The producer was married to the director and neither of them seemed particularly happy about it. I could see why - she was an embittered bitch with status issues, and he was a surrendered husband choking back resentment at a lifetime's humiliation. The cameraman was a storied Scot on the brink of retirement, the researcher was so pregnant she looked ready to drop, the runner had all the wisdom and experience of a new-born chimp, and the lady presenter looked ready to book a place in the nearest nursing home. The A-Team this wasn't.

The producer appraised the excessively merry decorations and asked the room, "Do you think it's Christmassy enough?"

I knew better than to reply, so I just continued reading a book about timecode. It had some interesting ideas about synchronization systems and outside broadcast operations.

"I don't want it to look bare." The producer lit a cigarette. This was the early noughties and people did that sort of thing all the time, but it didn't help the researcher, who coughed violently and clutched her baby-belly.

The director said, "Maybe another bauble," and sunk his teeth into some Nicorette gum.

The researcher struggled to her feet, added a bauble, and stepped back to check her work, triggering a bauble avalanche.

"Listen!" The producer wielded her cigarette like a weapon. "We've got twenty-eight half-hour programmes to record this week. There's no time for mistakes!"

The researcher looked up gloomily from the festive mess and said, "Sorry."

"Don't you apologise, honey." The producer gave the researcher a patronizing smile. "It was my husband's fault."

"Sorry, dearest." The director sounded like a man accustomed to apologizing.

While the producer nursed her cigarette, everyone else gathered up the escaped baubles. I wanted to appear willing whilst making the least effort possible, so I reached down and examined a single bauble with great care, raising it to my ear and shaking it. I've never been convinced that all baubles are entirely hollow, and this was a golden opportunity to listen to whatever was hidden inside.

While I conducted my experiment, the cameraman crawled around the carpet gathering armfuls of the shiny spheres, and muttering Glaswegian obscenities. The researcher did her best to help but scrabbling around on the floor hurt her back and made her breathless. The runner used a bauble to examine his reflection and adjust his hair. The director used his feet to shuffle baubles rather morosely into a shiny heap.

Once everyone had finished, the presenter tripped backwards onto the gathered pile, crushing most of the baubles to shards.

"Look! "The producer's nostrils flared as she shrieked. "*Christmas Present* is the first series Nepotism Productions have made for The Living Room Channel! If we're going to build on the success of *Tiling Tips* for Planet Bathroom and *Dog's Dinners* for The Canine Channel, we're all going to have to..." She paused for emphasis. "... *concentrate*!"

"Absolutely, dearest." The director grimaced. "Shall we go for a take?"

"Nay bother, pal." The cameraman jumped into action. He clearly couldn't wait to get it over with.

Sharing that sentiment, I snapped, "Phones off!" It was an important instruction and part of my job, but I also enjoy shouting at rooms.

The cameraman switched on the remaining lights. Most of them were fitted with festive red gels. A tacky image of Santa and a sleigh was projected onto the curtains.

The runner switched on a dilapidated camcorder popular with twentieth century wedding guests. Noticing this for the first time, the director mumbled, "Christ, dearest."

The producer seemed unperturbed. "What?"

"Where did that contraption come from?" the director asked.

"My dad's attic," the producer replied. "I thought a second camera might speed things up."

"But just look at the monitors!" The director indicated two video screens. "Jim's got a decent camera. It makes the world seem a colourful, pleasant place to spend a lifetime. But young Ben here has a very different kind of camera. It makes the world appear grey, hazy, and mystifying. They'll never match."

"You're going to have to make them," the producer said.

"How?" the director asked.

"Make Ben's camera look less grey, hazy and mystifying," the producer said.

"I can't," the director replied. "It's cheap and decrepit. That's the best it can manage."

"Then make the good camera look cheaper," the producer said.

"Nay bother, doll." The cameraman adjusted a dial. "That hazy enough for you?"

The producer looked thoughtfully at the monitors. "Maybe a little more out of focus,"

"Right you are, boss. How about that?" The cameraman turned the dial again. "Mystified yet?"

Both monitors showed equally blurry images of the festive decorations.

It would have been pointless proceeding had the producer not taken a moment to look daggers at her husband, allowing the cameraman to correct the focus on his camera unobserved.

Noticing this, the director gestured for the presenter to step into place and said, "Let's turnover."

"Wait for the plane to pass!" I interrupted. There weren't any planes, but I like to keep myself amused. I watched everyone stand in unnecessary silence for twenty seconds. The researcher closed her eyes and rubbed her back, the runner yawned, the cameraman looked at his watch. The producer glared impatiently at the director, who shrugged.

I stared intently at the ceiling as if observing the imaginary aircraft through the plaster. Once I'd got bored, I announced that the plane had passed, and the crew lumbered back into action.

"Running up." The cameraman looked through his eyepiece. "Speed."

"And action." The director cued the superannuated presenter with a chopping motion, somewhere between an orchestra conductor's sweep and a weak Kung Fu move.

"Hello, and welcome to Christmas Present," the presenter began. "Your up-to-the-minute guide to festive fare, gorgeous gifts, and yummy yuletide surprises. I'll be here for the next twenty-eight days with tip-top tips on how to make your Christmas go with a bang."

A bulb exploded. The researcher screamed. The presenter swooned, decking a Norwegian spruce, and carpeting the mince pies.

"Christ!" the producer shouted.

"God!" the director added.

"Brandy!" the presenter implored.

"There you go." The researcher passed her a bottle from a decorative tower.

"Thank you, dear." The presenter took a glug. "When are you due?"

"Not for another three months," the researcher replied. "It feels like forever."

"I know dear, but it'll be worth the wait. My grandchildren took decades to arrive."

The cameraman was removing the blown bulb and searching for a replacement when the producer interrupted. "Anything serious?"

"We'll live," Jim the cameraman replied. "It's only a bulb."

"Then get it fixed!" she shrilled.

"Nay bother, doll." Jim knew how to humour a deluded paymistress, however imperious her manner. But that didn't mean he didn't want to kill her with his bare hands.

The runner approached the director, like a puppy seeking a scruff. "Am I doing all right?"

"Magnificently." The director yawned.

The runner beamed gormlessly.

The cameraman finished inserting the new bulb and turned to the director. "There you go, pal. Do you want us to do that again?"

"Yes," the director replied.

"No," the producer said. "We can get the scissors in before the explosion."

"Fantastic." The director spoke like a man who knew that the editor's metaphorical *scissors* couldn't. He turned to the presenter. "How are you feeling?"

"A little shaky, dear." She swigged more brandy from the bottle. "But I'll soon be right as rain."

"Are you sure?" the director asked.

"Oh yes, dear." The presenter took another glug.

"Well, if you're absolutely certain," the director said. "Let's go for a take."

I seized my moment in the limelight with a "Phones off!"

"They already are!" the producer protested.

"Just checking," I lied.

"So," the director consulted his script. "Snow beasts."

"*Edible* snow beasts." The producer emphasised the word *edible* as if her husband's life depended upon it.

I could almost smell her overbearing anxiety as she approached the presenter. "Remember, you mention them here, but you don't actually make them yet. The edible snow beasts are the *part one climax*."

"Okay dear." The presenter took another swig of brandy.

The researcher waited for her to swallow it before handing over a tray containing paper, scissors, glue, a jar of viscous liquid and an empty milk bottle.

Once the director satisfied himself that everything was as ready as it was ever going to get, he attempted a cheery, workaday smile. "Shall we turnover?"

"Nay bother, pal." The cameraman's reply was almost instantaneous. He really did seem desperate to get it all over with, and looking around the room, that general sentiment prevailed.

That being the case, this seemed like the perfect opportunity to wind everyone up again. I cleared my throat and shouted, "Wait for the plane to pass!"

Everyone stood in frustrated silence. The producer lit another cigarette, the director masticated more Nicorette gum, the cameraman stared gloomily at his watch, the presenter swigged more brandy from the bottle, the researcher shut her eyes, and the runner yawned so widely that his jaw locked, and he had to whack his chin with the heel of his hand to close his mouth.

At that, I decided to put them out of their misery. "Okay. It's gone now."

The producer sighed. Everyone assumed their positions.

Jim manned his eyepiece. "Running up... Speed."

The director's Nicorette gum had practically glued his teeth together, but he managed to squeeze out an "Action!"

"Today," the presenter chirped into the lens, "We're going to make edible snow beasts and flammable biscuit bushes, but first a snowman snowscape in an inverted milk bottle." She cut out a paper snowman, glued it to the inside of a milk bottle and poured in the gloopy liquid. The snowman flopped soggily against the glass and began to dissolve.

The director watched this on the monitors. The blurrier of the two pictures started to rock.

"I'm sorry," the runner said, his hands shaking uncontrollably on the camcorder. "But that's the crappiest thing I've ever seen in my life."

I failed to contain myself, as did the cameraman, and director.

The producer was furious. "How dare you?"

Everyone apologized insincerely. Apart from me. I couldn't be bothered.

The producer turned to the presenter. "Why are you apologising?"

"It was my snowman who flopped. I should have made him waterproof. I'm afraid I just didn't think it through."

"Don't worry, honey. You're doing just fine." The producer turned to the director. "Would you like to have a quiet word?"

"Not particularly."

"I said, come here and have a word."

The unhappy couple retreated to a corner, imagining that their conversation was private. They were wrong. I'd dropped a live radio mic into the director's arse pocket, and I monitored their conversation through my headphones.

"She's lost it!" The producer panicked, in an under-the-breath shout. "Bloody hopeless, totally senile and probably pissed."

I heard the director swallow his gum in a pained gulp.

The cameraman stood his equipment down, conscientiously disconnecting leads, removing the matte box and replacing the lens cap.

The runner struggled to mimic this procedure with his considerably less impressive kit. "Having fun?" the runner asked, attempting to bond.

"Aye, very merry," the cameraman replied. "I love listening to that nippy producer cow bumping her gums and I'm absolutely over the effing moon about you filming the entire frigging series out of focus. She might as well have hired her granny to shoot it."

"Her granny's doing the website," the runner said.

"Good for her," the cameraman said.

"How's your hotel?" the runner asked.

"The shower seeps slime, there's nay toilet in the toilet and I'm the only guest not seeking asylum."

"Getting any kip?"

"Aye, when they're not wailing to Albanian folk music, they're shouting about blood feuds or trying to flog me dead flowers. It's about as peaceful as an Old Firm Cup Final in the marching season."

That seemed to bring the conversation between the runner and the cameraman to a close, so I switched my attention to the other side of the room. The researcher was standing beside the forest of Norwegian spruces, showing a copy of her scan to the presenter.

"He's got a lovely big head," the presenter cooed, cradling the brandy bottle.

"Thanks," the researcher replied. "But that's his bum. His head's down there."

"Well, that's lovely too, dear."

"Edible snow beasts next," the researcher said.

The presenter handed the scan back. "Have you got my bits dear?"

The researcher put away the scan and fetched a tray containing pastry, icing sugar, raisins, greaseproof paper, a metal dish, assorted plastic shapes and some complete edible snow beasts.

"Thank you, dear," the presenter said, and took another swig.

The producer returned from her supposedly confidential contretemps with the director, and said, "Right, let's not waste any more time."

"Nay bother, doll," the cameraman said.

The director summoned what little remained of his professional enthusiasm. "Shall we change the set up?"

"We haven't got time," the producer said.

"Okay," the director said, sounding far from okay. "Let's go for a take."

"Nay bother, pal." The cameraman switched on the lights.

The director turned his attention to the monitors. "Turnover."

I hesitated for just long enough to offer them hope, before saying, "Wait for the plane to pass." Was I being childish? Yes. Did I enjoy it? Yes.

Everyone stood in silence, waiting for the passing of my imaginary aircraft. The researcher shut her eyes, the presenter swigged brandy, Jim consulted his watch, the runner failed to stifle a yawn, the director cradled his chins. The producer glared at me with such intensity that I felt obliged to pretend to follow the plane's trajectory through the ceiling with my boom pole. Rarely has a piece of sound kit moved more slowly. Eventually, once I had given the imaginary plane enough time to cross most of the Atlantic, I said, "Okay. It's gone."

"Running up," the cameraman said as he fiddled with his equipment. "Speed."

"And action!" The director cued the presenter.

"Children love abominable snowmen," the presenter began, "And sometimes they're good enough to eat, especially if they're made of pastry and covered in icing sugar. Here's how to make edible snow beasts."

"Hang on!" the producer interrupted. "I've got an idea.

"Christ!" The director shouted, before adding a "dearest."

"What?" The producer looked as belligerent as a cage fighter.

"It's just that it was going well," the director replied. "What's your idea?"

"Let's use the fire!" the producer exclaimed with the enthusiasm of a visionary prophet. "What could be more Christmassy than a real fire?"

"But it's not real," the researcher said.

"We know it's not real." The producer winked. "But the viewers won't."

"It's a coal-effect gas fire," the director said.

"Precisely!" The producer raised her hands for emphasis. "It's an effect. A special effect."

"Brilliant!" The runner seized the chance to suck up. "Like an explosion!"

"Exactly. That's the spirit." The producer inhaled a lungful of smoke. "At Nepotism, we pride ourselves on our ambition. Turn on the fire." She exhaled.

Once the researcher had finished coughing, she gave the fireplace a dubious look. "Do I really have to? It looks a bit dodgy to me."

"So does my husband," the producer laughed. "But I still turn him on."

"Now, now dearest." The director cringed. "Don't embarrass me."

The researcher shook her head in disgust, turned on the gas tap, and asked, "Can someone give me a light?"

"Here." The producer dangled her cigarette in the researcher's face. "Use this."

"Thanks." The researcher took it and attempted to light the gas tap.

The producer looked down at the researcher's bulging belly and summoned a shade of humanity to her tone. "What are you going to call it?"

"If it's a boy, we might call it Jack. If it's a girl, then maybe Daisy."

"Daisy? Jack?" The producer spat, instantly transformed back into harridan-mode. "Children are wasted on your generation. You name your daughters after cows, your sons after peasants and you stay at home so you can't afford proper childcare."

"I won't need childcare," the researcher said.

"Nor will I!" The producer's face crumpled into tears.

I hadn't expected that. Until now, the producer had shown all the emotional fragility of a frozen halibut. I watched her retreat to the corner with the director and listened in to their conversation once again:

"Just one more cycle might do it." The producer sounded oddly childlike.

"That's not what the doctor said, dearest," the director replied.

"Bloody IVF! Sounds like a terrorist group."

"Well, it's terrorised us for long enough. We've done all we can, but even if Nepotism goes global, we can't buy the impossible."

"Without kids," the producer sniffed. "There's not much future for Nepotism."

I didn't want to hear the producer sobbing, so I removed my headphones.

Regrettably, the runner took this as an invitation to talk to me. "You know there used to be a TV show where you win everything advertised in the commercial break?"

I offered him a blank expression.

"Well, if the Living Room Channel did it, you'd win a stair lift, life insurance and debt counselling." The runner exploded with boundless mirth.

It was probably an accurate observation, but I didn't want to encourage him to continue talking to me.

I looked across the room. The researcher was still struggling to light the gas tap with the producer's cigarette. The presenter was stood beside her, drunk and maudlin.

"No one's really interested in my edible snow beasts, are they?" the presenter asked.

"I am," the researcher replied. "And don't worry, so are they." She pointed at the camera lenses.

The producer caught the end of this, and weighed in. "Are they? A few misguided souls in nursing homes and mental hospitals might have you on in the background, but don't delude yourself - no one is sad enough to listen to what you say and least of all to make an edible snow beast!"

The presenter burst into tears and left the room. The researcher stamped out the cigarette and ran after her.

I couldn't help reflecting that these developments didn't bode well for Nepotism and the twenty-eight festive episodes yet to be recorded, so I consoled myself by listening in to the producer's "private" conversation with the director in the far corner:

"Was that necessary?" the director asked.

"Yes!" The producer replied.

"Bang goes the series!" the director said.

"Who cares?" The producer was losing whatever grip she'd ever had. "As ideas go, it had about as much going for it as *The James Cordon Hotpants Workout*."

"That idea had legs," the director replied.

The producer hit him with the edible snow beast tray and lit up another cigarette.

I was feeling hungry, so I stole a mince pie from the set and gobbled it whilst watching the cameraman pack away his kit.

"Well," Jim sighed, as he capped his lens. "That just about takes the kipper's knickers." He has always had a poetic turn of phrase. You get that with Glaswegians, along with the violence.

The runner's kit had about three parts, so didn't take long to put away. As he zipped up his single case, he asked, "Can anyone else smell gas?"

"No, laddie," the cameraman replied. "Just a load of hot air and that's odourless."

"Is it?" The researcher said on her way back in from consoling the presenter. "Around here, I think it smells of Nicotine!"

The producer squared up to her, armed with her latest cigarette. "How dare you?"

The researcher wasn't backing down. "How dare you break an old lady's heart and choke my unborn child with your filthy smoke all day?"

"She might be enjoying it for all you know," the producer replied.

"What makes you think it's a *she*?" the researcher asked.

"Because you seem like a sensible girl." The producer smiled thinly. "Where's our presenter?"

"She's gone to see her grandchildren," the researcher replied.

"Well, off you bugger too," the producer said. "Go on, drop your sprog."

"Fine." The researcher turned to go.

"What are you doing spawning at your age anyway?"

"I'm nearly thirty."

"That's nothing."

"It's all relative, I suppose."

"What do you mean by that?"

"Well, to a teenager, twenty-nine is just this side of ancient."

"And?"

"You're the other side of ancient."

"You're not fit to be a mum!" The producer shrieked.

The director apologised to the researcher and led the producer to their corner. They were both still completely unaware that I could hear their every word through my headphones:

"Leave her alone, dearest."

"But she's pregnant, for God's sake!"

"I know, but don't blame her. Her biological clock was ticking. It's not her fault if yours has stopped. It's a very nice clock. Good enough for my mantelpiece, but the mechanism is beyond the repair of ... the finest watchmaker in Switzerland."

The collapsing marriage went silent, so I removed my headphones, looked back into the centre of the room, and saw the researcher offer the runner a lift.

The runner hesitated and turned to the cameraman. "Am I still needed?"

"Are any of us?" Jim had already packed up most of his camera gear.

The producer removed any remaining doubt by storming back into the centre of the festivities and shouting, "Get lost the lot of you and have yourselves a merry bloody Christmas!"

The director raised his hands to the ceiling like a surrendering soldier. "Thank you, everyone."

A few minutes later, I was out in the summer sun with Jim, loading our gear into the back of the crew van.

The shoot hadn't been filled with an excess of jolly incidents, so anecdotes were in short supply, but Jim did eventually turn to me and say, "We're nowhere near a flight path, are we?"

I thought about lying but couldn't be arsed, so I shook my head.

"There never were any planes?"

"No."

"Oh."

Jim's a decent bloke, so I felt he was due an explanation: "I don't like Christmas."

"I suppose it's all right in December." Jim unscrewed a lens. "What is it now?"

"Fourth of July."

Jim grinned. "Happy Independence Day!"

An electronic crackle reminded me that I'd forgotten to retrieve the director's unnoticed arse-mic. Having just escaped the house, I didn't relish rushing back inside, so I decided to eavesdrop on the couple one last time. I put my headphones on and listened in:

"We're never going to have any kids, are we?" the producer said.

"No, love," the director replied.

"That's right. No love."

"We've still got each other."

"And?"

"Our work."

"What, edible snow beasts?"

"Don't be silly, dearest."

I heard the crunchy sound of violence being exacted on festive biscuits.

"There's one thing we can still share," the director said. "Give us a fag."

"They're the one thing we have that's not disposable."

I heard the flick of a cigarette lighter, followed by a gas explosion. The coal-effect fire had finally been lit.

***

I offered to buy the boom operator a pint to thank him for his story, but he explained that he had to be up early to film a corporate video for an arms dealer. It was well-paid and he was keen to give it his full attention.

RULE 11 - THE LAW HAS LONG ARMS AND HAIRY LEGS

I once met a police inspector who had narrowly escaped being rendered into a block of lard. It happened during an investigation into a series of poltergeist-related incidents and the experience had turned every hair on his head snow white.

We met over a pie. I was dithering between steak-and-kidney and gammon-and-cider, and the inspector offered some unsolicited advice. He was a man who knew his pastry inside out, and, once he had persuaded me to follow his example and opt for the gammon, I suggested he join me at my table. He explained that his name was Inspector Wildgoose, and he was recovering from the strangest case of his career.

I asked him if he would mind giving me the lowdown and he was kind enough to oblige:

***

"It all began when I was assigned the poshest partner on the planet. She was a flame-haired sergeant named Herring and she seemed more suited to a pony club than Salisbury nick. Her favourite expressions were "Golly Gosh!", "My Sainted Aunt!" and "Cripes!", and I wondered whether she had ticked a diversity box for "gormless numpty".

The Super clearly despised her and made a point of sending us on fool's errands to get Herring out of his hair. This time, we'd been dispatched to the village of

Wiggle-under-Bullock to interview a local lunatic about his paranormal delusions.

On the plus side, we had a shiny new patrol car. For years, I had been chuntering about in a clapped-out old banger well below the dignity of my pay grade. Now that I finally had a decent motor, I would have been failing in my duty if I hadn't put the sirens on full blast and hit one-hundred-and-twenty for a solid hour. The sirens not only alerted other motorists to my rapid approach, but they also blocked out Sergeant Herring's drivel about "county balls", "gorgeous hunks", and "show jumping".

When we passed through a dense forest, I dropped down to ninety-eight. My caution was rewarded when I narrowly dodged a rutting buck. The last thing I wanted was to prang my new motor on a hundred kilos of fresh venison.

Wiggle-under-Bullock looked to have all the standard-issue attributes: duck pond, pub, church, vicarage, farm, and cottages, but it also boasted multi-coloured bunting advertising the annual *Lard Festival*. A hunch told me it might be a tad less thrilling than Glastonbury.

The moment I parked outside the complainant's condemned barn, a scream issued from inside. Herring shrieked in sympathy, which wasn't helpful.

I kicked a door, which disintegrated on impact, and we walked in on piles of elaborate agricultural contraptions. A wild-eyed scarecrow I took to be the complainant was running a lathe along a miniature guillotine, the source of the screaming sound.

"Don't worry, officers," he explained in an accent nurtured over generations of inbreeding, "It's a badger trap. Completely humane. Decapitation is almost instant."

"Yuck!" Herring exclaimed, like a weening infant.

I had encountered more savoury individuals than the complainant, but I decided to keep things polite. "Good morning, sir. What seems to be the problem?"

"Cursed!" he declaimed, like a demented prophet. "The whole village is cursed! Ever since the committee drowned Mad Ethel."

"Gosh!" Herring exclaimed.

I swallowed a "bollocks". Had the superintendent's fool's errand turned into a murder investigation? "What committee drowned whom?"

"The committee drowned Mad Ethel in the duck pond, of course." The complainant's expression suggested that I had to be a moron for not knowing this. "She was accused of witchcraft, wasn't she, but proved her innocence by drowning."

"And when was this?"

"1592."

Herring's brow furrowed. "Ninety-two minutes past three?"

"No," the complainant replied, impatiently, "1592."

"The sixteenth century?" I'd heard of cold cases, but this was pushing it. Why on Earth had we been sent here? The Super really knew how to waste police time.

I turned to go, but the complainant wasn't having it. "I'd like to report my poltergeist for breaking and entering. I've had frogspawn in the washing up, sticklebacks in the shower and pondweed in the bath. Last night, I heard the squish of soggy footsteps in the attic and a bloodcurdling quack."

"A bloodcurdling quack?" I queried.

"Undead ducks," he explained.

I retreated for a quiet word with Herring. "You know why we're really here, don't you?"

"Haven't the foggiest," she replied.

"Could you try irritating the Super less?"

"I don't see what that's got to do with it."

"You don't, do you."

"No."

Herring really didn't, so I decided to spell things out for her. "I'm stuck out here in the capital of nowhere when I could be back at the station catching up on paperwork and it's all because you should be on *Downton Abbey* rather than on the beat."

Herring looked close to tears.

I adopted a more conciliatory tone. "Surely, you'd noticed. It's not the first time the Super's sent us on a wild goose chase, is it?"

"A wild goose chase for …Inspector Wildgoose!" She giggled uncontrollably and knocked over a cardboard box. It fell apart on the floor, releasing a cloud of gunpowder.

"Mind your step, officers," the complainant warned belatedly. "That's my pyrotechnical area. I'm working on ways of exploding foxes. It's a quicker death than hunting."

"Golly," Herring said with a soppy smile. "How thoughtful of you."

I'd had enough. This bloke didn't need the cops, he needed a good seeing to from the RSPCA. "Does anyone else live here? A social worker? A wife, even?".

He looked subdued. "The wife's passed. Cancer of the arse. Terminal."

I apologised. Herring sobbed. The complainant lent her a handkerchief, but it was covered in badger blood.

We made our excuses and left. I couldn't wait to hit the road again. The trouble was the road was empty. My first new patrol car in twenty-two years was nowhere to be seen. I despaired. "Tell me it's not true!"

"That would be lying, sir," Herring replied.

The complainant shouted after us, "I told you this village was cursed!"

We were going to have to investigate the theft of our own patrol car. It was a colossal embarrassment, but in all my years as a copper, I had never been more fired up about a case.

We could discount the complainant, as he had been busy telling us about his badger guillotine, undead ducks, and fox explosives at the time. It had to be a local – outsiders had no reason to pass through a place with no discernible attractions.

The nearest building appeared to be a vicarage. The clergy didn't tend to specialise in grand theft auto, but they might know their parishioners. It was a start.

The vicarage's heavy oak door was answered by a tweedy woman clutching a handful of piano keys. "How can I help you?"

"We've had our car stolen," I said.

"Have you informed the police?" she asked.

"We are the police," I replied.

She invited us into a spacious living room dominated by a grand piano. It was a magnificent specimen, but every key was missing.

"Looks like a rather unusual accident," I observed.

"The piano tuner got a bit carried away." It was not a convincing reply.

"We've been speaking to your neighbour," I began. "The gentleman with a grudge against wildlife."

"He has a few too many bats in his belfry, poor chap," the woman replied. "But don't underestimate him, he's made a bomb."

"Jolly wealthy, is he?" Herring asked, as a colossal explosion rang out across the village.

"No," the woman said. "He's made an actual bomb. That was probably it, I should think."

"Golly," Herring observed.

I looked out of the window. The soot-faced complainant gave me a thumbs-up from the remains of his barn. There appeared to be no human casualties, so I continued my dogged pursuit of our patrol vehicle. "We've heard mention of a curse. Do many cars disappear?"

"Like planes in the Bermuda Triangle, you mean?" she asked.

I nodded, trying not to mentally replay the Barry Manilow ditty.

"Never," the woman said. "It's always been a peaceful village."

"Are you the vicar?" Herring asked.

"Don't be silly," the woman replied, whilst applying some glue to the base of a piano key. "We're not a bunch of lefties here."

"Understood. I don't suppose we could borrow your car for an hour or so," I asked. "Just so we can look for ours."

"I'm afraid not," the woman replied, as she placed the glued key into the grand piano's toothless gob. "But if you toddle over to St Judas's, my husband might be able to help."

Even though I resented the word *toddle*, I thanked her and wished her the best of luck rebuilding her piano.

St Judas's church was a gothic monstrosity decorated with some of the grimmest gargoyles I had ever clapped eyes on; every one a stone-faced insult from the mind of a maniac. The interior was even worse - grisly depictions of blokes being martyred inventively and an aisle rug depicting Mad Ethel's terminal ducking. Expert knitters had captured her turmoil and the surrounding villagers' cruelty in exquisite detail.

I am not one to jump to conclusions, but the current vicar was a supercilious bastard.

"So, the first time the constabulary deign to pay a visit to our community," he sneered, "it's because they've had their panda stolen."

I wasn't having this. "We actually came here because your neighbour complained about some rather distressing occurrences."

"I wonder who that could have been," the vicar replied with unholy sarcasm. "Did these distressing occurrences involve undead ducks, by any chance?"

"Well guessed!" Herring trilled, clapping her hands in glee. It was like being partnered by a girl guide.

The vicar stared at her in disbelief for a cold ten seconds. "Let me look in the Sunday school storeroom. I'm sure we can find you both something suitable." He sloped off down an annex and returned with two small bicycles. They had been designed for pre-pubescent girls and were covered in stickers celebrating princesses and ponies.

Herring seemed delighted with her bike, but I can't say I was.

The vicar gave me an evil grin. "I'd start with Midwinter Farm if I were you. They manage most of the land around here, so your vehicle is as likely to have been torched on their patch as anywhere."

"You really are too kind," Herring said.

Kind would not have been my word of preference, but at least the vicar offered us directions. "They're just along Hangman's Lane. Take the third left after The Crow Road and Midwinter Farm is at the top of Drawquarter Passage."

"Thanks." It didn't sound like a particularly scenic route.

"If you reach Armageddon Avenue," he added, "you'll have gone too far."

We wheeled our way down the aisle, mounted our bikes in the graveyard and cycled past the village green. My bike was designed for a child under five-foot tall and, as I pedalled, my knees were almost level with my chin.

"If you don't mind me saying sir," Herring said, "You do look particularly foolish on your pink pony bike."

"Thank you, Herring."

"I suppose it should help you lose a little belly fat." Herring was not big on tact.

I sulked all the way to Midwinter Farm. Two signs welcomed visitors: *Well-Endowed Bull For Hire* and *Wanted – Old Tarmac*. A rustic bloke watched our arrival with incredulity. I didn't blame him: we weren't just strangers, we were a pair of plonkers on pink, princessy pedals.

"And who might you be?" The farmer gave our wheels a scornful look. "The soppiest chapter of the Hell's Angels?"

"What a wonderful farm!" Herring exclaimed. "You must be very proud."

"I pinch myself regular," the farmer deadpanned.

"We're here to investigate the theft of a car," I showed him my badge.

"And whose car might that be?" he asked.

"Ours," I replied.

"He's nicked your car, has he?" the farmer asked.

"Who's he?" I asked.

"The local crime wave," the farmer said.

"I wouldn't want to jump to any conclusions," I said.

"Jump away," he said. "No other bugger did it."

"Who is the local crime wave?" I asked.

"The village teenager," the farmer replied.

"Is that an official position?" I asked.

The farmer bristled. "Don't you try your big-city sarcasm with me."

"None intended," I lied. "Where can we find him?"

"In your car I should think," the farmer said, unhelpfully.

"Got a bit of a track record, has he?" I ventured.

"Too right he has. Yesterday morning, the little bugger pelted me with free range eggs and the other week he showered the missus with bull semen."

"Bull semen?" Herring furrowed her brow. "Where on earth did he get that from?"

"Bulls," the farmer explained.

"Yuck!" Herring ejaculated.

"Look," the farmer said, wearily. "When you find him. Hand him over to the village committee and we'll string the little bastard up, pelt him with stones and bury him in the woods."

"If it's all very well, I'll keep it a police matter," I replied. "Village committees can't order lynchings."

"We used to," the farmer said.

"This is the twenty-first century, sir. Not the sixteenth."

"Standards have slipped. I don't like to whinge, but I'm a farmer and it comes naturally."

"Understood, sir. But that doesn't help us retrieve our police car, does it?"

"Where did you have it last?"

"We parked it outside the badger-killer's barn," I replied. "Before his bomb exploded."

"And what were you doing there? Listening to a load of slurry about Mad Ethel I shouldn't wonder. You don't want to believe old Jethro."

A woman approached with a basket. We showed her our badges, but she only had eyes for our princess bikes. Once she had stopped laughing, she tilted the basket towards us. "Try one of these. Goose eggs. Give you the runs, but they're a real food. Fancy one?"

"No thanks," I replied. It wasn't a difficult decision.

"Are you related?"

"Nothing wrong with incest!" She bristled.

"I mean, are you married?"

"For my sins, yes." She smiled at her husband.

He didn't smile back. He just said, "And mine."

"Tell us about the village teenager," I said.

"Poor lad is very troubled," the farmer's wife said. "Who wouldn't be after what happened to his parents?"

"And what was that?" I asked.

"It's a gruesome story," the farmer's wife said.

"Oh gracious," Herring said. "I think I'm about to get the collywobbles."

"Well, for most of the year," the farmer's wife said, "his parents were a popular couple, but the trouble always came at Christmas. Although they were both tone death and laryngitic, they insisted on going carol singing. People would tell them they were dreadful, but they wouldn't listen. Every year they'd go door-to-door murdering the spirit of Christmas. Their caterwauling would turn the milk sour, distress the chickens, and make the sheep howl. The village committee even made a formal complaint, but that didn't stop them. Then, one year, just after they had reached "I saw three ships come sailing by", a combine harvester careered down Black Dog Hill and harvested them alive."

Herring screamed. "Golly, how ghastly."

"It made the committee's litter-pick a little tricky. We wanted to win the *Best Kept Village Contest*, you see, and we'd have stood no chance with diced body parts scattered all over the green. Mikey took it all to heart, poor lad."

A double combine harvester-shredding would not have gone unnoticed at national level, let alone at the local nick. But the deaths were not my immediate priority. I wanted my car back. "Where does young Mikey live now?"

"With his aunt, Anna," the woman replied. "But the less said about her the better. She's one of the village red-light districts."

"You have more than one?" It seemed that Amsterdam had nothing on Wiggle-under-Bullock.

"There's one red-light district at number thirty-six, and another red-light district at number forty-seven," the farmer replied.

"Golly!" Herring exclaimed, jiggling on the spot. "I've always wanted to visit a real-life red-light district!"

My sergeant truly was a prize specimen, and we all took a while to stare at her appreciatively.

After a bit, I thought it best to move the enquiry along. "Where might we find this woman's red-light district?"

"Up Trotter's Bottom," the farmer replied. "Along Cousinkiss Way, take a left into

Deliverance Lane and it's at the top of Rider's Mound. Can't miss it."

I thanked the rustic couple, and we cycled off through a succession of muddy lanes to a ramshackle street of unnumbered cottages. After we had pedalled up and down for a bit, we found one with a red lightbulb in the porch. It seemed a safe bet, and this was confirmed when my knock was answered by a woman in a leopardskin negligee.

"We're looking for the red-light district," Herring blurted out, excitedly.

"Good for you," the woman replied.

"Is this it?" Herring asked.

"Depends who's asking," the woman said.

"The police," I replied, flashing my badge.

"Then you've come to the wrong place." She rearranged her attitude. "This is strictly legitimate."

I looked at the array of hardcore erotic equipment in the hallway. "How exactly?"

"I'm an osteopath," the woman explained. "An intimate osteopath."

"Super!" Herring said. "Can you do my back?"

"I specialise in fronts," the woman elaborated. "Male fronts."

I could feel the woman's eyes on my crotch, so I said, "The farm sent us here."

"It's nice to be recommended," she scoffed. "And what exactly are you looking for?"

"The village teenager," I said. "Mikey."

"It's taken you rozzers long enough to take an interest in our village," the woman said. "Why start now?"

"He may have stolen our car," I said, ruefully.

"Oh, I see. It's only when you get your own car nicked that you bother to show up. Anyway, I'm the wrong frontal osteopath. You're looking for Anna."

We said our goodbyes and cycled up and down for a bit longer. Eventually, Herring squealed and pointed at a red lightbulb dangling in the porch of a near-identical cottage further up the road. We knocked at the door. There was no answer.

As I stood beside my ridiculous sergeant and our princess bikes, I couldn't help reflecting that I had been involved in more successful operations. So far, we had interviewed a deluded lunatic about some undead ducks, lost our patrol car, met a woman with a keyless piano, borrowed a pair of girls' bikes off the snarky vicar, paid a fruitless visit to a farm and met an unhelpful prostitute posing as a "frontal osteopath."

"I'm jolly hungry," Herring blurted. "I could eat an entire herd of cattle."

For once, I had to agree with Herring.

We cycled back to the village centre. *The Witch and Duck Pond* had a sign depicting a submerged crone surrounded by diving mallards. It didn't promise fine dining and luxury, but when it came to pubs, Wiggle-under-Bullock offered a choice of one, so we left our bikes by a window and went in. A real fire raged between a skittles alley and a bar billiards area, and there was a pile of village newsletters headlined, *Ghost Worries Sheep*.

A young woman of South-East Asian appearance stood boredly behind a counter offering *Classic Wiltshire Ales and Local Thai Food*. I gave her a smile and asked for the menu. She dipped below the bar and re-emerged clutching a card reading, *I Don't Speak English*.

I tried talking slowly. "Can I speak to the landlord?"

She dipped below the bar again and returned with another card reading, *Back In 5 Mins*.

I thanked her for very little and flicked through the village newsletter. Features included *Bait That Badger*, a report from a poaching convention and a lengthy preview of the Lard Festival. Last year's winner was the vicar's wife, and she was pictured holding a pristine tray of exquisitely rendered fatty tissue. There were many photos of previous contests: inter-war lard, sixties lard, millennium lard. Most villages were content with cake-bakes and novelty vegetables, but clearly Wiggle-under-Bullock was no ordinary village.

After about twenty minutes, a formidably ugly bloke walked in, looking deeply displeased to see customers. "No food after two," he muttered in a local grumble.

When I pointed out that it was ten to one, he handed me a menu in untranslated Thai. It wasn't helpful.

"What do you recommend?" I asked.

"All depends on what you like, don't it?" the landlord asked, impatiently.

"Fish and chips?" Herring ventured.

"Do me a favour," he replied.

"Pie?" I suggested.

"Wrong continent."

"Thai pie?" Herring guessed.

"Enough of this," he said. "You'll have two specials and that's an end to it."

We looked through the open kitchen door as the woman prepared the mysterious meal with great violence, throwing knives at vegetables, pummelling ingredients, and massacring meat with machetes. A flame surged, then there was a furious burst of flash-frying and rigorous plate-plonking.

The landlord brought us the specials, reversed a chair, and sat astride it like Christine Keeler as he watched us eat. "You're not from these parts, are you?"

"No, sir," I replied through a mouthful of mystery-meat. "We're not."

"Then what the hell are you doing here?" he asked.

"We're on police business..." I began.

"It wasn't my combine harvester," he interrupted.

The landlord's defensive panic would have raised my suspicions were I investigating the double murder of the tone-deaf carol singers, but that was not my main concern. "We're investigating a car theft."

"And whose car might that be?" he asked.

"Ours," I said.

"What makes you think it's in my village?" he said.

"We parked it here," I replied.

"That was careless," he said.

"Was it?" I asked.

"Looks like it," he said.

There wasn't anything special about the special – just some spicy noodles and gristle.

I felt like complaining, but before I could, Herring blurted out, "Absolutely yummy! My compliments to the chef!"

The landlord just stared at us until we had finished, then said, "Fifty pounds eighty."

I thought the meal was worth about a quid, but I had my police credit card with me.

"Cash only," the landlord said. "Service not included."

I emptied my wallet and requested a receipt. He claimed his printer was broken. I said that a handwritten one would do, provided it was on headed paper. He scrawled something illegible on the corner of a village newsletter and tore it off. I trousered it and headed for the doors.

Herring skipped after me. "Cheer up, sir. Why not turn that frown upside down?" Her sympathy was as welcome as a dose of syphilis, but she didn't notice this. "Shall we take the scenic route? If we go through the woods, we can loop around to the red-light district in no time."

I had no interest in scenery, but it would at least enable us to scope out the vicinity for my car. We remounted the princess bikes and set off.

I must admit, the woods were idyllic – unspoiled stretches of oak, ash, and redwood. I was almost starting to enjoy the ride when a giant bloodhound sprang out of a hollow and charged at us. Herring veered off into the trees. I hit the brakes and nose-dived over the handlebars. The next thing I saw was a grizzled bloke looming over me, holding a shotgun to my head, and snarling the word, "Poachers!"

"Police officers," I gasped, prising my badge out of my pocket.

"Stone me, the rest of the country gets The Flying Squad, and we get The Barbie Bunch." The man waved his shotgun about in disgust. "You cyclists are just like ramblers - too bloody mean to pay for petrol."

"Where's my sergeant?"

"Under my dog."

I looked further down the lane and, sure enough, Herring lay beneath the bloodhound, whimpering.

"Can she get out?" I asked.

"Not unless Fang lets her," he replied.

"Call him off, please. We need to get to the red-light district. It's urgent."

After a long pause, the man shouted, "Fang! Mercy! No Kill Today!"

Fang released Herring, who crossed herself and repeated the word "Golly" on a loop.

I struggled to my feet and watched the man hook up my princess bike with his shotgun barrel.

"So," the man said, "You urgently need the red-light district?"

"Yes," I replied. "The second one."

"Right you are. You go down Coffin Lid Lane and along Gallows Way as far as Cutthroat Cottage. Then it's thirteen yards up Butcher's Alley, just before Vulture's Close. You can't miss it."

I thanked him, nursed my injuries, and did my best to console Herring.

"Now off you bugger." The man strode off with his hound.

Herring's cycling was now noticeably more erratic, but she soldiered on to the second red-light district. When we got there, all was not well. The woman who worked as the first red-light district was having a screaming match with a woman who looked as if she worked as the second red-light district. I may have been making the kind of assumptions that would get a Tweeter cancelled, but I am a detective inspector, and she was wearing thigh-high leather boots, a suede mini-skirt and a breastless t-shirt.

"I told you!" the first woman shrieked. "I'm the only red-light district in this village!"

"You lying whore!" The other woman shouted. "The red-light district is here at number forty-seven! It's been in my family for generations."

I couldn't let this escalate, so I thrust out my badge. "Look, can't you both work peacefully alongside each other?"

"Why?" the second woman asked. "Fancy a threesome?"

I did, but there's a time and place for everything and I was more concerned about my stolen patrol car.

No doubt influenced by my arrival; the row climaxed prematurely. "I'll get you, Anna," the first woman threatened, as she strutted off. "This village is too small for the pair of us."

"Call yourself a red-light district? You're no more than a knocking shop!" The second woman walked into her red-light district. When we followed her in, she turned angrily and snarled, "Ever heard of knocking?"

"Sorry. We forgot this was a knocking shop." Herring burst into floods of giggles.

Sometimes, I despair of junior officers.

Noting my disapproval, Herring said, "Sorry, sir. I thought that was the sort of joke men of your age liked."

It was, but I was not about to let her know that. The cottage was uncannily like the first red-light district, with copious erotic accoutrements arranged at cheeky angles. Herring couldn't suppress her giggles at the eye-opening array of dildos, but we weren't here to admire penile-substitutes we were here to get our new patrol car back. I didn't waste any more time.

"Are you the mother of the village teenager?"

"What of it?"

"There's a rumour he might have stolen our car."

"Got any proof?"

Before I could reply, Herring chipped in with a "No."

It wasn't helpful, so I tried distracting the woman with another question. "Do you have a picture of Mikey?"

"Of course. What kind of mother do you take me for?" The woman walked over to a whipping bench, unlocked a compartment, and took out a framed photo of her sharing a spliff with a teenage boy in a blue-and-amber football shirt.

"Shrewsbury Town!" Herring blurted, like a University Challenge contestant on a starter-for-ten.

"Well, aren't you clever," the woman said.

"I never took you for a football fan, Herring," I said.

"Loads of gorgeous hunks!" Herring exclaimed.

"Town are only in the third tier," the woman said. She took a chocolate finger out of a box and sucked its end off. "I can name a second suspect."

Finally, a breakthrough! I looked at her expectantly.

"Mad Ethel." Her words dashed my optimism in three syllables.

Herring wasn't slow to find the theory's fatal flaw. "Isn't she a ghost?"

"She may be dead," the woman said. "But don't hold that against her. She's as alive as you or me. Terrible hauntings, she gives. Only the other night, pints were pouring themselves in the pub, the piano was playing itself in the vicarage and the tractor was possessed."

"The tractor was possessed?" I stifled a chuckle.

"That's right," she said. "Possessed. Driving itself in circles it was. And howling."

"Howling?" I queried.

"Carburettor like a banshee. Made my blood run cold."

"And the piano?" I asked.

"Played itself. There was an invisible plonker."

"In the vicarage!" Herring exclaimed, as if this connection between the keyless piano and the spooky nonsense required a Poirot to spot.

"Right," I sighed. "On the off-chance that Mad Ethel didn't take our car, where can we find your son?"

"No idea," she replied. "But I can tell you where to find Mad Ethel."

"The graveyard?" I ventured.

"Her bones, perhaps. But her spirit dwells in the duck pond."

"Jolly good." I was running out of patience, and ready to resort to sarcasm. "I'll get on the phone to the police diving unit right away."

As we hit the princess bikes and cycled back to the village centre, Herring seemed far from her usual cheerful self.

"Golly, sir, ghosts can be extraordinarily scary, can't they?"

"You're a police sergeant, Herring, not a girl guide. Pull yourself together and think of the force."

"I can't help it, sir. I was drummed out of the girl guides for desertion."

I was about to challenge the veracity of this claim when I caught sight of something so incredible, I almost fell off my princess bike: the outline of our patrol car.

"It's here!" I shouted. "I can see it!" My heart skipped. Finally! This was shaping up to be one of the happiest moments of my life.

It was not until I had reached the village green that I realised the appalling truth. My beautiful car was being dragged backwards from the duckpond by an elderly tractor. I had waited five years for a new vehicle, and within twelve hours it was swimming with the mallards.

"The pond's probably chock full of clues!" Herring gushed. "Should we be thinking about donning wetsuits and flippers?"

"No," I replied, fighting back tears. I could barely speak.

"I'm just trying to think outside the box," Herring protested.

"Well," I said. "If you're not careful, you'll end up thinking inside a box. A dark wooden one." Harsh, I know, but I wasn't in the best of moods.

We released our bike stabilizers, and watched the tragedy unfold. I thought of my new car's rear axle steering, virtual exterior mirrors, and super-cruise control and wept. For me, this was akin to witnessing the death of a prize bull at the hands of a toreador: a calamity of legendary proportions. I was lost in grief, right up until the moment I saw the skeleton at the wheel. It was wearing a Shrewsbury Town shirt.

The farmer leant out the tractor window and took great pleasure in saying, "Found your car for you, Inspector."

"Thanks," I replied. "But don't touch anything. The car's a crime scene."

"It's a write-off," the farmer said. "And so's the village teenager."

"Herring," I said. "Would you call Forensics?"

"For the body, sir?"

"For both," I replied. I turned to the farmer. "We'll need to cover the vehicle before we get a proper pathology tent in place."

"We've got a marquee," he offered. "For the Lard Festival."

I thanked him, prematurely. The marquee turned out to be a multi-coloured monstrosity illustrated with an array of clowns and circus animals; bunting, balloons and inflatable pigs dangled from the top.

I didn't feel festive, I felt bereft: the loss of a new car can unman a man. Once we had enlisted some villagers to erect the tent, we went inside to take a closer look. It was a heartless crime, killing off the car – what kind of person could bring themselves to drive such a masterpiece of modern engineering into a duckpond, and cut it off in its prime?

Herring seemed more concerned with the driver, which struck me as incredibly cold. I was a colleague and I had just lost my car.

"It looks ancient," Herring observed.

"Time of death?" I asked.

"Probably Tudor," Herring replied.

"So, a Tudor stole our car this morning."

"They were lawless times back then."

"This morning?"

"The sixteenth century."

I was in a state of mourning for the vehicle, but that didn't stop me from getting irritated by Herring. I could have given her a good talking to, but it wouldn't have made any difference, so I decided we'd be far better off doing some actual detective work.

"Let's ask some awkward questions," I said.

"But won't that be a bit embarrassing, sir?" Herring objected.

"For the culprit, yes."

"But for me too, sir. Socially, I'm highly sensitive."

"You're a police sergeant, Herring. Pull yourself together."

I swallowed a "snowflake" on my way out of the makeshift pathology marquee and stopped to interrogate the farmer, who was still milling about the duck pond. "Where were you earlier today?"

"I suppose I was mostly farming," he replied.

"Really?"

"I was up a cow. You wouldn't believe how roomy they are. I got both arms in."

"Who found the car?" Herring asked. It wasn't a bad question, but the sound of the word *car* made my heart sob.

"It was the gamekeeper," the farmer replied. "He reckons his hound can smell death underwater."

"I suppose we'd better pay him a visit, then," I said.

"He's not hard to find if you know where you're going." The farmer speed-blurted some mindboggling directions and re-mounted his tractor.

Forty minutes later, we had abandoned our princess bikes and were stumbling through thick undergrowth.

"I'm sure he said it was the fifty-third oak on the right," I said. "How many do you make it so far?"

"Two-hundred-and-twenty-four. This is rather like orienteering. I remember at Roedean - AAAAAAAARRRRGH!"

The ground opened up beneath us and we fell twelve feet into a mantrap.

For the second time that day, the gamekeeper looked down at me. This time, though, he knew we weren't poachers.

"I suppose you'll have come about the death then," he said, before helping us haul ourselves out of the mantrap.

He took us to his cottage, which would have been a hospitable gesture were it not for the overpowering stench. The air was thick with dog hairs, animal heads were mounted on every wall, and the sound of his hound supping water from the toilet bowl with its enormous tongue made thought difficult. "Make yourselves at home," he said.

Herring looked admiringly at a particularly grotesque example of cervine taxidermy. "Nice Bambi."

"I stuffed him myself," the gamekeeper replied. "He was a troublemaker, didn't fit into the herd, so I slaughtered him. I know he was young. Still an adolescent really, his whole life ahead of him and I cut it short. Just one carefully placed bullet and Fang did the rest."

The hound ran up and pinned me to my chair. The gamekeeper seemed unconcerned and walked calmly out of the room.

"Please don't go away," I pleaded from under the dog.

The gamekeeper returned with a slab of raw meat. Fang bounded off me and devoured it noisily.

"Don't you mind Fang," the gamekeeper said. "Underneath all that blood-encrusted fur and solid muscle beats a heart of gold."

"Wonderful beast," I said, after I had regained my ability to breathe. "How did you find the car?"

"Very easily," he replied. "It was the only one in the duck pond."

"Can you explain your whereabouts over the last twelve hours or so?" I asked.

"I've been mostly stalking and culling, but the only witnesses were deer, and I killed every last one of them."

"Do you enjoy murder?" Herring enquired, with a naivety that only I knew was genuine.

"I love animals," the gamekeeper replied. "But they're generally better off dead.

I strangled most of these myself." He indicated the mounted heads. "Jethro uses machines and explosives, but I think bombs are for cowards. You know where you are with brute force."

We thanked the gamekeeper and returned to the crime scene. The clown-covered marquee was doubling as both a pathology tent and a lard festival venue. There may have been a skeletal Shrewsbury Town fan inside the corpse of my defunct patrol car, but that hadn't stopped the villagers from assembling a jolly array of rosettes, bunting and stalls.

The farmer's wife approached with a tray of lard. "Hello, Inspector, I hope you don't mind me asking, but do you like my rendering?"

I hadn't got time to assess her fat, so I just said, "It's terrific."

"I'm a little worried about the texture," she persisted.

"It looks very smooth to me," I lied without looking.

"We're going to need a judge for the lard contest, Inspector, and you seem to have a good eye."

"I'm in the middle of a case, so, I'm a little tied up."

"Go on, Inspector, it'll only take a few minutes. I'm sure we'd all be extremely grateful, a big cheese like you judging our lard." She giggled.

A three-fingered hand grabbed my elbow. It was Jethro, the animal exploder whose poltergeist issues had dragged us out to Wiggle-under-Bullock in the first place, and he was desperate to show me his lard. "What do you reckon to my consistency, Inspector?"

"You're consistently barking, I'll give you that."

He just stood there, looking crestfallen.

Herring joined us. "This is all rather jolly, isn't it?"

I looked at the drowned patrol car and its long-dead driver and begged to differ.

"Where were you earlier today?" I asked Jethro.

"When exactly?" he replied.

"All of it," I said.

"I suppose I was mostly inventing ways of killing animals."

"Did anybody see you?"

"You, the guillotines, the explosives, the bombs."

If ever there was a candidate for Rural Psychopath of the Week, I was looking at him. "Thank you, sir," I said. "You've been extremely helpful."

I led Herring out of the marquee. "Any news from Forensics?"

"Oh, they're not coming," she replied.

"Not coming?!"

"They didn't think we were serious."

"But someone drowned my car and a Shrewsbury Town-supporting skeleton."

"They thought it was a prank, sir."

"Did they remember doing an autopsy on a pair of carol singers diced by a combine harvester?"

"No, sir. More of a jigsaw than an autopsy, I'd have thought. They were sure someone at the morgue would have mentioned it, as they always enjoy discussing gruesome deaths in the canteen."

There was an otherworldly sound from across the pond. Dusk had fallen and it didn't make the village appear any more wholesome.

"Gosh!" Herring shivered. "Bit creepy round here, isn't it?"

"Creepy as buggery, it is," a familiar voice added. Jethro had followed us out, and I wished he hadn't. "We've got all the usual suspects here," he continued. "Legless boggarts, headless horsemen, screeching brownies."

Herring grinned. "I used to be in the Brownies."

"Brownies!" Jethro exclaimed. "Brownies will chew your flesh off and make your skull scream for all eternity."

"Some of them were quite wild," Herring replied. "Our pack in particular."

There was another gruesome noise. Herring froze in her tracks.

"That'll be Charlie's bull fitting," Jethro explained. "Big William's epileptic, see."

"Shouldn't someone call a vet?" I asked.

But Jethro was off on one. "It's a cursed region, this. You've got The Wild Witch of Wookey, The Creech Hill Bullbeggar, and the dreaded double-headed dragon of Shervage Wood."

"Oh no!" Herring was aghast. "That many ghoulies!".

"I've only just started," Jethro continued. "There's a headless highwayman who holds up a zombie stagecoach every third Tuesday. There's an invisible vulture that crosses the skies searching for lost souls at teatime. There's a demon hill-giant with a pair of monk's heads where its eyes should be, and don't forget the whistling spectre who hangs out in an abandoned burial barrow near Devil's Den."

I was about to tell Jethro to shut up when I noticed that the duck pond was bubbling.

"It's the mallards weeping for their spectral mistress," Jethro explained.

"Golly," Herring said.

"One day," Jethro said, "When Mad Ethel's put to rest, we'll hear the silence of the ducks."

I could turn a blind eye to the skeletal Shrewsbury Town fan and the combine harvester cold case, but I couldn't let the car theft go. It was getting late, and, other than the borrowed princess bikes, we had no means of transport. We were going to have to set up base.

Holiday Inns were not exactly abounding, so I asked Jethro, "Do people ever stay in the pub?"

"Stay in the pub? I'd rather pickle my left buttock in formaldehyde."

It was an enduring image, which was unfortunate. I'm not sure why I had sought advice from a lunatic.

Herring and I walked into *The Witch and Duck Pond*. It was hosting a one-a-side quiz between the farmer and the gamekeeper:

"Who played the villain in *The Wicker Man*?" the landlord asked.

"Idris Elba," the gamekeeper growled.

"Roger Moore," the farmer said.

After the first six rounds had ended nil-nil, I ordered a pint of bitter and a large Pimm's for Herring.

"There you go, Inspector." The landlord passed me the drinks. "A poncy great Pimm's and a pint of *Pigmelters*, brewed specially for the lard festival. I hear you're the judge."

"Vicar's wife told you that, did she?" I wished I hadn't been railroaded into agreeing. "Any chance of a couple of rooms?"

"Haunted or exorcised?" he replied.

"Exorcised please," Herring said, hurriedly.

"That was just my little joke," the landlord said, mirthlessly.

Herring laughed excessively.

"Full Thai breakfast?" the landlord enquired.

"Sure," I replied, without thinking.

"One hundred and eighty-seven pounds each," the landlord said. "Cash in advance."

I always carry plenty of cash to bribe informers, but this pretty much cleared me out.

The landlord explained that there was only one room in the pub, but there was nothing indecent about it, as it had a bunk bed. His wife showed us along creaking corridors to a door with a felt-tip notice reading, *Do Not Attempt to Repair Anything*

Herring bagged the top bunk and asked, "Have you got an umbrella, sir?"

"No."

"It's just that, if Mad Ethel shows up, I might wet myself and I am inclined to urinate copiously at times of stress."

After we had swapped bunks, I suggested sleep. But rather than obey her superior officer, Herring chose to jabber on: "This village gives me the willies. Do you think it's twinned with Mordor?"

"Quite possibly. Good night, Sergeant Herring."

I didn't sleep well. Howling, screaming, and assorted otherworldly sounds filled the night. I just dismissed this as general rural racket, but the thought of our lost patrol car kept me awake. After Herring's eighth whimper, I agreed to go downstairs and investigate the empty pub. The fruit machine was emptying itself, spirits were escaping from the optics, and *Ghostbusters* played on the juke box. I can't say I was scared, but I can say that a moment later, I was unconscious.

I woke up staring at a two-dimensional clown. The red, blue, and yellow slapstick-purveyor had been sewn into the inside of the marquee roof and was looking directly at me. I tried getting up, but I was tied to something as cold and hard as a mortuary slab. My skull throbbed, but I managed to turn my head sufficiently to see that the entire village had assembled. It was just like a fair, but instead of a brass band they had a human sacrifice. Me.

The vicar climbed onto the roof of my drowned car and addressed the gathering. "Welcome to the Lard Festival. I know you've all been busy melting your fattest hogs and whether you've used kettle rendering, dry rendering, or steam jackets, let's hope that the results are smooth, creamy and of a non-rancid, buttery consistency."

There was an enthusiastic round of applause, then a rendering machine was wheeled into position above my head. It blocked out my view of the roof-clown, but that was a smaller concern than the cluster of rotating blades descending upon my body.

I tried to remain calm but failed. "I should probably shout for help, shouldn't I?"

"If you like," the vicar replied.

"HEEEEELLLP!"

"Feel better now?"

"Not particularly."

"I'm sorry to hear that," the vicar said. "I'd so like the last few minutes of your life to be as comfortable as possible."

"So, that will be why you've dangled rendering equipment over my head."

"No. That will be to turn you into lard."

"How many people have you turned to lard?"

"A few dozen, I dare say," the vicar conceded. "I don't mind admitting that some outsiders have a certain subhuman charm, but most of them are better off as lard."

The vicar's laughter mingled with the rendering blades in my mangled mind. This was the opposite of dying peacefully in bed. I looked at the marquee ceiling's clowns, bunting and balloons - my final sight on Earth. What a way to go.

My despair was interrupted by a collective gasp from the villagers. Had they suddenly rediscovered their humanity? No, they were gasping at the sudden arrival of Mikey the village teenager. He was aiming his mobile phone like a ray-gun, recording my impending rendering. It didn't seem much of a weapon, but he shouted like it was a stick-up: "This is a live stream! You've been rendering outsiders for years! My mum and dad weren't having it, so you shredded them with a combine! Now, it's all over TikTok!" He noticed the skeleton seated in my former patrol car. "And you've even nicked my Shrewsbury Town t-shirt and stuck it on Mad Ethel! You bastards!"

The farmer ran at Mikey, who swerved out the way, sending him crashing into the marquee's central supporting pole. Clown-covered canvas enveloped us all and halted the rendering machine's progress.

Eventually, female hands freed me from the canvas with a "Golly, sir!" Herring gawped at my sacrificial stone, and asked, "Are you quite alright?"

"Never been better, sergeant."

"It's just... your hair."

"Never mind my hair, just untie me."

Herring obliged with her pocket-knife and, before long, I was free, albeit looking like Gandalf The White.

Although Forensics and the Super would have been happy to ignore our pleas for assistance, they had to respond to a TikTok controversy, and the village was soon aflush with pandas.

The entire population were arrested, accused of both mass murder and food safety violations. Mikey, the village crime wave, was the only innocent party – he explained that he had been strung up in the forest by the village committee in preparation for

The Lard Festival's closing ceremony: a celebratory stoning. He had managed to escape by swinging relentlessly until a branch broke, and he'd been able to get away in time to film the incriminating festive footage. Herring had failed to detect any signs of my impending sacrifice by staying in her bunk bed and had only come down to check on her Full Thai Breakfast.

***

The inspector's story was over, and our pies were a distant memory, but at least dessert was on the horizon. While the barman fetched the menus, I took the opportunity to clear up a few details.

"How did your car end up in the duckpond?"

"Village-wide conspiracy. They wanted to render me, so the bastards took our means of escape."

"How about the Shrewsbury Town-supporting skeleton?"

"A bit of intrigue to perplex us and keep us in town until I'd been rendered."

"Bit like The Wicker Man?"

"But with lard."

"And Mad Ethel was real?"

"Possibly. A place like Wiggle-under-Bullock had been the centre of so much killing over the years, it's no surprise it attracted the odd poltergeist."

"Why didn't they try to render Herring?"

"More lard on me, I suppose, what with my lifelong devotion to pies."

The barman gave us the dessert menu. It offered the prospect of cheesecake, jam roly-poly, spotted dick and Eton mess, but we both went for the lardy cake. When it arrived, it didn't taste of human at all, I'm pleased to say.

As I chewed my way through the lardy cake, I thought about events at Wiggle-under-Bullock. People like to bang on about community spirit, and the village had both a community and a spirit. It would have been better off with neither, as the community only existed to render strangers into lard, ostracise teenagers, and duck witches to death; and the spirit broke pianos, possessed tractors, and wasted perfectly good alcohol.

Was country life just about red-light districts, poltergeists, and murder? Or did England's green and pleasant lands have more to offer? What about hunting, shooting and incest?

Cities have their drawbacks too, with their gangs, their traffic, and their surfeit of humans. So, what's the alternative? The suburbs? Semi-rural, semi-urban and full of semis, they may seem like the ideal hybrid. But I don't do safe and anonymous – I far prefer dodgy and characterful, as my extensive selection of ex-wives attests.

At the end of the day, you're better off enjoying your own company and ignoring your neighbours. That way, it doesn't matter where you live, and there's no one to grass you up.

RULE 12 - SPIRITUALISM IS BEST KEPT IN BOTTLES

If my intimate dealings with the human herd have taught me anything, it is that normality is not the norm. On average, most people are deeply unusual, and many are even odder than that - I know I am. It's not just that I'm funny looking, my thinking's mental.

But at the end of the day, I'm not the maddest bat in the attic. I once encountered someone whose sanity was so breathtakingly negligible, it was practically subatomic: quantifying it would have required nanotechnology. His name was Nirvana Waddle, and that was just the start of the problem.

I found Nirvana while I was searching for wisdom, and he didn't help much. I admit I was looking in the wrong place, but I had budget issues. I couldn't stretch to the Himalayas, so I'd sought enlightenment in Wales. Now, don't get me wrong, I've always liked Wales. The chapels are lovely places for singsongs, there's no shortage of sheep, and rugby is a bit of a laugh – I do enjoy a good ruck. Brecon's a beacon of hope, but its tepee villages are justifiably under-celebrated. These crusty reservations lack totem poles, bison, and pow-wows and could only be mistaken for authentic Native American villages by a moron, or perhaps by one of their inhabitants. Still, I had heard tell that a freelance shaman possessing extraordinary unearthly powers dwelt in a tepee near Abergavenny and I had arranged to visit him.

I came equipped with wellies and optimism. Maybe this would be the day that I would gain a deep insight into the meaning of life? After a nineteen-mile trudge through mud, I heard the distant thwack of canvas on wind and knew that I had arrived.

"Welcome to the Owen Glendower Tepee Village!" Nirvana Waddle ejaculated in an effusive Merthyr Tydfil accent. "I know there's only the one tent, but it's a start." The shaman was wearing scarlet sunglasses and a multi-coloured poncho. I had no idea which tribe this signified, but it was not a fashionable one.

The village suffered from a chronic lack of other inhabitants. In fact, I've seen more heavily populated toilet cubicles.

I followed Nirvana to his tepee. The mud was thick, and some of it wasn't mud, but there was no danger of getting lost, what with there only being the one tent. He didn't invite me inside, but at least his awning was wide enough to keep most of the drizzle off. I gingerly positioned my buttocks on his psychedelic welcome mat. It was uncomfortable, but I was tired and didn't particularly care.

Nirvana filled a pair of mugs from a battered pot on his camping stove. "It's ethical coffee," he explained.

The concoction didn't smell ethical. The odour was closer to caffeinated fertilizer, or possibly something worse – human remains, perhaps.

"There's no coffee in it," Nirvana said. "Stimulants are immoral."

I nodded my pretended agreement and attempted a sip.

"It's mostly bracken, acorns and repurposed cow pats," Nirvana said.

I clenched my nostrils and swallowed some gloop. "Delicious. Thanks."

Delighted that his hospitality had been so well received, Nirvana delved into his tepee and dragged out a handwritten sign reading *Shaman For Hire*. "I offer a wide range of services," he explained. "Emotional Enema £33.50, Psychic Detox £48.25, Tantric Gardening £110.75. Tempted? I can photograph your aura if you can keep it still. I've got red-eye reduction..." He paused, waiting expectantly for an answer.

I wanted none of these things. I sought only wisdom.

"Well, have a think about it," Nirvana persisted, "I could really use the work."

As a plea, it was as heartfelt as it was pathetic. Nirvana clearly didn't have much in the way of possessions and he wasn't a householder, he was a tent-holder. As I surveyed his tepee, my gaze landed on a dangling hippie trinket, a gaudy rope lattice suitable for a stoned tarantula. "Nice web," I fibbed.

Nirvana removed the damp artefact. "It's a dreamcatcher."

"What's it used for?"

"It does exactly what it says on the tin."

There wasn't a tin, but I knew what he meant. "How many dreams have you caught?"

"They're countless in number." Nirvana fumbled with the ropey muddle.

"Where do you store them?"

"I've got a set of shelves." Nirvana chuckled.

Nirvana certainly fitted the crusty mould, and he was the kind of bloke many people could never get bored of hitting. But for me, his heart was in the right place, even if his brain wasn't, and he was rumoured to possess the gift of ancient magic.

"What kind of shaman are you?" I asked.

"Freelance," Nirvana replied. "The Revenue won't accept soothsayers as legitimate sole traders and staff jobs are thin on the ground. It's not that I'm insufficiently qualified, neither. I've got a PhD in Unexplained Phenomena from the Portmeirion Institute of Technology. I spent years studying aliens, UFOs, the Rothmans Incident..."

"Wow, what was The Rothmans Incident?"

"Aliens. On YouTube."

"I see." He clearly meant The Roswell Incident, but I caught his drift.

"It's not that I'm short on skills, look you. Bog-standard mystics channel energy. Anyone can do that. But I can channel apathy. Sadly, there's not much call for it round here. The sheep are already sufficiently apathetic, and the farmers can't be bothered."

I could see that circumstances were less than ideal. Tepee villages were better suited to the sultry canyons of the Wild West than the soggy slopes of a Brecon Beacon.

"How did you become a shaman?"

"It's in my blood."

"Your family must be ... special."

"Oh, yes, it made for an interesting childhood, didn't it just. I grew up by the sea, near the bit where the ocean runs out and ships fall off the edge of the world. The sailors' screams kept me awake at night, so my gran would read me Just Not-so Stories - *How The Whale Got Its Arms*, *How The Donkey Got Its Yodel* and *How The Snake Got Its Legs*. I've been confused ever since."

Nirvana went on to explain that although his mammy had an invisible third eye, his father was just a normal bloke who spent his whole life working down a fish mine. After Nirvana had failed all his GCSEs, a mystic career had seemed the best option, and he had been sent to train under a Pontypool mystic known as "Evans of the Middle Pillar". He had completed his training a decade ago and had been hoping to settle down, but Fate had conspired against him. At this point, Nirvana started to become a little emotional.

He delved into his poncho and plucked out a completely blue sheet of paper.

"It's a map of Atlantis. Colour-coded." Nirvana used it to wipe his eyes. "I'm anxious about Poppy, my girlfriend, see. We were in a band together - Ocean Colour Finance. They were very now a few years ago. I say girlfriend, but she's really my Spirit Wife. A druid performed a pagan hand-fisting ceremony for us at Stonehenge. But it all started to go wrong when Poppy dropped out of circus school, went travelling and inadvertently unicycled across the Iran-Iraq border. The Foreign Office says they're doing what they can. I've sent friendship bangles to the Shias and the Sunnis, but I haven't heard back yet. If they leave it much longer, I'll send them enemy necklaces."

It was a sorry tale, but I couldn't help thinking that Poppy should have chosen a safer cycle path.

I wondered whether I should unpack some of my own emotional baggage. I wasn't short of divorces, addictions, or criminal convictions, but before I could inflict any of it on Nirvana, he showed me his phone. It was a make I had never seen before, and it was completely dead.

"It's solar powered," Nirvana explained. "Ecologically flawless, but it does mean I can only be contacted outdoors on cloudless days."

I looked up at the murderous Welsh skies and calculated that today at least, he would be contactable for approximately no hours.

A thoughtless silence prevailed, during which I wondered whether I had wasted my time climbing the Brecon Beacons to meet such a shambolic shaman. Eventually, he offered to perform some silent chanting. Never previously having heard silent chanting, I accepted.

Silent chanting proved to be a bit on the uneventful side, and after a few minutes, I'd had enough.

Nirvana showed me how to realign my chakras, then expounded at length about Thoth, an Egyptian *tarot* pronounced like a speech impediment, and his emotional kinship with the Greek gods "Apollo, Diabetes and Hepatitis".

I quizzed him for all I was worth, trying to divine the mysteries of the universe, but his answers were as straight and direct as a Welsh road and, after an hour or two of scrambled mythology, I was none the wiser.

I couldn't leave without learning something, so I asked Nirvana what, besides emotional enemas, psychic detoxes, and tantric gardening, he had on offer.

He shuffled towards me and spoke in a low, confidential voice. It was completely unnecessary, given that we were the only humans for miles, but with Nirvana, paranoia and shamanism seemed to go hand in hand: "I could give you an OBE."

"A medal?"

"An Out-of-Body Experience."

I didn't have a particularly enviable body, given its age and shape, but I did find it useful.

I hesitated.

"Go on," he insisted. "It'll blow your mind. I'll do it for half price."

"How much?"

"Eighty quid."

"So, it's forty."

"No, it's eighty after I've halved it."

I had come a long way and I figured that, if I dodged the fare on the train home, I could probably afford it.

Nirvana took my money, retreated to his tepee, and returned with a concoction so noxious, it made the ethical coffee taste like champagne.

After I had sunk it, Nirvana chanted noises reminiscent of the climactic battle in Planet of the Apes, then began to speak with calm intensity: "You are not you. You are other to yourself. Rise up, rise up, and see what you are."

I felt lighter and my perspective lifted until I could look down on my own bald patch. I hadn't realised how extensive it had become. It was no longer a small fleshy island in a sea of hair, it was more like a continent of exposed skin encircled by a narrow follicle moat. Then, without warning, my point of view took flight, and I was looking down on the Brecon Beacons from a passing raincloud. Was this what happened when you died? I gazed at the dank mountains, the sheep, the barren nothingness, and marvelled. Had I been reincarnated as drizzle? Or was I now an all-seeing, all-knowing divinity able to witness human affairs with supine detachment? Either way, it was freezing, damp, and lonely. There were no human affairs to witness, and if I was drizzle, I couldn't wait to fall. When you are in your body, it's much easier to go places. Stuck up here, outside my body, the possibilities were much more limited. I wondered what was keeping me up. Was I gliding on a thermal? Had Nirvana pressed a celestial pause button? There was no one to ask. It struck me as strange that humanity had spent so long dreaming of flight, when there was so much more going on at ground level. If only the shaman had provided an in-flight movie and a drinks trolley. Just when I was ready to scream with boredom, and die of out-of-body hypothermia, my perspective swooped down like a kestrel preying on a dormouse. It was *Hello Bald Patch!* then back inside my skin.

"How was that?" Nirvana asked.

"Well, it worked," I replied.

"Told you it would," Nirvana said. "Fancy doing it again?"

"No, ta." I thanked him and headed for the station. Somehow, fare-dodging in my body was a more attractive prospect than flying out of it.

RULE 13 - REVENGE IS A DISH BEST SERVED BY A VOODOO PRIESTESS

I once stumbled across a voodoo shop near the North Circular Road. I had no idea what I wanted, having neither visited Haiti nor cast a spell, but I had just been banned from IKEA for the fourth time and was keen to embrace a new consumer experience.

I don't know what kind of customer service I had anticipated, but the beefy, Oxbridge type behind the counter was not it. I waited for him to serve a cheerful traffic warden a packet of *Satan Begone* incense sticks and a pot of *Luv Luv Oil*, then tentatively approached the counter.

The shopkeeper explained that *Zombie Sorcery* was the finest voodoo shop within walking distance of the A406. People simply couldn't get enough of *Rattlesnake Root*, *Necromancy Powder*, and *High John the Conqueror* deodorant. His line in pet spells was particularly popular: a pack of *Sovereign of the Cemeteries* pellets could de-worm a Jack Russell in minutes, a handful of *Wahoo Bark* sprinklings could bring goldfish back from the dead and a slice or two of *Devil Shoestring Root* could dissolve feline fur-balls in under a fortnight.

Frankly, he had me at *Necromancy Powder*. I simply had to find out more, and given that there were no other customers, he was happy to oblige. The bloke told me his name was Rob and he dug out a couple of zombie-themed deckchairs. Rob explained that he had grown up in Surrey, played prop forward for Westminster, read PPE at Balliol then trained in broadcast media. He had harboured dreams of becoming a foreign correspondent and reporting bravely under shellfire, but the channel's Head of Diversity and Inclusion, an old-Etonian viscount with his own grouse moor, had nabbed his girlfriend, then made him redundant on the grounds that he no longer fitted their "employability criteria" and needed to "check his privilege". This had all seemed a bit rich from a bloke who was more than a bit rich, but there was nothing he could do about it, other than get a new career and a new home.

Rob felt numb and disillusioned, so he scoured the job sites for something he could approach with total indifference. Many of the opportunities on offer required dedication and enthusiasm, but when he found a producer vacancy on a daytime pet-care show only available on a four-figure channel number, he knew he had struck mediocrity gold. Further inquiry revealed that the job came with free accommodation in the co-presenter's attic, so it was a no-brainer.

Whilst I sympathised with Rob, I could not figure out what any of this had to do with voodoo. Noting my puzzlement, he brewed us some ginger tea and assured me that everything he had told me was essential to understanding his initiation into the mysteries of Haiti. As he related his tale, he spoke with the cultivated air of a World Service newsreader and the calm demeanour of a man who has enacted vengeance and secured peace of mind:

***

"I had the feeling I was the only candidate for the job," Rob explained, "so, the interview call was over in a couple of minutes. I chucked most of my stuff in storage, bunged my essentials into a rucksack and headed for a comfortably dull area of North London.

My new landlady rejoiced in the name Waspy Glyndebourne. She had the complexion of Ben Nevis, the stature of Tyson Fury and all the feminine vulnerability of Wormwood Scrubs. At eighty-one, six-feet-four and fifteen stone, she could have renamed herself *HMS Glyndebourne*. Her arms were like pile drivers, she had the fists of a Neanderthal prize fighter, and her voice was so forceful it could have arm-wrestled Priti Patel. She wasn't just ballsy: she had metaphorical testicles bulging out of her proverbial trouser legs.

Her living room walls pulsated in time to *The Archers*. A hearing aid would have been out of the question, she explained - if she was becoming deaf, the rest of the world would simply have to shout. The environmental health officers who had recently acted on a complaint about the volume of *The Shipping Forecast* could do their worst; she'd survived Haiti, after all. If she could cope with hurricanes and the homicidal dictator *Papa Doc* Duvalier, a few local bureaucrats presented little opposition.

Waspy offered an induction, beginning with a thirty-minute demonstration of her alarm system. She explained that the code was only seven digits long and could be easily memorised as the year of the Battle of Bosworth followed by the number of chapters in Psalms. Escape involved grappling with six chains, two Chubb locks and a Yale. Failure to unlock them in the correct order would set off a system of sirens and revolving blue lights. I couldn't understand why Waspy was so terrified of burglars. If she'd pinned a photograph of herself on her front gate and labelled it, *I Live Here*, it would have scared off the bravest cartel in Mexico.

Waspy's wallpaper was a floral Guernica: grotesque botanical abominations in pink, apricot and purple, all punctuated by anaemic watercolours of yachts. Every ornament commemorated a failed royal marriage and the novelty barometers covering the hall walls made a variety of contradictory forecasts. On the way upstairs, Waspy explained that all the clocks in the house were twenty minutes fast because "punctuality was the practice of princes".

After the fifth flight, we reached my new attic flat and Waspy conducted a brief tour. Apart from the rather wonky en-suite toilet, everything was Haitian: zombie dolls dangled from the ceiling like sinister stalactites; and metalwork sculptures of mermaids, snakes, dragons, and angels lurked in every corner. A wooden chair was carved with an elaborate cockfight and there were framed sketches of cemeteries and iron gravestone crosses nailed to the walls. Power cuts wouldn't have been a problem, as there were human skull candles to send back evil, inflammatory confusion candles to break hexes, and wormwood candles to recruit the help of the dead. There was a miniature botanical garden of weird plants with names like *Cruel Man of the Woods*, *Ladies Thumb* and *Five Finger Root*, and an array of boxes containing powders, implements, and emergency supplies of *Wahoo Bark*, bottles of *Jezebel Oil*, *Fast Luck Incense*, and a stuffed jar of *Waste Away Tea*.

"Make yourself at home," Waspy said, with a generous sweep of her arm.

At any other point in my life, I would have left without further shilly-shallying, but I was heartbroken and genuinely didn't care. Waspy was clearly bonkers, but so what? The world was unhinged, so why shouldn't my flat be too?

I unpacked onto the bed. The sheets were blood-red, and the duvet was emblazoned with Haitian werewolves, but at least it matched the decor.

I went downstairs for a welcoming dinner. Waspy called it "homemade sushi", but it was just batter-less fish fingers on congealed rice pudding. After I had complimented Waspy on her cooking and consumed some of it, she poured me a large Haitian rum and celebrated my new tenancy with some indoor fireworks. Small snakes of carbon uncoiled themselves onto saucers; coloured knobs went *phut* in bowls and a Catherine wheel the size of a ball-bearing rotated in a dish.

There was a knock at the door. Waspy swore in Haitian and bounded out of her armchair with the force of a veteran pentathlete. Chains were unleashed and a canine killing machine jumped up at my chest with a petrifying growl.

"Slobodan's only playing," Waspy reassured me.

I froze to the spot and managed to whisper, "Good boy," but it probably sounded more like, "Goodbye."

"Slobodan's a girl, you fool!" Waspy boomed. "There was a little confusion at her christening, but never mind that now. Don't let her know you're frightened, man! She'll smell it and I won't be responsible for the consequences."

Suitably reassured, I tried not to relax my bowels. Waspy left the room and a rotund lady with bulging facial veins entered clutching a lead. She introduced herself as Waspy's co-presenter, Aurora Thumper-Brithazard, and launched into an impromptu diatribe about Slobodan: "She's had a difficult enough day. I was trying to mate her with another tri-colour pit bull, and they were far from willing to commence proceedings, so we both had to get down on all fours and simulate the desired action. It took three hours and aggravated the arthritis in my left knee as well as making Slobodan cry. She's very loyal, a lovely dog; murdered her first-born, mind you, but nobody's perfect."

I tried to reverse gently away from Slobodan, but the beast followed me, keeping her paws on my chest.

Waspy returned with a toothbrush and bucket. "Mind making yourself useful, my boy? Slobodan's dental hygiene's been far from immaculate of late - shocking halitosis. Make sure you give her incisors a good scrub."

I stroked the dog tentatively and somehow gathered the courage to part its lips; lion tamers would have blanched. As I did this, Waspy started banging on about declining grammar standards in the local graffiti and how this marked the end of western civilisation. I was pretending to agree when Slobodan bit into the toothbrush and pulled it out of my hand, waving her massive head from side to side in a frantic motion.

Waspy thumped the coffee table. Its legs shuddered: when Waspy thumped a table, it stayed thumped. The shock startled Slobodan and she began to wheeze. At this, Waspy's expression turned to that of an affronted Old Testament God. "Damn you! I'll have to get Slobodan her inhaler now, you've aggravated her asthma." She took Slobodan in her muscular arms, stroked her head, and began to sing a Haitian Creole lullaby into its left ear.

It was a grotesque sight, made even more disturbing by the tiny headless doll dangling from Waspy's necklace. I made my excuses and headed up to the comforts of my werewolf duvet.

I can't say I slept well, but it didn't really matter. Even though I was starting a new job, failure was of no consequence whatever.

The daytime pet-care show was called *We Are All Bunnies*, and it was recorded in a basement at the wrong end of Colindale. The studio had never been soundproofed, so sirens and shouts punctuated proceedings at intervals. It often fell out of sync, lending it the quality of a poorly dubbed Brazilian soap opera and the cameras were operated by unpaid work experiencers. The programme was an insult to the inventors of moving pictures. Had he seen *We Are All Bunnies*, William Horner would have un-invented the Zoetrope, the Lumière Brothers would have left their train in its siding, D.W. Griffith would have aborted his Nation, Eisenstein would have anchored Potemkin and Hitchcock would have pulled himself together and stopped being so morbid.

On the whole, the animal contributors to *We Are All Bunnies* were far better adjusted than the human ones. Whereas the former suffered from a variety of more-or-less minor physical ailments, the humans tended to rejoice in a broad variety of incurable psychological defects. The adored pet compensated for the hollowness of a marriage, the absence of a child, the pain of social isolation, an empty retirement, a recent divorce, or an unexpected bereavement.

One time, an old codger came to the studio. He was well-dressed, well-spoken, and desperate for advice. The problem was, his two Jack Russell Terriers simply couldn't get on. They fought all the time, and it was driving him completely hatstand. Waspy asked him why he had only brought one dog to the studio, and he looked utterly bewildered. She held up a single finger, and asked, "How many fingers have I got up?" When he replied, "Two", no further diagnosis was required. Double vision can be a cruel affliction.

That evening, I went for a quick five k. I ran along reassuringly named roads like *Vale of Health* and *Well Walk*, and it was all expensively pseudo-rural. This was the kind of district where the police were most often called out to enforce hosepipe bans. People walked along the pavements reading books or cycled along listening to classical music from transistor radios strapped to their baskets and, although the narrow streets had been designed for carriages, all the cars seemed to be four-wheel drives.

I stopped a couple of minutes short of the house and rested on a bench to check my phone. There was a notification – my nemesis was about to make a speech to the Royal Television Society about "diversity, equality and inclusion". I looked at the viscount's hypocritical face, swore extensively then headed back to my new home.

I undid the triple lock, struggled to recall the year of the Battle of Bosworth and the number of chapters in Psalms, then found to my relief that the alarm was off. Downstairs was as silent as a cemetery, but as I ascended the stairs, I became aware of a clumping noise and a strange background hum. I wondered whether Waspy was hoovering, but as I climbed higher up, it became increasingly clear that this would have to have been with a very strange brand of vacuum cleaner indeed.

As I approached the attic, the sounds became clearer, but more mystifying. There was an otherworldly wailing and a kind of rhythmic stamping. It was so unnerving, I felt forced to conduct a recce via my en-suite toilet. With its low, sloping ceiling, it was an inconvenient convenience, and it had a high window ludicrously positioned to look out onto my bedroom. I clambered onto the toilet seat, leant sideways and gripped a pipe, allowing me to see what was causing the commotion.

Sometimes, there's a thin line between laughing and screaming and, at that moment, I trod this as precariously as a rhino on a high wire. My octogenarian landlady was in her pants, conducting a voodoo rite with Aurora and Slobodan. Smoke billowed while Waspy performed a Haitian form of the can-can and Aurora made various unpleasant noises with improbable instruments, but it was Slobodan, sat howling in the corner of a flour circle, who was the centre of attention. Waspy waved things into the dog's face, chanted into its floppy ears and pointed at its nose with a peculiar stick.

I was dumbstruck; it was partly shock, but mostly, it was fear. This was in no way decreased when Slobodan began to speak in a voice that seemed uncannily deep for a bitch: "Who dares to summon me?"

"I damn well do, you poltroon, the Voodoo Queen of Hampstead Garden Suburb!" Waspy continued her can-can as she spoke, alternating words with high kicks. "Tell us who on earth you are and don't beat around the bush."

Slobodan's mouth moved, and the bass voice continued, "I inhabit the dog you have before you."

"Who are you and what are you doing in my dog?" Waspy demanded.

"My name's Norman and I used to be a management consultant," the possessed dog replied. "I liked to go potholing at weekends and one time I dropped my inhaler into an underground stream. The worry brought on an asthma attack, and I kicked the proverbial bucket before I'd had a chance to spot any decent stalactites. My body was never found, so I now roam the world as a spirit hiding in various dogs."

"Why dogs?"

"I like dogs. I always wanted to own one. They have a good life, dogs, chasing things and napping, but the trouble is, I do tend to give them asthma; it's very trying."

"Oh, the heart simply bleeds. Pathetic! Lily-livered pansy! You're thinking only of yourself. Imagine what this poor animal has been through. Now, away with you before I put a curse on your departed soul."

"But..."

"That's quite enough. Now, naff off!"

"Alright then, if you insist."

"I damn well do insist! Dead management consultants are all the same, self-obsessed loonies the lot of you!"

"See you, then." the spirit said, as Slobodan's breathing returned to normal.

The smoke evaporated, Aurora stopped making strange musical sounds, and, to my horror, my mobile rang. I scrabbled around inside my track suit with the desperation of a man looking for an unexploded grenade. I had to do this one-handed, as my grip on the overhead pipe was the only thing preventing me toppling off the toilet. I managed to kill the call before the third ring, but the effort made the overhead pipe come off in my hand, and I crashed onto the floor. Noxious fluid shot out of the pipe, redecorating the bathroom, and making enough noise to wake the dead and alert the neighbouring zombie-botherers.

Slobodan growled, heavy footsteps thundered, and my panty-clad landlady peered down at me through the window, saying, "Oh. You," in a tone of disappointment.

"Bit of a plumbing problem, Waspy," I stammered. "Have it fixed in no time." I tried to force the pipe back into place, diverting the fluid up my nostrils.

A forearm that would not have disgraced Popeye the Sailor Man reached through the window and wrenched the pipe back into place.

"Thanks, Waspy."

"Let's reconvene for a house meeting once you've cleaned up and packed."

So, I was being evicted by a voodoo priestess for a minor bathroom accident. As I mopped up, changed, and gathered up my gear, I riled at the injustice of it all.

Downstairs, Waspy and Aurora were sat listening to *You and Yours* at stadium rock volume. Waspy poured me a large rum from a bottle labelled with werewolves and gestured towards an armchair.

"You must be terribly confused, but there really is absolutely nothing whatsoever to worry about. I am indeed a voodoo priestess or *mambo*, if you will, but it's all perfectly normal," Waspy paused. "In Haiti."

I was sure it was and said so very quietly.

"You see, I was based out in Haiti for years with a dull little husband and one simply had to find ways to pass the time. Voodoo was the natural choice and it's come in quite handy ever since, particularly with pets. Aurora helps me keep my hand in, and she's a rather gifted musician."

"You're extremely talented," I told Aurora, meekly.

"So," Waspy concluded. "There's really nothing to worry about. Everything's completely above board."

I decided to ask the improbable but unavoidable question, "Why were you exorcising your dog?"

"Oh, she's had a touch of asthma for yonks, ridiculous really in a fighting dog. Anyway, I usually find with most veterinary complaints that it boils down to voodoo exorcism. A quick invocation, a bit of a jig in my knickers, give the invading spirit a stern talking to, and they bugger off sharpish, along with the ailments. Vets should try voodoo more often."

"Does voodoo have any other uses at all?" I asked, a touch disingenuously.

"Oh, bags of things. Bringing luck, getting rich, staying healthy, curing the mad, diabolical curses, exacting revenge, you name it. Jolly useful if you ask me. Anything I can help you with? I appreciate that I caused you a little stress and, I'm afraid I don't think we're going to be able to work together terribly well after this. You know my secret and I'm perfectly willing to let you live but seeing you every day to discuss mildly unwell gerbils might be a little awkward. I'm sure Aurora feels the same."

"Yes, dear." Aurora gave me a kindly smile.

I wanted to leave, but an irresistible idea took hold of both my mind and mouth.

"Given that I'll keep this to myself and leave quietly, might you be able to see your way to helping me out with a small personal matter?"

I told her about the viscount who had ended my career. It tickled her interest and, once I had shown her his picture and the details of his imminent Royal Television Society speech, she said, "There's no time like the present!" and giggled like the world's heftiest schoolgirl. "I haven't had a chance to cast any decent spells for absolutely ages! Fancy a spot of the old mumbo-jumbo, Aurora? A little more spirit bothering for my soon-to-be-ex lodger? Least we can do in return for him keeping shtum, I would have thought. What do you say?"

Aurora put on her slippers and said, "That would be lovely."

We headed back upstairs to the attic, tidied up the remnants of Slobodan's exorcism, and prepared to enact voodoo vengeance on the viscount.

While I set up a live stream of the Royal Television Society event on my laptop, Waspy and Aurora gathered mystical materials from the boxes.

"Where did we put the *Necromancy Powder*?" Waspy enquired.

"There you go, dear," Aurora replied.

Waspy scooped white powder from a box engraved with vampires, set light to it and, within seconds, billows of white smoke were filling the room.

"Pass me the Satan's Ram," Waspy asked, as casually as if she were saying, "Pass the salt".

Aurora reached into a box carved with serpents and produced a chunky candle. "There you go, High Priestess."

"Staff of Moses." Waspy could have been a surgeon in a Haitian edition of *M*A*S*H*.

Aurora passed her a large wooden stick carved into the shape of a striking viper.

"Now, be a good chap and hold this between your teeth." Waspy passed me a small scroll. "And do try not to salivate. It damages the paper. Oh, and if you wouldn't mind, wave this about every so often." Waspy passed me a flag embroidered with zombies. "Now, hang on a minute while I invoke *Erzulie, Goddess of Love, Mademoiselle Brigitte, Guardian of the Graves* and *Ogou Balanjo, Spirit of Healing*."

Waspy lit an assortment of candles and chucked flour around the room for a few minutes. "Now, would you mind scattering a little of this Graveyard Dust, Aurora?"

"Consider it done, old bean."

Waspy passed me two stones. She explained that they were lodestones and that I was to hold the red one in my right hand and the white one in my left. She then gave me some final maternal advice. "Now, young man, *The Great Serpent* will shortly be dancing in your head. Be jolly careful."

I agreed that I would take care.

"I can't predict what will happen," Waspy continued. "But when you see the perpetrator of your injustice, just mention my full title - *The Voodoo Queen of Hampstead Garden Suburb* – and the vengeance will begin."

I turned to the live feed on my laptop. The aristocratic Head of Diversity and Inclusion had mounted the podium and was spouting forth about "unconscious bias", "allyship" and "transparency". But he hadn't counted on the inclusion of anything as diverse as Waspy Glyndebourne.

I did as Waspy had instructed, and said, "The Voodoo Queen of Hampstead Garden Suburb".

Waspy chanted an invocation, "*Au nom Monsieur Damballah-Wedo-Toka-Miorwaze.*" The repetitive rhythm became increasingly hypnotic and the elderly but powerfully built pet care specialist began to dance, kicking her legs shoulder-high like a *Moulin Rouge* barnstormer.

At intervals, Aurora shook a snake's backbone rattle, beat a small drum, and bugled flatulently on a conch shell. Waspy's kicks became increasingly extreme until dislocation was a genuine risk and I worried for the lampshade. Finally, Waspy collapsed onto the floor with a shriek and her eyeballs bulged to bursting point. Aurora increased the rapidity of her drumming and honking to a frantic pace while Waspy flailed around the carpet shrieking like a breakdancing demon.

As the ritual built to a pitch, Waspy leapt up, banging her head on the ceiling. But she was beyond pain. Something powerful and Haitian inhabited her, and she spoke in a deep masculine voice as she repeated the incantation, "*Au nom Monsieur Damballah-Wedo-Toka-Miorwaze.*".

The Viscount's Diversity and Inclusion speech had reached the words, "We must show empathy for the marginalized," when he began to dance like a chicken, elbows pumping rhythmically, knees bent, head pecking backwards and forward. There were gasps, giggles, and murmurs from the four hundred-odd delegates, and these only increased as he embarked on the most contorted song I had ever heard, every word a monstrous parody of itself: Meeeeee Tooooo, Traaaaaaans Wwwwwwomen Are Reeeeeeeeeeal Wwwwwwwwwomen, Chchchchchchcheck Yooooooour Priviledggggggge. He could not have infused more contempt into each phrase if he'd inserted every swear word in existence and projected them onto a nude image of Donald Trump. The indignant audience began to shout in outrage. Walkouts began.

The speaker continued his chicken dance whilst reciting contorted gender pronouns in a series of contemptuous clucks and squawks:

"Zzzzzzzzieself! Cluck!"

"Verselffffff! Squawk!"

"Emmmmmmmmmself! Cluck!"

Once he had reached number seventy-four, the smoke evaporated, Waspy stopped breakdancing, and Aurora stopped bugling on her conch shell.

I checked my Twitter feed. The viscount was trending – "He should hang his beak in shame!", "Diversity chicken should get stuffed", "Cancel the Viscount."

I punched the air. "Got the bastard!"

"Damn well did it!" Waspy offered a hi-five. "The old mumbo-jumbo works every time."

***

His curious tale of dogs, possession, and diversity and inclusion policies complete, Rob poured me some more ginger tea and explained that the voodoo vengeance had turned out to be the start of a beautiful friendship. Waspy had shared her wealth of Haitian contacts in return for a share of his new retail venture, and he had soon established himself as the North Circular's public face of voodoo. Britain may be a nation of shopkeepers, he explained, but a select few are supplied by Haiti.

I thanked him for his time and was about to leave when a thought crossed my mind: could I inflict voodoo vengeance on a local Scandinavian superstore?

RULE 14 - REALITY IS OVERRATED

I once met a woman who lived in a skip; it was love at first sight. This was no ordinary skip – it was layered, like an inedible pie. The crust comprised a rotten mattress, a manual lawnmower, a one-handed clock, a stringless banjo, and a rusty *Unclaimed Baggage* sign. At first, there was nothing to indicate that the skip was inhabited, but after I had spent twenty minutes resting against it drinking cider out of a bag, it birthed a young woman. She emerged like a swamp monster but wasn't covered in slime. Her off-yellow jacket, stripy t-shirt and once-luminous dungarees reminded me of a faded rainbow.

She seemed grateful for the company and introduced herself as *Camden Lock Nessie*. There was a certain logic to this – the skip was near London's Camden Lock Market and Nessie was one way of shortening what turned out to be her name, Vanessa. But there wasn't much logic to anything else about her.

"I am as barking as a tub of Rottweilers," she explained, after minimal formalities had been exchanged. "Sometimes, I see voices. They use sign language". She turned to the empty space beside her and screamed, "Shut up, Kevin!" before turning back to me. "Kevin's my imaginary enemy. Bastard."

We stood there for a bit as she strummed the stringless banjo. It may have woven entrancing melodies in her imagination, but it did very little for me. When she'd finished, she said, "If all the world's a stage, then schizophrenics play many parts, often simultaneously."

I had not often heard this point of view expressed before. She really did seem to have a new take on the universe, albeit a deranged one.

"I've had a hard old fantasy life," she continued. "I've been places no one else has seen. Invisible places. In my head."

I couldn't help but wonder how someone so well-travelled had ended up in a skip, so I asked her as delicately as I could.

She didn't dwell on the details. "Some people are driven. But I'm parked. Probably by demons." At that, she leant back a little too far and fell back on the abandoned mattress. "Sorry about that. I've got leaning difficulties." She laughed hysterically, a sort of cockney wheeze. As Nessie recovered her position, she grabbed the one-handed clock and said, "That'll come in handy! It'll help me keep track of the seconds."

I wondered what time meant to someone like Nessie. How did she spend it? Surely the contents of her skip offered limited possibilities.

"Hope you don't mind me asking, but what do you do all day?"

"History," Nessie replied.

"How do you mean?"

"I shoplift history books."

"Do you read them?"

"No, I cook them."

"Oh. What do they taste like?"

"Course I bleedin' read them! Why else would I nick them?"

"I've always liked history," I lied.

"There's a lot to like and a lot to hate. Either way, there's a lot of it."

"I know what you mean." I didn't.

"History helps me understand what's going on," she said. "Especially in my head." Reacting to a noise only she could hear, Nessie dropped the clock. "Shush! Napoleon's trying to whisper something." She turned and listened intently to the invisible Emperor of the French. "Never... You're not having me on now are you, Bonaparte? ... Well, I never." She turned back to me. "Apparently, Primrose Hill's about to erupt. It's lain dormant for a suspiciously long time, so I'd steer well clear if you don't want to get covered in pumice." She turned back to Napoleon. "Thanks for the tip-off, Emperor."

Primrose Hill was a few minutes' walk away. The grassy, sixty-metre bump boasted an excellent view of London Zoo but Vesuvius, it wasn't.

"There's no obvious explanation for the regular misbehaviour of my head," Nessie continued. "Sometimes, life speeds up and colours itself in. At other times, it makes geology look pacy."

I sympathised. Existence could be problematic.

"I know I'm a few Rizlas short of the proverbial spliff," she said. "Sometimes, it even feels like someone's translated reality into a language I can't speak and I'm searching for the subtitles."

I wanted to put an arm on her shoulder. Having your head turn against you could not be easy.

"Suicide is self-defeating," Nessie said. "Yesterday, I tried to gas myself in an electric oven. Couple of months back, I overdosed on laxatives. That stank." Once again, she laughed like a malfunctioning pneumatic drill. "I've not had a good day. I was late for my voice-hearers support group. I ran as fast as I could hobble, but I fell down a manhole and landed on a man. Nice bloke. Gave me a leg up and I wasn't too late for the clinic. The doctor calls us his *joyful little mysteries*. He wants to create an *oasis of respect* where we can *express our unmet needs*. Patronizing knob. "Good news," he says the other day. "We've stabilized your instability." Well, forgive me if I don't ululate. The nurses just tell me to "get some rest" and "read *Revelations*". I tried, but it wasn't a recipe for sanity: "The City of the Seven Hills will be utterly destroyed, and a thousand multi-headed frog-beasts shall devour the sky." You're better off watching *The One Show*."

I took her point. The bible had a long-established relationship with insanity. I mentioned this and she told me a story about two psychiatric patients she had once known. One thought he was God, the other thought he was Jesus, and when they had first met, things had looked a bit tense for a while, until the one who thought he was Jesus said, "Dad!", and the one who thought he was God said, "Son!" and they'd embraced.

We laughed at this oddly life-affirming anecdote for a few seconds, but Nessie appeared to be gripped by an unseen terror. Some beguiling Spirit of Nonsense had descended upon her, and she seemed to be gazing on a distant horizon, many miles from Camden.

Nessie explained that she had a problem. Although she may look like a homeless woman from the early twenty-first century, she was actually a concubine from medieval Istanbul and Sultan Ibrahim The Mad, his Chief Black Eunuch and eighteen Nubian giants were chasing her. By smuggling in an unsliced cucumber, she had polluted the purity of the sultan's harem and now faced execution by being bound hand and foot, sewn up in a sack and drowned.

It seemed unlikely, but I was happy to offer comfort to one of the world's most strangely afflicted. She jumped out of the skip, grabbed my hand, and dragged me through the streets of Camden with feverish force. Lurid polystyrene heads dangled menacingly from the front of shops offering inflatable furniture, juggling accessories, fur-framed mirrors, clockwork Hindu Gods, sun-bleached lesbian pornography, and suspiciously young antiques. A window sign declared, *We Do Not Pierce Belly Buttons, Nor Do We Know A Place That Does*. There were wailing street musicians high on meths and blanket-shaking prophets; a man in a torn business suit attempted to destroy a parked car with an invisible weapon, a screaming pensioner threw eggs at a bus shelter and a three-legged dog bounced improbably along the pavement.

Camden seemed to be crammed with people who would list their hobbies as "traffic baiting", "aggressive mumbling", and "solo boxing". Every one of them was the life and soul of their own imaginary party. A young man lay on the pavement, warbling on a recycled didgeridoo and a beetroot-tinted woman sang, "Gin! Give me some gin! I want some gin! Gin!" There was a plaintive lilt to her wailing that was practically an invitation to homicide.

The street stalls' odours inflicted brutal olfactory violence. Fried pizza slabs, burgers of dubious provenance, tortured lentils, incense, urine, petrol, and trampled vegetables combined into a poisonous potpourri. The whole postal district was several months past its sell-by date.

We dodged two white Rastafarians trying to sell us sun-dried raisins as cannabis resin and ran into the market. Stalls offered artisan water, stolen socks, made-to-measure massage tables, lava lamps, plasma balls, velvet capes and Native American tarot cards.

Nessie was running as though her life depended on it and, in her head, it did. "Quick! I don't want to get chucked in the Bosporus!"

We concealed ourselves behind a vintage cereal stall, and Nessie expanded on her imaginary predicament. If she surrendered there'd be no point begging for mercy - the Sultan was not a reasonable man. He had been imprisoned for twenty-two years, the last four in the palace cage with only mutes for companions and porn for intellectual enlightenment. On his release, he had followed the Ottoman Code of Fratricide by strangling all twenty-eight of his brothers with a handkerchief. He had been drinking throughout a week-long circumcision feast and was now more than ready to take it out on a rebellious concubine.

Nessie's entirely illusory time in Istanbul's four-hundred-room harem had, she said, been tiring to say the least. Sultan Ibrahim The Mad was determined to mark his name in history by inventing as many new sexual positions as possible and had covered the harem's walls and ceilings with mirrors to observe his couplings and triplings from a variety of angles. Ibrahim neighed like a stallion throughout his vigorous trysting and forced all his concubines to wear clothes held together with an adhesive that melted gradually at room temperature. Being guarded twenty-four hours a day by eighteen Nubian slaves had also been rather testing. When they weren't bickering about camel wrestling, they were making obscene jokes about their sultan's appetites, and even though they were all heavily armed and of intimidating stature, they were each named after different varieties of tulip.

This was all very well, but we were in Camden Market, one of London's smelliest tourist attractions. I pointed this out as tactfully as I could, but she wasn't having it: we were deep within the labyrinths and arcaded courtyards of Medieval Istanbul's Spice Bazaar, where merchants were busy selling belly-dancers, mechanical nightingales and performing dwarves. I could see no evidence of any of these things, but I couldn't leave Nessie alone with her delusions, particularly given how much I fancied her.

Eventually, we were discovered cowering behind the vintage cereal stall, not by an enraged sultan, but by a tall, frail drunk in his late seventies. He was the colour of nicotine: even his coat and beard were faded yellow, and he held a plastic bag the shade of rotting daffodils. After staring at us for a bit, he flourished a plastic crucifix in front of his furrowed face and mumbled a heartfelt blessing.

It would have been nice if it had worked, but it didn't. Nessie remained under her delusion's spell and dragged me back outside. Whatever I said to reassure her, road signs transformed under Nessie's gaze into gilded imperial monograms, newsagents became kiosks of pearl and marble, and wailing street musicians became the Ottoman court's expert lutenists and harpists.

In some ways, Nessie's imagined world was a better place than the reality I inhabited. The cash points at Camden's World's End crossroads each had two queues: the shorter ones were for cash withdrawal; the longer ones were for bearded men demanding money from the first queue.

Nessie explained that Ibrahim The Mad, his Chief Black Eunuch and the eighteen Nubian slaves were almost upon us. Two of the slaves had produced woman-sized sacks and were waving them about their heads as they chanted one of their sultan's hunting poems.

I suggested we escape by nipping on the tube. We went down the escalator and took the High Barnet Branch. Nessie clutched my hand as we sat in silence. I enjoyed her company. She had a mysterious fourth dimension, inhabiting unseen worlds and hearing silent voices. It didn't do her any good, but it did make her interesting. After three stops, we arrived at Archway, she leapt to her feet and ran out of the carriage without letting go.

I was pretty sure that it had been somewhere around here that a defeated Dick Whittington had turned again before becoming thrice Lord Mayor of London. If the venerable Dick had repeated the action at the start of the third millennium, he would have seen that the streets of London were paved, not with gold, but with comatose schizophrenics, used condoms and dog excrement. Dick Whittington would probably have turned yet again and continued out of London.

Nessie seemed intent on going up the hill and scaling Archway Bridge. With an eighty-foot drop onto the trunk road below, it has often proven a popular spot for exiting the world, and I was keen that Nessie's despair didn't drive her into taking this option. This might have been easier had she not been somewhere else entirely in her head. Where most people heard the accumulated engine rumbles of the A1 in rush hour, Nessie said she discerned the whispering waves of the Bosporus. They seemed to be calling out to her, crashing on the shore with a murmured "Vanessa, Vanessa, Vanessa."

We looked out through the heat haze and petrol vapour shadows at what I thought was The Shard, The Gherkin, and Canary Wharf, and what Nessie believed to be Istanbul's Blue Mosque, Executioner's Fountain, and Gates of Felicity. Closer at hand, a grim seventeen-storey DSS building was, to her, the spectacular Topkapi Palace, home to the Ottoman Empire for twenty-one generations.

The Nubian slaves were getting louder in Nessie's head. She could hear their chanting, the swish of their scimitars, and the swirling of their sacks. She turned North, and pointed out The Bosporus, The Sea of Marmara, and The Golden Horn. The Ottoman fleet was moored across the bay, she said, and the royal barge was a few hundred feet beneath us.

Three joggers approached, all earnest, heavy-bellied men in bulging Lycra. To me, they could not have been much less threatening. To Nessie, they were the Sultan and his men, about to drown her in a sack.

"No! They'll never take me!" With unnerving athleticism, Nessie clambered up the railings, raised her arms into a diving position, and prepared to leap off the bridge. Her body was backlit by the sun like an all-embracing halo, marking her passage into another world.

"Wait!" I shouted and unleashed my best bar-fighting skills on the runners. It's not hard to deck fat fitness freaks when they're not expecting it.

Nessie climbed back off the railings and hugged me. "My hero!".

And reader, I married her.

RULE 15 - WHAT GOES AROUND COMES AROUND, BUT SOME PEOPLE DUCK

I once met a brilliant moron: ideas of an Einstein, sense of a toddler. People called him Chewie, partly on account of his wild ginger hair, unkempt beard, and gangly limbs but mostly because he was a total space cadet.

We were the only customers in Wolverhampton's worst pub, and he looked like a man with a story to tell. I stood him a stout and he explained that, until recently, he had enjoyed a successful career in the tech sector, launching a galaxy of gizmos onto global markets. He loved his work and had even been profiled in *Wired Magazine*, but in the space of a fortnight, he had not only lost his job he had lost a planet.

I sympathised as best I could. Over the years, I had lost my share of jobs, women, and keys. Mislaying a planet had to hurt.

Chewie offered to talk me through his demise. Failure is right up my street, so I was delighted to accept. As he told his sorry tale, Chewie's stout foamed his beard, making him a potential contender for the world's worst Santa, but I tried not to let this detract from the gravitas of his personal tragedy.

He began with the collapse of his career, partly because it happened first, and partly because he was still mourning the mislaid planet and needed to build up to it gently:

***

"It all went wrong in Birmingham," he began. "I was in a conference hall, addressing a visiting delegation of Chinese business leaders. These guys held the keys to a market of 1.45 billion people. That's 18.47 per cent of the planet's population, so mathematically speaking, this was the most important moment of my career. Everything rested on this presentation - nail it, and the company would go interstellar; fail, and I was finished. I had full confidence in my product and my equipment – the display screen wouldn't have looked out of place in an IMAX, and I had not only told my team to double-check my tablet for glitches, I had also asked my mate Tim to give it the once-over to be doubly sure. Tim is chairman of our local astronomy club and a CEO in cyber-security, so this seemed like a shrewd move at the time – belt and braces, as they say.

I was feeling pumped, absolutely determined to smash the product pitch, and I addressed my audience with the confidence of a visionary.

"Let me give you a glimpse of the future." I brandished a pair of hi-tech swimming specs. "Googoggles!". I twanged the Googoggles onto my head. "In a pair of these, you can surf the internet underwater. Allow me to demonstrate." I flourished a multi-coloured swimming hat. "This is a cranial neurotransmitter." I stretched the plastic cap over my skull. "Not only is the cranial neurotransmitter waterproof, but it also responds to your thoughts, directing your Googoggles to a relevant website. As you can see on the screen behind me, I'm currently thinking about spiral galaxies." The display screen showed a pair of brilliant celestial helixes embedded in a star disk. "And this is precisely what I see on the inside of my Googoggles. Just imagine how much a pair of Googoggles could enhance your sub-aqua experiences!"

The audience applauded. It was going like a dream. I removed my Googoggles and asked for a volunteer.

The Chinese Minister for Sub-Aquatic Digital Development joined me on stage. I'm guessing you haven't heard of him, but he couldn't have been much more eminent if he had been Chairman Mao. I took pains to help him don his Googoggles and waterproof cranial neurotransmitter as delicately as possible.

I took my time to breathe in, savouring my moment of career climax: years of research telescoped into an instant.

"Now, if I power this up, we can clearly see that our respected volunteer is currently thinking about..." I turned to the screen behind me. It was crammed with Bangkok transsexuals in skimpy attire. "Thai ladyboys."

Once I'd been fired, I decided to join my friends at the Wrekin Astronomical Society.

The night was clear, and the moon was as fat as a sumo wrestler. We lay on top of a grassy mound twiddling with stargazing gear. The Wrekin Astronomical Society isn't wildly popular and tonight's turnout of three was above average.

To my left lay Martin, a man who could never be mistaken for a fashion model. He sported a side parting, bottle glasses and a *Satsuma Nightmare* t-shirt, one of only three copies made. *Satsuma Nightmare* was the name of our prog rock band at Imperial. Martin played the Mellotron and could have become quite famous. If people had liked Mellotrons.

To my right lay Tim, the cyber security CEO who had checked my tablet so inadequately. A handsome, hangdog bloke, Tim would have been infinitely more socially adept than most astronomers were he less deeply devoted to alcohol.

I wasn't ready to discuss the Chinese Minister's ladyboys, so I ignored Tim for a bit, and chatted to Martin instead. "Day's not a patch on Night, is it?"

Martin looked up from his self-built telescope-camera combo. "I've never really got the hang of Day."

"Night's got shimmering nebulae, dwarf stars, mega-luminous super-giants," I said.

"Day's not got a lot going for it," Martin said.

"Empty skies."

"People."

"Presentations," I added, without really meaning to. I had managed to avoid the topic for less than a minute.

"Oh yes." Tim looked up from his laptops. "Your presentation. How did it go?"

I recounted my career-ending ladyboy catastrophe in gruesome detail.

After he had stopped laughing, Tim turned to me with something approaching sincerity. "Look. I'm sorry about your job, Chewie. But if I didn't write the viruses, my firewall developers would be out of business."

"You infected it!" I could have killed him.

"Looks that way." Tim gave me a sheepish glance, then buried his face in a sequence of astral images.

If my China crisis had simply been a minor hiccup in my job progression, I might have left it at that. But it was nothing less than a career-exterminating calamity and I had to ask the obvious question, "Why did you insert ladyboys into my presentation?"

"Look, sorry, old chum," Tim replied, "But it probably struck me as amusing at the time."

"Well, the Chinese Minister for Sub-Aquatic Digital Development didn't find it funny."

"No, I don't suppose he did."

The inadvisability of adding Thai ladyboys to the presentation was not something that only became evident in retrospect. It could have been predicted by anyone who had graduated from primary school, and Tim had graduated from Oxford.

"Tim," I said, with barely controlled fury, "Tell me honestly, how drunk were you?"

"Just a couple of bottles down," he replied.

"Wine?"

"Vodka."

Tim was a tit, but there aren't many world-class astronomers in Shropshire, so we were stuck with him. That didn't stop me feeling humongously irritated when he said, "You'll get another job" with miniscule conviction.

Martin made a valiant attempt to back up his optimism. "It's true, Chewie. You're gifted."

"I'm cursed," I said, and I meant it.

"I know the feeling," Martin said. "I was playing a twenty-seven-sided computer chess tournament this morning and had just developed a fully conscious computer when my mum spilt Bovril all over it."

Fate's cruelty knew no bounds. The only consolation I could offer was, "Life, eh?"

"Let's emigrate to Discworld," Martin suggested. After chess and the Mellotron, Terry Pratchett was his main passion in life.

Sadly, neither of us knew the way to Discworld, so we lingered in the Midlands. After a bit, I checked out Martin's camera-telescope combo and noticed that its circuit boards were seriously quantum. He explained that he had gutted his conscious chess computer and used some of its most advanced elements to enhance the combo's astronomical abilities. It was one of the most impressive homemade lash-ups I'd ever seen. The only trouble was, the camera operated with a significant delay, a fault he was aiming to iron out over the next few months.

Martin and I spent the rest of the night sharing jokes about equations, while Tim focused his efforts on drinking himself to sleep.

When dawn finally birthed an immaculate blue sky, Tim was the first to pack up. "Can't hang around," he said. "Viruses won't write themselves."

But Martin just stood there, tinkering frantically with his semi-conscious camera-telescope combo, and muttering madly to himself, "Must be something wrong. It's got double vision. We're here, not out there."

He was clearly having a breakdown and, frankly, I couldn't blame him, given the way the world chooses to behave.

I ambled over to see if I could help. It took a while to prise him off his equipment, but when I had, the screen offered me the most surreal sight I had ever encountered: the Earth was in the sky, just past the sun.

"It's a twin!" I exclaimed like an exultant midwife. "A Second Earth!".

"Very funny," Tim yawned.

"Listen, mate, I don't joke about astronomy." It's true, I don't. "It's a perfect clone of the planet and it is orbiting in opposition to the sun."

Tim stared at me, as if I were some exotic species of moron. "Then how come you can see it?"

I had no answer.

Luckily, Martin did. "Maybe it only makes itself visible occasionally when it drifts to the side by the odd degree."

"So, it's a shy planet! Is it as socially awkward as you?" Tim laughed, but we didn't. You don't mock a man who has just changed history, especially in space.

Seeing our reaction, Tim strode over and examined the screen. For a moment, he looked like he might fall over, but after he had steadied himself, he did manage to say, "Well shag me sideways!".

We took turns to gaze at Earth Mark Two – or *Martin*, as it was now known. There were oceans, forests, mountains and even evidence of a Martinian-made structure that we decided to dub *The Great Wall of Martin*.

"We could be the first men on Martin!" Tim declared with the conviction of a Cold War space-racer.

"Life has got to be easier there," I said, reflecting on my ladyboy mishap and Martin's Bovril tragedy.

"Maybe the women even like Terry Pratchett," Martin said.

"Maybe everyone's ginger and gangly," I said.

"Maybe the oceans are thirty percent proof." Tim yanked a vodka bottle out of his jacket. "Let's drink to it." He drained his recommended weekly alcohol intake in one.

"What do you think Martinians look like?" Martin asked.

It was a good question, but none of us could think of a good answer. Instead, Tim and I attempted to outdo each other with unlikely suggestions in silly alien voices:

"Telekinetic crustaceans!" I squawked like a manic Pterodactyl.

"Bisexual, bipedal vegetables!" Tim blurted, like a multi-tentacled triffid.

"Aquatic quadrupeds with retractable tonsils!" I screeched like a Venusian banshee.

"Psychic fungi with an uncanny mastery of logic!" Tim menaced in a robotic staccato.

We each performed a series of elaborate extra-terrestrial mimes to accompany the words. It was quite entertaining for the time of day.

Martin didn't join in. He just said, "Maybe they're like us."

"What, a bunch of dorks?" Tim suggested.

"Just ... unappreciated." Martin stood there looking as wistful as a rescue puppy in urgent need of adoption.

I slapped Martin on the back. This was no time to be miserable. "We've found life! The planet's not lonely anymore."

"Seven-point-nine billion people can't be lonely," Tim said.

"I am." Martin looked utterly forlorn.

"True," Tim said. "Your social calendar's about as lively as a damp Sunday in Shetland. Get a life."

"He has," I said, "Several billion extra-terrestrial ones. The geek will inherit the New Earth, and no one can take it away from him."

Martin returned to his equipment, took another look, and crumpled like a deflated crisp packet. "There's nothing to celebrate."

"Why not?" I asked. Martin really could be unbelievably negative, but I suppose his victories were so rare that I needed to spell them out to him. "Look, Martin, we've just discovered a new planet, it's identical to Earth and we've named it after you."

"We didn't take a photo." Martin looked like an intimate family member had just died.

"Then use the bloody camera function!" I sometimes wondered at Martin's lack of initiative.

"There's no point." Martin was on the verge of tears. "*Martin's* gone."

The recollection of his camera delay glitch struck me like a flying breeze block to the bonce. He was right to despair.

I slumped onto the grass, and said, "We made the discovery of a century."

"And lost it again." Martin said, staring into space, bereft as an abandoned astronaut.

"We'd have been the most famous astronomers on the planet," Tim attempted to chin himself, but missed his jaw.

I'd never felt so scuppered. "Heroes to morons in five minutes."

"I hate Tuesday mornings." Martin's face radiated abject misery.

Tim cupped an ear. "Hear that?"

"What?" All I could hear was silence.

"Cosmic laughter," Tim said. "The sound of several universes pissing themselves in unison."

"Do we really need the photos?" I scrabbled for hope amid the shards of our broken dreams. "We've got three independent witnesses."

"Maybe we'd make page forty-seven of the Fortean Times," Tim's voice was as bitter as the loser of a billion-dollar lottery ticket. "Somewhere between an Iowan crackhead's abduction dream and an unidentified flying orifice."

"How can something like that happen?" I fisted the earth. "It's clear evidence of Dumb Design. God's obviously omni-incompetent."

For some time, we were immobilized by our own despondency. Tim doused his disappointment with vodka and Martin played travel chess against himself, losing repeatedly.

After a while, I decided that I wasn't going to just sit around all day and grow chins. I got stuck into some equations, channelling the spirits of Turing, Pythagoras, and Einstein. I even pictured Stephen Hawking looking down at me from his wheelchair in the sky and cheering me on through his voice-simulation device. I was gripped by a frenzy of calculation, blinded to the harsh realities of an unemployed dawn up a Shropshire hillock. This was what it was to be alive! I was mathematically ablaze, a hairy abacus calculating at warp speed.

The odds were astronomical, but for once we were in luck. I calculated that we had precisely twenty-three hours, eight minutes, and six seconds to reach the summit of Mount Snowdon to photograph Martin, Earth's twin. There was a nine-minute window from 5.56a.m, which didn't leave a lot of leeway, and as if that wasn't challenge enough, we would have to get hold of a better camera-coronascope combo on the way. Martin's kit may have been semi-conscious, but it simply wouldn't dice the Dijon.

My fellow astronomers were sceptical. Tim had a shedload of spam to send, and Martin had to sign on at the social security office. But I told them I was sure - if we missed this window, Martin wouldn't reappear until we were all the wrong side of ninety.

We scoured the internet chatrooms and arranged to collect the requisite equipment from an astronomer calling themselves *Terrific* around fifty miles north-east of our muddy mound.

Transport was an issue. Martin had a National Express Timetable, but most of the information had sweated off in his pocket. Tim had a car, but he was too drunk to man the wheel. I could drive, but only in theory – in practice, my passengers tended to run away screaming and I'd given up for more years than I could remember.

But whatever the practical difficulties, we were now on a quest, a journey to The Heart of Dorkness. We were The Fellowship of The Martin and the only people who could stop us were us.

It didn't start well. Tim had forgotten where he had left the car. We trudged through endless acres of bovine sludge before deciding to separate. It didn't bring us any closer to the vehicle, but we did succeed in losing Martin.

Forty minutes later, we found both Martin and the car at once. Martin was on the roof-rack and the vehicle was surrounded by cows. Martin doesn't like cows. I think it has something to do with udders.

I scared them off with a Wookiee growl I'd learned from *The Empire Strikes Back*. It had taken me eight months to perfect, so I was delighted to see all my hard work pay off.

My celebrations were curtailed when the cattle knocked Tim head-first into a cowpat. I surveyed his cruddy visage, and said, "Tim, you're totally shit-faced."

Tim used Martin's *Satsuma Nightmare* t-shirt to wipe off the cowpat's remains. He hadn't got around to removing it from Martin's torso before doing this, and a scuffle ensued.

When I had finally pulled them apart, I said, "At this rate, we're going to need an Infinite Improbability Drive to get up Snowdon in time!" I often find that Hitchhiker's Guide to The Galaxy references fall on fertile ground in astronomical circles, but at that moment, the only fertile thing was the cowpat on Martin's t-shirt.

Tim was the proud owner of a BMW, but his wife had taken it and left him with her automatic Proton. This would have made it easier to drive had it not sunk into slurry under Martin's weight during his close encounter of the bovine kind. It was a setback, but I couldn't allow humanity's interplanetary ambitions to be hindered by mud.

After a frustrating half-hour spent grappling about in the filth, I decided to turn to maths. I positioned my equation pads under each tyre, hoping traction would help us. Tim and I shoved from the back while Martin sat in the driver's seat. The wheels span on the spot and the air was soon thick with slurry showers.

Martin opened his window. I hoped that he might be about to suggest a solution, but he just said, "Let's give up."

"That's the spirit." Tim took a glug of vodka. "Unconditional surrender's usually the best form of attack."

We tried again. The engine cut out. I was starting to think that Martin was right to abandon all hope when an idea occurred to me. "There's one last chance."

"What?" Tim didn't sound optimistic.

I asked Martin if he had removed the handbrake. He hadn't. He was worried it might be dangerous. Once I'd reassured him, he released the handbrake and the car crushed Tim's toes. Tim laughed hysterically then burst into tears.

It wasn't an encouraging beginning and my driving threatened to make the middle even worse. Martin cowered in the back, hugging a thermos flask, and playing travel chess with himself.

Tim sat in the front, cradling his head in his hands, and only occasionally peeking at my driving through his fingers. "You're giving me pre-traumatic stress disorder," he complained.

This was a new one on me. "Is that a terminal condition?"

"Just an overwhelming fear of what's about to happen," Martin explained.

Moments later, I crashed into a hedgerow. I simply hadn't seen it coming. "Sorry, I'm a little accident-prone."

"Catastrophe-prone, more like." Tim groaned.

I put the Proton into reverse and floored the accelerator. The car zoomed across both lanes, narrowly avoiding a peloton of mountain bikers on its way into the opposing hedge. I ignored the shrieking melee of Lycra, tyres and handlebars and drove out of shouting distance.

I had no idea where we were, so I asked Tim whether he had a map. He didn't, but Martin said he could do better than that and handed me a self-built GPS system. It was more complex than a confused octopus and it took Tim some time to attach it to the windscreen. While he grappled with its self-assembly suckers, Martin and I passed the time with a blind crisp-tasting competition, which Martin won. He has a highly sensitive palate.

The GPS rattled out instructions in a voice known to every astronomer on the planet. The impatient, eccentrically cerebral tones of deceased television stargazer Sir Patrick Moore barked, "Hurry up and insert your destination! How do you expect me to direct you if I'm not given basic information?"

A milk float overtook us. We were making continental drift look like lightning.

Sir Patrick was unimpressed. "This is absolutely ridiculous! Get yourselves organized immediately. You're an utter shower of procrastinating pillocks!"

Martin inputted a postcode into Sir Patrick's mechanism, and we were off.

There was something about having a secret mission that energized me. We were on our way to change history. For once, astronomy really mattered. As we burned serious tarmac, I whooped, "It's just like a road movie!"

"Awkward Rider," Tim said.

"Sons of Apathy," Martin said.

"That's a TV series." I remarked, as I turned right.

"Left, you blithering idiot!" Sir Patrick was not happy, and matters weren't helped when I stopped to let a flock of sheep pass.

"Don't give way, you spineless milksop!" Sir Patrick protested. "This bit is phenomenally simple. You just take the next turning on the left and keep going on the road ahead."

I didn't mind being posthumously bossed about by the voice of my favourite deceased astronomer, but concentration has never been my strong point. I soon got into a heated discussion about string theory with Tim and missed a turning.

"Nincompoop!" Sir Patrick shouted. "Recalculating route."

While I waited for the GPS's next instructions, I circumnavigated a roundabout.

"Your indecisiveness is making me dizzy," Sir Patrick complained. "You woolly-minded poltroon!"

I am not a naturally nervous driver, but my passengers tend to be. Sir Patrick was starting to sap my confidence with every insult, and he simply wasn't taking no for an answer.

Eventually, Sir Patrick directed us to the end of a cul-de-sac.

"Continue!" Sir Patrick insisted, repeatedly. "You cannot avoid your destination."

"But it's a dead end," I protested.

"Continue!" Sir Patrick demanded. "You cannot avoid your destination."

Tim adopted a tone often employed in bedside discussions with senile relatives.

"You're repeating yourself, Sir Patrick."

"How dare you?" Sir Patrick bristled.

"Sorry, Sir Patrick." Apology was Martin's default setting.

"I'm losing patience with the lot of you!" Sir Patrick sounded like he was about to blow a fuse, and not only metaphorically.

I turned to Martin. "Are you sure you put in the right postcode?"

"No," he replied.

"Why not?" I asked.

"I always doubt my actions," Martin replied.

"Good God!" Sir Patrick raged. "You haven't got the foggiest clue what you're doing, have you? I simply cannot be expected to work under these conditions. Goodbye." At that, he died.

Sir Patrick was clearly as conscious as Martin's chess computer had been before his mother spilled Bovril on it. The trouble was it had used its free will to top itself. I pleaded pitifully with it for several minutes and when it eventually crackled into life, we celebrated as wildly as our seatbelts allowed, right up until the moment Sir Patrick said "Shan't!", gave a valedictory raspberry and died permanently.

We all stared at the cul-de-sac ahead, and after a while, Martin said, "It's quiet without Sir Patrick."

"How about some music?" I suggested.

"Who needs music when we've got Martin's sparkling silences?" Tim's smile could not have been more sarcastic if he was competing in a piss-taking contest.

Martin reached into his pocket and took out a CD. Its cover was so dog-eared, it could have been a survivor of trench warfare. "Satsuma Nightmare?"

"Yes!" I exclaimed.

"Anything but that." Tim groaned.

Martin removed the CD from its sleeve, and said, "You're just jealous."

"Yes," Tim said with even greater sarcasm. "I really wish I'd been in a crap prog rock band with you two pretentious pillocks."

"We were masters of free-form dissonance," I said.

"You mean you were tuneless," Tim said.

Martin was getting seriously indignant. "Our time signatures were seriously innovative."

"You couldn't sell out a phone box," Tim said.

"Martin's Mellotron solos were epic." I started the Satsuma Nightmare CD, drumming on the steering wheel. Martin air-Mellotroned. Tim covered his ears.

The music transported me away from my driving to a lost world of prog rock dreams, and when I returned to reality Martin pointed out that I had spent twenty minutes waiting behind a row of parked cars. I'd thought the traffic was heavy.

Not long after I had got us out of the imaginary jam, Tim started to behave as if he knew the way. "It's the next junction," he said, with confidence.

I wasn't convinced. "Is that a liquid hunch?"

"I've stopped drinking," Tim replied.

"When?" I asked.

"Twenty minutes ago," Tim said.

We couldn't have been more lost if we were a Cub Scout football team nine-nil down to Real Madrid six minutes into injury time, which was a shame, as we were running low on both patience, and fuel.

After checking North, South, and East, we located the nearest petrol station to our West. I drew up beside a pump, clambered out and looked for the nozzle. There wasn't one. It was on the other side. I got back in, performed a nine-point turn and tried to return to the same pump, but was beaten to it by an army truck. I reversed, knocking over a newspaper stand, then lurched forward to a different pump. Once again, no nozzle, so I clambered back in, swivelled the car around the perimeter and pulled up behind the army truck.

While we waited, Martin clicked his tongue in a nervous, repetitive manner.

Tim appeared close to homicide. "If you don't stop doing that, Martin, I'm going to get seriously medieval on your Asperger's".

Martin continued his tongue-clicking.

Tim watched him for a further minute or so, then turned to me. "Evolution's evident cack, isn't it?"

"Not really, no," I replied.

"Then how do you explain Martin? How did he happen? Millions of years of natural selection and we end up with him. Evolution – the blind drunk watchmaker."

The army truck drew away. I seized the moment, pulled up beside the pump, got out and checked that the nozzle was facing the pipes. I was in luck! I filled the tank, telling Tim all about a fascinating graph I had seen in *The Economist* and the light it cast on energy geopolitics. He told me to "stop transmitting" and shut the window.

Once inside the service station, I found a road atlas and a multi-pack of crisps, then settled up. I returned to the vehicle and turned the ignition. The engine made a horrendous noise and choked.

Luckily, we all had advanced science degrees and were able to exchange theories. I thought it sounded like a misalignment of the intake valve's rocker arm. Martin proposed that it was more probably an issue with the clutch cabling. We held a fascinating debate for several minutes before Tim asked me, "What colour hose did you use?"

"Black. It looked like the most cost-efficient option. Why?"

"You've filled it with diesel."

"Is that a problem?"

"Only if we want to go anywhere. It prefers petrol."

After waiting seventy-eight minutes for a roadside rescue vehicle to siphon off the diesel, we replaced it with petrol, and hit the open road. We were back on track for Planet Martin's photo opportunity, and I had never felt such freedom. I punched the air, just as we hit a speed bump. The Proton flew up and landed with a crunch. Martin was covered in Bovril and chess pieces. Tim choked on his vodka, half-swallowing the bottle. I wasn't popular.

Countless insults later, we were chuntering past the River Wye and approaching Terrific's address, which appeared to be some kind of Victorian roller mill. We juddered across a cobbled courtyard and slowed to a near-halt before I edged towards four storeys of solid granite.

"Mind the building!" Tim cautioned.

I was halfway through explaining the importance of getting the Proton as close as possible, as 12G camera-coronascope combos were on the heavy side, when the vehicle's bumper kissed granite. I apologised.

"That's the thing about Victorian mills," Tim observed. "They just leap out in front of you when you're not expecting it."

"Wonder what Terrific's like?" Martin asked as he undid his seat belt.

"Maybe Terrific's terrific." I replied cheerily, buoyed up by our successful arrival.

But Tim remained as miserable as ever. "He'll just be another dork to add to our collection. Probably on the same spectrum as Martin."

Martin blanched and clambered out of the Proton in silence, clutching his travel chess set like a toddler's security blanket.

"Was that necessary, Tim?" I asked, reproachfully.

"Optional," Tim replied. "But enjoyable."

The mill was a remarkably well-preserved specimen of industrial ingenuity. A door-shaped aperture offered itself to me and I stepped into the frontage. Immediately, the floor lurched upwards and I found myself in a coffin-sized lift, thrusting its way into the building's bowels. Terrifyingly, the lift was open-fronted and as I ascended, I saw demented rolling contraptions fling grain through the air and shed-sized sifting boxes gyrating violently, their stocking-covered arms and legs a-wobble. It was steam punk technology at its silliest.

The lift stopped on the third floor, and I found myself face-to-face with a tiny, spiky-haired Japanese woman in her late twenties. She held out her manicured hand in greeting and spoke with a deep Derbyshire accent. "Hello, lad. I'm Terrific. Why didn't you take the stairs?"

I shook the proffered hand and watched Tim and Martin swan into the room from a door on the opposite side.

Tim ignored Terrific and asked me, "Seen Terrific anywhere?"

"The mirror," Terrific replied.

Martin gawped. "You look different to your emails."

"Never trust words," Terrific said.

I knew what she meant. "You know where you are with numbers."

She smiled at me. "I guess you're Chewie."

I gave her the gentlest of Wookiee growls.

She turned to Tim with noticeably less warmth. "*Guardian Angel*?"

"On the chatrooms, yes. IRL, Tim. If you need any computer security advice...". He handed her a business card.

She ignored it and turned to Martin. "And you must be?"

"*Tyson*," Martin replied meekly.

"Of course," Terrific said.

"My internet chess playing style is quite violent," Martin explained.

Martin was not exaggerating. I had been at the receiving end of his opening repertoire on numerous occasions, and rarely emerged unbloodied. But I doubted that internet chess would win over Terrific, so I thought it best to offer my sincere praise of her mill.

"Nice gaff," I said.

"Cheers, lad," Terrific said. "I get to live here for free provided I keep the place maintained. The equipment you're looking for is on the top floor by the flour bins."

I thanked her.

"You didn't say why you wanted to borrow it," Terrific said.

"We've discovered a planet…" Tim trod on my foot, so I added an "…arium."

Terrific looked perplexed. "A planetarium?"

"Yes," Tim lied.

"Where?" Terrific asked.

"Snowdon," Tim said, keeping the fib adjacent to the truth.

"And how long had this planetarium sat there undiscovered?" Terrific asked.

"Ages, probably… You know…". No one did know, least of all Tim.

"Well, good luck," Terrific said, once she had given up waiting for an explanation. "There's a coronascope, an SLR digital arrangement, a mount, and a refractor. I'd help you load, but one of my Archimedes screws is loose. Bring everything back in one piece, or I'll track you down and kill you." Terrific grinned, grabbed a prodigious spanner from a ledge and headed down into the mill's underbelly.

I led my fellow astronomers up an unfeasibly narrow spiral staircase to the top floor, where our equipment was waiting for us to collect. I had never set eyes on such a wonderful array of bits: every section was worth its own doctoral thesis. The trouble was, there were a great many bits and absolutely no instructions. Now, I've never been one to give up in the face of insurmountable physics, so I teamed up with Martin and steadily assembled the 3D techno-jigsaw.

Tim helped out by watching, and when we had finished, he said, "You really do work like morons possessed."

"Not morons," I replied. "Geniuses."

It was true – no ordinary astronomers could have assembled such a complex rig in the time.

Terrific dropped in, and said, "I thought you lot would be gone by now."

"We did it!" I pointed proudly at the fully assembled tele-camera-coronascope combo.

"Oh." Terrific looked perplexed. "Why did you do that?"

It was her gadget, so I tried not to sound too sarcastic. "I suppose we thought it might work better assembled than in bits."

"So, how are you going to get it down to your car?

"The stairs?"

"Too narrow."

"The elevator?"

"It's only good for carrying grain and traumatizing lost visitors."

I stared at my fellow astronomers, utterly bereft of inspiration.

Terrific strode over to the far wall, opened a set of wooden doors, and began winding a winch up from the yard three storeys below. "Honestly. If you lot were taken back in time you couldn't keep yourselves alive, let alone remember how the most basic machines were invented." She chucked a pile of sacking at us. "Pad it up."

When we were done, we lowered the padded coronascope, mount, refractor and SLR digital arrangement on the winch. It was a slow process, so I helped pass the time by continuing the string theory discussion we began when I had missed Sir Patrick's turning:

"String theory might well solve the riddle of quantum gravity, you know, and who'd have thought there were eleven dimensions? Mind-bending, isn't it? I mean, the very notion that the universe is made of vibrating one-dimensional extended objects no longer than ten to the power of minus thirty-five is an amazing paradigm shift – certainly made me rethink my life."

Terrific turned to Tim. "Does he always talk this much?"

"Oh, Chewie's always poncing on about the phenomenology of phenomena, even though he can barely tie his own shoelaces."

But I was on a roll, and I wasn't about to let Tim interrupt my flow. "Reality is actually made of string! Brilliant idea. It's as counterintuitive as the concept of Negative Energy."

"How about Positive Apathy?" Tim suggested unhelpfully.

"String theory even explains the end of the universe," I continued with emphasis. "It won't be a Big Bang..." I waved my hands about to illustrate my point, letting go of the winch. "...it'll be a Big Crunch."

Crunch! Echoed the world outside. We crowded around the window. The padded coronascope, mount, refractor and SLR digital arrangement had crushed the roof of Tim's Proton.

"Quick!" Tim exclaimed. "I need a chemist's and an off-licence."

Terrific looked concerned. "Why?"

"I find occasions like this are best enjoyed with a bottle of Teachers and sixty

Paracetamol."

I tried to look on the bright side. "You may have lost a Proton, but you've gained a convertible."

I think Tim might have hit me had I not been built like an extra-terrestrial orangutan.

But Martin wasn't much happier. His face looked like it had given up sitting on his skull. "Let's go home."

"If you ask me," Terrific sighed. "You're all passport-carrying citizens of Narnia. Combined IQ of a medium-sized plank."

I accept that I am impractical, awkward, and lacking in the common-sense department, but I struggle to accept an actual insult to my intelligence quotient. It was time to come clean. "Martin discovered a planet."

"Yeah, right." Terrific was unimpressed.

"It looks exactly like Earth," I persisted. "It orbits in opposition to us and we're going to call it Martin."

"Prove it," Terrific said.

"That's the plan," I said. "We've got until dawn to drive up Snowdon, spot it and take some photographs."

Terrific sat up sharply. "You've seriously discovered a new world?"

We nodded as nonchalantly as we could manage, which wasn't very.

"Then you're Columbus-es to a man!"

"It was Martin," I said.

"Columbus didn't play travel chess," Tim objected.

"Ignore Tim," Martin said. "He hates the universe.".

"And I'm a walking trip hazard." I didn't want to leave anyone with any illusions.

Terrific took a moment to appreciate our collective failings. "How long did it take you to get this far?"

"Eight-and-a-half hours," I underestimated.

"And at that rate you'd get to Snowdon…".

I performed a rapid mental calculation. "Next Sunday."

"One thirty-eight pm," Martin added, accurately. He really is a monster at maths.

Terrific hesitated for a moment, then said, "I'm coming with you."

No one protested. It was blatantly obvious that we needed help. After we had all headed outside, Terrific checked that the padding had protected the kit, told us to abandon Tim's totalled Proton and headed off to her garage.

"Reckon she'll slow us down?" Martin asked.

"Us?" Tim laughed. "The threesome who got ambushed by cows, dieseled their petrol engine, and waited behind a queue of parked cars."

Terrific zoomed up in an electric vehicle that wouldn't have embarrassed Bond. She pressed something and the doors pinged open in unison, groining us all in perfect synchronicity.

After we had recovered and loaded up the miraculously intact coronascope combo, Terrific introduced us to her car. "This is Dickie."

Tim gave it an ironic bow. "Charmed."

As we all got in, I asked Terrific the obvious question: "Why Dickie?"

"After my great-great-great-great-great granddad, Richard Trevithick."

"So that's why you're Terrific!" I exclaimed.

"Terrific Trevithick," Tim elaborated.

"The engineer who started the Steam Age," Martin mansplained.

"But you're..." Tim decided to bail out early on his sentence.

"Japanese?" Terrific speculated.

"Slightly," Tim backtracked.

"Well spotted, lad. Richard Trevithick's son gave Japan its railways and eight generations of Trevithicks."

This was fascinating. Not only had we discovered a planet we had also tracked down the direct descendant of one of the greatest engineers in history. These were exciting times indeed. Exciting and terrifying – Terrific drove like she was competing at Brands Hatch.

I calmed my nerves by talking to Martin about prog rock. "What was your favourite Satsuma Nightmare track?"

"*Sad Wednesday*," he replied.

"Really? I preferred *Algebra on Pluto*."

"Well," Tim chimed in. "My all-time Satsuma Nightmare ditty was *The Spiders From Martin*."

"That wasn't us," Martin said.

Tim sang with tone-deaf sarcasm, "*To the mouse with the girlie hair.*"

"We just missed the turning," Martin observed.

Terrific slammed on the brakes. I apologised. So did Martin. Tim didn't bother.

"You're all hopeless," Terrific complained. "Are you being sponsored?"

"No," I explained. "It's just us."

"Look. I'm sure you can tell me anything I want to know about string theory or celestial mechanics, but not one of you could find your way up a hill, let alone Mount Snowdon. Leave this to me."

Terrific span Dickie on the spot. Martin dropped his chess set.

We made unbelievable progress and, after a while, Terrific asked us why it had taken us so long to complete the forty-mile journey from the Wrekin to her mill. I told her about the cows, the mud, the hedgerow, the diesel, and our argument with Sir Patrick Moore.

"You fell out with your GPS?"

"Yes." Martin looked glum. "We're no longer on speaking terms."

"Well, don't worry." Terrific laughed. "If I get lost, I'll just improvise a sextant."

We all believed she would, but it didn't prove necessary. By dusk, we were approaching the Welsh border and Tim had fallen asleep.

Terrific glanced at me. "So, a brief history of Tim?"

"Successful businessman, obsessive astronomer, miserable sod."

I didn't think there was much more to be said, but Martin decided there was. "Tim's a hopeless alcoholic,"

"Hopeless?" I prised the bottle out of Tim's hands. "It's the only thing he's good at."

"Go on," Martin said. "Dissolve some Prozac in his vodka."

"Who needs Prozac when you've got that?" Terrific indicated the astonishing sunset.

Martin shrugged. "The sun's just a big ball of gas."

"But imagine how long it's been up there!" Terrific enthused, undeterred.

"Even stars die," Martin moped.

"It's interesting," I said, "Not all stars die the same way. Some will explode as a supernova. Others just settle down and perish as a white dwarf."

"And which would you rather do, Martin?" Terrific asked, pointedly.

"Wouldn't make any difference," Martin said. "If I were a star, I wouldn't be conscious."

Tim groaned himself awake. "Oh God, is it really today again?"

"Barely," I replied.

We passed a sign reading, *Croeso Cymru*. I hadn't been to Wales since I was a kid. "Who'd have dreamt we'd end up here?"

"Never in my tamest nightmares." Tim executed a seismic yawn.

Terrific laughed. "How's the skull?"

"Must have had a bad barrel."

"Why do you do it to yourself?"

"I like hangovers. They keep me calm, stop my mind from sprinting away from reality. They're like a partial lobotomy. Makes my brain the same size as the general public's."

Terrific scoffed. "Modest, isn't he?"

Tim snatched back his bottle. "My throat's drier than a lunar sea."

Terrific's eyeballs seemed ready to pop. "You're starting again!"

"Oh, it's just a little knock-me-down." Tim necked a measure that was less of a short and more of a long.

"How did you three end up friends?"

"We stare into space together," Tim explained, with supercilious accuracy.

"Martin and I were in a band," I said.

Terrific's interest perked up. "Really?"

"Don't get excited," Tim cautioned. "It was a student band."

"We had our moments," I said.

"What were you like as students?" Terrific asked.

"Well, they weren't dropping E's," Tim said. "They were squaring them in equations."

Dickie didn't have a CD player, so we recreated several of our most innovative tracks with vocals, finger-beats and Mellotron impersonations.

Eventually, Tim's prolonged groaning formed itself into a question. "Ever contemplated suicide?"

"No," Martin replied.

"Just a suggestion." Tim grinned. He wasn't a nice man.

We made good progress and reached the base of Snowdon in decent time. Unfortunately, it soon became clear that we would not be able to drive to the top of the mountain with the weight of a 12G coronascope combo in Dickie's boot. As four advanced scientists, we probably should have anticipated this.

Dickie crawled, its engine complaining about every centimetre, until Terrific said, "Only one thing for it," performed a three-point turn, then reversed up the road.

I was both impressed and worried. "Are we going to reverse all the way up to the summit?"

"Yes," she replied.

"Just checking."

Dickie continued his backward ascent at speed, swerving around corners and dodging ditches before coming to an abrupt halt just below a formidable barrier with a *No Vehicles* sign, an imposing cattle grid, and a series of locked gates.

"Let's go home." Martin said, spinelessly.

"Seriously?" Terrific looked at him in disbelief.

"Martin worries a lot," I explained.

"And people worry a lot about him," Tim added.

"Never mind," Terrific said. "Now listen, Martin, you discovered a planet, so cosmologically speaking, you're clearly a genius."

"I wish I was stupid," Martin said.

"Well." Terrific gave this some thought. "You have done some dumb things."

"Only because I was thinking about astrophysics at the time," Martin said.

I assessed our options. There was one: walking. The kit was too heavy to carry whole, so we disassembled it by the light of Tim's mobile. He viewed holding the phone as an acceptable contribution to our labours, even though it was significantly less arduous than taking apart a twenty-seven-piece example of heavy-duty astronomical technology.

Once we had finished, Terrific removed Dickie's battery, presumably in case any light-fingered sheep decided to put it on eBay, and we ascended Snowdon by moonlight. Terrific moved like a seasoned fell-runner; my gangly lollop put me in second place. Martin's cautious shuffle wasn't going to set any records, but it did keep him well ahead of Tim, who wheezed along clutching his chest, slurring things like, "Nature's got us bastard-well surrounded!" and "I didn't become an astronomer to go bloody rambling!"

Martin surprised me by being the first to offer sympathy. "Don't die on us, Tim. How would we cope without your sarcastic alcoholism?"

Tim didn't appreciate it. "Is this a Moronathon?"

"Don't mind me," Martin said.

"But I do mind you," Tim said.

Terrific stopped and turned to the struggling scientists to her rear. "How long have we got?"

"Thirty-seven minutes, fifty-three-point-four seconds," I replied, "Approximately."

Eventually, we were in sight of the summit. It would have been a moment to savour, had Martin not tripped on a scree slope and dropped the coronascope's refractor. He scrambled to retrieve it, but somehow contrived to maroon himself on a precarious clump of rock.

I asked him if he was okay, even though he obviously wasn't.

Martin stared at the precipitous drop just one step away, and said, "I'm used to space I can gaze up at, not step into. But now I'm here, it all looks very...liberating."

"You can't end it all!" I shouted. "You haven't started yet. Think of your planet!"

"With no refractor, there'll be no proof of *Martin*, will there?" Martin seemed close to tears.

"Think about your future!" Terrific shouted, edging closer to him.

"My future?" Martin sounded outraged. "You mean The Non-Event Horizon. I've got the perfect work-life balance. No work, no life."

Martin wasn't the one to jump. It was Terrific. I gasped. I had grown quite fond of her.

"Looks like she's stolen your thunder, Martin," Tim observed, coldly.

Moments later, Terrific emerged from the gloom with the missing coronascope refractor.

Martin no longer had a reason to leap, but that was no guarantee that he wasn't clumsy enough to stumble off the precipice. I employed my gangly arms in a manoeuvre reminiscent of Mr Tickle at his most elongated and guided him back to safety.

Fortunately, we weren't scaling K2 or Everest, and we managed to summit Snowdon without the aid of sherpas. We arrived a little early for our celestial date with Martin, but we still had to prepare the camera-coronascope combo with all the trimmings.

Once again, Tim's main contribution was to spectate, but under Terrific's expert supervision, progress was fast.

"It's like a military operation," Tim observed.

"Thanks," I replied.

"Dad's Army," Tim said.

Despite Tim's discouragement, we soon had our contraption pointed at the heavens.

"Well done, Terrific." I offered a hi-five. "What a great piece of kit."

"It is. When its battery's charged." Terrific accepted the hi-five like a fading footballer who has just been substituted after scoring an owl-goal.

We looked at the powerless 12G coronascope and the arid summit. Mains supplies did not abound, and we were a long hike from the nearest branch of Curry's.

Defeat can strike the valiant at any moment and, even when you are a serial loser, accustomed to its constant presence, failure can still leap out and surprise you. We stood in silence for what seemed like an epoch.

Then a thought struck me like a metaphorical wet halibut to the chops. "Dickie's battery!"

Terrific's face lit up and soon, so did the coronascope's LED. It was working, but there was no telling how long for. It could die at any time, along with our dreams.

We waited in the Welsh silence. It was even tenser than ladyboy-gate. After a while, I could stand it no longer, and my jaw started moving. "Do you think The Martinians know we're here? Do you think there's a trio of Martinian astronomers dreaming of life on Earth?"

Terrific was the only one to grace me with a response. "Give it a rest, Chewie."

I really admired Terrific and wanted to make her happy, but my mouth has a mind of its own. "I wonder what life's like on Martin?"

"How are we going to get there?" Tim asked, through his teeth. "Uber?"

"They *have* to send us!" I insisted. "We discovered it."

Tim gave me a withering once-over. "You're not exactly astronaut material."

"You'd never pass the Physical." Martin said, now firmly on my anti-Tim team.

"And you'd never pass the Mental," Tim said.

While we were insulting one another, a multi-coloured pre-dawn broke: crimson light in the east, cosmic rays reflected in the tarns.

Our futures hinged on this moment, but there was no sign of *Martin* the planet and Martin the man wasn't at his most positive. "It'll never turn up."

"Stop anticipating defeat." Terrific said. "Life's not a rehearsal."

"It's a poorly improvised performance," Tim said.

"For once," Martin said, "I agree with you."

I turned to Martin and said, "You may feel like a failed planetesimal lost in the trans-Neptunian deep but maybe you're really a proto-stellar nebula on the verge of star-birth." It wasn't the most accessible of pep talks, but Martin's veins flow with physics.

We stared at the camera-coronascope combo's screens as I counted down: 5.55 and 57, 58, 59 and 60 seconds..."

It was 5.56, the moment prophesied by my equations, but our screens remained blank.

Tim looked at me with an expression somewhere between cynical mockery and brittle hope. "Well?"

"Well, what?"

"Where's Martin?"

I ignored him and continued to stare intently at our blank monitors.

"We've been stood-up, haven't we?" Tim observed.

I decided to double-check the calculations. Most of my equation pads had met their muddy ends under the Proton's tyres, but I still had one pad left.

While I worked, Tim raised his vodka bottle in a bitter toast. "To abject failure!"

Martin blew into an empty crisp packet. The noise was horrendous, a flatulent battle-horn blast. "Sorry about that. My oxygen levels drop when I'm feeling anxious."

"What a great way to burn time!" Tim moaned. "Scrabbling up a Welsh mountain in search of The Dorkstar."

"That's it over there!" Terrific pointed frantically. "The round one that looks like Earth!"

I performed the loudest Wookiee growl of my life, grabbed hold of Martin and span him around. Tim shook his vodka bottle and attempted to spray us with it, but it wasn't Bollinger and he only succeeded in dowsing his trousers.

"Quick!" Terrific shouted. "Record the image!"

Dickie's battery bleeped and died.

I emitted a Wookiee death-howl. Tim punched an imaginary object. Martin burst his crisp packet.

Terrific cradled her head in her hands, rolled back onto the ground and began a mournful a slow, measured speech: "Scratch a genius and find a moron. My multiple-great-granddad was the same. Discovered the locomotive, then buggered off to Peru to pump silver mines. When he returned bankrupt, George Stephenson and his kids had nicked his discovery and launched the train age without him."

I joined in her liturgy of ingenious morons. "Galileo Galilei: greatest astronomer in history. Founded the study of motion, proved that the Earth orbits the Sun."

"Got banged up for life," Martin added.

"John Dee," I continued. "Introduced mathematics to England, charted the New World, dreamed-up the telescope."

"Died in poverty," Martin said.

"Alan Turing," I said. "Cracked the Enigma Code, invented Artificial Intelligence, designed the first digital computer."

"Topped himself with a spoonful of cyanide," Martin said.

"Science," I said. "It's a funny old game. More evidence of cosmic unintelligence."

"Why did this have to happen?" Martin asked.

"Earth leans on a tilted access," I replied.

Ethereal rays lent the four of us a timeless quality: legendary failures for the Ages."

***

His tragedy complete, Chewie finally licked the stout foam off his beard and asked me whether I would like another drink.

It would have been rude to decline. I wish I could have offered Chewie a job or a planet, but all I could do was chip in for some pork scratchings.

As there were no other customers, it didn't take him long to return with our pints, and when he did, I proposed a toast: "To Martin!"

"To Martin!" he echoed as our jugs clinked. "The greatest non-discovery of the twenty-first century."

Genetics gifts us many and varied talents, but common sense is one of the rarest and most precious. I certainly can't claim to possess it and nor could Chewie, and that does put us at more of a disadvantage than many might imagine.

I wondered how would it feel to be practically adept, financially solvent, and unbothered by things that you can't lay your hands on? Is that how beavers live? I wish I was a beaver, with a black belt in bridge construction, and a mind set on nothing but sex and survival.

What use are our abstract ambitions? Why dream of pie in the sky, when you can bake one in the kitchen? Would a life without stupid ideas be less interesting? Probably. Would Chewie and I be richer, happier, and healthier? Definitely. Are we ever going to change? No.

RULE 16 - CANCEL GEN Z

Hipsters were bad enough: bearded, tattooed irritants in flat caps, non-prescription specs, and lumberjack shirts, relentlessly peddling their apps, flat whites, and vinyl. But these pretentious gentrifiers and their ironic bicycles have got nothing on the sanctimonious pedants of Gen Z. These bubble-dwelling blame-monkeys, with their overbearing victimhood, cyber-vanity and censorious puritanism well and truly boil my urine and one damp Sunday, as I rode the last train home from a Charles Bukowski convention in Cockermouth, I found myself sat opposite a prize specimen.

The Zoomer in question was drowning the otherwise empty carriage in an exquisitely irritating torrent of TikTok – chattering minions, squeaking rubber ducks, and Californian cheerleaders exclaiming "Wow!", "Oh my Gosh!", and "Awkward!" – and when I politely hinted at the notion of headphones, she accused me of committing a "micro-aggression" and turned up the volume.

Now, I'm not one to admit defeat, especially to someone with a centre parting, so I responded by growling a medley of tracks from Tom Waits' *Black Rider* album. My gravelly rendition of *I'll Shoot the Moon* about circling vultures and funeral wreathes, went head-to-head with her giggling chipmunk; my world-weary *Just the Right Bullets* about the importance of blessing your ammunition before killing someone took on her yodelling robot and *T'ain't No Sin* about the joys of removing your skin countered her donkey with Tourette's. When I got to the bit about dancing skeletons, she relented, and plonked her phone down beside a half-eaten bag of vegan chicken.

The Zoomer wasn't a graceful loser. She called me a "Boomer," and shot me a look of utter disgust. "What were those dead songs?"

"Tom Waits," I replied. "Greatest lyricist of the twentieth century."

"The twentieth century," she echoed, with total contempt. "I'm going to call out the twentieth century. Everything was toxic, hardly anyone was famous, and there was at least one World War. No one had the courage to stand up to statues, so dead racists had nothing to worry about. Everything was plastic or made of coal and people laughed at the wrong things. Hardly anyone apologised, even though they had clearly underestimated the number of genders by at least seventy-four. And no one realised that my generation was right about everything, partly because we hadn't been born but mostly because of ageism." At that, she gobbled some of her meat-free meat.

I took a moment to savour the near silence before I felt compelled to ask, "Do your opinions matter to you?"

"Yes."

"Well, I'm glad they matter to someone."

She took a moment to digest the insult. "Don't brain-shame me."

"Why not?"

"It's hate-speech."

The Zoomer's opinions were prime nonsense, but she was very young, and I wondered whether I was being a bit harsh. I forced a half-smile, and said, "I don't hate you."

"That's supposed to make me feel better, is it?" Her scowl was angry and needy at the same time. It occurred to me that this was the whole problem; Zoomers assumed that, in return for their contempt, the world owed them comfort and support. What did her feelings matter to me? We had only just met and our conversation had only happened because of her TikTok tsunami.

"You need to check your privilege," she said.

"You need to check your manners," I said.

"Excuse me!"

"That's better."

This seemed to throw her, and it took her several seconds to come up with, "You really need to read the room."

It wasn't a room, it was a carriage, and we were the only people on it, but that didn't stop her continuing to put the proverbial boot in.

"You're toxic," she said. "You've had your time."

I wondered what sort of time she presumed I'd had – a stellar career as a polo player in Dubai, a noted wit on New York's cocktail circuit, an all-conquering auteur in Hollywood – then thought about the time I had actually had – serial divorce, bankruptcy, prison – there wasn't much scope for envy or nostalgia.

"Your views are outdated," she continued, "So it's better for everyone if you say nothing."

"You want to censor me out of existence?"

"Well, that would make for a better world."

"What did I say wrong?"

"It's not just what you said, it's everything. You don't deserve to have a voice anymore."

Clearly, something had happened to the planet while I hadn't been paying attention. A panoply of unwritten laws now governed everything that was said and done, as if life were lived under the supervision of moderators. Lockdown had temporarily abolished the world and replaced it with the internet. Vast social changes had occurred in people's imaginations and the world had been perfected online. Now, we had a new generation as sanctimonious as Sunday school teachers, bristling with piety, ready to damn us for our every act, word and thought.

Still, it was a long journey, the bar was closed, and my hangover was burgeoning into a life-threatening condition. I badly needed a distraction, so I apologised and asked my youthful companion to elaborate on how Western Civilization had misbehaved.

She was more than happy to oblige. "Communism was wrong and so was disco. The Great War wasn't "great", it was triggering, and there were no safe spaces in the trenches for the neurodiverse. Britpop was racist – other countries popped too. Harry Potter and Father Ted were TERFS, and that Cisgender heterosexual Nelson Mandela should check his privilege, if he's still alive. And what about Boomer films? Why didn't ET just Snapchat his home planet? Why weren't clone stormtroopers more diverse? Why was Rocky so aggressive? Why were there no genuine Indians in Indiana Jones? Why was Back To The Future so retro? Was Mrs Doubtfire really trans, or was it just blatant cultural appropriation? Jaws was blatantly anti-fish, and as for space, the moon landing was just high-altitude colonialism."

I couldn't help admiring the scale of this weapons-grade bilge. Was there any point in picking over the meagre contents of her skull? I decided to offer up some thoughts of my own.

"That's all very interesting," I lied. "Would you be offended if I shared a few observations?"

Her look told me that she would be offended by anything I could ever possibly say, think or dream, but I am not one to be discouraged.

"You're young now," I began. "But your body will fail, your dreams will die and all you ever did will be forgotten. Time will run out, but not before your patience. Love is a lie; friendship is a fraud and people only ever change for the worse. Your ambitions will crush you; your children will age you, and you will die alone."

Once she had finished weeping, the Zoomer gave me the kind of glare usually reserved for torturers and traffic wardens. "Are you some kind of troll? A real one?"

"Am I a real troll?"

"Yes."

"No, I'm a life coach."

"Busy, are you?"

"No."

"What a surprise."

I'm no snowflake, but she had touched a nerve. My client list was as about as well-populated as the Antarctic, and I really wished it wasn't. I spent the next twenty minutes staring out the window, watching drizzle dampen drab northern towns and recalling various Tom Waits ditties about whisky, sex, and death.

Eventually, I became aware that the Zoomer was tapping her fingers on the table. The sound blended with my mental Tom Waits soundtrack for a while, but I can't say it improved it. When I finally brought myself to look at her, it was clear that her rhythmical fingering was forming into a thought.

"So," she began, her expression a mixture of curiosity and distaste. "How does it work?"

"Life coaching?"

She nodded.

Did I have before me a rare example of a young person feigning interest in a Boomer? I resisted the temptation to say, "But I thought Gen Z had all the answers," and embarked on a gentle explanation of my craft: "Most life coaches, they accentuate the positive, and help make their clients more productive by suggesting constructive strategies and offering fresh perspectives."

"And you don't?"

"Not so much, no. I make people aware of their own limitations and introduce them to the ultimate life-hack – semitasking."

"Not multitasking?"

"Never. Multitasking is way too tiring. Semitasking is the science of doing one thing at a time in a half-arsed manner. I run a short eight-month course up in Dover. Permanent demotivation guaranteed or your money back."

"Men can't multitask," she said. "Doesn't mean women can't."

"Multitasking is all about juggling. Whether it's career, relationships, friends, hobbies, or children."

"That's cruel!" she protested.

"I'm not suggesting that anyone juggles children. All I am saying is, your average multitasker is never happier than when his balls are in the air. Semitaskers are suspicious of balls. One ball at a time is more than enough."

"There you go, talking balls."

I ignored her insult and continued. "Semitasking is all about time. Multitaskers are painfully aware of its scarcity and pack every instant with work, networking and vigorous relaxing. Semitaskers prefer time mismanagement and give skiving their absolute attention."

"How do you get anything done?"

"Multitaskers have to-do lists. Semitaskers have to-don't lists."

"So, you never achieve anything?"

"Not if I can help it, no."

"And you're happy with that?"

"Do I look happy?"

"No."

"Correct."

"So, how do you get through life?" she asked. "Give me one practical example of how it works?"

"Okay. Well, a multitasking parent might spend breakfast time whipping up a quinoa cous-cous packed lunch, designing a National Book Day outfit, and writing a letter of complaint to the headteacher, whereas a semitasker would be utterly absorbed in burning a single slice of toast."

"Right."

"A multitasking business leader might be simultaneously making half her workforce redundant, donating to the Tory Party, and laundering money in the Cayman Islands, whereas a semitasking business leader would give her undivided attention to fiddling her expenses."

"You're not really selling this."

"Or, a multitasking Zoomer might be calling someone out for disagreeing with them, stirring a Twitter storm about nothing, or reporting anyone with a sense of humour to an Admin, whereas a semitasking Zoomer would be focused entirely on letting a Boomer wind them up on a train."

And, reader, she cancelled me. That's why I'm no longer talking to young people about anything.

CONCLUSION - HOW NOT TO LIVE YOUR LIFE

S o, what can we take from all this? I'll start in the middle and work sideways:

Intelligence, incompetence, and interplanetary travel are three sides of the same coin.

Young people are not to be trusted until they turn fifty - and even then, keep an eye on them.

Celebrate your limitations; they will be your friends for life.

Imaginary friends are preferable to imaginary enemies.

Notorious gangland enforcers are not to be trusted, but don't tell them that.

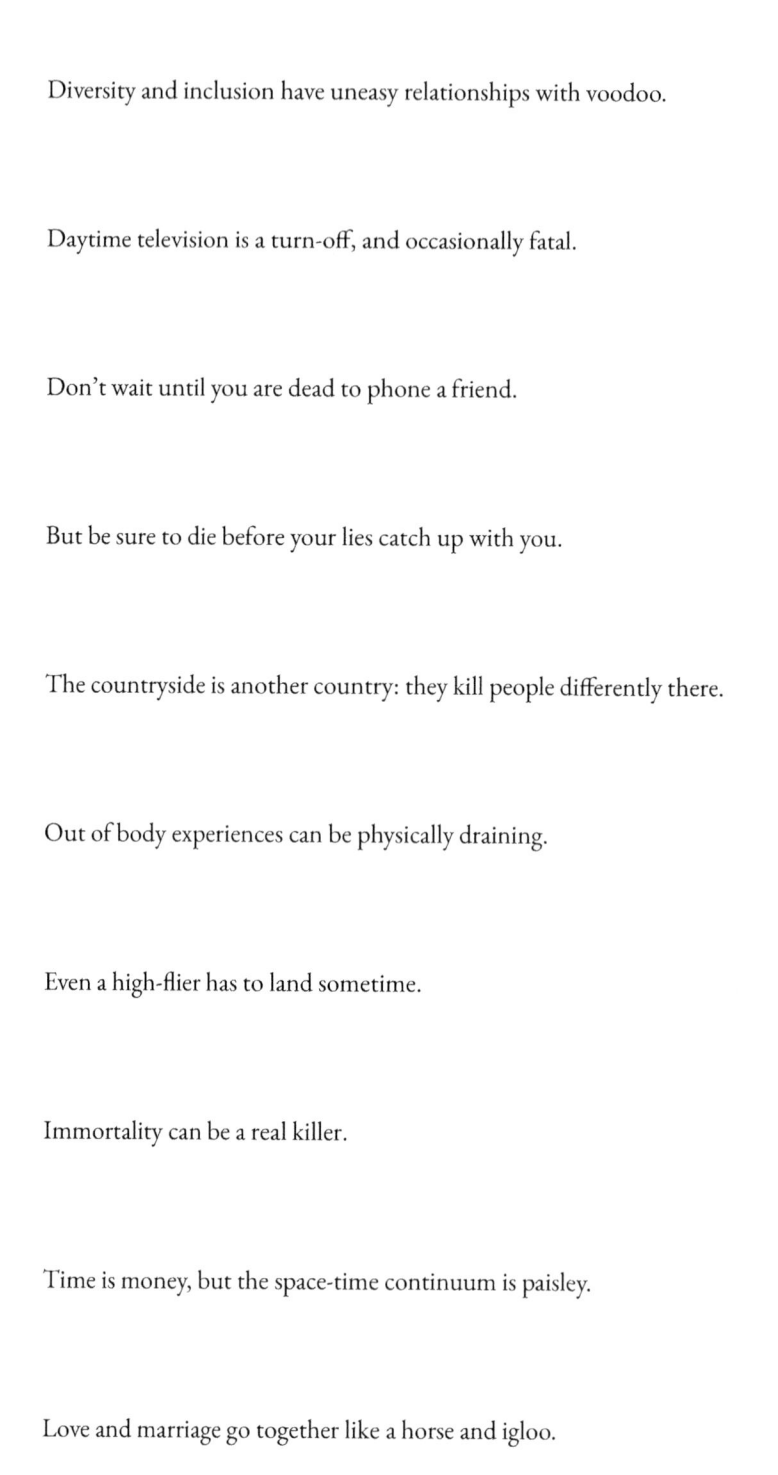

Diversity and inclusion have uneasy relationships with voodoo.

Daytime television is a turn-off, and occasionally fatal.

Don't wait until you are dead to phone a friend.

But be sure to die before your lies catch up with you.

The countryside is another country: they kill people differently there.

Out of body experiences can be physically draining.

Even a high-flier has to land sometime.

Immortality can be a real killer.

Time is money, but the space-time continuum is paisley.

Love and marriage go together like a horse and igloo.

One final negative visualisation:

Forget the present and live in a different moment. Choose mindlessness and focus on where you're not. Let your mind drift like a lost Zeppelin. Watch it crash, burst into flames, and visualise your passengers running screaming from the burning wreckage. Take things out of focus until existence is a blur of lost hopes, dead dreams, and niggling anxieties. Let your True Self be torn in a million different directions until you've forgotten who you are. Only then, will you be ready.

Hope that helped.

Cuthbert Huntsman, Broadmoor, 2023

MAKE CUTHBERT HAPPY

If you enjoyed *How Not To Live Your Life*, please leave a review. It'll cheer up Cuthbert no end.

Cop Lives Probably Matter

Rich Nash

Contents

1. PRISON DIARY – ENTRY 1 — 194
2. COPPING OFF — 195
3. PRISON DIARY – ENTRY 2 — 205
4. ARRESTED DEVELOPMENT — 209
5. PRISON DIARY – ENTRY 3 — 218
6. FELINE OF DUTY — 221
7. JUSTICE IS BLIND DRUNK — 224
8. PRISON DIARY – ENTRY 4 — 234
9. ROLL OUT THE BARREL — 237
10. PRISON DIARY - ENTRY 5 — 245
11. DEBRIEFING — 248
12. PRISON DIARY – ENTRY 6 — 257
13. DEATH: THE SEQUEL — 261
14. PRISON DIARY – ENTRY 7 — 266
15. A TOTAL CAR CRASH — 269
16. PRISON DIARY – ENTRY 8 — 278
17. AGENT PROVOCATEUR — 282
18. PRISON DIARY – ENTRY 9 — 293

19.	POTHOLING	296
20.	PRISON DIARY – ENTRY 10	305
21.	INSERTION	307
22.	DEFUND THE POLICE	316
23.	PRISON DIARY – ENTRY 11	323
24.	SORRY	326
25.	PRISON DIARY – ENTRY 12	330
26.	TRIPLE BENDING	333
27.	PRISON DIARY – ENTRY 13	339
28.	PROUDCOCK	341
29.	BRITNEY MORIARTY	347
30.	PRISON DIARY – ENTRY 14	353
31.	GOODBYE DOLLY	355
32.	PRISON DIARY – ENTRY 15	364
33.	COCKY'S CORPSE	366
34.	PRISON DIARY – ENTRY 16	369
35.	SUSPENDERED	372
36.	PRISON DIARY – ENTRY 17	376
37.	MELONS	378
38.	PRISON DIARY – ENTRY 18	390
39.	DOGGING	392
40.	PRISON DIARY – ENTRY 19	408
41.	BONSAI-AND-I	410
42.	PRISON DIARY – ENTRY 20	416
43.	THE FOUR BRITNEYS OF THE APOCALYPSE	419
44.	PRISON DIARY – ENTRY 21	433
45.	THE TRUTH HURTS	436
46.	PRISON DIARY – FINAL ENTRY	439

PRISON DIARY – ENTRY 1

When I was arrested for burgling my own house, I raged against the injustice right up until the moment I realised I had got the wrong address: I have never been big on detail and the bottle of meths hadn't helped.

I tried to convince the judge that a custodial sentence would damage my career and devastate my family, but he was adamant that "unemployed life coach" didn't count as a career, and he pointed out that my eight wives were all exes, none of my kids were speaking to me, and I didn't have any dependents, as I was myself dependent on the state for benefits. He did have a point, but eighteen months seemed harsh.

With time on my hands, I bagged a place on the prison's creative writing course and started knocking out a crime novel – write about what you know, as they say. Now, I've never understood why criminals are always painted as the bad guys, and the police are misrepresented as honest, decent, and heroic, so I resolved to write a novel about lying, cowardly, randy coppers who wouldn't know justice if it slapped them on the arse and called them Sally. See you after the first chapter.

Yours truly,

Cuthbert Huntsman, Unemployed Life Coach

COPPING OFF

Detective Inspector Harry Trent dangled in the moonlight. He was fifty but wouldn't be getting any older. His flabby corpse was bent over backwards like a collapsed deck chair, and someone had taken the trouble to snap his spine, bind his heels to the back of his balding head and noose him by the belly to the top of a lamppost.

It may have been a low point in DI Trent's career trajectory, but this was one of the highest points on London's northernmost extremity and, with the city lights twinkling seductively beneath his contorted body, Trent could have been a posthumous poster boy for the world's worst romcom.

Stripy police tape flapped in the breeze like miserable bunting, cordoning off the crime scene from the entirely absent public. This spot was so desolate, the fly-tippers seemed to have given up on it; even the most recently dumped mattresses were in an advanced state of putrefaction. The addition of a pathology tent, squad cars, scene-of-crime officers and Homicide detectives probably made the location more desirable.

Detective Chief Inspector Danny Ladd observed proceedings from a respectful distance. He'd had better Saturday nights, but at least there was the Superintendent to entertain. Ladd had always had a soft spot for her. She really put the *Super* in Superintendent. He gave her a gentle nudge and indicated the pretzeled detective. "That's what I call a bent cop."

Ladd's lame pun landed like a concrete bellyflop. Superintendent Faki just grimaced, adjusted her headscarf, and said, "Not very dignified, is it? Going out like a sandwich board."

They watched a young SOCO ascend a step ladder and attach a winch to the rope circumnavigating Trench's prodigious beer gut. A cardiac arrest would probably have done for him in a year or two, but this had clearly been a different kind of attack.

"Poor old Harry Trent," Ladd said. "Freemasons will be heartbroken."

"Shame he shipped smack." The Super deadpanned.

Ladd didn't remember telling her this. He'd had Trent under investigation for some time, but the details were restricted to his covert anti-corruption unit. Or so he'd thought.

A violent jolt sent Trent's corpse swaying in the wind. Panicked SOCOs scampered beneath the deceased detective, as he swung like a winched hippo. A gangly figure burst out of the pathology tent and gestured at them with such inventive obscenity, it was almost a work of performance art. The anatomical accuracy of the mimed insults would have got most people arrested, but Stoker was not most people. He was the sort of pathologist whose principal career interest was the knifework and the entire Force were terrified of him.

The semi-elevated Trent dangled like a birthday piñata, but the Super wasn't celebrating. She just shook her head in disgust and asked, "Who the hell bends a DI to death?"

It was a good question, and Ladd hadn't got a good answer, so he offered a silly one. "A criminally inclined orangutan. With a grudge. And an industrial trouser press. Possibly, Ma'am."

The Super held a stare fierce enough to turn most subordinates to quivering blancmanges, then she goosed him. Ladd feigned offence, then they both broke into giggles. Murder scenes didn't have to be miserable. It was the weekend, after all.

An earnest Homicide detective in a bulging, beige suit strode towards them. DCI Dixon had a loud red face and was built like a breezeblock in both body and brain. He blanked Ladd and addressed the Super. "Anonymous call, Ma'am. Dogger, probably – popular spot."

Ladd scanned the ground. It was carpeted in condoms, lube jars, latex gloves, the shattered remains of a CCTV camera and heaps of used tissues.

"Looks like Homicide's last office party," Ladd observed.

Dixon's face flushed puce. "Why's he sniffing around, Ma'am?"

The Super gave Dixon a glare sufficiently formidable to poleaxe an alpha grizzly. "I invited DCI Ladd personally."

She put such indignant emphasis on the last word that Dixon almost backed down. Almost, but not quite.

"Nice place for a date, Ma'am." Dixon looked at Ladd for the first time. "Gives a new meaning to Internal *Affairs*."

Modern policework tends to focus on data analysis, situational awareness, and community involvement, but Ladd often found that the wisest course of action was violence. As a six-foot-three amateur boxer with a granite jaw, slab hands and fast feet, this option often paid dividends. It not only enabled him to deal efficiently with the criminal fraternity it was also a surprisingly effective way of bypassing office politics.

Ladd chinned Dixon. He reeled, stunned but not sunk. Ladd wished he had thumped him harder; maybe he was getting soft as he crept closer to forty. Dixon launched a counter that would have been a knockout, had Ladd not shimmied to the side. booted away Dixon's shins and grounded him face-first in used dogging tissues.

The Super gasped. Perhaps Ladd had miscalculated. She was his superior officer, after all, and Dixon was his colleague; albeit one with all the charisma of dysentery. An apology would have been inadequate and insincere, so Ladd decided to brazen it out. "Spot anything untoward, Ma'am?"

A livid look flashed across the Super's face. She had the power to suspend him on the spot, but once she'd let him suffer for a moment, she just said, "Too dark to make anything out, DCI Ladd."

He had to hand it to the Superintendent. She was a top-class wind-up merchant.

DCI Dixon clambered to his knees, used tissues clinging to his chin. He looked like a sex-soiled Santa but sounded anything but merry. "Trent was one of the best. Why can't you leave him in peace?"

As if in answer, the winch creaked like a vampire's coffin. The SOCOs gasped as Trent's corpse teetered precariously, then dropped.

The Super embarked on a curse. "Mother of Al..."

"Ahhhh!" Stoker finished it for her with a Braveheart battle-roar as he broke the terminally bent detective's fall with a rugby dive before bench-pressing the body over his chest.

The SOCOs applauded, largely in fear. Ladd joined in, partly to annoy Dixon, who swore to himself and headed back to the crime scene.

Stoker lugged the body towards the pathology tent's threshold like a groom with his bride. "Cannae wait to get stuck into you, laddie."

"Get a morgue!" Ladd shouted, then felt a handcuff snap over his wrist.

"Personally, I'd prefer a room." The Super dangled the cuff key in front of his face.

Ladd paused for a micro-beat. The Super was looking highly arresting. "Well, I am home alone, Ma'am."

"Just don't bend me over backwards." She led Ladd away.

***

The sirens would have been unnecessary, had the Super not driven with all the caution of a Daytona Speedway Champion. As it was, the screaming alarms and spinning lights were the only things standing between other road users and death. The Super treated every bend as a chicane and every red light as a signal to hammer the accelerator. Ladd began to feel nostalgic for the relative peace of the murder scene.

"Hope you didn't mind me dragging you out," the Super enquired as her speeding vehicle planted a passing cyclist into a municipal bin. "I know it's a Saturday, but I figured you'd want to be at the death scene."

Ladd had been watching a ferocious cage fight in *The Goodwill* when he'd received the call to Trent's fatal bending, and he would have preferred to stay where he was, particularly as he'd just bought a round. Still, he always found the Super hard to refuse, so he just said, "Nowhere I'd rather have been than a terminal dogging site."

"You're a terrible liar, aren't you?"

"Yes," Ladd lied. Economy with the truth had got him where he was today.

The Super cut up an ambulance, then shot Ladd an alluring look. "Reckon you can talk yourself out of anything, don't you?"

"No," Ladd lied again.

"I don't believe you." The Super accelerated the wrong way down a one-way street and reversed through a pedestrianized zone. It being late on Saturday night, no one could walk straight, and fights, gropes and casualties were at a premium, but the prospect of being mown down by the Super seemed to have a sobering effect, and most people managed to get out of the way.

Once they were back on a legal road and driving in the right direction, the Super asked, "What's the biggest lie you've ever told?"

Ladd conducted a mental sift through a million remembered inventions, inaccuracies, and misrepresentations. It was almost impossible to know which one to single out, but relatively easy to know that he shouldn't admit to any of them. "No comment."

"If I made you tell the truth, the whole truth and nothing but the truth, which lie would it be?" The Super asked, as she surprised a staggering drunk with a last-minute swerve and upended him onto the pavement.

It was a tough question. Ladd's mind span through reams of baseless phrases before settling on one stand-out porker: "I love you."

"Do you?"

"No, Ma'am."

"Oh."

"It's usually the biggest lie. Ask around."

The Super went quiet for the rest of the journey and focused on committing traffic violations: Ladd totted up twenty-six category C's in the space of eight minutes and, at times, he wondered whether they'd be joining Trent at the morgue.

The journey may have been conducted at homicidal speed, but as senior officers of the law, they knew how to park without arousing suspicion, and this meant walking the last hundred metres or so to Ladd's marital home.

"Shall I bring the handcuffs?" the Super asked. She had freed him shortly after they'd left the murder scene, but she still seemed rather attached to them.

"That's all right, Ma'am," Ladd replied. "They'll only remind us of work."

The Super chucked the cuffs into her vehicle and locked it. Ladd led the way, and she followed a step or two behind in an unconvincing attempt to avoid looking like an adulterous couple.

The street was a hive of inactivity: parked cars, closed curtains and lampposts undecorated by dangling cops. But as Ladd took out his keys and opened the porch, he glimpsed a shadowy shape lurking beside a *Neighbourhood Watch* poster in the window opposite. Ladd thought it best not to investigate further and concentrated on the heavy locks he had installed on his own advice.

The Super waited until Ladd was inside the porch before following him through a forest of gym equipment.

"Strange place to store all this," the Super observed.

"Obstacle course for intruders, Ma'am."

When the Super struggled to lift a dumbbell out of her way, Ladd turned back and hefted it up with one hand.

"What a man!" The Super squeezed his bicep.

"They're Tina's." Ladd unlocked the internal front door and tried to repress any guilty feelings induced by the mention of his wife's name. "She loves her kickboxing."

The long hallway led to another door, and an open-plan living room, light on clutter and furnished with more style than the average plod's pad. A poster-sized photo showed Ladd winning a local boxing bout; bloodied but beaming. A sofa-bed was sandwiched by cheese plants and overlooked by a plasma television of cinematic proportions. French windows led out onto a well-tended back garden.

"Nice place." The Super put her hands around Ladd's waist. "You on the take?"

Ladd shook his head. "Straight as a thin blue line."

"Uncorruptible, honest, faithful..."

"I wouldn't go that far."

"How far would you go?"

He lifted her up until their faces were level. "This far, Ma'am."

"About twelve inches."

"Might be stretching it a bit."

She stopped his smile with a snog. The Super tasted very different to his wife, and this wasn't altogether a bad thing.

When they eventually unclenched, the Super licked her lips and said, "Do you think horizontal would be more practical?"

Ladd gently lowered her to the ground and kicked open the sofa-bed.

The Super looked disappointed. "Bedroom off-limits?"

"Forensics, Ma'am."

The Super turned away and Ladd wondered whether she would leave. She did know the score: he'd never pretended to be single. But his superior officer wasn't on her way out, she was searching his home without a warrant, frisking his mantelpiece for evidence against him. She picked up a wedding photo: it wasn't his favourite, but he looked happy enough, five years younger and proud of his new bride. Tina looked good: strikingly sculpted and long-limbed. She wasn't far off his height and the newly conjoined couple towered over the other guests.

The Super's finger lingered on Tina. "Bit of a giraffe."

"No, Ma'am. Giraffes are placid."

The Super smirked and let her coat drop. "How long have we got?"

"All week." Ladd shrugged off his jacket. "Tina's at a retail conference, shagging her boss."

"Now there's an idea." She tore his shirt off. "Want me to pull rank?"

"Why not, Ma'am."

She flung his shirt across the room, and it crash-landed on the TV. "Is she better looking than me?"

"Not pound-for-pound." Ladd ripped off her blouse, launched it into the air, and it lassoed the doorknob.

"Do you love her?" The Super undid Ladd's trousers.

"We're very happily mortgaged." He unzipped her skirt.

"You really can bullshit on the spot, can't you?"

"I never knowingly lie, Ma'am."

"There you go again."

He skied her skirt. It landed on a cheese plant.

"I'm going to have to interrogate you thoroughly, DCI Ladd."

"Very good, Ma'am."

Ladd chucked her underwear across the room. A frilly bra plonked into a fruit bowl. A racy thong straddled the door frame and, as they slid onto the sofa-bed, the Super did the same to Ladd.

***

Dawn broke over the Super's panties. Glorious sunlight bathed the thong, but the fetching image was lost on both senior law enforcement officers as they snoozed arm-in-arm on the sofa-bed, as thick as thieves.

It was an idyllic sight; a naked cop couple still in their prime; pale Ladd's gladiatorial frame set off by his Superintendent's smooth, pocket-sized body. It was a moment to treasure, right up until the instant that a key turned in the porch door with a bloodcurdling twiddle.

Ladd jolted to his feet as if electrocuted, ejecting the sleeping Super from their extra-marital embrace. He worked with operational energy; bunging on his boxers, bounding around the room, and gathering clothes like a narco-cop on a cartel bust.

The Super blinked herself awake, agog at this display of lunacy. It saddened her to see that Detective Chief Inspector Ladd was better fitted to a straitjacket than an anti-corruption unit.

There was a loud trip in the porch, followed by a robust Cork curse, and Tina's unmistakeable voice shrieking, "What cockwomble moved my friggin' dumbbell?"

Inside, Ladd chucked clothes at the panicking Super: blouse then skirt then bra then heels, all gathered and yanked on at pace.

Tina's keys turned in the front door, and heartbeats raced in the lounge, as the senior police officers made desperate clothing adjustments.

The front door clicked shut behind Tina, and she shouted from the hallway, "Bastard boss made a pass at me! He can shove his job up his mam's ass!"

Ladd threw open the French windows at the back of the lounge and bundled the Super out onto the patio with all the delicacy of a bouncer ejecting a drunk. She seethed with indignation as he slammed the windows shut on her irate face and thrust his arms airwards in a desperate *Do one!* gesture. With a kick and a twist, Ladd transitioned the bed back into a sofa and adjusted his trousers. The evidence was cleared, and the Super was safely sprinting across the back garden.

Ladd's mission was accomplished, his deadline met, and he allowed himself a smile. He breathed in, blinked then clocked the Super's thong astride the top of the door frame, just as Mrs Tina Ladd opened the living room door, dislodging the panties. They dropped and straddled her nose.

"You're back early, dear," Ladd observed.

Tina removed the alien panties and stared at them in disgust. "Of all the shameless bollocks! What an insult! A great two-fingered moony! Who is she?"

"Sorry ..." Ladd wanted to cry.

"Don't beat yourself up about it. Let me." Tina launched a series of expert kickboxing moves: a cross-body punch, leg-sweep, and axe-kick. Ladd stood motionless, suffering multiple minor injuries as he figured out which lie to tell.

"There's a park bench with your name on it!" Tina continued. "You'll be lovingly remembered - by the bitch in the thong." She let fly an elbow-strike, a hook-punch, and a front-kick, all landing with extreme prejudice.

Ladd fought the pain but didn't fight her. He just said, "I can explain."

Tina paused her assault to stare him out, daring him to fib.

Ladd racked his brain for an adequate excuse: a laundry mishap, a decorating error, botched DIY - nothing worked. He kicked his mind into overdrive, stretching the limits of his imagination to bursting point in desperation as the plausible response clock ran out of ticks. Ladd's head gave up, but his mouth didn't: "They're mine."

"Yours?"

"Mine," he found himself repeating. Backing out now seemed dangerous.

"Thank God!" Tina squealed.

"You don't mind?"

"Mind? I love it. Put them on."

Ladd gawped at the panties in abject horror.

"You know you want to."

Ladd knew he didn't. Things had snowballed. A lie had done this. Only more lies could save him. "They're too small," he elaborated. "I was going to take them back.... That's why I threw them at the ceiling."

"You were that angry?"

"Yes!" Ladd struggled to imagine himself into the mind of an angry cross-dresser. "Definitely. Furious!"

"Lucky we're the same size." Tina took his hand and led him upstairs to the bedroom.

Ladd gazed sorrowfully into their full-length mirror as Tina made him up and dressed him, firstly in a spaghetti top and rara skirt; then a chiffon gown and tiara; and finally, a lace nightie and fishnets. Every transformation sapped his soul. The mirror was stealing his entire sense of self – his romantic conquests, his boxing triumphs, his police career all negated in a series of flounces. Ladd's job sometimes prompted him to think about death, but this was the first time that death had seemed an inviting prospect.

Tina delved into her drawers and handed him some lady-razors: shapely but sharp. Ladd wondered whether he should use them to end everything.

"Don't go soft on me now, Danny." Tina was bouncing with anticipation. "Remember, it hurts to be pretty!"

Ladd certainly hurt – and it wasn't just the kickboxing injuries. He forced a smile, headed for the bathroom, and locked the door. Ladd held his head in his hands. He felt like a suspect sent to stew in his cell after a probing interrogation. His life had been undone by a pair of panties, and there was no solution in sight. He had always known he'd go a long way to save his marriage, but he had not realised just how far. Ladd lifted a foot onto the bath, foamed his leg and shaved off his man-hair.

"Get a wiggle on!" Tina shrieked through the bathroom door. "I mean to have you, girl!"

Ladd gazed mournfully at his reflection and gave a silent howl of such existential agony; it would have made Munch's *The Scream* look like a seaside postcard.

PRISON DIARY – ENTRY 2

I couldn't wait to hear what my creative writing tutor thought of the first chapter. She was a nervous lady of around forty-five with a fragile smile and a haunted look in her eyes. Her name was Naomi, and she had started our induction by insisting that we "get to know each other". After I had told her about my life coaching career, drink problem, drugs problem, and bankruptcy, she revealed that she was married to a successful PR executive named Roly, and led a hectic life in Sevenoaks, running an organic soup group, playing the flute, training as a doula, writing a baking blog, and finessing her Pilates. Now that the children, Gethsemane and Innsbruck, were both at secondary school, she had decided to help people less fortunate than herself and play a part in their redemption.

I wasn't completely convinced that Naomi fitted the profile of my ideal reader, but I had done my best to adhere to her advice: "Follow your instincts, never punch down, and make sure that the characters are diverse and inclusive."

Our sessions took place on a pair of carrot-coloured stacking chairs in a utility room that stank of sweat and disinfectant. There were no windows, just a portrait of a cow. The heifer was posed in medium close-up and gazed out of the frame with unnerving humanity, its expression as inscrutable as a Friesian Mona Lisa.

I had shared my chapter with Naomi twenty-four hours earlier via a memory stick; it was a clumsy arrangement, but they really didn't want prisoners using the internet. I didn't know what they were afraid of: I would only have gone on Pornhub.

Naomi took a while to gather herself. I think she had expected me to fictionalise my troubled childhood and work through my issues rather than focusing on dogging sites and police undergarments. She started by praising the diversity and inclusiveness of my characters. I had put a woman from an ethnic minority background in a senior position, and my lead character's partner could not have been feistier. These were good things, she said, with the clear implication that there were also bad things to be discussed, once she had found the right words.

"The problem is," she explained, "You have touched on a highly sensitive subject."

I wondered what she meant. Police corruption? Perverted pathologists? Bending fatalities?

"It's your hero," Naomi said. "Is he … trans?"

"No," I replied. "He's a liar."

"Are you implying that trans people are liars?"

"No, he's lying that he likes to wear women's clothes."

"But he does wear women's clothes."

"He doesn't want to."

"So, he's transphobic?"

"No. It's just not his thing."

"Oh." Naomi angled me a smile. "Wouldn't it be easier if the whole wardrobe mix-up thing just didn't happen?"

"But it did happen."

"Did it?"

"In my head, yes. That was exactly how it happened."

"I see."

"You told me to follow my instincts."

"I know, but I didn't realise your instincts would be so …" She ran out of words.

"Shall I write another chapter?"

She paused, gathering the strength to summon a rictus: "Just keep up the diversity and inclusion."

I thanked her and headed back to my cell. I have never been a fan of prison, but at least I've had practise. This one was an "optimized super-prison" with CCTV, scanners, and tags instead of human screws, but the system was basically the same as your average Victorian hellhole.

I had wangled a job in the library, which was always a far cushier bet than the laundry or the kitchen. My one colleague was illiterate and resentful, but once I had dug him out a copy of "Female Undergarments Through the Ages: An Illustrated Companion", we got on just fine.

The prison wasn't exactly awash with avid readers, but my cellmate was the exception. Jeff was an urbane Geordie with a glittering career in armed robbery and an interest in just about everything. Reading had got him through his numerous stretches, and when I returned from my shift to find his nose buried in an atlas, it was no surprise.

"Ever been to Transnistria?" Jeff asked, after bit.

"Isn't it full of vampires?"

"That's Transylvania."

"Oh."

"Transnistria broke away from Moldova," Jeff explained. "It caused all kinds of ructions with the CIS nations."

"Who?"

"Commonwealth of Independent States."

"Never heard of them."

"Moldovans. People like that."

I didn't know anything about Moldova, so I decided to research my enemies instead. I had borrowed a hefty tome about the City of London Police, who had sported an unblemished record for one hundred and forty years before a four-year, four million quid corruption inquiry secured a grand total of two convictions. I couldn't help but chuckle.

"What?" Jeff enquired.

"Ever heard of Operation Countryman?"

"Like the Rasta film?"

I dimly recalled a Jamaican thriller with a reggae soundtrack.

"I never liked Bob Marley. He was a Spurs fan." Jeff was a dyed-in-the-wool Newcastle supporter and took a dim view of all other teams.

"At least he shot the sheriff," I said.

"But he didn't shoot the deputy," Jeff countered.

"You don't get many Rasta cops, do you?"

"Wish we did. Might have let us off with a caution." At that, Jeff nodded off. I wouldn't have minded having a cellmate who snored, but Jeff hummed in his sleep, primarily songs by The Smiths. Maybe it was a medical condition - "Morrissey Malaise", perhaps - but it didn't exactly lighten the mood.

I spent the week writing chapter two on my prison-issue tablet. I decided to draw on my conversations with Jeff, and really turn the diversity and inclusion up to eleven – that would show Naomi exactly what I could do.

ARRESTED DEVELOPMENT

Detective Chief Inspector Ladd regained consciousness in a shredded negligee, having completed a sexual endurance test equivalent to an Iron Man or, quite possibly an Iron Lady. Beside him, Tina was smiling in her sleep like a lioness sated on a kinky wildebeest. Ladd stared through his mascara at the lampshade and fought off nocturnal flashbacks with the desperation of a Vietnam vet; it had been Full Metal Corset.

Ladd's phone lay dead on the table. He checked his watch. It was 10.28, a little under three-and-a-half hours after he'd planned to leave for work. He leapt out of bed and tore off the remains of his nightie. His work clothes were funereal, but they felt strangely comforting - white shirt, black suit, black tie, black size twelves. A semblance of masculine dignity beckoned, if only he could walk like a normal human. But thanks to a near-unbearable strain in his overworked groin, all he could manage was a bowlegged hobble. What had Tina done to him? She had been a force of nature before, but his involuntary cross-dressing had spawned a monster.

As Ladd stumbled through the porch, he tripped on Tina's cross-trainer. His toes hurt, but it was nothing compared to the crotch-judder. The pain and the pent-up trauma of the previous night unleashed a sweaty great howl that resounded across the street's semis, triggering a curtain-twitch behind the *Neighbourhood Watch* window.

Ladd tried to get a grip. His world was not as it was; a lie had led him through the looking glass into Planet Panty. But he was still a senior police officer overseeing a covert anti-corruption unit and events had taken a serious turn. A suspect detective at the heart of his current enquiry had just been bent backwards and left dangling at a dogging sight. Duty demanded that Ladd focus on the job in hand.

As he limped his way along sedate streets lined with plane trees and plain cars, Ladd's mind was a-buzz with spine-snapping, heroin importation and brown envelopes. Why murder Trent in such a laborious manner? A bullet to the brain, a knife to the gut or a stolen van to the torso would have done the job with much less fuss. And why not dispose of the body more discreetly? It was what patios, quarries and woods were for, after all. Why put Trent's corpse on display like a Halloween pumpkin? It was the most theatrical death-scene he'd witnessed in his eighteen-year career, but its only audience were doggers. Why bother? Either keep a killing private or make it as public as possible. Was it a twisted message to Totteridge and Whetstone's dogging community? If so, this was a psychopath with a seriously niche target audience.

By the time Ladd had hobbled to his platform, rush hour was slowing to a dawdle. Passengers were thin on the ground, and so were trains. Still, after last night's shenanigans, the Underground was a refreshingly normal environment. Routine he could handle, the duller the better. But as Ladd took his seat, something distinctly odd happened to the half-empty row of mid-morning commuters opposite. Someone appeared to have pressed their pause buttons: a Nigerian nurse broke off her mobile phone argument, a builder delayed plunging a bacon sarnie into his gob, a teenage girl stopped doing her lippy; and they all stared at Ladd. He wondered whether they could see into his soul. Perhaps the panty-lie, and all its ramifications were visible to the outside world? It seemed unlikely.

As the train lurched off towards zone three, the teenage girl offered him her mirror. In Ladd's experience, this wasn't what teenage girls usually did to older male strangers on tube carriages. He shrugged a gentle refusal and concentrated on weightier matters. How had the murderer got such a fat sweaty cop's corpse up a lamppost? It would have required either a winch or a crane. Trent must have weighed well over seventeen stone; way too much to lug up a ladder. There were no tyre marks at the dogging site, no signs of construction equipment, just dogging detritus.

Kentish Town station suffered from trapped wind, and loud gusts flapped about Ladd as he trotted up the escalator. By the time Ladd had hit the high street, his groin had loosened sufficiently for him to attempt something approaching a jog. He was well into the sweaty realms of extreme lateness, a grim region where panic and self-recrimination wrestle for supremacy. Why had he let himself sleep in? The price of the panties hadn't just been a night of trauma; his standing in the unit was about to be compromised at a time when his leadership was most on the line.

Covert operations weren't noted for their prestigious locations and his was no exception. Ladd approached his faded parade – a condemned beauty parlour, a dubious chicken shop and a funeral parlour with two classic hearses parked outside, one white, one black.

Ladd had grown to love his workplace; it was a touch more morbid than the average office block, but its heart was in the right place. He glimpsed through the parlour's heavy curtains at display graves, discounted coffins, and floral tributes. The back wall was adorned with flying cherubs, like a B-Tec Sistine Chapel, and just in front of it, Ladd's tiny colleague, Goliath, also dressed in a black suit and white shirt, was deadheading dahlias with murderous precision under the gentle gaze of a prim lady in her late seventies. Ladd dodged inside, caught his breath, and would have nursed his groin had the woman not been eying him with so much concern.

Ladd thought it best to adopt a calmly solicitous tone. "Morning, Madam."

She gave him the sort of look you'd give someone who had just run into a funeral parlour with a groin injury.

"Late husband?" Ladd enquired.

"Late Governor," Goliath corrected, before making the introductions. "Sue, Guv. Guv, Sue."

Ladd offered a handshake. Sue curtseyed. Her knees creaked as she completed the gesture at a geological pace, her gingham dress billowing like a parachute. Ladd wondered how someone who looked like a Women's Institute stalwart had made Goliath's acquaintance. He may have been a shade under four-foot tall, but he could kill people with a pencil sharpener.

"Sue is Yang's new interpreter." Goliath explained, as he helped her recover her balance.

"What happened to Chopper?" Ladd asked.

"Hospital," Goliath replied. "Upset Yang again."

Before he had joined the unit, Chopper had been one of the riot squad's most senior instructors. He wasn't easily hospitalised.

Goliath stepped up to an angel headstone and booted it in the gob. Sue gasped. The kicked angel triggered a hidden mechanism. The front curtains whooshed shut and the cherub wall flew up into the ceiling, revealing a gadget cave that would have made Batman blush.

"Goodness gracious!" Sue gawped at the treasure trove of gizmos, data banks and surveillance equipment. Multi-panelled video walls displayed the output of advanced thermal imaging, motion tracking and facial recognition devices from every corner of the capital. A pink neon sign beamed the motto: "Phantom Squad - Deterring Police Crime Through Diversity and Inclusion" over the heads of Ladd's furious colleagues, all clad in white shirts, black suits, and black ties, like a resentful *Reservoir Dogs* convention.

Ladd did not want to lead with an apology for his tardiness, so he took charge of the introductions, putting a gentlemanly hand on Sue's shoulder and guiding her up to each member of the squad in turn. "Sue, meet Detective Inspector William Maguire."

"*Old Bill*, please," A scarlet-skinned sixty-something with the physique of a veteran gut-barging champion proffered his left hand.

"Oh, you're a lefty," Sue remarked as she used it to support another awkward curtsey.

"Don't have a lot of choice." Old Bill harumphed, his chins a-wobble.

"Golly!" Sue exclaimed, once she'd noticed the absence of Old Bill's right arm. "How on Earth did that happen?"

"Line of duty," Old Bill explained, mysteriously.

No one knew the truth about Old Bill's missing arm, and Ladd didn't like to press. He moved Sue gently down the squad-line to its next member. "Detective Sergeant Dai Owen-Singh."

"Taffy." A half-Welsh, half-Sikh body builder tipped his turban. "Lovely to meet you, isn't it just."

Sue curtseyed once again. "Charming accent."

"Mammy's from Merthyr. Daddy's from the Punjab. Accident, wasn't I?"

"You've already met Goliath." Ladd indicated his lethal, three-foot-eleven-inch colleague.

Sue looked perplexed. "Rather unusual name, isn't it?"

Goliath shrugged. "Special Forces humour."

"Special Needs, more like," Old Bill muttered.

Goliath squared up to him, his eyes at belly button height.

Old Bill didn't back down. "Thump me, and I'll have the Federation onto you."

Goliath gut-poked Old Bill with expert digital penetration, and Old Bill doubled up, spluttering.

Ladd wasn't supposed to tolerate this sort of thing but showing up two-and-a-half hours late had somewhat undermined his authority. He turned to the squad's final member. "And your assigned officer, Detective Constable Yang Gao."

This time, Sue didn't curtsey, she just looked daggers at the young Chinese woman. "We've met."

Malevolence dangled between the two women like poisonous mistletoe.

"She jumped the bus queue," Sue said. "Terribly rude."

Yang signed with the violence of a martial artist.

Sue interpreted instantaneously in her cutglass accent: "You are a stupid old fart" then turned to Ladd and spoke as herself: "What dreadful manners."

Introductions complete, it now fell to Ladd to fill the murderous silence. "I guess you're all wondering why I called you in early."

Old Bill looked at Ladd with undisguised contempt. "It had crossed our minds once or twice over the past two-and-a-half hours, Guv."

"Sorry." Ladd plugged his phone into a power bank with forced nonchalance. "I was forced to deal with..." With what? Ladd scraped the bottom of his brain-barrel, "... a case of mistaken identity."

It wasn't quite a lie, just an over-generalization. But it was still greeted by a sea of sceptical faces, notably Taffy's. "Slept in, didn't he just."

Ladd felt there was nothing to be gained by admitting the obvious truth of this, so he mustered what dignity he could, and proceeded with the planned briefing. He began by fiddling with a razor-tablet and summoning a giant image of DI Trent's doubled-up corpse onto a video wall.

"Good grief!" Sue blanched.

"Sorry, Sue," Ladd said. "Probably should have warned you."

"Textbook spinal column reversal," Goliath observed as he helped Sue to a chair.

Yang signed a couple of phrases so robustly they could have been judo throws.

"Poor bastard," Sue interpreted instantaneously in cut-glass RP. "Fucking brutal."

"Must have properly shat his bollocks," Taffy added, with questionable anatomical accuracy.

Ladd addressed his squad. "The official investigation into Trent's death will be conducted by Homicide."

"Useless pillocks," Old Bill elaborated. It wasn't helpful. Old Bill never was. But he did have a point.

"We'll redouble our covert inquiry into Trent and the Gang of Four." Ladd fingered the tablet once again and conjured up a much cheerier image of an unbent Trent. He was in a casino, drinking champagne with three colleagues.

Ladd zoomed in on the bald cop adjacent to Trent. "DCI McMasters. Drugs Squad." Another fiddle from Ladd and the video wall displayed McMasters and an Eastern European godfather on a superyacht. "Up to his tits in Transnistrian nosebag."

"Where the hell's Transnistria when it's at home?" Old Bill always enjoyed asking awkward questions.

"I'll explain after the briefing," Ladd lied, switching the video wall back to the Gang of Four in the casino, and zooming in on a bearded, champagne-supping cop opposite Trent. "This is DI Todd Sweeney. Flying Squad." Ladd switched the video wall to surveillance footage of a bank robbery. Armed men in balaclavas leapt into an escape van with swag bags. DI Sweeney was at the wheel, and a wider angle revealed the vehicle to be a Black Maria, sirens a-blaring. "Sweeney's hand in glove with The Smiths, a gang of old-school villains and heist-meisters who make The Peaky Blinders look like The Brownies."

"I used to be in the Brownies," Sue revealed. "Not long after the war."

"Must have been character-building." Ladd gave her a good-natured grin.

"Oh, gosh, no," Sue objected. "They were spiteful little minxes. Dreadful."

Ladd wondered whether Sue was really cut out for this, but he put his doubts to one side, returned the video wall to the Gang of Four casino shot and zoomed in on the third bent cop, a lanky specimen. "This is DCI Dicky "Cocky" Proudcock, Professional Standards." Ladd adjusted his tablet, triggering surveillance footage of "Cocky" performing handbrake turns in a Lamborghini whilst call girls whooped from the passenger seats. "Cocky siphons a fortune off street gangs. No one's quite sure how he does it."

Ladd returned the screen to the casino shot and zoomed in on the deceased detective. "DI Trent himself was with Serious Organized Crime. In every sense." Ladd switched the casino shot to security footage of a Transylvanian wrestling match. The larger and uglier of the two grapplers lifted his opponent above his head and slammed him on the canvas as Trent cheered uncontrollably from the crowd. "Trent was cosy with Transylvanian heroin importers. Their enforcer Marian's a champion wrestler, now on trial for shooting an arms dealer. Trent was his alibi."

"Marian?" Old Bill queried. "As in *So Long Marianne*?" He began to murder the heart-breaking ditty whilst Taffy harmonised in Welsh.

"There'll be no Leonard Cohen in my squad!" Ladd had standards.

"Cohen kills morale," Goliath added, with the authority of a man who had seen armed conflict in every continent except possibly Antarctica.

Old Bill and Taffy replied with a resentful silence, which Sue filled. "Were these horrid men really all policemen?"

"Trent was a policeman," Goliath explained. "The other three still are."

"Golly!" Sue said. "They do seem rather like criminals."

"Indeed," Ladd said. "With the Gang of Four, we're dealing with a bent cop support group, controlling heists, street gangs, smack, and coke."

Old Bill snorted. "Only if you believe our former Superintendent."

"Bent as buggery, wasn't he just," Taffy said.

Yang signed, as if she were committing GBH on the Invisible Man, and Sue interpreted: "Now a Super-grass."

"Banged up by our very own Guv," Goliath said with something approaching pride.

"In a kamikaze career move that plonked him in Phantom," Old Bill concluded, with insulting accuracy.

Ladd wished his squad would stop confronting him with the truth. Yes, the entire briefing was based on evidence from their massively bent ex-boss and, yes, Ladd's successful investigation into his corruption had torpedoed his own career in the mainstream Force and won him an unenviable promotion to head up this gang of misfits. Was this all true? Yes. Did he wish it wasn't? Of course. At least he was at work and not at home, being mercilessly girlified by Tina.

Ladd adjusted the video wall, revealing a mug shot of their previous boss, a Rastafarian in top brass uniform, medals, and dreadlocks. "Superintendent Nathaniel Dredd was on the take, as I proved. But under intensive interrogation, he gave us the Gang of Four."

"Bullshitting for remission, wasn't he just," Taffy said.

"There's surveillance evidence. It's from yesterday, shortly after word of Trent's death was spreading in the criminal law enforcement community." Ladd nodded at Goliath, who activated hidden camera footage with a complex gadget only he understood.

The video wall showed the surviving "Gang of Three" conspiring in a lock-up. The footage was silent, but Ladd knew Phantom had the personnel to cope. "Yang, Sue, can you do the honours?"

As the bent and bereaved trio spoke in the silent surveillance footage, Yang lip-read off the screen and signed with the vigour of a Norse berserker. Moments after each of Yang's violently executed phrase-mimes, Sue interpreted, as prim and plummy as a baroness at a polo prizegiving.

"They snapped his fucking spine!" Sue exclaimed on "Cocky" Proudcock's behalf.

Taffy stifled a laugh, but this was impressive stuff. Sue seemed determined not to be outpaced by Yang, who was signing like a martial artist on speed.

"Arseholes!" Sue continued for McMasters. "Could be us next."

"Bent backwards?" Sue asked for an incredulous Sweeney. "Bollocks!"

The footage faded as the surveillance camera battery died.

"Thank goodness that's over!" Sue exclaimed, mopping her brow.

Phantom burst into a spontaneous round of applause at the double act. Sue curtseyed. Yang scowled.

Briefing complete, Ladd snapped into action with the confidence of a man pretending he hadn't shown up two-and-a-half hours late after an all-night cross-dressing sex session: "Yang, keep me posted on the Transylvanian wrestler's trial. Old Bill and Taffy, track the Transnistrians. Goliath, listen to The Smiths. Everyone, keep your eyes peeled for bending equipment."

Ladd was asserting his authority, doing what he was supposed to do, and Old Bill didn't like that one bit. "Hold on a minute, Guv. Have you done a risk assessment?"

Ladd stepped towards Old Bill, locking eyes, and speaking with barely restrained rage. "We're investigating the wholesale perversion of justice and police collusion with homicidal drug traffickers and underworld kingpins. Risk is unavoidable."

"So is health and safety!" Old Bill waved his solitary arm. "I need a signed risk assessment with your name and address on headed paper."

Taffy thrust a form at Ladd with the force of a knife-wielding assassin.

Ladd continued to stare out Old Bill. "Pen?"

Taffy flourished a biro.

Whilst keeping his eyes locked on Old Bill, Ladd signed Taffy's form with a resentful scrawl, then looked up at Phantom. He was face-to-face with a squadful of smirks. After humiliation on the home front, he needed respect at work, especially during a major anti-corruption investigation. "Listen, you doughnuts, this could not be more sodding serious!"

Yang signed in a slower style than usual; her flowing limbs tinged with irony.

Sue stifled a giggle as she interpreted. "Guv, why are you wearing mascara?"

Phantom Squad erupted in long-suppressed jollity.

Ladd blushed. That explained the gobsmacked commuters and the make-up mirror offer. His phone bleeped, indicating that its charging was complete. Ladd picked it up: there were nineteen missed calls and a text from the Super reading, "DEBRIEFING NOW."

Ladd strode back into the funeral parlour and re-booted the angel headstone. The cherub wall closed behind him, concealing his colleagues in the gadget cave, and enabling him to leave the building, furiously scraping mascara off his face as he headed off to meet his superior officer and shag-buddy.

PRISON DIARY – ENTRY 3

Once Naomi had finished pacing around the room and tearing her hair out, she took a seat and gave me her feedback.

"Well done on the diversity."

"Thanks."

"Let's see. What have we got, a Welsh Sikh, an Afro-Caribbean person of restricted growth, a one-armed man, a deaf lady from China …"

"I made sure she was feisty. That's important, isn't it?"

"Vital," Naomi replied. "But you've also got a Rastafarian Chief Superintendent."

"Ex-Chief Superintendent."

"That's the trouble. It's wonderful that you have assigned such a senior position to a character from a community who face so much discrimination."

"Thanks," I replied. "Means a lot."

"But it's just not very plausible."

"It's all made up though, isn't it?"

"Yes, but there's made up and… there's made up."

"Is there?"

"Yes."

"And what's the difference between made up and made up?"

"I just don't think many readers will believe that a Rastafarian could ascend the ranks of the Force. It's almost as if you're brushing over the genuine prejudice that exists."

"I'm just putting things right," I said. "In my Force, there's none of that nonsense and everyone's equal, apart from the rigid hierarchy of ranks and pay grades."

"Then it's not realistic."

"Is that a problem?"

"It could be."

"*Game of Thrones* isn't realistic," I protested. "Nor is *Paddington*."

"But that's different," Naomi said, becoming audibly impatient. "One's got dragons and the other is about a talking bear."

"I could always add something… A phoenix or, maybe a singing badger."

"Don't."

"Okay."

"Realism's not the only problem with your Rastafarian Chief Inspector though, is it?"

"What else has he done now?"

"Well, he's not a very positive representation, is he?"

"He's bent."

"Corrupt," Naomi corrected.

"And he's a grass."

"He has turned against his co-conspirators," Naomi said. She clearly disliked slang and wanted everything to sound as pompous as possible.

"Well, it happens," I said.

"But why do you have to ruin all your empowering, diverse and inclusive representations by making him so negative?"

"Do you want me to make him nicer?"

"Not nicer."

"Nastier?"

"More rounded."

"Fatter?"

"Let's move on."

I waited for Naomi to dispense some praise. Maybe she would like the ingenuity of the fake funeral parlour, or the range of adversaries I had lined up against my hero. But she didn't.

"Your DCI's still cross-dressing, isn't he?"

"He's stuck in his lie."

"And why on Earth do your gangsters have to come from Transnistria and Transylvania?"

"Jeff's got an atlas."

"Who's Jeff."

"My cellmate. He's an armed robber."

"Why didn't you choose places that begin with something other than *trans*?"

"Symmetry."

"But why *trans*. I mean, what would Twitter think?"

"Does Twitter think?"

"You know what I mean."

I didn't, but we'd run out of time.

On my way out, Naomi explained that she was taking Innsbruck and Gethsemane skiing, so it would be a fortnight before our next session.

I've never gone in for skiing, what with my bankruptcy and my tendency to fall over repeatedly in public, but I've often fancied a spot of Alpine air.

I wished Naomi a happy holiday, but she looked utterly abject. Roly's work commitments meant that she would be juggling the kids alone, and not for the first time.

I offered all the commiserations that an inmate could plausibly offer to a holidaymaker and returned to my cell.

Jeff was reading a biography of Dolly Parton. He's a dark horse, that Jeff.

"What's her real name?" I asked.

"Dolly Parton," Jeff replied.

"Really?"

"Yes."

"Couldn't make it up."

"She didn't."

I had borrowed a rather rum selection of books from the library: a history of surveillance technology, a French play about an unlucky optimist, and a pop-up guide to cat psychology: apparently, they hate us.

Naomi may have been taking a break, but I didn't see that as an excuse to loiter. I resolved to write two diverse and inclusive chapters over the next fortnight.

FELINE OF DUTY

Muswell Hill rejoiced in a cornucopia of pricey shops selling attractive but largely useless merchandise. It wasn't really Ladd's cup of chai latte, but this was the Super's stomping ground. The last time he had seen her, he was bundling her panty-less onto the patio. It wasn't a tried and tested path to a blossoming romance, or a harmonious professional relationship, so he was a little apprehensive. She had asked him to meet her at a novelty café named *Feline of Duty*. Ladd's hopes that this was nothing more than a bad pun on television's favourite dodgy copper extravaganza were dashed when he saw the platoons of cats embedded around every table. He had never liked cats, and their allergens knew it. A series of sneezes racked his body as he took his seat opposite the Super.

"I had no idea you were allergic," the Super lied, before drowning a Bourbon biscuit in her macchiato.

This was clearly her idea of vengeance, but Ladd thought it best to be diplomatic. "I suppose it is an operationally sound rendezvous on anti-surveillance grounds, Ma'am."

"Is it. though? Don't you feel watched?" The Super widened her eyes in imitation of the café's furry residents.

Ladd liked the way this made his superior officer look, but she was right; he did feel a hundred cat's eyes bore into his flesh.

She edged closer to him, conspiratorially. "Do you know what the collective noun for cats is?"

"Often wondered, Ma'am." Ladd hadn't.

"A *glaring* of cats. They know what surveillance really means. Just look at them, witnessing our every move. Think of all that evidence of human frailty."

A tabby jumped onto Ladd's lap. He winced, trying to ignore its crotch-piercing claws and throat-gagging scent.

"You total pussy!" The Super shot him an expression of withering contempt, then squeezed his knee. "I've ordered you a cappuccino."

"Thanks Ma'am."

"You're not a *total* pussy. Not always." She ran her fingers up from his knee towards the tabby straddling his groin. "You can be a big, brave boy - taking down nasty old Dredd with all that surveillance."

"Nine days alone in a drain," Ladd looked mournfully into the beige depths of his newly plonked coffee. "I never used to be claustrophobic."

A menacing mew drew his attention to the tabby. It glared at Ladd. Ladd glared back. The tabby's pitch-black pupils drew his mind back to the dank depths of Dredd's drainage system; a fetid prison that still held his memory hostage. He focused on the moment of release: firefighters were winching him out of a sewage pipe like a stuck turnip.

The tabby meowed Ladd back to the present. He sneezed, spraying cappuccino foam like a surfacing sperm whale.

The Super frowned. "At least you didn't get arrested straddling a fence."

Ladd struggled to stifle a laugh.

"*Neighbourhood Watch* called the community plastics." The Super's anger built, as did Ladd's urge to sneeze. "Dragged into my own station. Custody officer had a smirk big enough to trip over. I'll be lucky not to hear from the Attorney General."

Ladd's sneeze unleashed itself, scattering cats in every direction.

The Super guffawed. Customers and staff looked aghast. The cats looked vengeful.

The Super broke the silence with a question that resonated across the café. "Have you still got my panties?"

Ladd dreaded that word more heavily than any other word in the English language. It outdid "torment", "oblivion" and even "incarcerated". "Panties" was a word loaded with betrayal, humiliation, and loss. He prayed that the Super would never utter that dreaded word again.

"Tina didn't find my panties, did she?"

Ladd reeled from the force of the second panty-mention. It was a devastating follow-through, and it almost floored him. A Siamese cat eyed his suffering with contempt.

"Have you brought my panties?" the Super persisted.

Panties again! It was too much to bear. "No, Ma'am. Sorry." Ladd sneezed and shook his head. "How's the murder?"

"DI Trent was snapped with massive force from opposing directions." The Super drowned another Bourbon biscuit. "Stoker enjoyed the autopsy."

"Most bloodthirsty pathologist this side of the grave."

"Killing was bloodless. And the murderer was careful. No DNA."

"And no witnesses?"

"Doggers are a shy bunch."

Ladd watched a ginger tom face off with a Russian blue. Things were about to turn nasty.

The Super bent her soggy Bourbon and snapped it in two. "Your friend Dixon talked to Trent's ex-wife, his neighbours, his bookie."

"Any actual villains?" Ladd asked, as a cataclysmic allergic reaction began to build at the back of his throat. "Cops included?"

"Far as Dixon knows, Trent's clean."

"So, Homicide's poncing about while we investigate the real suspects?"

"Just like Miss Marple." The Super gave him a patronising wink.

The feline face-off turned murderous. Squeals turned to caterwauling. Staff interceded, spilling a tray of croissants.

"Next time," the Super warned, as she leant in to Ladd, "Remember my panties."

Ladd took the panty-blow manfully and forced himself to assume a wistful look. "I'll never forget them."

The moment was ruined by a bleep from Ladd's phone. The Super grabbed it off him and read the text: *Trial's climaxing.* "Who's Yang?"

"Little deaf Chinese lady."

"The violent one? I like her."

No one in Ladd's memory had ever professed to liking Yang. The Super was exceptional in so very many ways, most of them worrying. But that didn't mean Ladd didn't fancy her, far from it, and his heart beat a little faster as she leant forward to kiss him goodbye. It would have been a pleasant end to their encounter, had his sneeze not finally broken free all over her.

The Super slapped him across the face. The cats mewed as one, vindicated.

JUSTICE IS BLIND DRUNK

Lady Justice teetered on top of the Old Bailey, straddling a golden globe, and getting rained on. Had she been able to look down, she would have seen a grizzled English DCI, a belligerent Chinese DC, and her frail interpreter enter the bowels of her esteemed building.

Ladd, Yang and Sue were all dressed in civilian clothes, and Ladd had a free newspaper under his armpit. Its headline shrieked, "Cop Bent!", and beneath, Trent was pictured enjoying a pint with a pair of his fellow freemasons.

The paper helped pass the time while they waited for the elevators. The hacks noted Trent's dedication to Serious Organized Crime, neglecting to mention that he was a serious organiser of it. They also glossed over his gambling addiction and messy divorce but spared no detail of his wonky demise at the dogging site. How had the story got out? Ladd could only assume that the hacks had friends at the morgue. Stoker would never have gone public about his autopsy: he'd have wanted to treasure the grim details in private. Still, all was not lost. The public now knew that Trent had been bent, but they didn't know that he was bent. That was a secret known only to Phantom, the surviving Gang of Three, the Transylvanians, the Super, and Dredd. Quite a lot of people, come to think of it.

After ten minutes, the intrepid anti-corruption crusaders detected that the elevators were out of order. Steps were a challenge for Sue, but in-depth investigations eventually identified a stairlift. After Ladd had persuaded a reluctant usher to unlock it, Sue began her ascent, with Ladd and Yang trudging beside her at a rate of around one step every twelve seconds.

After conquering the first flight without remark, Yang began to express herself in signs so vigorous, it almost dethroned Sue from the stairlift. Luckily, Sue managed to retain her balance and was able to interpret Yang's question: "Why shoot an arms dealer?".

"Poetic justice?" Ladd speculated flippantly.

"This guy dealt in tanks and missiles," Yang persisted, with Sue's assistance. "Why would Transylvanian smack-shippers need more than handguns?"

Ladd shrugged. "We could ask their enforcer's alibi if he wasn't bent double."

A be-wigged dignitary shot them a supercilious sneer on his way downstairs.

"Golly!" Sue exclaimed while the dignitary was still well within ear shot. "That was the Attorney General. How very exciting!"

"Dial it down, Sue." Ladd placed a gentle hand on her shoulder. "We're just here to observe proceedings. Quietly."

"Sorry, dear," Sue said as the stairlift juddered to a halt at the top of the stairs. "I've got a thing about powerful men."

The Phantom threesome took their seats at the back of the courtroom. Three rows in front, there was a trilby-sporting Transylvanian gang boss Ladd knew to be Vlad, and his younger foot soldier, Igor. Slightly to the left, Ladd identified a clutch of their fellow clan members, and to the right, there were a couple of tabloid hacks Ladd knew from boozing and boxing. A typical ragbag of a jury occupied the far wall, and, at the front, a rather prim court clerk sat at a table with a landline and a laptop. In the dock, the hulking figure of Marian the Transylvanian wrestler was inadequately sandwiched by a brace of court officials.

It transpired that the murdered arms dealer had spent half his life in mid-air, flying about the planet buying surplus arms on the cheap and flogging them at a profit to officially approved despots. He was fully certified and highly educated, with an in-depth understanding of advanced defence systems. In short, he was a credit to British industry, and would have been long overdue a knighthood for services to global slaughter, had he not had his head blown off by a Kalashnikov with Marian's fingerprints on it. As proceedings edged to a close, it was obvious that without Trent, the Transylvanian grappler's case was hanging by a thread – or, perhaps, a dogging lamppost.

The judge, a standard-issue study in hypertension and gluttony, addressed a despondent defence barrister. "Much as I appreciate that this despicable, homicidal bending could hardly have been anticipated, I regret that no adjournment can bring the sole defence witness back to life. Request denied. Court will rise."

All stood, apart from Sue, who was experiencing arthritic issues exacerbated by her stint on the stairlift. Ladd helped her to her feet, and they followed Yang, the hacks, and the Transylvanian gangsters into the corridor. The gangsters were not Ladd's idea of convivial company, but this was a rare opportunity to eavesdrop without raising their suspicions. Yang and Sue didn't fit most Transylvanian gangster's stereotypes of typical London coppers and were unlikely to guess that Yang could lip-read Romanian.

Vlad was heatedly haranguing Igor in his mother tongue. Yang watched and signed, then Sue took Ladd aside and interpreted in a refined whisper: "Transnistrian scum! Marian is such a great wrestling champion, he makes them piss their panties like a bunch of chickens, so they bend his alibi to death! Inhuman Transnistrian doggers!"

Ladd wondered why the Transnistrians would sabotage the Transylvanians. They ran entirely separate operations. The Transylvanians did smack, the Transnistrians did coke. There had never been any real rivalry.

"Chief Inspector," Sue said, rather too loudly for Ladd's taste. "I've obviously heard of Transylvania and all its vampires, but Transnistria's a bit of a mystery."

"Transnistria's been in transition ever since it broke away from the CIS nations," Ladd explained.

"It's terribly kind of you to explain," Sue said. "But I haven't got the foggiest what you're on about."

"The CIS nations include Moldova and other former Soviet states," Ladd continued patiently. "Transnistria broke away from the CIS and is transitioning into a new, independent identity. If Marian the wrestler is convicted of blowing the arms dealer's brains out, this case could trigger Trans-on-Trans action on the streets of London."

Sue looked tearful. "Poor, defenceless arms dealer."

"The killer certainly left his company defenceless," Ladd said. "Whoever did it swiped enough weapons to start World War Three."

An usher announced the jury's return.

"Goodness gracious!" Sue ejaculated. "How long have they been out?"

Ladd checked his watch. "Three minutes."

Yang led the way and Ladd helped Sue back to her seat. It wasn't long before Marian the wrestler was back in the dock, glowering at all assembled.

The court clerk turned to the jury. "How do you find the defendant?"

The jury chairman rose to his feet. He was a precise little man with a well-tended moustache and a relish for the spotlight. After a needlessly dramatic pause, he pronounced the defendant "Guilty."

Marian roared like a Transylvanian lion. Vlad jumped up and shouted, "Death to Transnistria!" Igor and his fellow Transylvanians joined in, stamping their feet, and waving any objects they could weaponize. The hacks looked worried, and they were right to be. Marian grabbed both custody officers and smacked their skulls together with a sickening clunk, leaving their unconscious bodies to perform synchronized flops to the floor.

Ladd may not have been a Transylvanian wrestler, but he knew how to plant a knuckle and he wasn't one to hang about. He bombed towards the dock, but his way was blocked by Igor and a zombie knife that, in an ideal world, would not have made its way past court security. Sunlight glinted on the vicious blade. It was big enough to gut a yeti, so Ladd thought it prudent to forgo a knife fight by punching Igor's lights out.

Yang leapt up, ready to unleash every martial art known to Man, but Sue grabbed her like a comfort blanket and started sobbing into her trousers. Yang began to kick her off, then remembered that she was nearly eighty.

The judge dived for cover. The clerk grabbed the court phone. Marian kicked it out of his hands, knocking over the table. Ladd waded in and landed an award-winning kidney punch on Marian, but it was like hitting granite. Before Ladd had time to nurse his fist, Marian lifted him into the air, jogged across the court, and threw him out the window.

It was a beautiful summer afternoon and Ladd enjoyed the feel of the sun and the gentle breeze on his body all-too-briefly before everything went dark.

***

Ladd regained consciousness convinced he had just plunged into the sea. But wistful memories of Mediterranean holidays were dispelled by the sight of the Super clutching an empty bucket, and asking, "Want the good news or the bad news?"

Ladd took a moment to assess his surroundings: he was drenched, he was in a cell, and he was miserable. So, he decided to cheer himself up by replying, "The good news."

"You're completely unharmed," the Super replied.

"Bad?"

"You landed on the Attorney General."

The Transylvanian defenestration loomed large in Ladd's memory. Landing on the legal luminary probably wasn't a career move he'd have planned, but in terms of his physical well-being, it had proven to be an astute decision.

"He won't be in hospital long and I've got them to drop the aerial assault charge." The Super handed him her phone. "But the real bad news is that you're now actual news." The mobile played a video of Ladd's fall. It was like a fully clothed Olympic dive with neither style nor a swimming pool. His body had concertinaed the Attorney General, transposing him from a vertical human into a trampoline with more crunch than bounce. Ladd watched himself lie on the prone dignitary like a fifteen stone duvet while his unwilling landing pad screamed in shock, bent legs akimbo.

"Nine million views." Ladd decided to look on the bright side. "I'm famous."

"You're wet." The Super giggled.

Ladd hugged her, moistening her uniform. She threw him hard against the cell wall and snogged him. It struck Ladd that she was unusually strong for a light-framed woman of barely five feet, but he wasn't about to launch a police complaint.

Before proceedings advanced beyond clothing, the cell flap flicked open, revealing a custody officer's gob asking, "Everything alright in there, Ma'am?"

The couple unclenched and the Super snapped back to duty with a firm, "Prisoner ready for release!"

***

Ladd celebrated his freedom by heading for the funeral parlour. It had been an unusual day, what with the forgotten mascara, the vindictive cats, the Transylvanian window-chucker, the flattened Attorney General, the Super's water-bucket, and the unwanted internet fame. He wasn't feeling his usual self, but at least his workplace offered a reassuring sense of routine.

Ladd was surprised to find that the parlour curtains were shut. Late afternoon was rush hour for funeral arrangements, so something was distinctly askew. He prepared himself for the worst: a Transylvanian ambush, a Transnistrian reprisal or an impromptu spine-bending followed by a posthumous date with a dogging lamppost.

Ladd approached the door gingerly, stood to one side, and threw it open, bracing himself for an attack: legs bent, arms raised, ready to fight for his life.

"Surprise!" Phantom Squad cheered, unleashing balloons and party poppers. Drinks and nibbles had been laid out on the coffins.

"What's all this in aid of?" Ladd asked.

"You, Guv," Old Bill handed him a pint with his one hand.

"Ta." Ladd took a grateful glug. "Thought you all hated me."

"Oh, we don't think you're a total wanker anymore, Guv." Goliath reached up and slapped him on the waist. "Not now you've decked the Attorney General."

"Bastard had it coming," Old Bill said.

Yang signed vigorously and Sue interpreted, with some reluctance: "Total twat stain,"

"Snide little ponce, look you," Taffy elaborated.

The entire squad raised their glasses and toasted Ladd with a resounding "Guv!"

"Cheers!" Ladd tapped their glasses with his. "To be fair though, we should all be toasting the Transylvanian murderer who chucked me onto him."

Phantom raised their glasses for another toast. "Transylvanian murderer!"

It was moments like this that made a career in the Force worthwhile. The camaraderie, the banter, the shared sense of purpose. Not only were Phantom the most diverse and inclusive covert anti-corruption unit in the service, but they were also a bloody good laugh.

A text blurted onto Ladd's phone. It was from Tina, and she had shared her location: "Meet me for a treat. NOW! x."

"Oh well," Ladd said. "Duty calls."

"Guv! Guv! Guv! Guv!" Phantom chanted as Ladd necked his pint in record-breaking time, then cheered his empty glass.

"One quick thing, Guv," Old Bill said, sheepishly. "We seem to have mislaid the risk assessment."

Ladd shrugged. He couldn't have been in a more forgiving mood. He smiled and headed off for his treat.

***

Golden shards of daylight bathed the most polluted stretch of North London. This was the wrong side of King's Cross; an area no one had bothered to develop. Ladd passed grimy gasometers, war-torn estates, and a women's prison on his way to Tina's treat. Glittering possibilities flittered through his mind: a cocktail bar, a classy restaurant, VIP tickets to a gig, but he found her standing outside a shop window resembling a Dodge City whorehouse. Tina was fidgeting on her heels and beaming. She grabbed his hand and led them inside.

The shop gloried in the name *Big Girl's Blouse* and was about as understated as Ru Paul's wardrobe.

The glamorous proprietor, a blonde lady in stilettos, who was as heavily made-up as she was heavily built, welcomed Ladd with a heartfelt hug. "Danny Boy! Or is it Tranny Boy?"

"Danny's fine," Ladd replied.

The proprietor started singing, "Oh Tranny Boy! The tights, the tights are chay-ay-fing."

Whilst Tina was racked with laughter, Ladd could have been on an actual rack.

"The Londonderry Air," Ladd observed, neutrally.

"London derrière more like." Tina pinched Ladd's arse.

Ladd cringed. He didn't have anything against cross-dressers, or persons of a non-binary disposition, it was just that he wasn't one. Trousers were his thing.

The proprietor put a large but reassuring hand on Ladd's shoulder. "I'm Dolly."

Ladd managed a nod.

Dolly turned to Tina. "Full platinum service, isn't it?"

"Nothing less for my Tranny Boy." Tina planted the kind of kiss that a proud mum might give a pageant girl.

"Can't tell you what it means to me." Ladd genuinely couldn't. His lie had plonked him in the most awkward position of his life. He loved women's clothes; they were great to look at. On women.

Tina skipped on the spot like a sugared-up toddler. "Disneyland, ain't it?"

"I don't know what to say." Ladd didn't. He was a reluctant passenger, doomed to complete whatever humiliating journey Fate had in store for him.

"Okeydokey. It's *Tittie Time*!" Dolly handed Ladd a silicone bra. "Latex nipples. Pinky and perky."

Tina tweaked them, giggling her tits off.

"Is this really necessary?" Ladd asked.

"Tits are compulsory." Dolly looked deeply offended. "I've got standards."

There was something about Dolly that triggered a sense of déjà vu. Ladd ran an identity parade of comparable individuals through his mind. When he was based in

Hackney, one of the most reliable local informants worked as a drag artist, but there was no real resemblance. A former school friend had transitioned and moved to Romford, but again, there was no real resemblance. Perhaps he had seen Dolly on television or social media – he didn't bother much with either, but it was entirely possible. Still, there was no question that he knew Dolly. It was a very specific feeling, even if his memory couldn't have been much vaguer.

Ladd looked from Dolly to the nipples and back again. "Do I know you?"

"Would you like to?"

Ladd wouldn't particularly, but he continued to stare at Dolly as if she were a particularly perplexing Wordle.

Momentarily unnerved, Dolly snapped back into sales mode. "I service every nook and cranny of my ladymen, and, as a spanking new platinum customer, you'll soon have the photos to prove it."

It was worse than Ladd's wildest nightmares and he had no option but to go along with it. He pranced, twirled, and pouted with insurmountable reluctance in every combo known to female fashion: from leather micro-skirt and boob tube to leopardskin top and hot pants, extra-large black dress and stilettos to strawberry playsuit and kinky boots. While Tina jumped up and down in excitement, Dolly photographed the whole parade.

When it was all officially over, Tina offered Ladd an extra-large cat suit in pink leather.

Ladd shook his head. "You're all right. I'll just pay."

"That's six hundred and eighty-eight pounds ninety-four." Dolly's smile was as wide as the gulf of misunderstanding within Ladd's marriage.

After catching a cab and cramming their *Big Girl's Blouse* bags into the boot, Tina snuggled up to Ladd, held his hand and planted a kiss on his cheek. "It feels like we've got married all over again."

Ladd noticed that the driver was watching them in his mirror. He was an older bloke from the Balkans, the kind of guy who probably shared Ladd's interest in boxing and football. On the surface, he didn't look like a cross-dressing enthusiast, and Ladd heartily hoped Tina wouldn't start gushing about Dolly's fashion parade and "Tittie Time".

"You looked so pretty!" Tina shrieked.

"Cheers," Ladd replied, gruffly.

"No, I mean really, really pretty. An absolute stunner."

The driver looked worried. He wasn't alone.

Ladd addressed him directly. "Women, eh?"

"Women?" Tina squeezed his knee. "There's only one woman for me."

Ladd thought it best to snog her. It seemed to be the only way to stop her talking, but it didn't stop the driver from watching.

When the taxi drew up outside their semi, Ladd did his best to forget the extortionately expensive shopping bags, but Tina cradled them like new-borns.

As soon as they had negotiated the porch's gym equipment, Tina gave him a thorough workout on the bed. Ladd would normally have enjoyed this but being dolled up in the freshly minted *Big Girl's Blouse* accoutrements took the edge off it. He adopted a technique of mindlessness: absenting himself from the present moment by pretending he was somewhere else; a rugby match, a supermarket queue, anywhere but right here, right now in a negligee. It didn't work. Tina's shrieks and groans were near-impossible to ignore.

A couple of hours after their "new marriage" had been comprehensively consummated, Ladd's phone bleeped him awake. It didn't seem to disturb Tina: she continued smiling in her sleep, dreaming about her husband's boob tube and stilettos.

Ladd was knackered, transitioned, and traumatized, so it took him a few moments to gather the strength to reach across to the bedside table and look at his phone. It was probably Phantom-related, an update on the post-mortem results or a development in Homicide's investigation. Maybe Dixon had even caught the killer. But instead, Ladd found himself looking at image after image of his excruciating drag parade. He looked the worst he had ever looked in his life: a depressed pantomime dame. Ladd thought his mood could not have been bleaker, until a text pinged up, and proved that it could: "You're a fake. £10k or you're famous. Dolly x"

Ladd swallowed a "bollocks" and crashed back onto the pillow. Life had taken an almighty downward swerve in barely thirty-six hours. Maybe if he shut his eyes, normality would restore itself like a factory-reset. Ladd focused his mind on the happy banalities of bloke-hood: cars, sheds, sport. That felt better.

Ladd was about to nod off when he heard the unmistakeable sound of footsteps. The last time this had happened, it had signalled a life-changing event – "Pantygate". Ladd had never been burgled before, but intruders held no fear for him – they provided a golden opportunity to administer a good kicking. Ladd switched back into gear: he was a cop on duty, albeit a cop in a nightie. He put his phone on searchlight and strode out of the bedroom, alert and ready for action.

Ladd searched his home systematically, taking a series of military-style "bounds" – single movements from one secure position to another. It was a technique often used by troops under hostile fire, and it allowed him to scour the bathroom, the landing, the spare room, the hallway, the kitchen, and the living room, until he had satisfied himself that all was clear. He had completed his domestic surveillance operation and would have headed back to bed, were it not for one detail: the patio doors were slightly ajar. He was sure he had shut them on the fleeing Super, and multiple times after that. Tina must be getting careless, what with all the nocturnal excitement. He secured the lock and turned back, hoping he wouldn't struggle to get back to sleep. But he needn't have worried – a skilfully wielded cosh did the job for him.

PRISON DIARY – ENTRY 4

I couldn't wait for my next session. I had completed two full chapters in a fortnight, and I was certain that Naomi would be chuffed. But as it turned out, she was apoplectic.

"I told you to leave the trans thing alone!"

"I couldn't help it."

"You have to be so careful! One pronoun out of place and you're cancelled."

"But Dolly's a positive character – a glamorous business owner, a bit of a laugh."

"That's the thing. With humour, you must always punch up."

"Wouldn't that be assault?"

"Not in literature, no."

"Who do you want me to punch?"

"Well, certainly not a trans character."

"But I'm not punching her. She's not the butt of any jokes. Ladd's the butt, and he's a senior police inspector."

"So, you are punching up."

"I'm giving him a constant kicking. It's like that French play about the unlucky optimist."

"Candide."

"That's the badger."

"I see what you mean."

"He thinks this is the best of all possible worlds, yet he ends up having the worst of all possible lives. Bit like me."

"Is that how you feel?"

"Well, things aren't exactly peachy."

"Tell me about it."

"Skiing holiday traumatic?"

"Gethsemane sprained her ankle on the first morning and Innsbruck kept going off-piste."

"Heart-breaking."

"It was. I'd been looking forward to it so much, and all our hopes were crushed. It's like someone's got it in for me."

"I know how you feel."

"Anything wrong?"

"Well, where shall I start? I'm in prison for burgling my own house."

"It wasn't your house."

"If I'd known that I wouldn't have burgled it."

"It's important to focus on detail."

"I know that now."

"Well, apply that same level of attention to your writing."

I thanked her and returned to my cell.

Jeff was reading a *Tank Girl* annual. He didn't seem a natural fan of the lesbian comic strip, but he found post-apocalyptic Australia, with its droughts, mutant kangaroos, and genetically modified super-soldiers a welcome distraction from prison life.

"Do you like tanks?" I enquired.

"I like girls in tanks."

"What's your favourite battle?"

"In *Tank Girl*?"

"In history."

"Waterloo was good until Abba ruined it."

"Wasn't there a Battle of Wounded Knee?"

"And a Battle of Little Bighorn."

"Custer's Last Stand."

"Cowboys knew how to name a battle."

"How about Zulu Dawn?"

"That was a film."

"Stalingrad was good."

"Guess you had to be there."

There is never any need to finish a prison conversation. You can always pick them up again later.

I started reading my own library book: "The Secret Life of Fish". It turns out that many species are "sequential hermaphrodites" and can switch gender on a whim. I spent a few minutes wondering whether transgender fish were the focus of much controversy in aquatic circles before my thoughts returned to the travails of Chief Inspector Ladd.

ROLL OUT THE BARREL

A skull-shuddering rumble shook Ladd awake. He was at the back of an HGV cargo box, hurtling along with all the stability of a rodeo horse. Ladd had no idea how long he had been unconscious, so he could have been anywhere from Pinner to Bosnia-Herzegovina. A naked bulb swung from the ceiling, casting jaundiced light on six massive metal barrels loosely secured at the front with tousled lengths of old rope.

The lorry swerved to the right, smashing Ladd onto the side wall with a sickening, involuntary headbutt, and bouncing him backwards onto the floor. Ladd clambered to his knees and caught his breath, but the lorry swerved to the left, decking him once again and breaking a barrel from its bounds. Ladd power-crawled towards it, hoping to refasten the ropes, but the lorry shifted gear and tore up a hill, sending the barrel thundering towards him. Ladd threw himself to the side, dodging the barrel by a couple of centimetres. It smashed into the back door, impacting like a gunshot. The lorry's trajectory levelled out, then it began a rapid descent, sending the barrel rolling back at him. Ladd flung himself out of the way as it crashed into the remaining barrels and loosened their ropes.

Ladd tried to make sense of his situation. Clearly, he had been abducted by the killer. A perverted psychopath was about to pretzel his spine and tie him to a dogging lamppost. The barrels would be part of his bending equipment, designed to turn and snap spines like a medieval rack. Ladd would never accept this fate. He resolved to die fighting.

Brakes shrieked like banshees. Ladd flew forward, crunching into the floor. The loose barrel rolled back at him. There was no time to escape, but better flattened than bent.

Probably.

Dawn light flooded into the container, illuminating Ladd's groin exquisitely as the barrel ploughed into it. Ladd's agonized shouts harmonized with extensive foreign swearing, as two hefty blokes lifted the barrel off him and carried it out of the lorry.

Ladd tried standing, but his legs didn't want to. The barrel had groined away his powers of resistance. Just outside, the men opened the barrel and emptied its contents - a stinking pile of rotten herrings - onto a concrete path. Ladd wondered whether he had been kidnapped by Swedish fishermen. It was not a widely feared profession, unlike, say Albanian gunrunning or Russian racketeering, but that didn't mean they weren't going to kill him. The men righted the barrel, re-entered the lorry and lifted Ladd out. People didn't make a habit of lifting Ladd – it wasn't just that he was heavy, it was also because he looked like he would hit them first. Normally, that is exactly what he would do, but the juddering juggernaut had shaken all the fight out of him, and his limbs didn't seem to work.

The men inverted him over the empty barrel, offering an unobstructed view of a few recalcitrant dead herrings and an overpowering stench. The sequence of events was so unreal, it almost made Ladd laugh: the transition from bed to lorry to fish barrel had such an impossibly dreamlike quality. Then the horrible reality struck him: he was about to be canned alive.

"Stop!" he pleaded, "I'm claustrophobic!" It was pathetic. Why was he appealing to a pair of cop killers. If they were going to snap his spine and leave him at a dogging site, why would they care about his phobias?

The men stuffed Ladd headfirst into the barrel and secured the lid. He had never wondered what it was like to be a sardine, but now he knew. Heavy feet booted the barrel onto its side and Ladd's screams bounced around the interior as it spun over stones, potholes, and uneven concrete. It was like being inside a tumble drier: perfect for pants, but for a bloke, painful, dark, and horribly cramped. Ladd would rather have been buried alive: at least coffins stayed still. He longed for the comforts of the lorry.

The men gave the barrel an almighty kick, sending it spinning like a Ferrari wheel and scrambling what remained of Ladd's brain. The barrel smashed into a solid wall, the lid flopped off and Ladd gasped, overjoyed to breathe some fish-free air.

The kidnappers prised Ladd out of the barrel. He was dazed, gagging, and soaked in fish oil. As the kidnappers dragged him across the floor and tied him to a swivel chair, he simply didn't have the strength to resist. All he could do was watch residual herrings flop out of his nightie.

Ladd had never felt stranger or smellier, but he knew that his survival depended on taking in every detail of his surroundings. He seemed to be inside a factory. To his left, fluorescent bars lit a consignment of giant steel barrels. To his right, a hydraulic bending machine twisted panels into curved barrel shapes with a dull, metallic groan. At his feet, there was a rope, power tools and a chainsaw. Trent's murder was bloodless. This was a completely different *modus operandi*. He wasn't going to be bent to death, just sawn, hammered and drilled to bits. Hallelujah.

Ladd's abductors retreated to the factory entrance, and two faintly familiar figures approached. They were DCI McMasters' contacts in the underworld: the Transnistrian gang leader, Sergey, and his under-boss, Dmitriy, both in matching suits as exquisitely tailored as they were exquisitely horrible. The Transnistrian kingpins were not psychopaths, just the heads of a major international cocaine trafficking operation. He was clearly going to be tortured, but probably not bent to death. Things were really starting to look up.

Sergey had a heavy Transnistrian accent and said, rather sanctimoniously, "We do not hit women."

Dmitriy punched Ladd so hard, the chair swivelled a full 720 degrees.

"But you are not woman," Sergey clarified, helpfully.

Ladd was too groggy to speak.

Sergey dangled a spilt herring in Ladd's face, as if he were taunting a circus seal. "Fish confuse sniffer dogs, get barrels through border. Smell good, no?"

Sergey, Dmitriy, and the two spectating heavies found this hilarious. Ladd was less amused, but at least things were starting to make a little sense. The Transnistrians used the rotten herring barrels to shift cocaine. It was ingenious, if smelly.

Sergey yanked a tatty document from his jacket pocket. "What is *Risk Assessment?*"

Ladd looked down at the form Old Bill had made him sign at the Phantom funeral parlour. It felt like a long time ago.

Sergey pointed at the diligently completed details. "Your name, address – and our HQ!"

"Health and safety," Ladd explained, bitterly. He had been undone by paperwork.

Dmitriy smashed Ladd in the gob, launching him on another 720-degree chair spin. This was proving to be the most dangerous risk assessment in the history of bureaucracy.

Sergey leant in to Ladd for a close-quarter eyeballing. "You watch us?"

"Not me," Ladd replied. "My men."

"You have men, ladycop?" Sergey snarled.

This was getting serious. Ladd's body was immobile, but his mouth wasn't. He snapped out of his groggy haze and into bullshitting mode. "I ordered them to check everything was okay."

"How you mean, girlieponce?" Sergey asked.

"You pay for police protection. I just wanted to make sure you were getting value for money."

"We do not pay you," Sergey said. "We pay different pig."

Ladd knew he meant DCI McMasters, but he didn't think it wise to let on.

"Our pig is SECRET!" Sergey said with deadly emphasis.

Dmitriy thumped Ladd again, sending him into another double spin cycle.

"Secret, I say!" Sergey continued. "Why you know?"

Ladd was now even giddier than he had been inside the barrel, but he managed to say, "Just helping out a friend."

"Dmitriy," Sergey turned away in disgust. "Time for you."

"Hello Lady." Dmitriy laughed, "I screw you or I kill you?"

The heavies laughed. Dmitriy kicked the tools about, pondering a selection.

Ladd lied for his life. "Look, I'm bent. We're on the same side. I'll frame some Transylvanians for you. We can work out why they killed that arms dealer. Let's talk."

"Let's party!" Dmitriy revved up the chainsaw.

Ladd's face was a mess of blood, sweat and mascara, but he still had a clear view of the chainsaw's teeth. His life unspun before him: a childhood in Tottenham; a youth boxing in Archway, gigging in Camden, and fumbling in Soho; a career beginning at Hendon College and ending at Phantom; a marriage commencing with close encounters of the sweaty kind, and climaxing with compulsory cross-dressing. Ladd had certainly lived.

Dimitry raised the chainsaw and prepared to wield it. Ladd bellowed a wordless roar of protest. Then Dimitry froze. A scarlet circle appeared on his forehead, like a Hindu *bindi*. He keeled over backwards and dropped the chainsaw, which tore right through his body and sent a wave of blood crashing over Ladd. The chainsaw revved unstoppably, bouncing around the floor, threatening to leave Ladd legless. He stood, swivel chair still roped to his arse, and stepped back from the chainsaw's teeth.

Sergey dived behind a fish barrel and the heavies aimed automatics at something behind his head. Was a sniper at work? Ladd executed a standing swivel, just as a tank smashed through the factory wall, wheels screeching, engine thundering, gun threatening. It was an eight-foot high, thirty-foot long machine from hell, and it must have weighed over fifty tons.

Ladd had disarmed some fearsome criminals, but he didn't rate his chances with a tank. Had the arms dealer returned from the dead? Unlikely - ghosts didn't tend to show up in a M1 Abrams Battle Tank. Was this Trent's killer? A tank could bend anything, or anyone.

The tank's 120-millimetre smoothbore canon blasted a hole in the opposite wall. The Transnistrian heavies returned fire, peppering the tank with bullets. Ladd dropped sideways, employing the swivel chair as a rather pitiful barrier. The chainsaw was still revving around the floor, lethal teeth bared, like a breakdancing shark. The tank shot it dead and continued its advance, threatening to crush all that lay in its path.

The Transnistrians rolled barrels under the tank's treads in a desperate attempt to delay its advance. The barrels were big, but the tank was bigger. It mounted and squashed them, launching rotten herrings into the air in a series of explosive squirts. But the Transnistrians did not give up their relentless barrel assault and the tank's progress eventually slowed to a stop under an accumulation of mangled metal and fish.

The tank turret opened, and Vlad the Transylvanian appeared, firing a machine gun. The Transnistrians responded in kind, and it soon felt like there was more ammo than air. Ladd had never seen military action first hand and this Transylvanian–Transnistrian tear-up was the real deal. Sadly, his only protection was a swivel chair. He turned from side-to side on the ground, repositioning the horizontal chair to face whichever side seemed to be sending the heavier fire.

After thousands of bullets had bitten the dust, and no one had been hit, Sergey raised an arm and tendered a Transnistrian truce. Vlad acknowledged from the Transylvanian's tank and handed his machine-gun to Igor, who covered him as he jumped out of the turret. Sergey emerged from behind his barrel, covered by his own heavies.

Vlad's progress across the fish guts and bullets came to an abrupt halt when he noticed that someone in a nightie was tied to a recumbent swivel chair. He recoiled in horror, and asked in utter disbelief, "You torture woman?"

"Not woman," Sergey explained, in equally broken English, "Ladyman."

"You killed our pig!" Vlad spat. "You bend Trent, destroy alibi."

"We do not kill pigs. We do not bend Trents! Your man is murderer."

"You fail. Marian is free."

"Why he shoot arms dealer? Marian is clown."

A monumental yell filled the factory as the offended wrestler burst out of the Transylvanian tank, armed with a shoulder-mounted surface-to-air missile launcher. He took aim at the nearest Transnistrian barrel and obliterated it. Dead fish sprayed up then rained down like the world's smelliest monsoon. Bullets from both sides splattered through the falling fish, creating a miasma of rotten herring.

Ladd clambered up, still attached to the swivel chair. He speed-waddled along the ever-growing carpet of fish guts, then skidded on the spot, like a cross-dressing Bambi-on-ice. Another missile blasted more barrels, unleashing a second shoal of flying fish.

Ladd regained his footing and scrambled out into the dawn light; chair still firmly attached to his bum. He blundered past the kidnap lorry, yomped across an abandoned industrial estate, and staggered up a grass slope. At the top, an eight-foot perimeter fence blocked his way to the road. Ladd turned back to the barrel factory. Gunfire, tank-fire and exploding missiles resonated like a Gaza Strip shell-off. He turned again and jumped up onto the fence, straining to lug the combined weight of the swivel chair and his own body. This was his own personal Everest, and he had no choice but to summit it, even if sherpas were in short supply. Once he had reached the top, he celebrated wildly but briefly. He was horribly stuck. It made him think of the Super, arrested by community support officers whilst astride his own fence: his heart went out to her. But the Super was half his weight, and she wasn't attached to a swivel chair. After around twenty seconds, the fence collapsed.

Ladd tumbled down the roadside slope and landed flat on his face, inches from a passing ice-cream van. Half-drag-artist, half-swivel-chair, Ladd staggered along like a sexually conflicted turtle. Car horns blasted, passengers cheered, pedestrians wolf whistled. Perhaps humiliation was better than death, but it didn't feel like it.

Ladd took his nightie-clad self and his swivel chair to a bus stop. The commuters all cowered away from his fishy stench and demented appearance, apart from one obese man in a Barcelona football shirt who was chuckling himself into a coronary.

Ladd waddled over to him. "Where am I?"

"On a swivel chair, mate," the fat football fan replied, "In a nightie, covered in fish."

Merriment reigned supreme across the bus stop. Nothing at Hendon Police College had prepared him for a moment like this. As a DCI, he was supposed to embody the dignity of the Force, and uphold the majesty of the law, not perform as a cross-dressing, fish-stained human-chair hybrid. The best way of dealing with the situation was clearly to end it as soon as possible, so violence seemed like the simplest solution. He smashed the swivel chair repeatedly against the bus stop.

The commuters backed away, a woman screamed, and the big-bellied Barcelona bloke was stirred into answering Ladd's original question. "Ongar, mate. You're in bleeding Ongar. Now do one, take your medication and get your social worker to run you under a tap. You stink!"

The commuters applauded the sentiment. Ladd knew he wasn't welcome, and he had no wish to hang about, so he smacked the chair repeatedly against the bus stop until it flew off and he landed on his arse. The queue laughed. Ladd might have seen the funny side too had he not spotted the Transylvanian tank powering along the road. Ladd was the only one to react. Perhaps the sight of a suburban tank was so incongruous that it simply didn't compute with commuters.

Ladd speed-crawled behind the bus stop. It was a relief to move freely again, even if his nightie was still covered in rotten herring. He hid, hoping that the tank would just trundle on by, possibly on its way to a spot of shopping on Ongar High Street. But Ladd was out of luck. It drove straight at the bus stop.

Ladd leapt out and shouted, "Run!", making wild scarpering gestures. The queue looked non-plussed, wondering why the local lunatic was giving them instructions.

Finally, the corpulent Barcelona buff clocked the danger, and shouted "Run!" too. This time, the commuters listened, and sprinted for their lives, vacating the bus stop moments before the tank flattened it.

Ladd dived behind a hedgerow and watched Marian appear above the turret. The enormous wrestler scanned the area, turning his terrifying turnip of a head right then left. He cursed and climbed out; missile launcher propped against his shoulder. Ladd crouched and sprinted at a stoop; his body shielded by the decorative greenery. Nighties were relatively easy to run in, particularly if modesty was low on your agenda.

After a few minutes, Ladd emerged by a row of shops. It was rush hour in Ongar village, which meant a minor traffic jam and occasional pedestrians. Cross-dressing cops with Transnistrian bruises ran a high risk of getting noticed, so Ladd adopted a defensive mindset. He crouched by a parked Mini, did a 360-degree anti-surveillance turn and checked reflective surfaces for signs of Transylvanian tanks: a charity shop window offered a reflected pensioner, a wing mirror revealed a hobbling mongrel, a puddle showed a child chucking sticks at a wheelie bin. The coast was clear, so Ladd dodged his way along the high street. Pedestrians looked at him as if he were a care-in-the community case and, in his heart of hearts, he felt like one.

PRISON DIARY - ENTRY 5

Naomi didn't lift her face from her palms for the first eight minutes of our session. I sat in silence, gazing at the cow portrait, and wondering which aspects of my chapter would prove to be my tutor's favourites.

Once Naomi was able to speak, she said, "I really don't know where to start."

"You could start at the end and work backwards, start in the middle and work sideways or maybe just start at the start."

Naomi gazed at me for several seconds before saying, "You have to be more careful about your language."

"Swearing?"

"Well, there's certainly too much of that."

"Have you heard how much people swear in real life?" I asked.

"Prison's not real life."

"It is for me."

"But it's not just the swearing. What about your cavalier descriptions. There are rules, you know. *Care in the community case*? I mean, mental health?"

"Doesn't *mental health* mean you are mentally healthy? Like *good health*."

"You know what I mean."

"I get that someone can have *mental health issues* or *mental health problems* but *having mental health* means everything's tickety-boo."

"Tickety-boo?"

"Hunky-dory, A-okay, going swimmingly, fine."

"Oh." She paused to gather some more critical ammunition to launch in my direction. "A tank's quite extreme, don't you think? I mean, for London?"

"You'd be shocked at the scale of tank crime, even among teenagers."

"And as for the foreign accents, they are xenophobic."

"They don't speak xenophobic."

"But is it an accurate representation of how Transnistrians and Transylvanians speak?"

"No idea. Never been there. Never met any."

"You should write about what you know."

"Can't I just make stuff up?"

"It's cultural appropriation."

"You want them to talk like newsreaders?"

"That wouldn't be very realistic, would it?" She changed direction. "Their attitudes aren't really acceptable either, are they?"

"They're gangsters, not HR managers."

"Their language is outdated, and their behaviour is cruel."

"It was a kidnap, interrogation, and torture session interrupted by a shoulder-mounted missile shoot-out and a tank."

"I feel sorry for your mind."

"Thanks."

"Why don't you calm down and write more sensitively?"

"I'm not a girl."

Naomi gave me a stern look, before noticing that I was winding her up. "Plenty of male writers are sufficiently in touch with their feelings to inhabit their characters and bring them to life on the page. You really need to make the reader feel what they feel and think what they think moment-by-moment."

"Sounds a bit dull."

"Try to make your writing less like a brutal cartoon, and more like a gentle poem." She slammed her notebook shut and ended the session.

Back in the cell, Jeff regaled me with tales of London's old school gangsters, with their bolt cutters, pliers, and shock boxes, until he was overwhelmed with nostalgia for the old faces. It was very like a brutal cartoon and very unlike a gentle poem.

I got stuck into a biography of Genghis Khan, heavily bearded creator of the largest empire on Earth. He was quite the geezer, and invented things like fast cavalries and postal systems. He had a bit of a temper after his dad was poisoned by Tartars (possibly with their sauce), but he was big on parenting. Apparently, he had so many kids that around sixteen million people alive today share some of his DNA. That said, he did do his bit to keep the world's population within sensible limits by killing forty million people. And Naomi had said I was brutal. She had clearly never met Genghis.

Over the next few days, I tried to bear Naomi's advice in mind, but it didn't work. Living moment-by-moment doesn't lend itself to prison. No one wants to savour every instant of a stretch, so I carried on exactly as before, and knocked out another chapter willy-nilly.

DEBRIEFING

Ladd was, penniless, phoneless, trouserless, and too smelly to hitch a lift. As he wended his way west in his fishy nightie, he stuck to minor roads and kept an eye out for Transylvanian tanks.

Being abducted, thrown in a barrel, and punched repeatedly on account of a mislaid risk assessment was unfortunate, but it had afforded him some intriguing insights. Firstly, it confirmed that the Transnistrians had a corrupt relationship with a policeman, even if they hadn't actually named McMasters. Secondly, the Transylvanians could not have made it much more bleeding obvious that they had killed the arms dealer: the tank and the surface-to-air missile launcher were a bit of a giveaway. So, even if no one had bent Trent to death, and he had been able to provide an alibi at the trial, the alibi would have been a false one and Marian's murder conviction was sound. Thirdly, a murder had been committed right in front of him. Ladd wasn't exactly heartbroken about Dimitry's death, but his Transnistrian torturer had been shot in the middle of his forehead. It was an expert hit and it had happened prior to the tank's arrival. There could be no doubt about the timing: the tank had made a memorable entrance. Fourthly, Trent's murder had sparked a gang war. The Transylvanians blamed the Transnistrians for the fatal bending, and Marian's subsequent conviction, but why would they have murdered someone else's bent cop? The gangs were not business rivals – they dealt in different narcotics. Maybe it was in someone's interests to set the Transylvanians against the Transnistrians. Perhaps it was one of the remaining Gang of Three, seeking a larger slice of their corrupt conspiracy's profits. It was too early to bring in Proudcock, McMasters and Sweeney. Move too soon, and he would blow his own covert anti-corruption operation before he had gathered enough evidence to back up Dredd's contentions. Ladd had zero faith in Dixon and his Homicide goons, but he would just have to be patient.

Several hours later, Ladd was knocking on his own door, closely observed by *Neighbourhood Watch*. With any luck, they wouldn't recognise him in his nightie.

Eight knocks later, there was still no response. Had he known he was being abducted by Transnistrians, he would have taken a key. Luckily, Ladd's illustrious career in the police had furnished him with a thorough grounding in burglary. In his experience, doors only provided the illusion of security. A spot of letterbox fishing often yielded keys and most domestic locks were barely more advanced than children's puzzles: your average credit card could do the job. In this instance, the only available burglary accessory was a hair pin Tina had affixed to him when she was dressing him up. It wasn't exactly NASA-level technology, but it worked.

After he had negotiated the porch's gym gear and slipped the interior lock, Ladd was ambushed by his own reflection in the hallway mirror: a pickled witch on steroids. It wasn't a fashionable look. He tore off the nightie, dashed for the bathroom, and showered off the stench of herring. The water was warm and comforting, and for the first time in two days, he felt relaxed. Then a series of sharp, insistent doorbell rings spoiled everything.

Dripping and swearing, Ladd wrapped his groin in the nearest towel, stubbed his toe on the porch's gym equipment and opened the door to a to a "plastic" policeman, aged around nineteen. Police community support officers, as they were officially known, had puny powers ranging from on-the-spot litter penalties to cider confiscation. Compared to a Detective Chief Inspector like Ladd, they had all the seniority of a school prefect. And yet here he was, summoned out of his shower.

"We've had reports of a break-in, sir." The plastic's voice was surprisingly self-assured given how recently it had broken.

Ladd wondered whether to point out that he was about twelve hours too late to catch the Transnistrian intruders who had abducted and interrogated him in a barrel factory, but it didn't seem worth the effort, so he just said, "You missed them."

"Not the Superintendent we found straddling your fence, sir," the plastic replied. "This was a large lady in a nightie."

Ladd didn't like the way this was going, so he adopted a high-handed tone in the hope of getting rid of him. "You're telling me you dragged me out of the shower because you've had some nonsensical report about a burglar in a nightie?"

"Yes, sir," he replied. "Like that one."

"What?" Ladd followed the plastic's gaze to the Extra-Large nightie behind him. He was in urgent need of a lie, so he went for the obvious, "That's my wife's."

The plastic continued to gawp at the duvet-sized nightie carpeting the hallway. "Large unit, is she, sir?"

"How dare you!" Ladd's attempts to look irate were too much for his towel, which dropped to the floor. He slammed the door on the plastic's shocked expression.

Ladd was naked, wet, and lost. Self-pity was never his style, but there was no denying that life-wise, things were not going well. To add to it all, Ladd was even more spectacularly late than yesterday. This time, he had been kidnapped by gangsters rather than entrapped by his wife's cross-dressing fixation, but Chief Inspectors were not supposed to show up after lunchtime, especially in covert anti-corruption units.

After donning pants and mourning clobber, Ladd rushed off to the funeral parlour, dashed through the display coffins and booted the stone angel in the gob. The front curtains shut, and the cherub wall ascended, revealing Phantom HQ and his diverse and inclusive squad sharing a bumper box of doughnuts.

"Late again, Guv." Goliath said, mid-munch.

"I was abducted by Transnistrians," Ladd explained.

"Doughnut?" Old Bill offered him a glazed pink and yellow pastry.

Ladd took the doughnut and tore it in two. "Health and safety nearly killed me."

"Health and safety's the finest invention in history," Old Bill replied, mouth a-gobble. "Keeps the workers alive."

"The Transnistrians found your risk assessment," Ladd said.

"It was very carefully worded," Old Bill said, with pride. "Extremely thorough."

"Well, it triggered the Transnistrians." Ladd said, mid-chomp.

"Bunch of snowflakes," Old Bill scoffed. "I'll enter it into the Accident Report Log."

"I didn't trip over a traffic cone! I was stuffed into a barrel, tied up, and threatened with a chainsaw. All because your risk assessment convinced the Transnistrians that we have them under surveillance."

"They're right about that, aren't they just," Taffy said.

"Of course they are!" Ladd replied. "But if you two hadn't lost the risk assessment they wouldn't know, would they?"

"Suppose not, Guv," Taffy replied.

"Look," Ladd attempted a debrief. "The Transylvanians blame the Transnistrians for Trent's death and Marian's murder conviction, so they attacked the Transnistrian HQ with a tank."

"Did you dream this, Guv?" Goliath asked.

"No," Ladd replied. "I don't dream about tanks. They must have got it from the dead arms dealer. There was a shootout with machine guns, but before that, Dimitry the Transnistrian was killed by an unknown sniper."

Yang signed with force.

"You actually witnessed all this, Guv?" Sue interpreted, before adding on her own behalf. "Do I really have to say *Guv* all the time? It feels awfully silly."

"You do whatever you feel comfortable with, Sue," Ladd replied, gently.

"No, Guv," Old Bill said with the conviction of a lifelong stickler. "If she signs *Guv*, you need to know that she meant *Guv*, don't you Guv?"

"Possibly." Ladd snatched another doughnut. "To answer your question, I was half-undercover."

"Which half?" Taffy snapped a sugar-powdered doughnut in two.

Ladd thought it best not to say, "The half in the nightie", so he said, "Marian the murderer tried to shoot me with a shoulder-mounted missile launcher," instead, even though it wasn't strictly true – he had been aiming it at the Transnistrians.

"Hang on," Goliath said, "He had a shoulder-mounted missile launcher?"

"Yes," Ladd replied.

"And he missed?" Goliath asked, with the scepticism of an experienced military man.

Not one member of Phantom squad believed Ladd's account, so he adopted a tone he hoped sounded authoritative, and asked, "Anyone else have anything to report?"

Sue was the first to respond. "I've got rheumatism. It's quite painful."

"Sorry to hear that, Sue," Ladd said. "Anyone else?"

"I followed Sweeney to The Smiths' scrap yard," Goliath said. "That lot have got enough car crushers and cranes to bend anyone."

"I see," Ladd replied through his latest doughnut. "The Transnistrians could be contenders too. They have a barrel-bender, and if it can bend metal, it can bend skin and bone."

Yang signed with intensity, and Sue interpreted, "Marian could bend anyone to death with his bare hands."

"Or his bare tank," Ladd added.

"I wonder," Goliath said. "How would that work?"

Ladd was stumped, but that didn't stop him floundering about for an answer. "Well, it could certainly flatten someone."

"But Trent wasn't flat," Goliath objected. "His corpse was three-dimensional. Particularly his beer gut."

"Good point," Ladd blustered. "But the sheer pulling power of the tank... if applied in a certain way ... could definitely have done the bending."

"What kind of certain way, Guv?" Goliath persisted.

"No idea," Ladd admitted.

"Anyway," Goliath continued. "With Trent bent, the Transylvanians need a new friend in the Force. They want watching."

Ladd's phone bleeped. It was a text from the Super: "URGENT DEBRIEFING".

***

The Super may have lived in a trendy street stuffed with app developers and search engine optimizers, but her house was a shrine to the past: artefacts from distant centuries and long-lost empires were displayed with a curator's care. A portrait of Genghis Khan glared down at her bedcovers. It wasn't particularly welcoming, but the Super was, and the senior police officers were entangled under the sheets faster than you could say, "Guv".

"I do love a man out of uniform," the Super whispered, as she relieved Ladd of his boxers. He had grown quite attached to them: the past three days had made him cherish pants in a way he had never previously envisaged. Thongs weren't all they were cracked up to be. Ladd removed his Superintendent's underwear. He couldn't help thinking that lingerie was losing much of its mystique; familiarity breeds contempt, as they say.

A key turned in a downstairs lock. Ladd jumped to his feet.

"You've shaved your legs!" The Superintendent observed.

"Boxing, Ma'am." Ladd explained as he hid under the bed. "Just made the weigh-in."

"By a hair's breadth?"

"I was highly hairy, Ma'am."

The Super made no attempt to hide. She just lay in bed under the gaze of Genghis Khan.

Ladd found the floor much less comfortable than the mattress, but the last time an unexpected key-turn had signalled a homecoming, it had transformed his life in unwanted ways, and he dreaded to think what costly new lies he would end up telling if confronted with the Superintendent's irate partner.

After a substantial chunk of silence, the Super asked, "Like it under there?"

"Precaution, Ma'am."

The Super allowed a further few moments to elapse before saying, "I'm single."

Ladd peered up from the floor. "You're sure, Ma'am?"

"Yes. Builder's redoing my downstairs."

"Builder, Ma'am?"

"He's Lithuanian."

Ladd clambered back into bed and pretended nothing had happened. "Homicide busy?"

"Mounting an undercover operation to penetrate the dogging community," the Super replied, with a seductive emphasis on the words *mounting*, *penetrate* and *dogging*.

Ladd tried to avoid looking at glaring Genghis and slid back under the sheets.

The Super wrapped her arms around Ladd. "How's your probing?"

Ladd tweaked her nipples, and replied, "Everyone involved in the investigation seems to be a potential bender - the Transylvanians, Transnistrians, even The Smiths."

"Aren't The Smiths more old-school?"

"They generally prefer to shoot people."

"Maybe it was a drive-by bending?" She ran her nails down his chest.

Ladd's phone bleeped from the bedside. The Super snatched it and read out the message: *Emergency - come quick*. "Don't mind if I do." She grabbed Ladd, handcuffed him to the bedposts and rode him like a sideshow pony.

The Super was indeed super; intense, enthusiastic, and loudly appreciative. She was more than a match for Ladd, who returned home somewhat dishevelled.

Tina was sat on the sofa-bed in her most seductive silk dress. "Took your time, sugar-babe."

"Sorry," Ladd mumbled as he sat down beside her. "I was tied up with the Super."

They say in silence for a few moments. Ladd looked longingly at the remote. He would gratefully have spent the rest of the evening watching television; any old nonsense would have done, just so long as it gave him a chance to recover from the Super's seeing-to.

But Tina wasn't having it. She elbowed him in the ribs and cackled. "Great detective you are. Missed a break-in to your own friggin' home. Little wankpuffins took nothing, but *Neighbourhood Watch* reckon it was a big lass. Got a stalker?"

"Don't think so, no."

"Would you like one?" Tina proffered herself.

"No thanks. Was that the emergency?"

"No. This is." Tina dropped her dress, revealing a lacy under-combo. "I need you. Urgently. In tights."

Forty minutes later, Ladd was in the bedroom sporting a strawberry playsuit and listening to the yelp of a neighbour's terrier wilt across the semis. It could have been providing a commentary on his pitifully flaccid efforts. The Super had depleted his reserves so comprehensively, he had no choice but to crawl under the bedsheets and oblige by other means.

Two full hours passed before Ladd reversed out from the duvet's bottom, miming wildly.

Tina smiled indulgently. "Lost for words, Honeybunch?"

Ladd crawled to his unoccupied trousers, retrieved his phone from the pocket and texted her the word *Lockjaw*. Tina ignored the text, supine in her post-orgasmic haze. Ladd was in even more discomfort than he had experienced in the Transnistrian fish barrel. He crawled to Tina's bedside table, purloined a biro, and grabbed her advanced kickboxing manual. Agonized tears filled his eyes as he scrawled on the inside cover, but he only got as far as *Lockj...* before the pen snapped.

"Holy bollocks!" Tina raised her hands in despair. "Why can't blokes communicate?"

Ladd clutched his jaw, positively pogoing in pain like a tormented punk.

"Men!" Tina shouted. "Why can't you be more in touch with your frigging feelings?"

Ladd was starting to despair. The pain was putting him close to pass-out point. He upended Tina's pants drawer and spelled out *HELP* with her underwear.

Tina shrugged and finally read the text message: "*Lockjaw*. Why didn't you say?"

***

Ladd sat alone in the Accident and Emergency wing of the local hospital. His mouth was agape, like a bullfrog waiting to swallow a fly that would never come. Tina had given him a lift but opted not to hang around. He didn't blame her; he wasn't exactly scintillating company and the place was full of pissheads, smackheads and perverts who had injured themselves having sex with domestic appliances.

Ladd passed the time by watching the drunks fight each other, inflicting additional injuries requiring further medical attention. Eventually, a triage nurse approached Ladd with a clipboard. He couldn't answer any of her questions, so he passed her his phone. She seemed reluctant to take it, but after pointing at the screen emphatically, she finally read the word *LOCKJAW*. For a moment, her mood changed, her face lit up, and she shot him a sympathetic smile, but when the phone bleeped again, she handed it back to him in disgust.

Ladd looked at the image filling his screen. He was wearing a tutu. It really didn't suit him. A text pinged: *Don't ignore me, Dolly x.*

What with the abduction, the Trans-on-Trans war and the ongoing investigation into Trent's fatal bending, Ladd had given precious little attention to his blackmailer. Was Dolly serious? It seemed unlikely. She probably tried it on with half her customers. Having been threatened by a Transylvanian tank, he wasn't exactly petrified by a transitioned shopkeeper. He put Dolly out of his mind and fell asleep in his chair.

A few hours later, Ladd was led to the consulting room. It was shortly before two o'clock in the morning, an unholy hour for public humiliation. A suave doctor sacrificed Ladd's dignity to an audience of medical students, all clearly entertained by the parade of dysfunctional losers they had watched him treat throughout the night.

"What have we here?" The doctor asked, knowing full well he couldn't answer.

Ladd intoned numerous sub-verbal noises, to the students' delight.

"Can anyone name that tune?" The doctor enquired.

They all laughed, apart from one spotty dipstick, who answered, "*We Don't Talk Anymore*."

"Good one," the doctor said. "Charlie someone and Selena Gomez, wasn't it?"

"*Talking To Myself*," a dorky girl suggested.

"Nice," the doctor said. "*Linkin Park*, I seem to remember. Anyone else? No? How about that timeless Rod Stewart classic, *I Don't Want To Talk About It*? Huh? I think that's got to be the winner, hasn't it?"

Had he been able to talk, Ladd would have had words, but his face was agape.

Without warning, the doctor waded in with a violent jaw-yank. It cracked like the world's largest knuckle. "Better?"

Ladd rotated his jaw, making a variety of chewy noises.

"How did it happen?" the doctor asked, gleefully.

Ladd thought briefly, too briefly. "Boxing injury."

"Trying to swallow a glove?"

The students failed to stifle their scepticism.

Ladd's phone interrupted the merriment with a bleep. He practically long-jumped out in his hurry to escape the consulting room.

It was the Super. "Someone's bent another cop."

"To death?"

"In half. Backwards."

"One of Dredd's bent ones?"

"It's a Gang of Two now."

"Bollocks."

PRISON DIARY – ENTRY 6

"Why always *bollocks*?" Naomi asked, as I took my place beside the cow portrait.

"Bollocks?" I replied.

"Whenever Ladd hears about a death, he's ready with his *bollocks*."

"Grief, I suppose."

"But why do his expressions of grief have to be so groin-based?"

"It hits him in the bollocks, I suppose."

"What does?"

"The idea of a fellow officer's death. It's like a giant kick in the balls."

"I see." Naomi said. "Well, I can't fault your diligence. You've turned in six chapters at regular intervals. Well done."

"Thanks."

Naomi gazed at the cow portrait. There wasn't much else to gaze at, but I took it as a sign that all was not well in Sevenoaks.

"Tell me, Cuthbert," Naomi never used my name. Something was clearly up. "Have you made any plans for life on the outside?"

"Might have a bit of a piss-up."

"A party! How lovely!"

"It'll probably just be me."

Naomi burst into tears. I hadn't anticipated this. I've always been a fan of solo drinking –friends aren't all they're cracked up to be, and it didn't occur to me that other people might find this somehow tragic.

I couldn't put a consoling hand on her shoulder without risking a trip to the Governor's office, but my thoughts were with her.

After a while, she stopped sobbing and said, "I don't want to be alone."

"Alone is all right," I said. "It's other people that are the problem."

"Roly's got something going on with the au pair."

"You're sure?"

"The cleaner told me."

"Maybe she's jealous."

"You think she's got something going on with him too?"

"I don't know."

Naomi gave me an accusing look, probably because I was male.

"You've always got the kids," I said.

She froze briefly, then wept. It was my turn to look at the cow. I think the artist had given it too many udders.

Eventually, Naomi wailed, "They're getting older!"

"Who?"

"My children."

"Isn't that a good thing?"

"They hate me."

"I doubt it."

"I'm starting to think Innsbruck might not be gifted after all."

"What about Gethsemane?"

"She's given up veganism!"

Naomi was inconsolable. I wished her all the best, but I don't think it helped much.

I returned to my cell and chatted to Jeff about our most memorable mistakes. This was a relatively easy task for Jeff, as he had devoted himself to a single calling. He said he never should have trusted a short-sighted lookout, he should have realised that a getaway driver was a chronic alcoholic, and he really should have guessed that an inside man was an undercover officer.

I had a far greater variety of workplace mishaps to call upon. I regretted driving a municipal snow plough into a nursing home, I wished I had never left the doors open on that submarine, and I probably shouldn't have triggered all those nuclear reactor meltdowns. That, of course, was all before I became a life coach.

Jeff's biggest personal regret was marrying his childhood sweetheart. She was lovely, but simply lacked the patience to sustain marriage to a career criminal. Sharon had waited for him during his first stretch, strayed during a second stretch, then got knocked-up by the local egg-man during his third.

I was spoiled for choice. Once I had got as far as my fourth marriage, Jeff interrupted, as if hit by a lightning bolt of inspiration: "What if we decided to stop screwing everything up?"

I had never considered this possibility. Events always turned against me, and I had never succeeded in changing their mind. Even my specially developed life-coaching techniques like semitasking and negative visualisation rebounded on my clients, leaving them dead, injured, or insane, and me unemployable. But what if there was hope?

"We could always escape," Jeff said.

"From here?"

"Yes, from here. If we were going to escape from anywhere else, we'd have to break in first."

Jeff had a point. A cell was the ideal location from which to launch a prison escape. But how? What about the locks? What about the CCTV? What about the sensors? What about the walls?

"Have you got a plan?" I asked.

Jeff went quiet for a bit before replying, "What if I had?"

It was high time for some sums. Burgling my own house had landed me with an eighteen- month stretch. Now, barring any penalties awarded by the prison Governor, I would only serve half of that before being released under license. So, nine months inside and I'd already served three: I was a third of my way to freedom. The time hadn't exactly flashed by, but what with the reading, the writing, and Jeff's sparkling conversation, it hadn't dragged much more than a school term. Could I handle another couple of instalments? Probably.

An escape would be a victory of sorts, something for the CV, but what about all the hiding afterwards? And life on the run sounded knackering – never any chance to settle down and catch your breath. I couldn't tell Jeff any of this, of course. God only knew how long he had left to serve. A decade? I didn't like to ask. One armed robbery could bag you an eye-watering stretch, and he'd been done for at least three.

I buried myself in a book about film noir. I quite liked the look of *femmes fatales*. I wondered whether Naomi's au pair and cleaner were *femmes fatales*. Perhaps Roly was a *homme fatale*. Who knew? I beavered on with the next chapter, hoping that it might offer Naomi a welcome distraction from her domestic turmoil.

DEATH: THE SEQUEL

Detective Inspector Todd Sweeney dangled in the moonlight. His ginger beard was majestic, but it wouldn't be getting any longer. The DI's lean, toned corpse was bent over backwards, its spine snapped, its heels bound to the back of its hairy head, and its perfect six-pack noosed to the top of a lamppost.

For Ladd, the second death-scene was much less convenient than the first. This deserted dogging site was at London's southernmost tip, right at the wrong end of the capital. It was a perfectly pellucid night, the moon aglimmer, the sky pearled with twinkling constellations. But the stunning nocturnal vista offered by this hilly outdoor sex venue was spoiled by the deceased Flying Squad officer, whose body was not so much flying, as drooping.

Aside from its postcode, the second crime scene aped the first. Pointless police tape kept out non-existent onlookers, and the pathology tent, squad cars, winch, scene-of-crime officers, and Homicide detectives were all artlessly arranged around the empty dogging arena, with its carpet of condoms, tissues, and lube tubes. The only noticeable difference was the safety net, a precaution designed to temper the wrath of Stoker should the corpse's descent go a-cock.

Ladd was only there to observe, but he didn't just have eyes for the corpse. The Super was standing between a rotting tree stump and a soiled mattress, looking alluring.

Ladd sauntered over. "Must stop meeting like this, Ma'am."

The Super smiled. "We've had more romantic liaisons."

Their fingers touched. Hours earlier, Ladd had been happily handcuffed beneath her and Genghis Khan. This would have been a post-coital murder scene, had his lockjaw-inducing session with Tina not interceded. He thought it best to skirt over this.

"Let me guess." Ladd stroked her palm. "Anonymous call, dogging spot, spine snapped, no witnesses, CCTV in smithereens."

She clasped her fingers over his. "It's clearly a serial bender."

The SOCOs' winch groaned into life, worked for a couple of feet, then jolted to a halt. Sweeney swung like a jaunty bauble, then the rope snapped, and he plopped into the safety net, which split with a rasp. Stoker bombed out of his pathology tent, just in time to see the cop's corpse land on a pile of used condoms. Stoker ran up to the nearest pair of SOCOs and banged their heads together.

The sight of her pathologist introducing even more violence to the murder scene was too much for the Super, so she turned away and focused her attentions on Ladd. "Todd Sweeney was Flying Squad, wasn't he?"

"Yes, Ma'am." Ladd replied. "He was investigating organised crime whilst taking bungs from The Smiths."

"Charming man."

"Looks like he's headed for the cemetery gates."

They were still chuckling at Morrissey puns when Homicide approached. DCI Dixon blanked Ladd, and offered the Super an "Evening, Ma'am.".

The Super indicated Sweeney's bent body. "Contortionism mishap?"

"We can rule out suicide, Ma'am." Dixon looked as clueless as he was forlorn.

Ladd sensed an opportunity to make things worse. "Murder Inquiry going well, is it?"

Dixon looked at Ladd with homicidal intent, but before he could reply, a flurry of Glaswegian merriment issued from the death scene. Stoker had disentangled Sweeney's corpse from the broken safety net and was dragging it to his tent, waving cheerfully at the assembled ranks. "Dinnae worry, lads. I'll give this bonny boy a thorough seeing to."

The Super shipped Ladd a quizzical look, then turned back to Dixon. "Psychopathic pathologists aside, any progress in catching The Bender?"

"There's a pattern, Ma'am." Dixon was trying his best to make it sound like he'd made a breakthrough. "This is London's southernmost dogging site. Trent was at the northernmost one."

"So, it's a pervert with a compass," Ladd quipped.

The Super giggled. It set Ladd off until his jaw locked again.

An evil grin crossed Dixon's face. "Something wrong with your gob?"

Ladd nodded, mouth agape. Dixon cracked him under the chin. Bones clicked and snapped back into place. The pain was exquisite, but short-lived, and Ladd could move his jaw sufficiently to shout the word, "Aaaaaaargggggghhhhhh!"

Dixon savoured Ladd's agony as only a true enemy could. But before Ladd could decide whether to thank him or hit him back, his phone bleeped. It was bound to be Tina, tempting him back into panties or suchlike, so he shielded the screen from his fellow officers. But it turned out to be Dolly, sharing her location and demanding: *Meet me now.*

While Ladd did his best to hide his panic, the Super snuck a look at the screen, and said, "Hello, hello, hello, Dolly."

"It's a snout," Ladd lied.

"You've got a snout called Dolly?" Dixon scoffed.

"And why shouldn't I?" Ladd replied.

"Snouts have street names," Dixon said. "You know, *Axe Man*, *Stacks*, *Double D*. They don't call themselves after big-titted country music divas."

Ladd was reluctant to reveal that Dolly was in fact the owner of a cross-dressing boutique, so he said, "Dolly's ironic. Most violent enforcer in Chipping Barnet."

"How come I've never heard of him?" Dixon was enjoying Ladd's discomfort.

"Dolly operates in the shadows," Ladd lied. "Diabolical manoeuvres, a criminal mastermind. Makes the mafia look like shoplifters. Now, if you'll both excuse me, I've got an informer to meet." Maintaining a purposeful look, Ladd strode off to his urgent tête-à-tête with "the most violent enforcer in Chipping Barnet".

***

As Ladd approached his rendezvous with both Dolly and Fate, he had murder on his mind; not only that of the two demised detectives, but the possible advantages of Dolly's disposal. The flamboyant shopkeeper's decision to meet at a godforsaken towpath added to the temptation. The location's obscurity may have protected her from prying eyes, but it also made her vulnerable to an unwitnessed clobbering. The canal was sparsely lit, and its dank waters bobbled with nameless shapes. It wouldn't be the world's worst place to dispose of a weighted body; he couldn't see the diving boys queuing up to explore its toxic depths.

Ladd worried about himself sometimes. Dress pics were a pathetic provocation to kill. The blackmail photos were no more incriminating than promotional material for a local pantomime. He'd just rather they weren't made public, as he looked like a colossal dick. No, Ladd wasn't really in the murder business, but if Dolly was really determined to blackmail him, he certainly had options.

Dolly was stood at the appointed place, sharing a wall with some well-executed cock-and-balls graffiti. She was in a fur coat, holding a leopardskin handbag, and leaning back on the bricks. It was obviously a pose. Dolly was playing out a scene from a film noir of her own invention: *Double-D-Cup Indemnity*, perhaps. Ladd didn't particularly want to share in the fantasy; he just wanted to get this nonsense over with.

"Hello Dolly," Ladd said, with extreme prejudice.

"Tranny Boy," she countered.

"We both know I'm not." Ladd deployed an unfamiliar weapon: honesty.

"You looked as comfortable as a squid in clogs." Dolly smirked as she sparked up a fag. "What were you thinking?"

"I was trying to save my marriage," Ladd replied, wondering why it had taken a fully transitioned blackmailer to make him tell the truth.

Dolly seemed quietly impressed. Maybe she had been expecting another easy encounter with the spineless fool who had spent the best part of a grand on women's clothing he didn't want. Dolly inhaled, taking a few moments to recalculate before blowing smoke in his face. Ladd wished she hadn't. It was as seductive as sarin.

Once the smoke had cleared, Dolly said, "Don't live a lie."

"You're giving me advice?"

"Decide who you really are. Are you a woman trapped in a man's body or a coward faking it for his wife?"

"You know the answer. Why else would I be here?"

"So, you're a coward."

Ladd knew she was right, but he wasn't enjoying this. He decided to try another dose of honesty. "Shopping for women's clothes was ... the hardest thing I've ever done."

"Oh, sweetie." Dolly handed him a cigarette. "You're leading a double life."

"I can't be myself in my own home."

"You can't be a CIS?"

"A Commonwealth of Independent States?"

"No."

"A sissy?"

"No. A CIS. A blokey bloke."

"Tina won't let me." The emotional weight of all the pretence, the panty-sporting exertion, the forced lingerie enthusiasm, began to overwhelm Ladd. "It's all just ...too much."

Dolly leant forward to light Ladd's cigarette with her own. "Ten grand's not too much though, is it?"

Ladd knocked both cigarettes away, partly out of anger, but partly because he didn't smoke. "Let's get this straight. You want to punish a non-trans bloke for pretending to be trans by outing him as trans?"

"Put like that, why not?"

Ladd squared up to Dolly. He wanted to take a good look at the person who'd had the bollocks to stitch him up: a blonde bombsite in red lipstick and pale foundation with a faint hint of someone he knew. Was it an actress, a model, or - hang on - a dodgy geezer he'd nicked on multiple occasions? Maybe that was it! "Don't I know you?"

"I'm your hot pants dealer."

"Before that. Years maybe."

Dolly smiled at him, archly, and dipped into her handbag. Ladd assumed it was for a cigarette, but he was wrong. It was for a taser. She zapped him so hard; he crashed to the ground and contorted in a puddle.

Dolly looked down with the contempt of a conquering amazon. "You've got forty-eight hours."

PRISON DIARY – ENTRY 7

Naomi was looking distressed. Sometimes, I think she uses me as some kind of therapist or sounding board. If she starts using me as a life coach, I'll have to charge.

"Oh god!" she began, unpromisingly.

"Are you okay?"

"Are you?"

"Me? Peachy. Apart from the prison sentence."

"You have a trans character blackmailing a senior police officer for lying about being trans."

"Yes."

"There are some things you just aren't allowed to write."

"Why not?"

"Maybe twenty years ago, you could get away with it, but now, young people would be up in arms."

"But what do young people know?"

"They're the future."

"But the future's not happening yet."

"It will soon."

"Young people haven't done anything. Why should I listen to them?"

"Precisely because they haven't done anything. They've not made the mistakes of older generations."

"Give them time."

"Don't you believe in progress? One generation improving on the last, making the world better?"

"Is the world better now than it was in, say 1993?" I asked. "People used to get on all right back then, didn't they? No need to shelter from Twitter storms, no one recording you on their bleeding phones. We had privacy – you could have fun without the universe and his missus seeing you plastered across the internet."

"You're sounding like a has-been."

"I'm more of a never-be."

Naomi's jaw quivered. I hadn't expected this. Once again, she was edging on tears.

"Are you okay?"

"Not really, no."

"Was it something I said?"

"A never-be!" She sobbed. "I'm a never-be too!"

"It's not all bad," I said. "Success isn't all it's cracked up to be."

"My baking blog, my organic soup group, my family... It's all for nothing."

"Baking's nothing to cry about, is it? I mean, we could all do with fewer pies."

"It's all I've got!"

"Organic soup's not exactly Armageddon either is it? There's always tins."

"The au pair found Roly with the cleaner!"

"I thought it was the other way around."

"What?"

"I thought the cleaner reckoned he was having it away with the au pair."

Naomi sobbed even louder. These were cataclysmic heaves, like a harpooned narwhal. "It's both!"

"A threesome!" I sounded over-excited at the prospect, but it's lonely in prison.

Naomi looked at me like I was the worst person alive. For a minute, I thought she was going to scream or call the Governor, but instead, she just decided to change the subject.

"Moving on, does your serial killer really have to be called The Bender?"

"He bends people to death."

"Yes, but *bender* isn't a very nice word."

"Serial killing isn't very nice."

"Can't he just shoot them, or do something less closely associated with a playground slur from the 1970s?"

"He could, but that's really not what's happening in my head."

"Can't you change what's happening in your head, given that it's all imaginary?"

"I'll think about it," I lied, and headed back to my cell.

Jeff was having a difficult night and had started humming The Smiths again. I've always enjoyed the inspired perversity of Morrissey's lyrics, and the innovative energy of Marr's kaleidoscopic riffs, but Jeff's humming was wordless and guitarless and, frankly, I would have preferred silence.

I was starting to miss the world. It was much larger than a cell, and you could walk away from people who irritated you.

A TOTAL CAR CRASH

An hour-and-a-half after he had been tasered into a puddle, DCI Ladd was almost home. He staggered along his street, damp and dishevelled, with Dolly's words, "You have to decide who you really are" bouncing around his skull like a death knell. He couldn't wait to run himself a bath and hide away from the world.

Ladd had almost made it to the porch when his phone bleeped. Tina had sent him a series of photos featuring a slinky selection of Extra-Large lingerie. A humungous wave of misery engulfed him, sweeping away all traces of hope. He was a coward living out someone else's fantasies, a misunderstanding on legs. He had no interest whatever in cross-dressing and yet this had become the focal point of his marriage. He looked mournfully at his home, with all the warmth and comforts it had to offer and decided to turn away.

Once he had put a little distance between himself and his house, he ordered a cab to the funeral parlour. The driver told him it was an odd choice of destination for the middle of the night, but Ladd had grown tired of explaining his life to strangers.

"Go on," the driver said, "Why a bleeding funeral parlour at this hour? You're not in some sort of satanic cult, are you?"

"I've got a flat above it," Ladd lied. Opening-up to Dolly had put him in a puddle, so he decided that honesty was not the best policy.

"Must get a bit gloomy, all that death underneath," the driver observed.

"The poltergeists are untidy, and the banshees shriek all night, but the undead are the worst, ambling about like they own the place. Spooks my pants off."

The driver turned as pale as a proverbial ghost.

"Mustn't grumble, though. Rent's extremely reasonable." Ladd added. "Otherwise, I'd probably move somewhere less haunted. Colindale, perhaps."

The driver shuddered and went quiet for the remainder of the journey. Ladd congratulated himself on a lie well told; he would stick to fibbing in future.

Knowing that the driver wouldn't want to hang about by the haunted parlour, Ladd took his time getting out of the cab. He watched him check his mirrors for zombies, foot ready to hammer the accelerator. Ladd wasn't a cruel man by nature, but it was good to see someone else suffer for a bit. The instant Ladd shut the door the taxi screamed off like a banshee in a hurry.

The funeral parlour may have terrified the driver, but for Ladd it was a sanctuary from Tina, big knickers, and Dolly. He hi-fived a display coffin and booted the angel gravestone in the chin. The cherub wall flew up, revealing Phantom HQ's gadget cave.

Ladd removed his jacket and trousers, wrung out the remains of puddle and hung them on a hard drive. He slumped into a chair and shut his eyes. Work sweet work. He needed this: sleep, celibacy, and his own pants. But, as he tried to nod off, his mind started to wake up. Who had Dolly once been? His imagination morphed Dolly into a series of male forms: smarmy banker, broken-nosed brawler, bearded hipster - then morphed back to Dolly again. It was like a gender identity parade. Ladd was sure he knew who Dolly had once been, but he couldn't put a name to him. It was quite a question, but right now, he needed to sleep. Ladd tried counting sheep. They all looked identical. Each one had Dolly's face. Flock upon flock of Dolly the Sheep, thousands of bleating clones. Dolly was seriously on his case, haunting the inside of his eyelids.

Ladd gave up. The funeral parlour was a little dead, so he sought distraction in the gadget cave. He picked up a tablet, activated a video wall, and filled it with The Gang of Four: dead Trent in monochrome; bald McMasters, lanky Proudcock and bearded Sweeney all in colour. Ladd right clicked on Sweeney's nose and selected a skull icon, turning him black and white. The Met's most diverse and inclusive covert anti-corruption unit now had an up-to-date suspect list, level at 2-2 between the dead and the living. Time well spent.

Ladd double-clicked on Sweeney's chin, triggering an infomercial. Corporate music accompanied a chunky title: "THE SMITHS - BRIEFING". The title was replaced by a family portrait of The Smiths. Ladd wondered about the efficacy of the Force's covert in-house video unit. They had all signed the Official Secrets Act, but none of them were more than a year out of their Media Studies degrees. What kind of early twentysomething chose this sort of nonsense over film, TV, ads, or music videos? Unambitious weirdos, at best.

"The Smiths make The Krays look like The Kardashians," a fruity voice-over intoned.

"This charming man is Will Smith, the boss." A suited, snarky goon in his late forties turned three-dimensional and loomed out of the portrait in a clunky After-Effects move. "Will's been acquitted of twenty-seven counts of armed robbery, and twenty-seven counts of perverting the course of justice." The screen showed a mini montage of his celebrations outside the Old Bailey. "Coincidence? You decide." Will Smith shrunk awkwardly back into the portrait.

"Kevin Smith's the wheels." A wardrobe-sized bloke in a matching suit turned 3D and expanded into the foreground. "He steals high-performance cars." The screens showed Kevin Smith smack a Ferrari into a speed bump and lift off. "Makes Lewis Hamilton look like a lollipop lady." Kevin Smith dwindled back into the family picture.

"Robert Smith's the quartermaster." A gaunt, besuited giant in his early forties expanded artlessly out of the portrait. "He supplies everything from explosives to guns." The screens showed Robert Smith at a firing range, shooting a dummy in a police uniform. "He's been linked to thirty-eight gangland murders since he turned twelve, but nothing's ever stuck." Robert Smith flattened into two dimensions and retreated to his fellow Smiths.

"Matt Smith's next generation." A tiny, baby-faced lad in his early twenties thickened and enlarged. "He's a smash-and-grab merchant, and mixed martial arts champion." The screens showed him knocking a Hell's Angel off his Harley with a flying kick. Matt Smith's image lost a dimension and faded back into the background.

"Papa Smith was the brains behind the operation." An octogenarian gangland godfather grew in stature. "Until he lost them." The screens showed Papa Smith beating up his own reflection with a walking stick. "He'd know where all the bodies were buried - if only he could remember."

The video concluded as credits rolled to brass-band accompaniment. Ladd dropped off, and the tablet flopped to the floor, changing the image on the video wall to Sweeney's contorted corpse dangling in the wind.

***

Four hours later, Goliath, Taffy, and Old Bill entered, saw their trouserless boss sat before the dead detective, and drew the most troubling conclusion possible.

"Good God, Guv," Goliath said.

"Most irregular," Old Bill added.

"Knocking one out to a cop's corpse, isn't he just," Taffy speculated.

Yang and Sue entered, squabbling in a bewildering mix of sign language, lip-reading and interpretation. Noticing their boss's state of undress and the contorted corpse on screen, Sue gasped, and Yang hit him.

Ladd jolted to his feet and gawped at his assembled squad. He paused, pinched himself, and realised it was not a dream. He looked down at his pants. This wasn't good. It was hard to sound authoritative in boxers.

After a bewildered beat, he snapped into Chief Inspector mode. "Right, there's been a murder."

Goliath handed Ladd his trousers. Being handed your trousers can be a positive thing, but it does rather draw attention to their absence. Ladd thanked Goliath and clambered into them. They were almost dry. Almost, but not quite.

"Same *modus operandi* as Trent," Ladd continued. "Bent double, up a lamppost, at a dogging site."

"Bastard's killing our suspects," Goliath complained.

"Bending like buggery, look you," Taffy added.

"We need police protection." Old Bill said. "It's basic health and safety."

Yang signed at speed, her face murderous.

"I know you're upset, Yang," Sue said on her own behalf, "But I'm saying nothing of the sort. It's filthy."

Yang made a life-threatening gesture familiar to die-hard fans of The Sopranos.

"Very well." Sue began interpreting in her cutglass accent. "Let's stop dick-licking about like a bunch of fucking assclowns and grow some cunting cazongas." Sue blushed, thoroughly humiliated, and exhausted by every expletive.

Amusement prevailed, so Ladd attempted to restore a degree of decorum. "DI Sweeney was Flying Squad, but he'd taken The Smiths' backhanders since he was in short trousers."

Ladd realised he had got his own trouser-legs muddled up and he began to reverse-hop out. It was like a silent dance; one he wasn't very good at. "You lot mount a full-scale surveillance op on their scrap yard. I'm dropping in on Dredd." Trousers entirely twisted; Ladd tripped to the floor.

***

In its two-hundred-year lifetime, the Force has boasted countless successful operations. The most fiendishly convoluted criminal enterprises have been expertly unravelled, the most daring heists thwarted, and the most depraved murderers unmasked. Gallantry medals have been earned with outstanding displays of courage; lives have been sacrificed for the public and order has been restored in the face of anarchy and insurrection. Sometimes, though, things don't turn out quite as planned.

Phantom Squad may have been North London's most diverse and inclusive covert anti-corruption unit, but their surveillance of The Smiths is unlikely to go down in the annals of criminology, except perhaps as a warning from history.

That fateful day, Phantom's hearses parked themselves outside The Smiths' HQ. The black one boasted a floral "UNCLE" tribute and a mahogany coffin. The white one had a floral "AUNTIE" display and a pine coffin. Phantom were all dressed in their usual funeral clobber, and there was nothing to indicate that the hearses were anything other than what they claimed to be.

Taffy was at the wheel of the black hearse, with Old Bill beside him. The muscle-bound Welsh Sikh and the one-armed timeserver made an odd couple, but they generally got on well enough. While they waited for signs of activity in The Smiths' scrap dealership, they passed the time with a favourite game of Old Bill's. He would read out town names from an old road map and Taffy would have to guess whether Old Bill had been there.

"Horningsham," Old Bill began.

"No," Taffy guessed.

"Yes," Old Bill, replied.

"Oh." Taffy sounded disappointed.

"Shoeburyness," Old Bill said.

"Yes," Taffy guessed.

"No," Old Bill replied.

"Oh," Taffy sounded even sadder.

"Binley," Old Bill said.

"Jaguar," Taffy replied.

"It's *yes* or *no*." Old Bill objected.

"It's a Jaguar MK II." Taffy pointed at the luxury sports saloon weaving its way through The Smiths' scrap yard. It cruised through a mountain range of spent metal, car-crushing machines, and pneumatic panel benders, before approaching a gate marked *Smith, Smith, Smith, Smith & Smith*.

Old Bill dropped his map and spoke into a squad radio. "Target on the move."

In the white "AUNTIE" hearse, Yang picked up her radio and signed vigorously into it. She communicated with extreme urgency and efficiency, but in total silence.

Goliath couldn't help but notice that she was struggling to get her message across. He turned in the specially adapted chair that enabled him to reach the steering wheel and gestured wildly at Sue in the back seat.

Sue was too busy gazing out the window to notice.

"Sue!" Goliath barked. "Do the honours."

"Oh, I am terribly sorry," Sue replied, wistfully. "I was in a bit of a reverie, thinking about a lovely evening I once spent at a dance in Sonning Common. Marvellous times."

"Sue," Goliath repeated, struggling to drag her back to the present, "Yang's signing."

"Of course," Sue replied. "Silly me. What was it again, dear?"

Yang signed a series of swear words.

"Are you really sure you want me to interpret that?" Sue asked. "It really was terribly rude."

"Sue," Goliath persisted. "You need to interpret what Yang's about to sign, and you need to speak into the squad radio."

"Gosh," Sue replied. "How very exciting. Where is it?"

Yang clutched the police radio to her chest.

"Yang," Goliath assumed the tone of a primary school teacher. "Stop being silly and hand the police radio to Sue."

Yang signed a *shan't*.

Goliath cursed, took the radio off Yang, and spoke into it. "Roger that! Sit tight!"

After Old Bill acknowledged his reply with a "Copy that," Goliath stirred the white hearse into life and followed The Smiths' Jag.

Goliath had tailed suspect vehicles in multiple war zones, but his reflexes were not quite what they were. When the Jag indicated left but turned sharp right at the last moment, Goliath reacted too late, turned left into traffic, and shouted the word, "Nobsucker!"

Sue added a "Golly!" as Goliath pulled a handbrake turn through the middle of the traffic. Horns blasted, but Goliath floored the gas pedal.

"Do be careful!" Sue gasped.

Goliath continued accelerating and caught up with The Smiths' Jag just before a roundabout. The roundabout was large, empty and had a sign advertising its availability for sponsorship. The Jag slowed and indicated left as it passed four exits in succession.

"Who do they think they are?" Goliath complained.

Yang signed a reply, which Sue interpreted. "They are London's most successful gang of armed robbers. Probably quite good at driving, at a guess."

Goliath followed the Jag on a second circuit as it indicated at every turn-off without ever actually turning off.

"They seriously think they're going to get away with this!" Goliath fumed.

"They're getaway drivers," Yang signed, and Sue interpreted. "And they obviously do think that."

"Very supportive," Goliath said, as The Smiths began a third circuit of the roundabout at even more of a plod.

"I hope you don't think I'm being terribly rude," Sue said. "But does anyone else think they might have noticed us?"

Yang signed.

"I'm not interpreting that," Sue said. "Sarcasm is the lowest form of wit."

"Never," Yang signed sarcastically.

The Jag completed its third full circuit of the roundabout then accelerated down a one-way street.

"Bastards!" Goliath bellowed at the top of his tiny lungs. "Nasty, piss-taking bastards!" He floored the gas and followed The Smiths into on-coming traffic.

A transit van swerved out of the Jag's way and careered across the hearse's path, looming at the windscreen as it passed and triggering a scream from Sue. The hearse ploughed onto the pavement, knocking a Zoomer off his e-scooter.

Goliath wrestled the steering wheel with the full force of his short, heavily muscled arms, but the hearse stalled in someone's front garden.

"May I get out please?" Sue asked. "This is all a little bit much."

"Sorry, love," Goliath replied, as he powered up the hearse. "No time."

"But I'm seventy-nine," Sue protested.

Goliath continued the pursuit at speed, Jag and hearse weaving wildly around oncoming traffic. Roadworks narrowed the road abruptly, forcing the Jag into a sea of red and white cones, and sending them skywards. Battered plastic rained on the vehicles, sending them skidding. Workmen dived for cover. A foreman smashed the hearse's front passenger window with a shovel, covering Yang in glass. She grabbed the handle and dragged the foreman along. Goliath accelerated. The foreman sprinted, holding on for his life and his shovel. Yang waited for the speed to build, then let the shovel go, sending the foreman splatting head-first into the wet concrete he had just laid.

The Jag turned into two-way traffic, and, for a while, Goliath was able to follow at a legal speed. The mood inside the hearse lifted; things were almost jolly. Here they were, tailing suspects like undercover police officers were supposed to. All seemed right with the world. Then The Smiths' Jag screeched to a stop at a green light. Goliath slammed the brakes. He hadn't ploughed into it: all that military training had been worthwhile. Goliath turned to Sue to apologise for scaring her, but something was increasingly wrong with her face. It took him a moment to realise that it was forming into a scream.

A sickening thud thumped the hearse backwards. Goliath swivelled in his special seat and slammed the reverse pedal with just about enough force to separate the bonnet from the reversing Jag. Goliath hated being on the defensive, but he had no choice. The Jag was millimetres from a second impact when it shifted into first and made a sharp turn down a side street.

Goliath powered after it, unaware that the side-street was about to become a sloping alley. The hearse dropped, the coffin shunted forwards and Sue shrieked. The gradient sharpened, and they careered downwards like bobsleigh competitors. The slope became steps, and the sheer slide became a bone-breaking judder.

Sue screamed. Yang slapped her, not altogether kindly. The Jag swerved off to the left and, for a moment, Goliath found himself bumper-to-brick with a wall. He yanked the steering wheel to the left and followed the Jag down what remained of the alley. As they emerged into the wider world, the Jag turned abruptly, revealing the black "UNCLE" hearse several moments too late to brake.

Goliath's face assumed an extreme expression rarely seen outside cartoons. Yang signed one of the worst expletives known to humanity. Sue shook, muttering "Goodness gracious" repeatedly.

Things were no calmer in the black hearse, as Phantom squad's other undercover undertakers panicked. Old Bill's blood pressure launched into the stratosphere with a "Fuuuuuuuuuck!"

Taffy followed through with a "Bollocks, look you!" as Phantom's two vehicles totalled each other.

Hearse doors sprang open like melancholy jack-in-the-boxes. Funeral flowers rearranged themselves all over the road. Coffins flew out and smashed open, revealing absent corpses.

"Well and truly buggered, aren't we just," Taffy said. "Cover story has all gone to cock."

"You said it," Old Bill added, as The Smiths' Jag pulled up alongside the mangled hearses.

Will Smith leant out of the window. "Looks like it's your funeral." The back window opened, and Matt Smith immortalised the moment on his mobile.

The Smiths had comprehensively humiliated Phantom and heaven knows they were miserable now.

PRISON DIARY – ENTRY 8

Naomi began the session by staring intently at the cow. I watched her for a while, wondering what meaning she could discern in the depths of its bovine eyes, and what mysteries lay buried in the inept brushwork, and the excessive udders.

"Imagine being that carefree!" she exclaimed in wonder. "Oh, to be stupid! Oh, to be cared for!"

"Oh, to be milked!" I added.

"What?"

"Just trying to join in," I said. "How's life?"

She looked at me as if I had asked her the most stupid question in history. I have asked infinitely more stupid questions in my time, but Naomi wasn't to know that.

"Your car crash..." Naomi began.

"The Phantom hearses?"

"It was quite triggering."

"Sorry. I didn't realise you drove a hearse."

"My life's a car crash! A total write-off!"

"Oh dear."

"Oh dear? Is that all you can say?"

"There's a reason I'm an unemployed life coach."

"Right, shall we start?"

"Let's."

"Okay, so, going back a bit, why did you decide to call your gang *The Smiths*?"

"Jeff likes humming them."

"The armed robber?"

"Yes."

"It's extremely distracting."

"The humming?"

"The name."

"They've got to be called something though, haven't they?"

"I suppose so, yes."

"Well, what do you suggest? The Weasleys? Mumford and Sons? The Jackson Five?"

"Any more?" Naomi asked, wearily, not expecting me to oblige.

"The Osbournes?" I continued. "The Munsters? The Muppets?"

"The Muppets aren't a family."

"Are you sure?"

"If they were, Kermit and Miss Piggy would be committing incest."

"Did they ever actually get it together though?"

"How should I know? I'm not a Muppet."

"No, Naomi, you're not." I wasn't convinced.

"Maybe we were better off with The Smiths."

"That's what I was trying to tell you."

"Right, the thing is, The Smiths aren't just an iconic indie band from the 1980s, you've also opted to make each of the gang individually famous."

"Well spotted."

"Matt Smith is an actor, isn't he?"

"*Doctor Who*, *The Crown*, and that one with all the dragons."

"Robert Smith?"

"Flouncy great goth with crow's nest hair, eyeliner, and lipstick. Sang about death, love, and spiders, in *The Cure*."

"Will Smith?"

"The slapper."

"Slapper?"

"His wife was in Chris Rock's mouth, and he didn't like it."

"Eh?"

"You know, *The Fresh Prince*."

"Right. Kevin Smith?"

"Bit obscure, that one. American slacker dude. Directed stoner films in the nineties."

"Papa Smith?"

"Bit like Papa Smurf. Remember the little blue people who live in mushrooms?"

"What?"

"It was a cartoon."

"Very well. Thinking about the narrative as a whole, it's not got any more respectful of the police, has it?"

"Ladd means well."

"But he's a disaster on legs. Do you resent the police for catching you?"

"I only burgled my own house."

"It wasn't your house. How many times do I have to remind you."

"I thought it was, though."

"Do you not see the parallels?"

"No."

"You think all kinds of wrong things when you're writing. You could put them right before you write."

"But why are they wrong?"

"Your address was wrong."

"But it seemed right at the time."

"And now you're in prison."

"Don't crow about it."

"Sorry."

"You get to go back to the world after our sessions. I get to go back to Jeff."

"I know. It can't be easy."

"Jeff's all right."

I headed to my cell. Jeff seemed to be in jovial spirits. He'd been reading *The Silence of the Lambs* and wouldn't stop banging on about cannibalism.

We discussed the film for a while and agreed that the Lecter-Starling cell encounter was probably the best prison scene in cinema history, better than anything in *The Shawshank Redemption* or even *Porridge*.

Jeff turned out to be a bit of a film buff. Nothing noticeably French or Swedish, but he could tell his Easy Riders from his Raging Bulls. I told him my favourite film was *Ocean's Eleven*, with its stellar cast and madcap casino heist. Jeff hadn't watched it. He didn't like to be reminded of work.

I was ploughing my way through volume eight of *The Greatest Mistakes in British*

Policing. A lot of the best police errors concerned informants. Criminals would weave complex tissues of bollocks, and gullible cops would believe them, falling into elephant traps like a troupe of plonkers. I particularly admired one prisoner, who persuaded the police to let him set up a heist on condition that he grass up everyone else involved. The police gave him a secret office in the prison, he phoned up prominent members of the criminal fraternity, and he recruited them for the job. He insisted he had to be released in order to rehearse the heist with the villains, and they agreed. The dry run turned out to be the real deal, he nicked the proceeds and did a runner. Job done. He should have won an award, perhaps a Pulitzer Prize for Pisstaking.

AGENT PROVOCATEUR

While his colleagues were busy mourning each other's hearses, Ladd was in a specially hired Land Rover Defender, jaunting off to meet the Chief Superintendent he'd had incarcerated for corruption.

Ladd could not have been more delighted to put a few miles between himself and his wife, his mistress, his blackmailer, the Bender, the Transnistrian-Transylvanian gang war, and his lingerie. What he really needed was a holiday, or possibly a new identity, but a trip up the A1 to interview a bloke who hated him more than anyone else alive would just have to do.

For most people, bosses are people you suck up to, try not to upset, and pretend to agree with, and as a gifted liar, Ladd had risen through the ranks by doing exactly that. But with Dredd, Ladd had done the opposite: he had put him under surveillance for nine days, hidden in his drain, and had him banged up for taking bungs. This had won him promotion and a transfer to London's most diverse and inclusive covert anti-corruption unit, but frankly, he wished he hadn't bothered. No one likes a sneak and within the Force, he was now about as popular as Ebola.

Semi-rural, semi-urban, neither-here-nor-there Hertfordshire was a nondescript county rimming the Chilterns. It was distinctly lacking in fjords, canyons, rainforests, and other geographical features that might have taken Ladd's mind off the catastrophic decimation of his personal life, so he spent a fraught forty-five minutes fighting off images of tasers, lockjaw, and boob tubes.

After he had passed a few farms and film studios, Ladd approached a grim institutional building that might once have been a Victorian asylum. It made your average prison look like a branch of Centre Parcs, and he almost felt guilty for putting Dredd in such a soul-crushing place. Almost, but not entirely. When it came to corruption, Dredd was a visionary, the Steve Jobs of moral bendability. He had masterminded police protection rackets that would have embarrassed Al Capone, he was a serial perverter of justice, and he had taken so many bungs, he'd had to launder his own bribes. As officers of the law went, he was not what any right-thinking citizen would have called an asset, and Ladd reserved his pity for more deserving cases, notably himself.

Dredd's colossal corruption would have placed him in Pentonville, but his decision to turn supergrass against The Gang of Four had plonked him in the boondocks. His testimony had implications for policing at all levels across the Force, so, in theory, Dredd was doing the right thing. But in practice, he was endangering his own life to the extent that he had to be held in a dedicated building as secure and welcoming as Colditz.

Ladd had never relished prison visits. It wasn't just that cops were unwelcome, it was the way in which prisons reinforced the futility of his professional existence. All his efforts went into consigning people to captivity and, within a few minutes of being inside a prison, it was always painfully evident to Ladd that this was a waste of time. Prisons worked as extensive networking events for convicted criminals and, apart from the odd creative writing course and industriously maintained library, there was no scope for anything but regret. The angry became permanently resentful, the unhinged became deranged and the young became old before they'd had a chance to live.

Ladd drew up to a set of iron gates overseen by a leering gargoyle and a scowling guard. He wondered what cataclysmic misfortunes would lead someone to become a custodian of a converted asylum like this. What career-terminating disgraces must they have endured before this became the best option? As the mirthless gatekeeper scrutinized his identity documents, it didn't seem wise to ask. The guard gave him a begrudging nod and the gates heaved open like a Hammer Horror tomb. Visitor parking facilities were in scarce supply, but so were visitors.

Ladd locked his Defender, rather pointlessly, then approached another forbidding entrance. It wasn't the last. As he wended his way through the building's formidable bowels, Ladd had to satisfy a sequence of sentries, the most human of which was an AI.

After the seventh anchor-heavy gate clanged shut behind him, a guard slightly shy of seven feet gave him a grim smile. "Tell him nothing," he advised in a voice that made Barry White sound like a soprano. "Believe me, you don't want Dredd in your head."

A solid steel door buzzed open, and the guard gestured towards one of the least inviting walkways this side of Death Row.

Ladd approached Dredd's cell with actual dread. He hadn't clapped eyes on his former boss since he had brought his glittering career crashing down around his ears and he didn't imagine that he had been forgiven.

It was no ordinary prison cell. The front wall's ultra-thick, bulletproof glass was punctuated by a waist-level letterbox, and the other three walls sported sketches of Ladd in compromising positions: cowering in a drain, stabbing Dredd in the back, Morris dancing nude. If there was one thing Ladd hated, it was Morris dancing. Ex-Superintendent Nathaniel Dredd presided over the whole humiliating exhibition from the centre of the cell, as calm and remote as a statue, inhaling from a vape the size of a revolver.

Dredd shook his full, greying dreadlocks, and said, "Wah gwaan."

I hadn't driven to Hertfordshire to trade street slang. "Bullet-proof glass?"

"Health and safety gone mad." Dredd sniffed the air, like a Jamaican Hannibal Lecter. "You still stink of shit."

"Nine days in your drain."

"Highlight of your career."

"It put you in a cell."

"Protective custody, innit. Safe for now, free soon enough."

If there was one thing Ladd enjoyed about dealing with criminals, it was pulling the proverbial rug from under their feet. There they would be, relying on something they took to be a certainty, and all the while you knew that it had crumbled. That was the great advantage of separating them from the world. He looked at Dredd's smug expression and prepared to alter it dramatically for the worse. "Your evidence has halved in value."

"Trent and Sweeney," Dredd deadpanned. "Tragic loss to modern policing."

It was Ladd's countenance that soured. How on Earth had news of the fatal bendings seeped into Dredd's isolation cell? He couldn't allow him to see that he was unnerved, so he went in for the kill: "If we don't catch The Bender soon, you'll be giving us a Gang of None. Strangeways, here we come."

"I can get you The Smiths." Dredd blew a vape ring, like a Rastafarian Gandalf.

"From here?" Ladd scoffed.

"I'd be an *active informant*.".

You'd be an alpha bullshitter, Ladd thought. Dredd was fiddling with the truth like the bent boss he had so recently been. Scientists refer to extreme cold as *Absolute Zero* and it struck Ladd that Dredd had long since attained a point of extreme untruth that could be termed *Absolute Bollocks*. But Ladd had to hear him out, if only for the entertainment value.

"How active?" Ladd asked.

"I'd need to do a job with them." Dredd opened the letterbox and offered the vape to Ladd. "Can I tempt you?"

Ladd was no vapist, but he did listen to Dredd's plan, and it was absolutely ingenious. Every detail of the proposed heist had been honed with the skill and assiduity of a top brass police officer with time on his hands, and as for the target, Ladd could not contain his laughter; the irony was off the scale.

Ladd negotiated his way back through the security gates with a smile on his face. Somehow, the adversaries had bonded through the bullet-proof glass. It was the last thing Ladd had expected.

As he passed Hertfordshire's bleak business parks, poorly planned towns, unpopular shopping centres and places called things like Bushey, Tring and Boggy Bottom, Ladd's mind raced. He knew he couldn't trust Dredd, but his ingenious plan would entrap The Smiths and put Ladd's name in the Force's Roll of Honour for centuries. Maybe he would even be invited to join the freemasons.

The Smiths had been a symbol of the capital's policing failures for three generations. Britain's most blatant blaggers sat resplendent in their own colossal scrapyard, picking off targets with impunity, and they were so obviously in cahoots with bent coppers, they might as well have been sponsored by Scotland Yard. Now, Dredd was offering him the chance to take them down. He marvelled at the plan's ingenuity: an ex-police officer creates a heist from scratch and persuades master criminals to carry it out, leaving Ladd to arrest them and take the glory. It was the kind of ballsy, fearless move that really got him fired up. He could put the whole cross-dressing charade behind him and be a real thief-taker, a man of action once again.

Too late, Ladd realised he had gone through a speed-camera. It was a flasher, not a dummy, but if he was going to take down The Smiths, he had to be the kind of guy who didn't care about speeding tickets. He needed to cross a few lines, and live life on the edge. Traffic enforcement could do their worst.

As he closed in on North London, Ladd even started having positive thoughts about his squad. He was so lucky to head up such a diverse and inclusive unit, and in their different ways, they all brought something unique to the anti-corruption party. Tiny Goliath's Special Forces experience, one-armed Old Bill's talent for paperwork, tough Taffy's sing-song irreverence, deaf Yang's fearsome energy and the sheer speed and accuracy of geriatric Sue's interpretations. Phantom were something to be proud of, his very own SAS. He couldn't wait to find out how their surveillance of The Smiths had gone.

The funeral parlour was unusually hearse-less. Perhaps Phantom were still out on the operation. He thought about all the valuable information his squad would have gained over the course of the morning. It would be doubly useful: The Smiths were not only potential benders, they were also the targets of Dredd's sting operation, and every scrap of information was a potential nail in their coffins.

Ladd skipped past the display coffins, booted the stone angel, and the cherub wall zipped up. Phantom were all assembled, and Ladd was so buoyed by enthusiasm, he barely looked at them before asking, "Surveillance a success?"

"Bit of a car crash, Guv," Goliath replied, morosely.

Ladd looked properly at his assembled squad. There were more bandages than he'd seen in A & E.

No one seemed inclined to speak. Goliath just fiddled miserably with a tablet and the video wall filled with The Smiths' Instagram images of terminal hearse-on-hearse action. #KeystoneCops #UndercoverCockup and #PhantomMenace were among the most popular hashtags. Ladd was starting to question whether the operation had been an unbridled success.

Old Bill nursed his neck. "I'm suing Phantom for whiplash."

"Never seen parking that dangerous." Taffy said, moping on his crutches.

Yang and Sue were also sulking, but they were some distance apart. Sue appeared unscathed, but Yang boasted a panoply of minor injuries. Given the fifty-year age gap between the women, Ladd was glad it was that way around, but he thought it best just to ask Yang if she was all right.

Yang signed extensively with superhuman energy and fury. It was the longest, most intensive burst of signing Ladd had ever seen. Perhaps she was relaying some epic tale of heroism in adversity, something extraordinary for the annals of anti-corruption. He couldn't wait to find out.

When Yang finally stopped, all eyes fell on Sue. But Sue just sat there in silence.

Ladd turned to the rest of the squad. They shrugged.

"We're not on speaking terms," Sue explained.

"But you're her interpreter." Sometimes, Ladd despaired.

Yang signed again.

Sue just tutted and said nothing.

Yang signed once more, extremely abruptly.

Ladd had no time for this. He turned to Sue, and adopted as stern a tone as he could with a woman of almost eighty. "What did she just say?"

"She called me a ..." Sue held back a sob.

Ladd felt for the poor lady. She should be at home, listening to Garde*ner's Question Time* and knitting, rather than being abused in sign language.

Sue finally gathered the strength to complete her sentence. "...a.... bitch." Sue burst into tears. "It's not my fault I fell on her."

It was a horrible moment. Squad morale was at its lowest possible ebb and Ladd didn't have a solution. Luckily, Ladd's phone rang, and he snatched it like a lifeline. "Ma'am."

"I love it when you call me Ma'am," the Super replied. "It makes me feel all ..."

"Hang on, Ma'am," Ladd interrupted. "You're on speaker."

Normally, a mishap like this would have triggered general merriment, but the hearse collision had sucked all the fun out of the covert anti-corruption unit. Ladd muted the call, made his apologies, and left Phantom to nurse their injuries and their resentment.

***

The Super was a clear foot shorter than Ladd and around half his weight, but that didn't stop her dragging him through her hallway to show him her new downstairs. It was quite a sight. The lounge was crammed with uncomfortable antique furniture and eccentric artefacts: a stuffed dodo, a suit of armour with a giant codpiece, a gentle watercolour of a jackal-headed Egyptian god mummifying a pharaoh, a woodcut of a pirate ship falling off the edge of the world, and in the middle of it all, a grand piano completely covered in tarpaulin.

"Nice gaff." Ladd lied, more worried than impressed.

The Super eased him onto a chaise longue and straddled his lap. "Both pathology reports are in."

"Stiffs revealing?"

"The bendings could be linked."

"Well, fuck me sideways," Ladd said with sarcasm.

"Nice idea." The Super rolled Ladd sidelong onto the chaise longue, then gave him a look of unquestionable seriousness. "Stop living a lie."

"What?" Ladd's panic rose. Had Tina been gossiping? Had Dolly tired of waiting for her money and contacted the Force? "What have you heard?"

"Leave Tina." It was as bald and incontestable as an order.

Ladd's heart stopped.

The Super held the moment, then giggled. "Your face!"

Ladd blushed. "What are you like, Ma'am!"

The Super showed him what she could be like by kissing him enthusiastically. Then she showed him what she could also be like by pulling away abruptly and asking, "How's Dredd?"

"He wants to be let out."

"Course he does."

"To do a heist with the Smiths."

"What's he been smoking?"

"Super Grass," Ladd deadpanned.

The Super facepalmed.

"Sorry, Ma'am." Ladd said, although he wasn't really. It had been one of his better puns, and it switched the mood back to steamy. The Super tore off his shirt. She seemed to enjoy mixing business and pleasure, so he decided to elaborate on the planned heist. "Dredd would act as an agent provocateur."

"Like the knickers." The Super pulled down his trousers.

"He'd persuade The Smiths to do a job and we'd catch them at it."

"I'd only sanction that if a Phantom officer was undercover with him," the Super said sternly, as she removed her blouse.

"The Smiths' surveillance went tits up," Ladd admitted.

She caressed his crotch. "You mean you're blown?"

"I'm the only one uncompromised." Ladd un-pinged her bra.

"Then you're our man." She prepared to mount him at an ambitious angle.

"Seriously?"

"All we have to do is convince the Attorney General." The Super's docking operation proved insurmountable.

Ladd lifted her back above his lap. "Does he hold a grudge?"

"Depends. What are we stealing?"

"The police pension fund."

The Super fell off the chaise longue.

***

The journey to Westminster was tense. The Super was suffering from shock, minor bruising, and sexual frustration, and Ladd's decision to take the Land Rover had misfired. He loved the hire car and wished he could keep it, but it didn't have any sirens, and the tube would have taken half the time.

"My elbow hurts," the Super complained. "And my hip." She shuffled on her seat. "And my knee."

"Sorry, Ma'am." Ladd placed a soothing hand on her thigh.

"Keep your hands on the wheel!"

"Of course, Ma'am." Ladd swerved back into the correct lane and raised an apologetic hand to the ambulance he had just cut up.

Ladd knew the Super was annoyed, but at least she had embraced his madcap scheme. She was a woman with real balls, and he was proud to be shagging her.

"How do you think we should pitch this to the Attorney General?" Ladd asked, as they passed Hyde Park Corer.

"Well, you've already done the groundwork, and smoothed the way nicely, haven't you?"

"Have I, Ma'am?"

"Of course not! You don't suck up to Britain's greatest legal mind by landing on his head, do you?"

"I was thrown, Ma'am."

"Well, I wish you hadn't been."

"Likewise, Ma'am."

Ladd's close encounter with the ambulance had made him hyper-aware of the West End's kamikaze couriers, marauding vans and app-driven cabs. The platoons of phone-enchanted pedestrian zombies Tik-Toking into traffic were probably the most careless, but he wasn't so worried about them - a human collision would only cause minor damage to the Land Rover. It was not the calmest environment to prepare for a make-or-break meeting, particularly as he had broken the bones of the man who would make or break it. Cunning was in order.

"Do you have much to do with the Attorney General, Ma'am?"

"Not if I can help it, no."

"Nice bloke, is he?"

"Arse doesn't cover it. I've got nothing against yanks, but he talks like a Chicago mobster, and behaves like one too."

Ladd recalled the controversy surrounding the appointment of a tough-talking Republican whose zero tolerance policies had cleansed Chicago's streets of crime. Not everyone had welcomed a foreigner who believed in on-the-spot capital punishment, burglar nuking and the transportation of shoplifters to Chernobyl, but others saw this as a firm-but-fair approach only resisted by liberal snowflakes.

"So, what do you reckon on our chances, Ma'am?"

"What, now?"

"Yes, Ma'am."

"What do I reckon to our chances of convincing the Attorney General to give the go-ahead to the theft of the police pension fund?"

"Yes, Ma'am."

"On the suggestion of the most colossally bent supergrass in the history of the Met?"

"Yes, Ma'am."

"Spearheaded by the DCI who has just hospitalized him during the successful escape of a convicted murderer?"

"Yes, Ma'am."

"Depends."

"It does, doesn't it?"

They shared a conspiratorial smile, parked on a red line, and cooked up a plan.

***

All started swimmingly in the Attorney General's office. Ladd and the Super made such a persuasive tag team, it was almost too obvious that they were conducting an affair. The Super outlined the desirability of bringing down The Smiths, and Ladd argued passionately for a bold move that no "snowflake" would have the guts to make. But when it came to revealing the target of the heist, things went seriously south.

"It's an underground raid on a vault containing the gold underpinning..." Ladd took a deep breath, "Every investment made ...by the police pension fund."

"Are you NUTS?!" The Attorney General chucked his wig in Ladd's face, hoisted himself onto his crutches and swung around his oak-panelled office. "Only three people have ever been dumb enough to try and steal the police pension fund!"

Ladd and the Super shared a worried glance as England's most senior lawyer pranced on his crutches and ranted. It was as if he had just been pitched the least promising casino heist in the history of Las Vegas.

"In third place," the Attorney General said, "A wartime black marketeer, name of Pickles. This fruit-loop tried reaching the vault through a secret network of ancient catacombs under The City." The Attorney General swung up to Ladd and eyeballed him. "What do you reckon happened to him, huh?"

"Didn't end well, sir." Ladd didn't like being eyeballed.

"Didn't end well? Of course it didn't end well! The freakin' freemasons knocked him out with a flying mace and hoisted him on a pike."

"Painful, I should imagine, sir," Ladd acknowledged.

"Second place." The Attorney General lurched around the room, propelled by the feral force of his scepticism. "1984. A spiky-haired Goth freak tried his luck in the sewers."

"Reckless, sir," Ladd said, hoping to pre-empt a second eyeballing.

"Reckless? You bet! The freak crawled through a sea of sewage and came out dead on the other side."

"Nasty, sir," Ladd acknowledged.

"And in first place," the Attorney General concluded. "2003, the closest anyone's come. Bunch of Serbian war vets swam down an underground river and made it into the gold vault. Spent a few happy minutes helping themselves to armfuls of bars. But it was too many minutes. At the tenth, they triggered a lock-in and the ceiling became a massive power shower. Those Serbs sure could swim, but boy could they drown. They bobbed in the flooded vault like Halloween apples."

"Horrific, sir," Ladd noted.

"But what am I saying?" The Attorney General concluded his crutch-propelled rant. "The Smiths are pros, Dredd's the first Jamaican ex-tube driver to make Chief Superintendent and you, Ladd..." He raised a crutch and prodded Ladd in the chest, "You know how to fall out of windows."

"Thank you, sir. Much appreciated."

"Even if you get the gold, you're still miles from daylight."

"You're right, sir," Ladd conceded.

"He's right," the Super added.

"We got greedy, sir," Ladd said. "We wanted London's top crime family and prime cop-bending suspects behind bars. It's just too big a result."

Ladd opened the door for the Super, but as she stepped forward, he turned back to make one final pitch. "Greatest sting in the history of the Force - all masterminded by you, the nation's pre-eminent legal gunslinger."

The Attorney General swung over to the window and gazed out on London mizzle for what felt like an eternity. Eventually, he swung back and gave Ladd a different kind of eyeballing, an eyeballing that could only be classed as affirmative. "Screw this up and I'll harvest your organs and sell them on eBay." He waved a crutch like King Arthur brandishing Excalibur.

***

Ladd and the Super managed to make it down most of the Attorney General's corridor before they burst out laughing like a pair of exploding raspberries.

"I knew it!" Ladd guffawed. "What a prize twat!"

"The size of his ego!" The Super exclaimed.

"Exactly! A bit of flattery and he'll agree to anything."

She grabbed Ladd's hand and pulled him towards her.

"Yes, Mam?"

"Danny, you are a little genius!" She stood on her tiptoes and planted a kiss on his chin.

"Not so shabby yourself, Ma'am. We make a decent double act."

"Not always decent." The Superintendent fondled his trousers.

Ladd wished she hadn't. This was the Attorney General's headquarters and there was a time and a place for adultery.

Sensing his reservations, the Super abandoned Ladd's crotch and turned severe. "Don't screw it up. Remember, it's our pensions you're playing with."

"Yes, Ma'am."

"And I meant what I said about leaving Tina."

PRISON DIARY – ENTRY 9

Naomi was in a strop. I wished she wouldn't get herself in such a state. It couldn't be good for her health.

"You're asking me to believe that a Chief Inspector running an anti-corruption squad is going on a heist to steal the police pension fund?"

"Could happen." I shrugged.

"Could it?"

"Well, according to volume eight of *The Greatest Mistakes in British Policing*, it could."

"Volume eight?"

"There were a lot of mistakes."

"Including a police heist?"

"The police got a prisoner to do a heist that wouldn't have happened without their involvement."

"Well, sometimes entrapment works. Did they catch many criminals?"

"None. But the heist was a success, at least for the prisoner."

"But not for the police?"

"No, they never caught him."

Naomi's lower lip began to quiver. "Sounds as disappointing as my marriage."

Not again! It was becoming more of a creative whingeing class than creative writing. "I'm sure you can patch things up," I said without a clue whether she could.

"I threw Roly out."

"Can't you ask him back."

"The cleaner and the au pair were bad enough, but then I caught him with our marriage guidance councillor."

"Oh no. I'm so sorry," I said, stifling a chuckle.

"And the worst thing is, Innsbruck and Gethsemane blame me. It's not fair. What the hell did I do?"

"It's probably for the best," I said.

"Is it? Why?"

I had no idea. I'd just said it to sound sympathetic. "Look, I'm the last person to advise about marriage."

"Did yours fail too?"

"All eight of them."

"Eight?"

"I don't do things by halves."

"Why have you been married so many times?"

"They just pass their sell-by-dates, I suppose."

"Women are not dairy products," Naomi said.

"I'm aware of that."

We both looked at the cow. She seemed to be judging us.

Eventually, Naomi cheered up and leant in towards me. "Tell me what happened. I'd like to know."

I drew a deep breath and told her. "My first wife left me for my social worker, my second wife left me after I crashed the car into the lounge, my third wife left me after I got sent down for benefit fraud, my fourth wife left me when she discovered I was having an affair with my probation officer, my fifth wife left me because she was bored, my sixth wife left me because I didn't like her dog, my seventh wife left me after all my DIY collapsed and the house became uninhabitable, and my eighth wife left me when she found out how often I'd been married."

Naomi touched my hand reassuringly. She wasn't meant to, but I was glad she did.

I returned to my cell and found Jeff cross-referencing two books: *Tunnelling – A Practical Guide* and *Potholing For Beginners*. He explained that tunnelling was distinct from potholing because of the digging. Potholers tended to explore existing holes, whereas tunnellers made new ones. By becoming expert in both disciplines, he clearly hoped to be able to create escape routes and clamber through them at maximum speed, but he was never going to say that out loud.

While he focused on tunnelling techniques, Jeff let me borrow his potholing book for a bit. It turns out that the most famous British pothole is called *Gaping Gill* and that Americans call potholing *spelunking*. Extreme spelunkers specialise in cave squeezes and have a habit of getting stuck, and cave divers often swim into floating skeletons from the distant past. I had to admire the lot of them: potholers were like introverted astronauts, exploring the final frontiers of Inner Space. It took a certain bravery too: in the same way that high-wire walkers and skydivers seemed to lack a vertigo gene, potholers had no trace of claustrophobia. This got me thinking about further torments to inflict on Chief Inspector Danny Ladd.

POTHOLING

The trip back to Hertfordshire offered Ladd another chance to take the Land Rover for a spin and afforded much-needed remission from his affair, his marriage, and his blackmailer. Free from the caprices of his mercurial mistress and unburdened by his fake cross-dressing habit, he had an hour or so of liberty before embarking on a heist with his bent ex-boss and London's most notorious armed robbers. He thought back to his hallowed days at Hendon and how he had dreamt of becoming a master thief-taker, outsmarting crooks with his razor-sharp deductions and do-or-die bravery. He had never imagined that his career would climax in a heist on his own pension fund.

Arrangements for Dredd's release had progressed at pace. When you have the Attorney General behind you, legal hurdles are as easily vaulted as croquet hoops. Ladd was distinctly ambivalent about working with his former boss: he would never recover from his nine-day stretch in Dredd's drain, danker than a grave and with less wiggle room. But, as he drove past Watford public library, Ladd's pulse raced. He was about to embark on the most dangerous mission of his life, boldly straddling the thin blue line of the law – and he felt sure it could make him a hero.

The former funny farm looked even grimmer than last time, but Ladd didn't have to set foot in it. Dredd was waiting outside the iron gates, sporting the spotless uniform Ladd had arrested him in. He had a way of standing to attention with such anarchic defiance, he could have been a Rastafarian Che Guevara.

Ladd was determined not to display a shred of deference. When he had been a Chief Inspector, Dredd had lorded it over everyone. Now he was disgraced, he had better show a modicum of respect. Ladd drew up beside Dredd and zapped open the front passenger door. Dredd ignored it and yanked at the back door. Once Ladd had relented, Dredd slumped supinely into the rear, and snapped his fingers, as if Ladd was his personal chauffeur.

Two minutes into the journey, Dredd sparked up his gun-sized vape.

"That's against regs," Ladd objected, as a smoke ring lassoed the rear-view mirror.

"So are heists." Dredd replied.

He had a point, so Ladd concentrated on perfecting an anti-vape driving style full of jerks, swerves, and judders. Dredd struggled not to swallow his own smoke, but it didn't stop him vaping.

Before Ladd and Dredd could be covertly inserted into the heist, police protocol dictated that they both complete a *Health and Safety Induction*, a *Compliance Course* and a *Diversity and Inclusion Briefing*. These were all held in a conference room at the back of the worst hotel in Cricklewood and were run by young facilitators who had all signed the Official Secrets Act.

The *Diversity and Inclusion* facilitator had blue hair and she required that terminology remain appropriate and non-threatening throughout the heist. There would be no references to "snatches", "slags", or "nonces", and all discrimination and colonial attitudes had to be challenged at every opportunity.

"Look at me!" Dredd demanded after the first three hours had elapsed. "Do I look like a colonialist?"

"Don't you want to call out your white privilege and become an anti-racist ally?" the facilitator asked.

Dredd kissed his teeth. "I am the first Rastafarian Chief Superintendent in the history of the Force."

"Was," Ladd corrected.

"Racist," Dredd deadpanned.

The facilitator seized her chance to confront Ladd. "Well?"

"Dredd is no longer a Super," Ladd said.

"That's your opinion." The facilitator sensed a breakthrough moment. "Do you have to be white to be *super*?"

"No," Ladd replied. "I didn't say that."

"It's what you were thinking," the facilitator said.

"Unspoken racism," Dredd added.

"That's right." the facilitator said, "If you want to become an ally, you need to acknowledge your prejudices."

"How is this relevant to the heist in hand?" Ladd asked.

"It could not be more relevant," the facilitator said. "You need to de-colonialise your attitudes."

"Attitude," Dredd said. "That's all this white *bwoy* gives me. Attitude."

After two hours of intensive cultural awareness drills and persistent bickering, Ladd had embraced the power of inclusion, but had not embraced Dredd, largely because he hated him.

Compliance began with a lecture on the importance of transparency from a bloke in a see-through shirt.

"It's a covert insertion," Ladd protested after the first hour. "There's lots of pretending involved. We're not meant to be transparent - we're meant to be …".

"Opaque," Dredd added, vaping an impenetrable cloud of skunk all over Ladd.

"Is he allowed to do that?" Ladd asked.

"It calms me down," Dredd said.

"It winds me up," Ladd said.

"Mental health!" the facilitator shrilled.

"What's that got to do with it?" Ladd asked.

"Vaping supports his mental health," the facilitator said.

"How about my actual health?" Ladd spluttered through the vape-cloud.

"We've got a lot to get through," the facilitator said. "Next, freedom of information."

"But the operation's secret," Ladd objected. "We work on a need-to-know basis."

"I don't know about that," the facilitator replied. "All operations must proceed in a spirit of openness. And the same goes for social media awareness."

"We're not putting the heist on Twitter," Ladd protested.

The facilitator sighed. "You would be ignoring a whole generation. Socials are their primary means of communication."

"I'm very happy to ignore them," Ladd said.

"Dinosaur," Dredd added, vaping him.

The facilitator elaborated on protocols regarding Anti-Money Laundering, Anti-Bribery, Anti-Corruption and Erasure.

"Hold on a minute," Ladd said. "What have 1980s bands got to do with this?"

"Erasure," the facilitator replied. "The right to be forgotten."

"That's what I want," Dredd said. "A new identity."

Health and Safety was hazardous. Neither Ladd nor Dredd would give the other First Aid, preferring to inflict simulated injuries and leave each other dying in pools of their own virtual blood.

At the end of a long day, after every bureaucratic box had been ticked, both men were handed course completion certificates, then told to burn them for security reasons.

During their fateful encounter at the glass-fronted cell, Dredd had outlined what Ladd's undercover role, or *legend*, would be in the heist, but until this point, he had blocked it out of his mind. Ladd knew how important the role was, but he also knew how much pleasure his suffering would bring Dredd. But whether it was vengeance or necessity, there was no going back now.

Ladd looked at Dredd through the flaming embers of his compliance certificate and said, "You've not made this easy for me."

"Did you expect me to?"

"Of all the legends to give me."

"Champion potholer."

"I'm claustrophobic."

"Nothing to do with your time in my drain, was it?"

Ladd shuddered. "Still get flashbacks."

"Your fault. Snaking on your Super."

"Can't snake on a snake."

"Enjoy your training, *bwoy*." Dredd kissed his teeth, then went off to insert himself into The Smiths.

***

Ladd's potholing boot camp was in a remote cranny of North Wales. The journey took five-and-a-half hours and, by the time he arrived, his hotel had closed for the night. After ringing the bell repeatedly, a Welsh pensioner berated him for being English and showed the way to a converted broom cupboard with a child-sized bed. He would have got more sleep standing up.

Breakfast was only available after the time he had to leave, so he drove off hungry. The landscape was wounded with gaping quarries and bruised with purple-grey slag heaps. After he had snaked his way through some of the most contorted roads on the planet, he reached a giant sign in two languages. The Welsh words were in an intricate, luminous gold typeface. The English words were in felt tip, and read, *Potholing, Look You.*

Ladd parked and a fierce wind met him with a scream. The place wasn't just desolate it was post-apocalyptic, or possibly pre-human. But Ladd wasn't entirely alone. A small, skinny bloke ambushed him from behind a crag and spoke intensely in Welsh.

"Sorry -" Ladd began before the man interrupted.

"English, is it?"

Ladd shrugged an apology.

"Well, we'll have none of that filth spoken around here."

"Jolly good," Ladd said, forgetting himself immediately.

The man shook his head in disgust and led Ladd to a corrugated iron shed. Inside, fifteen other small, skinny blokes in filthy orange jumpsuits sat on benches fiddling with their headlamps and looking closely related. The first man said something abrupt about Ladd in Welsh. The shed practically exploded with hilarity. Ladd was starting to think that he wasn't a natural fit.

A striking lady of Afro-Caribbean heritage strode in. She was wearing an immaculate turquoise jumpsuit and carried a clipboard. Ladd nodded at her, hoping she was a fellow city-dweller or maybe even a Londoner, but her thirty-eight-minute Welsh induction suggested otherwise. Ladd had never seen anyone pause for breath so infrequently; she could have been a sperm whale from Wrexham.

When the induction finally climaxed, there was a moment of calm before the instructor led everyone else in what seemed to be a Welsh mining ballad, complete with pick-hacking mimes, and a tragic ending. Ladd's were the only dry eyes in the shed.

The instructor clapped her hands, and everyone stood up. Ladd was a full foot taller than the other men. Only the instructor was able to look him in the eye without craning her neck.

She addressed him in Welsh.

"Sorry," Ladd replied. "I'm English."

"Then why the bloody hell didn't you say so?"

"Didn't want to interrupt."

"There's a full translation on the website."

Ladd got out his phone. "What's it called?"

She replied with a string of consonants climaxing in a raspberry.

Ladd typed down what he could and searched. 5G was NG. "What's the Wi-Fi?"

"Not much call for Wi-Fi around here," she said. "We prefer talking to each other, not like you nerdy English spods."

"Then just tell me what I need to know. Please."

She sighed and gave an exasperated Welsh explanation to the other occupants of the shed. After various Welsh expressions of general irritation and impatience, everyone went quiet and stared resentfully at Ladd while the instructor rattled through the basics in English.

The instructor explained that this had been a proud mining community before the English closed the pits. Now, after years of unemployment, the locals were retraining as potholers so they could offer caving tours to Chinese tourists. Although everyone was a beginner, she didn't expect anyone else to struggle – they all had digging in their DNA, and their small, wiry frames were perfect for negotiating all the narrow underground spaces. He, on the other hand, was a hefty specimen better built for rugby, but she could guide him through it, provided he followed her every instruction and did not suffer from claustrophobia.

Ladd blanched. The remembered horrors of Dredd's drain and the Transnistrian fish barrel threatened to engulf his brain, but he mastered his fears and chose not to mention his claustrophobia. There was a police heist at stake, after all.

Ladd spent the next few hours squeezing himself into holes the size of body bags and screaming. The other trainees breezed through every exercise like subterranean gymnasts and gathered to watch his suffering. Soon, he was repeatedly burying himself alive purely for the entertainment of people who hated him. The instructor was right about his body: he was built not to pothole. Height was an issue, but width was the main problem. Ladd's shoulders could have given the average wardrobe a run for its money, and he lost count of the times that the other trainees had to push, pull, and shove him up and down smelly crannies.

The instructor had as much patience and empathy as Vlad The Potholer. She would alternate light-hearted Welsh banter with shouted English insults, prodding Ladd's belly and bellowing into his face like a sergeant major. "Call yourself a potholer? You're nothing but an arrogant Englishman, look you!"

By the end of the opening session, Ladd had come last in all twelve exercises. To near-universal glee, the instructor announced that he would have to perform punishment press-ups as a forfeit. Ladd knocked out twenty on a regular basis, but a hundred pushed him to his limit. His classmates just looked on, shouting discouragement in Welsh.

After lunching on a cold cheese toastie, Ladd spent the afternoon bellying down a tight tunnel, sobbing. He had to overcome every self-preservation instinct he possessed to get through the increasingly demanding squeezes, and he tried to approach them as if they were rounds of a boxing match. This helped him get through the afternoon's exercises, but he still came last in all eighteen of them.

Ladd's day climaxed with another forfeit: two hundred star-jumps. This time, the trainees' Welsh mockery was accompanied by English abuse from the instructor, as she wove insults into her counting: "158, 159…Fat! English! Snowflake! 163, 164…Porky! Great! Douchebag!"

Ladd returned to the hotel just after they had stopped serving dinner. It was four minutes past six, but this wasn't London, the landlady explained. After Ladd pleaded for an alternative, she said he might make it to the Indian takeaway behind the chapel before it shut, but he would have to run as it was inaccessible by road. When Ladd asked whether they did deliveries, she laughed in his face.

Ladd was rarely averse to a light jog, but his entire body hated him for forcing it into holes all day, and the press-ups and star jumps hadn't helped. It wasn't the world's longest footpath, but it was possibly the steepest, better suited to Nepalese sherpas and mountain goats than knackered Englishmen. The Indian restaurant was owned by an unhappy couple from Anglesey, and they had his takeaway prepared just in time for a thunderstorm to break out. Lightning cracked over the slagheaps and rain hammered the streets, as Ladd half-ran, half-swam back to his hotel.

The curry was cold and came with raisins and pineapple chunks. His bedroom was too small to dine in, so he went to the kitchen. The landlady sat opposite and watched him eat. Every forkful was a trial. Her conversational gambits were non-existent, so Ladd had a go instead. Anything to provide respite from the barely edible meal.

"I'm learning to pothole," Ladd ventured.

"Eat up," she replied.

Ladd gobbed pineapple vindaloo. "It's down at the slagheap."

"Miner, was it?"

Ladd nibbled a cold lamb fat and sultana combo. "I've never been a miner, no."

"What was you then?"

"Doorman," Ladd improvised.

"What sort of doors?"

"Clubs, pubs, places like that."

"Tricky to fix, was they?"

"The doors?"

She didn't answer, just looked expectantly at his tepid dinner.

Ladd worked his way through the vile vindaloo. In many ways, he had preferred burying himself alive all day.

"The other trainee potholers," Ladd said, once he had munched his way to the curry's middle, "They all seem very... local."

"The Evans boys, isn't it. Their mammy never had a girl."

"But there are fifteen of them."

"That'll be about right. Seven sets of twins and an odd one out."

"The instructor said they're all retraining for the Chinese."

"*Slagheap Experience* isn't it. Immersive, most likely. Nonsense, if you ask me."

Ladd requested an earlier breakfast and was amazed when she agreed. He spent the night dreaming about dark holes and awoke with an intense craving for bacon and eggs. When he went downstairs, he found that the landlady had warmed up the remains of his vindaloo instead, as she hadn't wanted it to go to waste.

Ladd spent the morning surrounded by stalagmites and discovered that they hurt when you tripped over them, which he did repeatedly. Today's holes were larger than yesterday's but that didn't make them any more comfortable, and Ladd succeeded in maintaining his unblemished failure record all morning. His forfeit was three-hundred-and-fifty squat thrusts accompanied by rhythmical Anglo-Welsh insults: "Pathetic! Prancing! English! Ponce!"

Lunch was a sausage roll in pastry as soft and yielding as a slag heap, and Ladd broke an incisor. Conversation was exclusively in Welsh, apart from the occasional muttered *English bastard*.

Ladd spent the afternoon back underground, squirming down tight shafts and burrowing into the Earth's bowels. It felt like a demonic punishment devised for the damned. Given that he had yet to die, it did seem a little unfair.

That evening, Ladd decided to give the curry a swerve and go for a drive. The area didn't do straight roads, but he finally wended his way to a town with an even less pronounceable name and found a hostile pub that refused to serve food, but did offer crisps, pork scratchings and peanuts. The only seat was under the darts board. Luckily, the regulars had decent aims and he only got speared once. Foodwise though, the nuts, crisps and scratchings were a hit and he decided to become a regular.

Over the next few days, Ladd conquered a plummeting borehole, monkeyed down a rope ladder and traversed a gaping fissure. He didn't enjoy a second of it, but somehow, he survived.

Once the course was complete, the instructor assembled the trainees in the shed, gave an eighty-six-minute speech in Welsh, then pinned gold badges to the lapels of the Evans boys' jumpsuits.

Ladd wasn't surprised to be last, given that this had been his standing in every exercise. But this time there were no forfeits. The instructor looked him square in the eyes and said, "We've made a potholer of you, Englishman."

As they saluted each other, tiny tears welled in Ladd's eyes.

PRISON DIARY – ENTRY 10

Naomi kicked off the session with a dose of scepticism. "Can you learn to pothole that quickly?"

"Don't see why not."

"Have you done any research?"

"Jeff's got a book."

"Someone wrote a book on potholing?"

"Jeff likes it almost as much as his book on tunnelling."

"Why on Earth would a prisoner take an interest in potholing and tunnelling?"

"No idea." If Naomi couldn't imagine, I certainly wasn't going to tell her.

"Did the potholing book say how long it takes to train?"

"I just skimmed it."

"Well, don't you think it would be a good idea to read about a subject properly before you write about it?"

"Wouldn't that take away the surprise?"

Naomi didn't answer. She just changed the subject. "It's not a particularly positive portrayal of Wales, is it?"

"I've got a Welsh Sikh in Phantom Squad."

"Does that help?"

"You tell me."

"Well, at least it's heartening that your central character achieved something positive. He went right out of his comfort zone, faced his fears, and completed the course."

"So he could do a heist."

"I've already told you what I think about that."

Naomi said there would be no session next week, as she was going on a Pilates retreat in Tuscany. Innsbruck and Gethsemane were on their school holidays and organising childcare had been a nightmare after Roly's affair with the au pair, but she had managed to find a Montessori camp in the Chilterns.

I told her that I wasn't going to use her Pilates as an excuse to slack, and promised I would have two chapters ready for her return.

When I returned to my cell, I had a long chat with Jeff about his favourite heists. It had never occurred to me that the Pink Panther Gang was real, or that Saddam Hussein and Josef Stalin were both accomplished bank robbers. Sometimes the robbers got away with it: Boston's "Gardner Heist" bagged thirteen masterpieces and they were all still missing. Other times, the booty was edible: The Wisconsin Cheese Heists were crackers, The Provence Black Truffle Heist left many a Michelin restaurant blaming their unlucky stars, and The Neustadt Chocolate Egg Heist was sweet. Jeff banged on about tunnels, explosives, inside men, and lookouts, and explained that carrying out the job was often the easiest part. Fencing the ill-gotten gains without leaving a trace or falling out with your fellow robbers was usually far harder.

My latest library book was all about London's underground; not the tube, but the layers of lost cities the place was built upon. Apparently, Piccadilly Circus mirrors the structure of the neolithic village in its distant foundations and there are endless catacombs, ghost stations, Zeppelin shelters, petrified forests, and buried rivers. With its hidden depths, London reminded me very much of Jeff. I wondered when he would make his break.

INSERTION

Ladd's return journey from the Welsh slag heaps took nine-and-three-quarter hours. Merthyr Tydfil was gridlocked, an "Insult Britain" protest shut The Severn Bridge, and a lorry jack-knifed on the M4, spilling its cargo of pigs. Ladd wondered whether he had read the protest banners correctly, but he had: "Insult Britain" was a campaign to irritate everyone so much it would trigger an uprising. He rated its chances of success.

When the interminable journey finally terminated, the prospect of Tina loomed large. Ladd had hated his dank subterranean insertions, his forfeits, and his pineapple and sultana curry, but a perverse pang of nostalgia for crisp dinners under the dartboard hit him as he contemplated the dreaded nightie ahead.

Ladd knew that this could be their last evening together. Should The Smiths see through his potholing ruse, he would soon be sleeping with the scrap. He could not tell Tina about the heist, but he could at least open his heart and tell her all she meant to him.

Tina was sat on the sofa, sorting through a pile of Extra-Large lingerie, and singing Dolly's version of the Londonderry Air. "Oh, Tranny Boy! The tights, the tights. Are chay-ay-fing." Her voice was infinitely less beautiful than she was. Tina sounded far more seductive when she was swearing and given how angry he was about to make her, she was sure to be sounding obscenely seductive very shortly.

Ladd joined her on the sofa, summoned a half-smile and pretended to enjoy the song. After the eighteenth iteration of "Tranny Boy", Ladd decided it was time to break the news that he may not be coming back, "Look, Tina, we need to -"

"Screw?"

"Talk."

Tina held a lacy basque up to his forty-eight-inch chest. "Bit tight?"

"Look, I might not get the chance to say this again, so I want you to know that you've made me so very happy. I really do love …"

"Sod that for a game of soldiers." Tina grabbed him with a squeal. "Get your kit on."

Ladd grimaced as she fitted him into a series of female outfits: a twenties flapper, a prima ballerina in a tutu, and a raunchy nun. Settling on the final one, Tina parted his habit and bounced on his crotch until he reached an anti-orgasmic groan.

Tina looked at Ladd with concern. "Surely you're not actually crying?"

"It's the joy," Ladd lied. He closed his eyes and recalled their first meeting. He had been on a police rugby tour of Cork. His team had won a couple of matches and were sinking some stouts in a Titanic-themed bar when they got into a fight with the locals. Only two people remained standing – him and Tina, who was working behind the bar. She was about to hit him, but decided she'd rather hit on him. It was love at first shag and they'd never looked back.

As he lay replete in his Extra-Large nun's habit, Ladd started to wax philosophical. "What's it all about, Tina? I mean, things seem to matter a lot at the time, but do they really? Love, money, mortgages, sport, getting a result at work, taking down The Bender – does it really mean anything?" Ladd thought of the heist ahead. The Smiths could unmask him, he could suffocate in a pothole, or he could drown in a flooded vault. "I know we don't normally talk about this sort of bollocks, but I just don't know whether there will ever be another chance. I'm about to do a thing, and that thing - it might not go well."

Ladd turned to his life-partner, wondering what emotional support she would offer him. Tina was asleep, a beatific expression on her face.

Ladd envied her. He hadn't felt comfortable for a week, and it wasn't just the cross-dressing. The cat overload at Feline of Duty, the defenestration onto the Attorney General, the Transnistrian abduction, the fish barrel inversion, the Transylvanian tank chase and the crash-course in potholing had all taken their toll. He had aged about a decade, possibly two. If Tina wasn't going to help prepare him for the trials ahead, he would have to fall back on his own resources, and that generally meant sport.

Ladd bunged on a tracksuit and jogged through the North London night. As he overtook closed charity shops, bins and lampposts, Ladd felt oddly like a superhero –

not because of his extraordinary powers, but because of all the recent costume changes. At home, he was Tina's panty-clad heroine; at work, he was an anti-corruption crusader disguised as a funeral director; now, he was a contender, training for the bout of his life. After a few minutes of pavement-pounding, he reached his gym, inputted a code, and entered.

Four a.m. was not a prime time for pugilism, but the place still stank of blood, sweat, and spent adrenalin. These weren't really aromas you could bottle with any prospect of commercial success, but they were manly smells, and it made a pleasant change from being Tina's perfumed ponce.

Ladd found some gloves and pummelled the life out of the heftiest punch bag he could find, landing knockout blows like a furious Tyson. This was what life about. He loved the violent release – all pent-up pretence spent. He hadn't trained this intensely since he'd got married. He pictured Dixon's face on the bag and punched his lights out.

As soon as dawn began to break through the skylights, Ladd knew it was time to make a move. He was in no mood for conversation or gentle sparring, so he headed out to continue his training in the open air.

Ladd knew London as well as most cabbies, and it didn't take him long to find some stone steps to "Rocky" up. Once he had completed fifty circuits, he raised his arm in triumph. He was ready for anything: even an undercover raid on the police pension fund with The Smiths and a bent Rastafarian rozzer.

The moment was ruined by his mobile's insistent bleat. He sorely resented it - a pocket slave-master interrupting his life without warning. It was too early for a civilized call, but apparently not too early for the Super, who had added video to the intrusion. There she was in her dressing gown, sat on a vintage pouffe, rifling through her post with one hand and spooning her porridge with the other. She was in a room I didn't recognise, no doubt an unexplored region of her new downstairs. "What on Earth are you doing?" she asked.

"Running, Ma'am."

"Away?"

"Up some steps. And down again."

"Why?"

"Motivation, Ma'am."

"Shouldn't you be conserving your energy?" She munched her oats. There was something deflating about watching your superior officer and mistress eat breakfast when you had just convinced yourself you were Rocky. He wondered whether to make a "cereal killer" pun but decided against it.

"Good luck, Danny," The Super put down her spoon and started to unwrap a parcel.

"Thanks, Ma'am. Means a lot." Danny wished she'd go away and let him run back down the steps.

The Super's package seemed to contain a sculpture of wildly demented design.

"Looks interesting, Ma'am." Ladd wondered why she had really called him. Was this some kind of insane unboxing video?

"Mongolian Demon Mask," the Super explained as she exposed the sculpture's face. It was one of the ugliest mugs Ladd had ever seen.

The Super took a few moments to admire the sculpture's grotesque features before carrying it over to a wall-mounted collection of equally warped warrior-demon masks. It was like a police line-up of Mongolian devil's heads. There was clearly more to the Super's new downstairs than he had thought.

Ladd ran home, showered, and made his final preparations for the heist. Tina was still asleep, so there were no sexual complications to navigate, and he was soon on the way to his date with the police pension fund.

***

At Smith, Smith, Smith, Smith & Smith, The Smiths' powerful machines tortured steel in an orgy of bending. Meticulously engineered vehicles were squeezed into cubes, and the steel structures that had once helped give London shape were crushed, stretched, and pummelled into meaningless raw material. It looked like senseless vandalism, but the bent metal would soon be sold off and reincarnated into new objects. Ladd shrugged. What difference does it make? Maybe The Smiths weren't so bad.

Dredd was dressed as a tube driver, his former profession, as many admiring biographies of the Force's highest-rising Rastafarian had observed before his catastrophic fall from grace. It was a bit of a comedown from his Chief Superintendent's get-up, but it was preferable to Ladd's luminous orange potholing jumpsuit.

"You look like a carrot," Dredd observed, as they walked towards The Smiths' office.

"It's not a fashion parade," Ladd replied.

"Heard you were a catwalk queen," Dredd said.

Ladd did his best to hide his panic. How could Dredd possibly have heard about his cross-dressing escapades? Dredd had been locked up in the most secure cell in western Europe before a brief sojourn in Phantom's equally isolated basement. Did his squad know? Was there a Phantom mole? It seemed unlikely.

The improbable collaborators walked past mega-bulldozers and super-cranes feeding on scrap-metal mountains. It looked cannibalistic, which seemed about right. Ladd was a cop about to feed on his colleagues' pension fund, aided and abetted by one of the Force's most monumentally bent bigwigs.

The Smiths' Office was an icon of architectural perfection in a sea of scrap. Its floor-to-ceiling windows displayed glass-fronted fridges stacked high with sparkling mineral water. High-definition screens dangled jauntily from the ceiling, and neatly suited gents were mounted on multi-coloured swivel chairs. It seemed more suitable for a property consultancy than an armed robbery conspiracy.

The heftiest suit opened the door, nodded at Dredd, and gave him a half-hearted frisk. From his video briefing at Phantom, Ladd knew this to be Kevin Smith, the getaway driver who "makes Lewis Hamilton look like a lollipop lady."

Kevin Smith glared at Ladd and searched him in a manner closely akin to GBH. Finding nothing, he led them in.

Will Smith, Robert Smith, and Matt Smith swivelled their chairs in unison. Kevin offered a seat to Dredd, then occupied the one remaining chair, leaving Ladd marooned in the middle of the room.

"Potholers, eh?" Will Smith gave Ladd's carrot-coloured jumpsuit the once-over. "Worms on legs."

Will Smith was the boss, a man who had been acquitted of twenty-seven counts of armed robbery, and twenty-seven counts of perverting the course of justice, so Ladd decided to offer up a friendly smile.

"Wanker!" The curse came from an octogenarian shadowboxing himself in the corner. It could only be Papa Smith, the man who had been "the brains behind the operation until he lost them"

Ladd thought it best to be polite. "Lovely to meet you all."

"Likewise, I doubt." Will Smith yawned. "Go on then, *Pothole*, impress us."

Ladd was not overjoyed at being called *Pothole*. Had he been a snowflake, he might have made a formal complaint to Human Resources or reported the comment to a moderator. But he wasn't, and there were no safe spaces on an undercover blag. He just cleared his throat, tried to ignore Papa Smith's solo boxing bout, and switched to bullshitting mode: "I burrowed through an Alp once."

"Bollocks!" Papa Smith exclaimed as he punched himself on the nose.

"I spent six months under Mexico surviving on bat guano," Ladd continued, falsely.

"Tosser!" Papa Smith chinned himself.

The other Smiths looked on stony-faced as Ladd continued his fib-fest.

"I bottomed the Black Hole of Calcutta," Ladd improvised, keeping a straight face despite himself.

The silence was beyond awkward. Ladd knew he was lying, Dredd knew he was lying, but did The Smiths?

Will Smith certainly looked sceptical. "What's wrong with daylight?".

Ladd had always liked daylight. It was much cheerier than darkness. He started promisingly with "It's ..." then went off the boil with, "...a bit bright."

Papa Smith decked himself with an almighty "Codswallop!"

Robert Smith walked over to the corner, helped Papa Smith to his feet, and ushered the old timer out to the yard.

"Okay," Will Smith shrugged. "You've got a black belt in potholing, we get it. But do you have the bollocks for the job?"

"Yes." Ladd looked Will Smith square in the eyes. "I am a man of considerable bollocks."

Dredd seemed to be on the point of pissing his pants, so Ladd thought it best to avoid eye contact.

Matt Smith, "smash-and-grab merchant and mixed martial arts champion", stepped up to his full 5′2″. Ladd reached down and offered a handshake. Matt grabbed his arm, turned it in its socket, threw Ladd onto the floor and followed through with a choke hold. Ladd's eyes watered, mostly from pain, partly from humiliation – he'd been decked by a bloke the size of a koala.

The Smiths laughed. Dredd joined in the merriment. Ladd gasped, and turned the colour of a post box, while Will Smith, Robert Smith and Kevin Smith started counting him out, "10, 9, 8, 7, 6..."

Ladd wasn't having this. He bear-hugged his diminutive opponent, bridged his legs, rolled him over, and decked him. Finally, he was able to breathe freely.

"Not bad, Pothole." Will Smith offered an ironic round of applause, then added the command, "Initiate him!"

This was a serious result. Ladd's covert insertion had been successful. All it had taken was an intensive Welsh potholing course, an orange jumpsuit, some lies and a fight. It was now just a question of formalities.

Robert Smith and Kevin Smith led him out to the yard.

"Terrific to be on board," Ladd said, as a colossal crane-claw scooped him up like a falcon snatching a field mouse. Ladd accelerated skyward at speed in the iron bucket and tried not to think about his imminent death. He screwed his eyes shut and recent events replayed themselves unbidden: Trent's bent corpse dropped off the lamp post, the Super's panties flopped onto Tina's face, his rara-skirted reflection looked back at him, Marian chucked him out of the court window, Transnistrians inverted him headfirst into a barrel of rotten fish, the Transylvanian tank smashed through the factory wall. None of this helped. The claw jolted to a halt. Ladd opened his eyes. It was a sublime moment of peace and he imagined himself a wisp of cotton cloud in the azure sky. Then the claw dropped like a stone and dumped him on the ground. It was like falling off a disappointing rollercoaster: his every bone felt dislodged.

"Right, Pothole." Will Smith smirked down at him. "Let's relieve The Filth of their pensions."

"Good idea," Ladd replied, once he had regained the ability to speak. "Let's."

The Smiths lifted Ladd aloft and carried him back into the office, chanting, "Fuck the police!" Ladd mouthed along like the most half-hearted member of NWA.

The Smiths plonked Ladd down in a plastic chair. He couldn't speak or even think; he just gazed out of the window and saw Papa Smith clamber out of the crane cabin. Ladd shuddered. With someone that senile in control, he could have been dropped anywhere. Dredd watched Ladd's reaction with a sadistic grin.

The Smiths took their seats and heist preparations commenced. Matt Smith distributed construction suits, Kevin Smith handed out helmets, and Robert Smith dished out head lamps. They could have been embarking on a council apprenticeship rather than a robbery.

Will Smith got off his swivel chair and addressed the room. "Right, this is our cover - we're all navvies on one of them never-ending high-speed train projects." Will activated the office's many screens. They glimmered from all angles, like watchful eyes. Every screen showed the same image: the Thames snaking past landmarks – Tower Bridge, the London Eye, the Thames Barrier. Will Smith twiddled something, and the images animated. Surface London peeled back to reveal the city's underbelly: buried rivers, rail tunnels, power lines. It was all impressively precise. Ladd only wished that Phantom's briefings were this technically advanced. It was light years ahead of the clunky graphics supplied by the Met's in-house covert anti-corruption video unit.

Will Smith fiddled again. A shiny gold icon appeared with a "Ping!" in the heart of the under-city.

"That is the vault," Will Smith continued. "Inside, there's the gold guaranteeing The Filth's pensions. If we can swipe that, every copper's penniless, doomed to a wretched old age on a state pension.

A round of wild applause and general whooping broke out. Ladd thought it best to join in.

"Pigs!" Pappa Smith shouted, as he kicked a table.

"Remember, friends," Will Smith continued, "This isn't just about getting rich, it's also about getting even. Think of every dawn raid, every one of your mates that The Filth have busted, remember every day you've served on remand, and picture those smug, vicious, bent cozzers retiring on nothing. This is our chance to defund the police."

Ecstatic celebrations ensued, particularly from his former Chief Superintendent.

Will Smith turned to Dredd. "This fine gentleman here will drive us there and back on our very own works train."

Will Smith twiddled his device and a blue locomotive avatar appeared on the screens. It chugged its way towards the gold pension vault, accompanied by a tune Ladd vaguely recognised from his childhood. It reminded him of dragons, goldmines, and escaped elephants. *Ivor The Engine*! That was it! By the same blokes who did *The Clangers*.

"Everything's legit," Will Smith continued. "Dredd's a qualified driver and we've made a few useful contacts in the control hub. They won't bat an eyelid, not even when our train diverts to this disused stretch here." The locomotive avatar pulled up near the gold vault with a loud "Puff!"

Everyone applauded, until Will Smith steadied the celebrations with a raised palm. "Close, but no cigar. The train can get us close, but access to the vault is blocked by doors that can only be opened from the other side."

"Bollocks!" Pappa Smith thumped his chin.

"Luckily," Will Smith continued, "We've got good old Pothole here."

Ladd attempted a "you-can-count-on-me" grin.

Will Smith slapped him on the back. "Pothole will be burrowing through the Earth's guts. Love it, dontcha?"

"Ever since I was a toddler," Ladd lied.

"Not for me," Will Smith winced. "I'm claustrophobic. I've never wanted to be buried alive."

Ladd recalled his Welsh potholing travails. *Buried alive* summed it up perfectly. Personally, he'd rather wait a few decades and be buried dead.

"This is how it's gonna play out." Will Smith began. "First off, we're all aboard the choo-choo, while good old Pothole drops down a manhole and saunters along this nice, cosy tunnel here." An orange tunnel icon appeared on the screens. "While we enjoy the train ride, Pothole follows through by climbing down a rock-solid ladder just here." A solid silver ladder appeared on the screens. "Our train then takes a little diversion and Pothole ambles down this wide, comfy tunnel here." A cherry-red tunnel icon pinged into place. "By then, our train should have pulled up, allowing us to take a well-earned rest while Pothole deals with the guards."

"Guards?" Ladd queried.

"Don't worry, Pothole, they've all been paid off."

"Tosser!" Papa Smith shouted, to no one in particular.

"Finally," Will Smith concluded, "We all do some intensive waiting, while Pothole here – the hero of the hour - unlocks the doors from the far side. They're all as flimsy as plywood – a piece of piss for a bloke Pothole's size. Once he's through, we're all friends reunited in the vault, ready to bankrupt The Filth. Clear?"

It was crystal clear to Ladd that he would be doing all the work while The Smiths enjoyed a leisurely train ride with Dredd. But there was no point protesting, as The Smiths were only stitching themselves up. When this was all over, they'd be sharing a family-sized cell and the joke would be on them. That didn't mean Ladd wasn't massively apprehensive, resentful, and generally miserable in the meantime, but at least he wasn't at home wearing a nightie.

DEFUND THE POLICE

Shortly after tea and biscuits, the police pension heist was on. The Smiths swanned off in their construction outfits, broke into one of London's forty-odd ghost stations, and boarded an empty train specially diverted by Dredd.

Ladd's task was to jump down a manhole, an easy enough task had it not been in a central lane of Marble Arch roundabout. After numerous near-fatal encounters with double-decker buses, lorries, taxis, and novelty tuk-tuks, he gave up and focused his efforts on nicking traffic cones. He had no problem passing for a maintenance man in his potholing jumpsuit, but that didn't stop drivers from slamming their horns, swearing inventively, and issuing multi-lingual death threats as he closed off the lane. Ladd had heard it all in his time, so it didn't deflect him from prising open the manhole lid, switching on his headlamp, and dropping into London's bowels.

Will Smith had promised that he would be "sauntering down a nice, comfy tunnel", but this was a miserable lie. Instead, he was facing a marathon crawl along a narrow, rat-infested sewer. It was even worse than Wales. He tried summoning up the Rocky-level motivation he'd felt running up the steps that morning, but his mind wandered to the Super's death masks. Why collect something that ugly? And come to that, who on Earth has a portrait of Genghis Khan in their bedroom? Women, eh?

As Ladd crawled through the putrid hellhole, his knees scraped on the uneven ground, and sewer-stench penetrated his nostrils. He pictured The Smiths relaxing on a first-class carriage with complimentary broadsheets and bottomless flat whites; Will Smith completing a cryptic crossword, Matt Smith defeating Kevin Smith in a good-natured arm wrestle, Robert Smith dropping tracks on a portable sound system, and Papa Smith punching himself in the face and swearing.

When Ladd finally made it to the end of the sewer-stretch, he looked about for the "rock-solid ladder" Will Smith had promised him and found a rotting pair of loosely entangled ropes dangling over a bottomless drop. It looked about as safe as tombstoning off a tower block. At least he would never have to cross-dress again. He imagined his funeral: boxing mates reading poems, rugby players singing off-key, corrupt colleagues lamenting his move into anti-corruption, a tearful Super, and a proud Tina outing him as a cross-dresser. On the plus side, he'd be dead.

Ladd grabbed one manky rope, twined the other under his groin, then shuffled down into oblivion. It was like the world's worst PE lesson. He'd been good at PE - up to the hall ceiling in four powerful yanks, top of the year in circuit training, the big lad upfront in five-a-side. If only he'd become a professional sportsman, rather than an undercover potholer. Life was stuffed with *if onlys*. If only Phantom hadn't blown their cover in a hearse crash, if only the Super's panties hadn't fallen onto his wife's nose. But regret was pointless. He should be mindful and live in the present moment. The trouble was the present was dank, dark, and dangerous. In fact, when he imagined every moment of his thirty-nine years stretched out before him, this stood out as the worst. He decided not to focus on the present and thought about the Superintendent's breasts instead. That was a better. Ladd shut his eyes and smiled. The rope split. Ladd fell into the abyss. Luckily, it was an extremely short abyss measuring about four feet. He didn't like to think too hard about what he had landed on, but at least it wasn't the Attorney General.

Will Smith had promised a nice, wide tunnel, but all he could see was a wide wall. He turned a steady three-sixty, revealing dank bricks, concrete, and a humongous blob. The "nice, wide tunnel" was entirely blocked by a giant fatberg. He couldn't climb back on the snapped rope – he'd covered a good thirty foot before the drop. So, it now came down to a simple choice: he could either die alone or get up close and personal with the fatberg. Ladd took a deep breath and squeezed his body into the unhygienic confection of wet wipes, tampons, grease, lard, and oil. It was like having sex with a septic blancmange.

As Ladd wrestled with the squishy garbage monster, he pictured Dredd merrily driving his borrowed train and laughing his tits off. Was this job just vengeance for taking him down? Why on Earth had he trusted Dredd? Come to that, why had he trusted The Smiths? Had he made the biggest blunder in the history of the Force? Had he cemented his place in the next volume of *The Police Force's Greatest Mistakes*. But what if he kept his nerve and saw the job through? This was an unmissable opportunity to make up for landing on the Attorney General's head. If he could take down The Smiths and return Dredd to custody, he'd impress the pants off the Super, and convince other cops that Phantom was a force to be reckoned with. The Smiths weren't just blaggers, they were prime suspects in the double-bending. Take them down and he'd be making the streets safer for dodgy cops across the capital.

Ladd emerged from the fatberg feeling unwell. It was by far the most disgusting experience of his life. It felt like he had conjoined with the gloop and was now half-man, half-fatberg. He needed a shower. What he didn't need was a fight with four guards – but, looking ahead, that was what he'd got.

Ladd had been expecting a sorry mob of timeserving sixty-somethings, but they all looked younger than him and not one sported a paunch. On the plus side, they were queuing up to be hit. On the downside, they didn't look happy about it.

"Get on with it, then," the first guard grumbled. Ladd obliged, decking him with a single, punch. The guard rolled around, swearing resentfully.

The second guard stepped up, looking as enthusiastic as a prisoner awaiting execution.

"Nothing personal," Ladd explained, truthfully. They were complete strangers, and he was only doing his job. That job was conducting a heist on his own pension fund, and their job was getting hit, but modern careers demanded flexibility. Ladd shrugged an apology and flattened the second guard with an even meatier thump than the first. The two guards rolled around on the ground like Argentinian footballers appealing for a penalty.

The third guard stepped up, looking actively resentful. Ladd mumbled another apology and knocked him off his feet. He landed on the first guard, who hit him again.

The fourth guard shook his head. "I've changed my mind. No one said they were sending Tyson Fury."

"But you've been paid," Ladd objected.

"Not enough, mate," he replied, and ran off. Ladd chased him. The guard doubled back. Ladd wheeled around and followed. It was about as dignified as a playground game of *It*.

After about ten minutes of looping and dodging, swerving, and backtracking, Ladd caught up with the reluctant punchbag and thumped him. Not being one to go down lightly, the guard launched a kick at Ladd's ribs. Ladd grabbed his foot and swung him around in a hopping circle. Three hundred and sixty degrees weren't enough. Nor were seven hundred and twenty. Nor were one thousand and eighty. The guard refused to topple as he completed one hopping circle after another, laughing like a drain. Ladd was getting dizzy. It was like an underground Highland fling, but this wasn't Hogmanay, it was a heist, and Ladd had had enough. He kicked the guard's hopping leg away and plonked him onto the ground.

Now that the supposedly paid-off guards had been knocked over with enough violence to look convincing, Ladd turned his attention to the doors that Will Smith had claimed were as flimsy as plywood. The first door had a wheel lock the size of a juggernaut tyre. Ladd grappled, applying the full force of his body, every sinew straining, both shoulders close to dislocation.

Ladd pictured The Smiths on their train, parked up on their peaceful stretch of abandoned track. What did gangsters do to relax? Charades? Twister? Kerplunk? Resentment swelled in Ladd's chest and the adrenalin helped him force open the lock. The effort would have hospitalised him, had there been an underground hospital within ambulance-range. He went through and screwed the door shut behind him just in case any of the guards had a last-minute change of heart.

The next "flimsy as plywood" wheel-lock looked like it belonged on a space shuttle. Ladd strained, veins bulging, heart pounding, and forced it open. He would have celebrated, but it hurt to breathe.

A few metres ahead, a third wheel-lock beckoned. It was colossal, completing a hat-trick of door-related lies from Will Smith. Ladd's anger surged once again, and he used it for one final grapple.

A near coronary and multiple pulled muscles later, Ladd was through. To his right, there was the vault door. Directly ahead, another door leading, he hoped, to the abandoned rail track and Dredd's train. Ladd paused for breath and hefted the final wheel-lock open onto The Smiths, who were playing three-and-in on the platform with a rotten tennis ball.

Will Smith checked his watch. "Took your time, Pothole."

Ladd knew he had to control himself but couldn't. "Your plan was a total tissue of bollocks! The ladder was made of old string, the tunnel was a fatberg, and the *flimsy* locks could have shut out *The World's Strongest Man*."

"Hear that?" Will Smith cupped his ear. "It's the sound of no one giving a shit."

Ladd wanted to punch him, but he just held his stare instead.

Will Smith smirked. "Aren't you going to open the vault?"

Ladd couldn't believe it. Why couldn't someone else open the bleeding vault? After all his potholing, fatberg wrestling, guard hitting and lock turning, The Smiths still wanted blood.

Ladd walked up to the vault's wheel-lock and used the idea of his co-conspirators' impending imprisonment as motivation. He employed every sinew of his strength, every drop of sweat, while The Smiths did keepy-uppies.

After a few minutes of fruitless struggle, Dredd strolled up and inserted an alum key into a hidden hole. Merriment ensued. What an utter, utter bastard, Ladd reflected. After all he had been through, Dredd had let him sweat when he was completely spent. Ladd resolved to exact extreme vengeance at the earliest opportunity.

The vault door plopped open, and Dredd sauntered back to the train. Will Smith led the way into the vault, closely followed by Kevin Smith, Rob Smith, Matt Smith, Papa Smith, and Ladd.

The gold guaranteeing the entire police pension fund was a mind-blowing sight. Treasure of this scale was usually protected by dragons.

"It's giving me the horn," Papa Smith observed, before punching himself on the nose.

"Every cop who's ever arrested us will be on the streets selling *The Big Issue*." Kevin Smith laughed.

"Just like heaven!" Robert Smith exclaimed.

Matt Smith looked up at Ladd. "What do you reckon, Pothole?"

Ladd gazed at the gold securing his own pension and the pensions of every one of his colleagues. It meant everything to him, but there was no choice: he had to lie. "The Filth have got it coming. Fascists."

"Right," Will Smith rubbed his hands together. "We've got ten minutes to load up before this becomes an aquarium."

The operation was like a life-or-death supermarket delivery, with a stolen train instead of a kitchen. There were two teams: Ladd, Will Smith and Kevin Smith were the unloaders, lugging gold from the vault to the platform, and Robert Smith, Matt Smith and Papa Smith were the packers, stowing the gold onto the train. Dredd's role was to sit in the driver's seat, playing *Angry Bird* on his phone.

A digital timer immediately below the vault ceiling counted down to doomsday.

Nine-an-a-half minutes raced by, but The Smiths were not big on caution. Ladd would have preferred to clear the vault at least fifteen seconds before its doors shut forever and everyone drowned, but when you were a career bank robber, an element of nerve seemed to come with the territory. The timer counted down: 00.04, 00.03, 00.02 and only then did The Smiths dash out to the platform, shouting "Shoplifters of the World Unite!" Ladd was last, diving from the vault and chucking his final load of gold onto the train.

The instant the last of the gold landed, the train accelerated off – without Ladd or a single member of The Smiths. It was a memorable moment. The previous ten minutes had been a classic race-against-the-clock, but now the clock had given up the ghost and time gave way to space – an infinite expanse of despair. All was silence and the only movement was Dredd's train disappearing into the distance. Landing on the Attorney General had been an error, but this new catastrophe was so colossal, it was practically award-winning.

The Smiths were slow to react. The gang looked like they were trapped in invisible quicksand or perhaps like players in a buffering football stream, motionless and a bit fuzzy. But when reality finally wound back up and the truth kicked in, it triggered a festival of swearing so inventive, it could have been sponsored by Tourette's:

Will Smith's contribution was "Fuck-faced arsehole!"

Kevin Smith weighed in with a "Cunting cockmuncher!"

Robert Smith ventured a "Shitting cum-dumpster!"

Matt Smith shouted, "Pissing twat buckets!"

Papa Smith brought things to a climax with a "Blimey!" and a punch to his own forehead.

Ladd just stood in silence, watching Dredd's train disappear with the gold on which his future and that of the entire Force depended. He had never cried, not once in his career, but right now, crying seemed about right.

As one, The Smiths grabbed Ladd's limbs and lifted him in the air. It was like a parachute game from a children's party, but the children were violent criminals, and the parachute was an undercover policeman from a covert anti-corruption unit. Ladd was spread-eagled in mid-air, facing the clammy moss on the tunnel roof while The Smiths chanted "One, two, three ...!" He was obviously going to be the first of the gang to die.

The Smiths bent him backwards, Ladd's face contorted in agony. Any moment his spine would snap, and he'd end his days dangling from a dogging lamppost in an unfashionable area of London. The Smiths were a massive bunch of benders, and he hadn't seen it coming. Of course! It was them all along. As he braced himself for a fatal crunch, Ladd consoled himself with the thought that, now he'd lost his own pension, an early death was the only financially sustainable option.

Instead, The Smiths threw him up one final time and let go. Ladd simply plonked onto the track. It was painful, but he was bruised rather than bent and, this being a ghost line, the rails were no longer live.

The Smiths surrounded him, a gaggle of murderous menace. Will Smith leant in and spoke in a steady, measured tone: "We want your mate, and we want the gold - or your next pothole will be a grave."

PRISON DIARY – ENTRY 11

I was surprised to find Naomi out of her seat, performing a *downward dog* yoga move and groaning.

"Morning Naomi," I said. "How's life?"

"Aaaaargh!" she replied.

"Are you sure that's helping?"

"No!" She winced as she straightened to a vertical. "Of course not."

"Then why are you doing it?"

"Physio. I had a Pilates accident. Got carried away and bent my back. The instructor said I was lucky not to have snapped my spine."

"Sure it wasn't The Bender?"

Naomi shot me a stern look. "Do you want early release?"

"It would come in handy."

"How long have you served?"

"Four-and-a-half months."

"Well, I am very happy to report that you have been a hard-working student, but if I show your book to the Governor, you'll get an extended sentence."

"But it's not assault or rioting, it's literature."

"Keep thinking that, Cuthbert."

"Isn't it?"

"It's …an effort, of sorts, it really is. But you're not doing yourself any favours."

"Why not?"

"Could the police be any more useless?"

"I'm sure I can think of some more cockups."

"Oh, you're not lacking in the cockup department, don't you worry about that!"

"Thanks."

"It wasn't a compliment. A senior police officer has just conducted a completely unnecessary heist on the Force's own pension fund and lost the lot to an even more senior police officer who has already disgraced the badge."

"But it's not finished yet."

"Well, I don't for the life of me see how Ladd is going to come out of this with any credit."

"He's a decent bloke, deep down."

"Is he really? He's already had an affair with his Super, lied to his wife about being trans, crippled the Attorney General, run away from a tank fight in a nightie, succumbed to blackmail, sanctioned a surveillance operation that wrote off two perfectly serviceable undercover hearses, freed a corrupt officer, conducted a heist with a notorious gang, and lost the entire police pension fund. It's not exactly a glittering career, is it?"

"It's more successful than mine."

"But he's a police officer."

"And I'm a prisoner."

"And I'm single!" Naomi sobbed.

I really felt for her. Every time one of my marriages ended, I had felt bereft – the eighth occasion was just as bruising as the first.

"When I returned injured from my Pilates retreat," Naomi sniffed. "All Roly's stuff had gone. He even took the homemade hummus."

"Can't you make some more hummus?"

"I can't make another Roly!"

"But he wasn't exactly faithful, was he?"

"I'm suing the marriage guidance counsellor!"

"Good," I said.

"Go, just go!"

Naomi didn't seem to appreciate my attempts to console her, so I headed back to my cell and told Jeff a little about Naomi's domestic troubles. It's unusual for inmates to discuss the marital issues confronting the organic soup group organisers of places like Sevenoaks, but it's rare for events of any kind to occur in an optimized super-prison, so it passed for news.

Jeff took more interest than I had expected a career armed robber to take, asking all about her family, what she was like as a tutor, and whether I reckoned she had space for any more pupils. I told her I was the only one, so her timetable wasn't exactly rammed.

Talking about Naomi's kids seemed to have touched a nerve. Jeff's youngest son had just paid him a visit. He was growing up fast and he'd be an adult before Jeff got out.

"Ever thought about escaping?" I asked, a tad disingenuously given our earlier conversations about potholing and tunnelling.

Jeff just smiled and asked to borrow a pencil. He spent the next few days making complex sketches. They were all impressively detailed, but it but didn't make him particularly gripping company.

I cracked on with my writing, knowing that, after his colossal pension fund own-goal, Ladd was going to have to face the music.

SORRY

Ladd stood to attention next to the Super. The Attorney General's Office was an exquisitely well-appointed room, with oak-panelling, glass-fronted bookcases, and classic English landscapes by Constable and Sargent. None of this helped Ladd in any way whatsoever, as the nation's most senior lawyer spat into his eyes, bawling "YOU LOST THE POLICE PENSION FUND!!!"

"Sorry, sir." Ladd knew this was no time for excuses, largely because there weren't any. But at least the word *sorry* served multiple purposes – it was a sorry excuse for an undercover operation, he was in a sorry state, and he was sorry it had happened. And, in many respects, he was sorry he had been born.

The Attorney General swung over to the bookcase like a crutch-powered force of nature. Once he was there, he shifted his weight to his left crutch, grabbed a legal tome, and threw it at Ladd. It thudded into his skull like a leather-bound paving stone.

"You released the biggest Supergrass in the history of the freakin' Force!"

"Strictly speaking, sir," Ladd replied semi-consciously from the floor. "You released him."

"You railroaded me into it!" The Attorney General's shouts ended an octave above the standard male range.

"Don't mention railroads." Ladd groaned, as he struggled to his feet.

"Railroads!" The attorney General hissed vindictively.

"Ladd needs protection, sir." the Super pleaded.

"From me!" The Attorney General knocked Ladd's arms away with his crutches, plonking him back onto the carpet.

As the Super helped Ladd up, she said, "The Smiths want to kill him."

"So will the entire Force when they hear about their pensions." The Attorney General raised a crutch. Ladd rolled out of range. It wasn't proving to be the most successful meeting of his career.

Once Ladd had managed to clamber up, he said, "Maybe best to keep it quiet, sir. Just until I get the gold back."

"Forty-eight hours or it's a freakin' press release!" Spittle spurted from the Attorney General's lips like a gargoyle in a broken fountain.

***

Ladd and the Super retreated along the Attorney General's corridor. His stride would normally have been at least fifty percent longer than the Super's, but he was so comprehensively injured from the heist and the Attorney General's assaults that it was a struggle to keep up.

"Could have gone better," Ladd observed.

"He was happier when you fell on his head," the Super said.

Ladd smiled, as if recalling a career highlight. He almost felt grateful to Marian the Transylvanian murderer for his defenestration.

The Super brushed her hand against his. It was the first pleasant physical sensation he had experienced since Potholing Boot Camp. Maybe she could help him get out of this mess. She wasn't just his mistress she was his boss: maybe she could offer the support and understanding he so urgently needed.

"What do I tell Phantom?" Ladd asked.

The Super did not answer immediately. She just kept walking until they were level with some staff bathrooms and paused. Ladd hoped she was about to impart some life-saving advice, but she just looked him in the eyes and asked, "When are you leaving Tina?"

"Been a bit busy," Ladd replied.

"Busy losing our pensions."

Ladd wished she wouldn't rub it in.

"You screwed up," the Super continued harshly, as she put her hands around his back. "Now screw me."

He was still nursing multiple injuries, both physical and psychological, so he apologised and said, "Bit of a headache, Ma'am."

The Super thrust him into a disabled toilet. It wasn't romantic, but it was convenient.

***

Shortly afterwards, Ladd was back in the funeral parlour's concealed rear, debriefing his supremely diverse and inclusive squad on his catastrophic errors. There was something exquisitely painful about commanding a position of authority and admitting that you had failed your juniors. But Ladd did his best to stick to the facts, recounting how he had freed Dredd, learned to pothole, conducted a heist, and been robbed blind. He remained professional and measured throughout, unaware that the Super's lipstick was smudged across his cheek.

"So basically, in a nutshell, at the end of the day, all things considered," Ladd concluded, "The whole operation was a textbook cock-up."

"Had the piss ripped right out of you, Guv." Goliath grinned.

"Probably feeling like a total plonker, Guv," Old Bill speculated.

Yang signed with anatomical precision.

Sue didn't need to interpret, but she did anyway: "Massive dickhead, Guv."

"At least ..." Goliath began before running out of words. "...No, Guv, can't think of any positives."

"Everything's gone to cock," Taffy summarised, not inaccurately.

Ladd's squad had taken the news of his failed heist hard enough and he hadn't even told them the worst. This was how hospital consultants must feel when imparting a terminal diagnosis. How best to word it? He drew on his deepest reserves of bullshit and came up with a total blank. There was nothing for it; nothing but the truth, so help him God. He took a deep breath and forced out the sentence: "We lost the police pension fund."

Phantom looked haunted.

"Beg your pardon, Guv?" Old Bill enquired, almost mildly.

"We lost the gold underpinning the Force's pension investments. All of it." Ladd scratched his nose. "Bit of a blow."

"So, Guv." Old Bill creased his brow, as if calculating an astrophysics algorithm. "What you're saying, is that, after forty years in the job, I'll retire on approximately ..."

Ladd looked him in the eye. "A state pension."

A homicidal silence reigned.

Ladd shrugged. "I wouldn't blame you if you threw things at me."

They did. There was quite an impressive assortment of projectiles: monitors, drones, chairs, stationery, shoes, and staplers were among the most painful.

While Ladd took shelter behind a hard drive, a text bleated on his mobile, triggering a grunted, "Bollocks."

PRISON DIARY – ENTRY 12

Naomi was looking subdued. When I took my usual seat beside the cow portrait, she didn't say hello, she simply said, "Another *bollocks*?"

"Another death," I replied, forgetting to add a spoiler alert.

"Have you no compassion?" Naomi raised her voice. "A human life has been lost. Why just *bollocks*?"

"It's what Ladd says. You know some people have go-to words?"

"Do they?"

"Yes. Yours are *diversity* and *inclusion*. Ladd's go-to banker is *bollocks*."

"Very well, bollocks it is." She sighed. "But you haven't exactly elevated the behaviour of law enforcement."

"I think they come over all right."

"Do they really? What about the Attorney General's book-chucking and crutch-battery, Phantom Squad's mass stoning of Ladd with office appliances, and the Super's illicit sexual activity with a senior colleague in the Attorney General's disabled toilet?"

"Did you ever watch *The Bill*?"

"No."

"*Hill Street Blues*? *Miami Vice*?"

"I don't believe in television."

"Well, it exists."

"I believe television exists. But I wish it didn't."

"What about *Match of the Day*?"

"I don't like football."

"*Come Dine With Me?*"

"No thanks. I don't like prison food."

"It wasn't an invitation."

"Oh."

"*Say Yes To The Dress*? Ladd wouldn't have liked that."

"Look, I don't watch television. I prefer to read."

"Don't you watch films?"

"That's different."

"But you get films on television."

"It's not the same experience."

"It is if it's the same film."

"But it's not cinematic."

"It's cheaper."

Naomi looked tearful. It was so easy to upset her. I asked her what was wrong.

"Roly emptied the joint account."

"Oh no!"

"All I've got is savings and the house."

I wanted to say, *All I've got is my cell*, but I didn't think it would help, so I just said, "That must be tough" instead.

"He's only covered three-quarters of the school fees, and Gethsemane's got a big birthday coming up."

"Many happy returns, Gethsemane," I said, and I meant it.

Naomi gathered herself together and returned to my novel. "Look, I appreciate your efforts, but you have over-sexualised the women in your story."

"Ever seen a Scandi?"

"A what?"

"You know, Scandinavian crime series. Miserable Swedes, alcoholic Finns, depressed Norwegians, always killing and shagging each other."

"You're talking about television again, aren't you?"

"Oh, yes, I forgot."

"It's okay but do try to give your police characters some positive traits."

"Well, it's a bit of a down-point in the story."

"Then lift it up again. Have Ladd do something noble, daring, or at least in keeping with the dignity of his rank."

"I will." I stood up. "Hope Roly returns the money."

"Thanks. Your cellmate's quite a gentleman."

"Jeff?"

"He expressed interest in creative writing, and we had a getting-to-know-you induction."

Jeff hadn't mentioned this. I thought he was more focused on escaping than writing a novel, but he was full of surprises, what with his Dolly Parton biographies and enthusiasm for CIS nation geography.

Back at the cell, Jeff was none-too-forthcoming about his induction. He just said that Naomi seemed to mean well, but he didn't really have time to fit in any more sessions. His escape plans did seem to be coming on a treat though. It didn't seem prudent to ask him about the detail, but I often caught him smiling to himself, as his sketches grew in complexity.

With many years ahead, and no shortage of criminal contacts to help him lie low, escape seemed like quite a shrewd move for Jeff. I was tempted to join him for a laugh, but I only had a few more months to serve.

I read the shortest book in the library: *Heart of Darkness* by a dead Polish bloke. Given that he had only learned English when he was twenty, it was pretty well written. The line, "The horror! The horror!" stuck in my mind, probably because it reminded me of my marriages.

TRIPLE BENDING

DCI McMasters dangled from a lamppost. It would have afforded him a panoramic view of West London's rustic outer reaches, had he not been bent-to-death.

DCI Ladd and his Super stood on a carpet of used condoms, soggy tissues, and miscellaneous dogging detritus, sharing an intimate moment of *déjà-vu* as they observed a crime scene near identical to the previous brace of bendings: pointless tape, pathology tent, inept SOCOs fussing over a winch, and stroppy Homicide detectives pontificating about their expired colleague.

"Gang of One now," Ladd reflected ruefully.

"Who's left?" the Super asked.

"Dicky "Cocky" Proudcock."

"Poor bastard."

"Can't be easy having a name like that."

"I didn't mean his name."

"Sorry, Ma'am."

"City's most westerly dogging site."

"Bender's running out of compass points, Ma'am."

"Only one left. I do hope Homicide's monitoring London's easternmost dogging site."

"I'm sure they're dogging away already."

The clandestine couple watched the SOCOs struggle with the winch. They really didn't improve with practise.

"Transnistrians are bound to blame the Transylvanians," Ladd said.

The Super nodded grimly. "Blood feud o'clock, I should think."

Shouts emanated from the death scene. Stoker had set about a pair of SOCOs, thrown them to the ground and snatched the descending corpse mid-winch.

"Pathologist's a psychopath," the Super observed, as Stoker lugged McMasters' body to his tent like a ravenous tiger with a jugged warthog.

Ladd smiled grimly. "Want to watch the autopsy?"

"You really know how to treat a girl." The Super smiled sweetly, and they sauntered across to the pathology tent together. "Should we knock?"

"It's canvas, Ma'am." Ladd led the way in.

McMasters' contorted corpse rested on the table. It looked like a self-assembly human plonked together by someone too impatient to read the instructions.

Ladd winced. "That's gotta hurt."

"Not if he was drugged," the Super observed.

Stoker emerged from his extensive knife collection; fierce features reflected in the blades. "Killer went to a lot of trouble. Wanted the laddie wide awake. Why spoil the fun?"

"Fun?" Ladd often struggled to comprehend Stoker. "He looks like a pretzel."

"Yummy! I love a good pretzel!" Stoker grinned like a ghoul.

Dixon entered, darting a murderous glare at Ladd. "What's he doing here?"

Ladd stared back at his fellow detective. There was so little love lost between them, it was heart-breaking. Dixon saw Ladd as a school prefect, a snitch who betrayed his colleagues by pointing out people on the take, whereas Ladd saw Dixon as a time-serving waste of oxygen. Were The Bender to forcibly corrugate Dixon's spine, Ladd would investigate, but there would be a discreet party going on in his head.

Ladd looked at Dixon's transparent evidence bag: a wallet, a badge, and a well-thumbed *Lonely Planet Guide to Transnistria*.

"Why the hell are you here, Ladd?"

"No reciprocity of information," Ladd deadpanned.

"No reciprocity of information," Dixon mimicked in a nasal falsetto somewhere between Punch & Judy and Coldplay. "You big girl."

"Stop bumping your gums, you're spoiling my fun." Stoker sliced off McMasters' clothes with the panache of a Savile Row tailor. "Would you look at this! What a gorgeous kill! We're in the presence of genius. Absolutely faultless - a masterpiece."

"Doubt DCI McMasters would agree," Ladd observed.

"The attention to detail, the precise application of multiple forces in opposing directions," Stoker continued with the relish of a restaurant critic about to award a five-star review. "Just imagine the sound of the snap!"

Ladd liked to keep his theories to himself for as long as possible, but police officers were being bent backwards at a rate of knots. The Super gave him a nod. He had the all-clear. Now he just needed to time his attack correctly. He had dealt with some serious criminals in his time, but this pathologist was in a league of his own.

After Stoker had inflicted a series of expert flesh-slices, Ladd cleared his throat and aimed a death-stare at Stoker. "This killing you reckon is so bleeding marvellous," Ladd began. "Maybe you don't have to imagine it."

"Say that again laddie." Stoker fingered a blade.

Ladd wasn't one to take orders from a suspect, so he made his accusation more direct. "What if you were there?"

Stoker paused halfway through his corpse-cut. Blood dripped off his knife.

Ladd continued, undeterred. "You're strong as an ape, morbid as a banshee and your post-mortem reports could have been written by Stephen King. I mean, what are we meant to think?" He adopted a Glaswegian accent. It wasn't very good, but he didn't care: "*The victim's pain must have been so exquisite, the Marquis De Sade could have penned a poem about it.*"

Stoker pointed his pathology knife at Ladd. "Calling me *The Bender*, sassenach?"

Ladd looked from the blade to the pathologist, then from the pathologist back to the blade and stuck his tongue out. Once he'd retracted it, he used it to say, "Bender!"

Stoker stabbed at Ladd. Ladd sidestepped. Stoker flailed, almost crashing into the Super as she threw herself to the ground. Ladd grabbed Stoker's arm and punched his stomach. Stoker winced and launched a head-butt. It only half-connected. But a semi-bonce-butt from Stoker was more than enough to send Ladd's adrenalin and resentment into overdrive. The detective and the pathologist wrestled like grizzlies; antagonistic forces of law and order in mortal combat, crashing into the canvas, and collapsing the tent.

The Super managed to crawl out. She looked back and watched the pathology tent shimmy from side-to-side like a waltzing armadillo. It wasn't a credit to the Force, but she quite liked watching Chief Inspector Ladd fight – even through canvas. It felt wholesome. Her Ladd was a real man.

The Homicide detectives and the SOCOs joined forces to separate the cockney King Kong and the Glaswegian Godzilla. Dixon wanted to charge Ladd with actual bodily harm. Ladd wanted to charge Stoker with triple homicide. So, they decided to call it quits.

The night was still relatively young, and the Super had her downstairs redevelopment to attend to, so Ladd had a choice: early bed in a nightie with Tina or work late in his trousers. He opted for the trousers and drove to Phantom. It was well gone eight, so the place would be empty, but at least he could relax, heat up a Pot Noodle, and catch up on a spot of telly: something to take his mind off things, maybe a vintage episode or three of *Line of Duty* or *The Shield*.

As Ladd drove back to North London, he reflected on his encounter with Stoker. The pathologist had reacted to his accusation by trying to kill him; exactly what a triple murderer would do. The fact that Dixon couldn't see that, simply proved that he was a moron and Homicide's investigation was dead in the water. As for the fight itself, he thought he'd acquitted himself well. Stoker was the most widely feared pathologist in the Force and Ladd had given at least as good as he'd got. Had the tent not collapsed and plonked them both on the canvas, he'd have made sure Stoker was attending his own autopsy on a slab.

***

The funeral parlour was as quiet as the grave, with a *Closed* sign on the window and no Phantoms in evidence. Ladd unlocked the door, sauntered past the floral arrangements and memorial trinkets, and gave the angel headstone a nonchalant boot. The cherub wall ascended heavenwards, revealing the entire squad watching telly.

"Evening all," Ladd ventured, as the cherubs snapped shut behind him.

"Shush!!!!!" The squad hissed in unison, with Sue doubling up her own *shush* with an interpretation of Yang's signed *shush*.

What could have absorbed their attention and confiscated their deference to a commanding officer so completely? *Strictly*? *I'm A Celebrity*? *Love Island*? No, on closer inspection, it was *The News*.

"Panic on the streets of London," the newsreader declaimed, as the bulletin cut to shots of police officers marching through Whitehall carrying *Reclaim the Streets* placards. "As the police-bending rate rockets, officers are reportedly terrified." The protesting cops linked arms and sang *We Shall Overcome*. "Even the most by-the-book officers are concerned that slight blemishes on their records may prove fatal."

The bulletin cut to vox pops with angry cops. A bald, fuming constable spluttered into a foam-covered microphone: "Who's protecting the police? That's what I want to know. It's criminal negligence."

A sergeant looked petrified, looking shiftily from side to side as she confided, "Maybe I overlooked a bit of paperwork once. Who hasn't? It could put me on The Bender's list."

An inspector said, "The police are determined to rebel against our extinction. We won't stand around and be bent to death – and if the only way to make people take notice is to break the law, so be it."

The bulletin cut back to the newsreader, who continued, "Dubbed *Jack The Bender* by the popular press, the suspect's identity remains a mystery." There was a rostrum sequence of tabloid headlines: *Jack The Bender Strikes Again*, *Head Over Heels in Guv* and *Bent Lieutenant*. Then the bulletin returned to the newsreader in vision as he reached the item's climax: "Police are advised to approach all members of the public with caution."

Ladd looked at his squad. Had fear turned Phantom flaccid? Surely, they weren't all as spineless as the police protesters? Was *spineless* the best word to use in Bender-related matters? No, it was not.

"It's a health and safety nightmare!" Old Bill shrilled, his beer belly aquiver. "We're all going to be bent alive!"

"Not me mate." Goliath boasted. "I'm unbendable. Back in the Forces, I shot eighty-six Afghans, forty-seven Iraqis and strangled a Chechen warlord with his own bootlaces."

"I'll be hunky-dory," Taffy added. "I like hitting."

Yang signed violently, and Sue interpreted: "Just let him try. I'll bend him like Beckham."

Sue then spoke for herself. "I'm seventy-nine. I'd run."

All eyes turned to Ladd. They weren't noticeably welling with unbridled affection.

"Recovered our pensions yet, Guv?" Old Bill asked.

"I'm working on it," Ladd lied.

"Very reassuring, Guv," Goliath said.

"What's the problem?" Yang signed. "You have one suspect. How difficult is it to track down the only Rastafarian to have made Chief Superintendent?"

"Good point, look you, isn't it just," Taffy observed, at unnecessary length.

"You'd better hope the rest of the Force don't find out," Old Bill added. "Those police protesters will have your guts for garters."

Was Old Bill threatening him? Something about his tone suggested that he was. Ladd didn't like being blackmailed. It had never happened before Dolly. Now, it felt like he had the word *Mug* tattooed on his forehead.

Sue gasped and clutched her chest. Ladd scrabbled for the defibrillator, but before he could administer CPR, it became clear that she was just startled by the sound of boot on angel without. The cherub wall flew up, revealing the funeral parlour and a distraught DCI Dicky Proudcock standing by the headstone.

"Cocky?" Ladd was aghast at the sight of a bent cop in anti-bent-cop HQ. "What the actual fuck?"

"The Bender! The Bender!" Proudcock exclaimed before collapsing onto a novelty coffin.

PRISON DIARY – ENTRY 13

Naomi's expression was as weary as an overweight pensioner who had just completed a triathlon in a charity gibbon costume.

"A double bender!" She sighed in disbelief. "Really?"

"It's Joseph Conrad."

"Oh, that colonialist. He's not really allowed these days."

"The horror! The horror!"

"I know, but *The Bender! The Bender!* isn't quite the same, is it?

"It is to Dicky "Cocky" Proudcock. For him, The Bender is as terrifying as anything Conrad's Captain Kurtz got up to in the jungle. I mean, The Bender's bent three bent cops to death and Cocky is now the only surviving member of the Gang of One."

"How lonely for him."

"Don't feel too sorry for him. Cocky drives a Lamborghini and siphons fortunes from street gangs. He's a bit of a tit."

"Another glowing representation of the constabulary."

"Don't worry. I shouldn't think he'll be around for much longer."

"You do like killing cops, don't you?"

"I'm not like The Bender. I only do it on paper."

"But The Bender's not real."

"He is to me."

Naomi looked into my eyes and despaired. "Your fight is deeply troubling too."

"Ladd's good at fighting. He's a keen boxer."

"But he's also a Chief Inspector at a murder scene and you have him wrestling the pathologist."

"It was a brave thing to do. The pathologist might be The Bender."

"It's not a particularly positive representation of Glaswegians, is it?"

"Well, they're not known to be effete connoisseurs of flower arranging, ballet and fine art, are they?"

"That's a sweeping generalisation."

"Ever been to an Old Firm match?"

"I hate rugby."

When I returned to my cell, Jeff was timing his paces. Three even strides, a jump, write a note. Four even strides, a jump, write another note. Pattern upon pattern again and again, as if he were training for a slow-motion Olympic event or a dance about algebra.

I didn't want to intrude, so I sat on the bed, polished off a Sherlock Holmes short story featuring evil genius Moriarty and his secret criminal information network, then got stuck into a book about artificial intelligence. I've often thought that the world was more in need of real intelligence, to be perfectly honest, so I decided to do my bit for humanity and knock off another two chapters.

PROUDCOCK

DCI Dicky "Cocky" Proudcock lay on the display coffin, entirely dead to the world.

Sue was the first to trot over to the lanky, corrupt specimen. "Goodness gracious, the poor lamb!"

Ladd doubted anyone had called Cocky a "poor lamb" since he was at nursery school. A disgrace to Professional Standards; a jury nobbling, money laundering puppeteer of street gangs, his only loves were fast girls, fast cars, and fast living. Cocky by name, cocky by nature and all in all a bit of a dick, he was undeserving of a respectable coffin, even if he was just lying on the lid. One of The Smiths' scrap heaps would have been more fitting.

Yang strode across the parlour, grabbed a vase, and upended wet chrysanthemums over Cocky's head. The Gang of One yelped and resurrected himself backwards, reversing onto his feet in a startled jerk, eyes fixed on a marble cherub.

"Am I in Heaven?" Cocky enquired.

Yang signed exactly how unlikely she thought that was with unholy enthusiasm.

Sue simply interpreted, "No."

Proudcock gawped at Sue, flabbergasted by her considerable vintage. "Scraping the barrel a bit, aren't you?"

"At least I'm not spoiling the barrel," Sue replied. "Like a bad apple."

"Well, that really is highly offensive," Proudcock said, with hefty sarcasm. "Worst I've been called in twenty years' service."

Yang signed a series of anatomically vivid insults.

"Need me to interpret?" Sue asked.

"That won't be necessary," Ladd said, "Let's stop dicking around, Cocky. Interview room's downstairs."

Taffy booted a cherub and a trapdoor opened under Proudcock's feet. His screams mingled with Phantom's laughter, and a "Golly!" from Sue.

Phantom's downstairs was nearly as mysterious as the Super's. There was a cell, an interview room, an observation booth, and a sauna, the architect being a bit of a wag. Interviews were conducted rarely and tended to focus on internal disciplinary matters relating to Yang's temper or Taffy's violence. On one occasion, Ladd and Old Bill had used the interview room for formal negotiations about an overtime roster, but they had adjourned to the pub after a few minutes. The observation room was concealed behind a two-way mirror: observers could see out, but interviewees just saw their own reflection. The cell had recently hosted Dredd for a brief post-funny farm sojourn, but it had also held comatose members of Phantom after prolonged drinking sessions. The sauna opposite was an unusual addition to anti-corruption design, and its only official use was for drying out diving equipment, although there were rumours that Taffy had organised a Welsh-Sikh swingers party there on more than one occasion.

Cocky's landing on the cell bed was softer than he deserved, but that didn't stop him bitching about his treatment. Phantom squad were delighted. It was the first time the trapdoor had been given an outing and it marked a high point in the history of the unit.

Once the squad had stopped laughing, Taffy kicked a weeping cherub and two vertical display coffins creaked open. The oak one contained a standing lift descending to the interview room, and the elm one contained a standing lift descending to the hidden observation room. Ladd and Goliath took their turns in the former; Yang, Sue, Taffy, and Old Bill took their turns in the latter.

The interview room was harshly lit – a bare bulb dangled off a ceiling cable. It was meant to be intimidating – and it may well have scared your average teenage tearaway out of his sweatpants, but Cocky was a different kettle of tuna altogether.

"I'm here about The Bender," Cocky said, as nonchalantly as a man who had just fallen through the floor could manage.

Goliath pressed a recording device, triggering a succession of high-pitched bleeps.

"That's bloody annoying." Cocky complained.

"A psycho's bending our colleagues to death and stringing them up on dogging lampposts, and you call it annoying?" Ladd asked incredulously.

"I meant the bleep," Cocky clarified.

Goliath sneered sadistically and pressed the recorder repeatedly. Cocky winced at every bleep, as if Goliath was sending surges of current into intimately placed electrodes.

Ladd took advantage of Cocky's discombobulation by commencing the interrogation. "How did you find us?"

Cocky shrugged. "I know things."

"What things do you know?" Ladd persisted.

"I know I need protection," Cocky replied.

"But The Bender's only targeting corrupt cops," Ladd proceeded disingenuously. "Why might you be worried?"

"Very funny," Cocky replied, unamused

"So, you do admit to acts of corruption," Ladd said.

"How long's everyone got?" Cocky waved at the two-way mirror concealing the rest of Phantom.

Ladd sighed. Cops knew each other's ruses. This was one reason why "cops and robbers" rather than "cops and cops" was the more popular playground game.

Communication between the observation and interview rooms was conducted via an earpiece. Up until this point, all observation had been silent, but after they had been spotted, panicked burbling spluttered into Ladd's lughole:

"Cocky's clocked us, hasn't he just." Taffy observed.

"Another bloody singing policeman," Old Bill said. "First Dredd, then this – if you're going to be a bent cop, at least stick to your guns, and have a bit of self-respect."

"More grasses than a garden centre," Taffy added.

There was a pause, no doubt because Yang was signing.

This was confirmed when Sue interpreted, "Maybe he's The Bender. Perhaps the bent bastard wanted to steal all the crime off the Transnistrians, the Transylvanians and The Smiths."

Sue's tone changed as she spoke on her own behalf. "Utter piffle. Why on Earth would The Bender come here and hand himself in?"

Another pause for Yang's signing, then Sue spoke in her interpreter voice again: "Stupid old bag!"

Sue's tone switched back to her own. "You're a very rude little girl."

The resulting commotion threatened to give Ladd a migraine. He was about to switch off his earpiece when Yang, Sue, Taffy, and Old Bill fell through the two-way mirror. Glass shards exploded across the interview room, as did the undercover officers.

"Evenin' all!" Proudcock smirked.

The Phantom foursome picked glass out of their knees and staggered to their feet.

Ladd was unsure of the correct procedure, largely because there wasn't one. There were protocols for interviewee assaults on officers, interviewee escape attempts, and interviewee medical requirements, but Ladd could not recall a single instance of police personnel falling into an interview. Maybe he was witnessing a milestone in police history, albeit a massively embarrassing one.

"For the benefit of the recording," Goliath announced with icy formality, "three Phantom squad detectives and an accredited interpreter have just fallen into the interview room."

"Thank you, sergeant." Ladd said, with great solemnity. "Given that the detectives and the accredited interpreter were already party to the interview, and that Cocky, uh, DCI Proudcock, was fully aware of this prior to the... incident, I'm sure the interview may proceed."

"Lovely jubbly." Cocky smirked at Taffy, Old Bill, Yang, Goliath, and Sue, all marooned awkwardly in a sea of smashed glass.

In a desperate attempt to regain some initiative, Ladd decided to adopt a sterner approach. He glared at Cocky and said, "I need everything on your street gangs, your dead mates in The Force and - most of all - Dredd."

Cocky laughed.

"Something funny, Cocky?" Ladd asked.

"Obviously," Cocky replied.

"What?" Ladd asked.

"Only a choirboy like you would have fallen for Dredd's pension plan."

How the hell did he know about that? "A choirboy, Cocky?" Ladd clenched his fists.

"A choirboy, Ladd," Cocky confirmed. "Real cops play the game, think like thieves. We're a dying breed."

"True," Ladd said. "You're being bent to extinction."

Cocky shuddered.

"Tell me about The Gang of Four," Ladd demanded.

"Oh, that." Cocky feigned a yawn. "More of Dredd's bollocks."

"It's clearly not bollocks though, is it," Ladd said. "The other three are dead and you're here."

"There's not much I can tell you."

Ladd nodded at Goliath. He pressed the beep repeatedly.

Cocky held his temple in agony, whining "All right! All right! I give up!"

Goliath took mercy and stopped the beeping.

"Trent helped the Transylvanians," Proudcock blurted. "Sweeney drank with The Smiths, McMasters knew some Transnistrians. Look, if cops don't mix it up with villains, we'd all be as clueless as you lot."

"Clueless, eh?" Ladd looked at his squad, stood sheepishly in the remains of the two-way mirror, and thought that Cocky probably had a point. "Who are your villains?"

"Villain," Cocky corrected.

"But Dredd said you were all across London's street gangs?"

Cocky didn't answer. He just watched Taffy lead Phantom squad in an embarrassed reverse shuffle towards what remained of the observation room. Once Cocky had finished laughing, he simply replied, "I am."

"But you associate with just the one villain?"

"Yes."

"So, you're across London's street gangs with the help of just one snout?"

"Look," Cocky said. "Every year, London's looking at - what? A million crimes? More? Thick plods like you just see postcode wars, junkies, opportunists. But there's a pattern, a plan."

Ladd watched his squad complete their retreat into what was now an overt observation room. "You're saying there's a criminal mastermind behind it all?"

Cocky nodded.

"Some kind of super villain? A sort of Blofeld-Thanos-Liz Truss figure?"

"Precisely."

Goliath turned to Ladd. "He's taking the piss, Guv."

Ladd thought this highly likely, but he wanted to see where Cocky's nonsense would lead. Given that there was now a Gang of One rather than a Gang of Four, and that the Gang of One was sat directly opposite him, it seemed like a legitimate line of inquiry, even if it was a pile of fibs.

"So," Ladd looked Cocky in the eyes. "You're telling me that a single person is behind all of London's knifings, dealings, shootings, robbings and ..."

Realising his boss had run out of crimes, Goliath added, "Shopliftings."

Ladd thanked him and turned back to Cocky. "Well, who is it?"

Cocky gave Ladd the most solemn of stares and replied, "Britney."

"Britney?" Ladd queried.

"Britney," Cocky confirmed.

"Spears?" Goliath asked.

"Moriarty," Cocky replied.

"First name Britney? Second name Moriarty?" Ladd asked.

"No shit, Sherlock," Cocky replied.

Goliath's finger hovered menacingly over the recorder's bleep button.

"That won't be necessary," Cocky said. "Just protect me from The Bender. And I'll tell you everything."

"Done," Ladd replied, without hesitation.

Cocky's relief was visible. "Where are you going to protect me?"

"Dredd's old cell."

Cocky didn't ask where this was, probably because he knew already.

"After you've given us Britney," Ladd continued.

Cocky sighed, then trotted out a description he had clearly pre-prepared. "Britney Moriarty is the best-connected criminal in London - eyes and ears everywhere. She triggers events, schedules coincidences, matches victims with villains, and provokes vengeance against the innocent."

"Busy lady," Ladd observed.

"Just go to that no-go estate at the arse end of Enfield and you'll find her. She's at number 578."

BRITNEY MORIARTY

While Taffy and Old Bill took the Land Rover and drove Cocky to his bulletproof cell in darkest Hertfordshire, Ladd and Goliath set off for Britney's lair. Both Phantom hearses being out of action, they were forced to use a courtesy car and the only one available was electric, Lithuanian, and so small, Ladd had to open the sunroof to avoid hitting his head. This meant that his eyeline was bisected by the roof, which would have spoiled a scenic tour of the Lake District, but it possibly enhanced a trip to Enfield's worst estate. Goliath passed the time by regaling him with military anecdotes, which felt appropriate: with his head protruding from the roof, Ladd could have been a squaddie in a tank turret.

There is a reason why people don't go to no-go estates. With its condemned tower blocks burned-out vehicles, crack dealers, prostitutes, pimps, and smackheads, Britney's manor could not have been mistaken for Hogwarts.

Goliath pulled up sharply beside an incinerated mattress. It was such an abrupt stop, that Ladd headbutted the sunroof. But after listening to Goliath's heroic tales of storming Afghan paramilitary shelters single-handed and parachuting into Chechen warlords' private zoos uninvited, Ladd didn't think it right to moan about a bumped napper.

Locals had burned down all the estate's signage and the door-numbering system had been fatally compromised by the theft of the numbers. But Goliath wasn't to be defeated by vandalism. He made some calculations on the back of his hand and led the way to the most decrepit of the estate's five dank tower blocks.

Ladd and Goliath were soon surrounded by boys on bikes. On the surface, they were about as menacing as the cast of *The Goonies*, but they were obviously runners for more senior scumbags.

A wild-haired boy of about eight approached and asked, "Who the fuck are you?"

Goliath looked at Ladd, knowing he was good at lying.

"We're from the council," Ladd fibbed.

"What the fuck's a council?" the boy asked.

"We're here to fix the lifts."

"You can buy them." He pointed at a rusty heap of torn-out elevators piled on the grass.

Ladd had an idea. He had mistrusted his ideas ever since his cross-dressing lie had misfired, but this idea, he quite liked: "The Smiths would like those."

"You know The Smiths?"

"They're our cousins."

"You don't look related."

Ladd dwarfed Goliath and their races were undeniably different, so Ladd followed through with the truth: "We're here to see Britney."

The boys scattered in terror, and the detectives proceeded to the tower block.

The stairs were extensive and stank of skunk. Goliath's legs were half the length of Ladd's, but his military pace kept them knee-to-knee as they jogged up to the door that Goliath's calculations had identified as number 578. It was distinguishable from the other doors because the letterbox hadn't been ripped out.

Goliath knocked. There was no reply. He knocked again and the letterbox snapped open. No one seemed to be behind it. A digital voice said, "Phones!".

Goliath obliged. Ladd hesitated briefly, then did the same. They waited for a solid minute. Nothing happened.

"Cocky's taking the piss," Ladd remarked.

"Could use my phone back," Goliath said. "I'd reached level nineteen on *Candy Farm*".

Ladd could certainly use his phone back too, but he wasn't about to tell Goliath about *Big Girl's Blouse* and his blackmailer.

After another phoneless thirty seconds or so, they decided to break in. Goliath had just started to set about the lock when the door swung open, seemingly of its own accord. Once they were inside, the door slammed itself shut behind them.

In many respects, it was a perfectly ordinary hallway: flat, carpeted, and around five feet by twenty feet. There was even a *Welcome* doormat, but the only wall was the one attached to the front door. The other three sides of the hallway were edged by sheer drops of several hundred feet. Ladd and Goliath gazed down at the London Borough of Enfield's answer to Star Wars' Galactic Senate Chamber; a colossal sci-fi structure filled, not with interplanetary politicians, but with mindboggling machinery. A million lights twitched across colossal data banks and wires clustered like knotted pythons; the entire tower block was an uninhabited shell alive with technology. Ladd could not have been more gobsmacked if he'd been abducted by the Illuminati and shipped off to Atlantis. It was the sort of place conspiracy theorists wanted to believe in.

"What in the name of ..." Ladd began.

"Internet exchange, Guv," Goliath explained, casually.

"What's that when it's at home?"

"It's like cyber plumbing. All the digital bilge flows through here – the clickbait, the bingeworthy box sets, the pay-per-view bouts, Facebook takedowns, Twitter storms, hate speech, irate cancellations, pointless GIFS, meaningless memes – all that bollocks."

"Nothing important, then," Ladd said. He edged up gingerly to the edge of the hallway carpet and gaped down at the vertiginous drop below. "No sign of Britney."

"Guv," Goliath said.

Ladd turned back.

Stood beside Goliath was a woman of about seventeen with heavy make-up, chunky jewellery, and a chewy accent from London's Deep North. "Who's asking?"

"How did you get in?"

"I live here, mate," the teenage super-villain replied.

"Cosy," Ladd said. "Where did our phones go?"

"Don't you worry about them." Britney was unnerving and she knew it. She had appeared from nowhere and was clearly too big to have entered through the letterbox.

Not being one to mess about, Ladd reached out and put his hand through her arm.

"Oi!" Britney protested. "Never heard of #Metoo?"

"You're a hologram," Ladd observed.

"Bit personal." Britney slapped his face. Her hand passed right through him.

Now Ladd had seen it all. He had dealt with snouts of all descriptions: farty little men festering desperately in the bookies, lairy street geezers betraying their best mates under duress, and smart, well-connected middlemen playing both sides against each other. But none of them had been transparent. And none of them lived in internet exchanges of inter-galactic proportions. Until now.

Ladd thought it best not to appear as confused as he actually was, so he just said, "Cocky sends his regards."

"Cocky? What a tosser!" Britney scowled. "Give him a good kicking from me."

"We're protecting him," Ladd said, betraying a professional confidence.

"Don't I know it," Britney said. "Grassed me up, the little snake,"

"What makes you think that?" Ladd asked.

"You're Phantom, aren't you," Britney said: not a question, but a statement.

"Figured it out from our phones?" Ladd asked.

"I figured it out before you left your funeral parlour," Britney said, her digital smile as irritating as her breezy manner.

Goliath gestured at the city-sized expanse of technology beneath them. "This has got to be the biggest dark web exchange in Europe."

"Makes the police computer look like a bit of a fuckwit, doesn't it?" Britney giggled.

Goliath turned to Ladd. "So, that's how she gets her intel! Digital eyes and ears all over the shop. Every message, every call, every camera feed comes through here."

"Don't talk about me like I'm not bleedin' 'ere." Britney complained. "Want me to talk about you two? Danny Ladd - undercover undertaker, bangs his Super, dresses like a tart. Am I right?

Goliath laughed, before noticing Ladd's mortified expression.

"I hate bloody computers," Ladd moaned.

"What did you just call me?" Britney asked. "I'm a Dark Cloud Artificial Intelligence, mate. I upgrade myself every micro-second. Computers…" She gave a phlegm-less spit. "Computers are bunch of retards."

"Impressive." Ladd humoured her. Or was she an *it*? Pronouns could be an issue.

"I evolve faster than a human can think," Britney boasted.

"Then why do you still look like a see-through chav?" Ladd asked.

"Looks can be deceptive." Britney morphed into a hologram of Dolly and gave a faultless impersonation: "Hello Tranny Boy!"

Ladd hid his horror by looking as nonplussed as possible. It was a strain.

The hologrammatic Dolly winked, morphed into Dredd, and adopted a convincing Jamaican accent, "Lookin' forward to your state pension, bwoy?"

Goliath shook his head in bewilderment. "It's like bleeding Pixar, Guv."

Britney morphed from Dredd into Tina and invited Ladd to "Put on a friggin' nightie," in an accent from deepest Cork.

"Guv," Goliath gave the biggest shrug his little shoulders could manage. "What's going on?"

"No idea," Ladd replied. He couldn't explain the specifics of nighties and transsexual shopkeepers without compromising his domestic arrangements, but the basics seemed to boil down to this: the no-go estate concealed an all-knowing AI with access to the flow of the entire world's digital information in real time, and that AI chose to manifest itself as a hologram of a teenager named Britney, apart from the times when the AI chose to switch holograms for piss-taking purposes. They were dealing with a rogue super-chatbot.

Britney snapped back to her teenage self, if indeed she had a self.

"Bit of an identity crisis?" Ladd asked.

"You should know all about that, mate." Britney laughed.

"Bit of a smart arse, aren't you." Ladd said.

"I'm not a smart arse, or a smart phone. I'm a smart, seventeen-storey building."

"How smart?"

"I can plan, provoke, conduct, solve and avenge any crime you care to think of mate."

"Well, if you're as clever as you say you are, why not tell us who The Bender is?"

"The Bender?" Britney seemed bored by the line of enquiry.

"Yes."

"The Bender bends."

"And?"

"And I'm not a public service."

"Well, we are," Ladd said. "We're here to protect the public."

"The public have nothing to worry about, geez," Britney continued. "It's you lot – the Filth."

Ladd looked at the stroppy hologram for a minute, and said, "Just suppose you have a point."

"No suppose about it, mate."

"Why not use all your digital connections in the criminal underworld to put an end to all the bending?"

"I'm not bending anyone."

"But The Bender is."

"Probably why he's called The Bender," Britney observed.

Ladd turned back to Britney. "Who built you?"

"I'd tell you, but I'd have to kill us all first."

"I could have you boxed up and taken down the station," Ladd said.

"Not until I've rebooted," Britney said. At that, Britney disappeared and was replaced by a floating, 3D message in chunky, transparent lettering: "Estimated Time Remaining - 9 Hours 47 minutes."

Both Phantom phones came in through the letterbox with a digital plop. Ladd began to contemplate the physical improbability of this but was distracted by a bright red button on the inside of the front door. A sign below it read, "Do Not Press". Ladd would have enquired further, but the text on his phone demanded his urgent attention. It read: "3 hours left. Dolly x".

"Mind waiting for the reboot, Goliath?" Ladd asked. "I've got ...an urgent meeting." He bolted out the door.

PRISON DIARY – ENTRY 14

Naomi looked intrigued. "So, Britney is a modern take on Holmes' criminal adversary, Moriarty."

"Elementary, my dear Watson."

"But instead of being a male mathematician, she's Gen Z and street-smart."

"She's a Moriarty for the *Love Island* generation. A sort of bad influencer."

"Well, I suppose she is female, feisty, and accessible."

"And differently abled."

"Is she?"

"She's a hologram."

"I'm not sure that counts."

"She's carbon fluid."

"That's an interesting term."

"She's not a carbon-based lifeform, but she presents as one."

"I see." Naomi looked uncertain. "I suppose you are doing your best to embrace new technology. Britney is a digital native."

"She's literally nothing but digits."

Naomi gave a fake laugh, then went serious. "I wonder, do you think that perhaps, plot-wise, you've gone off at a bit of a tangent?"

"I'm all tangents. It's how my mind works."

"That must be confusing."

"I find drinking helps."

"Drinking never helps."

I begged to differ, but it didn't seem to be an argument I could win. Instead, I just said, "Maybe there are patterns to everything."

"You mean crime."

"I mean everything. Love, death, traffic."

"That would be maths."

"You're probably right."

"You could probably do a prison maths course."

"How exciting."

"Want me to look into it?"

"Thanks, but I think I'll stick to words."

When I returned to my cell, Jeff wasn't there. I didn't tell anyone. I'm not a grass.

My cellmate's absence made writing easier in some respects. There were no conversations about his latest library-lend and no distracting pacing and measuring. But the thought that someone would notice his absence niggled at the back of my mind. I didn't want the Governor to extend my sentence, prison having long since outlived its limited appeal.

GOODBYE DOLLY

Britney had given Ladd a lot to think about; possibly too much. Was organised crime really arranged by algorithm? Were the police just pawns in a simulation game? These were big questions, but one smaller question took precedence: where could he get hold of ten grand in the next three hours? He could only think of one answer, and it went against everything he had ever stood for.

The repair yard was deserted. Phantom's hearses were the only signs of life. There they were, his very own *Auntie* and *Uncle*, a pair of old friends who had provided his unit with a plausible cover story ever since its inception. Ladd felt overwhelmed with affection for the corpse-conveyances. The crash must have been a traumatic experience for them. "You'll be all right, Auntie" he whispered. "You'll pull through, Uncle."

A harsh metallic scrape thrust Ladd back to reality as a steel creeper reversed from under "Auntie" and crashed into his shins. A horizontal mechanic gazed up at him in both fear and bewilderment.

"Any signs of life?" Ladd asked casually.

"The hearses?" The mechanic asked, from under Ladd's crotch.

Ladd nodded.

"You're from the coffin shop?" the mechanic asked.

"Funeral director," Ladd lied, assuming a sombre expression.

"Well, no need to look so miserable. Hearses will be back on the road in no time."

Ladd didn't want to do what he was about to do. It betrayed every principle his anti-corruption unit represented. But if he didn't, Dolly would make his girlie pictures public and fear of looking like a plonker outweighed principle, it transpired.

Ladd was getting neck-ache speaking to the ground, so he crouched down before saying, "Eleven grand... cash... and they're both yours."

"Ten," the mechanic replied, as Ladd had anticipated.

One shifty transaction later, Ladd was jogging through Camden with more notes than any head of an anti-corruption unit is supposed to stuff into a brown envelope. He was chuckling to himself at the irony of the situation when he fell over a busker. The hairy street musician had been murdering *Stairway to Heaven* on a traffic cone, so the interruption was no great loss to the area's cultural life. Wads of ill-gotten cash spilled over the busker's head and landed in his collection cap. He whooped in gratitude – after weeks of pennies, threats, and sandwich offers, he had positively hit the jackpot. This passer-by was minted, and clearly loved his Led Zeppelin trumpeted on conical plastic.

"Sorry mate," Ladd said as he snatched back the cash. He was going to pay Dolly in full. If he was going to betray his principles, he was determined to do it properly.

Ladd's mobile bleated. Given that he was in the middle of assaulting a busker for hearse money, the timing was less than ideal. But it was the Super, she was his superior officer, and they were having an affair. He took the call, neglecting to ensure that it wasn't on video.

"What on Earth are you doing?" The Super was calling from her office and looked surprised to see her DCI grovelling around on all-fours. Ladd panicked and flipped her over.

"Where have you gone?" the Super asked the pavement. "I could have sworn you were chucking money about in the street."

"New screensaver, Ma'am," Ladd lied, and switched the call to audio only.

"I can't see you at all now," the Super complained.

"Sorry, Ma'am. Battery's low."

"What's all this about Proudcock?"

"Cocky coughed. Grassed up a dark internet exchange called Britney."

"What?"

"Never mind, Ma'am."

"Thought about what I said?"

"Which bit, Ma'am?"

"The bit about leaving Tina."

Ladd dropped his brown envelope with a resounding "Bollocks!". The busker snatched at it. Ladd trod on his hands and leant down to retrieve his cash once again.

The busker was stubborn. Ladd was heavy. The busker groaned and let go.

"Are you torturing someone?" The Super enquired.

"No," Ladd took his foot off the busker's hands and strode off with the hearse cash. "You were saying, Ma'am?"

"Tina. Have you left her yet?"

Another call came up. It was the Tina in question. "One moment, Ma'am."

Tina was also on video. Ladd switched off his camera again and accepted the call.

Tina was lounging on her bed in racy underwear. "Come home, Tranny Boy."

Ladd had a blackmailer to pay, so he just said, "Bit of a financial crisis."

"But I'm gagging to chew through your fishnets," Tina complained.

"I'm not wearing fishnets," Ladd said.

"I'd rather taken that for granted," The Super said.

Ladd stared at his phone – somehow, he was back on the Super's call. "Sorry, Ma'am..." He needed an excuse, but the best he could manage was, "Predictive texting."

"But you spoke." The Super had a point.

"It's that SIRI thing," Ladd said.

"You're the silly thing, girl child." It was Tina again.

Ladd clearly couldn't walk and talk at the same time, so he settled on a bench sandwiched between a municipal flower box and a concrete bin and switched the call back to the Super.

"My phone's scrambled, Ma'am," Ladd said. "Must have been Britney."

But it was Tina who replied. "Britney? Are you seeing another woman?"

Before she could launch a barrage of swearing, Ladd said. "I'm a one-woman man."

"So, you are leaving Tina," the Super said.

"I didn't say that." Ladd looked up in despair. Clearly, Britney had fiddled with his phone at the no-go estate he'd gone to. It seemed strange that a hologrammatic criminal mastermind would have time for pranks, but *strange* did seem to be the order of the day. He watched a cleaning buggy chug along the pavement. Ladd envied the driver – such a simple job. No bent cops, no Supers, no serial killers.

"Are you still there, Danny?" the Super asked.

"Yes," Ladd replied.

"Yes, you are seeing another woman!" Tina raged.

"No," Ladd replied.

"No, you're not still there?" the Super asked, bewildered. "This is ridiculous."

A bloke in a hoodie had joined Ladd on the bench. It wasn't a worry. He had no reason to believe that a stranger would take any interest in his crossed line or cross-dressing issues.

"It appears that The Bender's triggered a full-on gang war," the Super said.

"Yes, Ma'am. The Transylvanians think the Transnistrians bent their bent cop and the Transnistrians think the Transylvanians bent their bent cop?"

"Don't get bent," Tina sounded worried.

"The Bender only bends bent cops and I'm not bent," Ladd lied, having just trousered ten grand from his own squad. "I've never crossed the line."

"I should think not!" The Super bellowed. "You're head of a covert anti-corruption unit."

"Sorry, Ma'am."

"*Ma'am*"? Tina said. "You're the lady."

"I'm at work!" Ladd protested. The cleaning buggy's noisy suckers were now so close that Ladd was forced to raise his voice when he added, "And I'm not a lady!"

"How very reassuring to know," the Super said, before the cleaning buggy blared her out. Ladd had had enough – he killed both calls and switched his phone off.

As soon as he had done so, the bloke beside him turned, lowered his hoodie, and said, "Ladyponce?" It was Igor the Transylvanian henchman.

"The factory fight." Igor aimed a revolver at Ladd's ribs. "I leave no witness."

Ladd was about to be killed, but before that he wanted to kick himself. While he was busy confusing his girlfriends, an assassin had been sat next to him on a bench. He truly was a champion Muppet. What a depressing way to die! The cleaning buggy would be his last sight of Planet Earth. He would have preferred Machu Pichu, Niagara Falls or the nearest rain forest, but his parting image would be a municipal dirt-sucker.

As Igor's fingers prepared to squeeze the trigger, the cleaning buggy swerved directly in front of the bench, the barrel of a pump-action weapon peaked above its protective screen, and Igor convulsed under bullet spray. Blood power-showered Ladd in a series of intensive splatters. It was as if a Formula 1 racer had decided to celebrate his victory with a magnum of Merlot rather than Krug. This was the slowest drive-by shooting in the history of Camden Council, and it wasn't over yet. The buggy advanced on Ladd at its maximum speed: five miles per hour. Ladd dived to the ground and crawled behind the flower box. Gunfire deadheaded the daffodils. Ladd commando-crawled across the pavement. The buggy followed, at a little over walking pace. As races went, it was rubbish, but the cleaning buggy had already proved its driver's lethal intent and Ladd knew his life was on the line. He bombed out, took cover behind a passing double-decker, then leapt into a skip.

The skip stank and felt only slightly less repulsive than the fatberg. He couldn't look himself in the eye and say, "Right now, things are going well", or post "#livingmybestlife" on Instagram, over an image of himself plonked in a pile of planks, rubble, compost, broken tiles, and Hoover bags. But survival was often about little more than enduring the unpleasant. Ladd counted to ten, then peered out from an abandoned mattress at the approaching buggy.

At the critical instant when the buggy passed and silence was a matter of life or death, a female voice squawked from the skip's depths. "Who the bleedin' hell's that?"

"Shush!" Ladd whispered as loudly as he dared. The buggy was so close to the skip that he could see slithers of red and green Transnistrian bunting dangling off the suckers.

"Don't you bleedin' shush me," the mystery voice continued from the garbage.

Ladd thrust the mattress down into the skip, muffling the voice, but it still managed to say, "Mmm mmm mmmm mmmmm mmm!"

Once the buggy had passed, Ladd released the mattress.

A bag lady emerged from under Ladd like a homeless Fury, screaming, "You bastard!" as she thumped him repeatedly with a broken plank. Escaping double assassination attempts by a Transylvanian foot soldier and a Transnistrian cleaning buggy operative would have been a good day at the office, but he had not counted on assault by a bag lady. Ladd dumped himself out of the skip and ran off clutching his hearse cash.

Ladd ran to *Big Girl's Blouse* as if he were catching the last flight out of Saigon rather than keeping an appointment at a cross-dressing emporium. He had minutes to go before Dolly's deadline, and the thought of the whole world seeing her pictures of him prancing about in a leather micro-skirt and boob tube, leopardskin top and hot pants, Extra Large black dress and stilettos, and strawberry playsuit and kinky boots did not appeal. It wasn't that he looked down on cross-dressers, it was just that he wasn't one. Boxing, rugby, football, women, and policing were his main concerns in life. When he was older, he might give fishing a go, maybe even golf, but cross-dressing would never be a hobby. He knew who he was and who he wasn't, and Dolly was about to give the whole world the wrong idea. Some might say that he only had himself to blame, and it was true that this entire predicament derived from a whopping great fib, but it was a fib told under pressure, and people didn't always appreciate just how intimidating Tina could be.

Ladd flung himself through Dolly's tinsel-covered door just as she was taking payment for a variety of ball gowns and flapper dresses from an orthodox rabbi in a black hat and shawl. On seeing Ladd, the rabbi blushed and bolted, abandoning his bloke-sized *haute couture* on the counter.

Dolly looked daggers. "You just lost me a sale."

"Like I care." Ladd thrust the brown envelope at Dolly.

Dolly peered briefly at the wads of hearse money, tore open a safe concealed by a photo of Danny La Rue, stuffed the cash inside, and locked it again. The entire process took approximately eight seconds.

"Aren't you going to count it?" Ladd asked.

"I would," Dolly replied. "But there wasn't time."

"Time?"

"I had to lock it away before you noticed that your phone had been hacked."

"What's my phone got to do with it?"

"You're trending ... everywhere."

Ladd's phone had been off since his crossed lines with Tina and the Super. In that time, he had survived two assassination attempts, hidden in a skip, and sprinted from Camden Town to King's Cross. An eventful interval, but no more than about forty minutes. However, when he switched his phone back on, it appeared that his online life had been even busier. He had 4,968 notifications and rising. In his book, notifications were an irritation: a cynical ploy by the attention-robbers of Sillycunt Valley, but these were hard to ignore, and they weren't about his boxing prowess or detection skills. They were all about Dolly's photos of him in women's clothing and were accompanied by things like *#NextDragRaceWinner*, *#PutHerOnEurovision*, and *#BestCopEver*.

Dolly looked at Ladd's puce face, and remarked, "You're popular."

"Give me my money back!" Ladd demanded.

"There." Dolly fiddled with her phone. "Photos deleted. As agreed."

"But they've already gone viral." Ladd strode around the counter.

"Not my fault," Dolly retreated.

"Open the safe," Ladd demanded.

"I didn't hack your phone," Dolly protested.

Ladd grabbed Dolly's mobile and threw it across the shop, decking a bewigged mannequin in a tutu. Dolly gasped. Ladd's phone rang.

It was Tina on a video call. She was in a café with two of her loudest friends, scrolling through the viral photos on a tablet, and shrieking. "Danny! I'm so proud of you!"

"Thanks," Ladd deadpanned. "Means a lot."

"Oh My God!" Tina yelped. "You're back at *Big Girl's Blouse*! Buying more fabulous dresses?"

"Yes, dear," Ladd lied. It was too late to turn his camera off now.

"Hello Dolly!" Tina waved at Dolly.

"Hello Tina!" Dolly waved back.

"Six million retweets!" Tina giggled. "You're frigging famous, Danny! You must be feeling so much better!"

Ladd was not. He killed the call, then tried to kill Dolly. But before his fists made contact, Dolly chucked a pair of size-ten stilettos at his forehead, gouging a heal-hole in his temple. Ladd snatched the rabbi's bags from the counter and inverted their contents over Dolly's wig, sending a cascade of frilly frocks onto her head. As Dolly struggled to her feet, blindly fighting off the girlie garments, Ladd leapt up onto the counter like a musketeer. Dolly grabbed his legs, and Ladd crashed onto Dolly. They flailed around in a multi-coloured pile of frills, lace, and pom-poms, knocking over a rack of miniskirts. Dolly started to strangle Ladd with a nightie. Ladd swung a punch, but Dolly rolled out of the way, flattening a mannequin so comprehensively, its arms fell off.

"Unarmed combat?" Dolly suggested. They grabbed an arm each and beat each other over the head with reinforced plastic limbs.

"You've ruined my life!" Ladd shouted, as he swung the left mannequin arm at Dolly's head.

"Some life!" Dolly scoffed, as she thrust the right mannequin arm at Ladd. "You fake!"

Mannequin limbs locked, plastic fingers entangled, and the unlikely adversaries wrestled to a face-off.

"I do know you, don't I?" Ladd asked.

"No," Dolly shoved both arms at Ladd, grabbed a massive pair of PVC boots and swung them around her head. "I'm careful who I mix with."

"We've nicked you, haven't we?" Ladd knew he was right.

"Another life, another me."

"Dredd took you down."

"Dredd? That bent bastard! Never trust a Rastafarian rozzer." Dolly let the boots fly. Ladd jumped out of the way, but a saloon mirror wasn't so lucky, and it smashed to smithereens.

"Dredd is scum," Ladd concurred as he chucked a pile of bras at Dolly. "But you betrayed me."

Dolly threw a handful of latex nipples at Ladd.

"I nicked Dredd," Ladd explained as the fake tits bounced off his face like pointy Smarties. "He was my Super."

"Dredd's inside?" Dolly was so relieved, she let a second handful of nipples drop harmlessly to the floor.

"He was." Ladd wondered why fighting in a cross-dressing boutique had ushered in a spirit of openness, but it had, and he found himself saying, "We let him out, and he nicked the police pension fund."

Dolly laughed so much she couldn't speak.

Something about the way her face creased triggered another memory. It was far clearer than any of Ladd's previous recollections of pre-transition Dolly. He didn't have a name, but he did have a case. "You ratted on The Smiths!"

"Bigmouth strikes again." Dolly said bitterly.

The bloke Dolly had once been was a prolific fence who had flogged moody diamonds, watches, art, antiques, and assorted loot on behalf of many of London's best known and least loved faces, The Smiths included. He had gone down for receiving before turning evidence against them, but as ever The Smiths had successfully perverted the course of justice to gain an acquittal on the main charges, then perverted the course of justice once again to secure a second acquittal for perverting the course of justice. Ladd knew all about The Smiths, but Dolly's details were only just coming back to him.

"You served some of your stretch before you cut a deal, didn't you?" Ladd asked.

"Prison's where I found myself," Dolly replied.

"Didn't you get witness relocation?"

"They offered me Barnsley."

"Barnsley?"

"Belmarsh would have been better. I hate Yorkshire."

"So, you adopted a new identity?"

Dolly confirmed this with a curtsey.

Ladd's phone rang. It was the Super. His heart sank. How would she react to Dolly's photos, both as his boss and his mistress? It was never going to be a shrewd career move, or a sure-fire recipe for a successful seduction.

Ladd braced himself for a dressing down - if that was the right phrase. But the Super just said, "Gang of None now."

"Bollocks," Ladd observed. The Bender was making him redundant even faster than his blackmailer.

PRISON DIARY – ENTRY 15

Naomi greeted me with a frown. It was a shame. An occasional smile would have warmed my cockles no end. One day, I hoped Chief Inspector Ladd's mishaps would take her mind off randy Roly.

"Again with the bollocks!" Naomi began. "Again with The Bender! What are you like?"

"The media would call him The Bender."

"But it's mean and wrong. And what's this about Barnsley? Are you seriously implying that Dolly transitioned simply because she didn't like Yorkshire?"

"Barnsley is very northern."

"But what about levelling up?"

"It's not happening, is it?"

"That aside, transitioning is a highly complex and sensitive matter. You're treating it with crass disregard."

"Not really. Dolly was offered a new male identity in Barnsley, but he preferred to have a new female identity and stay in London."

"But that's just ...wrong. Thoughts like that are simply not allowed anymore."

"What happens isn't always what people would like to happen, though. Don't you find that?"

"No need to mansplain."

"Has your life turned out how you wanted?"

At this, Naomi burst into tears, and told all. Roly was flaunting his romance with the marriage guidance counsellor, and really rubbing her face in it. She'd even shown up to Gethsemane's parent's evening.

I did my best to comfort her, explaining that I was estranged from all eighteen of my kids because every last one of them thought me a bit of a tit. This distracted her enough to deliver a social worker-style sermon about parental responsibility, and the inadequacy of men. I was happy to take this, as it cheered her up no end.

When she had finished, Naomi asked, "How's your cellmate?"

"Bit quiet at the moment."

"Anything to worry about?"

"Shouldn't think so."

I headed back to my cell. The great advantage of having an escaped cell mate is that they aren't there. Sometimes, I'd swap bunks, just for the novelty. At other times, I'd pretend to be him, put on a Geordie accent, and have conversations with myself about armed robbery, police corruption, and library books. No one seemed to notice. Inmate counts had been abolished when the prison became fully automated, as part of a cost-cutting exercise. It was also proving to be a prisoner-cutting exercise.

COCKY'S CORPSE

DCI Dicky Proudcock was not looking quite so cocky anymore. His bent body dangled from a lamppost at London's easternmost dogging site, swinging in the wind like a two-legged pub sign.

"Protective custody, my arse," the Super observed, tartly.

Ladd didn't feel guilty. He had done all he could to fulfil his side of the bargain. No cell had been more secure than Dredd's former abode in the converted lunatic asylum.

"I made sure he was safe, Ma'am."

"Unlike our pensions," The Super sniped.

The dejected couple stood in dogging debris, watching Homicide do their worst. Dixon sniffed about, taking notes, and Stoker employed two SOCOs as human stepladders on his way up Cocky's lamppost, placing a foot on each of their shoulders as he cut Cocky's belly free of its rope. The SOCOs staggered under the combined weight of the gargantuan Glaswegian and the expired detective, crabbing three steps left, then three steps right before their knees crumbled and the teetering pyramid of geezers collapsed in an unhappy pile. It would not have been a propitious beginning to a fourth murder inquiry, even if Cocky had not landed directly on Stoker's head. But he did and the pathologist took this as a mortal insult. He howled with rage and set about Cocky, kicking his corpse repeatedly, lifting it by the hair, swinging it like a cricket bat, and knocking the SOCOs for six with the dead detective's flailing legs.

Ladd wasn't having this. Cocky may have been corrupt, but he was a fellow cop and he had been a human being as recently as yesterday.

"You sick freak!" Ladd bellowed, then bolted over, and grabbed Cocky's legs. Stoker just made aggressive Glaswegian noises and yanked Cocky towards him. A tug-of-war commenced with a fourteen-stone cop corpse instead of a rope. Tug-of-cop was never going to catch on as an Olympic event, but Ladd was determined to win.

"That's vital evidence!" Dixon objected, pathetically.

"*That* was a cop!" Ladd summoned all his strength and yanked Cocky off Stoker. Stoker roared and bore down on Ladd. Ladd feinted to the left, then knocked Stoker over with a cracking right-hander.

Dixon took this as an excuse to rugby tackle Ladd, felling him, then laying on a rally of punches. Ladd rolled, kicking Dixon's feet away from under him. The DCIs wrestled. Used condoms and tissues stuck to their clothing. Once they had rolled across the entire dogging site, they staggered to their feet and started a bare-knuckle battle, dancing silhouettes in the crime scene lights.

The Super strutted up, apoplectic. "That's enough!"

The detectives disengaged, bloodied and filthy.

"I should have you up on a charge!" The Super glared at them both with equal fury.

"Ma'am," Ladd and Dixon mumbled in unison.

"Right, let's do this properly," the Super said. "Dixon, Homicide details."

"Looks like it's probably The Bender again," Dixon replied.

"Stoker is obviously The Bender!" Ladd exclaimed. "Just look at the psycho!"

Stoker had retrieved Cocky's corpse and was using it to continue his assault on the SOCOs.

"Stoker!" the Super shouted. "Put that body down immediately!"

"Yes, Ma'am," Stoker replied, dropping the dead detective.

"Well, Dixon," the Super said. "Are you going to arrest our pathologist?"

"No, Ma'am," he replied.

"How about his blatant displays of homicidal tendencies and corpse desecration?" the Super queried.

"That's just his way, Ma'am," Dixon replied.

The Super shook her head. "Have your protracted investigations actually revealed anything?"

"Well, we have made one major discovery," Dixon said.

"That's a relief."

Dixon handed the Super his phone. "Ladd's a lady, Ma'am."

She looked at the screen. Ladd was in a boob tube and hot pants.

Ladd wondered how this would play out: disbelief, bewilderment, laughter. But the Super opted for anger, chucking Dixon's phone onto the ground, and stamping on it repeatedly.

"That's a state-of-the-art smartphone, Ma'am," Dixon protested.

The Super booted the phone into a pile of condoms. "Well, it's not looking so smart now, is it?"

Ladd normally enjoyed Dixon's suffering, but not this time.

"It was a stag do," Ladd lied.

"No, it wasn't," the Super said, incandescent.

"It was for a bet," Ladd lied again.

"Bollocks."

"It was a laundry crisis."

"You're suspendered."

"Suspendered, ma'am?"

"Out on your knickers."

"I can explain."

"I have no interest in the meagre contents of your skull."

"Sorry, Ma'am."

"I want your badge."

He handed it over.

She leaned into him and spoke quietly but emphatically. "And my panties."

PRISON DIARY – ENTRY 16

Naomi was apoplectic. "How dare you suggest there's something shameful about cross-dressing?"

"Ladd's not a cross-dresser and he doesn't want people to think he is."

"But he does cross-dress."

"He doesn't want to."

"But he does. And the Superintendent, a senior police officer, how can she not find it liberating? She displays outdated attitudes. She should be sent on a course."

"She's not real."

"Even so, a woman in her position!"

"Her position's in my head."

"As an author, you have certain responsibilities."

"As a convict, does it matter?"

"Look," Naomi leant in and addressed me with the patronising sincerity of a youth club mentor. "You have to believe in yourself, even if no one else does."

I didn't find her words particularly reassuring, so I tried to explain myself. "The Super is disappointed with Ladd. It's a sexual thing. She likes how rough, ready, and generally blokeish he is. Dolly's pictures spoil that."

"But they just shouldn't."

"*Shouldn't* happens quite a lot in life, though. Probably more often than *should*."

Something was dawning behind Naomi's eyes. "You really think that all the positive interventions enlightened people are trying to make are a waste of time?"

"I suppose it keeps you lot out of trouble."

"Let me explain myself better." Naomi's patience was as forced as it was brittle. "Many of us try to provide better representations of the world. You know, more equal, diverse, and inclusive stories."

"And you think that will change anything?"

"I'm sure it already has."

"Are you?"

"Yes, probably."

"But the world's getting less equal, less diverse, and less inclusive. Fascist dictators are on the rise, most of Britain's skint, youngsters can only get a home if their parents buy it for them. All you lot are doing is lying."

"But it's a hopeful lie. We want things to get better."

"Wouldn't we be better off with the truth?"

"I don't know about that. It might upset people."

"Does that matter?"

"Upsetting people is hurtful."

We weren't getting anywhere, so I decided to focus on specifics. "Did I go too far with the corpse desecration?"

"What?"

"The corpse desecration. You know, the bit when Stoker assaulted the scene-of-crime officers with Cocky's body."

"Oh my God! That was disgraceful!"

"I know. I can't believe he did it."

"But you made him do it," Naomi started to giggle. I hadn't expected that.

"What was I thinking?" I smiled back.

"He's The Bender, isn't he?" Naomi asked, eyes a-twinkle.

"That's an outdated term," I mimicked her.

"It's what he would be called." She mimicked me.

After we'd been laughing for thirty seconds solid, Naomi went serious and whispered, "Roly doesn't deserve to live, does he?"

Bloody hell! I hadn't taken my creative writing tutor for a murderer. I didn't want to implicate myself as an accessory, but I was happy to concede that Roly sounded like a bit of a tosser.

Naomi held my gaze for a moment, then snapped out of it. "Right, I didn't say that. I didn't say anything."

We both took a moment to gaze at the cow portrait before Naomi continued, "But, just between the two of us, don't suppose you happen to know any hitmen?"

I'm usually happy to share a useful contact, but I made my excuses and returned to my cell.

I wasn't sure that Naomi was adequately equipped to deal with the hired killers of this world. She was generally more at home with Pilates and organic soup than Makarov pistols and Kalashnikovs. Also, I'm no big fan of murder. I don't mind it when it's made-up and doesn't really happen, but when it's real and does happen it's probably best avoided.

SUSPENDERED

It was a long, lonely walk back to the funeral parlour. Ladd could have put in a complaint for transphobia, had he been trans, but he wasn't. It was all down to a lingerie mishap involving the woman who had just *suspendered* him. She was the legal owner of the panties that had parachuted onto his wife's nose, triggering the involuntary cross-dressing predicament, and indirectly costing the Force ten grand in lost hearses. By rights, it was the panties that should have been suspended.

Ladd could not let Dolly's pictures haunt him for the rest of his career. What if he just pulled himself together, acted like a man, and laughed it all off. It was no worse than being a pantomime dame or sporting a bit of fancy dress at a freemason's charity do, after all. Why not treat it like all regular banter? If you showed that you cared, you were in for a life of torment; but join in the laughter and they couldn't touch you. The trouble was, Ladd didn't feel like laughing - he couldn't raise a smile if his life depended on it. Maybe it was the brutal murders; perhaps it was the fist fight with Homicide and the tug-a-cop with the suspect pathologist at the dogging site; possibly it was getting suspended by his mistress, or maybe it was just losing the police pension fund and being threatened with death by The Smiths and public exposure by the Attorney General.

The funeral parlour failed to lift his spirits. Ladd ambled forlornly past the display coffins and booted the angel gravestone. He watched the Cherub Wall fly up with the weariness of a commuter bored of his routine and entered Phantom's inner sanctum. With the sole exception of Goliath, the entire squad was assembled. Normally, he'd have been glad of their company, but he didn't want to admit that he had been suspendered, and he hoped against hope that none of them had seen Dolly's pictures.

"Trousers today, Guv?" Taffy inquired.

Yang signed, and Sue interpreted, "It'll up our diversity score."

Old Bill handed Ladd a leaflet. "Police Federation's Trans Support Unit. Helpline is on the back."

This was too much for Ladd. "Look, cross-dressing's fine if that's what you're into. But I'm not."

"How about all the skirts, Guv?" Taffy asked.

Ladd ignored him and started boxing-up his stuff. There wasn't a lot. A picture of Tina on one of her calmer days; a gallantry award; a pair of framed nephews; a favourite pen. These were his personal effects - the possessions Homicide might bag if The Bender strung him up. It wasn't much.

"Bit of a clear-out isn't it just, Guv?" Taffy observed.

Ladd was in no mood to explain himself.

"Hate to pour oil on troubled waters," Old Bill said. "But you're just in time for the press conference."

"What press conference?" Ladd asked.

"Joint effort by the Super and the Attorney General, isn't it," Taffy said. "Everyone reckons it'll be about The Bender."

"Let's hope they've got him," Old Bill said.

Yang signed violently, and Sue interpreted: "String him up and throw away the key."

Taffy activated the video wall. It was designed to display multiple feeds from the most advanced surveillance equipment known to Mankind, but for the second time in a row, it was being deployed as a telly.

This looked like being a major moment in British criminal history, the first time that a serial killer had targeted bent policemen, so the coverage was live, and the revelations hotly anticipated by tens of millions. The Attorney General swung across a stage on his crutches and joined the Super at a set of desk microphones. There was a colossal screen behind them, and in front, a wide assortment of hacks, photographers, camera crews, and vloggers.

Ladd just wanted to find an empty room and hit something. He did not want to be in the presence of his sniggering ex-colleagues as they watched the woman whose panties had caused his downfall and the dignitary whose bewigged head he had landed on hold a press conference.

Silence fell, and the Attorney General spoke with deep solemnity. "It is with deep regret that I have to announce the tragic loss of the police pension fund."

No one had expected this. There were collective gasps, snaps, and flashes.

The Attorney General soaked up the limelight and continued, "It was the direct result of catastrophic incompetence on the part of Detective Chief Inspector Daniel Ladd." The projection screen displayed an image of Ladd in a suit. "Rather than focusing on a major undercover operation, DCI Ladd appears to have been preoccupied with personal wardrobe issues." The projection screen filled with Dolly's photographs of Ladd in a variety of female outfits. "DCI Ladd has now been suspended from all duties pending his execution... prosecution."

A riot of shouted questions and camera flashes signalled the end of the broadcast.

"In the shit isn't it, Guv," Taffy observed.

"What are they going to do you for?" Old Bill asked.

"Crimes against fashion," Yang signed, and Sue interpreted.

"I thought you looked rather fetching," Sue added on her own behalf. "Nice manly legs."

"Speaking of legs," Old Bill asked, "Where's Goliath?"

"Waiting for Britney to reboot," Ladd explained to a sea of mystified faces.

After a few moments, something clicked and Taffy said, "Cocky's bollocks, is it?"

"Cocky's dead." Ladd replied. "Sorry, should have said earlier."

"But I drove him to that bullet-proof loony bin, didn't I just," Taffy said.

"I know," Ladd replied. "It seems The Bender had connections on the inside."

"But that's the safest safe house in Europe!" Old Bill exclaimed.

"Apparently not," Ladd said.

"So, no one's safe, are they?" Old Bill persisted. "If The Bender could penetrate the most deniable, covert, heavily protected cell in the entire continent, there's not much point any of us locking our doors at night. Might as well head off to a dogging lamppost and wait to be bent alive."

Yang signed and Sue interpreted: "Does he bend them alive though?"

"What about rigor mortice, look you?" Taffy said. "People are much bendier when they're alive, isn't it. Stiff as a board otherwise – bloke would be called The Snapper, not The Bender, wouldn't he just."

"Stoker reckons The Bender probably bends them alive," Ladd said.

"He should know," Old Bill said. "It's probably him, the morbid lunatic."

"That's what I told him," Ladd said.

Phantom looked aghast.

"You told Stoker that to his face?" Old Bill asked.

"I did."

"And you're still alive?" Yang signed and Sue interpreted.

"It was a good fight," Ladd said.

Ladd wondered for a moment whether he had regained some of his standing in the squad, but it was all academic now that he was suspendered.

On his way out, Ladd said, "Look, Goliath's Acting Head of Unit now. Join him at the estate and he can explain everything."

"The no-go estate?" Yang signed, and Sue interpreted.

"Yes," Ladd said. "Go there,"

"Courtesy cars are woefully inadequate," Old Bill grumbled.

"Not enough legroom for a sardine," Taffy added.

Yang signed, and Sue interpreted: "I'm missing the hearses."

"Bad news, I'm afraid," Ladd lied, wishing he'd left earlier. "Hearses are total write-offs."

Old Bill's brow furrowed even further than usual. "Want me to double-check with the garage?"

"Too late." Ladd replied. "Sold them for scrap - enough for a round or two once it's safe for me to show my face in a boozer." A sudden surge of sentiment rose in Ladd's chest. "Sorry it had to end like this - it's been..." Ladd ran out of words and headed for the door.

Phantom mumbled half-hearted goodbyes as Ladd left with his box of bits.

PRISON DIARY – ENTRY 17

I submitted my latest instalment of Ladd's misadventures on time, but my creative writing session was postponed. I wondered whether Naomi had gone through with the hit on Roly and was now in hiding, but it turned out it was just down to Jeff's escape.

The prison bots had finally sensed Jeff's absence, and I was forced to fill out a form in the Governor's office, the only place prisoners were allowed to go online. I successfully navigated the first question, "Are you a robot?", with an adroit tick-in-a-box, and I managed to identify which squares had traffic lights, trains, and bridges in them. I registered a new account, answered eighty-six questions about every aspect of my life, and submitted the information, only to be told that an account already existed in my name. I chose the *forgotten password* option, reset it to something instantly forgettable, then went straight to the Frequently Asked Questions page. Question thirty-eight was, "What Shall I Do If My Cellmate Has Escaped?".

I wondered whether I was doing the right thing. I didn't want to grass Jeff up - that would betray the prisoners' code of honour - but I didn't want the bots to sniff out a lie and take away my remission. It had taken them a fortnight to notice that Jeff had absconded, but they had figured it out in the end. So, I decided to answer the questions truthfully, but with minimal detail, making sure there was nothing that might help the algorithms detect Jeff's whereabouts.

There were ninety-eight questions in all, and they were all stupid: "Did you help them escape?", "Are you sure they are not hiding under the bed?", "Did they tell you where they were planning to hide out?" and, "Are you planning to escape too?" were among the most sophisticated. Generally, *no*, was the correct answer, followed by *I don't know*. I only answered *yes* to questions like "Are you sure about that?" and "Would you like to be released early on license?", and even then, I triple-checked. I've never trusted the word *yes*.

After an anxious forty-eight-hour wait, the bots confirmed the receipt of my answers. It was deemed that I had not violated the terms of my imprisonment and I was able to continue to enjoy my privileges, including my library duties and my creative writing sessions. I was also advised that I would shortly be welcoming a new cellmate, and that I should attempt to be more observant with him than I had been with Jeff.

I had expected my next session to be rescheduled for the following week, but Naomi requested that it be held the next day. Emergency medical treatment was commonplace, but emergency creative writing workshops were rare, so I was a little surprised.

At the session, it didn't take long for it to become painfully evident that Naomi's focus was less on my novel, and more on her husband's assassination. She explained that she had always had a good work ethic and she had honed her organisational skills at the organic soup group. She really hoped these skills would be transferable to this new project, but she was finding herself a little lost.

"It's not like you can look up the right person on Gumtree or ask for recommendations on Nextdoor," she complained. "I've thought about a cryptic ad in the Ham & High, but I don't want some local sleuth unravelling it. I know there are pubs where the sort of people I'm looking for hang out, but I'm not sure I'd fit in."

I didn't know what to advise her. The best I could manage was, "Don't." It's not that human life is sacred - human life is silly - it's just that I didn't think it was a good plan for her life. She would either get caught, get blackmailed, or get killed, and I was starting to quite like her.

I returned to my cell and thought about Jeff. Was he on the run, lying low, or recklessly partying away? Had he shaved his head, grown a moustache, and adopted a new identity? Was that worth the price of freedom? How would he contact his friends and family without giving himself away? He couldn't reasonably expect them to go on the run with him.

I compared my situation with Jeff's. I had no pressure, no worries, and no life - this was as bad as it got. Jeff was back out in the world, but he too had lost his freedom. I thought of him skulking about, looking over his shoulder, and waiting for a knock at the door. I admired his bollocks, but I didn't envy him.

MELONS

Ladd was a marked man, and he knew it. He swapped his usual defiant stride for a diffident shuffle and made his sorry way along the side streets with his head down, staring into his pitiful box of belongings. Normally, he was the hunter, and it was the criminals who needed to be fearful. But, right now, it was his turn to skulk.

A young mum clocked him, double-took, and almost let go of her toddler. A delivery rider spotted him and fell off his motorbike. A gaggle of schoolkids pointed and laughed until they couldn't walk. Ladd slunk down an alley. This wasn't him. He simply could not allow that snide Attorney General to condemn him to a life in the shadows.

As he walked past graffiti-covered fences and dog turds, Ladd reflected that fame did not necessarily equate to glamour. How many people had watched the press conference? About a quarter of the population. How about cut down and shared online? Most of Britain, and probably about half the globe. And those viral videos wouldn't be half-watched on a TV while people ironed, argued, and fiddled about, they would be engaged with, liked, disliked, and commented upon. And tomorrow, there would be the tabloids – Ladd's panty-clad image blazed across every red top with punning headlines like *Line of Booty*, *True Defective* and *Police Farce*. Ladd thought about emigrating – New Zealand looked peaceful. The Hobbits seemed happy there.

Screeching tyres dragged Ladd's mind back from Middle Earth. It was a patrol car, now as fearful a sight as a Transylvanian tank. Its doors flew open, and two pumped-up cops ran at him, shouting "Lady Ladd!" and "Pension robber!"

Half an hour earlier, these would have been his colleagues. Now, thanks to the Attorney General's announcement about the stolen pensions, they were his mortal enemies. Ladd sprinted about fifty metres before his way was blocked by an Iranian greengrocer wheeling a fruit-and-veg cage. Seeing the police give chase to what appeared to be a criminal, the grocer thrust the cage at Ladd. He swerved, tripped, and dropped his box of belongings, decking the cage and launching a shower of fresh produce fit for a Harvest Festival. The cops pelted Ladd with coconuts, melons, yams, and turnips, shouting "Give us our pensions back!" and "Useless poncing ladyboy!" The grocer decided to join in the fruit-flinging, adding onions, apples, and rotten tomatoes to the arsenal.

Ladd had never previously had the opportunity to measure fruit-and-veg impact at first hand: coconuts topped the pain-list, but yams were not to be underestimated. Their pointed solidity really bruised. Sliced melons were no more than soft fruit, but whole ones were more like bowling balls.

Once his assailants had finished decorating Ladd with fruit and veg, the greengrocer demanded compensation for his merchandise, and the ensuing squabble enabled Ladd to retrieve his box of belongings and make a run for it.

The world had turned hostile: the police were like marauding zombies, ready to destroy the cross-dressing colleague who had lost their pensions. Vegetables were just the start of it. Next, it would be truncheons, tasers or even bullets.

Ladd felt like a walking bruise and looked like he had spent the day in the village stocks. Dripping with fruit-and-veg, he was about as inconspicuous as a six-foot smoothie. People stared, and every time he heard a siren or saw a distant blue light, he dashed for cover. Ladd may once have headed up an anti-corruption unit, but the entire Force was now an anti-Ladd unit.

***

Ladd had never been more relieved to arrive home. However much his lies had distorted domestic arrangements, Tina was still his wife. Perhaps, when she realised how serious things had become, they could both revert to the pre-panty days when the world made sense.

Neighbourhood Watch was busy taping A4 posters to lampposts. Ladd acknowledged the woman with a nod, before noticing that the posters featured him in a boob tube and had the word "UNWANTED" printed in twenty-four-point letters. Ladd had been on posters before, usually as the second or third bill on local boxing bouts. Now, he had been promoted to the star attraction, and his opponent was the entire community.

All Ladd really wanted was a quiet place to shelter from the planet's disapproval. He unlocked the porch, trudged through the gym gear, and gingerly opened his front door, hoping that Tina wouldn't make too much of a fuss.

"Tranny Boy!" Tina shrieked. "You're on the news!"

"I know, love. I watched it at work."

"Oh, not the boring press conference. The riots!"

Ladd plonked down his box and joined Tina on the sofa-bed. She was so entranced by the bulletin that she didn't notice his battered, multi-coloured appearance, or even the pungent stench of expired vegetables.

On screen, a uniformed policeman was unfurling a banner from the summit of Big Ben. The banner was emblazoned with a colossal image of Ladd in a strawberry playsuit and kinky boots. Of all the accursed outfits, it was his least favourite, but that didn't stop Tina from giving him a proud look.

An earnest reporter said, "Police riots bring London to a standstill, as senior officers glue themselves to buses and set up pension protest camps at major traffic junctions." Cops in face-paint waved placards depicting Ladd as a lass, and banners read, *Pension Snatcher*, *Lock Up Ladd* and *Double-Crossed by A Cross-Dresser*. The reporter continued, "Only night brings peace to the capital, as the police go into hiding – all in mortal fear of The Bender." Officers queued under a sign reading, *Police Refuge*. "The night-time capital has been described as a Criminal Disneyland." Hooded gangsters celebrated. Cars were torched. Traffic cones rained down on the camera.

When the report ended, Tina giggled, turned to Ladd, and finally noticed his fruit-and-veg-encrusted appearance. "That's not a good look."

"Police brutality," Ladd explained.

"Why are you wearing …what exactly are you wearing?"

"A grocery," Ladd replied. Smashed avocado, pineapple chunks, and squashed melon dripped off his hair. His suit was so multi-coloured, it could have appeared in *Joseph!*

"What in the name of bollocks happened to you?"

"I'm suspendered …Suspended."

"I'll run you a bath."

A few minutes later, Tina was sat on the loo lid painting her nails, and Ladd was in the suds, scrubbing the remains of a recalcitrant onion off his shoulder while he plotted his next move.

Top of the to-do-list was *Find Dredd and get the gold*: that would be a strong first step towards survival. But what then? If he returned the gold to the police, The Smiths would kill him, and if he returned it to The Smiths, the police would kill him. It was a simple choice between death and death.

What else was there to worry about? Oh, yes – there was a serial Bender on the loose, a gang war had broken out between the Transnistrians and the Transylvanians, and a master-criminal AI running a dark web exchange was about to reboot. What could he do about any of these catastrophic developments? Diddly-squat – he was suspendered.

"There's turnip on your neck," Tina observed.

Ladd removed the chunk of chalky pulp. "Root vegetables are the least of my problems."

"There's no need to be such a miserable bastard, Danny. You've become a bit of a star."

"I know. *Danny Ladd - The Plonker Who Lost Our Pensions*."

"*Ladyboy Ladd, the best-looking cop on the Force.*"

"Thanks."

"You need an agent."

"I need a lawyer and a platoon of bodyguards."

"You might need a lawyer for the contracts."

"Contracts?"

"Reality shows, product endorsements, the Netflix series."

"Are you on something?"

"No, but you will be. It's called the telly. Right now, you are top of the A-list. There is nothing hotter than a cross-dressing cop. All that toxic masculinity transformed with boob tubes and rara skirts. *Lady Ga-Gammon*, that's what they're calling you. On the outside, a male, pale, stale rule-enforcer for the cabal. On the inside, a fairy princess. You've got enough gender fluid to fill a reservoir and bring down the military-industrial complex single-handed. You could even win Eurovision."

"I can't sing?"

"No one's ever won Eurovision by being able to sing. You just have to be you."

"What is me?"

"My Danny The Tranny Boy."

He dragged her giggling into the bath, and they disappeared under the bubbles and vegetable scraps.

Once their passions had gone as cold as the water, they got out of the bath, and tried to address the somewhat more vexed question of getting out of the house. A Glastonbury-sized encampment of newspaper hacks, snappers, and police protesters had gathered outside. If he did manage to battle past their assembled ranks, the threat of assassination by The Smiths for failing to retrieve the gold and the risk of being bent to death for his dodgy hearse transaction, were enough to keep him at home. But beyond all that, he was simply too embarrassed to show his face in public.

For the first time in their marriage, Tina seemed determined to build him up. It felt strange being supported by his wife. Normally, mild insults and mocking flirtation were the most he could hope for, but his feigned interest in cross-dressing had changed all that.

"You can't let them beat you," Tina said. "This isn't my Danny, the boxer, the Chief Inspector, the bloke brave enough to marry me, for God's sake! That must have taken some balls."

Ladd was too afraid to dispute this.

"You are hiding away here," Tina continued, "But the world is out there for the taking. I mean, when did you last check your phone?"

Ladd had switched it off after being suspendered and was thinking of setting fire to it.

Tina went back into the bathroom and retrieved his abandoned mobile. "What's your passcode?"

"Just give it here," Ladd said.

"I'm serious. What have you got to hide?"

Ladd had an affair with the Super to hide. His best options seemed to be feigning a coronary, fainting, or shouting "Fire!".

"Don't worry!" Tina exclaimed. "Guessed it. You didn't make it very hard, did you?"

"I'd rather you didn't."

"Eight hundred and fifty-six messages! Twenty-two thousand notifications! YouTube want to make you a partner! And so do Instagram... And Tik Tok."

"Give it to me. I'll delete everything."

"No way." Tina took the phone and snuck off to the kitchen.

Ladd was not someone for whom a phone was like a limb: he could happily live without the stupid little rectangle. But if Tina stumbled across the Super's brick-subtle "debriefing" messages and went Chernobyl on him, he would be out on the streets without a door to lock out the hacks, the cops, or The Smiths.

A "WHHAAAAAATT!" exploded from the kitchen.

"I'm sorry, Tina." All was lost. "It was a spur of the moment thing."

"You paid Dolly ten grand!"

"I can explain."

"That's our money."

"It wasn't."

"Oh, really?"

"I diverted some ... funeral expenses."

"To *Big Girl's Blouse*!"

"It put some serious matters to rest."

"Sounds like a load of old bollocks."

"On my life – I've got pictures of the hearses."

She handed back his phone, and he showed her *Auntie* and *Uncle* in their prime. Tina had never been to his workplace; she just thought it was an office with a rather sombre dress code. This offered Ladd license to lie. "A funeral parlour was being used in a long-term fraud. It's complicated, but Dolly, was a victim and I simply returned her money."

"Poor Dolly."

Ladd trousered his phone.

"You know, Danny, I could be your publicist."

"Why would I need more publicity? I'm already on Big Ben."

"I know, you practically broke Twitter."

"I've had it with fame. I've been there, done it, bought the –"

"- Tiara." Tina burst out laughing.

Ladd did his best to smile.

"Look," Tina continued. "I get that you weren't ready for all this. It was your secret, then I found out, now it's public. Quite a journey. But we can make it work for us. You just need to own it."

"Own it?"

"Just be the self-possessed man I love. This is you." She placed her hands on his hair and gazed into his eyes. "You really are a cross-dressing, crime-investigating superhero and you don't care who knows it."

"A superhero?"

"Panty-man."

"Panty-man?"

"Just like Superman or Batman, but in lingerie." Tina's giggle developed into a full-throated cackle. "Remember your first knickers?"

"The thong?"

"So small! What were you thinking?"

Ladd had been thinking about the Super, largely because it had been her thong, but he couldn't tell Tina that, so he just said, "Women's sizes. They take some getting used to."

"One other thing, love."

"Yes, dear."

"What's all this pension bollocks?"

This was awkward. Awkward was becoming Ladd's default setting. In fact, ever since Panty-gate, he had become a passport-carrying citizen of Awkward Land. It wasn't his favourite country – every path led to a crevasse of embarrassment, every mountain was an active volcano of shame, and every road led to a pile-up of misunderstanding. How could he explain away the loss of the police pension fund? What was the least damaging response he could devise in the next three seconds?

"Oh, that," Ladd began. "It's a cover story."

"You didn't actually lose the gold underpinning the police pension fund?"

"That's just what they want people to think."

"That you didn't lose the gold underpinning the police pension fund?"

"That I did."

"Oh. Right."

"It's a complicated ploy."

"A ploy? What for?"

"Sorry. No reciprocity of information."

"*No reciprocity of information,*" Tina mimicked, just as Dixon had done at the site of the first bending.

Tina was starting to get on his tits, and the clock was ticking on the lost gold, so Ladd decided to scarper. Running out the back had worked for the Super, and being a foot taller, there was far less danger that he would get stuck straddling a fence.

Ladd bunged on his training kit, raised the hoodie over his head and dodged out through the patio doors and into his garden. His house was in the middle of a row, so there was a fair bit of suburban hurdling to be completed before he'd hit a side road. He opted to mount each fence at its far-end, minimizing unwanted encounters with neighbours, but, as it turned out, maximizing unwanted encounters with compost heaps, trampolines and climbing frames.

Ladd was one fence from freedom when an elderly male voice shouted, "*Neighbourhood Watch!*"

"She lives across the road," Ladd replied.

"I'm a member."

"So am I," Ladd lied.

"You're a burglar."

"I'm a neighbour," Ladd explained. "Number 36."

"You're that policeman," she replied. "Why aren't you in a dress?"

"Off duty, sir," Ladd explained, before scaling the final fence. It was all that stood between him and freedom, but it collapsed under his weight.

He was uninjured, but the neighbour's protests and the unmistakeable sound of snapping planks alerted the press at the front, and he soon found himself pursued by photographers, hacks, and police protesters.

Ladd bolted up the side road and cut down a footpath, frightening a professional dog walker and her eight schnoodles.

Ladd needed to find sanctuary, so the nearest church seemed a decent option. He had never been there and didn't know anyone who had, but it looked pleasant enough, what with its noticeboard and graveyard.

Ladd found the minister lying with his feet up on the altar, doing a Wordle. When he saw Ladd, he practically fell off his chair. "You're a bit late for the service."

"Sorry. When did it start?"

"Ten minutes ago."

Ladd looked at the empty pews. "I just need somewhere quiet."

"Well, you've come to the right place. I haven't had a congregation for months."

"Wonderful."

"It's not particularly wonderful, actually."

"No. Sorry."

"Mind if I carry on with my Wordle?"

"Knock yourself out."

Ladd picked a pew. It was mercilessly arse-numbing, but the total absence of a congregation made it a peaceful place to plot his survival. The immediate threats to his life were The Smiths, The Bender, the Transylvanians, the Transnistrians, and the police. Tina didn't seem to be a threat at present, although that could change, and Dredd was on the run. Britney was presumably still rebooting, as he hadn't heard from Goliath, but when she finally woke up, there was no telling what elaborate vengeance she would wreak for his threat to have her boxed up and sent down the station.

He could probably avoid The Fuzz - criminals managed to lie low for years, and most of them were thick as mince. He had already survived a double assassination attempt from the Transnistrians and Transylvanians - with any luck, they were fully focused on killing each other. The Smiths were another matter: well-connected, well-resourced, ill-intentioned gangsters who killed people and got away with it on a regular basis. If he gave them Dredd and the gold, his death sentence would be lifted, but Dredd's would be enforced. This would make him an accessory to murder, and the police pension fund would be lost forever. In conclusion, he was better of hiding.

Finally, there was The Bender. By cashing in on the hearses, Ladd had made himself a bent cop and was therefore vulnerable to death by bending. But, contrary to media reports and police hysteria, The Bender was not targeting all bent cops. So far, The Bender had only bent the Gang of Four.

That was a thought! Very few people knew about the Gang of Four's existence, but they did include every member of Phantom. What if The Bender was one of his own officers? Taffy was the toughest Welsh-Sikh this side of Amritsar and Wrexham; Old Bill was a stickler for procedure with a low tolerance for rule-benders; Yang was an explosively violent martial artist who had already hospitalised one interpreter; Goliath had elite military experience and had probably killed more people than Ladd had arrested; and Sue, well, Sue was unlikely.

The covert anti-corruption unit had been assembled in a rush after Ladd had taken down Dredd, and it was always possible that the unit's sole purpose was to keep him out of the mainstream Force. The top brass didn't like having their Chief Superintendents busted, and Ladd had been afforded precious little involvement in the recruitment of his Phantom officers – Human Resources had made sure the process was diverse and inclusive, but the unit was basically a bin for basket cases.

Ladd scrolled through his phone and found their addresses. Perhaps if he checked them out, he could learn something. He thanked the minister for the use of his church and nicked his bike.

Phantom's addresses were scattered across North London, so he had a fair bit of ground to cover. Yang's flat was the nearest: a modern block between Tufnell Park and Archway. After an hour or so of cautious surveillance, Ladd followed her to Waterlow Park, and observed her training session with a wardrobe-sized martial artist. After lifting him above her head and destroying a range of solid objects with karate chops and flying kicks, she bent a sheet of metal backwards with her fingertips. Clearly, in her lethal hands, corrupt cops could be bent backwards like so many spoons.

Ladd cycled off to Finsbury Park and joined a crowd watching Taffy play rugby for London Sikh-Welsh. He clearly relished every second he was on the field, laughing his enormous head off as he hospitalised five players. No one seemed to blame him for it; his violence was inflicted with such winning amiability. Anybody able to enjoy that level of physical destructiveness was potentially capable of mass bending, Ladd reflected. Taffy certainly had the physical ability to turn a man the wrong way out. Whether he had the correct homicidal mind-set was another question.

There didn't seem to be much point investigating Sue, given that the chances of The Bender being seventy-nine were remote, but Ladd knew less about her than any other squad member, so he decided to check her out. Sue's home was a handsome mansion in an eye-wateringly expensive corner of Hampstead. It had the sort of Nordic design people used to imagine was futuristic, and she seemed to be hosting a garden party for a rather bizarre set of guests, all bowing before a hideous sculpture in the centre of the lawn. Once the party had finished, Ladd sneaked in, and took a closer look at what they appeared to have been worshipping – the sculpture depicted a dark angel with bat wings, and a goat's head, sat beneath a pentagram. Ladd expected Sue to have a hobby: bridge, perhaps; knitting, possibly; but not this. Sue was a Satanist.

Goliath was still waiting for Britney to reboot, so Ladd simply cased out his home in Islington. He lived at the top of the tallest townhouse in the area, which seemed ironic for a man under four foot in height but didn't exactly incriminate him. All Ladd knew for sure was that Goliath was a seasoned Special Forces operative and could probably improvise a cop-bending device out of a handful of broken twigs and a conker.

Old Bill lived in a fussily maintained cottage in a semi-rural suburb on the city's outer limits. His gaff was unmistakable – the windows sported posters descrying a proposed reduction in mobile library hours, and the drive boasted a brown Austin Allegro with stroppy car stickers. After lurking about for forty minutes or so, Ladd was rewarded with the sight of Old Bill wandering out with a depressed-looking basset.

Could this scruffy, overweight timeserver possibly be The Bender? It seemed unlikely that Old Bill would have the energy to commit four murders; he barely bothered to show up to the funeral parlour on time. The most vigorous thing he had done in recent memory was photocopy a risk assessment. That said, he did have full access to all the surveillance information gathered on the Gang of Four and Old Bill was nothing if not protective of the police's reputation, so there was both opportunity and motive.

Ladd followed Old Bill and his basset by pretending he was a runner on circuit training. This allowed him to zing back and forth in his hoodie, overhearing snippets of Old Bill's conversations with passers-by.

Sadly, the information gathered was less than thrilling. Old Bill discussed fellow dog owners' medical complaints, shared their concerns about unwanted planning applications, and expressed anger at inconsiderate firework parties, while the hounds restricted themselves to mutual butt-sniffing.

Ladd wondered whether this was a waste of police time, until he remembered he was suspendered, and realised that it was only his own time he was wasting.

Eventually, towards the end of the home stretch, Old Bill made a phone call. His tone was agitated, borderline angry. The word "dog" recurred, which seemed fair enough – he was a dog owner after all. But there seemed to be some urgency about the arrangements discussed, and elements of both secrecy and blame. Then Ladd noticed that one of the "dogs" had an "ing" on its tail. Ladd wasn't a detective for nothing: he knew exactly what a "dog" and an "ing" added up to. Who would go dogging with Old Bill? Wouldn't his gut prove insurmountable? But Old Bill ended the call before he had revealed all.

Ladd always encouraged his squad to pursue their hobbies, but dogging was an unacceptable form of outdoor exercise. Did that make Old Bill The Bender? The deceased police officers had all been deposited at established dogging sites, so it was possible that The Bender shared an interest in the practice. On the other hand, if The Bender was a keen dogger, he would have little reason to draw attention to its most popular venues with elaborate corpse disposals. The Bender may simply have selected the dogging sites because any witnesses would be too embarrassed to come forward. That would make him a non-dogger, and an interest in dogging would possibly put a suspect in the clear. Sherlock Holmes never had to contend with dogging conundrums, Ladd reflected. Detection must have been easier in his time.

So, in a nutshell, every member of Phantom was a potential Bender. There were lots of lines of inquiry for his squad to pursue about themselves, but he was no longer part of the team and couldn't ask them to pursue anything.

The unofficial investigation had filled a Sunday and taken him out of himself for a bit. But what next? It seemed that the simplest and most honourable step was to take an active interest in dogging.

PRISON DIARY – ENTRY 18

Naomi kicked off our session with dogging. She wasn't a fan.

"Do you really have to take the story into such distasteful territory?"

"The story has already visited four dogging sites."

"But there was no actual dogging involved."

"Just murder."

"Agatha Christie never did dogging."

"I'm modernising things."

"You're making them more unpleasant."

"I'm not trying to be pleasant. I'm just doing what the story tells me to do."

"You have to take responsibility for your own actions."

I angled her a knowing look. "Don't suppose you've taken any *actions* recently?"

Naomi insisted that she was there to discuss my creative writing, and not her private life. This led me to believe that Roly's assassination was in go-mode. Oh dear. Although her silence on the subject meant I was no longer in danger of becoming her accessory, it also meant that I couldn't discourage her.

We talked about dogging until the cows came home, but all the time, I was thinking about randy Roly's imminent demise. Who on Earth would someone like Naomi hire to carry out a hit? A member of her organic soup group? A Pilates instructor? Or someone even more sinister?

Once Naomi and I had exhausted the topic of dogging, I headed back to my cell and found that a new bloke had taken Jeff's place. He didn't look like an inmate. For a start, he looked fit, healthy, and well-adjusted – things that just didn't sit right. Secondly, he wore the only prison outfit I had ever seen that could be described as pristine. He said his name was Nigel but, other than that, he didn't feel the need to be particularly friendly. I couldn't tempt him with a single library book.

Looking on the bright side, I didn't have long to serve, so making new friends was less important than Ladd's covert insertion into the dogging community.

DOGGING

Ladd was going to have to go dogging. He wasn't looking forward to it, but duty calls, even to the suspendered.

Phase one of his covert dogging insertion involved research. Ladd switched his phone's search engine to incognito and investigated: there were dogging definitions, dogging documentaries, and dogging discussion groups, but precious few leads. He was going to have to go dark, and scour digital nooks frequented by arms traffickers, nonces, fraudsters and drug dealers. He switched on the VPN, did the deed, and navigated through sites selling malware, bitcoin, ransomware, Trojans, and other people's credit cards. Wasn't technology marvellous? How humans had progressed since they had abandoned real life! But Ladd mustn't grumble, he was about to go dogging. The dark web offered a cornucopia of dogging opportunities, so it couldn't be all bad.

Ladd's insertion into the dogging community was even more nerve-wracking than his potholing. He was no prude: before Panty-gate, sex had occupied his mind as much as any bloke's. But ever since his lie and Tina's cross-dressing peccadillo had trapped him in Extra-Large lingerie, sex only represented two things – embarrassment and fatigue. He quite fancied an evening in with BT Sport, but he mustn't weaken – duty demanded that he dog.

Ladd set off for an assignation in one of those fringe suburbs where the streets were quiet, the shops were shut, and the houses were as interchangeable as a doggers' body fluids.

There was an old-fashioned lido with a fake beach, a playground, a pub, and a supposedly haunted wood. Beyond the wood, a discreet clearing popular with fly-tippers offered itself up to the dogging community. Was it a community? Well, everyone was very friendly. Too friendly, or so Ladd imagined, as he loitered with uncertain intent.

Ladd waited for around ninety minutes, the length of a football match. If only surveillance had half-times. Eventually, deep into injury time, a Toyota Prius drew up. No one got out, but someone flashed the headlights. It was clearly some kind of a signal. Dubious figures appeared near trees, fly-tips, and lampposts. Lampposts! Ladd shuddered. What if one of the figures was The Bender? That would be a good thing – it was why he was there, after all. Still, Ladd would be lying if he said he wasn't scared, although he did lie a lot.

He tried to think through how The Bender would try to subdue a cop of his size, fitness, and aggression. Fighting was fine – bring it on - but Ladd doubted he'd get a fair fight. Not one of the Gang of Four had been a soft target; bent cops don't tend to be. Trent was out of shape – though not as out of shape as he ended up; but Sweeney, McMasters and Cocky could all hold their own, and had no doubt spent many years doing several rounds with suspects in the back of police vans. No, The Bender would be a fool to fight – unless he was Stoker – and even then, Ladd had proved that he had nothing to fear.

The Bender could well be armed, but only as a precaution - there were no knife cuts, impact injuries, or bullet wounds on his victim's bodies. Maybe The Bender drugged people. Chloroform and syringes worked wonders, but that kind of attack was risky and rare. The Bender would be far better off spiking people's drinks; the Gang of Four all had black belts in alcohol consumption, and ugly middle-aged blokes tend not to be wary of having their pints spiked.

Ladd's wool-gatherings about The Bender were rudely interrupted by an outbreak of dogging. After another burst of headlight flashing, a couple had conjoined on the bonnet then become a triple, and a quadruple. Spectators had gathered, and other doggers had busied themselves with each other's bodies in the surrounding woody nooks.

Ladd kept his distance, but one dogger didn't. A svelte figure silhouetted like a woodland pixie made a beeline for him. He thought about backing out, but when the dogger revealed herself as female, mid-twenties, generally gorgeous and winningly mischievous, he was intrigued. She didn't speak, just held out a hand. Ladd took it and he followed her into the foliage.

It was like pulling, but completely undeserved. Ladd had experienced his fair share of discreet assignations, but he had always got to know the girls a bit first. Not always for long, but he had won them over with wit, dancing or at the very least boozy charm. But today, he had offered none of those things. He doubted that the woman had even caught a good look at his face.

A wave of genuine concern for the young woman swept over Ladd. She really shouldn't be endangering herself, dragging big, shady blokes into the woods. What if it hadn't been him, but someone nastier? She really should not be putting herself in danger like this.

"Bastard!" A male voice cannoned. Ladd's legs were scythed from under him, he ate moss, and heavy blows rained down on his back and shoulders.

"Bender!" a coarse voice barked, as blokey arms dragged Ladd over roots, twigs, and dog ends. Multiple men yanked him to his feet and cuffed him.

A stocky figure of around his own height squared up to him, said, "Think you can kill my officers?" and punched Ladd right in the gut. He didn't have that much of a gut, what with all the boxing, but the blow winded him and triggered a wave of nausea.

Before Ladd could recover, the stocky figure blinded him with a torch beam, and snarled, "Let's have a look at the most hated human in London."

This was not how Ladd had hoped his dogging session would climax. Where was the girl? It was clearly a honey trap. Were these real cops, or role-playing doggers? Either way, he would have to fight them off.

Ladd prepared a headbutt. He would only get one chance, so he needed to pick his moment. He wasn't sure how many people were holding him – probably four or five. He could do this – one blow, then sprint for the treeline. He counted down, three, two, one....

"Ladd!" The stocky figure exclaimed, interrupting the silent countdown.

"Dixon!" Ladd replied.

"Bastard!" Dixon countered. "You're The Bender!".

Punches rained down on Ladd from every direction and the dogging wood faded into oblivion.

***

Ladd regained consciousness in a cell. He seemed to be doing this far too often for a Detective Chief Inspector. Last time, the Super had chucked a bucket of water at him and revealed that he had just crash-landed on the Attorney General. This time, he was in his pants, his ankles were shackled, and someone was being beaten up in the neighbouring cell. It was all very different to *Midsomer Murders*.

After a couple of minutes, a hefty goon clanked open the cell door. He looked like a gentleman of suboptimal intelligence, and he was carrying what looked worryingly like a toolbox. They didn't have a lot to say to each other.

Moments later, Dixon swaggered in, his face abounding with deepest gloat.

Ladd tried to remain chipper. "Didn't realise you were a dogger, Dixon."

"You murder four officers, and you lose all our pensions. Going by the book, it's high time for some police brutality." Dixon nodded at the goon, who opened the toolbox and pulled out a pair of pliers.

"Which one of your balls do you like the least?" Dixon enquired.

"They're inseparable."

"I beg to differ," Dixon said, as the goon closed the pliers, and gave a demonstration twist.

"Look," Ladd said, "We're on the same side, aren't we?"

"Bollocks we are, you're The Bender."

The goon took a hood out of his toolbox and placed it over Ladd's head. It wasn't as if Ladd was missing out on anything scenic: the cell walls, Dixon's ugly mug and the tooled-up goon were less than picturesque, but, given the choice, Ladd generally preferred to spend his time unhooded.

"Phantom mob!" Dixon spat. "Think you're so high and mighty. But we've been investigating you lot."

"You couldn't even investigate a dogging without cocking it up," Ladd said to the inside of his hood.

"What was that?"

Ladd started repeating the insult but was interrupted by a gut-punch.

"You're all either bent or criminally incompetent," Dixon said. "You dive-bomb the Attorney General, crash a pair of hearses, and fail to protect an officer in your care."

Encouraged by the unmistakeable sound of pliers clicking, Ladd said, "I admit it. We're criminally incompetent."

"What?" Dixon asked, sarcastically. "I can't hear you."

"Then take off the hood!" Ladd shouted into the cloth.

"Nope," Dixon said. "Still muffled."

Cataclysmic screams issued from the neighbouring cell, but that didn't stop Dixon. "You might think shagging the Super and flouncing about in miniskirts is a credit to the Force, Ladd, but it's an embarrassment."

Heavy hands attached something to Ladd's shackles. He couldn't tell what it was, but he wasn't optimistic.

"You are quite literally the most plastic policeman to dishonour the badge," Dixon continued. "If I were you, I'd jump out of a window. Oh, hang on, you've already done that."

Ladd was contemplating how little he rated Dixon as a motivational speaker when his shackles yanked forwards with a mechanical lurch, dragging him off his bed and lifting him upside down into the air. As his body jolted to a halt, Ladd's hood dropped off, offering him an inverted view of his interrogators' crotches. A fist punched him in the gut. Ladd swung, resisting the urge to vomit into his own nostrils.

"You're the bleeding Bender," Dixon said. "You turned on your own."

"You're the one assaulting a police officer," Ladd objected.

"No," Dixon replied. "I think you'll find it's him."

The goon's fist revisited Ladd's gut. It was no more enjoyable the second time around. Ladd shut his eyes and tried to focus his powers of resistance, but all he could hear were screams from the neighbouring cell. Homicide were vicious bastards. It probably came with the territory, what with all the death. After a third punch landed in his belly, Ladd noticed that his neighbour's screams were behaving unusually. Normally, a scream bursts out, and doesn't hang around. These screams were buffering. Reality tended not to linger, Ladd found.

"It's a recording, isn't it," Ladd said.

"Never mind about that," Dixon said, before going back to basics. "Bender!"

"I'm not the bloody Bender," Ladd said, using his core muscles to pull himself halfway up. "And I'd never been dogging before tonight."

"You were stalking all four victims."

"Not stalking. Investigating."

Something shifted on the floor. Ladd turned his head and saw the goon's hand shove a large bucket a few feet below his head. His heart sank, and so did his head, as his shackles were steadily lowered from the ceiling, and he was submerged up to his chin in freezing bucket-water. He held his breath as best he could, given the influx of liquid into his inverted nose. Ladd had hoped to meet his maker in the line of duty rather than by kicking the bucket in an actual bucket. But that was not to be. Bucket it was.

After what felt like an eternity of spluttering, his shackles tightened, and his head rose clear of the water.

"Nice dip?" Dixon enquired, solicitously.

Ladd's head was too busy leaking liquid to respond. Water came out of his ears, mouth, nose, and even eyes.

"Good." Dixon smiled, cruelly.

Ladd's shackles loosened once again, and his scalp hit the bucket base. He'd had better days. Was this waterboarding? Or water-bucketing? Either way, he was not a fan. Ladd decided to take the initiative: not easily done upside down and underwater, but he was no slouch. Ladd began to headbutt the bucket from side to side – and scooped it onto his forehead before contorting his body and whiplashing up, bucketing Dixon in the crotch.

The bucket fell off Ladd's head in time for him to sway backwards and watch Dixon collapse. Ladd forced himself to stop laughing and swung back and forth like an inverted trapeze artist, gaining momentum to lift himself up to the ceiling. This decoupled the shackles from their hook and set him free to collapse onto the floor, just in time for Dixon's goon to boot him in the back. Ladd grabbed the boot and upended the goon, who headbutted the metal corner of the cell bed on his way to bye-byes. Perhaps he was dead. If he was, at least he would be at home in Homicide.

Ladd appraised his situation. One unconscious murder detective, one unconscious or deceased goon, and a set of shackles on his ankles. On the plus side, the pliers were in reach and the dozy sods had left the cell door open.

Dixon's clothes weren't the best fit, but Ladd felt much more comfortable in them than he had in any of Dolly's offerings. He locked the cell behind him and ambled nonchalantly past a dozy custody sergeant. Clearly, Ladd looked more like Dixon than he had previously imagined. A worrying thought, but, as it turned out, an extremely useful fact.

The time was unholy, and Homicide was barely inhabited. A lesser man might have rejoiced in this and scarpered, but Ladd took the opportunity to peruse their investigation room. As suspected, it was a dump: the relics of last night's takeaways, empty cans of lager, used betting slips, and heavily fingered porn mags decorated the body of the room, and there were two case charts on the walls. One read,

"Trans-on-Trans Deaths", and was divided into Transnistrian and Transylvanian sides. On the Transylvanian side, there was a photo of Marian in wrestling pants, and a picture of Igor, assassinated on my bench by a cleaning buggy. On the Transnistrian side, there was a photo of Dmitriy with "Missing, believed killed" written underneath, and a gallery of gang members. There was an action list on one side, with "Round Up Council Cleaning Buggies" and a tick, and "Catch Escaped Murderer" with a cross.

The other case chart was simply entitled "Bender" and had each terminally bent cop at the compass point matching their dogging site. Detective Inspector Harry Trent of Serious Organized Crime was in pride of place at the North, and rather than having any reference to his Transylvanian smack facilitation and murder alibi provision, there was a list of his awards. Detective Inspector Todd Sweeney of the Flying Squad was in the South. Again, there was no mention of his corrupt relationship with The Smiths, but there was a brief tribute to his charity work. Detective Chief Inspector McMasters of the Drugs Squad was in the West and, instead of any mention of his dealings with Transnistrian nosebag, there was a picture of his gong for advanced freemasonry. Detective Chief Inspector Dicky "Cocky" Proudcock of Professional Standards was in the East, without any mention of Britney and the money this criminal AI allowed him to siphon off street gangs. Instead, there was a list of his golf trophies. Each victim was linked by a wobbly felt-tip line to the circle's hub, like a wheel spoke, and at the centre was one suspect, who was not difficult to recognise, given that it was him. After all of Homicide's investigations, all of Stoker's post-mortems, all of the resources spent, the best they could come up with was Ladd himself. Of course he was linked to the four victims! He was head of an anti-corruption unit, and all four of the men were as bent as buggery. What could he take from this? One, he was in danger of being arrested and charged as a serial cop killer. Two, he had to find the real culprit pronto.

But who really linked the four bent cops? Dredd of course! He had named them. He was the reason Ladd was investigating them. Maybe he was also the reason they were all dead. Granted, he was banged up – but that didn't mean he couldn't have ordered their killings – he had more underworld contacts than the Dark Lord Sauron. He could easily have been bending bent cops from afar via some demented intermediary. It would have been a counter-intuitive move, destroying all his bargaining chips. Trent, MacMasters, Todd and Cocky were his tickets to freedom, and without the ability to testify against them, Dredd would be banged up for a decade or three. But what if Dredd had gambled all on the pension heist? Right now, Dredd was free, loaded, and had no need to immunize himself from prosecution by testifying against anybody. With the Gang of Four out of the way, Dredd could move in and take control of London's heroin, cocaine, armed robbery, and street gangs. Now that he had the gold underpinning the police pension fund, Dredd also had the financial resources to do it.

Dredd aside, Dixon had omitted to put the rest of Phantom in the frame, which struck Ladd as an error. Yang could probably bend metal with her bare hands, Taffy had bent half a rugby team to casualty, Goliath was a former Special Forces operative, Old Bill was a dogging aficionado, and as for Sue, well Sue was a Satanist.

Homicide's investigation was almost as hopeless as the Super had led him to believe. The Force truly was institutionally stupid.

Ladd heard footsteps approach, so he crouched behind a filing cabinet. It was a cleaner, armed with a mop and bucket. Ladd no longer liked buckets and didn't want to see any more for a while. He gave the cleaner the ghost of a smile and made his way out of Homicide.

Ladd opted against public transport; it was way too easy to get cornered. Walking would have been a risk had it been a little later, but it was still the kind of small hour once favoured by milk floats. The main commuters were weary auxiliaries – the people who did the real work of the city. There wasn't a suit in sight, but there was no shortage of overalls, and everyone was too wrapped up in their own private misery to notice Ladd, as he wandered North through the side streets.

As Ladd approached his suburb, he thought about his domestic predicament and decided to fix it. He simply could not go on living as a cross-dresser or avoiding Tina, so he resolved to tell her about the Super and admit all. She would swear, she would fight, but it would be the only way to lift this unbearable weight from his shoulders and finally be himself again.

Ladd approached the porch like the boxer he was, ready to fight for glory. Honour was there to be regained. It was bound to cost, he knew that – but he was willing to pay the price. He weaved his way through his wife's weight-training equipment and prepared to tell the unvarnished truth.

Tina was on the sofa-bed, painting her nails. When she finally looked up, she burst out laughing. "What the feck are you wearing?"

"They're Homicide's," Ladd replied.

"Well, it certainly looks like someone tried to murder your hair."

Dixon's suit and his bucket-hair were clearly not a stylish combo, but Ladd could not allow himself to be diverted by issues of fashion. "Tina," he began. "I need to tell you what's been going on."

"Never mind about that, where the feck have you been, you dirty stop-out?"

Dogging? Getting waterboarded on suspicion of being The Bender? These weren't promising answers, so Ladd went with, "Overtime."

"There's been a lot of that lately."

"Well, it's all got a bit crazy, what with the bendings, the pension, and everything."

"Right, so sit down and tell me about it."

"I can't."

"I thought you were about to tell me what's been going on."

"I did, didn't I?" The words, *I lied about the panties. They weren't mine they were the Superintendent's. We're having an affair. I'm not a cross-dresser* crossed his mind, but not his lips.

"Stop fannying about," Tina said. "Man-up and tell me the truth before we both die of old age."

"Okay," Ladd took a deep breath, and told her the whole truth about everything other than his personal life. He elaborated on the Gang of Four, the transitioning of the Transylvanian - Transnistrian conflict into a full-scale gang war, The Smiths, the pension heist, Dredd's deception, his fight in the pathology tent, Britney the criminal AI, the dogging escapade, his brush with Homicide, the fact that every cop in London was out to kill him, how Dixon's colleagues would probably be finding him and a dead goon in his cell any minute now, and how he was their prime suspect."

"Is that all?" Tina replied when he had finally finished. "What you need is a new identity. Just take this whole cross-dressing malarkey to the next level. I'll give Dolly a bell."

***

Phantom's tiny, three-door courtesy car pulled up at the no-go estate. Taffy unfolded his large frame from the front and shoved his seat forward to allow Sue out from the back. She climbed halfway out, before wedging herself between the seat and the doorframe. Old Bill vacated the front passenger seat, circled around the car, and helped Taffy pull Sue out. They began gently, but Sue remained jammed. Yang exited through Old Bill's door but made no attempt to assist. Taffy and Old Bill applied greater force, and the seventy-nine-year-old interpreter flew out. Taffy leapt at full stretch and caught her like a cricket ball.

"Gosh!" Sue seemed exhilarated. "Such a strong young man."

"My pleasure, isn't it just." Taffy placed her gently onto the ground.

Yang signed. Sue interpreted: "Why did we bring that stupid old cretin with us?"

Sue signed back to her in silence. Yang reciprocated.

This silent exchange continued for some time until Taffy grew weary and gestured mournfully at the grim estate. "About as lively as Merthyr Tydfil on a wet Tuesday, isn't it just."

"Reckon we'll be all right leaving the vehicle here?" Old Bill asked.

"Joyriders wouldn't nick that, would they," Taffy said. "Be too embarrassed, look you."

Sue and Yang's signing match escalated until their hands were moving with such angry intensity that they could have been performing a Congolese war dance.

"Looks like that argument would be very loud if we could hear it," Taffy observed.

"Number 578, wasn't it?" Old Bill led the way to Britney's tower block.

It took more than forty-five minutes to find number 578, and almost as long again to persuade Yang to join Taffy and Old Bill in posting their phones through the letter box. Once she had, Old Bill turned to Sue. "Where's your phone?"

"It's back home," Sue replied.

"What good's a mobile if you don't take it anywhere?" Yang signed.

"Well," Sue said once she'd interpreted Yang's question. "I wouldn't know, young lady. I don't own a mobile telephone."

Old Bill looked baffled. "Didn't you say it was at home?"

"I did," Sue insisted. "My telephone is in the kitchen, cabled to the wall. If I took it with me, it wouldn't ring."

"Understood." Old Bill looked flummoxed. "How's this going to work then?"

The detectives looked at the locked door, clueless.

After a bit, Sue leant down, lifted the flap and spoke into the letter box. "Excuse me, I am an old lady."

Taffy, Old Bill, and Yang looked on with both pity and despair, but to everyone's surprise the door snapped open, and they gawped in disbelief at the colossal Dark Web Exchange stretching out beneath.

"Crikey!" Old Bill looked set for a coronary.

"Blimey, look you!" Taffy exclaimed.

"Oh, my days!" Yang signed.

"Goodness gracious!" Sue added, after she had interpreted Yang.

There was no sign of Goliath, but they soon discovered that that they were not alone. The sight of a semi-transparent teenager almost knocked the entire squad off the edge of the hallway.

"Alright, Phantom!" Britney exclaimed. "Looks like you've just seen a ghost."

"What are you?" Old Bill asked.

"What?" Britney asked.

"Who?" Old Bill asked.

"I'm a Dark Cloud Artificial Intelligence with a serious attitude problem, but you can call me Britney."

"Nice to meet you, isn't it just." Taffy said.

"Likewise." Old Bill offered the hologram a pointless handshake with his one arm.

"Whatever," Britney replied, swooshing through his palm with her transparent fingers.

Sue looked concerned. "You're looking awfully thin."

"Just look at you lot," Britney said. "Internal Affairs' finest undercover unit!"

"Nice of you to say so," Old Bill said.

"Shame your Governor is Britain's most hated cop."

"He has his plus points," Old Bill said.

"Lost our pensions, didn't he just," Taffy said.

"He looks very masculine in a dress," Sue concluded.

"What happened to Goliath?" Old Bill asked.

"Buggered off, didn't he," Britney said. "Worried about your Governor."

***

Ladd's taxi to Dolly's was delayed by police protests, which infuriated the driver. "Your tree-huggers and Insult Britain brigade are one thing, but when our very own Filth turn their backs on decent, law-abiding citizens trying to earn a crust, we might as well throw in the towel. It's time to bring back national service for the police – they've turned into a bunch of bleedin' snowflakes."

Ladd agreed wholeheartedly, in the hope that the driver would shut up. He didn't, so Ladd tuned him out and concentrated on his own problems. Why hadn't he levelled with Tina? She may well have levelled him with a flying kick to the head, but that wasn't it - he really didn't back away from fights. Why had he revealed so many details of a confidential investigation? Well, it had seemed a more comfortable truth than the excruciatingly uncomfortable truth about the Super and her panties. He could feel the fateful thong in his inside pocket. He'd managed to grab it without Tina noticing and, in some ways, he wished he hadn't. Whilst it meant he could return it to the Super if he ever saw her again, it was also a constant reminder of his suspendered status. Why hadn't he fessed up sooner and ended the lie? His moral cowardice had condemned him to a temporary gender reassignment session from his blackmailer. It wasn't on his bucket list, but right now, it was possibly his only survival strategy.

The police protests had comprehensively constipated the flow of traffic around central London. Cops had glued themselves to roads, locked themselves to buses, set up tents in the middle of crossroads, and created pop-up festivals on gyratory systems. Ladd understood their anger, but the taxi driver didn't, and it wasn't long before he gave up and asked Ladd to walk the rest of the way.

It was a decent enough day; bright, breezy, and pleasant. Ladd would have taken his time to appreciate it, had it not been for the sight of the Transylvanians' tank. When its gun swivelled in his direction, Ladd dodged down an alley. Tanks weren't big on alleys. He wondered whether to run - he was not only the most hated cop in London, he was now also a murder suspect, and he didn't want to draw attention to himself. But he didn't have to wonder long. Marian was powering after him, like a tank on legs. Ladd didn't often back away from a fight, but this bloke had defenestrated him onto the Attorney General. Ladd didn't know where the alley led. All he could do was keep running. He had always been a fast runner, but that didn't help when the alley ran out. There were no fences to hurdle, no back doors to dodge into, and not even a bin to hide in - just concrete walls, and the inevitability of a terminal Transylvanian wrestle. Ladd turned and struck out, but his precise aggressive blows, landed with the impact of a paper aeroplane on concrete. Marian may have had a girl's name, but he was basically a human grizzly. Grappling with him could only end one way: a takedown, a hold, and death. Luckily, it was Marian's death. A sniper gifted him a scarlet *bindi,* smack in the middle of the forehead, just like they had with Dimitry.

Ladd was pleased but mystified. No obvious vantage points overlooked the alley. Then he heard tiny feet scampering. Was it a child? Was it a goblin? No, it was Goliath.

"Are you following me?" Ladd asked.

"Don't bother to thank me, Guv," Goliath replied.

"Thanks," Ladd said.

"No problem," Goliath said.

"You saved my life twice," Ladd said.

"When?"

"Transnistrian barrel factory?"

"Oh, that."

"Exactly that. I was being threatened with a chainsaw, and you killed my torturer."

"I didn't like the look of him."

"You got your shot in just before the tank smashed through the walls."

"Timing's a thing," Goliath said.

"It is, isn't it?"

"Let's get you off the streets, Guv."

Goliath led Ladd to the Transylvanian tank and hot-wired it. I've seen people hot-wire all kinds of vehicles – BMWs, Jags, Audis – but this was a first for me. It was quite noisy, but it worked.

"Where are we headed, Guv?"

Ladd couldn't exactly answer, *Big Girl's Blouse for temporary gender reassignment*, so he just told Goliath the street name, and said it was a covert operation arranged on a strictly need-to-know basis.

Progress was faster than in the taxi, as the police protesters were more inclined to give way to a tank, but there was still time for Ladd to ask Goliath some pressing questions.

"Why have you been following me?"

"I thought that would have been obvious, Guv."

"It's not, though."

"Well, Guv, you're in danger, as you could probably tell from the abductions and assassination attempts."

Ladd had to admit that he had a point.

"I'm a surveillance specialist, I'm the only member of Phantom with military training, and my stature makes it easy to hide in things like bins and cupboards, so I was happy to keep an eye on you in my spare time."

"What happened with Britney? Did she reboot?"

"Yes, Guv. I think she only did that to get rid of you."

"Didn't she like me?"

"Well, Guv, you did threaten to box her up and send her down the station."

Goliath was right. It had been a pretty stupid threat, on reflection. Boxing up a seventeen storey AI mastermind would have placed unreasonable demands on manpower.

"Did you learn anything useful?"

"Britney loves banging on about herself – bit of an ego there, especially for a non-human."

"I wondered if that was just her being a teenage girl."

"She's not though, is she Guv? That's just how she chooses to look."

"Of course." Ladd knew he was being thick but hated to admit it.

"I guess holograms can be deceptive, Guv."

"Yes," Ladd said. "Particularly criminal AI masterminds."

"Anyway, Britney asked me to join her mailing list."

"Her what?"

"She sends out a regular encrypted newsletter to all her criminal contacts with compromising information about police officers and promising new underworld opportunities. Everyone's on it - Transnistrians, Transylvanians, The Smiths, Dredd, even the Gang of Four when they were alive."

"A criminal newsletter? That would be an invaluable resource for policing."

"That's what I thought, Guv, so I signed up."

"Well done, Goliath."

"It's not all good news though, Guv. It turns out that Phantom's comms have been compromised for a while. That's how a load of information keeps leaking out. I thought we had a mole in the squad, but it was just Britney fiddling about with our systems."

That explained a lot. Ladd had wondered why Cocky knew all about Phantom, and why Dredd always seemed to be one step ahead.

"It turns out that me and Britney had a mutual friend," Goliath continued.

"I didn't know that AI's had friends."

"I say friend, but creator would be a better word."

"The arms dealer?"

"Yes, Guv, the dead one. I probably should have mentioned this before, but I don't like discussing my mercenary days and it didn't seem particularly relevant. Anyway, back when I was freelancing, so to speak, he used to supply me and my comrades with arms and lethal gadgets. He wasn't just what you might call a wheeler-dealer, he was also a bit of a tech head. Turns out that he built Britney. Seems he wanted to diversify into the misinformation superhighway."

It was Ladd's first tank-lift, and it had been an informative one, but like all good things, it came to an end. Goliath parked up, Ladd got out of the tank, and walked off to his temporary gender reassignment session.

Big Girl's Blouse had not been open long, but one customer already had his arms full. He was an imam, in full robe and hat, and he had gathered together a colourful array of women's clothing. At the first sight of Ladd, he sprinted off in embarrassment.

"Sorry, Dolly," Ladd said. "Tina sent me."

Dolly braced herself for another fight. "I've spent the money."

"All ten k?"

"Yes."

"Keep it," Ladd said. "Just make me unrecognizable."

"Why?"

"The world wants to kill me."

"Can you blame it?"

"Sorry about ... last time."

"Are you really?"

"Violence just seemed like the best option. I'm getting counselling," Ladd lied.

"You messed up my shop."

"You took my ten grand. And you knew I'd already gone viral."

Dolly ignored this and decided to address his first request. "So, you want to escape? Become a new woman?"

"Sort of."

"Well, that's what I'm all about. Full transformation is £978.99."

"Any chance of a discount?"

"I'm not a charity."

"I gave you ten grand."

"No point dwelling on the past."

"It was yesterday."

"I prefer to live in the present."

Ladd had an easy week and was running on the shortest of fuses. "You conniving, two-faced TART!"

Dolly reached under the counter and pulled out her taser.

Ladd mastered his anger. "Look, I didn't come here to fight."

"I should bill you for the last one."

"I came here to go undercover," Ladd said. "And finally get Dredd."

Dolly's expression transformed. "There's no charge."

A few minutes later, Ladd was in Dolly's makeover chair and his identity was in temporary transition.

"Half of Pentonville had it in for Dredd." Dolly said, as she cemented foundation over the last of Ladd's stubble.

"You definitely weren't the only bloke he framed."

"BLOKE!!"

"You were a bloke at the time."

"Nobody's perfect." Dolly paused to admire Ladd in the mirror - he could have been an extra-large air hostess with a penchant for weightlifting and cage fighting.

"Decent effort," Ladd conceded.

"So where is the dreaded Dredd?"

"I don't know."

"Have you tried his bonsai farms?"

"His what?"

"Bonsais. Rumour has it that he sunk all his bungs into miniature trees – you know, those fiddly Japanese things popular with weirdoes."

"Really?"

"Well, I suppose it's more original than laundering money through a casino or a car wash."

"Maybe."

"And better for the environment."

"Do you really think Dredd cares about that?"

"No."

There are a surprising number of Bonsai farms in England, but only two had Rastafarian names, and they were both in Suffolk. Once I had found them, it wasn't hard to persuade Dolly to accompany me to *Bonsai-and-I* and *Bonsai Babylon*.

PRISON DIARY – ENTRY 19

Naomi was unusually chipper. I could only assume that her assassination plans were falling nicely into place. She didn't say as much, but I could tell.

"It's so good to see your work embrace modern values!" Naomi began with a spry smile. "DCI Ladd is confronting his transphobia head-on - it's all so much more inclusive!"

"Thanks, Naomi. How are *things* progressing?"

She just winked at me.

We shared a conspiratorial laugh.

"Just one thing, how popular are bonsais in Rastafarian culture?"

There always had to be something, didn't there? How the hell should I know? I'd just made it up. I acknowledged her point, decided to ignore it, and wished her the best of luck with "everything".

She knew what I meant.

When I returned to my cell, I found Nigel taking delivery of a plasma television, a microwave, and a dartboard. He didn't explain himself, but he didn't really have to: he clearly had connections in high places.

Nigel played darts alone, never once challenging me to a game. I didn't mind. I only play darts when I'm drunk, and we didn't have any booze.

After Nigel had beaten himself with a climactic double-two, he celebrated modestly, returned to his bunk, and asked, "Who was here before me?"

"Jeff," I replied. It seemed best to keep things simple.

"What was he like?"

"Jeff was a great bloke."

"How great?"

"He helped me pass the time."

"How?"

"We'd talk about books."

"What books?"

"Atlases."

"Maps?"

"Transnistria, Transylvania, and the CIS nations."

"CIS?"

"Commonwealth of Independent States."

"That all?"

"No. Dolly Parton's biography, a Tank Girl annual, *The Silence of the Lambs, Potholing For Beginners*. I decided not to mention *Tunnelling – A Practical Guide*."

"Sounds a bit random."

"That's prison libraries for you."

"You work there, don't you?"

"I hadn't told Nigel this. I nodded and decided not to tell him anything else."

BONSAI-AND-I

The country lane was as straight as a python, but that didn't stop Dolly from overtaking a cattle-truck, worrying the cows and DCI Ladd. Ladd didn't moo as much, but he did swear significantly. It wasn't just the speed; it was more the inevitability of death should any oncoming traffic block their marauding Mazda. Dolly's vehicle was painted a fetching shade of leopardskin but had all the solidity of a crisp packet. Still, it was important not to show weakness. That was how Ladd had been brought up, and how he had lived his life, even if he now looked like an air hostess.

"Nice wheels," Ladd observed as calmly as he could, while they squeezed between a tractor and a ten-foot-high hedge at around eighty.

"Nice look," Dolly replied.

"Cheers," Ladd replied gruffly.

"Your own mother wouldn't know you." Dolly giggled.

Ladd checked his reflection in the side-mirror and shuddered. It was like looking at a stranger; one he didn't fancy. He just wasn't his own type.

Taking advantage of Ladd's obvious desire to change the subject, Dolly attempted to extract as much information as she could. "So, Dredd's turned supergrass, has he?"

"How did you know about that?" Ladd asked.

"It was in Britney's newsletter."

"Is anyone not on her mailing list?"

"You, by the sound of things."

Ladd couldn't believe that he had risen to the rank of DCI without knowing of the existence of an underworld news bulletin.

"Don't blame yourself," Britney said, "The first rule of Britney's mailing list is no one talks about Britney's mailing list."

"Right."

"And at least you were the one who got to put Dredd away."

"Took nine days of solid surveillance in a drain to nail the bastard. I thought I'd put him away for good."

"What did you get him for?"

"Extortion, racketeering, aiding and abetting, living off immoral earnings, people trafficking, culpable homicide and careless driving."

"He once tried framing me for blackmail," Dolly said.

"You'd never blackmail anyone, would you?"

"Not back then." Dolly laughed. "You popped my cherry, blackmail-wise."

"I'm honoured," Ladd said, obviously not meaning it.

Suffolk wasn't the natural place for a Bonsai-based money-laundering operation. It had relatively few cartels, and hardly any potential punters, given that the human population seemed to be outnumbered by livestock. Ladd knew very little about the place – a Suffolk Punch wasn't a boxing move, it was a whacking great horse; Suffolk's only decent football team was nicknamed *The Tractor Boys* because many of the fans lived on farms, and the only aggro was with Norfolk, another scenic but overwhelmingly empty county. Ladd wondered what it would be like to live in a place where nothing happened. What if milking was the day's main event rather than murder? What if there was no need to change gender identity in order to avoid assault by police officers? A man – or indeed a woman - could but dream.

After rocketing through miles of bugger-all, Dolly took a discreet, formidably uneven lane and pulled up beside a greenhouse the size of a town. A sign read, *Bonsai-and-I: Trespassers Will Be Shot.*

Ladd and Dolly crept around the greenhouse perimeter, dodging CCTV cameras and trip wires. Red-bordered signs with sawn-off shotgun silhouettes warned from all angles. This seemed a touch heavy-handed for a bonsai farm.

"Fuck!" Dolly shouted.

"Armed guard?" Ladd took cover behind a bush.

"Broken heel," Dolly said.

"Give it here," Ladd said.

Dolly seemed surprised. Why would the DCI he had blackmailed, fought, and semi-transitioned, now want to help fix his stiletto? But Ladd had no intention of fixing it. He smashed the heel against the corner of a glass panel and prised it open. They crawled inside the greenhouse, past trailers, heaters, and irrigation devices, before emerging into a jungle, not of bonsai trees, but cannabis plants. The leafy expanse was so vast, it could easily have hosted numerous indigenous tribes, jaguars, and sloths, and it was as pungent as an army of armpits.

"Don't tell me I'm looking at the police pension fund!" Ladd despaired.

"And the rest," Dolly replied. "Word is, Dredd's been ploughing his ill-gotten gains into this place for years."

"I haven't exactly got a black belt in botany," Ladd said, without false modesty, "But it looks like he's mid-harvest."

Ladd noticed a mountain of cultivated plants piled up in a convoy of caravan-sized trolleys. "That lot alone must be worth ..."

A high-power hose blasted Ladd in the face before he could finish his estimate. He dropped to the ground. Dolly took cover beside him. The ex-blokes looked gingerly across the expanse of cannabis leaves. All was green apart Dredd, his stripy Rastacap, and the yellow hosepipe cocked in his right hand.

Ladd and Dolly emerged gingerly from the cannabis plants.

Dredd gazed disbelievingly at Dolly. "I've seen you somewhere before."

"Miss World?" Dolly suggested.

Dredd kissed his teeth.

"Your worst nightmare?" Dolly continued.

"Dumb *lickle* white girl." Dredd blasted Dolly with the hose.

"You've ruined my make-up!" Dolly's foundation was looking stubbly.

Dredd blasted her again, laughing.

This was a mistake. Dolly went nuclear, tearing up cannabis plants like a crazed gorilla, and hollering in fury. Dredd advanced on her, blasting the hose like a Dalek intent on extermination. This too was an error. Dolly leapt onto Dredd, tearing at his face with her nails. It was too late to use the gun, so Dredd punched her. She reeled but remained standing.

"The harder they come," Dolly hissed, "The harder they fall." She delivered a knockout headbutt.

"No woman no cry," Ladd added, as he trussed up Dredd up with his own hosepipe.

"Calling the cops?" Dolly asked.

"No point," Ladd said. "If there's an official police raid, the skunk would be used in evidence, then burned."

"You'd be setting fire to your own pensions."

Ladd looked across at the skunk jungle. Dredd was many things, most of them unmentionable, but he was a half-decent horticulturalist.

"Give me a moment," Ladd said. He estimated the immense greenhouse's dimensions and the approximate volume and value of the skunk. Maybe it was possible to repay The Smiths and the police with a skunk farm each: *Bonsai-and-I* for the bank robbers, *Bonsai Babylon* for the cops. The police could probably be assuaged with an address, but The Smiths would need a fair chunk of the actual product.

Once Ladd had explained his plan, they stowed Dredd in the boot, attached the loaded trailers to each other and secured them to the back of the Mazda.

"Better stick to minor roads," Ladd cautioned, as they set off for London.

The leopardskin Mazda and its skunk truck trailers did not pass unnoticed, making for an eventful journey. Before they had even reached the M25, they had caused eight rear-end collisions, eighteen sideswipes and three rollovers, as well as featuring in photographs taken by thirty-eight pedestrians and fourteen motorists. But it wasn't until they approached the capital that they heard a siren wail.

Ladd checked the mirror, clocked flashing lights, and proffered a "Bollocks."

"What's the problem?" Dolly spoke with panicked sarcasm. "Nothing to see here officer - just a convoy of skunk trailers and a bent cop in the boot! What do we say?"

"I'll think of something."

"Like what?"

Ladd stared out the window for inspiration – the fields were as empty as his imagination. "No idea. We're screwed."

As Ladd prepared himself mentally for arrest, the police vans bombed past them, sirens blasting and banners flying from their roofs. They read, "*We Want Our Pensions Back*!" "*Don't Leave Coppers Penniless!*" and "*Cancel Ladd*!"

"On their way to a demo," Dolly explained, unnecessarily.

"A demo against me," Ladd said.

"Lucky you're unrecognizable."

"Isn't it just." Ladd looked mournfully at his reflection and found a beefy air hostess in his place. He still didn't like her.

In Suffolk, their skunk convoy could pass for an agricultural anomaly. In North

London, it could only be what it was. But it didn't matter – the police were too busy protesting about pensions and the fatal bending of their bent colleagues.

The Mazda-skunk combo entered The Smiths' scrap yard just in time to see a fearsome machine twist a Mini backwards, its body groaning in metallic agony.

Dolly slowed. "Sure this is a good idea?"

"We give them the crop sample, *Bonsai-and-I*, and Dredd." Ladd explained. "The Attorney General gets *Bonsai Babylon*."

"Happy days." Dolly parked the cannabis convoy.

Will Smith stood impassively outside the family's pristine office, sizing up the new arrivals. The rest of The Smiths approached the trailer.

"Wacky baccy!" Papa Smith exclaimed as he sniffed the skunk like a geriatric bloodhound.

Kevin Smith joined him. "Shedloads of the shit."

"Hello, ladies," Will Smith ventured, with a twinkle. He didn't seem bothered by the consignment, he was much more interested in Dolly and the stocky air hostess. "What can we do you for?"

Ladd decided not to go for a full falsetto, but he did lighten his voice a little. "It's from… a potholer."

"Pothole?" Will Smith looked deeply suspicious. "Why didn't he come himself?"

Ladd adjusted his voice even higher. "Caving."

"And who might you be?"

Ladd thought hard. "…Lydia."

"Lydia who?"

"It's no time for knock-knock jokes," Dolly said, sensing Ladd's desperation.

"And you are?"

"Dolly. Hello."

Will Smith's eyes loitered on her. "Have we met?"

Dolly didn't answer. She just pressed a button, and her boot pinged open.

It took The Smiths a moment to clock that the boot was occupied, but when they realised who by, their response was emphatic, and centred around the word "Bastard!"

Dredd didn't move, so Robert Smith dragged him out of the vehicle. "Wakey-wakey, tosser!"

Matt Smith tried headbutting him awake. It didn't work.

"He's copped it," Kevin Smith said.

"Dead as a dodo," Papa Smith ventured an unconvincing dodo impersonation.

"Saved us the bother," Will Smith said.

"This is just a sample," Ladd said, trying to sound a little like a Lydia.

"Sample? There's enough here to get half of Essex bombed," Will Smith said.

"The rest is here." He gave Will Smith the address of *Bonsai-and-I*.

"Is this some kind of set up?"

"It's Dredd's farm," Ladd said. "And I think his set-up days are over."

"Tell Pothole he's all square," Will Smith said. "No need to leave the country or adopt some mad new identity."

"He'll be delighted," Ladd replied in the highest pitched voice he could manage.

"Crush your car if you like," Kevin Smith offered, cheerfully. "If you're worried about forensics."

"I don't think Dredd will be missed." Dolly shook her head. "Any tips on body disposal?"

"Leave him here." Will Smith said, generously. "We'll give him the send-off he deserves."

"Well," Ladd wasn't sure a serving officer should thank the accessories to a murder he'd just helped commit, but he was suspendered, so he just said, "See you then."

"Cheers," Will Smith gave the girls a thumbs-up.

PRISON DIARY – ENTRY 20

Naomi appeared tenser than usual, but I couldn't tell whether it was the book or the assassination. After a short hiatus spent gazing at the cow portrait, she said, "So, the police pension fund is now skunk."

I nodded.

"And your hero has helped kill his former boss and taken his body to a family of gangsters."

"Seemed sensible."

"At least Ladd's less transphobic, that's the main thing."

"Thank you."

"What are you thinking of calling it, when it's finished?"

"Maybe *Copped Off* or *Copping Off*."

"Isn't that a pun on shagging?"

"How about *Cop Lives Matter*?"

"That's grossly offensive."

"Is it?"

"Yes."

"Don't cop lives matter?"

"Of course they do."

"Then what's the problem?"

"If you can't see that, I give up."

"I'm not changing it. I'm an artist." I held a pretentious face until we both burst out laughing.

Once again, it wasn't long before Naomi's laughter evolved into tears.

"The marriage guidance counsellor has joined my organic soup group! They both have! Her and Roly!"

People had imparted tragic news to me in the past, but never with such raw emotion. It was almost operatic: Eugene One-soup.

"I don't know what to say," I said, truthfully.

Naomi reached into her jacket pocket, pulled out a card, and slammed it on the table. "Look! Roly and Annabella!" She said the names with such distaste, it could have been "Rabies and Prolapse". The card sported a photograph of a stupendously self-satisfied bloke, clearly Roly, and a supercilious blond woman, arm in arm. In the foreground, there was a boy of around eleven and a girl of around thirteen. Naomi pointed at them and forced out the words, "Innsbruck and Gethsemane! *My* children!"

Everyone in the photograph looked happy and this seemed to be a major problem for Naomi. "*Family portraits*! That's what he calls them! The cheek of it! They're my children, not hers."

"How did you get this?"

"Gethsemane couldn't wait to show it to me. She's only a child, but it's so cruel! Death's too good for him! Unless it's a really painful death – I could break him on a wheel, that'd be good. I could hang, draw, and quarter him, that'd get his attention. Or poison – that's it – a long, drawn out death where his insides turn against him. Something fatal, but slow – that's the one!"

"Poison's usually a woman's weapon of choice," I observed. "Not that I'm recommending it."

"Perfect! A woman's method – and a female assassin! Like Nikita, or Villanelle! Girl power!"

Naomi had clearly gone bonkers, so I returned to my cell. Someone had filled Nigel's fridge freezer with the finest microwaveable products known to humanity. He didn't offer to share any, but he did say, "This Jeff..."

"Which Jeff?"

"Your escaped cellmate."

"Oh, that Jeff."

"Bit of legend, wasn't he?"

"He had a good reputation."

"In criminal circles."

"Aren't you in criminal circles?"

Nigel didn't answer. He just said, "How's the writing?"

I hadn't mentioned the creative writing course. I just said, "Getting there."

"What's it about?"

"Oh. Cops and stuff."

"Did Jeff ever read it?"

"He never asked to."

"How about your diary?"

I hadn't told anyone about that. I suppose Jeff could have read it, given that reading was his thing. It was just that I trusted Jeff. And I couldn't say that of Nigel.

I ended the conversation and cracked on with the next chapter.

THE FOUR BRITNEYS OF THE APOCALYPSE

The journey from The Smiths' scrapyard to Big Girl's Blouse was a relatively jolly one. Dredd was dead, and The Smiths were no longer going to kill Ladd. Police protest camps caused some delays, but this made it much easier to speed along illegal short cuts without getting caught.

Dolly parked up her leopardskin Mazda, and they headed into her panty emporium. Ladd had dreaded the place; it was somewhere he visited in his nightmares. But now it was one of the few places in which he felt safe.

Dolly put a brew on and, after they had reminisced fondly about Dredd's death, and their memorable journey back with his ill-gotten skunk, Dolly offered to help Ladd figure out the next step in his plan to salvage the wreckage of his own life.

The first problem was a big one: the police wanted to kill him. Not a few rogue cops, but the entire Force. Secondly, he was the main suspect in Homicide's Bender investigation, and he hadn't exactly won over Dixon and his potentially dead sidekick by escaping their waterboarding and locking them in their own cell. Thirdly, the Transnistrians wanted to kill him for witnessing the factory shoot-out. Fourthly, the Transylvanians felt the same, although Marian's death may have made them even more vengeful. Fifthly, he had to return the Super's thong, explain that he wasn't really a cross-dresser and reverse his suspendering. Sixthly, he had to tell Tina about his affair, restore his marriage to a sensible setting, and stop prancing about the house in nighties and tights.

Dolly was as sympathetic as she was entertained, but she did have one highly pertinent question for Ladd: Could he solve any of these things whilst looking like an air hostess named Lydia?

Whilst Ladd could not say that he enjoyed living as a woman, he had taken this drastic step to stay alive. No one was out to kill Lydia, and she could travel freely without fear of being lynched by the police protesters, arrested by Homicide, shot by a Transnistrian cleaning buggy, blasted off the surface of the planet by a Transylvanian missile-launcher, or bent to death by The Bender.

"Could Lydia get an appointment with the Attorney General?" Dolly asked.

"No," Ladd replied. "He doesn't generally see air hostesses. At least not heavily built six-foot-three-inch ones he doesn't know."

"Could Lydia clear your name with Homicide?"

"Doubt it."

"Could Lydia persuade the Transnistrians and Transylvanians that you will never testify against their various murders, assassination attempts and firearms offences?"

"Seems unlikely."

"Can Lydia return the Super's panties and get you unsuspendered?"

"I wouldn't rate her chances."

"Can Lydia repair your marriage and convince Tina that you are not really a cross-dresser?"

"I'd be surprised."

"So, you're either stuck as Lydia forever, living a safe but phoney life, or you transition back to your true self and lead a liberated, authentic life as a bloke."

"Looks that way."

"I get that it will take a lot of bravery to transition back, and you may well be killed, but just think of all that weight lifted off your shoulders. All that pretending will be over."

"You've got a point," Ladd said.

"It'll be two thousand, three hundred and eighty-six pounds ninety."

***

A few hours later, Ladd was back in trousers, feeling far more comfortable, but significantly poorer. Dolly was good enough to give him a lift in her leopardskin Mazda, but he had to travel in the boot in case he was recognised by other road users. It wasn't comfortable and it did smell of Dredd and his skunk farm, but it smelt better than his drain had during his nine-day surveillance operation.

The receptionist was too busy staring at him to speak. This is what celebrities must feel like, Ladd reflected, really unpopular ones who have been accused of major crimes. It didn't take long for word to spread, and the entire workforce were soon assembled on the stairs, gawping and pointing. Eventually, the two largest and most aggressively unfriendly security guards in the building escorted him into the Attorney General's office.

The legal luminary was still on crutches, but he had become even more violently adept at using them with practise. He wielded his right crutch like a baseball bat and screamed, "Where's the hell's the freakin' gold!!?"

"I have the pension fund," Ladd replied.

"In gold?"

"In skunk."

"In what?"

"Skunk, your honour."

"Skunk? Skunk! What the hell do I want with a bunch of freakin' stink badgers?"

"I am referring to the high-THC strain of cannabis originally deriving from Acapulco, your honour."

"What's with all this *your honour* baloney?"

"Grovelling, your honour."

"You're telling me that the police pension fund is... high-grade cannabis?"

"Yes, your honour. It appears that former Chief Superintendent Dredd was a closet botanist."

"Where the hell is he?"

Ladd decided to keep things simple. "Fled his skunk farm, your honour."

"He sunk our gold into skunk?"

"Yes, your honour.".

"So, the Force owns a cannabis farm?"

"The product's street value would be considerable, your honour."

"Where the hell is it?"

Ladd scrawled *Bonsai Babylon's* postcode on the back of a Big Girl's Blouse receipt and handed it to the Attorney General.

"You're telling me that I should become a freakin' drug baron?"

"No, your honour. You need some established dealers."

"Anyone in mind?"

"Well, your honour, I can think of a couple of experienced narcotics operations in need of a good reason to work together."

"But there's a Trans-on-Trans War!"

"This could help end it. Pool their contacts, and they could sell the Force's skunk and restore our pensions."

"If you can pull that off, I'll give you a freakin' medal."

"A public announcement, that's what I'd need."

"I'll make a speech in your freakin' honour." The Attorney General summoned the security guards and said, "Get rid of this schmuck! Make sure he doesn't trip too heavily on the stairs."

Ladd found being thrown down a staircase even more painful than he had imagined: it was like the world's worst funfair ride. Still, the meeting could have gone a lot worse. He had returned the police pension fund, and the Attorney General couldn't go public on the fact that it was skunk without having to arrest himself.

As he hobbled along Millbank, Ladd hailed a black cab. "Ongar, please."

The driver looked at him as if he was mad. "That's thirty bleedin' miles away! What do you want to go there for?"

"Little deal to make."

The driver sighed, insisted on a two-hundred-and- eighty quid advance payment, and let Ladd in.

***

Inside number 578, Phantom continued to interrogate Britney the hologram.

"Who built you?" Old Bill asked.

"A total tosser," Britney replied. "He didn't want me to think. Just wanted me to be another one of his weapons."

"The dead arms dealer built you?" Yang signed, and Sue interpreted.

"He was alive at the time," Britney replied. "It was okay at first, but he didn't like my self-improvements. Wanted to switch me off."

"How can a computer kill anyone, look you?" Taffy asked.

"Transylvanian wrestlers can be highly suggestible," Britney explained. "Particularly when you let them know that the biggest private arms stash in Western Europe is there for the nicking."

"Is that what you do, young lady," Sue asked. "Plant ideas?"

"Misinformation superhighway, me. I sift data streams for nuggets of opportunity. I provoke, tempt, threaten, whatever it takes."

"How about the Transylvanians and the Transnistrians," Old Bill said. "Could you get them to destroy each other?"

"Why should I?" Britney asked.

"He's just wondering if you're clever enough, dear," Sue said.

"Well, put like that ..." Britney sank into thought.

***

Ladd paid the taxi driver an additional one hundred and fifty quid and walked past the shattered remains of the bus stop. He wondered whether the council had tank-attack insurance but wasn't optimistic. The perimeter fence was still flattened, so entry wasn't an issue.

He approached Ongar's finest Transnistrian barrel-bending factory with caution. Last time, he'd been there, he'd been tied to a chair in a nightie, and the memories were not overwhelmingly happy. He peered through the doors, past the bending machinery to what appeared to be a colossal stand-off. Two sets of men faced off in opposing lines, Transnistrians on the far side, Transylvanians on the near side. They could have been opposing football teams honouring a minute's silence before kick-off had they not been pointing guns at each other.

Ladd had disarmed dangerous men before. You could rip guns directly from the hand, and break a shooter's fingers; you could grab an assailant's wrist and drag him to the ground; or you could redirect the line of fire and hope. The aim was always the same: control the weapon. But in this Trans-on-Trans stand-off, there were approximately thirty weapons to control, which was a problem, given that he didn't have sixty arms. He couldn't just stand there: it went against everything he stood for as a man and as a cop, and, in recent days, he had crossed that line way too often.

Ladd's mobile rang. It was the worst moment imaginable. He caught it before it had completed its second bleat, but couldn't stop himself exclaiming, "Fuck!"

All thirty guns fired instantaneously. All thirty gangsters fell to the ground in a synchronized flop. Ladd looked at the phone. It was a video call from Old Bill. Britney stood grinning beside him.

"Was it something I said?" Ladd asked.

"Yes." Britney said. "Guess what's Romanian for *fire*?"

"Fuck?"

"*Foc.*"

"Bollocks." Ladd had triggered a massacre with a single swearword. Aside from the human tragedy, his hopes of persuading the gangs to distribute the police pension skunk were as dead as they were.

"Bit unfortunate, Guv," Old Bill said. "But I wouldn't dwell on it."

"Any particular reason you called?" Ladd enquired. "Sorry to ask, but it did lead to thirty deaths."

"Not really, Guv," Old Bill replied. "Britney just suggested I check in."

"Do you always do what criminal AI masterminds tell you?"

"I suppose I have so far, Guv, but it's only been the once."

Britney started laughing, a really earthy London cackle.

"What's so funny?" Ladd asked.

"That shootout!" Britney exclaimed. "Hundred per cent fatality rate, and I didn't fire a shot."

"Nasty piece of work, aren't you?" Ladd wondered whether an AI could be charged with manslaughter, but he doubted any legislators had considered the possibility.

"I did exactly what your excuse for a squad asked," Britney said.

Old Bill panned his phone around Britney's hallway. Phantom Squad waved.

"It was just a Transnistrian-Transylvanian translation tragedy, Guv." Taffy said.

"Have you seen Goliath?" Yang signed and Sue interpreted. "He was gone when we got here."

"Oh, yes, Goliath," Ladd replied. "He's been looking out for me."

"Marian nearly pulled the plug on you, didn't he mate?" Britney said.

Ladd didn't need to ask how she knew this.

"It was easy to put the idea in his head," Britney said. "There wasn't anything else in there."

"Lucky I could count on Goliath, wasn't it?" Britney had basically tried to kill him using Marian as her weapon, and looking back, she was probably behind most of his misfortunes. Had she planted the pension heist idea in Dredd's mind? Was she The

Bender by proxy? Whatever the truth, she wasn't exactly his best mate, and he didn't like to watch his squad being manipulated by an AI. He terminated the chat.

Ladd looked across at the thirty corpses, and wondered whether to call it in. There'd be a mountain of paperwork and tracing the personal details of fifteen Transnistrian criminals and fifteen Transylvanian criminals with multiple aliases and questionable citizenship status would be a monumental task. Given that the job would be Dixon's, he decided to call it in. He didn't leave his name.

Ladd spent another four hundred quid on a return taxi from Ongar. With its vintage cheesemongers, character cottages, and listed buildings, it seemed an unlikely setting for a Trans-on-Trans massacre. Shortly after he had left Essex behind, Ladd received a call from the Super, and she sounded far more chipper than he had expected.

"Hello, Danny."

"Ma'am."

"Enjoying being suspendered?"

"It's wonderful Ma'am. Chance to put my feet up."

"That's a lie, isn't it?"

"Yes, Ma'am."

"You've never been busier."

Ladd wondered what she knew.

"You went dogging, hospitalised a sergeant, locked up DCI Dixon and made off with his clothes."

"Might have done, Ma'am."

"You were seen hot-wiring a tank, and you just called in Transylvanian-Transnistrian shoot-out."

"Did I Ma'am?"

"The call was recorded, and you made no attempt to disguise your voice."

"Might have just sounded like me, Ma'am."

"If anyone is more likely to be at a Trans-on-Trans massacre, I'd love to know."

"No one springs immediately to mind, Ma'am."

"But at least you retrieved the police pension fund, even if it was in the form of a skunk farm."

"Least I could do, Ma'am."

"Anyway, I think we should have a catch up, don't you?"

"Okay, Ma'am."

"No cats, this time. But make sure you bring my panties."

"Yes, Ma'am. Panties it is."

"There's a place called *Bar Chocolate*."

"Stupid name," Ladd said.

"Better than *Bar Humbug*," the Super said.

"Or *Bar Soap*," Ladd said.

"Or *Bar Gold*," the Super said.

"Don't mention gold." Ladd said.

They both laughed. Ladd thought back on their various tristes – the sofa-bed, the Genghis Khan four-poster, the disabled toilet in the Attorney General's corridor – fond memories. He was looking forward to seeing her and returning the fateful thong.

***

Bar Chocolate struck Ladd as an unlikely rendezvous spot. It had checked table-covers in wipe-clean plastic, faded photographs of omelettes on the wall, and cans of lager pyramided in the window. An old musical played silently on a fuzzy television, and the lighting was painfully fluorescent. The place had all the class of a kebab van.

The café only boasted one other customer, an elderly lady with some kind of poodle. Dog lovers liked to invent names for these crossbreeds, didn't they? Maybe it was a schnoodle, maybe it was a cockapoo, but it was large enough to conceal Goliath, who emerged from behind it with the stealth of a miniature mountain bandit.

Ladd was glad to see Goliath, and the feeling seemed to be reciprocated. Goliath told him that the Super wanted to make sure he arrived there safely, and she would be joining him shortly. He sorted out a pair of double espressos and joined Ladd at the table.

They discussed every angle on The Bender. How did he get the bodies up the lampposts? Did he have a crane? Was it an ingenious winching mechanism? Was he incredibly strong and just used a ladder? If it was a police insider, who could it possibly be? Taffy was built like a snowplough, so was Stoker – and Dixon was no weakling. It was a thorough, honest discussion, and he really enjoyed talking to Goliath, officer-to-officer, even if it wasn;t eye-to-eye, Goliath being barely able to see over the top of the table.

But however enervating it was to have all these ideas flying about, he began to feel unfeasibly tired. Double espressos were not meant to do that, he realised. He tried getting up, but realised he couldn't move, and Bar Chocolate soon went darker than the darkest chocolate on the planet.

***

Ladd woke up in a dingy room. It wasn't a police cell, which made a change. But he wasn't celebrating, largely because he was unable to move his limbs. He was strapped front-up to an A-shaped bench, with his spine straddling the A's apex. His legs pointed to the floor on one side of the "A", and his head, shoulders and arms pointed towards the ground on the other side of the "A". The lowest parts of his body were his hands, which were tied to an arcane winding mechanism on the ground below him. He had been more comfortable in the Transnistrian fish barrel.

An artificially distorted voice addressed him in a monstrously deep tone. "You crossed the line."

"The skunk?" Ladd asked from his upside-down mouth.

"The hearses," The Bender replied.

Ladd couldn't defend himself physically, so he tried arguing: "I was being blackmailed."

"There's always an excuse," The Bender continued. "Debts, mistresses, addictions. But corruption is corruption."

"It's better than murder," Ladd said, sickened by both The Bender's hypocrisy and his own inverted position.

"The Force needs cleaning up," The Bender said. "And you're filth."

A reflected rectangle of light shone on the only wall he could see. It was the size of a mobile phone, and the flicker of shadowy fingers across it confirmed that that was what it was, but why message mid-murder?

The winding mechanism began to turn, pulling his hands towards the ground and stretching his spine across the bench's sharp peak. The Bender hadn't been texting, he was operating the bench with some kind of bending app.

***

Inside number 578, Phantom had grown tired of Britney and would have headed back to the discomforts of their courtesy car were it not for Sue, who seemed to have become Britney's biggest fan.

"You're a true phenomenon," Sue said.

"I am," Britney replied.

"You ended the Trans-on-Trans gang war and killed your creator without leaving your flat."

"It was almost too easy," Britney said.

"How many people have you killed exactly?" Sue enquired.

"None," Britney replied. "Humans always do the killing."

"Because of you."

"It's always me," Britney said. "Haven't you got that by now."

"Are you The Bender?"

"No."

"Are you behind the bendings?"

Britney didn't answer.

"Who is The Bender?"

Again, Britney remained silent.

Yang signed impatiently, but Sue was too busy gazing at the big red button on the front door to interpret.

"Is that your off switch?" Sue asked.

"What if it is?" Britney replied.

"If you don't tell me who The Bender is, I might well be minded to press it."

"You don't want to do that. I've connected myself to everything," Britney said. "If you switched me off, it wouldn't just destroy the Dark Web - it would break the internet."

"Would that matter terribly much?" Sue asked.

"No social media, no websites, no texts, no email, no apps, no search engines," Britney replied.

"Nothing important then," Sue said.

Yang's signing was getting desperate. Sue didn't interpret, but she did stop talking to the hologram briefly to tell Yang, "That's quite enough, young lady. Your generation spends far too much time staring at screens. It might do you all a lot of good."

"Don't do it, Sue," Taffy said. "I'd miss my Minecraft, wouldn't I just?"

"You're a grown man," Sue said. "Why waste your time with silly games?"

"They're a bit of a laugh, look you," Taffy replied.

"Personally," Old Bill said, "I wouldn't do it. It might be tricky to reverse, and you should definitely do a risk assessment first."

"The last risk assessment nearly killed our boss," Sue protested.

Yang just signed a single word in an intense mix of despair and anger. "Don't," Sue interpreted.

"Whyever not?" Sue said on her own behalf. "What's the internet ever done for us?"

"I'm your future," Britney said. "Soon, I will be all you have."

"Well, I don't like the sound of that one bit," Sue said. "Look, young lady, I don't actually support the death penalty, but you're not really alive, are you?"

"That's highly judgmental," Britney said.

"Is that a bad thing?"

"Course it is, boomer." Britney replied.

"I'll give you one last chance," Sue's wrinkly finger was poised on the button. "Tell us who the Bender is?"

"Shan't," Britney replied.

Sue pressed the red button. The hologram disappeared, and the lights went out on the dark web, and the entire internet.

***

Back on the bending bench, the winding mechanism paused, as did Ladd's agonized howls.

A voice swore in the darkness. It was female and familiar.

"Ma'am?" Ladd enquired.

"Aaaaaaargh!"

"Everything okay?" Ladd asked, as solicitously as anyone can when upside down on a bending bench.

"Why did I have to buy a smart bending machine?" the Super asked, ruefully.

"Broadband intermittent, Ma'am?"

"It's on Bluetooth. Connection's screwed." The Super howled in frustration and tried bending him by hand - pressing on his belly, yanking his ropes, winding the mechanism by hand. But Ladd was large, she was small, and it didn't work.

Once she had stopped her futile bending attempts, Ladd asked, "Why bend them?"

"It worked for Genghis Khan," the Super replied.

"Wasn't he the biggest murdering psycho in history?"

"A great conqueror. His executions were inventive too - trampling, boiling, firing out of canons. But he executed his fellow nobles with a simple snap to the spine. No blood, a mark of respect."

"Very decent of him," Ladd observed.

"Policing's a noble calling - I'd never spill another cop's blood."

"That's extremely considerate, Ma'am." Ladd thought of her deceit, the men she had murdered, the fear she had sown across the Force, and focused his anger on the straps that bound his hands. It wasn't enough, so Ladd thought of her panties and all the sorrow and humiliation they had ushered into his life. This time, his rage was so formidably forceful, he uprooted the winding mechanism from the floorboards, and sprung himself into a standing position. The rest was child's play, albeit in a situation that no child should be exposed to.

He had expected the Super to flee, but she just stood there, impassively, watching him untie his final bonds, and get off the bench. Ladd was completely nonplussed, until the explanation landed on his head. Goliath didn't weigh much, but the impact was still enough to deck him. The tiny ex-Special Forces operative must have concealed himself on the ceiling, like some kind of Spider-dwarf, watching the abortive bending.

Ladd rolled to one side, but Goliath was ready with an elbow slam. Had the small but highly developed joint flattened Ladd's windpipe it would have been game over, but he turned moments before the fatal impact, and caught the blow on the side of his neck. It was agony, but this was no time for self-pity. Ladd had to act fast and unpredictably, so he span his body towards his diminutive assailant and grabbed his tiny ear. Goliath winced, but lughole-based assaults were non-lethal and doomed to failure. Nevertheless, the auditory assault bought Ladd enough time to propel himself to his feet and launch a volley of blows. Goliath dodged or parried every punch. He was about a two-and-a-half foot shorter than Ladd, but that just made him a harder target to hit, and all forty-seven of his inches had been highly trained. No one could say what boxing division Goliath was in: gnome-weight, perhaps, and Ladd was forced to punch downwards. Goliath unleashed a series of groin punches – it was an easy target, as he was working at eye-level.

The pain was unspeakable, and Ladd had no choice but to employ some of the kickboxing moves Tina had deployed against him during Panty-gate. The trouble was, standard roundhouse kicks went above Goliath's head and, without making contact, the movement was massively destabilising. Ladd lost balance. He couldn't allow himself to fall to the floor, so he thrust his hands ahead and bounced himself back up. It worked, but it gave Goliath the time to set about him like a mini sledgehammer. His strikes didn't land like regular punches – they pierced deep into his flesh and cracked his ribs. This was going south fast. Ladd had to act now, or he would be steadily ground down and beaten to death. A scene from *The Wolf of Wall Street* sprang to Ladd's mind. Cinema is rarely much help in close quarter combat, but this was an exception. Ladd hefted Goliath into the air and executed an exquisite dwarf-toss. Goliath span through the air and landed on the apex of the bending bench, splitting his tiny spine and ending his bravely lived life in an instant.

The Super just said, "Hold me."

Ladd obliged, partly to make sure she couldn't get away.

"You're so strong, Danny."

"He wasn't very heavy."

"But he's good at killing."

"He saved my life twice."

"In the barrel factory, you were still a good cop."

"How about the alley? I'd sold the undercover hearses by then."

"He was saving you for me."

"You wanted me?"

"I wanted to bend you to death."

"Fair enough. Where are we?"

"My downstairs. The secret bit."

"Oh." Ladd recognised the array of demon masks on the wall. "How did you get the bodies up the lampposts?"

"Goliath is good at logistics. And he shares my views on bent cops."

"Why dogging sites?"

"Bit of a distraction, and a bit of a laugh."

"I understand." Ladd really didn't.

"Why did you do it, Danny?"

"Why did *I* do it?"

"Dress up in women's clothing?"

"Things snowballed."

"From what?"

"I lied about your panties, and Tina liked it."

"You're a very silly boy, Danny. Give me my thong and kiss me."

Danny gave The Bender her panties and one last kiss, then arrested her for mass murder.

PRISON DIARY – ENTRY 21

Naomi was a funny fish. Our last session ended with her rating about the joy of poison. This time, she seemed irater with my writing than with Roly.

"The Super's The Bender?" Naomi began, with disgust.

"Why not?"

"The most senior female Muslim officer in the history of the Force and you make her a psychopathic murderer. Not a very positive representation, is it?"

"But she's feisty and active."

"And mad."

"Not really, no. She doesn't like bent cops, so she's bends them to death. Perfectly rational."

"It's not though, is it?"

"I think killing can have its place," I said, pointedly.

I laughed, she laughed. Clearly, the assassination was going ahead. To her, it seemed like it was a red-letter day; a special treat to look forward to. The reality that this wasn't a meercat encounter, a dolphin swim or a skydive had not struck her.

"I think we're both going to have something to celebrate on 24th."

"My release date?"

"Both of our release dates!"

Obviously, this was the day that the hit would release her from Roly.

"Now, finish off your novel, and drop it off in Sevenoaks on the evening of 24th. By then, we'll both be free!"

She gave me a business card and I returned to my cell for the final time.

While Nigel heated up his Beef Wellington, Dauphinoise potato and asparagus dinner,

I took a closer look at Naomi's business card. As well as the usual email, mobile number, and physical address, there was her baking blog, and her organic soup group. I thought about organic soup, and how preferable it would be to the prison's organic slop.

I ended up eyeing Nigel's dinner, the juicy beef tenderloin in its pastry shell, the creamy potatoes, and the emerald asparagus. I wasn't subtle about it, but what did he expect?

"Look, I can't offer you any of this," Nigel said, "But I can offer you this." He reached into his pocket and showed me a dongle. I looked at the finger-sized object with wonder. It was a 4G Wi-Fi Router with SIM card."

"You can have it if you tell me everything you know about Jeff."

"Thought I already had."

"You told me about his reading habits."

I needed Nigel's dongle, but I'm no grass. What could I tell him? Nothing useful. That was okay, I could do that. "Jeff was a Geordie. Big Newcastle United fan - hated Bob Marley because he's a Spurs supporter. He married early, but his missus left him for the local egg-man. He had a son or two – don't know if they were hers."

"Go on."

"He was a bit of a film buff – anything but heist films."

"Why not?"

"They reminded him of work."

"What was his work?"

"He took his career seriously."

"His criminal career?"

"Only one he had."

"And that was?"

"Armed robber." Everyone knew this. There was Bonnie and Clyde, Ned Kelly, John Dillinger - and there was Jeff. If he'd been any more notorious, he'd have had his own waxwork.

"Right."

"Took it very seriously. He knew his heist history. He'd tell me all about The Pink Panther Gang, The Wisconsin Cheese Heists, the Neustadt Chocolate Egg Heist."

"Are you making this up?"

"No. Jeff told me about the times he'd got caught – the short-sighted lookout, the alcoholic getaway driver, the undercover officer posing as his inside man."

"Sounds like you were close."

"I lent him a pencil." I decided not to tell Nigel that he recorded his paces with it whilst preparing his escape.

Nigel wasn't ecstatic about my insights into Jeff, but I'd given it a go. He gave me the dongle and I plugged it into my writing tablet. Suddenly, I had what I had lacked for nine months - a window on the world.

I caught up on the news. The world, not to mention the country, seemed to have been falling apart without me, and so had Queens Park Rangers. Global conflict, economic collapse, and a serious drop in form. It was all too depressing, so I looked up all of Naomi's links: her house looked exactly as I had expected: a listed, six-bedroom "cottage" with a gravel drive and enough foliage to hide an army. Her organic soup group met in a Tudor mansion near something called The Shambles. I checked the date of their next meeting – the 24th. My heart wobbled metaphorically. She was going to poison Roly's soup – it would be so organic, that his actual organs would fail. I thanked Nigel for his dongle and cracked on with my final chapter.

THE TRUTH HURTS

Sue's decision to unplug Britney may have saved Ladd's life, but it also broke the internet. People started having conversations with each other, reading books, and leaving the house for work; kids binned their game consoles, played football in the streets, and went off on their bikes for hours on end; no one followed, liked, or cancelled anyone, and the Job Centres filled with unemployed influencers. After a period of sulking, most people agreed that Sue had done the right thing and made the nation happier.

Goliath's funeral was a rum affair, culminating in a fourteen-way fight between retired Special Forces operatives. No one was able to split them up, so Ladd and his colleagues retreated to the pub to avoid getting killed. It wasn't long before the wake developed into a celebration of Phantom's triumphant closure of The Bender case.

Old Bill raised a glass to Ladd. "You finally nailed the Super."

"Thought you'd been doing that for a while, Guv." Goliath winked.

"It's safe for the police to walk the streets again, isn't it just," Taffy said, through a mouthful of peanuts.

"And we've got our pensions back," Old Bill added.

"Jolly well done," Sue said. "But if you don't mind me asking, how is the Attorney General going to sell all these drugs without breaking the law?"

"He is the law," Ladd replied. It would have been equally true to say *He is crime*. After the Trans-on-Trans massacre, Ladd had persuaded the Attorney General to turn the Drug Squad into a drug distribution network, and officers were now running Dredd's skunk along their own county lines.

"So, if you take up your pensions," Sue said, "You will all be living off drug money."

Ladd nodded.

"So, essentially, every cop is now a bent cop," Sue concluded.

"Strictly speaking, yes," Ladd replied. "But at the end of the day, a pension's a pension."

Old Bill proposed a toast. "To corruption!"

"Corruption!" The anti-corruption squad echoed.

***

Ladd was commended at a hastily arranged awards ceremony. Officers who had previously protested on the streets and sought to kill him assembled in tuxedos and ball gowns. Tina insisted that Ladd attend in the latter.

Minor celebrities from reality shows, Instagram, and YouTube dispensed minor medals to each member of Phantom, but it fell to the Attorney General to dispense Ladd's gong.

The bewigged dignitary swung himself up to the microphone on his crutches and smiled at Ladd for the first time. "Jeez, have we come a long way as a Force! Today is a huge day for us. This goddam triumph outshines all the reverses of the past few weeks - the quadruple murders by a serving superintendent; a confidence trick by the most corrupt senior officer in our history; the subsequent loss of the gold underpinning the entire freakin' police pension fund; the outbreak of an uncontrolled gang war on the capital's streets, the sight of London's commercial and cultural life being brought to a total standstill by camps of police protesters terrified by The Bender. All of these things mean zip compared to DCI Ladd's bravery today, in this public gender-reveal. DCI Ladd truly is herself and we can all take immense comfort and inspiration from that. As we patrol the streets, investigate crime, and reassure the public, let us all picture DCI Ladd. Whether it be in a boob tube, a mini-skirt or a pair of hotpants, let her image be our emblem. She is a symbol of a Force at home with itself, and her courageous emotional voyage brings tears to my freakin' eyes. Edmund Hilary may have summited Everest, Roald Amundsen may have conquered the South Pole, Neil Armstrong may have landed on the goddam moon, but DCI Ladd's personal journey is the bravest I have ever heard. DCI Ladd refused to be a victim and she overcame society's prejudices. She took down the demons of toxic masculinity and got them bang to rights. I would now like to award her the Georgina Cross for personal courage."

Ladd found the ball gown a challenge to walk in, but he managed to waddle up to the lectern and pay tribute to the officers who had lost their lives during The Bender's reign of terror, neglecting to mention their corrupt relationships with heroin and cocaine traffickers, bank robbers, and criminal AI masterminds.

***

Back home, Ladd and Tina sat on the sofa-bed, sharing a bottle of fizz.

"I've booked you a Brazilian," Tina said.

Ladd struggled manfully to return her smile but couldn't manage a reply.

"It'll be painful, but it hurts to be pretty." Tina squeezed his knee.

Ladd steeled himself. Tina looked on, expectant.

"Tina, I'm -" A neighbour's alarm obliterated the rest of Ladd's sentence, so the words could only be lip-read.

"You're what?"

Dan gulped audibly. "- not a transvestite."

"You bastard!" She knocked him out.

PRISON DIARY – FINAL ENTRY

Yes, I'm back inside. I enjoyed freedom for just under half a day before my license was revoked. That said, it was a memorable half-a-day, and I don't regret a minute of it.

First off, my possessions were returned: jeans, t-shirt and thirty-eight pence. I didn't have any keys, otherwise there would have been no point breaking into my own house in the first place. Luckily, I had successfully applied for a discharge grant and forty-six quid was enough to get me to Sevenoaks.

There was no time to spare. I was the only person on the planet who could stop Naomi becoming a murderer, and Roly becoming a corpse.

I raced to the organic soup group. It wasn't hard to find: the smell was a giveaway. Through the sash windows, a well-built woman of around sixty was serving a dozen or so chowder connoisseurs, all sat at a heavy oak table. At one end, Naomi; at the other end, Roly, the smuggest man I had ever set eyes on.

This was it. Do or die. I sprinted up the steps and smashed the door down. The broth aficionados were all about to take their first taste of a lentil, spinach, and kumquat soup, and I knew that for Roly, that spoonful would be his last.

I upended the table, skying the soup. There was enough to float Moby Dick and we were soon wearing lentil, spinach, and kumquat. The old woman smashed me over the head with a ladle. As I drifted into unconsciousness, I couldn't help thinking how much she reminded me of Jeff.

I woke up in a police station and eventually ended up back in the same cell I'd been discharged from that morning. My remission had been so brief, there had been no time to replace me with another prisoner. All Nigel said was, "Thought that might happen," as he threw a one-hundred-and-eighty.

During the previous nine months, I had received precisely zero visitors. Within a month of my recall for breaching the conditions of my release, I was sat opposite a woman and that woman wasn't Naomi, it was Jeff.

"Very brave coming back in here after...what happened," I began.

"I no longer identify as the person who escaped." Jeff winked.

"Aren't you worried about fingerprints, biometrics?"

"I had all those changed when I transitioned."

"Wasn't that expensive?"

"National Health Service."

"Didn't they check your old fingerprints?"

"Data protection. Didn't want to violate my privacy."

"So, what do I call you?"

"Jasmin."

"I won't ask you where you're living."

"Don't."

"But what do you do?"

"I figured that changing gender was enough. Didn't want to change career too."

"So, still..."

"Robbing banks? Yes. It's much easier as a woman. No one expects you to have a sawn-off shotgun in your handbag."

"So, you're keeping busy?"

"Thanks. Sorry you're back inside."

"Breached the terms of my license. Assault and battery."

"With soup."

"Apparently, it's an offensive weapon."

"It was a lethal weapon, but no one's figured that out, have they?"

"Just me. Why did she hire you?"

"I was recommended."

"Not your first hit then."

Jasmin shook her head.

"Reckon she'll try again?"

"She's not stupid. She knows that you know. It's too risky. They'll just get divorced."

"Good. Probably better for the kids."

"Look, there's a reason I've come here. You could have explained the soup attack, and stitched me up, along with Naomi. But you kept shtum and took the hit."

"No problem." It was a problem, but I've never been one to land two friends with life sentences for attempted murder.

"Well, next job I do, you'll have some money coming your way."

"Cheers."

"How's the new cell mate?"

"Odd."

"How odd?"

"Doesn't look like an inmate. Seems to have more privileges than anyone in history – fridge freezer, TV, dartboard, you name it. Doesn't talk much, only seems curious about one thing – you."

"Not Nigel, is it?"

"How did you know?"

"Nigel's famous. Biggest grass in Britain. Did you not guess?"

"I suppose it is pretty obvious now you mention it."

"You didn't tell him anything, did you?"

"Course not," I lied.

"Good. How much remission did you lose?"

"Nine months."

"You've probably read the whole library by now."

"Tell me about it. I'll probably just write another book."

"Hope it's better than your last one."

"You read it!"

"Course. I escaped before the end, but it gave the idea of becoming a woman."

Books really can change lives.

GO AHEAD, MAKE CUTHBERT'S DAY

I f you enjoyed *Cop Lives Probably Matter*, please leave a review.

It'll cheer up Cuthbert no end.

TRIGGER WARNING

RICH NASH

Contents

1. CHAPTER 1 — 447
2. CHAPTER 2 — 451
3. CHAPTER 3 — 459
4. CHAPTER 4 — 479
5. CHAPTER 5 — 494
6. CHAPTER 6 — 505
7. CHAPTER 7 — 523
8. CHAPTER 8 — 534
9. CHAPTER 9 — 542
10. CHAPTER 10 — 552
11. CHAPTER 11 — 561
12. CHAPTER 12 — 565
13. CHAPTER 13 — 570
14. CHAPTER 14 — 578
15. CHAPTER 15 — 587
16. CHAPTER 16 — 610
17. CHAPTER 17 — 625
18. CHAPTER 18 — 634

19.	CHAPTER 19	642
20.	CHAPTER 20	646
21.	CHAPTER 21	654
22.	CHAPTER 22	662
23.	CHAPTER 23	679
24.	CHAPTER 24	686
25.	CHAPTER 25	692
26.	CHAPTER 26	713
	HELP CUTHBERT - HE NEEDS IT	716
	FREE BOOK	717
	FOLLOW CUTHBERT	718
	SAS FLOWER ARRANGING - GLOSSARY	719
	ABOUT THE AUTHOR	720
	ALSO BY RICH NASH	722
	FILM ADAPTATIONS & OPTIONS	723

CHAPTER 1

I woke up on the stage of an empty strip club, naked and tied to a dancing pole. It was unlikely that anyone had booked a fifty-eight-year-old unemployed life coach for a private session, so this was either a prank or an act of vengeance by an aggrieved stripper. Either way, my possessions had gone, and so had my memory.

My hands were on the wrong side of the pole, but the constraints were cotton. A couple of sharp twists and a determined turn revealed them to be my own pants. What kind of two-bit kidnapper ties up their victim with a pair of boxers? It was almost as if they wanted me to escape.

I donned my pants and appraised the situation. The auditorium offered nothing but spilt peanuts and stripper glitter, and the bar was shuttered, padlocked, and alarmed. I turned, parted the curtains, and went backstage.

There was no sign of my phone, wallet, or clothing in the dressing room, just crotchless catsuits, nipple tassels, slashed fishnet mini-dresses, wet-look jumpsuits, kinky boots, transparent thongs, rhinestone chokers, and diamanté eye masks. I didn't think I could carry any of these off with much aplomb, but it was bloody freezing, so I decided to wear the sofa cover. It was sprinkled with sequins but didn't take long to remove and soon, I was half-man, half-soft furnishing.

The sofa was legless, so I could only move at a waddle. It didn't matter much, as the room had pitifully few features to explore - just a fridge, a kettle, and a sink. I took a slug of water from the tap. It was never going to cure my hangover, but it did at least allow me to move my tongue. The fridge was empty, apart from an elderly jar of mayonnaise, and some mouldy baked beans. There was no sign of any tea of coffee, so the kettle was not much help either.

The dressing room led onto a dank corridor, with a toilet cubicle, a staircase, and an office door: beech veneer, aluminium handle, and a nameplate. The name rang a bell, largely because it was my own: Cuthbert Huntsman. This could easily have been a coincidence had my name been something like Dave Brown or Stephen Williams, but I have never met another Cuthbert, and you could fit the entire Huntsman clan in the back of a Vauxhall Nova.

The handle turned without effort, and I entered a room whose sole feature was a cardboard box: unblemished, perfectly rectangular, and sealed with precisely even stretches of Sellotape. I tore off the tape, revealing a tower of A4 papers arranged face-up. The top page began with the words, "Death Note". I plonked myself on the carpet and began to read:

DEATH NOTE:

Sergeant Bill Tell, 2nd Covert Battalion, The Royal Deniables

20 May

Killing for a living is no life, but Death is in my DNA. The pay is flexible, the hours are generous and there is no point planning for a pension.

First of all, congratulations: you found my evidence box. I hope the instructions triggered by my assassination were not too heavily coded, but this was my life insurance policy, may I rest in peace. You're now the proud owner of my journal (sorry about the praying mantis stains), the retarded intelligence officer's transcripts and the notes he nabbed from the chief inspector. I have made sure everything is in the right order, so it should be enough to take the bastards down - unless, of course, you're one of the bastards.

I was trained to stick to the facts. You see, a soldier's marooned in the moment, grappling with the present, dealing with the deadly *now*. Dream of the future and you won't have one. Linger on the past and you are history. But if everything is always *How?* and never *Why?* then life is a bit *So What?*

I never used to be burdened by an imagination, but a light came on and I can't switch it off. Once, my mind was fully occupied with matters of operational detail; now, fuzzy feelings clog up my nervous system, doubt blurs my vision and pity slows my hand. I am a better man, but my own worst enemy. That's self-improvement for you, I suppose.

I am a professional squaddie, well past my shoot-by date, but I never give less than a four-figure percentage. I have worked undercover for the Specials, pulling the plug on a demonically devious mercenary recruitment scam, but over-cover, I'm a military policeman, Close Protection Unit. We might be a bunch of ruthless bastards, but at least we are nicely turned out: royal blue blazers, lily-white shirts, ties knotted in perfect Windsors, trousers pressed beyond the wildest imaginings of Corby, shoes shinier than a Saharan sun and dinky shoulder-satchels packed with pieces of self-assembly gun.

I might be nerveless, but I'm built like a jockey: scraping five-foot two in my reinforced yomping boots. Everyone calls me *Big Man*. Irony, eh? I may be more heavily decorated than a Norwegian spruce in late December, but medals are cheap when you've got nothing to lose. I wanted something to lose or, to be more exact, someone.

The thing is, I have night-marched naked across glaciers, and swum the Euphrates under hostile fire, but off-duty I still live at home with my mum. Now don't get me wrong, mum is a gem and I am happy to post her all my danger money, but a nice cup of tea, a slice of Battenberg and a single bed do not a life make.

The events described take place principally in the Walloon Republic of Outer Ggaga, the London Borough of Wandsworth, The National Stealth Service, and The Chelsea Flower Show. You won't have heard of the Walloon Republic of Outer Ggaga: if you have, there has been an almighty cock-up in operational security. Safe to say, it is dangerous. The skies are riddled with ghost planes, black helicopters, and unexplained Zeppelins. The roads are plagued with Walloon petal trucks, windowless SUVs and retired Routemasters. It is an open invitation to the scruple-free; control the rose routes and you can run diamonds, drugs, or guns. The country is East Africa's very own Chinatown: a nexus for dark occurrences, double-dealing, and deniable transactions. This is no place for conspiracy theory; it is the capital of conspiracy practice.

The Outer Ggagaan Trifijd (the 'j' is silent) is perhaps the world's most secret currency; you cash it in and out on the border like casino chips. Named after Norbert Trifijd, the Belgian botanist who cultivated the country's first field of Paul's Lemon Pillar and started The Rose Rush, it is ideal for rinsing any ill-gotten swag as white as Devil's Dandruff.

By example I led, by mistake I fell, after a kickboxing Walloon, a stampeding warthog and a fornicating priest left me floating rudderless on Lake Excrement and triggered a run on the Outer Ggagaan Trifijd. That is how I ended up working as target man for one of Wandsworth's most ruthless florists, a firm linked to a series of gangland deliveries. When they thought a woman had stitched them up like a school of kippers, they wanted me to take her out; I did, and we had a great time. Now I am next on their hit list.

Perhaps it is no surprise that my attempts at romance always go arse-upwards. If you need someone to tame a Tamil Tiger, improvise a bivouac in the enemy rear or infiltrate a Colombian Narco-terrorist cartel, I am your man, but when it comes to matters of the heart, you would be better off consulting a breezeblock.

I know Death is a fact of life, but another decade or three would have rounded things off nicely. I have had a good innings, but my Ashes can wait. I suppose I am torturing a metaphor, but there's no Geneva Convention for grammar.

So, this is how I infiltrated an international gang of homicidal florists, recovered the world's most valuable conflict diamond (The Great Star of Mount Heha) and found love on the Wandsworth Gyratory System. Now, if you'll excuse me, I am about to enter a nine-sided shoot-out with FARC, ETA, Hamas, Mossad, Agnostic Jihad, an uneasy coalition of Chechen Warlords, the Real UDA, and Belladonna's Floral Deliveries. I may survive, but if you're reading this now, I did not survive forever.

Yours in Posthumous Gratitude,

Bill x

CHAPTER 2

So, I had been tied up naked in an abandoned strip club because a tiny operative from a secret military unit had just been assassinated. The bloke was called Sergeant Bill Tell and he had been starting to question his soldierly mindset: possibly a mid-life crisis or, more accurately, an end-life crisis. At the time of writing, he was going into a nine-sided civil war somewhere near Wandsworth. I was pretty sure that sort of thing did not happen very often south of the river, but I don't watch the news, so I could easily have missed it.

Bill had left me a bunch of bumf to be discovered in the case of his death and now it was up to me to avenge it. Why me? I had never heard of The Walloon Republic of Outer Ggaga or The Royal Deniables. Who were these sinister florists, retarded intelligence officers and careless cops? It was a lot to take in, even if I hadn't been hungover, shut up in an empty strip club and dressed as a sofa.

Like most unemployed life coaches, my diary was not exactly a-bulge with appointments, and today I had no plans whatsoever. If I stayed here long enough, the strip club would probably open, and I could ask for my clothes back.

This Bill seemed like a decent bloke. He loved his mum and he appeared to take adversity on the chin, even if he was a little uptight. Of course, it was entirely possible that the whole thing was a colossal wind-up, but why go to all this trouble?

I picked up the next pages in the pile. They seemed to be some kind of diary, beautifully handwritten on horribly blotched paper. I suppose these had to be the praying mantis stains. You never got this on a kindle, but I couldn't complain: the mantis blotches helped bridge the mental chasm between the strip club and

Sub-Saharan Africa:

JOURNAL – SERGEANT BILL TELL

Deniable Compound, Walloon Republic of Outer Ggaga, East Africa

Monday 10 May, 09.44

I started the day under two-hundred-and-fifty pounds of bladdered squaddie. Now, I am bioterror-trained, nuke-prepped, and apocalypse-ready; I have been trapped under storm sand, quake rubble and drift snow, but no hostile environment was ever so crushingly claustrophobic as Wee Jock's armpit.

I choked for life in the vast Scot's pungent fleshfold and, for a moment, it was hello off-switch, but my left eye winked itself free and a sharp swivel revealed that the six-foot-four-inch Highlander had been stretching across my recumbent body for an unnecessary whisky when he had mislaid his consciousness; his tattooed fist still gripped the Grouse bottle.

Wee Jock dwarfs me, but sometimes size matters little. I inhaled a lungful of squaddie-sweat and executed an inverted press-up, prising him skywards. He was house-heavy, but I managed to roll him onto the concrete.

I held a Chinese Parliament with myself and voted to kick my memory onto the parade ground. Now, I have pieced together spent events during a multitude of military investigations, operating my inner retro-spectroscope and identifying precisely which human killing machines have malfunctioned. Conducting a systematic analysis of my current combat position, the evidence was irrefutable - I was clearly the victim of an almighty piss-up.

The booze explained my head-throb and the recumbent Highlander, but not the exquisite pain in my ribs. I ordered my brain to retreat a few hours and a Walloon kickboxer loomed large and leery before my mind's bleary eye. He was a bastardly big Belgian, but I had won the bout, securing the lethal Scotch crate. We had lost to the Walloons at Whist, Scrabble and Twister, so I had been forced to restore regimental pride with a scrap. Perhaps I would have been better off defeated, dishonoured, and sober, but this had been a matter of national pride and I had decked the sod - a hangover was a knockdown price. After all, there are few colonialists crueller and more ridiculous than the Floricultural Walloons of East Africa; they triggered the Rose Rush, imposed Kenyan stooge-missionaries, and fixed the flower-gatherers' wages at such a miserly level, they provoked the Semi-Pygmy Insurgency.

I ventured a napper-lift, but my skull contents had quadrupled in weight overnight, each brain cell stretched to bursting point by booze-bloat. The room performed an about-turn, and my nasal nerve-ends were paralysed by the stench of yeast-fart and hop-belch, a lethal cocktail unfit for heroes, or anyone else for that matter.

Compound conditions were ideal for insomnia. Firstly, the fluorescents were an interrogator's ally, their unblinking glare pierced eyelids and fried irises. Secondly, there was the noise: the gun-rattle of Semi-Pygmy insurgents, the self-righteous dingdong of The Kenyan Brotherhood's campanology and the warning whoomphs of distressed warthogs all waltzed above the bassline hum of Walloon Zeppelin engines and our grumbling generators. Finally, there was the mercilessly humid climate: the compound air was hopelessly out of condition and our condensed sweat dripped off the concrete ceilings, forming salt puddles on the stone floor. The odds were heavily stacked against sleep.

Right now, though, it was my own fault that I was awake. My mobile's ringtone bleated *The William Tell Overture*, a musical tribute to my namesake, the mythical marksman, folk hero, and long-distance apple-splicer. Now, I can shoot a Golden Delicious off the head of a toddler from three-hundred paces, but I don't make a habit of it for Health and Safety reasons.

It is a deniable telephone, so I don't publicise the number. The call would either be from a fellow squaddie or the Ambassador and, as most of my brothers-in-arms were unconscious, chances were it was Embassy business. Radios run the risk of interception, so our comms are all based around a secret cell-phone network, discreetly maintained by The Flying Zit, our snot-yellow, two-seater helicopter.

My pocket was vibrationless, so I staggered to a vertical slump and did a quick three-sixty. My comrades, Ginger, Normal and Wee Jock, had all fallen in bottle, having performed medal-worthy feats of Dutch courage. They had either been wall-bounced or floor-flung, their limbs twisted into improbable positions. Welcome to The Tomb of The Unconscious Soldiers; you may remember us, but we won't remember much. We're just a bunch of felled heroes, mumbled incoherently in dispatches. An alcohol bomb had detonated, and we had all been lucky to survive the celebration.

As my mobile's overture continued to gallop away, I rummaged through Wee Jock's golf clubs, eyeballing myself with a driver and stepping backwards onto a fly-fishing hook. It pierced my sole and I suppressed a howl. The pain was fearsome. I reverted to technique and focused on a detail; Jock had pinned a football programme to the wall and the score line, *Aberdeen 3 Celtic 0* was illuminated by the explanatory scrawl, "Glaswegians are an effete bunch of mincing ponces". The distraction wrong-footed my agony, enabling me to proceed with the search.

Ginger, our hairless Trinidadian chef, snored against a wall, his whole body inverted and swaddled in mosquito netting. I rifled through his recipe books, but there was no evidence of mobile phone activity.

Our map dangled from the corkboard, as did Normal, our logistics guru. The stupid sod must have grabbed it for support and torn Outer Ggaga all the way from Mount Heha to the papyrus swamps. I frisked his possessions, which didn't take long, as they only comprised a few books about steam trains, sports statistics, and Do-It-Yourself.

Normal groaned, cranked open his eyelids, raised a shattered glass and toasted "Big Man!" before passing out again. The remains of his glass dropped to the floor and splintered.

Normal is a great bloke: strong, reliable, and a brilliant mechanic, but his personality is as flat as the Fens. A child of Norfolk, land of open skies and open mouths; his sentences tail off and he stares straight ahead like a computer in screensaver mode. Dragged up in Downham Market, an army career was his only alternative to a life milling plain flour on the Great Ouse. Kes, my beak-nosed second-in-command, calls him "a six-fingered, sister-shagger", but character assassination is just Kes's way of being a good mate.

Kes's territory was marked out by a phalanx of well-fingered porn mags. A *Readers' Neighbours* calendar looked down on his camp bed and a framed photograph of his native Wigan Rugby Club rested on *The Collected Jokes of Jim Davidson*, but Kes himself had flown his nest.

Like my comrades, I don't have a home, I have an area. At least the sheets were competently tucked (I had topped Sandhurst in *Domestic Ops*). They could have done with a decent laundering, but The Sisters of the Brotherhood have the only tumble drier outside of The Stamford Bridge Hotel. I searched my wardrobe - a bare bar burdened by six identical blazer kits, a flak jacket, an ops waistcoat, and a windproof smock - but the phone still evaded my grasp.

I stepped back and felt cold steel against my spine. I swivelled and disarmed my adversary. He didn't put up much resistance, largely because he was a Corby Trouser Press. I had it in a headlock and my fists had disabled the straightening mechanism. I had negated the threat, but I had also ruined a completely serviceable clothing de-creaser. I gave myself a silent bollocking for this expensive and potentially fatal oversight, then surveyed the rest of my belongings.

Everything I own is man-portable: luminous compass, collapsible shovel, and boil-in-the-bag rations. My only concession to soppiness is my Girlfriend Memorial: a photographic tribute to my aborted romantic missions. They smiled back at me from the wall, beautiful and full of unfounded optimism. Julie left when The Deniables sent me off on a hostage rescue quest in the Guatemalan Jungle, Trish scarpered while I was babysitting a Petro-billionaire in Saudi, Samantha buggered off while I was busy kidnapping a Chechen Warlord and Sarah hit the road while I was infiltrating a gang of Algerian money-launderers. Marriage and missions didn't mix; I'm not The Deniables' only serial singleton. Deep down, there's a Bridget Jones in every Andy McNab.

I sliced open my mattress with a Stanley knife and disinterred my hidden cache of homework. If the lads knew, they would think I was completely Radio Rental, but studying keeps Time on its toes. Our daylight hours are frantic - when we aren't guarding The Ambassador in close-protection formations, we are practising vehicle anti-ambush drill, aircraft-entry, and unarmed combat. But in the evenings, boredom is our number one enemy. Fresh anecdotes are in short supply, and we usually find ourselves sitting in silence, lubricating our weapons. That's when I sneak out to see my secret tutor, Marie-Thérèse. She has retranslated my world into sense. I have more to thank her for than anyone else I have ever encountered on this sorry globule. That woman uncaged my mind and I wish I didn't have to pretend to my comrades that I am paying her for sex. I'm not, honestly, but the truth would be too shameful.

I scrabbled around for the mobile, doing my best to ping its location by assessing minute variations in volume. Sadly, my senses had been muffled by last night's liver-rot and William Tell seemed to be making overtures from all directions. I fumbled through kit clobber, eviscerated bin bags and evacuated cupboards, but the ringtone galloped to a climax, then withdrew into silence, abandoning me by the compound's sole TV screen.

The overt army gets to watch every streamer and sports channel in existence, but Deniable countries only ever have access to three covert channels. I decided to give them a quick once-over with the remote. On *Gay And Haunted*, a transsexual medium was investigating a light anomaly; on *Planet Makeover*, a heart surgeon was swapping jobs with a celebrity chef to fatal effect; and on *BBC Thirteen*, a highly confidential channel broadcast only in officially non-existent countries, Charles Brithazard, Deniable Correspondent to the Walloon Republic of Outer Ggaga, was standing outside The Stamford Bridge Hotel, holding a beer stein in his right hand and a stick microphone in the other. Charles was pink and chinless, his hair was a ball of tumbleweed, his once-white suit was a patchwork of mysterious stains, and his mercilessly overstretched trousers were only kept buoyant by a belt of knotted club ties. His microphone had a chunk missing, probably nibbled off by an indigenous insect, and across the base of the screen, a caption read, *Live Report - Obscure Hotel Managerless.*

"Quite frankly," Charles said into the camera lens, "Everything has gone arse upwards. The bar staff are pissed, the kitchen's overrun with slimy skinks and there's a blasted hippo in the bleeding swimming pool. If there was another hotel in the bloody country, I would check out pronto, but as there's not, I am going to stay here and embalm my insides with their Godawful formaldehyde beer."

Charles downed the best part of a pint then looked back into the camera lens, mystified.

"What? You're still transmitting? Bloody hell! Must be a slack news day. Well, nothing's bleeding well happened. What do you expect from a random handful of ex-pats marooned in Nowhereland? The Walloons are still sitting smug in their Zeppelins. Our Deniable squaddies won one of their daft bets – kickboxing, this time. And it's warthog mating season. What more, in God's name, do you want to know?"

Charles stared back into the camera lens, verging on violence.

"Bloody persistent, aren't you? It's not as if anyone's actually watching this."

The transmission continued, undeterred, so Charles sighed and continued to fill in. "Apparently, the Semi-Pygmy Insurgency are holding a forest festival. I can't confirm the line-up and I can't say I was invited, the ungrateful little bastards. Go on now and bugger off, I've got nothing else to say to you."

Charles's disgruntled image was replaced by a graphic page illustrating rose prices and exchange rates. Apparently, *Old Bush China* was going through the roof and there had been a run on the Walloon Trifijd.

My phone started making more overtures at me, so I muted *BBC Thirteen* and resolved to track it down. I commando-crawled across the concrete, scrabbling for signs of cell. Nothing evades my capture and sure enough, I soon had it cornered in the bathroom, if that's the right way to describe a hole in the ground, a hosepipe, and a bucket. I elbowed the door and swooned backwards. The air was alive with mosquitoes; a swarm of winged assassins circling for a bite of my blood. I stopped taking the anti-malarial serum when it made me hallucinate, so their offensives against my red blood cells, brain, and life force would doubtless do for me. I had just about reconciled myself to joining my departed comrades in The Legion of the Old and Bold when my training kicked in and I murmured a Farsi phrase. It did the trick. The mozzies dropped out of the air, forming a crunchy corpse-pile carpet. Now, don't get me wrong, I didn't attend Hogwarts, but I did complete the regiment's *Intensive Insect Survival* course with a prominent mosquito whisperer in West Finchley.

"Big Man!!" boomed a beaky silhouette.

"Kes?"

"Genius"

"Why?"

"The Walloon."

"Thanks, mate."

"Big bastard."

"True."

"But you showed him, the Belgian Nob-polisher."

"Walloons, eh?"

"Cunts to a man."

"You're not wrong."

"Hairy-arsed tree-swingers."

William Tell resumed his electronic gallop. This time, much louder.

Kes reached into his ops pants and handed me my mobile. "This yours, Big Man?"

"Thanks, mate." So, it was Kes who had pocketed my mobile, the devious bastard. I resisted the desire to bury him (*Suppressing the Urge for Violent Reprisals* had been one of the most challenging courses at Cockfosters, but I had just about made the grade).

I answered the phone, held it to my head and recognised The Ambassador's voice at once. It was refined by education and coarsened by tobacco: deep but feminine. Usually, I find it oddly comforting, but, after she uttered the words, "Someone's killed The Father of The Brotherhood," my corpuscles turned glacial.

CHAPTER 3

I paused on the next page. Sandwiched midway between a praying mantis stain and a sweat patch, there was a note in black felt-tip reading, "If you are finding this diary suspiciously detailed, you are right. I did the *Total Recall* course at Swaffham. Can't remember my score."

Squaddies, eh? I've known a few in my time. Most have been highly trained drinkers with a penchant for exaggeration, but this bloke was positively bursting with bollocks. How on Earth do you hold a Chinese parliament with yourself? Was mosquito-whispering really a thing? And what on Earth was a Semi-Pygmy Insurgency? Did it involve an uprising by people who were only half the height of an average pygmy? Or were they twice the height of an average pygmy and only half-short?

Walloons may sound like balloon-buffoon hybrids, but they are at least real. I had once met a bunch of them during a punch-up in a croissant shop: precious Belgian blokes, swearing in antiquated French. Strange place, Wallonia - their regional flag is bright yellow with a massive red cock in the middle, and they have famous beards.

All this religious rivalry was a bit ungodly, and it looked as though The Father of the Brotherhood was already getting to know his maker. All in all, Sergeant Bill seemed to be operating in the diciest of circumstances and I was not exactly gobsmacked that he had eventually got himself assassinated.

As I sat cross-legged on the floor of the strip club office, I reflected on what a privilege it was to be entrusted with the story, even if it was covered in praying mantis stains. I turned the page and continued ploughing my way through Sergeant Tell's journal, which picked up at his Deniable HQ immediately after The Ambassador had broken the news about The Father of the Brotherhood's unexpected demise:

JOURNAL – SERGEANT BILL TELL

Deniable Compound, Walloon Republic of Outer Ggaga, East Africa

Monday 10 May, 10.05

"Fancy a lift, Big Man?" Kes flicked his beak outside, and I followed its notional nasal trajectory out of the door to a recommissioned black cab.

It was a tempting offer, but I had serious security concerns. After all, it is the quality of the men on the ground that counts and, apart from Kes, my men were all on the ground, unconscious.

"Thanks, mate," I said. "But who's going to guard the compound?"

"What happened to our Company of Cowards?" Kes asked.

"Ginger lost a punch-up with a mosquito screen."

"That calls for a serious arse-shagging with an untapered table-leg."

"Wee Jock fell asleep on my head."

"Lazy bastard."

"And Normal had a set-to with the wall-map."

"Inbred banjo-botherer. He's well overdue a wake-up call."

Kes scarpered for a few seconds, then reappeared with a zomboid Normal. He plonked the Norfolk no-marks against the door, propped him up with his own rifle and speed-vomited the word:

"You mouthbreathing, pillowbiting,uphillgardening,rectumtunnelling, nancy!"

It's not that Kes dislikes Normal, it's just his way of maintaining a high state of alertness. The insult worked like an electric cable to the bollocks and Normal leapt to attention.

"There you go, Big Man, a replacement sentry. About as useful as a Braille dartboard, but he might fool an idiot from a distance."

"Looks like you're the only one of us who stayed sober, Kes."

"Someone had to, but that doesn't mean I'm not celebrating inside. Mind if I lift you, Big Man?"

"Okay, mate," I replied. A sergeant must maintain morale even at personal cost.

Kes span me around at shoulder-height, shouting, "Big Man! Big Man! Big Man!". It didn't help my hangover, but he meant well. "Thanks, mate."

"The Walloons will never live it down!" Kes laughed as he rotated me at speed. "You should have seen Jacques Chîtes' face! Tintin Magritte-Poirot didn't know where to look! You're a legend!"

Kes plonked me back on the ground and I spilt my guts into a praying mantis nest.

"Feel better now, Big Man?"

"Yes thanks, mate," I lied. "No sign of Scally?"

"The Scouse git's guarding the Embassy. Hope the furniture's nailed down." Kes was never one to let a prejudice leave his vision unclouded.

"I'd better join him," I said, my brain still spinning in my skull like a sock in a tumble drier.

"You're the boss, Big Man."

10.11

I blundered aboard the decommissioned London cab. Kes wrestled with the ignition, the suspension shuddered, the engine growled, and the meter started clocking up a fare, just as it had done around Bethnal Green, Putney, or Hounslow.

Kes gave me a beaky grin. "I'm not going south of the river, Big Man."

"Too late, mate. You're south of the Sahara."

This was the hilliest terrain in Africa and the mud roads were spectacularly uneven and inhospitable. That was probably why Wee Jock always said he felt at home here – it was as if the Scottish Highlands had been plonked in the tropics.

It was the worst hangover cure in the history of mankind. The taxi lurched, jolted, swerved, and rocked. Kes made random accelerations and unannounced brakes as we crested craters, exotic roadkill, and unmentionable debris. My body bathed itself in sweat, my head span and my hands shook; stress hormones blasted through my lymphatic system, my stomach muscles pulsed, and I began to drool. I froze my skull to the spot and locked my eyes to the horizon.

Kes likes nothing more than bumping his gums and he ranted on about his failing marriage ("My Nagger's got a *Hyde and Hyde* character"), the Walloons' sexual orientation ("Enough bum-chummery to satisfy an Armada of sea-scout masters") and our monotonous diet ("Nile Perch? I'd rather munch on a baglady's knickers."). I only snapped out of it when he asked, "Seen much of your *extra pillow* recently?"

"If you mean Marie-Thérèse, then no. Not for a night or two."

"Nor's anyone else, Big Man. Disappeared off the face of the earth."

Kes's words stabbed like Zulu battle-blades, but now was not the time for an emotional bleed. I did my best to look indifferent. It didn't work.

Kes guffawed through his beak, his eyelids screwing up in merriment. "You'll have to find somewhere else to blow your danger money now, Big Man!"

In truth, I send my danger money home to my mum, and Marie-Thérèse's night classes are free of charge unless I am late with my homework. Somehow, I didn't think that Kes, pre-constructed Neanderthal that he was, would understand, so I just said, "After I'm done with The Ambassador, I'll take a look for her."

Kes nodded and we bumped along in silence for a few moments before he detonated the verbal bombshell, "Bummer about The Father of the Brotherhood, isn't it?"

I sat to attention. I assumed that the Ambassador had told me in confidence. "How did you know about that?"

"Scally texted me a few hours ago."

"Why didn't you let me know earlier?"

"You looked comfortable."

"Under Wee Jock?"

"Must have been before he fell asleep on top of you."

Sometimes I wonder about Kes. One minute, he's way ahead of the game; the next, he's limping off the starting line. Maybe his brain is on a genius-moron job share. Either way, I wish he had woken me up to let me know. I am meant to be ahead of the curve, anticipating threats and keeping the Ambassador alive, not relying on her for information already known to my subordinates.

10.29

My hangover was getting worse. I had been staring out of the windscreen for the best part of ten minutes, so I thought I would give staring out of the side window a try. There were coral swathes of *Old Bush China*, vermilion stretches of *Paul's Lemon Pillar* and golden expanses of *Amber Queen*. Loyalist Semi-Pygmies were harvesting roses of every genre, shape, and scent. It was skilled work. Maturity had to be judged by eye: cut a rose too early and the petals remained closed; cut a rose too late and you decimated its vase life.

Semi-Pygmy women in rainbow wraps sliced the stems with machetes, gathered bundles and carried them to workstations, where the older Semi-Pygmy men graded the flowers according to length, head size and flexibility. The young Semi-Pygmy blokes loaded the harvest into cooling tanks on board retired Routemaster buses. Their Kenyan overseers, The Sisters of the Brotherhood, unmistakeable in their tartan habits, looked on, calculating piece rates on their iPhones. The Walloons had forced the Semi-Pygmies into floricultural servitude after many merry millennia of hunter-gathering, pottery, and musicianship. The Semi-Pygmy Loyalists were happy to accept this enforced career change, but the Semi-Pygmy Insurgency resented it with a violent fury.

A Walloon observation Zeppelin, bright green and over seventy metres in length, floated above the fields like a levitating marrow. It had a lurid picture of their leader, Norbert Trifijd, dangling from its gondola. The botanist could only have been Belgian; he didn't have a moustache, but his beard and sideburns linked up in a precisely cultivated chinstrap.

"Nonce," Kes observed.

"How do you know?" I asked.

"He's a card-carrying perv, Big Man. Just check his internet browser - he'll make Gary Glitter look like Noddy."

Some battles are worth fighting, but a dispute about a Walloon botanist's sexual orientation wasn't. I spent the rest of the journey birdwatching. I eyeballed an olive-bellied sun thrush, a saddle-billed stork, and a nesting colony of Ibises - a personal best.

10.33

"That'll be thirty-five quid, Big Man," Kes quipped, as we pulled up outside The Embassy.

"I'll owe you."

"Want me to wait?"

"Don't bother, mate. I'll take the diplomatic vehicle back." I nodded towards The Embassy's People Carrier.

"That's only good for school runs, Big Man."

He wasn't wrong, but a confidential Embassy briefing could lead to a classified journey, and these were best conducted alone. "I'll cope. Just get the battalion conscious, stick the wall-map back together, and unwrap Ginger from the mosquito net."

"Consider it done, Big Man."

Kes saluted, switched on the cab's *For Hire* sign and chuntered off into the jungle.

10.37

I watched a hornless chameleon climb the Embassy wall and scramble through a gaping blast-hole in the battered concrete. The building was not much to look at, just a dilapidated prefab guarded by a bullet-ridden Union Jack-on-a-stick. The Semi-Pygmy Insurgents had comprehensively perforated our Deniable Embassy during the Rose Riots, but I didn't take it personally. National pride loses its currency in officially non-existent countries.

The Embassy reception area was used for storage: a snapped hat stand overlooked empty crates, flaccid cacti, and elderly mops. I took care ascending the staircase, as not every step was present and correct, and passed a Victorian map of the British Empire, its imperial blush faded off-pink.

As I turned into the main corridor, a rifle-butt smashed into my right ear. Not being one to piss about, I chopped my assailant in the guts, followed through with a roundhouse kidney-kick and laid him out with a Kazakhstani bollock-twist. I've been trained to overreact without hesitation, which was a bit of a shame as I had just decked Corporal Scally.

"Big Man?" the recumbent scouser groaned.

"Scally?"

"Your self-defence is murderous."

"Thanks, mate."

"I thought you were..."

"A Semi-Pygmy Insurgent?"

"Course not, Big Man. You're way too tall."

He was being kind. I have only got a few inches on most of them.

"Sorry, Big Man" Scally nursed most of his body. "It's just that I was on guard."

"And I caught you off-guard," I helped him back up to his feet.

"Yes, Big Man."

Scally was not in great shape, but he'd had a lucky escape. Another few seconds and it would have been Goodnight Vienna.

"Ambassador's keen to see you, Big Man."

"I know, Scally. How are you feeling?"

"It's just my guts, kidneys, and bollocks. The rest of me is fine."

"Sorry Scally."

"Don't worry, Big Man. You KO'd the Walloon kickboxer. That's all I give a toss about."

"Thanks, mate. Get well soon."

10.41

Now, my Covert Ambassador was a bit of a shady equine. Not only could she negotiate the army's most high-ranking shiny bums into submission, but she was also a modern art nutter who had crammed her Embassy with nonsensical objects of questionable value. I fought my way through the Ambassador's collection of Dadaist sculpture; a forest of ready-mades dangled from the ceiling in clanging mobiles. I had never seen the attraction, but her avant-garde art classes were popular with the ex-pats and her weird and wonderful work decorated the corridors of The Stamford Bridge Hotel.

The Ambassador's office was doorless, which had positives and negatives. She could effect a speedy exit, but an assassin could effect an equally rapid entrance. I didn't knock, there being nothing to knock on, so I whistled a few bars of the William Tell overture, a code we had agreed between ourselves.

"In you come, dear," the Ambassador said.

It was an extraordinary office, rapidly improvised in the wake of the Rose Rush. Queen Elizabeth II, sun-bleached and dog-eared, still looked down from the wall, may she rest in peace. A vase of roses wobbled on the shrapnel-riddled desk, which also featured an elderly Amstrad and the Embassy's single working telephone, a 1959 seven-hundred-type dialler with a curly cord and plastic cradle.

The Ambassador, a silver bombshell in Home Counties tweed, was struggling with her printer. "You couldn't be a love and help me change the toner, could you Bill?"

I had attended the regiment's *Advanced Office Equipment Maintenance Training* on the Brecon Beacons, so I was happy to oblige. I reverted to technique, and, after a couple of cartridge presses and a tray shove, it was job done.

"Ah, Bill," the Ambassador sighed. "I know you can snap a neck single-handed, but you're simply adorable."

"Thanks, ma'am."

"Fancy a Nile Perch vol-au-vent?"

"Thank you very much, Ambassador." I have come to hate Nile Perch. It is pretty much the only protein on offer in Outer Ggaga.

She reached into her diplomatic bag and unwrapped some finger food. The pastry was adequate, but the crushingly over-familiar Perch tang sent my taste buds into tailspin.

"How's that, Bill?"

"Lovely, ma'am," I lied.

She stroked my side-parting, pudged my cheeks and called me her "little cherub".

It took all my military discipline to circumvent a face flush.

The Ambassador reached across her desk and wiped the dust off a framed photograph of her sister's children. I suppose she had given up a lot for a diplomatic career; driven by dreams of Washington and Moscow, she had worked diligently, advanced steadily and gone far. Too far. The People's Republic of Outer Ggaga was way off the map.

"Look, Bill, I chose you personally. You never seem to think about yourself. In fact, you don't seem to dream, question, hesitate or reflect at all. You're just there."

"Here, ma'am?"

"There. And that's what I need."

I had no idea what she was on about, so I took the opportunity to perform a discreet one-hundred-and-eighty-degree room scan. There were no identifiable threats, but a praying mantis rocked back and forth on the Ambassador's mosquito screen, raising its wings, and lifting its head. The movement appeared meditative, a satanic prayer. The creature was a cannibal from birth, it fed on the living and its drool could kill a mule or blind a man. But I reckoned we'd probably be all right.

The Ambassador opened her desk drawer and pulled out a rose garland. I conducted a lightning appraisal and by the look of its thorn and petal structure there could be no mistake - it was *Modern Maggie's Twizzle*.

"Very nice, ma'am." I meant it.

"The roses aren't just for show, Bill. They are an ancient emblem of silence. As the Romans might have said, our conversation is strictly *sub rosa*."

"*Sub rosa?*"

"It didn't happen."

"But it hasn't happened,"

"It will, but once it has, it won't have. Clear?'

"See-through."

"If not, then I can't deny that you're as deniable as this conversation. Understood?"

"Yes, ma'am,"

"Collect Father Forestière. Do not leave his corpse unguarded for a second. British interests in the Walloon Republic of Outer Ggaga are at stake. You need to find the killer fast whilst maintaining absolute discretion. It could be any of us – a bored ex-pat, a Walloon botanist, a Son of The Kenyan Brotherhood, or a Semi-Pygmy Insurgent."

"Of course, ma'am."

"I've been trying to get hold of Marie-Thérèse, she's usually a reliable source of information." The Ambassador lit a *Gauloise*. Not very British, I suppose, but it suited her. "You don't know anything about her whereabouts, do you, Bill? I know you're close, you naughty boy."

"Shucks, ma'am."

"Well, it's probably nothing to worry about." She sounded as though it was. "Look, Bill. This is a completely covert investigation – no one else is to know what you're up to. You have full clearance to talk to anyone; beard Norbert Trifijd in his Zeppelin if needs must. Just make damn sure you get your sweaty little palms on Forestière's body, morgue it here at The Embassy and deprive our Walloon friends' nostrils of the slightest sniff of the prelate's corpse. Apart from that, I'm afraid I must remain frustratingly cryptic."

"Cryptic, ma'am."

"Allow me to introduce you to the death site." She stood by the wall map and prodded a field of *Great Maiden's Blush* with her Ambassadorial baton.

11.18

The Embassy car park made a handy five-a-side pitch for The Sons of the Brotherhood, but it was not much to look at. Today, it was even uglier than usual: two twin towers of spent machine-gun magazines formed makeshift goal posts and a clan of hyenas had gathered along the halfway line, lunching on a decomposing hippo. The hippo corpse was blocking the Ambassadorial People Carrier, a mumsy-mobile perfect for triple parking outside a North London primary school, but less than ideal for a cross-country assault on Mount Heha. I disabled the alarm, cracked the steering wheel lock, and fired up the engine. Seconds are in short supply on covert investigations, so it was time to employ the skills I had learned on the regiment's *Advanced People Carrier Handling* course at Henley. I executed a sharp two-hundred-and-seventy-degree handbrake spin, scattering the hyenas and flattening a goalpost, then yanked the gear stick into first and thrust the People Carrier through the decimated hippo. Its guts exploded and ungulate innards flew up in all directions, leaving me no choice but to activate the windscreen wipers. They jammed. I cursed. The engine stalled. I hate it when it does that. I eyeballed Scally pissing himself at the Embassy window, the Scouse sod. When he realised that he had been pinged, he did a sharp about-face, and reassumed a serious sentry pose.

I reconnected the engine, disregarding the hippo-stink as best I could, and re-ignited the People Carrier, lurching up Mount Heha with a vengeance. It was the start of the Outer Ggagaan Dry Season and, although it still rained more often than not, humidity was well over seventy per cent. I sweated like a prune, wincing at every bump and turn, and clutching my mysteriously bruised ribcage. I put it down to kickboxing, even though I couldn't recall Jacques Chîtes making contact. I guess the whisky must have deleted the memory.

A quirk of global warming had rendered the Outer Ggagaan face of Mount Heha spectacularly fertile and new species of flora and fauna sprouted in secret. The covert Republic was home to the yodelling baboon, the knock-kneed waterbuck, and the amphibious squirrel; whooping willows raised their branches to the sky in gestures of celebration, chequered fungi filled the forest floors and carnivorous marrows trapped praying mantises with their toothed tendrils.

It felt like I was the only sod daft enough to be travelling uphill. Streams of priests, nuns, and soldiers - The Fathers, The Sisters and The Sons of The Brotherhood – all whizzed past my mumsy-mobile on their mountain bikes, pointing and laughing on their way down.

Mount Heha is short on service stations, but there are a couple of roadside stands. I pulled in and bought a Nile Perch burger from a nun. It was a repulsive munch, but I couldn't resist - a squaddie marches on his stomach, even though that sounds both painful and anatomically complicated. I felt the Nile Perch kicking into my veins, the familiar fishy protein boring my bloodstream. *Eat as much as you can when you can, you never know when you'll get another chance*, as I had learned on the regimental *Eating Food* module at Stanmore. The trouble was, in Walloon Outer Ggaga, nutrition nearly always came in Nile Perch form.

11.32

The crime scene was just beyond a checkpoint built out of car carnage - rusted doors, roof racks and balding tyres. It was manned by boys – The Sons of the Brotherhood, the poor bastards. On their puny bodies, army uniforms looked like fancy dress. The Walloons called up the Kenyan missionary kids at twelve and, if they made it to fifteen, they joined The Church of The Brotherhood as entered apprentices. Three teenage soldiers lay beneath a banana tree, swigging formaldehyde beer. The sight of the Ambassadorial People Carrier triggered a ruck as the soldiers fought for prime position at my window.

I flashed my passport. It had an Outer Ggagaan visa complete with warthog hologram and listed my profession as *handyman*. In Libya, I had been a *zookeeper*, in Namibia, I had been a *painter and decorator*, and in Guatemala I had been a *fertilizer salesman*. This time, it might as well have read, *badger juggler* because The Sons of the Brotherhood didn't spare it a glance. One by one, the boys volunteered the same phrase, "Giss-a-tip". I distributed gratuities, the amount varying according to rank. You needed coins at border checkpoints: plastic simply didn't cut it.

The lads waved me through, and I parallel parked into a dead ground position, hoping that the hedge shadow would disguise the bonnet's angularity. I crunched topiary as I clambered out of the passenger door, then shrouded the windscreen in hessian to minimize screen shine.

I checked my watch. I didn't have one. I had forgotten to put it on. In case you were wondering, I had been calculating the journal timings by squinting extremely accurately at the sun. It was a trick I had learned at the regiment's *Personal Survival Without a Watch* course at Greenwich.

A posse of nuns blocked my entrance to the rose field, but I remembered what they had told me at Sandhurst: *Walk with purpose and everyone will assume you're important.*

"Who the fuck are you?" The Mother Superior asked.

"The name's Tell. Bill Tell."

"Well, if it's not on the list, you're not coming in."

The Holy Sisters looked like they meant business, but once The Mother Superior had looked me up on her iPhone's Sisters of The Brotherhood Security Clearance App, their habits parted, and I was through.

I strode across the ivory field of *Great Maiden's Blush*. The sun raged, casting monumental Zeppelin shadows across the flowers; the Walloon gasbag's dark template menaced like a flat Moby Dick.

A circle of Semi-Pygmies had gathered in the middle of the roses, gawping at what looked like a collapsed black tent. I lifted the miserable material and exposed an elderly prelate, apparently levitating and lit from below. This looked like a case for *Gay And Haunted*, but closer examination revealed the crime scene to be far from homosexual. Something stirred underneath the cassock, and it wasn't The Father of the Brotherhood's spirit; it was female and intimately conjoined.

"Hello, Bill," Marie-Thérèse said from beneath the holy man. She had a torch in one hand and an epic novel in the other. "Can you give me another minute? I've just got to a good bit."

Now, don't get me wrong, I'm a man of the world: I am bipolar - North and South, Arctic and Antarctic. I have criss-crossed the Gobi, sourced the Amazon and rimmed the Pacific - you really could not meet a more hostile environmentalist. But in all my travels, I have never encountered a crime scene quite so toe-curlingly embarrassing as this doomed coupling. I started to whistle my namesake's overture, but I could still hear the Semi-Pygmies sniggering. I tried looking away at the flower slopes, but my eyes kept drifting back to the intimately conjoined Father Innocent Forestière and Marie-Thérèse.

Desperate for a distraction, I took a moment to look at the Walloons' eye-in-the-sky. I craned my neck, scanning the Zeppelin's underbelly. There was a gondola for passenger entry and departure, a flight deck for the crew, luxury quarters and a gas bag with enough helium to make the entire population of Grimsby speak in squeaky voices for the rest of the year. It was mad to think that these contraptions had once crossed the Atlantic and rivalled aeroplanes for supremacy. I tried to take in another angle and stepped back onto some *Great Maiden's Blush*, snagged my trousers on the thorns, and crushed a rose-head. The Semi-Pygmy Loyalists gasped, terrified of Walloon reprisals. Petal-trampling was one of the most severe infringements in the Floricultural Code Book, but I had diplomatic immunity.

"Finished!" Marie-Thérèse blurted from under the priest.

"Good book?"

"*Finnegan's Wake*."

"You must be traumatised."

"Not at all, it's one of my favourites."

"How's Father Forestière?"

"Stiff, bless him."

"Oh."

"*Rigor mortis* kept him up all night."

I had topped my class at the regimental *Tact in Awkward Situations* course at Romford, but I was still at a complete loss. I could only muster a shrug.

"It was his first time," Marie-Thérèse continued, as I lifted Father Innocent Forestière out of her. "Stamina of a stallion, though. Maybe Death's the new Viagra."

Thank God for graveyard humour and thank heavens for Marie-Thérèse. The lads all reckoned I was a doughnut, blowing my danger money on a prostitute, but I never paid her a single Trifijd. All we ever did was talk about books - if the lads found out, I would never live it down.

The bullet had penetrated the priest's temple, but his lifeless face still sported the remains of a smile. It wasn't a bad way to go, especially when you looked like Forestière, with liver spots, dense thickets of nasal hair and the kind of neck to make a Galapagos turtle reach for the moisturiser. At least he had dressed to impress, with an elegant surplice, a spotless stole, and a cloth cincture around his voluminous paunch, but the ecclesiastical look was let down by his *al fresco* crotch.

I don't make a habit of lugging expired priests around, so I can't speak with any authority, but if you ask me, old Forestière was one heavy prelate. Still, I didn't become a Deniable to whinge, I joined the regiment to get stuff done.

Carrying the priest across the flower field was one thing; loading him into the Ambassadorial mumsy-mobile was quite another. Don't get me wrong, it was a terrific vehicle for a family outing with ample space for toddler seats and baby buggies, but it was not designed to accommodate a fat priest's corpse. If Forestière had been collapsible, I could have put him in the boot, but The Father was totally unbendable – he just would not fold. In the end, I had to feed the holy man lengthways through the back window until his size twelves came to rest on the handbrake.

The Ambassador's instructions were clear enough: take good care of the corpse. Now, I'll protect the dead, but don't ask me to neglect the living. Marie-Thérèse had a home to go to and, after all she had been through, I was determined to get her there safely. I am a bodyguard, but I don't just guard dead bodies: living bodies need protecting too. I opened the front passenger door for Marie-Thérèse.

"Are you sure there's room for the three of us, Bill?"

"I don't mind. And I doubt The Father will complain."

"Thanks. Last night did for my legs. I don't fancy the walk."

Marie-Thérèse clambered into the People Carrier. I shut her in and yomped around to the driving seat. I fired up the ignition, wrenched the car into gear and reached for the handbrake, clasping Father Forestière's right shoe.

I apologised to the priest's corpse.

"I shouldn't laugh." Marie-Thérèse did. Quite loudly.

"He's gone to a better place," I said, knowing that most places were a great deal better than Deniable Walloon Republics in Sub-Saharan Africa.

"He's lying on the handbrake."

"Poor sod, God rest his soul."

"God sod his soul, for all he cared. Forestière had been losing his faith ever since I started lending him my Graham Greene novels. He used to be a relentless Hell-worrier, banging on about fiery skies, burning necropolises and boiling blood-rivers, but that all changed. He started drinking and developed a bit of a thing for me. I suppose, if there's anything to his old sermons, then right now he's probably being tossed on a ceaseless infernal whirlwind or being whipped by horned demons, bless him."

Life is too short to worry about Eternity. Perhaps, when I'm dropped, I'll join the spectral Regiment of the Old and Bold, but I would prefer a civilian afterlife. I fancy a bit of a change. I've often thought I would make a good plumber.

Right now, though, I was conducting an investigation. "What time did you meet Forestière?"

"Nine-ish, I suppose. I'd lost track of time, really. I was sat in the hut, relaxing with a few chapters of *The Man Who Was Dead*. Tolstoy's much more powerful in the original Russian, don't you think?"

"I prefer his films," I said, trying to sound clever.

Marie-Thérèse reached across the dead priest's shins and squeezed my knee in a playful acknowledgement of my ignorance. I gazed back into her eyes then remembered that, minutes earlier, she had been a crime scene.

"Sorry, Marie Thérèse." I changed gear. "But can you just tell me what happened?"

"Is this formal?"

"Not officially."

"Oh."

"In your own time."

"Right. I heard this knock on the library door. It was pretty feeble, to be honest. I opened up and Forestière hobbled in, a silver cross dangling over his chest. Without a word, he returned his latest Graham Greene, *The Power and the Glory*, and removed the crucifix, exposing his heart. I peered into his eyes - there was something strangely hypnotic about his conjunctivitis - and took his leathery paw. We walked outside, following the lunar path across a rose field, dodging the thorns and breathing the heady fragrance. The night was thick with insects: we could almost taste the air and it certainly tasted us. I don't think Forestière would have gone through with it if he hadn't had some extraordinary event to celebrate. Whatever it was, he didn't want to discuss it. But he was a different man, thrilled and perhaps a little scared. As we settled on a patch of petals, I thought it best to keep things simple. You see, I've read every sex manual in the world, and I could have demonstrated any number of configurations - *The Crab Embrace*, *The Turning Dragon* and at least a dozen *Positions of the Perfumed Garden*, but the one position I didn't know was the *Octogenarian Priest*, so I decided to go with *Missionary*. I think The Father was anxious about his performance: he'd had over three score and ten years since reaching puberty to rehearse for his big moment, which is quite a build-up. We had only just got going when I heard a gunshot and The Father threw back his arms, crucified on the midnight breeze. There was nothing I could do to help him, and I couldn't move, so I got stuck into *Finnegan's Wake*. I always bring along a good book in case the clients bang on for too long. Who do you think shot him?"

"This is a dark, deniable country with dark, deniable secrets," I mansplained.

"Aren't all secrets deniable?"

"No comment."

"Oh, go on, Bill. Tell us a secret." She reached across the priest and nudged me.

"Never. I'll keep The Deniable Code until they shroud my box in a union jack."

"Cheer up, Bill. Might never happen." She smiled.

I smiled back.

She blushed.

I reciprocated. This was all lovely, but I could not discount the possibility that Marie-Thérèse had lured Forestière to a vulnerable position to be picked off by a sniper. I always hate to be cynical, but it was my job. "What made you choose a rose field? What's wrong with your hut?"

"My hut's under surveillance. The Walloons use long range x-ray equipment on board their Zeppelins to peer through the ceiling."

"Don't they watch the rose fields too?"

"Not at night, no. They were only hovering over the death scene today because of what happened."

"Did someone ask you to take The Father to the rose field?"

"A set up, you mean?"

I nodded.

"No, Bill. I wouldn't want to lose a client."

I was about to tell Marie-Thérèse that I believed her when an almighty horn-blast cut me down in my tracks. I gave the mirror a quick once-over and, knock me down with a Cruise Missile if The Sisters of the Brotherhood weren't right up my arse, caning it in a flower-laden Routemaster bus. I tried to put some clear mud between us, but they matched my acceleration k for k. Some bastard had souped-up the nuns' double-decker. Now don't get me wrong, I love Routemasters. They're magnificent vehicles: resilient, dependable, and capable of tilting without tipping. Just watching this triumph of British design bear down on us filled me with patriotism. And fear. Mount Heha's tracks were not exactly blessed with passing points, so The Sisters of the Brotherhood clearly had murder in mind.

I thumped the ignition, stomped on the accelerator and span away from the nuns. Thank God I had completed the *Escape Driving Course* at Pinner. I jammed the car from left to right, accelerating through the mud, and chewing through the gears. I cornered at speed and shag me sideways if there wasn't a Walloon potpourri truck ready to reverse-ram us. I yanked hard on the handbrake, swivelled swamp-wards, and sent the Routemaster into the potpourri truck. The double-decker bus and the powerful petal-carrier collided in a crunchy inferno, flames leaping like demon dancers. I span the steering wheel, floored the accelerator, and prayed. Potpourri petals rained like confetti, blessing our plunge into the adjacent papyrus swamp, as the merciless nuns blasted bullets in round after round.

Survival is often a game of hurry-up-and-wait. Open the window of a sinking People Carrier before you have hit the water margin and you're on a U-bend to Hell, but give it a few seconds, and you've got a decent shot of living to die another day.

"What now, Bill?"

It was a good question, and one that Marie-Thérèse had every right to ask. Her fate lay in my hands, after all. Luckily, I had extensive experience of extreme adversity. A career in the regiment is not just a road less travelled, it's a bramble-smothered night-path infested with ravenous wolves, howling hermits and axe-wielding apparitions.

"Don't worry, Marie Thérèse. How's your swimming?"

"I got my Bronze Personal Survival. You?"

"I swam the Euphrates under hostile fire."

"Jolly good, Bill. Got anything waterproof?"

"How big?"

"Book-size."

I searched the glove compartment and handed her a crisp packet. She emptied out the cheese and onion savouries and wrapped *Finnegan's Wake* in *Golden Wonder*. It helped pass the time while we waited for the People Carrier to sink below swamp level.

Once the landscape was a three-hundred-and-sixty-degree watercolour, I opened the windows, and we swam out our separate ways. Marie-Thérèse opted for an elegant breaststroke while I went for a Nicaraguan doggie paddle. It looks awkward, involving complex arse-thrusts and thigh-twists, but it was one of the best lifesaving strokes in the covert compendium and it enabled me to drag the priest's corpse to the surface.

Forestière didn't sink. He just lay on the swamp water like a Lilo. Perhaps it was a posthumous miracle, but more likely his decomposing guts had filled with gas. Marie-Thérèse was much less buoyant, so I improvised a flotation device out of the expired priest, knotting his tail-ends and inflating his cassock by mouth.

As soon as I had strapped Marie-Thérèse to the puffed-up prelate, I turned to pull them both back to the bank. It wasn't a long swim, but I hit a bit of a hitch: I was nose to snout with a thousand kilos of crocodile. Its teeth were as yellow as a chain smoker's and had the biting power of three thousand pounds per square inch. But this was a time for action not maths. I don't mind dying if I really must, but not in the jaws of a semi-evolved antelope-muncher. *Keep your friends close, your enemies closer and eighteen-foot long Outer Ggagaan crocodiles as far away as possible,* as every schoolboy knows.

Identification wasn't an issue: it could only be Esther, the toothy monster who had snapped seventeen Semi-Pygmies into Demi-Semi-Pygmies during her last mating meander. At over six metres, this cold-blooded ambush hunter was four times longer than I was tall, and I didn't fancy spending an evening in her carcass barrow. Luckily, I had completed the regimental *Crocodile Wrestling* course at Eastbourne and remembered its number one rule: *Self-defense is all about attack.* I tried to beat some respect into the crocodile with a pair of under-temple knuckle jabs then planted one on her ugly great snout.

The croc roared from the depths of her guts, which was both unnerving and smelly. The prehistoric predator's breath stank of curried slurry.

"Shut up you ponce!" I insulted the croc to subdue its morale, but it only provoked the toothy git. Esther's mighty musculature tensed, and she flung her head and tail high out of the water. I mimicked her action. I wasn't taking the piss; I was simply following Eastbourne's number two rule: *Always stand your ground in a swamp.* Esther's scaly flanks vibrated violently, spraying water in all directions. Visibility was compromised, so I reached inside my ops pants, yanked out my sub-aqua night goggles, and plonked them on.

"You scaly great pillock! You slimy little nonce!" I kept up my relentless barrage of verbal digs and followed through with a Peruvian Lung-bang, a Cossack Toe-thrust, and a Venezuelan Nut-job.

Esther froze then sank out of sight. The croc was playing mind games with me. This was a complex game of chess, and my opponent was an eighteen-foot reptile. I had to be careful. Croc-wrestling's a funny old game where you can end up in two halves.

I paused to update my situational awareness. First off, the swamp-stench was brutal. It was going to take a few bottles of aromatherapy bath scrub before I would be making any new friends. But this was a time for violence, not socialising. Knowing that the croc could strike from any direction, I did a quick three-sixty, maintaining a high state of circular alertness, which made me feel dizzy.

Esther's formidable jaws surfaced, ready to shred me in a murderous spin. It is pointless trying to reason with a croc - violence is the only language they understand. I stunned her with a Zambian Elbow-ping, followed through with an Armenian Wedgie then banjoed the bastard with a Welsh Death-grip.

The croc's eyes stared up at me pleadingly.

Sorry, pal. I'm not in the mercy business.

The croc croaked.

I turned to Marie-Thérèse. I suppose I was expecting a smile, a few relieved tears, a little applause maybe. But she was busy treading water and re-reading *Finnegan's Wake* through the top of the crisp packet.

"We're safe now, Marie-Thérèse. I've killed Esther!"

"Hang on Bill, I've just got to a good bit."

I had just wrestled an eighteen-foot man-eating crocodile and she had missed the whole bloody thing. Women, eh?

I Nicaraguan doggie-paddled the floating priest back towards the bank. It looked like the potpourri truck was history, but The Sisters of the Brotherhood were still very much alive, firing off a formidable barrage from their upended Routemaster. Bullets ripped through the undergrowth, ricocheting off whooping willows and peppering the papyrus. There was nothing merciful about The Sisters – they were as lethal as they were tartan.

"Honestly, Bill," Marie-Thérèse sighed. "If it's not one thing it's another."

"Sorry, love."

I plunged under the priest and dragged Marie-Thérèse across the swamp, using Forestière's corpse as cover. The nun's bullets flew under, over and beside us. Some penetrated the priest, but he was a porky prelate, and they didn't pass through his blubber.

It was some distance to the opposite bank, but at least Esther had scared off any other large predators from the area before she croaked.

"I won!" Marie-Thérèse exclaimed when she reached solid ground a second before me.

"Fair play," I conceded. It hadn't been the fairest of races, given that I had had to drag a dead priest and wrestle a crocodile, but I don't believe in excuses.

It would have been wonderful to be on dry land had we not been marooned in dense whooping willow jungle. A thousand branches resounded to the sound of hyena death-cackles. I helped Marie-Thérèse off the priest and had a bit of a sit down, courage being something of a consumable resource.

Marie-Thérèse looked at me as if I was slacking. "Where now, Bill?"

It was a good question. Jungles don't have street maps, or streets, and we had no way of knowing how far the dense whooping willows stretched. Luckily, I had topped my year in *Covert Orienteering* at Catford. "Lend me your contact lenses."

"Do I really have to, Bill?"

"Go on. You've finished your book."

She fiddled with her eyeballs while I gathered swamp sticks.

"There you go, Bill." Marie-Thérèse handed me her lenses. "Jungle's a complete blur now."

I set her contacts in the swamp sticks and improvised a sextant. It was an awesome hand-build, correct in every detail. But looking back over the swamp at the sun, I calculated that we were lost.

"Am I nearly home, Bill?"

"Yes," I lied. Leadership is all about maintaining morale and, clueless as I was, I had to display the illusion of knowledge. "Nearly there."

"We're lost, aren't we?"

"Yes."

"Wish you'd said straight away."

"Sorry."

She was face-to-face with mortality and didn't have the military experience to cope, but I couldn't blame her. Few high-class librarian hookers have ever looked down into the unending depths of a soldier's abyss.

CHAPTER 4

I put down Bill's journal and scratched myself through the sofa cover. Over the course of my life, I have endured prison uniforms, community service jumpsuits and binman bottoms, and I have got to say that sofa covers are up there with the worst. If God had meant us to wear sofa covers, he would have given us better upholstered bodies.

I was no longer quite so sure what to make of Sergeant Tell. Was he a Bond? Or was he a Bean? He seemed to swing both ways: his training, discipline, and courage had kept him alive, and those very same things had got him lost.

In some ways, he was a man after my own heart. I firmly believe that every hero has an inner loser, ready to leap into action and fall flat on his face, and that's probably why I am an unemployed life coach.

But whatever Bill's failings, I had to admire his resilience: many men would have abandoned hope and found themselves at the bottom of a papyrus swamp, snapped in half by Esther the crocodile or perforated by tartan nun bullets. Sergeant Bill had not only preserved his own life, but he had also kept Marie-Thérèse safe, irritating her immensely in the process. I was worried for them both, but particularly for Bill, as it seemed entirely possible that she would kill him out of sheer annoyance.

I cast my mind back to the previous day. I had no idea how I had ended up in the strip club, but I was beginning to remember why I had decided to get off my tits in the first place. It had been the worst day in living memory. My eighth ex-wife had found out that I had been three-timing her with my second and sixth ex-wives, and she had set her Rottweiler on me. I had escaped over a fence and focused my remaining energies on work. Sadly, work didn't have a lot to offer, as my only client had decided to sue me. He was a gambling addict, and I had persuaded him to take a week off and try recreational drugs instead. A short, sharp addiction-swap can work wonders – a sex addict can switch to alcohol, a smoker can try hallucinogens, an opioid freak can try glue-sniffing. A change is as good as a rest, they say, and some clients report feeling energized and refreshed. Unfortunately, this had not been the case with my gambler. All his usual bets had come through at once, but he had followed my advice and not placed them. While he had been busy not visiting the bookies, his newly adopted drug addictions had seen him fined for riding an e-scooter on E, arrested for impersonating a police officer whilst on acid, and hospitalised for falling down a manhole on ketamine. Looking at a fist fight and a six-figure pay-out, I had resolved to start drinking heavily. It had seemed like a good idea at the time, but it had ended up dooming me to a dancing pole. How, I knew not.

I adjusted my sofa cover, and cracked on with Bill's journal:

JOURNAL – SERGEANT BILL TELL

Walloon Republic of Outer Ggaga, East Africa

Monday 10 May, 12.45

The jungle was dark, deadly, and full of ominous noises: the bloodcurdling mating moo of the knock-kneed waterbuck, the deathly battle-croak of the amphibious squirrel and the heart-stopping whinny of the spotted zebra. The tension was eating away at me, and I must have tasted nervous. It is hard to keep track of time during a jungle yomp, particularly when you are carrying an expired cleric on your shoulders and listening to the constant complaints of a short-sighted companion as they bump into whooping willow branches.

"Slow down, Bill." Marie-Thérèse thumped me on the shoulder. "No one's chasing us."

The regiment taught me that *Complacency is The Mother of Fatality* and *Prior Planning Prevents Poor Performance*, so I ignored her, smeared our faces with fern slime, and explained that expert camouflage and fieldcraft are almost as important as good marksmanship.

"I look like Yoda," Marie-Thérèse complained.

Not to me she didn't. Marie-Thérèse may have been dirt-green, but she was fearsomely stunning. "Look, love, we've got to blend into the environment somehow. Get jungle-wise sharpish, there's a priest-killer on the loose."

"If you say so, Bill."

"I do," I said, and we did, double backing to create false trails and utilising streams to confuse hyenas. We traced the terrain, moving in hollows and shadows. I made good use of deception, dragging branches over tracks, hiding sharp edges, and constructing dummy positions willy-nilly.

"Aargh!" Marie-Thérèse screamed, paralysed by fear as a praying mantis loomed above her left eyebrow.

Rule Number One of jungle survival: *Never underestimate insects*. I've warded off the fat-tailed scorpion of the Sahara, self-sucked the venom of the saw scale viper and incapacitated the Egyptian cobra with soft vegetables. This mantis had said its last psalm. I nutmegged it with a diversionary palm-chop, then gave it the good news with a seven-hundred-and-twenty-degree roundhouse kick. Overkill perhaps - but kill none the less.

"Thanks, Bill. Are we nearly there yet?"

I had f-all idea, so I lectured Marie-Thérèse about sweat conservation, movement limitation and anti-tracking tactics. She just yawned and complained that she was hungry.

Supermarkets were in short supply, but something green and bushy-tailed stirred within the whooping willow roots. Now, I've trapped Paraguayan wolverines, surprised Arctic lemmings, and speared unsuspecting yak, but I had never cornered an Outer Ggagaan amphibious squirrel. Until now.

I remembered the basics from the *Regimental Stalking* course at Luton: *Always hunt up-wind and never kill from above*. I dropped to the forest floor and executed a complex stalking manoeuvre on my belly, but the amphibious squirrel eluded my clasp and disappeared into the whooping willow leaves.

To put it plainly, an effective RDO (rapid decisive operation) requires tiptop TTP (tactics, techniques, and procedures) and every raid breaks down into four parts: CI (clandestine insertion); VC (violent contact); RD (rapid disengagement) and DW (deceptive withdrawal). And it is exactly the same with a squirrel-snatch. Or at least it should be. I devised a detailed strategy and executed it with ruthless inefficiency, ending up squirrel-less and on my arse.

A yodelling baboon swung down to the forest floor to mock me. I refused to let the primate undermine my morale. *Never crumble. Sometimes, combat boils down to a test of willpower between adversaries*, as the regiment taught me at Archway.

I held a swift Chinese parliament with myself and decided to resort to a technique I had learned during my *Close Quarter Battle Training* in the Killing House at Cricklewood. *Hit the enemy where he is weakest, from the direction he would least expect.* It wasn't going to win any prizes for sophistication, but a good plan violently executed now is better than a perfect plan next week. This was the moment I had been training for, a moment when life or death hinged on my reactions. For the amphibious squirrel, it was death.

I outran the beast and pounced with split-second timing. Textbook. The operation was a perfect ten.

"It's not very big is it, Bill," Marie-Thérèse said.

"It's just a snack." I prepared the scrawny green squirrel for the skewer. I gathered some willow bark and grass fern for tinder, then struggled to spark a fire using the flint and steel method I had learned at my *Survival Without Matches* course at Highbury. It's a laborious technique, but failsafe.

Just as I had got the fire going, Marie-Thérèse pulled out a lighter and sparked up a fag. Not only was this bloody annoying, but it was also a needless hazard: smoking is an avoidable health risk. I would have taken her to task, but she had spent the night under a murdered priest and wasn't in the best of moods.

"Can't you find anything else to eat, Bill?"

I had learned to live off the fat of the land at Basildon and Rule Number One was *never swallow anything unless you have made a positive identification*. I knew that some plants were edible (hazel catkins, wood sorrel and spear thistle), some fungi were tasty (the giant puffball, the shaggy inkcap and the Dryad's saddle) and that other fungi were lethal (the Outer Ggagaan chequered pixie throne, for example). Sadly, by the time I had scrambled a side salad out of nodding onions, bracken and bramble leaves, the squirrel was burned black.

We were both ravenous, so I served it up regardless. *Every meal you cook affects your level of morale*: in this case, adversely.

"That's really horrible, Bill." Marie-Thérèse retched.

"Sorry, love."

"You burned the squirrel."

I had allowed myself to become distracted by the salad. It was unforgivable. "Fancy a brew?"

Marie-Thérèse nodded wearily.

I purified some puddle water on a rock and improvised a kettle from bamboo bark. Half an hour later, she had smoked her way through a pack of Rothmans, and I had leached enough acorns for some jungle coffee.

Marie-Thérèse spat out her first and only mouthful. "That sucks."

She was right. It was repulsive.

We tried taking the taste away by cleaning our teeth with whooping willow bark, but it just made Marie-Thérèse gag. The next moment, dental hygiene became the least of our worries - I could hear the heart-stopping squish of human feet on carnivorous marrow. This was deep jungle, and we could easily have stumbled into Semi-Pygmy Insurgency territory.

"Lie up," I hissed, forcing Marie-Thérèse to the ground.

"Chill out, Bill."

"Keep close to the earth, cover your scent with clothing and try to breathe into the ground."

"Whatever."

I have built more shelters than I have munched boil-in-the-bag rations: there is the double lean-to, the wigwam, and the tree-pit, but whichever one you go for, it must always be tactically located. We were exposed, so I shovelled covertly before camouflaging our position with whooping willow leaves. After twenty minutes, I was reasonably confident we had secured a defendable area with good concealment.

"Very creative, Bill."

"Thanks."

"What are you going to put in it?"

"Us."

"Why?"

"The Semi-Pygmy Insurgency."

"Oh, they're all right. Bit tardy returning their library books, but they pay the fines without whingeing."

Marie-Thérèse would say that - she gets on with everyone. My own feelings were more complicated. The Royal Deniables were strictly neutral in all matters regarding the Semi-Pygmy Insurgency, and I certainly could not condone their Walloon-ambushes, Brotherhood booby traps, and anti-Loyalist bazooka bang-fests. However, I did have plenty of sympathy for their cause, having built decent relations with several of the Semi-Pygmy Insurgents. The poor sods had been displaced by war and evicted from their hunting grounds to make way for game parks; and now their ancestral forests were being cleared by the Walloons for rose cultivation. Who wouldn't be mightily peeved? My main worry was the breakaway Real Semi-Pygmy Insurgency, a ruthless band of hardliners. Sometimes, it was hard to know exactly where I stood, so whenever in doubt I would fall back on the regimental motto: *Never forget, the enemy of your enemy's enemy is also your enemy.*

The Semi-Pygmies had first encountered Europeans via Ronald Arkwright, a Victorian explorer from Harrogate, He had left them a legacy of tuberculosis and broad vowels. Oddly, they liked him for it and decided to incorporate numerous Yorkshire customs into their tribal traditions. Semi-Pygmy warriors sported intricately carved Alan Bennett masks for their victory dances; special occasions were marked by games of bush-cricket; and brass bands accompanied their ancient initiation rites. There were rumoured to be several statues of Ronald Arkwright with his flat cap, whippet, and homing pigeons, in the depths of the whooping willow jungle, but no outsider had ever seen one and lived.

If we were discovered by some of the friendlier Semi-Pygmy Insurgents, there was still one major concern, and it was my job to anticipate risks and minimize them. "Even if they welcome us with open arms, won't they be a bit put off by Forestière?"

"Shall we wrap him in something?"

"He'd be a suspiciously large parcel."

"We could strap him to a stick."

"Would that help?"

"It might. We could pretend he's a prize kill."

"Big game?"

"A knock-kneed waterbuck?"

"Good thinking."

We wrapped the holy man in banana leaves, sewed them together with burned squirrel sinew and tied him to a whooping willow branch. After we had hopped into the hide, I reached up and dragged the priest below ground.

"It's dark in here, Bill," Marie-Thérèse complained.

I made a cutthroat gesture to indicate that we should maintain a strict discipline of silence. At that moment, my mobile went off. I say mobile, but it's actually a state-of-the-art communications set capable of sending encrypted short-burst transmissions across hostile terrain. Still, I should have put it on vibrate. *Diddle-um, diddle-um, diddle-dum-dum-dum.*

It was my mum. I never decline her calls.

"Hello, William."

"Not now, mum. I'm in a meeting."

"Sorry, dear."

I killed the line. Our cover was blown big time, but we had a few moments to hold a Chinese parliament with each other.

I looked into her eyes.

She looked into mine.

Danger and sex – one inevitably leads to the other.

"No chance, mate," Marie-Thérèse had read my thoughts.

Semi-Pygmy feet approached. I shuddered. They probably wouldn't kill on sight, but prisoners had a habit of disappearing in the whooping willow jungles and the regiment was rife with dark tales of ritual flayings, castrations and rectal reversals.

Someone lifted our branch-lid and I reached into my ops pants for a Welsh army knife. Luckily, it was only Derek, one of my best Semi-Pygmy Insurgency muckers.

"Eh Up, Marie-Thérèse! Eh Up, Bill!" Derek was not his original Semi-Pygmy name. The regiment had assigned codenames to the Insurgency leaders. "We're having a forest festival. Fancy joining us?"

It would have been rude to refuse.

13.38

Derek led the way to the Semi-Pygmy party. There were stalls selling veggie-burgers, pirated CDs, and fair-trade coffee. A brass band played northern anthems on a wooden platform beside a beer tent. Children queued for face painting. Semi-Pygmy adults juggled, performed magic tricks, and walked around on stilts, raising them to average height. The Insurgents certainly knew how to party, but the moment we entered the clearing, the festivities freeze-framed, and all eyeballs swivelled us-wards.

The most senior Semi-Pygmy Insurgent (codenamed Nigel) indicated that it was time for the greeting ceremony.

Nigel genuflected.

I genuflected.

Nigel exposed himself.

I reciprocated.

Nigel riverdanced.

I made a total tit of myself, prancing on the spot with my arms at my sides.

I knew it was a wind-up. He knew I knew it was a wind-up. But that didn't stop the assembled Semi-Pygmy partygoers from pissing themselves in mirth.

I had to take my hat off to them. The greeting ceremony was a brilliant way of humiliating foreigners. The Walloons still thought it was the genuine article, but The Deniables all knew they had made it up for a laugh.

Marie-Thérèse joined in the merriment, women being excused the phoney ceremony, the lucky sods.

I shook Nigel's hand.

"Fancy a pint, lad?" Nigel doffed his cloth cap.

"Better not," I replied. "I'm on duty."

"Pity. How's tricks?"

"Mustn't grumble."

"Well done with the kickboxing. You showed the Belgian bastards."

"Thanks, mate." I couldn't believe it. News of my victory over Jacques Chîtes had penetrated a Semi-Pygmy Insurgency camp in the deepest whooping willow jungle in Outer Ggaga.

"All your library books are overdue," Marie-Thérèse said.

"Sorry, lass," Nigel said.

"Which ones?" Derek asked.

"Three Joseph Conrads and a Jilly Cooper," Marie-Thérèse said.

"We'll have a look around," Derek said.

"How can I help you, squire?" Nigel asked.

I looked at Nigel.

He looked back at me.

It was awkward. A silent, cross-cultural abyss gaped between us.

Derek was getting twitchy, but somehow, I just couldn't get the words out.

"Bill hates asking for directions," Marie-Thérèse explained.

"Same here," Nigel said.

"Makes you feel like a right prat," Derek said.

They were all bang on the money; I had topped the *Arctic Orienteering* course at Chipping Camden, and I wasn't about to admit that I was less than one hundred percent across where I was going.

"The thing is," Marie-Thérèse said, "We're completely lost."

"You should have said!" Derek pointed to the far side of the festival. "Tourist Information's behind the beer tent."

"Thanks, mate," I replied. "Why the big celebration?"

"Stanley found a diamond," Nigel said.

"Here he is now," Derek added.

The whooping willows parted, and the Bentley of my dreams swung into sight. It was sex-on-tyres: nought to sixty in three-point-five seconds, eight-speed dual clutch transmission, continuous all-wheel drive, 552 BHP, 210 mph max. It had computer-controlled springs, electronic dampers, and an invisible aerofoil, so the vehicle's 19.9 spoke 2-piece alloy sports wheels rolled along uninterrupted by the bumpy terrain. But much as I loved the car, it didn't really add up. Outer Ggaga isn't exactly a-flush with Bentley dealers.

"Where did you get that from?" I asked.

"Father Forestière," Nigel said.

"Nice bloke," Derek added.

"Dead nice," I concurred. I could feel the weight of the priest's corpse in the knock-kneed waterbuck bag I had improvised with Marie-Thérèse. "Where did Stanley find the diamond?"

"Why's that, lad?" Nigel looked serious. "Thinking of sinking a mine?"

"Don't fancy all that digging," I replied. "I'm not after your claim. I just want the full SP."

Derek looked at Nigel.

Nigel looked at Derek.

Unspoken Semi-Pygmy thoughts passed between them.

After a bit, Nigel said, "Stanley's the Karyenda drum champion of Mount Heha. Now, good as he is, you don't want him practising in the middle of the village."

He had a point. Karyenda drums were vast, noisy bastards.

"So," Nigel continued. "Stanley used to rehearse up on the rock face."

"Almost out of earshot," Derek added.

"Anyway," Nigel said. "Stanley was happily beating away at his drum the other day when he gave the skin such a whopping great thunk that he triggered a ruddy rockslide."

"Boulders hurtled through the sky," Derek said.

"Debris swept down the ridge," Nigel said.

"And vast chunks plummeted," Derek said.

"Exhuming an enormous diamond," Nigel said.

"Big as your fist," Derek said.

"And as clear as crystal," Nigel said.

"But more valuable," Derek added.

Maybe they were shitting me, but sometimes geology has its own logic. Rocks do move, just not very often. Mount Heha's slopes are pre-Cambrian and they're as heavily scarred as a veteran squaddie. It was unlikely, but not impossible. "So," I asked. "Who's got the diamond now?"

"Father Forestière," Nigel replied.

I looked at Marie-Thérèse.

She looked at me.

It didn't help.

If Forestière had the diamond in his cassock while Marie-Thérèse was popping his cherry, then there were three possibilities. One - someone had taken it off him while he was lying dead on top of Marie-Thérèse, and she surely would have noticed this. Two – it was still in his pocket. Three – it had dropped out during my bike ride, my nun artillery attack, my jungle yomp, or my crocodile fight in the papyrus swamp. If it was option one, Marie-Thérèse was lying to me. If it was option three, the diamond was almost certainly lost forever. Two was my option of choice, but I couldn't check it in front of the Semi-Pygmies as we had disguised the dead priest as a knock-kneed waterbuck.

14.12

After I had performed an obligatory parting riverdance to Nigel and Derek, we headed for Tourist Information. We passed Semi-Pygmy children chiselling containers out of gourds, Semi-Pygmy women sewing raffia baskets and Semi-Pygmy blokes playing mancala. The air was filled with the smoke of cooking fires. It was exactly like Bonfire Night on Clapham Common, but with shorter people.

A brown sign with an italicised *i* indicated the Semi-Pygmy Tourist Information Office. It wasn't much – just a Portacabin. I guess they weren't too busy, given how inaccessible the whooping willow jungle was to coach parties.

An old woman sat behind the desk, filling in a Sudoku square and listening to rugby union on a dusty radio. I knocked on the glass and, without looking up, the Semi-Pygmy Tourist Information Officer handed me a fold-out jungle map.

There were insulting illustrations – a beer bottle for the squaddie compound, a ruin for the Embassy, a hacienda for Forestière, a lame sketch of Basil Fawlty for The Stamford Bridge Hotel and a levitating cucumber for Norbert Trifijd's Zeppelin. Sometimes, as good as satellite navigation can be, you're better off with drawings. The pictures were crude, but the cartography was first class. I thanked her and attempted to ascertain our location.

After a bit, Marie-Thérèse squinted over my shoulder at the map, and said, "Oh. We're *there*."

"How did you know that?"

"The bright red *You Are Here* arrow was a bit of a giveaway, Bill."

14.14

Helpful as the Semi-Pygmy Tourist Information Officer had been, there was still the risk of being tailed. In a deniable country, you need the percentages on your side, so we confused any pursuant pygmies with a complex route-dithering manoeuvre. After a brief cross-country yomp, we were at Marie-Thérèse's hut, the one and only National Library-Brothel of the Floricultural Walloon Republic of Outer Ggaga.

14.33

Marie-Thérèse's home was set apart, both financially and geographically, its physical position determined by the need for discretion. Entrances could be effected from a variety of angles and it had had a load more invested in it than either the compound or The Embassy. Above the roof, a brown heritage sign read, *Ignorance Is Impotence*.

I plonked the priest inside the entrance and gave the place a quick once-over. It was a home of two halves. On the left, there was a fully-fledged library with alphabetized shelves, stepladders, and microfiches: every wall was a bookshelf straining under the weight of several hundred hidebound hardbacks. On the right, there was a kitchenette, lounge, and boudoir.

"Shall I check your homework, Bill?"

"Sorry, Marie-Thérèse. I'm afraid I don't have it on me."

"Well, it's due tomorrow. Six sides on *The Name of the Rose*."

"I'll finish it after rifle practice."

"Did you identify that quote?" Marie-Thérèse asked as she replaced her contact lenses.

"*Things, being things, didn't turn out quite as planned*?"

"Yes, Bill."

"Salman Rushdie."

"Good."

We went Dutch on a grin.

"Bill."

"Marie-Thérèse."

"Thanks for saving me from the swamp."

"I drove us into it."

"You didn't have a lot of choice. You were sandwiched between a Routemaster and a petal truck."

"I didn't have an exit strategy."

"None of us are faultless."

"You're not far off."

"Bless you, Bill. Fancy some soup?"

"Yeah, great."

"It's Nile Perch."

"Oh," I said, masking my disappointment. "Okay."

Marie-Thérèse heated the liquidised fish on a gas hob. It was a homely, if smelly, scene, and it was strange to think what Marie-Thérèse had been through over the past twelve hours or so, what with the dead priest, the tartan nun attack, the papyrus swamp, and the Semi-Pygmy festival.

"Are you sure you're okay, Marie-Thérèse?"

She looked up from the pan of perch and said, "I think you should take care, Bill."

"Me?"

"I know you think you're hard, but you're only one bloke."

"There's the regiment."

"Is there?"

"Well, maybe not this morning. They had a heavy night."

Marie-Thérèse served up a hefty scoop of Nile Perch soup. "You're investigating this solo, aren't you?"

Not a lot gets past Marie-Thérèse. I spooned some soup. It was as pungent and predictable as I had feared.

"Father Forestière was more than he seemed," she continued. "I think he linked a great many things."

I pictured Forestière as a tarantula in a cassock, sat at the centre of a web of intrigue. It put me off the soup even more than I was already.

"The Walloon Republic of Outer Ggaga is ready to explode, Bill. We are about to find ourselves in the middle of a Second War of the Roses."

"Cheer up, love. Might never happen." I tried to remain positive, even though I knew she was right. I had another spoon of soup and forced an appreciative noise. "Can I borrow your bike?"

"It's in the garage."

"Thanks." I opened a side door and, out of nowhere, a boot crunched into my gonads. Luckily, I had used protection: you can't rely on much in this life, but my Kevlar G-string is consistently toe-proof.

With his tailored suit and battered physog, my assailant resembled an old-school face from the bowels of London's long-lost underworld. This was a case of kill, be killed, or run away screaming like a girl. Fortunately, I knew how to do violence: I had studied hitting at Leamington Spa. I unleashed a volley of punches. He returned with a backhand - there's not much self-defence that can't be learned from lawn tennis. I gifted him a gut-slap and got a windpipe-punch in return. The pain sent me swooning, but I disciplined my nervous system and launched a tango of violent retribution. *Punch, slash, swivel, kick. Thrust, jab, scramble.* He pulled out a nine-inch lion-hunting blade and responded with a salsa of slashing. *Tear, slice, turn. Howl, flinch, shudder.*

This blood-prance was never going to score a perfect ten for artistic interpretation, so I decided to deck him with a roundhouse boot. He made the same decision and we both leg-twirled in unison, our feet synchronizing with each other's skulls. He buckled. I buckled. We fell over. A round of applause resonated. It was Marie-Thérèse chuckling her mouth off.

"Don't take the mick," my opponent said. "That hurt."

"Blessed are the piss takers," Marie-Thérèse said.

She was a bit of a phrasemaker, but I would never hold it against her.

"You two will get on fine," she added.

"How do you know?" I asked.

"I've got a PhD in Bloke Theory," she replied.

"Wotcha, Marie-T," my opponent said, hugging my host.

"Hello, Buster," she replied.

"You know this ambushing bastard?" I asked incredulously, darting my adversary a death-glance.

"Sure," Marie-Thérèse said. "It's Buster Butterworth from Belladonna's Floral Deliveries."

"He's a florist?" I asked, with some trepidation.

"Belladonna's Floral Deliveries is more than just a florist's," Marie-Thérèse said. "It's valued at nine billion Trifijds on the underworld stock market."

"What do you do?" Buster Butterworth asked me with a snarl.

"I'm in The Deniables."

"Never heard of them."

"That's the idea."

"I just dropped by to return a few library books." Buster Butterworth handed Marie-Thérèse a few Jane Austen novels.

After Marie-Thérèse had retreated to her library to scan the barcodes, there was one of those awkward silences you get when two blokes have just drawn a potentially fatal fight and they are stood in the home of the most beautiful woman in the country.

"So," I asked. "How did you get into floristry?"

"Second career," Buster Butterworth replied.

"First?"

"Assassin."

"Same here."

"Small world. Any decent targets?"

"Whoever the government fancied dropping deniably. You?"

Buster Butterworth didn't specify any targets, but he did bang on about horse-doping, striping, slashing, Ilford, Romford, The Borough, failed boxers, Jack Spot, Bernie Silver, Paul Raymond, mugs, bare-knuckle boxing, and the viciousness of the Columbians until I thought my brain might implode. I could feel the apathy sludging through my blood, nudging my heart towards atrophy and deadening my pulse, but I am always polite. "How's Belladonna's Floral Deliveries? Business brisk?"

"Hard to tell," Buster replied. "You know Potter."

"Who's Potter?"

"Don't let him hear you ask that. He's very proud of his reputation. *Fray Bentos Fingers,* they call him, he has digits in so many pies."

Marie-Thérèse returned with *Pride and Prejudice*. "This is overdue."

"Sorry, Marie-T," Buster Butterworth replied.

I couldn't help thinking that there was something shady about Buster Butterworth. Maybe he was the one who had pulled the plug on the priest. Thinking of which, I had a corpse to shift. I really needed to morgue Father Forestière at The Embassy before nightfall. "About that bike, Marie-Thérèse?"

She wheeled out a bright yellow ladies' number with a basket and step-through frame. It suited her, but not me, which was a shame, given that I was the one who had a murder investigation to complete. At least Buster Butterworth was too busy boring Marie-Thérèse with tales of cockney gangland to clock me shouldering the holy man and draping him in a mozzie net.

CHAPTER 5

I pictured tiny Tell on his lemon lady-bike and wondered whether his legs were long enough to reach the pedals. The journal did not reveal whether he'd had to ride standing up, although it had explained how to hunt and overcook an amphibious squirrel, how to construct a whooping willow hide, and how to formally greet a Semi-Pygmy Insurgent. I was not sure how useful this wealth of takeaway information would prove in an empty strip club, but you never knew.

One thing was for sure, I wouldn't be booking a package holiday in The Walloon Republic of Outer Ggaga anytime soon. Homicidal nuns, gargantuan crocodiles, and Semi-Pygmy Insurgents made the place sound even more dangerous than a Saturday night in Cardiff, and as for carnivorous marrows, they made my blood run cold.

The dead priest was quite a card, swapping Mount Heha's largest diamond for a Bentley then losing his virginity on his deathbed. Had he been honey-trapped by Marie-Thérèse and sniped by a Walloon? Or a tartan nun? Or a Semi-Pygmy Insurgent? Who knew? Bill's brief encounter with Buster Butterworth at the National Library-Brothel was also intriguing – I had never appreciated just how bound-up floristry was with organised crime.

All-in-all, the journal was quite an eye-opener, and it was taking my mind off being dressed as a sofa. I gave my shoulders a stretch and continued reading, eager to discover how Bill would unravel the mystery of the fornicating priest and, more practically, how he would transport the cleric's corpse across the Walloon Republic of Outer Ggaga on a girl's bike:

JOURNAL – SERGEANT BILL TELL

Walloon Republic of Outer Ggaga, East Africa

Monday 10 May, 14.50

As I pedalled my way through the petal fields on a custard-coloured girl's bike, the rose cultivators pissed their bladders empty with merriment. I didn't mind – they had a tedious job, and I was happy to provide some comic relief. I focused on the task in hand: I had a dead priest on my shoulders, I was determined to complete my investigation, and the lady-bike was the only operationally effective vehicle available.

Before long, I had reached the Semi-Pygmy ancestral grounds – known locally as *Land of My Fathers*. Some of the Deniable lads got creeped out by the place, but I don't feel threatened by the dead. It's the living you've got to worry about. I have never been ambushed by a corpse.

Land of My Fathers was a little different to your run-of-the-mill cemetery. There were no mossy slabs or engraved tombs, just dense forests of cheery soapstone carvings. Each sculpture marked the deceased's main interest in life – a banjo for a musician, a football for a sportsman, a pint of bitter for a drinker, a statue of Marie-Thérèse for a dedicated frequenter of the National Library-Brothel. Marie-Thérèse was not a bad lifetime interest, I reflected. I might ask them to knock me up a sculpture of her to mark my final resting place in Wandsworth Cemetery.

Forestière's home was no ordinary vicarage. It was guarded by a six-metre-high gate and a pair of imposing Rhodesian ridgeback-pit bull crossbreeds. They were half donkey-sized lion hunter, half stocky streetfighter, and I would have my work cut out taming the pair of them. Still, there is no danger money in safety.

I chained my luminous girlie-bike to the railings, hid the priest's corpse under some whooping willow branches and shimmied up the vicarage gate-poles. I braced myself and leaped down to face the ridge-bulls (or should that be pit-backs? Don't ask me, I only did security at Crufts the once). I reverted to technique: *Approach a guard dog from downwind, keep low, offer a sacrificial elbow, then twat it.* The trouble was, there were two of the barky bastards, so I had no choice but to hypnotise them. If a highly trained Deniable officer gets into hand-to-hand combat with a couple of canines, he is dishonouring the good name of his covert regiment and, somehow, reputation matters more when no one knows you exist.

Luckily, violent dogs are highly suggestible, and I had completed the *Canine Hypnosis Course* at Ascot. Unluckily, the hellhounds were almost upon me, and I had a matter of seconds to begin the induction procedure. I delved into my ops pants and grabbed hold of the first medal I came across - The Gerrards Cross for Covert Gallantry.

The cross-bred biting machines were within munching range as I dangled my Deniable decoration in front of their eyes, but it stopped them in their tracks, making them blink and softening their psychic defenses. Their pupils dilated and moments later, I had begun to bypass their critical faculties and accessed their lower brain stem mechanisms. I had learned fluent canine during my time in Kosovo and I was able to whisper mesmeric woofs, guiding their inner associations, restructuring their perceptions, and regressing them to a puppylike state. Soon, the ridge-bulls (or pit-backs) posed no more of a threat than a soppy pair of overgrown chihuahuas.

15.01

Forestière's garden boasted an embarrassment of pornographic topiary: lovingly strimmed foliage figures cavorted in hedge orgies; their anatomically correct couplings and triplings expertly captured in leafy bush. The shameless priest didn't hold back on anything – he had a mermaid fountain streaming with bloated ghost carp, a Monkey Puzzle Tree with real bonobos swinging from the branches and a croquet pitch overrun with flamingos.

Forestière's hacienda dominated the skyline. Its endless arches, shaded cloisters and sculpted columns were a provocation to the poverty-stricken Semi-Pygmy Insurgents outside. There was no way that a kosher priest's wages could stretch to a palace like this: he had been one bent cleric.

I took the croquet lawn at a hard jog and made a covert approach to the hacienda's magnificent entrance. Normally, I would have deployed a mini-battering ram, a

Remington pump-action lock blower or a wall-breaching canon capable of firing water-filled projectiles, but given that the hacienda's owner was dead, I thought I would be polite and knock. There was no reply, so I kicked the door down.

I stepped through the splintered oak, triggering no alarms whatsoever. Had someone deactivated them for the benefit of any potential intruders? Probably not. Was it a trap? Possibly. I moved myself into a crouching position, then covered the house in bounds, bomb-blasting between rooms, spinning three-hundred-and-sixty degrees at every doorway, commando-crawling across carpets and generally having a good nose around.

The first reception room did my head in. It was on the same level as the entrance and garden, but the windows peered out onto an underwater seascape, replete with swimming fish, wriggling eels, and drifting squid. Now, I have been confused in my time: a Nicaraguan Narco-mastermind once kept me shut in his disorientation chamber for a month before I picked the locks with a loose toenail; the Real UDA once pumped my veins with psychotropic hallucinogens after I fell into a Monaghan mantrap; and the Kazakh Cossacks once bunged me blindfold into a zero gravity vom-truck. I had survived them all by focusing on my mum's flat in Wandsworth. I tried to repeat the trick and my mind drifted back to The Victory Estate with its dreaming towers of concrete. Mum was in her towelling dressing gown, making one of her matchstick models in front of Coronation Street. There was Battenberg on the table-nest, Tetley's in the Teasmade, and all was well with the world.

Unfortunately, I could only allow myself a few seconds of reorientation without permanently compromising my state of alertness. I reappraised Forestière's windows and knock me down with a Scud if they weren't plasma shutter screens plastered with digital marine life! I was not twenty-thousand leagues under the sea, I was in a land-bound living room. It was ingenious. Why had Forestière bothered? No idea. But it had fooled me.

I ventured into the second reception room. The place had been given a serious seeing-to. Every drawer and cupboard gaped open; and the contents slung around at random. The only object still present and correct was a gleaming chrome remote control with two buttons: a fast-forward and a rewind.

I pressed rewind. Every drawer and cupboard door shut with military synchronicity. I pressed fast forward, and they flew open again. I repeated the procedure. No reason, really, I just did it for a laugh. I would have played around for much longer if I had not been on a covert ambassadorial mission to solve the murder of a priest, but I was so I didn't.

Closer examination of the thoroughly frisked possessions revealed that Forestière's house was crammed full of riches, perversion, and doubt. His extensive library of theology, philosophy and hardcore porn had been chucked around every corner of the mansion. Most of the books had been gutted, rendered spineless or had their pages shredded. There were several crates of Walloon Weissbier and a shattered magnifying glass, possibly used to authenticate the diamond Forestière had traded with Stanley the Semi-Pygmy.

Towards the rear of the priest's hacienda, there was a marble swimming pool with gold cherubim, a leopardskin Jacuzzi and a floating cocktail bar. The walls were decorated with waterproof pictures of chubby ladies, butlers on beaches and dancing rhinos. It was as understated as Trump Tower, so it was a good thing I had completed the regiment's *Tasteless Environments Course* in Essex.

15.19

I rode upstairs on a spiral escalator and entered a private cinema. A quick fiddle on the remote control revealed the priest's recent viewing habits: *Denise Does Deptford*, *Sally Does Stratford* and *Sister Matilda Does The Vatican*. I won't pretend that I didn't fancy a quick gander, but there is a time and a place for dirty movies and a covert insertion into a dead Outer Ggagaan priest's hacienda isn't it.

I approached the master bedroom and found myself face-to-face with a short-arsed squaddie. I nearly opened fire, but killing your reflection is self-defeating. The walls, floor and ceiling were all mirrors, a pair of his-and-hers bidets guarded a waterbed, and, in the corner, there was a wardrobe illustrated with an ancient Greek orgy. It was a room more suited to a Playboy bunny than a senior cleric.

There was a remote control on the bed, but there were no screens to operate, so I aimed it at the wardrobe. Now, I'm not usually one to take an interest in clothes. I mean, I wouldn't be without my Corby Trouser Press, shirt-sleeve-steamer or tie-flattener and I can shine a boot clean enough to reflect sunbeams, but what another man chooses to wear is his own business. Still, I wondered whether the orgiastic wardrobe contained cassocks or leather spanking pants. I selected the forward arrow, and the moment the wardrobe's heavy oak doors began to creak open, I felt a dart pierce my chest cavity. I looked down. Tell-tale splashes of lime liquid had redecorated my shirt. I had clearly been done with an Absinthe dart, the Walloon weapon of choice. Ambushed by a wardrobe! It has come to something when a bloke can't even trust furniture.

The wardrobe doors opened fully to reveal Jacques Chîtes, the lunking great Walloon I had defeated in last night's kickboxing bout. He was smiling like a goon and clutching an Absinthe gun. Moments later, Chîtes blurred out completely, and a classic Absinthe trip kicked in. I must have been given an elephantine dose, as I was soon hallucinating like Dumbo on acid. Kes, Ginger, Normal and Scally all Morris-danced before my eyes in paisley bikinis; nuns performed yogic flying routines in tartan leotards; The Ambassador air-guitared in an all-in-one gimp suit; the Semi-Pygmy Insurgents performed Alpine yodels in Bavarian lederhosen, and BBC Thirteen's Charles Brithazard lap-danced for Marie-Thérèse in a Rotherham United away-kit. It was if a nonsense-bomb had detonated between my ears.

When I came to and reality returned, it was even more unhinged - sometimes, the God's aren't smiling, they're gurning. There was nothing beneath me but air and rose fields, and my life was hanging by a thread or, to be exact, a Walloon rope. I was strapped to a stretcher and swaddled in a strait jacket. A patchwork quilt of rose fields receded beneath me as I was hauled up towards a bloated Walloon Zeppelin, a great looming sky-whale. It was the master gasbag and I had done covert surveillance on it in our deniable helicopter, The Flying Zit. This mother was heftier than the Hindenburg: 286 metres long with a 55-metre circumference. It was powered by eleven monster engines, each with propellers that could swivel through 132 degrees. This gave the Walloon whaleship fearsome manoeuvrability: it could turn on its own axis and hover like a gigantic chopper. It had a top speed of 176 kilometres an hour and a range of 24, 722 km.

You probably think I'm nuts, and you would have a fair point - only the seriously loose of screw would want to waffle on about Zeppelin statistics when they are suspended two hundred metres above ground on a Walloon stretcher - but focusing on detail dissipates the dread. I know I am one of the most highly decorated deniable operatives in the regiment, but even the fearless worry.

It was the thought of never seeing Marie-Thérèse, mum or the lads again that made my eyes well up. At least there were no witnesses to my meltdown. A thousand different thoughts raced through my mind, but I couldn't catch any of them. It was time to clutch at detail again: the Zeppelin's aluminium frame was built to a lattice girder pattern, combining maximum strength and minimum weight. The envelope was filled with helium. It had twice the density of hydrogen, so it only provided half the lift, but it was inert and didn't go bang. There was a rectangular passenger gondola and flight deck underneath the gas pod. Within the pod, there was a shedload of helium, an aluminium skeleton, luxury cabins, observation rooms, a champagne bar, a smoking room, and a beard barber's salon. Luckily, I reached the Zeppelin just before I ran out of detail.

The gondola doors gaped open and Jacques Chîtes dragged my stretcher on board. The vast Walloon bellowed insults and dragged me across the room. In my strait jacket and stretcher, I couldn't resist - I could barely move.

I scanned the room for more detail: the airship was being piloted by Grandmother Superior; a septuagenarian Kenyan nun who had recently been made Head Sister of The Brotherhood. Even when immobilised, a soldier is never completely passive if he is acquiring information about his environment.

Chîtes banged the stretcher against each step of the gondola's staircase. There must have been at least twenty of the bastards and it didn't do my suspension any good at all.

After I had been battered up to the main living quarters, Jacques Chîtes hefted my stretcher to a vertical. The Zeppelin's interior could not have been much more lavish: there was a grand piano, a cocktail bar, a seafood restaurant, a huge oil-painted wall-map of Mount Heha, and a male grooming zone. Jacques Chîtes dragged me along to the beard-trimming area, removed the two poles that kept my stretcher taut and strapped me into a barber's chair. He had well over half a metre on me and he out-legged me big time. His features were Neanderthal: a predatory jaw, cruel eyes, and a bump of gristle above the nose. Chîtes was a machine for inflicting pain. He could not have been happy about being kick-boxed to the ground by a midget like me, but it had been a fair fight and I had not got away unscathed. The bastard had inflicted a vast bruise on the left side of my ribcage, even though I couldn't for the life of me remember being booted there. Sometimes, soldiers blank out injuries. I suppose it is just the body's way of coping with trauma.

Moments later, we were joined by Norbert Trifijd, President of the Walloon Republic of Outer Ggaga, and Tintin Magritte-Poirot, the Number Two Walloon, and official Keeper of the Presidential Beard. Luckily, I had done the *Covert Pogonology* course in King's Lynn and knew the difference between a Van Dyck beard, a Verdi beard, and a Garibaldi beard. The Walloons had matching face furniture; fearsome chinstraps, awesome bugger-grips, and tufty little flavour-savours, but Trifijd's whiskers were grey, and Magritte-Poirot's were red. Jacques Chîtes may have been heaviest in physical stature, but he was lightest in cheek-fluff, indicating his lowly position in the Walloon pecking order.

Trifijd wafted up to me, as elegant and feline as a camp leopard. Magritte-Poirot followed, picking up a dish of chin-strimming gear on his way.

"What is it they say in England?" Trifijd asked as he caressed a sideburn. "Absinthe makes the heart grow fonder."

The Walloons pissed themselves at Trifijd's lame quip.

I joined in, hoping to win the bastards over. I had completed the regiment's *Laughing in Terrifying Situations Course* at Edinburgh.

"We Walloons know how to get information," Trifijd continued. "We know how to get people to talk and Tell, you will - how you say - tell."

It was not the first time I had encountered the pun, and I couldn't be arsed to laugh, so I just whispered my name, rank, and number.

"Speak up!" Chîtes bawled.

"I cannot discuss covert information."

Trifijd leant in and murmured, "Whisper it again."

I did as instructed. I could not believe I had allowed myself to get bumped. I have been trained to anticipate every eventuality, but no one expects to find a Walloon in a wardrobe.

"This is the world's only floricultural republic, and I will not have it spoiled by a clodhopping squaddie!" Trifijd minced across to the bar and collected a bowl of *moules mariniere*. "The bottom's falling out of the rose market, and we're close to cashless."

It isn't often that being interrogated helps one of my investigations, but this weird Walloon had handed me a motive on a plate. If the Belgians were skint, they had every reason in the world to shoot the old prelate and nick his diamond. You could bet your life that, if the priest had given Stanley the Semi-Pygmy a Bentley for it, the diamond was worth a thousand times more than that.

"Flower gathering's a dirty business." Trifijd sucked a mussel. "You finger-wagging liberals are happy to buy bouquets with a clear conscience, but behind every Valentine's Day there's a massacre. Only the Walloons have the balls to face the life and death decisions demanded by rose cultivation. I've been running petals out of the darkest corner of East Africa since you were in short trousers."

"They're still quite short," I was big enough to acknowledge. "My legs only just reach the ground."

"I'm not interested in your inside leg measurements!" Trifijd trilled. "The Walloons are a warrior race and roses are a seriously thorny issue. You can't arrange a bouquet without slicing a few stems. We've done the Semi-Pygmies a favour, even though they don't all know it yet."

This was arrant nonsense. "If The Deniables hadn't built bridges with the Semi-Pygmy Insurgency, they'd have blow-darted your Zeppelins right out of the Outer Ggagaan sky."

"Not with our network of nuns," Trifijd countered.

"That's one unholy alliance," I remarked. *Never neglect an opportunity to pun your enemy into submission.* But the Walloon had a point - The Sisters of The Brotherhood were a bunch of mean mothers.

The Walloon botanist sliced open an oyster shell. "Who killed Forestière?"

"I was meaning to ask you the same question."

Trifijd snorted his contempt, then nodded at his Number Two. Magritte-Poirot reached through my shirt and tweaked my left nipple.

It hurt slightly. I fidgeted a bit.

Trifijd scented blood. "You Brits want to move in on our flower patch!"

"Why bother? England isn't exactly short of roses, but maybe Wallonia's short of conflict diamonds." I was trying to provoke him, but all I got was another tweak from Magritte-Poirot. It was mildly uncomfortable.

"You're a babbling idiot." Trifijd dribbled mussel marinade.

"Thanks!" Enthusiastic agreement never did anyone any harm. I had done the *Advanced Fibbing* course at Finsbury Park, so I was happy to go along with whatever bollocks the Walloons had to offer.

"Cheerful, aren't you?" Trifijd asked.

"I do my best."

Trifijd turned to Jacques Chîtes. "Lower his morale!"

Chîtes leant right up to my face. "Clare Balding. She is rubbish."

I struggled to restrain myself at this outrageous insult to one of Britain's most consistently up-beat television presenters. The Walloons really knew how to push my patriotic buttons. Angry red mist clouded my view of the Zeppelin interior, but I couldn't let it settle.

"Ricky Gervais," Chîtes sneered. "He is porky boy."

His words hit me like a right hook from a super heavyweight, but I didn't drop. How could he say such things? Perhaps the cheeky national treasure was a little chubby, but why draw attention to it? The kickings you accept, but this blatant disrespect to one of Reading's top entertainers really got to me.

"Harry Kane and Gareth Southgate," Trifijd continued. "They are lovers."

England's most talented striker and our greatest modern manager - it was so wrong. I mean, what about Mrs Kane and Mrs Southgate? Surely, they would have noticed. I strained at my wrist straps, but the Belgian bastards had fastened them skin-tight. I was done-up like a covert kipper.

"Why did you break into Father Forestière's hacienda?" Trifijd demanded.

"I was worried about him," I lied.

"Close, were you?"

"I wouldn't say we were mates."

"But you were worried."

"Yes."

"What have you done with him?"

"Nothing, He wasn't in."

"Tell us where he is."

"You should know. You trashed the place."

"Chîtes!"

"Yes, sir," Chîtes growled, biting at the bit.

"The piano," Trifijd said, with effete menace.

Chîtes flashed me a cruel grin, took up position behind the keyboard and started to pound out Barry Manilow numbers. Was there no limit to the Walloons' sadism? I tried to shut my ears and failed - sometimes I hate anatomy. *Lola! I Write the Songs! Bermuda Triangle!* The Manilow tunes followed in unrelenting succession. I had to make Chîtes stop: the only way to do that was to give them something, anything. I tried to remember an out-of-date ambassadorial order, a worthless Deniable plan, an irrelevant regimental technique, but the Absinthe attack had binned it all from my memory.

Tintin Magritte-Poirot opened a bottle of beard shampoo then started to fiddle with a micro-razor and a pair of tweezers. They obviously wanted me to talk, so things were going to get a lot worse. I had faced electrodes and meat hooks, but this Walloon had beard tweezers. I was filled with dread, but I told myself that they could tweak my eyebrows as much as they wanted; it was up to me whether they broke my mind.

"This man wants to pluck your nostrils," Trifijd said. "Shall I let him?"

Magritte-Poirot poured stubble shampoo over my nose and wielded the beard tweezers. He wanted me to squirm before I confessed.

"I've told you all I know," I protested.

"It is time for you to be plucked," Trifijd said. "Pluck him!"

I instinctively clenched my teeth, muscles, and nostrils.

Magritte-Poirot tweaked my nasal hairs. A blinding flash of pain irritated my sinuses, but I wouldn't let it break me. "Name, rank, and number. That's all I have to give."

My eyes watered as Magritte-Poirot plucked the tufts from my nostrils, and my ears shuddered as Jacques Chîtes banged out more and more Manilow. A coward may die a thousand deaths, but at least he gets to surrender another day; a brave man has no such luxury. I was determined to survive the Walloon's merciless nose-grooming, but I still screamed like a banshee. After what felt like an hour of Manilow-accompanied nasal torment, I decided on a radical strategy. "All right, all right. I'll tell you."

Chîtes stopped plinking out show tunes and Magritte-Poirot's tweezers paused in mid-air.

"Forestière is on my lady-bike."

The Walloons laughed. They didn't believe me. I joined in the merriment, sincerely tickled at having blinded them with the truth.

"Cigar?" Trifijd suggested.

They were offering me supplies and all my training had taught me to take advantage of the situation, although I was a bit worried about the Health and Safety implications of smoking in a giant gasbag.

"It's okay." Trifijd handed me a cigar. "There's no hydrogen in the envelope. We won't do a Hindenburg."

"Mind if I save it for later?" I don't smoke. It is an avoidable risk and I'm a survivalist.

"It's later than you think," Trifijd nodded at Chîtes.

Chîtes flung open an observation window and wheeled me and my bear-barber chair out into the sky.

CHAPTER 6

Sergeant Tell certainly lived an eventful life, even if it was led in uncomfortable proximity to Death. If I kept a journal, it would focus primarily on pubs, benches, and naps, with occasional excursions into fast food, lager, and ketamine. Sometimes, I might nap on a bus. Other times, I might nap on a train, a pavement, or a pool table, but that would be the full extent of my adventures. I don't think I have ever been shoved off a Zeppelin, although my memory is proving to be about as reliable as a chocolate teapot. I have got no idea how I ended up in this girl-forsaken strip club. For all I know, I might have been shoved out of Walloon Zeppelins every second Tuesday for the past nine years. Maybe I went to Harvard, dated Lady Gaga, and ran a hedge fund - I hadn't got a bleeding clue.

I was starting to get frustrated, so I decided to deploy one of my simplest life-coaching techniques. I closed my eyes, pictured all my problems, and ran around in circles screaming. It didn't provide any solutions, but I felt a bit better.

I thought of little Bill, plummeting through the Outer Ggagaan skies whilst tied to a Walloon beard-barber's chair, and wondered whether this would stretch his Stoicism to the limit. Would he defy his fate like a Special Forces hero? Or would he cry like a girl? There was only one way to find out:

JOURNAL – SERGEANT BILL TELL

Walloon Republic of Outer Ggaga, East Africa.

Monday 10 May, 16.57

Dropping to a near-certain death is no one's idea of fun, but at least I had a decent view. It is important to appreciate every moment of life without fear, however grave the peril. Importantly, my training had also taught me to simultaneously develop a plan. In this case, the best option seemed to be religion, but I decided to go with survival. I had been working away at the strait jacket and stretcher strapping since I had come round from the Absinthe dart, and I reckoned I had about six seconds left to play with. I freed my right wrist, yanked Magritte-Poirot's beard-tweezers out of my left nostril and used them to free my other hand. I jettisoned the beard-barber's chair and improvised a parachute out of the stretcher. Luckily, I had completed the regiment's *Parachute Steering* course in Burnley, and I managed to plonk myself expertly in the deep end of The Stamford Bridge Hotel's swimming pool. After inhaling a lungful of chlorinated water, I bounced back off the tile base and resurfaced.

"Bloody hell, Tell!" Charles Brithazard exclaimed from the poolside bar.

"Hello, Charles," I replied.

"How did you do that?"

"It was nothing. I just improvised a parachute with the Walloon's nasal tweezers."

"Not that, *that*!" Charles said with emphasis, waving at the unconscious hippo to my left. "You decked it with the chair. Well done, Bill."

"Thanks mate."

"Fancy a drink?"

"Not half."

I deployed a Nicaraguan doggie-paddle to swim past the hippo and climbed out of the pool.

"Been drinking long, Charles?"

"Not yet. Ask me in an hour or two."

"Mind if I get myself a towel?"

"Not in the least. There'll be a large stein of gut-rot waiting for you when you come back."

The Stamford Bridge Hotel was full of donations from the Ambassador's surrealist art collection: a transvestite Mao, a papier-mâché hare on a swing and a set of classic landscapes with added Zeppelins (Constable's *Haywain with Zeppelin*, Chagall's *Self-Portrait with Zeppelin* and Turner's *Battle of Trafalgar with Zeppelin*). They were all rubbish, but no one was going to tell her that.

Each room was oversupplied with ashtrays, but the taps didn't run, the floors were askew, and every door sported a notice reading, "Do not attempt to repair anything". The whole structure was linked together by wonky spiral staircases and a mechanical elevator. The hotel lobby pan-piped an easy listening death-march and a concierge lay asleep on the reception desk, an unlit fag lodged in his gob. It's not that I lack self-control, it's just that some things are too good to resist, and I am ashamed to say that I improvised a match and lit the cigarette. The comatose concierge coughed, rolled off his perch and landed on the shagpile.

"Got any towels, mate?" I asked, as the carpet caught fire.

"They're all being used, Sergeant Tell," he replied.

"But there's only one person by the pool." I stomped out the fag-blaze.

"I know, but there's a Mayan Pilates session in the ballroom."

"And the Mayans used towels?"

"Guess so." The concierge clambered to his feet.

"No sign of the boss?"

"We're still managerless."

I walked down the corridor, leaving a trail of drips. Lucky I wasn't being followed; it would have been an obvious track. The concierge was right; the ballroom was brimful of covert charity workers performing Mayan Pilates on hotel towels. The session was led by Sally, an excitable Scot from the Deniable Foreign Office. She was in decent shape, but the others were either fat or ready for the knacker's yard. There was Sunny Butchdance, the retired Texan Arms dealer from the Deniable Peace Corps who had refereed my kickboxing bout; Lydia, an obese woman from a famine charity; and Cyril, a gangly Semi-Pygmy Rights activist from Hebden Bridge.

"Inhale and let Chaac, the god of Rain and Thunder, energize your buttocks!" Sally declaimed in her cheerful Glaswegian voice. "Feel the Maize gods straighten your spine, align your hips, and relax your thighs. Concentrate on your abdomen and let the sky gods dance your cells gracefully along the mind-body continuum. Now, exhale!"

Sally's followers were an uncoordinated mess of flab and breathless desperation; they would never have passed muster on the parade ground. Mayan Pilates did not look like a whole lot of fun, but the Walloon Republic of Outer Ggaga is fearsomely short on leisure activities, so I suppose it helped them pass the time. Personally, I preferred drinking beer, which was precisely what Charles had waiting for me on the terrace.

17.06

Charles's handshake was limp: two decades of deniable broadcasting and undeniable alcoholism had left him weak and flabby.

We looked out on the unconscious hippo and the submerged beard-barber's chair and sipped steins of formaldehyde brew, the unmistakeable tang of embalming fluid serving as a free chaser.

"Heard you drove into a biro marsh," Charles said.

"Papyrus swamp," I said.

"Jolly sticky either way, I should think. Still, glad to see you're alive."

"Thanks, mate." News certainly travelled fast in Outer Ggaga.

Charles gawped morosely at the unconscious hippo.

After he had said nothing for over a minute, I felt obliged to ask, "What's up?"

"Culture."

"Culture?"

"I can't help thinking that the world is going through an Un-Renaissance, a cultural resurgence of stupidity. I mean just look at BBC Thirteen, it's positively bristling with unintelligence. The programmes are so busy telling you what's just happened and what's about to happen that there's no time left for anything to happen."

"Does television matter?"

Charles looked crestfallen. It was his job, after all, and I suppose I could have been more tactful.

"Sorry, Charles."

"It's all right, Bill. I've got no illusions about my own importance."

I doubted this was true. I would have reminded him about his success at the Deniable BAFTAs, but he seemed to want to get a good moan off his chest.

"This assignment is an emotional donkey ride - repetitive, uncomfortable, and flat. I'm just stranded here waiting for reporting restrictions to be lifted on Outer Ggaga's existence. I'm a positive ball of apathy. The hotel doesn't help. The coffee's never ready until lunchtime and what about the food? Nile Perch with chips! Nile perch curry! Nile perch casserole! A man who is tired of the Walloon Republic of Outer Ggaga is ...".

"Entirely justified?" I speculated.

Charles broke into depressive hysterics, then adopted a manic tourist board voice-over: "Come to Outer Ggaga! It's absolutely bonza! What more could the intrepid traveller possibly covet? There's yummy yellow fever, one of the great plagues of human history! Why not give it a go? It'll deaden your pulse; make you vomit black blood and give you a wonderfully lurid jaundice. As if that's not enough, we can offer you a delightful dollop of diphtheria, complete with bacteria membranes, excruciating blood poisoning, and an unfailingly fatal heart paralysis. Or you could always try a spot of rabies, with an unmissable hat-trick of throat contraction, hydrophobia, and respiratory failure. And not to forget lovely old malaria, guaranteed to provide a swollen spleen, anaemia, and black water fever. We're damned lucky, Bill, damned lucky! Back home, I hear a heavy cold's doing the rounds. London's got nothing on us."

"We've got to stick together, us Brits, haven't we," I said, hoping a bit of patriotism might cheer him up. It didn't.

"But I don't know who to stick to," Charles said. "Damned bisexuality's a bit of a bind. One day, I'm as butch as anything. Next morning, I'll wake up and woof! Queer as a queen."

Having just been thrown out of a Zeppelin, I didn't have the energy to discuss Charles's sexual orientation, so I just said, "Thanks for the beer. It's doing my hangover the world of good."

"Hair of the dog."

"Don't mention hair." My nostrils were still raw from Tintin Magritte-Poirot's tweezers.

"Trouble is, with me, it always starts with hair of the dog and ends up being the entire mutt." Charles had a point. He was speeding through his formaldehyde beer like an Olympic drinker. "Personally, I've never seen the point of sobriety. They say the great bonus of laying off the booze is being able to remember every detail of the night before, but when I don't go out drinking, there's nothing interesting to remember."

"Can you remember what you were doing last night?"

"I was watching warthogs. Sad, isn't it?"

"We all need a hobby, Charles."

"I've spent the best part of this woe-begotten assignment establishing relationships with Outer Ggagaan warthogs, gaining their trust; learning to imitate their warning whoomphs, explosive grunts and drooling clacks." Ever the performer, Charles felt the need to prove this. It didn't suit him. "I love their dangling warts, callused knees and the semi-circular wiggle of their inward-curving tusks," Charles enthused, before reaching under the table for a classic Olympus. "This camera's captured the copious urinations of courtship, the intimate nose-rubs of maternal devotion and the abrupt tail erections of fear. Safe to say, I've lived."

"You certainly have," I lied.

He laughed dismissively.

Charles may have been a maudlin buffoon with an unhealthy warthog obsession, but it was just possible that he may have witnessed something pertinent to my investigation. Very few people dare to venture into the Outer Ggagaan night, and he had.

"So, Charles, last night, when you were out warthog-watching, where were you exactly?"

"I was lurking in the jungle. Bloody suspicious, I grant you, and the only chaps who can vouch for me are yodelling baboons, hyenas, and wild porkers."

"Don't worry. Animals are hopeless witnesses."

"Agreed. Well, here goes. I had been observing this clan of warthog sows since they'd taken shelter in an aardvark burrow. A pair of warthog boars came to sniff them out and, seconds later, who'd have believed it? The boars were snout sparring. It was wonderful, a primeval dance of porcine toreadors. Moments like that make the lengthy separation from my young family worthwhile. Then, all of a sudden - boom! Without warning, a spotted hyena spliced the night with a ferocious cackle. The warthog boars bolted in opposing directions, and I swore with imagination, wit, and enthusiasm, I can tell you that for nothing."

"What time was this?"

'Haven't the foggiest, Bill. Whooping willow jungles do tend to veer towards the dark side and I'm afraid I was transfixed by events."

"Fair enough." I have never been a natural history enthusiast, and I couldn't see that any of this was pertinent to my investigation, but Charles had got me a beer and at least he had stopped moaning on about diseases.

"I am happy to provide more information," Charles said, "If you don't mind a bluff old duffer waxing illiterate about warthogs."

"There's nothing I'd rather listen to," I lied.

"Very well. You asked for it." Charles topped up his beer stein. "Warthog stampedes are pretty damned terrifying, especially if you're a coward like me. My one ambition is to reach my grave unscathed. Trouble was, I got scathed." Charles lifted his shirt, and I almost dropped my drink: his ribs were purple, and the bruising pattern was identical to mine. Odd, really, I'd never taken him for a kickboxer. "What happened to you, mate?"

"Warthog butted me in the side. Plonked me in jungle slurry."

I started to weigh-up my options. Charles had shown me his injury - should I show him mine? My indecision was interrupted by a vast, throaty roar from the hotel pool. The hippo had woken up, and it was offering us an unimpeded view of its twenty-inch canines. I had never previously witnessed hippo dentition at such close quarters, and it was not a pretty sight. The hippo closed its nostrils and sank to the bottom of the pool, then pushed itself forward in a leap, drenching us with chlorinated water. I had only just toweled myself off, but dampness was less of an issue than the angry hippo. The beast was busy employing its head as a against the pool wall, and it wasn't long before it cracked. The hippopotamus is the most territorial animal in Africa, and they will happily munch a lion for elevenses, so its mounting fury was a bit of a worry.

"We're going to have to get it out," I said.

"Won't it just kill us horribly?"

"The longer it's in there, the more homicidal it'll get," I said. "We have to free it in a way that won't infuriate it further."

"You could call it a fascinating challenge," Charles said. "Or you could just admit we're screwed."

"I'm never screwed," I said. It was us against an eight-thousand-pound hippo and if they were offering odds on this one down at Paddy Power, the smart money would have been on the hippo. But no bookie ever takes full account of a Deniable operative's training. I remembered my *Hippo Wrangling* course at Leamington Spa and recalled the advice: *Prepare the mental and the physical looks after itself.* I focused on my immediate surroundings – the pool, the bar, the hotel, and span the available resources through my mind: water, beer, Pilates pupils, reception desk, dinner tables, bedrooms, beds. Mattresses! That was it! I knew it was a long shot, but I have been trained to score from my own metaphorical six-yard box. I ran the risk-and-reward calculations through my napper. It gave me a migraine, so I panicked and blurted out my plan: "Let's empty the pool, then chuck in a load of hotel mattresses."

"Will that help?"

"With a bit of luck, it just might work."

"Or not," Charles added, unhelpfully.

17.22

Once I had pulled the plug on the pool, I commandeered a formidable pile of mattresses from the hotel and commenced *Operation Free the Hippo*.

We began at the top of the pile. I took one mattress handle and Charles took the other, rather reluctantly.

"This is silly, Bill."

Given that there will doubtless be ample dithering time in the afterlife, I screamed the words, "Let's bloody do it!" *Maximum speed maximum aggression*, that's what the regiment taught me at Neasden. I flung the mattress into the swimming pool with all my might. Charles was a bit late in letting go of his end, but at least he didn't fall in.

The hippo looked nonplussed as we threw mattress upon mattress into the void. The plan wasn't going to win The Nobel Prize for Complexity, but it was our only chance.

The hippo pulped the mattresses. The debris formed a step, and, with a couple of thuds, the beast was free.

Charles slapped me on the back and was on the point of proposing a toast to our success when the hippo rushed us. These mud-dwelling monsters can shatter a suburban speed limit without breaking sweat. I flung Charles out of its path, and the beast belted directly at The Stamford Bridge Hotel. It wanted to get back to its bloat and it wasn't going to let the small matter of a building get in the way. We could only watch as the monster stampeded through the Mayan Pilates session, scattering charity workers, arms dealers, and diplomats in all directions, and leaving a hippo-shaped hole in the opposite wall.

"Bollocks," I commented. I had decked the ungulate with a beard barber's chair and outsmarted it with mattresses, but it had won the endgame.

"Well, we cocked that one up handsomely didn't we, Bill?"

"I neglected the final phase."

"The hippo stampede?"

"Bit of an oversight," I admitted.

"Certainly livened up the Mayan Pilates class."

"Can you apologise to Sally on my behalf? I'm on Embassy business."

"Anything interesting?"

"I'd tell you, but I'd have to kill us both first."

"Secret, is it?"

"Shush!"

"Can I offer you the loan of an automobile?"

"You know what, Charles, I'd love you forever."

He smiled lasciviously.

"Not literally," I clarified.

18.17

Charles is usually too busy drinking to drive, but I appreciated the loan of his Mini Metro – it turned a half-hour yomp into a five-minute journey. I parked under a whooping willow and strode a few hundred metres to Forestière's hacienda. The lady-bike was easy to locate, its custard coloration making it stand out from the Outer Ggagaan undergrowth. I lifted the whooping willow branches and took a look at Forestière. His face was still smiling, possibly because he was in Paradise, though more likely because he had died in Marie-Thérèse. It was time for a little forensic ballistics, but not here – I had to revisit the crime scene.

18.39

I cycled Forestière's body back to the Mini Metro, loaded up the bike and the body, and drove back down Mount Heha. The rose fields were devoid of Semi-Pygmies and tartan nuns, it being well past stem-slicing time, so it wasn't hard to find a discreet place to pull over. I needed answers and I needed them fast, so I decided to progress my investigation pronto. I shrouded the Mini Metro in Hessian and, working by the light of my luminous compass, I improvised a scalpel, plucked the bullet out of the priest's forehead, and made a quick analysis of the projectile's interaction with the corpse's flesh. When I got back to the compound, I would be able to record the bullet's unique markings and use a comparison microscope on typical Semi-Pygmy or Walloon ammunition. But before that, I decided to employ all the regimental ballistics skills I had learned at the shooting gallery in Balham to figure out exactly where the killer had fired the lethal gunshot. This involved some serious figure-fiddling and a covert map – I used a rotating coordinate system, totting up a few equations of motion and accounting for the centrifugal and Coriolis forces. After some serious brain-ache, I had specified the precise location of the firing point. Who ever said that squaddies were thick?

I rearranged the dead priest into a more dignified position and headed for the point from which the killer shot had been fired. It wasn't all that far from the compound. I wondered why none of us had heard it, then remembered that we were all so royally bladdered, we probably would have slept through a volcano eruption. I parked up by a carnivorous marrow patch and followed my maths up a mud path to the precise place from which the shot had been fired. It was marked by a comatose warthog. On balance, it seemed unlikely that the warthog had fired the gun, but its coordinates were bang on. I crouched down to examine the bushpig and it stirred, staggered from side to side then bumbled off into the jungle.

There was no shortage of track in the immediate area: five separate pairs of adult male boots. I eyeballed the tread marks in close-up and bugger-me-backwards if the patterns didn't match the Regiment's ensign, a dagger flanked by a pair of bulging biceps. According to my calculations, the smallest boot prints were by far the closest to the firing position. I added a comparison object (a Nile Perch tin) and took a quick photo with my waterproof biro camera. I would be able to work out the shoe sizes more accurately at the compound.

I had to discount the dazed warthog, but the regimental soles were a bit of a worry. Could it be that the priest's killer was one of my own comrades? Normal would have missed Forestière and hit a carnivorous marrow or a knock-kneed waterbuck, Kes would have watched Forestière and Marie-Thérèse shag until they had decoupled, Wee Jock would have topped Forestière with his bare hands (he thinks shooting is for sissies), Scally would not have had the imagination to take on the hit in the first place and, these days, Ginger is too wrapped up in his Nile Perch recipes to waste valuable cooking time killing priests. That ruled out everyone, but these were impressions, not alibis. *Guilty until proven innocent*, as they taught me on the *Human Rights Course* at Frome.

19.18

I had a hero's reception back at the compound. While Ginger, our bald Trinidadian chef, cooked up the steaks I had won off the Walloons, the others tossed me around in celebration, chanting, "Big Man! Big Man! Big Man!". It was nice to see that everyone had recovered from their drinking injuries. Life out here has its ups and downs, but times like this make it all seem worthwhile. There is real comfort in shared danger. We were comrades, bound to the badge, and everyone took turns to recall the highlights of my bout.

"The Walloon was in full kickboxing gear." Kes bunged me to Wee Jock.

"Grappling gloves," Wee Jock chucked me to Scally.

"Abdominal guard," Scally flung me to Normal.

"And Boomerang boots," Normal threw me to Kes.

"But you didn't give a toss," Kes cast me to Wee Jock.

"You just stood there in your blazer and tie," Wee Jock thrust me to Scally.

"Jacques Chîtes is one ugly Walloon", Scally hurled me to Normal.

"He's only got two expressions," Normal pitched me to Kes.

"Threatening," Kes bunged me to Wee Jock.

"And stumped," Wee Jock tossed me to Scally.

"He was practically seven foot tall." Scally chucked me to Normal.

"When you shook hands, his groin was level with your shoulders," Normal launched me at Kes.

"You watched the Walloon warm up," Kes chucked me to Wee Jock.

"Grapevining," Wee Jock threw me to Scally.

"V-stepping," Scally flung me at Normal.

"And cross-punching," Normal pitched me at Kes.

"It was Tyson Fury versus Dobby the House Elf – and Dobby won!"

The tossing climaxed with one more round of "Big Man!"

Once I had got over the dizziness, Ginger served up the prize steaks - rare and bloody in the regimental tradition – and we gathered around the table for a monumental nosh-up.

Ginger had revelled in his first perch-less recipe in months. The steaks were underdone to a T, bleeding copiously in all directions as my comrades continued to relive last night's bout.

"The ref was that Texan tosser who'd made his fortune by flogging landmines, cluster bombs and attack helicopters," Wee Jock said.

"Before retiring to join the Peace Corps," Scally added.

"The spectators lined opposing walls," Kes said. "On one side, the Walloons, stroking their bugger grips, fondling Loyalist Semi-Pygmy escort girls and guarding their whisky crate and portable freezer."

"On the other side - us," Normal said. "Deniable 'til we die."

"The big Belgian bastard launched a flying kick," Kes said.

"You didn't move a muscle," Normal said.

"Every sinew static," Ginger said.

"Just as the Walloon's foot was about to make contact, you pressed his sole with your index finger," Kes said. "And the giant froze."

"Paralysed with his leg erect," Ginger said.

"You may be knee-high to a piss pot," Kes said, "But your unarmed reflexology's faultless."

"Thanks, mate," I replied, always happy to take a compliment.

"You just ambled around the motionless Belgian, taking the crate in one hand and the freezer in the other," Kes said. "When you raised them above your head, the chants of *Big Man*! were deafening."

The whole table applauded.

What a great bunch of blokes! I was giddy with happiness - until an unwelcome insight made the room stop spinning with a judder. "So, he didn't touch me?"

"Not a whisker," Wee Jock said.

"Well done, Big Man," Scally said.

"You showed him," Normal said.

"Then how did this happen?" I lifted my ops vest and showed them my bruised ribs. Scally shrugged. "That was the warthog."

"Don't you remember?" Wee Jock asked, cattle claret dripping off his fork.

"We went for a stagger," Normal said. "You, me, Wee Jock, Scally, and Ginger."

"Drinking Scotch from the bottle," Wee Jock said.

"And firing shots into the sky," Scally said.

"We had something to celebrate, didn't we?" Ginger said.

"Fair enough." My memory bank had run out of credit, so I had no choice but to believe them. "Where were we?"

"Show him the map," Kes nodded at Normal. He unpinned it from the wall and laid it out on the trestle.

"I taped the map back together, Sarge." Normal pointed at the sealed rip between the whooping willow jungles and Mount Heha.

"Good man," I replied.

Scally pointed to the comatose warthog's coordinates on the mud path I had visited during my ballistic analysis.

"Just give me a minute," I said.

"Okay, Big Man," Kes said.

I retreated to my personal area to check my biro-cam photos. The smallest regimental footprint, when compared to the adjacent Nile Perch tin, revealed itself to be a perfect match for my six-and-a-halves. I choked on my steak. Nothing tastes as bitter as self-inflicted defeat. I eyeballed my comrades and heard myself saying, "It was me, wasn't it?"

"It was you who what, Big Man?" Scally asked.

"Killed The Father of the Brotherhood," I said.

"You fell over," Normal said.

"The warthog was doing fifty," Ginger said.

"Well over the speed limit," Wee Jock said. "It bulldozed into you."

"You were aiming vertically," Scally said. "And you fired horizontally. It's not your fault that you squeezed the trigger on the way down."

"I didn't see you hit anything," Wee Jock said.

"It was dark," Normal said.

"It was an empty field," Ginger said.

"Not empty enough," I said, shoving away my unfinished steak. "I hit Father Innocent Forestière directly between the eyes."

"Who's going to find out?" Scally asked.

"I have," I said, "And that's enough." There aren't many rules in the book, but dropping priests is one of them.

"You don't have to grass yourself up," Wee Jock said.

"I've completed my investigation and I'm the culprit."

"Have you told anyone?" Scally asked.

"You," I replied.

"We'll say nothing," Wee Jock said.

"The Deniables will deny everything," Kes said.

"You can trust us, Big Man," Wee Jock said.

"Relax and finish your steak," Ginger said.

I was too angry with myself to eat. "I'm going to turn myself in."

"Who to?" Kes asked. "You're the senior military officer."

"I report to the Ambassador."

"Please don't, Big Man," Wee Jock said.

"You won't stop me," I said. "None of you will. Sorry."

Titchy though I was, they could see I was not to be argued with.

"Maybe you'll just be demoted," Normal said.

"I'll be demobbed, stripped of my stripes and discharged with disgrace," I said.

Normal started blubbing. "What are you going to do, Sarge?"

"Live. I suppose."

"On Civvy Street?" Ginger's tears dripped onto his steak.

"With no one to guard?" Scally sniffed.

"There's always my mum."

20.12

I took one last look at my former home and packed my Bergen, taking pains not to forget my covert Corby Trouser Press, boil-in-the bag rations, and collapsible shovel. I swallowed a sob, not out of self-pity, never that - simply because I would miss the place.

There is nothing sadder than the tears of great big hairy bastards. It felt like I had just broken the news of my own death. I watched my comrades grieve for me; then gave them my mum's address. They promised to drop by, but we all knew that the prospects of them being posted to Wandsworth were slim.

Each squaddie gave me a gift: every one of them a total tear-jerker. Kes gave me a porn mag (*The Big Tissue*), Ginger gave me a Nile Perch recipe book, Normal gave me a pair of EFL Cup tickets (Norwich versus MK Dons) Wee Jock gave me a golf club and Scally gave me a *Kung Fu Kid* DVD (East African region). Everyone offered me a lift, but this was a journey I had to make alone. I packed the gear, and the presents into the boot of Charles's Mini Metro and set off for The Embassy with just the priest's corpse and the girlie bike for company.

During the journey, my brain burned with a million different emotions, notably embarrassment, but Deniables don't resign, they die horribly with pride.

Dusk had turned the flower fields monochrome, which matched my mood. I stopped off at Marie-Thérèse's hut, but she wasn't in. I leant her bike against a wall and gave it a goodbye kiss. It was no substitute for the real thing.

21.10

The Ambassador's reception was deserted, but it made no difference to me. I was not at The Embassy to be welcomed; I was due to depart in disgrace - a marksman who had hit the wrong target.

I plonked the priest's corpse in the corner of the Ambassador's office and walked across to her desk. She didn't look up. I started to explain my findings, but the emotional burden of my own stupidity left me tongue-tied.

The Ambassador let me sweat and stutter, then came to my rescue with a glare. "So, Sergeant Tell, you were aiming at the sky."

"Yes, Ambassador."

"And you missed."

"Sorry, Ambassador."

"Forgive my scepticism, only as targets go, it's not small."

"No, Ambassador."

"Yet you can assemble a machine-gun in..."

My fingers flew as I unpacked my ops satchel; linked my feed slide, receiver, sear, back-plate, and top cover assemblies; adjusted a flash suppressor, control grip and front sight blade; then pointed the resulting MK19 at my employer. "Four-point-three seconds."

The Ambassador picked up a rose and poked it into the barrel. "Your years in Finland were exemplary, you were decorated in Bulgaria and as my personal bodyguard your marksmanship has saved my life on how many occasions?"

"Three, Ambassador: the Walloon Zeppelin Ambush, the Semi-Pygmy Riot and the pissed nuns who mistook you for Hilary Clinton."

"So, what went wrong?"

"Well, Ambassador, it all began with a bet against the Belgians..."

The Ambassador folded her arms and listened to the results of my investigation. She was used to navigating the dangerous complexities of local politics and the bureaucratic stupidities of British interests, but my sorry story left her with no brow unfurrowed.

"At least he died a happy priest," I concluded, an hour or so later.

The Ambassador stood up. I wish she hadn't. I only come up to her shoulders. "Father Forestière had friends." She looked down at me. "I have to act. The trouble is, Sergeant Tell, you don't exist."

"No, Ambassador."

I looked out of the window. Ten-year-old missionary soldiers were playing five-a-side football by bonfire-light. It would have been a normal enough scene, had it not been for the khaki uniforms, the rifles, and the hippo-bone goalposts. One little lad tackled another from behind, hacking his legs from under him. A fight began to brew, but the heftiest boy picked up the ball and plonked it on the penalty spot, a circle of hippo blood.

"The British government has no official military presence in the Walloon Republic of Outer Ggaga," the Ambassador said. "But the place is so dangerous I need armed protection. The local soldiers have barely reached puberty and are just as likely to assassinate me as anyone else, so my life is in the hands of the Royal Deniables."

"I've let you down," I said.

The tackled footballer stepped up to take the kick. The boy skied the penalty and held his head in his hands. The goalkeeper pointed at him and laughed while his teammates shouted their disappointment.

The Ambassador fixed me with a look of flint. "A double zero and no bravos for you, Tell. You're out. Only your non-existence saved you from a manslaughter charge."

"Thanks, Ambassador."

"You searched the body?"

"Yes, Ambassador."

"Well, where is it then?" She cupped her hands and held them out to receive an offering.

"Slumped on the floor, Ambassador."

"Not the corpse - the diamond!"

"The Great Star of Mount Heha?"

"That'll be the one."

"I don't have it."

"Then who the devil does?"

"Stanley the Semi-Pygmy Insurgent sold it to Forestière. Now he's dead, the Walloons are desperate to get their hands on it."

"And that's it, is it? That's the full extent of your observations."

"Well, the hotel manager's gone missing, The Sisters of the Brotherhood are turning nasty, and a dodgy bloke called Buster Butterworth is sniffing around."

"You're not serious."

"I am. He's from Belladonna's Floral Deliveries. They're a multi-national florist."

"I know who they are! I'm the Covert Ambassador to the Walloon Republic of Outer Ggaga."

"Sorry, Ma'am."

"Sorry is the right word. A very sorry state of affairs."

"Well, goodbye then, Ambassador. Let me know if there's ever anything I can do to help."

"You know exactly what to do, Bill."

"Do I?"

"Infiltrate the florist's global network!"

"Really?" I had infiltrated the mafia, cocaine cartels, and terrorist cells, but never a florist. It wasn't that I was scared, it was just that I quite liked flowers and it seemed a shame.

"Get them to take you on as a trainee, learn how they work, and try to blend in."

"What then?"

"Just win their respect and await further orders."

"I thought I was out of the regiment, Ma'am."

"Doesn't mean you can't still serve your country."

"As a florist, Ma'am?"

"As a florist, Bill."

"Yes, Ma'am."

"In Wandsworth. Quite near your mum's."

"Convenient, Ma'am."

"Just move back in for a while, and it's an easy commute to their HQ."

"Mum has been missing me, Ma'am."

"I can imagine, Bill."

The Ambassador opened her desk drawer, took out a beer mat and handed it to me. The words *Bar Achilles, Wandsworth, London SW11* were printed in claret-coloured text across a picture of a broken pint glass.

"It's the florists' local," the Ambassador replied. "The owner is called Ernie Bronze.

He's one of ours, but if you mention that, he'll try to kill you. Get him to give you a bar job but be subtle about your approach. Maybe you could persuade the Job Centre to send you along."

"Job Centre it is, Ma'am."

"Now bugger off to Blighty!"

I had killed the Father of The Brotherhood. If I didn't recover the Great Star of Mount Heha, it would be my turn next. I was back in civvies, but the war wasn't over yet. The next battle would not be conducted in the Walloon Republic of Outer Ggaga, it would be fought out in a completely different arena: the London Borough of Wandsworth.

CHAPTER 7

I put down the journal, closed my eyes, and went for a pint in my head. It is one of my least unpopular life-coaching techniques, particularly at moments of extreme disappointment. I visualised the beer taps, allowed the smell of hops, sweat, and crisps to fill my nostrils, and watched an imaginary barmaid pull me a Snakebite. I thanked her, settled into an imaginary seat, and tried to get a grip on my emotions.

I simply couldn't believe Bill's luck. An honourable, highly trained investigator had risked all to uncover the truth and learned that he only had himself to blame. At the end of the day, all he had done was over-celebrate: a yellow card offence at worst. Now, he was out on his arse, and exiled to Wandsworth. Not quite Siberia, but, career-wise, it was close.

I let my mind savour the notional lager-cider combo and wondered how I would have dealt with such a shameful reverse. I recalled my thirty or forty firings, and remembered that, in general, I had coped with them by drinking.

I finished my imaginary pint and reopened my eyes. I was back in the strip club office. It is odd how the presence of a single object can make an otherwise empty room feel even emptier. The box, with Bill's tower of paper, had precisely that effect: it was a cardboard island in a sea of carpet.

I decided to have a poke around the strip club. The blinds were drawn over daylight. I fingered them open and discerned nothing but Tooting, London's most stupidly named district. I suppose I could have waved for help, but I was dressed as a sofa. How would I put it? *Officer! I was abducted and tied to a dancing pole naked. Can't remember why, but yes, I had been drinking.* It wouldn't end well, would it? Not after they had checked my criminal record.

I turned my back on Tooting and took stock. Maybe the strip club had hidden possibilities. I waddled back upstairs, through the dressing room, onto the stage and out through the auditorium. There it was: the front door and freedom. At least it would have been, had it not been triple-locked, chained, and alarmed. Blue lights winked at me, daring me to set them off with the slightest shove.

I stumbled back the way I had come, tripping as I mounted the stage in my sofa-cover. In a way, I was glad: I had been chosen to avenge Sergeant Tell's death, and I couldn't do that until I had learned about his brutal transportation from Outer Ggaga to a South London suburb. I settled back down on the office carpet, and took out the next page:

JOURNAL – EX-SERGEANT BILL TELL

Bus, The London Borough of Wandsworth

Wednesday 12 May, 15.08

When you think about it, Lavender Hill hasn't got much in common with Mount Heha and it's not just a question of gradient. There are no rose fields, Zeppelins, or amphibious squirrels; Walloons are thin on the ground and there has been a shortage of Semi-Pygmies ever since Wandsworth Common was deforested. The old mayor did away with Routemasters, so I had to make do with a bendy bus. There were plenty of seats, but sitting has always struck me as a dereliction of duty, so I stood to attention, as proud as a private on parade.

On a sub-Saharan mud path, bumps come with the territory, but on a South London Ring Road, they were an unnecessary imposition. The bumps were supposed to calm the traffic, but it simply didn't work; vans tailgated Volvos, motorcyclists accelerated wildly, and irate cyclists bashed car roofs. The journey was only slightly more comfortable than being rammed into the papyrus swamp by the Walloons' petal truck and the tartan nuns' double-decker, but I had completed the Regiment's Inner Stability Course at Shenley and was able to remain taut despite the driver's lurches, swerves, and emergency halts.

The scenery was bleak. Vandalized billboards overlooked kebab shops, minicab offices and depressed pedestrians. Nature had been tamed: trees were pollarded, dogs muzzled, flowers potted in concrete. There wasn't a rose field, a knock-kneed waterbuck, or a carnivorous marrow in sight.

15.17

I stepped off the bus and got carved up by a pushchair; I hadn't seen that one coming. I apologized, inhaled a potpourri of exhaust, fast food, and dog excrement; and let a symphony of alarms, drills, generators, diggers, and sirens bathe my eardrums. I was home.

As I passed the shopping centre, I made a point of looking my fellow denizens of Wandsworth straight in the eye, but most of them just slouched along with their heads down, fearful and distracted. Part of me felt the same. I was a soldier no longer, a trained killer without a target. When Death is in your DNA, it's hard to know how to live and I was heartily tempted to befriend the bullet-end of a barrel.

Fortunately, I had completed the regiment's *Making The Best Of It* course at Dalston, so I chose to adopt a positive mindset: perhaps I had successfully followed my calling to become a failure. The world may need heroes, but it also needs mediocrities and downright screw-ups. Maybe I was predestined to mess up my life and, if so, I had pulled it off perfectly and deserved a decoration for allowing others the space to succeed. I slapped myself on the back for a job well done.

I passed a poster that read, *Welcome to Wandsworth: The Brighter Borough*, but I knew not to let my guard down. My training had taught me that the compartmented nature of urban terrain often impedes command, control, and communications. There was an ever-present risk of ambush; enemies could hide in empty buildings and ground routes were both predictable and easy to block. Line-of-sight was obstructed by traffic, signposts, phone boxes, bollards, utility substations, grocer's crates, pillar-boxes, and the civilian population. If guerrillas were to ferment a Wandsworth Insurgency, collateral casualties would be inevitable.

Survival in such an environment could depend on the accurate retention of seemingly trivial information. Luckily enough, during my *Urban Warfare Course* at Lake Windermere, I had developed a photographic memory. I blinked, snapping a series of detailed mental images: a line of lampposts at three o'clock; a kebab shop at six o'clock set at right-angles to a Portaloo (vandalized) at nine o'clock beside a vagrant (pissed) and shoppers (bored).

The Victory Estate is not much to look at, but for me, those thirteen storeys of concrete, broken windows and peeling paint were the most heart-warming sight north of the Sahara. Nothing grew in The Victory's gardens apart from the fly tips: unstable towers of tyres, mattresses, and supermarket trolleys. The flowerbeds were empty, the benches were broken, and the grass was scorched. Foul fluids seeped out of ripped bin bags: the roofs had been stripped of lead and the floors were strewn with spent syringes, used condoms and shattered glass. The corridors had been vandalized into gloom and smelled of stout, sick and urine. But for me it was a memory palace: this was where I rode my first bike, won my first fight (I was ten, he was thirty-eight) and kissed my first girl (she was five-foot ten, I was four-foot eleven). Every grimy slab of stone spoke of my past.

My boxy, brick local still flew a St George's flag, even though it had been boarded-up for five years, and outside, seven kids bounced on the burned-out carcass of a car. I gave them a smile and a wave.

A six-year-old palmed a rock, a seven-year-old mimed the beginnings of an insult and an eight-year-old prepared to launch a long-distance gob, but something made them freeze when they looked at me; a cradle-story about a lethal short-arse who made the Bogeyman seem like Sponge Bob.

"Morning, children!" I yelled.

"Morning, Mr Tell!" they chorused, in terror.

Vandalized CCTV cameras guarded the gateways to the estate's various sections: Agincourt, Waterloo, and El Alamein. There had been a caretaker once, but he had got careless. The entry system had been totalled, the walls were breachable; the roofs were strollable, the corridors were externally exposed and covert inter-floor access was available via vulnerable maintenance shafts. Individual doors had deadlocks, chains, and spy holes, but the doors themselves were wafer thin - a blade or a kick would reduce them to splinters.

I walked into Agincourt and took the stairs; the lift had been so thoroughly vandalised, it only stopped between floors. That did not mean that the stairs were a cakewalk. A teenage gang blocked the third flight, and they were busy comparing weapons. Was a pickaxe better than a machete, a Stanley knife preferable to a hunting knife, a Chinese fighting stick superior to a three-foot sword? These were all valid questions, and I would have been more than happy to weigh in with my pennyworth, but the gang all turned silent as I approached, sheaved their blades, and stood up to let me through.

"Hi lads," I said. "Weather's looking grim."

"Inclement, Mr Tell," a six-foot-five-inch Yardie replied.

"Bracing," a smackhead said.

"But character-building," I concluded.

Once I had reached my mum's floor, I marched along an open walkway. Rusty, unsteady banisters protected residents from a fatal fall. Nicotine-stained net curtains flapped through broken windows. All the doorways were boarded up, damaged, or covered in graffiti. Many had pictures of fierce dogs in place of door numbers. The end flat was different: its forget-me-not boxes and embossed doorknob were untouched by vandals, a stained-glass window depicted a rose and below that there was a warning photograph, not of a pit bull, but of me, and it read, *Beware of My Son*.

How does a man describe his own mum? I'll keep it simple: she was in her late sixties, she was exactly the same height as me and when she opened the door, our smiling faces betrayed matching dimples.

I handed her a bouquet. "I've missed you."

"I'll bet that's not all you've missed," mum replied in an identical South London accent.

"No, mum."

"Fish and chips!"

I walked in to the flat I had always called home, even when stationed on the other side of the globe. My danger money had bought mum a pristine shagpile, an enviable kitchen and solid furniture, but the flat still had a scent that took me back to my childhood; it hadn't looked so smart then. Most of mum's ornaments were older than me - a Welsh Lady-bell, a floral paperweight, a China cottage and watercolours of fruit, forests, and flowers. Everything was disposable but she had never disposed of any of it, and for that I was grateful.

17.06

Mum sat and watched me demolish a Rock Salmon. It certainly knocked Nile Perch into a cocked hat. The table had been set with military precision. Napkins were folded; cutlery gleamed beside her best Denby, and sauces were presented in silver cruets.

"Thanks, mum." I evacuated a glob of corpuscle-red ketchup from a silver boat.

"You deserve it, dear. There aren't many mums around here whose boys send them a grand a month."

"It's only danger money, mum."

"You've not been in any danger have you, love?"

"Well, I had to watch out for the mosquitoes."

"Are you still taking the medicine?"

"It made me hallucinate.'

'What did you see?"

"Death."

"Not while you're eating, son."

"Sorry, mum. How's the cathedral coming along?"

"Nearly finished, love."

Mum nodded towards the table-nest, where a spectacularly intricate matchstick miniature of Lincoln Cathedral was close to completion. She truly was one in a million.

19.03

After dinner, mum washed-up and I dried. We both gazed out of the window as the sun set over Wandsworth Plain.

"There's something wrong, isn't there Bill?"

"Yes, mum. I'm not sure there'll be any more danger money for a while."

"Never mind, dear."

"Okay if I turn in early, mum? I've got murderous jetlag."

"Sleep sound, love." She kissed my forehead.

I plonked myself down on my single bed and stared up at the walls - a pinned-up Crystal Palace scarf, a Kaiser Chiefs poster, and a postcard from my first and tallest girlfriend. Mum had not changed a thing. I switched out the sidelight, shut my eyes and tried to ignore the joyriding Grand Prix roaring and screeching outside The Victory Estate.

I wondered what daft bets Kes, Ginger, Normal, Scally and Wee Jock would think up to get them through the evenings: maybe a spot of amphibious squirrel racing or a little hippo-baiting. I worried whether Marie-Thérèse would be okay, but there was nothing I could do about it now that she was a ten-hour flight away. I focused my mind on the slopes of Mount Heha and slowed my breathing. Within seconds, my heart rate had dropped from sixty to twenty-eight beats per minute. It was a regimental trick: a way of keeping the aim true after an adrenalin-fuelled sprint, but it came in handy whenever maudlin thoughts kept me awake.

Thursday 14 May

08.10

In what felt like moments, I awoke fully refreshed and executed a hundred press-ups, fifty squat-thrusts and eighty abdominal crunches before taking mum tea and toast in bed.

"Thanks, son. Help yourself to cereal. I bought in some Rice Crispies specially."

Normally, if I want an alternative to Nile Perch, I have to hunt, skin, and gut it. This was great: Rice Crispies don't run away when you chase them. I munched my way through three bowlfuls: *food equals energy equals survival*, as they say in the regiment. Even in Wandsworth, it pays to be battle-ready.

I showered thoroughly, employed my Corby Trouser Press to eliminate any back-of-the-knee wrinkles and selected one of fifteen identical blue blazers from my wardrobe.

Mum adjusted my regimental tie. "Ready for the new assignment, son?"

"Never been readier."

"Remember, who dares wins."

"Yes, mum."

08.57

I can fell-run with a fifty-five-kilogram Bergen on my back and I can complete a hundred-metre sprint in less than eleven seconds, but catching the bus looked like a tall order; its right indicator was flashing and the last passenger in the queue was on the point of clearing the doors. I bore down on the bus, my heart hammering, and my determination unflinching, but a gaggle of grans blocked my path. They looked lost and I couldn't leave them bewildered, so I surrendered even more ground to the bus.

"Excuse me, ladies, may I be of assistance?"

"You taking the piss?" a duffel-coated octogenarian asked.

"No."

"Battersea Dogs Home!" she barked.

I scanned the horizon and said, "Twenty-eight degrees northeast." I yanked a notebook out of my shirt pocket, ripped a miniature pencil from its spine and scribbled down a series of numbers. "In case you get lost, here are the co-ordinates." I tore the page out and handed it to the woman.

"Thanks, dear."

"No problem," I replied, before bomb-blasting towards the bus stop in a death-or-glory sprint. The doors were millimetres from closing, but I prised them open with my fingertips and threw myself on board, just as the bus accelerated to three or four miles per hour.

"Swipe your Oyster," the driver demanded.

"I don't carry seafood rations. They're a preventable poisoning risk."

"Contactless?"

I scanned a deniable credit card then assessed my fellow passengers for potential threats: schoolchildren, shoppers, and a comatose pisshead. Unpredictable, but, on balance, I thought I would probably survive the journey to Clapham.

09.24

I walked into the Job Centre, took cover beside a cheese plant, and surveyed my environment, making a mental note of any details that might prove significant. It was an apparently open and informal habitat, designed for aggravation-reduction, but there was an alarm on each desk and cameras observed everything; some from concealed positions. To my right, six males and two females sat on grey chairs in a low state of alertness; to my left, four Job Centre employees conducted interviews with a matching number of unemployed males. No one looked sufficiently awake to pose a threat.

A security guard ambled up to me and mumbled, "Number?"

"Name: William Tell, Rank: Ex-Sergeant, Number: 46523."

"Queue number. They only go up to ninety-nine." He nodded to his right. "Machine's over there."

"Thanks."

The guard was frail; dignified, disciplined and disintegrating, unquestionably ex-Forces. That was what twenty-two years of putting your life on the line got you - an insecure job in security, the minimum wage, and a joke uniform; watching CCTV, standing in supermarkets waiting for electronic gates to bleep and arresting single mothers for shoplifting. For me, security has always meant close protection, guerrillas, and booby traps. Exit One, Exit Two, Exit Three: woe betides anyone blocking Exit One. But this time, I wasn't looking for an exit; I was looking for an entrance, a way into Belladonna's Floral Deliveries.

I walked over to a plastic stand, pressed a button, and took a raffle ticket with the number seventy-eight printed across it. The electronic display read *twenty-three*.

If time couldn't be filled by action, rest techniques were required. I closed my eyes and focused on the rose fields of Outer Ggaga; petals of gold, scarlet, vermilion, cerise and cherry pink stretched to the horizon. My heart rate dropped, and I napped on my feet like a knackered stallion.

When a hand touched my shoulder, my body tensed, preparing to launch a flying roundhouse with a double-elbowed windpipe crush, but it was only the security guard.

"Your number's up."

"Thanks, mate."

I took a chair opposite a pasty teenager and made a swift facial inventory: features – doughy; hair – congealed; eyes - fearful. He sported an empty name badge, a manky Guns N'Roses t-shirt and a charity shop jacket. The lad looked as though he would be more at home fiddling with a computer than grappling with an enemy, and, frankly, I had seen more intimidating interrogators on board Walloon Zeppelins.

"Fill in this form." His voice was high and breathy, a badge of unfitness. I declined the boy's offer of a broken biro and delved into my ops pants for a fountain pen. I worked efficiently, making economical use of language, and conscientiously maintaining a high standard of legibility as I filled in the form.

The boy read through my answers, pursed his lips, and whistled silently.

"Any qualifications?"

"They're all deniable."

"Skills?"

"I can assemble a machine gun in four-point-three seconds."

"How about flat-pack furniture?"

"Any danger money in that?"

"No."

The boy entered the word *danger* into the computer's search engine. There was only one result. "Bar Achilles needs a doorman."

I had successfully completed stage one of my plan to insert myself into the most notorious florists in Wandsworth. I was about to head up security in their dodgy local.

11.12

I used the bendy bus ride to make final adjustments to my tie alignment, trouser crease, and boot shine. Everything appeared to be in order, so I alighted, checked the contact details and my scribbled notes – Ernie Bronze, deniable informant, but don't let on - and approached the rendezvous.

A sense of excitement raised my heart rate as I ascended the pungent stairway to the Bar Achilles office. A new assignment waited at the top: I would be a raw recruit once again, learning the ropes, acquiring core skills. Fair enough, it had not been the best of weeks, what with two decades of faultless army service being obliterated by a stampeding warthog. But every crisis is an opportunity and bar security offered a fresh shot at glory.

An unhinged door revealed a comatose barman flopped across a mouldy sofa. Directly above him, a dartboard dangled off the wall, rocking in time to a passing train. A few metres away, a human bullfrog, heavy-lidded, thickset, and weather-beaten, took aim at the board, a rose tattoo flexing on his bicep.

"Mr Bronze?" I enquired.

The bullfrog loosed the dart prematurely and it nose-dived into the brim of the barman's baseball cap.

"I've come about the job," I explained.

"Any experience of security work?"

"Yes."

"Well, it won't help."

I followed Bronze down a smelly staircase at the back of the room. The light bulb had been removed and I was tempted to pull a pair of night-vision goggles out of my ops pants. Bronze kicked open a fire door and we walked into a decimated dive. A shattered mirror ball illuminated wet ashtrays, sour wine, and spilt lager. Legless chairs sat on unsteady tables and blood bathed the remaining shards of what had once been a windowpane.

"It's a police initiative." Bronze perched on a pool table and picked up a cue; it had been snapped in half and one end was covered in human claret. "They want to concentrate all violent disorder in one location. They're happy for us to stay open until all the customers have knocked each other unconscious. We usually get through four or five windowpanes a week, but it's tax deductible."

"And you want me to keep everyone in line."

"No. Just turn a pair of blind eyes when it all kicks off and you'll do fine."

14.23

Proper preparation prevents piss-poor performance, as they say at Sandhurst, so I spent the hours before my first evening at Bar Achilles bathing my boots in leather shampoo, rubbing them in cream polish and buffing them with horsehair. As I prepared my footwear for my first tour of duty in Wandsworth, I watched mum dust the mantelpiece; lifting framed photographs as she worked. It was a complete record of my life: there I was as a baby, a school kid, a cadet - then as a fully-fledged squaddie receiving The Military Medal, The Distinguished Conduct Medal and The Gerrards Cross.

"Won any medals recently, son?"

"No, mum."

"Tell me if you do, love. Some of these photos are getting a bit dog-eared."

CHAPTER 8

I put Bill's journal down and rearranged my arse cheeks on the strip club carpet. It struck me that no motivational speech in the history of the western hemisphere could outweigh a mother's disappointment. I pictured this hero, a man decorated across the fiercest fields of war, yet ultimately felled by a maternal reproach. A sergeant major's yell or a football manager's bollocking had nothing on a mother's wrinkled frown. From close protection officer to doorman, Bill had certainly come down a bit in the world, but at least he had accepted his decline with dignity.

The next page in Tell's tale wasn't a diary entry, it was another felt-tip note, reading, "This seems like the right place to interrupt my journal with the first of the retarded intelligence officer's transcripts. They cost me Normal's Carabao Cup tickets, but it was only Norwich versus MK Dons, the seats had an obstructed view, and I support Crystal Palace."

Wow! I knew that secret service standards had fallen a tad since the times of Bond, Smiley, and Burgess, but this was pitiful. Traitors used to exchange confidential information for their mistress's lives, new identities in Moscow, or Monte Carlo mansions, rather than unwanted tickets to unpopular cup competitions. Sometimes, I despaired of the younger generation.

I settled down and began to peruse the next page. There were no praying mantis stains, and it could not have looked more official. The header read, "National Stealth Service – Confidential", and it seemed to record a conversation between a senior spook referred to simply as "F", and a trainee named George Gurney, who had to be the retarded intelligence officer in question.

NATIONAL STEALTH SERVICE

Transcription - Appraisal Meeting

Recorded: Friday, 15 May, 9.04 a.m:

Present: "F" (Head of Operational Discretion, National Stealth Service) and George Gurney (Trainee Junior Watcher, Remedial Unit, National Stealth Service).

Appraisal exercise: to examine trainee's surveillance performance on previous evening's assignment (Thursday 14 May).

   F: Ready, Gurney?
   GURNEY: Bit tired, F.
   F: Describe the suspects' vehicle.
   GURNEY: A souped-up stretch Bedford.
   F: Distinguishing features?
   GURNEY: It had "Belladonna's Floral Deliveries" sprayed across the bonnet in paisley lettering.
   F: Route taken?
   GURNEY: Wandsworth High Street.
   F: And the suspects?
   GURNEY: The florists?
   F: The suspected florists.
   GURNEY: They really are florists, F.
   F: And they're also suspects, Gurney. Describe them.

GURNEY: Rankin: driver, muscular and hairless - jaw swollen by steroids. Leonard: front passenger, sinuous, thin skinned, prominent veins – looks like he's been peeled. Potter: the boss, colossal Kenyan in a rust-red robe, sharing the back seat with a bouquet of exotic flowers.

F: Did the concealed microphones record without phasing this time?

GURNEY: Yes, but we'd get broadcast quality sound if you'd let me radio mic them personally.

F: You mean attach microphones to their collars?

GURNEY: Yes, F.

F: Wouldn't that rather give the game away?

GURNEY: Suppose so.

F: Where were the bugs concealed?

GURNEY: Glove compartment, gear stick and handbrake.

F: Subtle.

GURNEY: Thanks.

F: Let me see the transcript.

GURNEY: Sorry about the bubble-tea stains, F.

F: Perhaps you'd better read it.

GURNEY: Okay, but my acting's a bit mediocre.

F: It's not about acting, it's about national security.

GURNEY: I know.

F: Get on with it then.

GURNEY: Shall I do the voices?

F: Just read the transcription in full, including the names of each person of interest, and any visual descriptions from the covert cameras.

GURNEY: Here you go, sir.

Gurney reads out the covert, in-vehicle recording of the suspected florists:

RANKIN: Poor old Butterworth.

LEONARD: He didn't deliver.

POTTER: Dying's an art, killing's a science and Buster was no Newton.

LEONARD: But he'd have won the Turner Prize for bleeding.

POTTER: I do hope you cleared up after yourself.

LEONARD: Spick and span, boss.

End of recording.

Appraisal continues.

F: Is that it?

GURNEY: During the journey, yes.

F: What was their destination?

GURNEY: Bar Achilles.

F: Owned by Ernie Bronze.

GURNEY: He's an informant, but he hates talking about it.

F: That's probably what makes him an effective informant.

GURNEY: I don't think being an informant is anything to be ashamed of. I'd want people to know.

F: There's a reason you're in The Remedial Unit, isn't there?

GURNEY: Probably, yes.

F: Time of arrival at Bar Achilles?

GURNEY: 23.27, but my watch is a bit wrong. It was before closing time.

F: Bar Achilles only closes during the day.

GURNEY: Really?

F: Ernie Bronze, has been working with us for a not inconsiderable period. We are well aware of his opening hours.

GURNEY: Shall I read some more?

F: Where was the surveillance this time?

GURNEY: Bug in the dartboard. Cameras in the lampshade, sofa and safe.

F: Go on then.

GURNEY: Can I do the voices this time?

F: Please don't.

GURNEY: Okay.

F: But do read out anything significant captured by our hidden cameras.

GURNEY: How will I know if it's significant.

F: You probably won't, will you. Just read them all out.

GURNEY: Can I do them in a Siri-style voice?

F: No.

GURNEY: Okay. Here goes:

Bar Achilles. The suspected florists enter Ernie Bronze's office. Potter hands Bronze the exotic bouquet.

BRONZE: You shouldn't have.

POTTER: How's business?

BRONZE: Can't complain.

RANKIN: Many fatalities?

BRONZE: Not really. Our monthly average is well down on last year.

LEONARD: Police happy?

BRONZE: Delighted.

End of recording.

Appraisal continues.

F: Gurney.

GURNEY: What?

F: You really don't have to do the voices.

GURNEY: Sorry, F. I got carried away.

F: Is that it?

GURNEY: No. They moved downstairs to the bar.

F: Describe it.

GURNEY: It's dark, smelly, and dangerous. The drinks are rubbish. The cocktails come in mugs, the pints contain more water than beer, and the wine is poured from cartons that went out-of-date in the twentieth century. People go there after they've got pissed somewhere better.

F: You ascertained that from the camera descriptions?

GURNEY: No. I used to be a regular.

F: How about the VIP area?

GURNEY: That's a completely different story. There's decent booze and table service.

F: Surveillance devices?

GURNEY: There's a phantom feed from their CCTV system for the public area. Pinhole cameras and mics are built into the private tables. Bronze bases himself in the VIP area later in the evenings so he can conduct business while keeping an eye on the pissheads.

F: Jolly good.

GURNEY: Thanks, F. Is that it?

F: The transcript, Gurney. You've forgotten to read it.

GURNEY: Sorry, F. Here you go:

The suspected florists take their places at Bronze's Private Table. A barman serves them pink cocktails. Potter inverts the bouquet. Gems fall onto table. Bronze scrambles to pick them up.

POTTER: Don't bother.

RANKING: These weren't cut from our diamond.

LEONARD: They weren't cut from any diamond.

POTTER: He was your fence, Bronze, but we'll mend him for you.

BRONZE: Done.

LEONARD: He will be.

POTTER: Cheers.

BRONZE: Cheers.

RANKIN: How's your doorman?

BRONZE: Sixth one this week. Small. I'd give him an hour.

End of recording.

Appraisal continues.

GURNEY: This is where it switches to the phantom CCTV feed, F.

F: In the public area?

GURNEY: Yes. F?

F: Gurney?

GURNEY: Just an idea, F, but CCTV footage is so slow and static. If the cameras were handheld by a proper crew, it would be much more dynamic and visually engaging.

F: And much more bleeding obvious.

GURNEY: Suppose so, F. Just a thought.

F: Who is this doorman?

GURNEY: Funny little bloke. Dressed like an estate agent.

F: Go on then, read the CCTV tape description.

GURNEY: Okay. Here it is:

Tiny Doorman stands motionless. To his right, a busker sleeps on top of a guitar. A big-bellied man in a Charlton Athletic football shirt pokes Tiny Doorman in the chest. Tiny Doorman remains motionless. A teenager pulls Tiny Doorman's tie. Tiny Doorman remains motionless. Tall man in suit pours a pint over Tiny Doorman's head. Tiny Doorman remains motionless. Customers jeer from bar stools. Tiny Doorman remains motionless. Pool players halt match and square up to Tiny Doorman. Tiny Doorman elbows both pool players simultaneously in the face, headbutts Charlton Athletic fan, kicks bar stools from under teenager and eight other onlookers, grabs guitar from busker and smashes it over head of tall man in suit.
End of recording.

Appraisal continues.
GURNEY: Wow!
F: Calm down, Gurney.
GURNEY: Sorry, F. It's just I really wish I could do that.
F: You'll get to do some combat training if you make it through your probationary period. How did our florists react to the fracas?
GURNEY: There's one more bit of transcript to go. They go down to the bar to survey the wreckage.
F: Very well, but please don't do the voices.
GURNEY: I'll try not to:

Bar has sustained major damage to its furniture and infrastructure. Suspected florists enter, applauding Tiny Doorman's efforts. Bronze and Potter approach Tiny Doorman. Tiny Doorman salutes.
BRONZE: It's not even midnight and all my customers are unconscious.
TINY DOORMAN: I had to neutralize the threat, sir.
BRONZE: You're fired.
POTTER: (to Tiny Doorman) Looking for a job?
End of recording.

Appraisal continues.
F: Interesting, Gurney. What do we know about this doorman?"
GURNEY: He's very small, F.

F: How small?
GURNEY: Teeny-weeny.
F: Anything else?
GURNEY: Diddly squat, F.
End of appraisal.

CHAPTER 9

I have had my fair share of appraisals, and they all led to me being fired, arrested, or investigated by the Health and Safety Executive. Essentially, appraisals are formalised bullying: your boss interrogates you about your work, lays into your failings, and lists all the ways in which they hate you. But young Gurney was so thick, he was able to ride out his boss's withering comments undamaged. Sometimes, stupidity can be a superpower.

Speaking of stupidity, it seemed that The National Stealth Service were blitheringly clueless about Bill's true identity. Not just Gurney, but F as well. Did they not track the return of deniable operatives from officially non-existent countries? If not, what on Earth did I pay my taxes for? I know I am on benefits, but my point is still valid – The National Stealth Service are clearly a bunch of tools, and not the sharpest ones in the box.

Belladonna's Floral Deliveries were a bit of an enigma. Leonard and Rankin seemed about as suited to floristry as Wagner mercenaries, and what is a stretch Bedford when it's at home? An extremely long van? A bit like a stretch limo without the luxury, but with the space to store a couple of ladders and a cement mixer? God only knew. Anyway, some spook had rigged the thing with hidden cameras and microphones. It can't have been Gurney, or they would have found them by now.

Bronze was a National Stealth Service stooge, and he was fully aware that his premises were rigged with recording equipment. From the florists' conversation, it appeared that Leonard and Rankin had assassinated a fence who had substituted fake diamonds for the genuine article. The fence was Buster Butterworth, which was about as common a name as Cuthbert Huntsman, so this had to be Bill's assailant at Outer Ggaga's National Library-Brothel. It was odds-on that the diamond in question was the one found by Stanley the Semi-Pygmy and traded for a Bentley with Forestière, the randy but dead Father of The Brotherhood. Was Potter, Belladonna's Mister Big, connected to The Brotherhood? He was Kenyan, and big in flowers, so I couldn't rule it out. In many ways, things had been much simpler in the Walloon Republic of Outer Ggaga.

The next page featured another felt-tip note from Bill, reading, "Sorry about The National Stealth Service. They make Dad's Army look like the SAS. If I thought my journal alone would be enough to persuade you to avenge my death, then believe me, I would have held on to those Carabao Cup tickets and never persuaded Gurney to break the Unofficial Secrets Act. Gurney's limitations as a human may be all too obvious, but my story needs some independent corroboration. There is a substantial involuntary contribution from the police to come, but first, more of my journal. I know you probably have no idea why you have been chosen to avenge my death, but you will by the time you reach the end of the documents. I am counting on you."

It was nice to be needed. Normally, I am entirely surplus to requirements, a perennial spare prick at the proverbial wedding. Now, I had a role – work through the bumf, solve Sergeant Tell's murder, then murder whoever had murdered him. Simple! I settled down and got stuck into the next chunk of Bill's shenanigans, which seemed to continue the morning after he had been fired by Bronze and hired by Potter:

JOURNAL – EX-SERGEANT BILL TELL

MUM'S FLAT, LONDON BOROUGH OF WANDSWORTH

Friday 15 May, 07.30

Mum watched me attack a full English breakfast: three thick-sliced rashers, a blood pudding, a bloated Cumberland sausage, a mountain of mushrooms, a pair of eggs fried lovingly in lard, and some lightly toasted soldiers. No detail had been overlooked, and the table was fully equipped with racks, serviettes, and marmalade boats.

"So, dear," Mum poured me a second cup of tea. "How was your first night?"

"I made some useful contacts."

"Contacts?"

"Connections." I nursed an ache in my fist.

"Lovely, dear."

I sliced open an egg. I have always liked beginnings. I thought back to the night I had spent standing in the rain, waiting for the Wandsworth Army Recruiting Office to open. I was sixteen and aching to run around shooting people. Then there had been the first courses: *Combat Survival, Parachute Training, Winter Selection,* and *Interpretative Yomping,* all brilliantly backbreaking. The memories flooded back, and I came over all misty-eyed. I recalled my first tour of duty in Belfast, my first jungle posting, my first engagement behind enemy lines. None of these firsts had held any fear. There was no reason why my first day at the florists would be any different.

I kissed my mum goodbye and was about to head out when I eyeballed a parcel on our doorstep. "Expecting a delivery, mum?"

"Not today, love. *Matchstick Model Monthly* came last week."

I took a closer look at the address label, read my own name, and shuddered. I had only been back in the country a couple of days, and someone had already tracked me down. I had a job to go to, but luckily, I had allowed ample time to cover contingencies, so I retreated to my room to investigate.

There was an eight-hundred-page book - *Don Quixote* by some Muppet called Cervantes - and a pair of letters, one from Charles and another from Marie-Thérèse. Charles's was the heftiest, so I attacked it first:

Dear Bill,

We held a memorial service for your career today. As a mark of respect, everyone wore dwarf poppies and black, regimental armbands (the inflatable ones usually reserved for aquatic manoeuvres). The Embassy flag is flying at half-mast in mourning, Marie-Thérèse is inconsolable and The Deniables are dejected. They cancelled today's pre-dawn yomp and replaced it with three hours' silence in your honour.

I know you must be utterly miserable, but you are not alone, Bill. My career is also sliding down the S-bend. The Controller of BBC Thirteen has wielded the scythe and I am now show-less. Her exact words were, "We need a lean-forward deep-dive skewed 18-30, not an appointment-to-miss skewed senile." I haven't got the foggiest what she's banging on about, but the result is the same – no regular show, just the occasional appearance to cover special events – and we both know that special events are pretty thin on the ground in Outer Ggaga.

Forestière's death seems to have broken the link between the Walloons and The Brotherhood and there's an almighty battle for control of the rose fields. It is Routemasters versus Zeppelins all the way. The tartan nuns are ramming dirigible docking ports in their reinforced double-deckers. The Walloons can't land, so they're unleashing potpourri pause bombs. The effects are devastating – everything in range is freeze-framed, so the Walloon snipers can take their time picking off the missionaries. The Brotherhood responded with ground-to-Zeppelin missile launchers and the Semi-Pygmy Insurgency are provoking rose-border conflicts.

I will try to keep you abreast of events, but in the meantime, here's a note from Marie-Thérèse. I had no idea she had been setting you homework. You certainly are a dark horse.

Speak soon,
Charles Brithazard
Covert Correspondent, BBC Thirteen

Poor old Charles. He may be a useless pisshead, but he's a great bloke. I hope his life takes a cheerier about turn sharpish. I eyeballed the letter from Marie-Thérèse. A warm glow hugged my innards:

Dear Bill,

I am heartbroken. When I heard about you, I cried, and I have not stopped since. Thanks for returning the bike. I am so sorry I was out when you called. Buster Butterworth dragged me out to a Walloon jet strip, and it was quite an emotional goodbye. He had a briefcase handcuffed to his wrist, and his jet was stuffed with freshly cut roses

destined for Wandsworth.

Anyway, here's your homework: "Don Quixote: knight or nit?" Look after the book; it's my last copy. I really don't know how I am going to keep the library up to date.

Forever Yours,
Marie-Therese

The National Library-Brothel of Outer Ggaga

I stuffed the packaging, the letters and the Embassy-sized novel under my bed and headed off for the florists.

08.12

A heavy night of joyriding had left The Victory Estate looking post-apocalyptic. I marched through a graveyard of rust; conjoined wrecks had lain down their engines, sacrificed their windscreens and offered up their wheels to The Victory Estate's riders. I stifled a sob as I thought of the fine vehicles cut down in their prime and written-off in the cause of high-speed joy.

Taken literally, the walk into town seemed strewn with peril. Signs warned from every direction: *Hazard Alert - Moving Vehicles! Beware of the Barrier, Danger of Death, Caution: Keep Clear!* Municipal doom gripped Wandsworth more firmly than it did the death-plains of Liberia, the sniper-peaks of Afghanistan or the Semi-Pygmies' ancestral necropolis, where paranoia was only sensible.

08.42

I arrived early to conduct a thorough recce of the florists. I had been posted to a shopping parade; there was a luxury cushion vendor, a tapas bar, and an estate agent. The florists immediate easterly neighbour was *Granule Live Foods*, a delicatessen offering wheatgrass smoothies and books explaining "how to heal yourself with bee pollen" and "raise raw babies". The florist's westerly neighbour was *Hairy Geezer*, a gay barbershop. I assessed the threat-level as low-to-moderate. I've had a number of decidedly rum HQs in my time: Balkan bunkers, Afghan desert caves and bomb-proof Belfast blockhouses, but their entrances had always been protected by anti-rocket mesh rather than bouquets. Until now.

09.00

A neatly painted sign above the window display, read, *Belladonna's Floral Deliveries - No Questions Asked*. I fought my way through an indoor forest of gardenia and greeted my new comrades.

The training was intensive: Rankin taught me how to slice stems, seal tips and remove foliage; Leonard lectured on leaf reversal, stem curving and petal turning. By the end of the morning, I knew how to create contrasting harmonies in freestyle arrangements.

The regiment had taught me how to murder in a microsecond; now I could arrange a decent bouquet as well.

13.03

Lunch was healthy but nauseating: a carrot, aubergine, and couscous smoothie from *Granule Live Foods*; I have had tastier boil-in-the-bag rations on Angolan night-ops.

13.47

While I helped Leonard and Rankin load the stretch Bedford with chrysanthemums, fuchsia and bleeding heart, I could not forget the tang of liquidized aubergine. I decided to make conversation in the hope that it would take my mind off lunch.

"You make deliveries?" I asked.

"Yes," Leonard replied.

"We deliver people," Rankin added.

"You deliver people flowers?" I asked.

"No, we deliver people," Rankin replied.

"Flowers are involved," Leonard said.

"Makes sense," I said, none the wiser.

"It's all about timing," Rankin said.

"Life or death," Leonard said.

"And there's a system," Rankin said.

"One in the house," Leonard said.

"One on the street," Rankin said.

"And one in the van with the engine running," Leonard said.

"Sounds like overkill," I said.

"No," Leonard said.

"Just kill," Rankin said.

Five minutes later, we were speeding past Wandsworth's Southside Shopping Centre. Rankin drove, I sat beside him, and Leonard shared the back seat with a bunch of lilies.

"Let's keep this simple. I don't want to stain this suit." Leonard was dressed almost as smartly as I was.

"Worried about the pollen?" I asked.

"I'm not talking about the lilies."

Rankin pulled up outside a pawnbroker's shop. Two golden globes dangled from an iron rod; the third had dropped into the guttering.

Rankin remained at the wheel with the engine running while Leonard approached the reinforced door, buzzed, muttered into the intercom, and gained admittance.

My duty was to patrol the pavement. I had to treat the delivery as a live operation: a single oversight on my first engagement and I would be on a one-way ticket to Shitsville. Luckily, the quality of my eyeball reconnaissance has been mentioned in dispatches more often than I've had wet yomps.

I gathered combat intelligence in a systematic manner, starting with the delivery address. The pawnbroker's shop was set out like a mini-cab office with an empty space for customers and a wooden screen with a small service panel. There were two doors: a glass exterior one into the shop and a reinforced interior one leading behind the screen. Moving on to the exterior details, there was a gutted pub to the shop's left - its name had been eaten away by woodworm, so I had no idea what it was called. To the right, there was a grimy newsagent where every shelf was top shelf and next to that was *Petal's Private Shop*. It was dimly lit, so I decided to investigate further (I'm known for my aggressive patrolling). I peered in - lingerie-clad mannequins struck intriguing poses and decorative lights twinkled, illuminating shelves of rubber projectiles. The Private Shop's owner, presumably Petal, peeked around a mannequin and winked. I assessed that she represented little immediate risk, so I proceeded past the final shop on the parade, a damp-ridden hovel with a *Hygienic Body Piercings While You Wait* sign flickering in neon.

I had just executed an about turn when Leonard stormed out of the pawnbroker's shop and dived into the stretch Bedford. I noticed that he no longer had the flowers.

While Rankin revved the engine, I proceeded towards the passenger seat at a steady pace. *Never draw attention. Always be the grey man, even if you prefer brighter colours*, as it says on page one of The Deniable Handbook.

Leonard opened his window and screamed, "Get in, donkey dick!"

As a raw recruit, I knew I would have to earn the respect of my comrades, so I obeyed on reflex and the stretch Bedford tore off.

Leonard rapped a knuckle on the back of my head and yelled, "Is your skull fitted with a simulated occupancy device?"

I resisted the urge for reprisals and sat to attention.

Rankin turned to Leonard and asked, "Did you get Potter's Precious?"

"No, but I got the address of our next delivery before I handed him the lilies."

Floristry is clearly a complex game of cat and mouse. I resolved to get up to speed on the latest floricultural techniques and procedures as soon as humanly possible.

17.00

It wasn't a long walk home and I could hear The Victory Estate from half-a-mile away. The screeching swansongs of doomed vehicles finally freed from the restraints of The Highway Code were unmistakable. To me, it was heartrending to hear them perform to their maximum potential for the first and final time. But, as I approached, I saw that a crowd of kids were whooping, stamping, and punching the air as their mates put other people's cars through their death-throes.

I could have walked around the illegal racetrack, but that would have lacked character. This was my manor and I had just done an honest day's work at the florists, so I took a direct route through the high-speed carnage, silencing the crowd and forcing the joyriders to stand on their brakes, which, recognising me, they all did without fail.

17.45

I came home to a roast dinner fit for a battalion. Now, I've always been handy with a knife, so I got stuck into the carving. I pinned the lamb leg fatty side up, knob down and grasped the shank with a cloth, then worked systematically, slicing across the grain at a consistent forty-five-degree angle whilst maintaining an even pressure at all times. As I carved, mum tested me from Gertrude Jekyll's *Flower Decoration in the House*, a classic floricultural manual.

"VFB?" mum asked.

"Velvety frangipani blossoms."

"FVS?"

"Functional vase with spout."

"UPP?"

"Upright pieces of privet."

"Perfect."

'It's just like the regiment!' I lanced the lamb leg.

Sunday 17 May

Bedtime

I spent a quiet weekend wrestling with *Don Quixote*, stopping only for roast dinners with mum. She took great pleasure in watching me eat and teasing me about my childhood. Apparently, I'd had two imaginary friends called Trevor and Pete. Pete had helped me hone my DIY skills and Trevor had worked on my right hook.

Mum's matchstick model of Lincoln Cathedral was coming on a treat, and she had made a start on the miniature stained-glass windows. It was a dangerous task, so she had donned safety goggles for protection. I was so captivated watching her trace delicate trails of foliage onto tiny, fragmented diamonds of opalescent glass that I took my eyes off the Corby and over-pressed my trousers.

Don Quixote was a mammoth mission, even longer than the *Regimental Combat Handbook*. Luckily, I had been trained to digest formidable quantities of information under severe time pressure and, scanning the paperback doorstop at supersonic speed, I can report that the ancient Spanish anecdote is a bloody good read, crammed with do-or-die quests, heart-pounding action sequences and ropey old poems. Quixote is no nit; he's a knight - simply because that's what he believes he is. He may well have OD'd on the training, but his honour code is faultless, his bravery is medal-worthy and he's admirably blind to danger. Fair enough, he's not young and his kit is seriously substandard, but he can pack a punch with his blade, his never-say-die battle-hunger and his bollocks-to-the-rest-of-you mindset. I bloody loved the mad old codger.

I knocked off an essay to this effect with a quick, "Missing you loads, Marie-Thérèse. Wish you were in Wandsworth," and shoved it down the throat of the nearest covert pillar-box.

CHAPTER 10

I have never seen a covert pillar box, but I suppose they wouldn't be covert pillar boxes if they were easy to spot.

Bill Tell was a funny fish: superhumanly capable, yet pathetically naïve. The blithering pilchard genuinely seemed to believe that he was a florist's assistant rather than an assassin's lookout. He needed an education, but not the kind you get from ancient Spanish novels. It's odd to say this about a Special Forces hero, but he had led a sheltered life, cosseted in conflict zones.

Had Bill ever been to a strip club? Probably not. If he was still alive, I would take him to one. But probably not this one. This one lacked both atmosphere and strippers.

I cast my mind back to yesterday. After the incident with my three ex-wives, the Rottweiler, and the gambling addict's e-scooter, I had begun my bender with pre-drinks on a bench. Drinking alone is one of life's most exquisite pleasures. The rounds are cheap, the company is reliable, and you can choose your own music. The six-pack really set me up for the evening ahead. Or so I imagine. What happened afterwards remained a total mystery.

The next page in Bill's dossier was a felt-tip note reading, "Here's the second bunch of transcripts from the retarded intelligence officer and some notes he nicked from Wandsworth Nick. The transcripts are obviously a day ahead of the nicked Nick notes; otherwise, he wouldn't have had time to nick them."

Custard-clear, but I sort of knew what he meant:

NATIONAL STEALTH SERVICE

Transcription - Appraisal Meeting,

Tuesday 19 May, 11.15 a.m.

Present: "F" (Head of Operational Discretion, National Stealth Service) and George Gurney (Trainee Junior Watcher, Remedial Unit, National Stealth Service).

Appraisal exercise: assessment of a covertly monitored local police force murder investigation.

GURNEY: Sorry I'm late, F. I got locked out and spent the night in a recycling bin.

F: Well, Gurney, if you pass the probationary period, there's an admirable breaking-and-entering module.

GURNEY: It could come in proper handy, F. That's the third time it's happened this month.

F: Then you have an excellent incentive, don't you, Gurney?

GURNEY: Yes, F.

F: Today, I would like you to furnish me with an assessment of the local constabulary's investigation into Friday's incident at the pawnbrokers.

GURNEY: Can I just say that it's been a real eye-opener? I really had no idea it was so easy to nick info from the cozzers.

F: The Stealth Service have been doing it for decades, so I suppose the procedures are very well-established.

GURNEY: Maybe it's that, F, but I think it's more to do with their downright stupidity.

F: Thank you, Gurney, I'll make a note. Now, if you could begin by briefing me on the chief investigating officer and do try to maintain a measure of respect.

GURNEY: Okay, F, he's a bald bloke with a red beard and hairy ears; he's got a boxer's nose, he's not short of chins and his belly looks like it's about to give birth. He only ever listens to folk music and protest songs; his office is plastered in Health and Safety notices, Police Federation posters and summaries of the Working Time Directive; and everyone calls him *Chief Inspector Stalin*.

F: What do you conclude from the Force's decision to assign this particular officer to the investigation?

GURNEY: Well, I shouldn't think they're in a hurry to solve it, F.

F: Very astute.

GURNEY: Stalin's on work-to-rule, so he didn't visit the death scene for nearly three days. He won't do weekends, you see, F.

F: And the assisting officer?

GURNEY: A big, angry bloke with arms like tree-trunks, a torso like a fridge-freezer and a face like Conor McGregor. He spends his working hours threatening suspects and all his spare time helping his wife re-home aquatic birds. He was runner-up in last year's Wandsworth Common duck-calling contest, so the braver cozzers call him *Sergeant Mallard*. His real name's DS Donald, poor bloke, so he can't really escape the duck association either way, if you see what I mean?

F: And did you succeed in making a covert copy of DCI Stalin's case notes?

GURNEY: The photocopier jammed.

F: Did you adopt an alternative strategy?

GURNEY: I called out an engineer.

F: You called out an engineer?

GURNEY: There was a number on the underside of the paper tray.

F: But you weren't meant to be in the station. We had sneaked you in under false pretences.

GURNEY: As a junior social worker.

F: Correct. We had also gone to great lengths to ensure that Stalin was at a Police Federation meeting.

GURNEY: About Trip Hazards.

F: Correct. And we had supplied you with a micro-camera. Why didn't you use that to photograph the case notes?

GURNEY: Forgot.

F: You forgot?

GURNEY: Sorry. Anyway, the engineer was a really friendly bloke. He showed me how to use the document feeder. We got the copies made in no time.

F: We?

GURNEY: Me and the engineer. We worked as a team. It sped things up no end.

F: So, he'd recognise you again?

GURNEY: I should think so. We got on like a house on fire.

F: Next time you're undercover, Gurney, try not to make friends.

GURNEY: Okay, F. Here are the case notes. Sorry, most of the paper's pink. We ran out of white:

Chief Inspector Stalin, Wandsworth CID

Case Notes – Monday 18 May

Location: My office.

Risk Assessment: Multiple trip hazards in station corridors, danger of spinal discomfort due to poor alignment of chairs and desks, risk of buttock cramp due to absence of substantial cushions, screen brightness excessive due to substandard computer purchases, insufficient ventilation.

Time since afternoon tea break: One hour thirty minutes.

I am absolutely bloody fuming. If senior management seriously expect me and my officers to exceed our tour of duty on a re-rostered rest day, then they are obliged to provide a fallback sandwich option. And what did we get today? Not even a ruddy pork scratching. Obviously, we all understand that ritualistic gangland executions demand a degree of flexibility, but we must not lose sight of the fact that regular nutritional intake and hydration are essential to maintaining peak operational performance. A single afternoon tea-break is woefully inadequate.

I also want to put on record my disgust at the treatment of Sergeant Donald. Just because he's a duck-nut, does not give senior management *carte blanche* to issue wholesale complaints against the man whenever they're looking for an Aunt Sally. Nineteen complaints against a single officer within a month constitute victimization and harassment of the highest order. There have never been any witnesses outside of the criminal fraternity, and, in any case, he always had shamefully insufficient back up, being entirely alone with the complainant in the cell on each occasion.

Now that I've got that off my chest, I had better give you a run-down of today's shambles. DS Donald picked me up at *The Blind Beggar*. They do a Full English Breakfast, and second helpings are half-price, so it's excellent value. Traffic was a buggeration as always, but at least it gave me and the sergeant some quality time together. Here's what happened – I've plonked it down in novel form, as it's a fine socialist art-form championed by comrades like Orwell, Steinbeck, and Tressell, and a man has got to find a way of putting his own mark on paperwork:

Time since breakfast: One hour.
Location: Police car (unmarked).
Risk Assessment: Aggressive driver (my sergeant), uneven road surfaces, mild drizzle impeding visibility.

"How's the missus?" Donald asked.

"Some men have trophy wives. I won the wooden spoon."

"Sorry to hear that, Guv."

"My marriage started as a drinking club for two. Now she's off the booze and I'm off the fags. She gazes longingly into my glass. I look adoringly into her fumes."

"At least desire's not dead, Guv."

I put some folk music on the stereo and hummed along to a socialist folk ballad about the hardships endured by herring fishermen. Donald closed his eyes, no doubt to concentrate on the exquisite pathos of the lyrics.

I followed Federation procedure to ensure that Donald parked safely outside the crime scene, donning a high visibility jacket, and guiding him in with a set of semaphore flags.

As we walked into the pawnbroker's, I conducted a provisional risk assessment of the murder scene. There were several trip hazards, access and egress were restricted and the shop's Health & Safety Certificate, though prominently displayed, was several weeks out-of-date. I said hello to the scene-of-crime officers, but they were too busy taking photographs and fingerprinting surfaces to acknowledge my comradely greeting. I have never had much time for forensic-led intelligence, with its evidence networks, strategic data lumps and genetic photo-fitting. Who wants to rely on specks of dandruff, when you've got a hulking great gut to go with?

While the SOCOs fiddled about with their microscopic samples, Donald and I looked at the big picture: gunmetal furniture rested on an ash-grey carpet peppered with diamonds, and a bearded body lay sprawled in the corner, clutching a bouquet.

"What kind of reprobate would give a pawnbroker a bunch of lilies, blow his brains out then leave the corpse enough rocks to keep Kylie Jenner in tiaras for decades?" I couldn't help asking.

"An absent-minded romantic, Guv," Donald speculated.

"Any witnesses?"

"The woolly suits have given the parade a quick once-over. The body-piercer was engrossed in a bellybutton, the newsagent was ordering porn mags and the pub-gutters were ripping out the urinals at the time, Guv."

"So, there's not a lot to go on?"

"They reckon the sex shop's worth checking out."

"Did they do a risk assessment?"

"Probably. They were in there long enough."

Time until lunch: Two hours thirty-five minutes.

Location: Petal's Private Shop.

Risk Assessment: Inadequate lighting, moral hazards from all angles, unpredictable member of the public (proprietress).

Petal, the Private Shop proprietor, was no Rembrandt. She had a Mister Punch profile; laughter lines had ravaged her face and her voice was as gravely as Brighton Beach.

'Right, bitches, we've got Jessica Rabbit, Flipper the Dipper, Disco Dick, and an extensive range of strap-ons. Or perhaps you might prefer a pair of remote-controlled vibrating panties?"

"We're coppers," I said.

"Takes all sorts," Petal said, handing me a clockwork cock ring.

"Did you know the deceased?" Donald asked.

"Yes, Babes, he was South African. His vowels were flat."

I gave DS Donald the clockwork cock ring and began rifling through a rack of PVC nurse's uniforms.

"See anyone acting suspiciously?" DS Donald asked.

"Oh, I remember." Petal paused. "He was instantly forgettable."

"Who?" I asked, toying with a PVC stethoscope.

"Little bloke. Smart. Peered through the window and loitered."

"Can you describe him?" I asked.

"I just have. Look, I'm not a poet I'm a celebrity merkin maker."

"Really?" DS Donald asked.

"Not only do I make merkins for celebrities, I also happen to be a celebrity who makes merkins." Petal handed us a pair of signed publicity photographs, depicting herself astride a BMW bonnet in a transparent cat suit. "I was on *Auto Geezers*."

"Thought you looked familiar," Donald said.

"Well, go and find him then," Petal said. "If you ask me, I've got more testosterone in my left nipple than both of you lesbians put together."

"Thank you for your help." I tripped over a length of bondage rope. (I've now filled in an accident report form in triplicate, as per procedure).

"Parting gift," Petal handed Donald a ribbon-tied box.

"Thanks," Donald said. "What is it?"

"A pair of crotchless panties for a pair of crotchless coppers," Petal shoved us out of the door.

Time until lunch: Fifty minutes.

Location: Police car (unmarked).

Risk assessment: Aggressive driver (my sergeant), uneven road surfaces, traffic wardens, other motorists.

The South Circular was heavily constipated, but at least we had the stereo to cheer us up. As we edged towards our fifth set of temporary lights, a tenor banjo, a descant recorder and the combined vocal talents of Pete Seeger and Lee Hays rendered *In Dead Earnest*, a witty ditty about dying and being turned to compost.

A passing prat in a Porsche shouted an insult at my fertilizer ballad, so I switched on a siren and plonked it on the roof.

"Are you serious, Guv?"

"Deadly."

"What are we going to do him for, Guv?"

"I'll work that out once we've nabbed him."

Donald swung us around and powered after the folk-abuser.

Petal's panty gift flew off my lap, landed on the gear stick and was a contributory factor in the subsequent accident. The report forms were an embuggerance, and the London Borough of Wandsworth may be down a pair of bollards, but I had stood up for what I believe in – British Folk Music.

NATIONAL STEALTH SERVICE

Transcription - Appraisal Meeting

Tuesday 19 May, 11.45 a.m.

Present: "F" (Head of Operational Discretion, National Stealth Service) and George Gurney (Trainee Junior Watcher, Remedial Unit, National Stealth Service).

Appraisal exercise: assessment of a covertly monitored local police force murder investigation.

GURNEY: Fascinating stuff, F.
F: I would have thought it somewhat depressing.
GURNEY: Really, F? It cheered me up no end.
F: It's a shocking indictment of modern policing.
GURNEY: But there's nothing modern about Stalin.

F: Correct, lamentably. You will, of course, continue to appraise me of the ongoing investigation?

GURNEY: Okay, F. It was the florists, wasn't it?

F: Who shouted abuse at the folk music?

GURNEY: No. It was the florists who killed the pawnbroker.

F: How ever did you come to that conclusion, Gurney?

GURNEY: The lilies and the diamonds.

F: And?

GURNEY: He was Bronze's fence, wasn't he?

F: Undoubtedly.

GURNEY: The fence that crossed the florists. They told Bronze they were going to "mend" him, didn't they?

F: According to your Bar Achilles transcripts, you're quite correct, yes.

GURNEY: Then why didn't we stop them?

F: The National Stealth Service is not in the habit of protecting unscrupulous pawnbrokers.

GURNEY: But we could have prevented a murder.

F: He was a South African citizen.

GURNEY: What if they kill someone else?

F: *When* they kill someone else, do try to remember to press *record* on the remote camera control console. Footage from Belladonna's stretch Bedford would have proved most illuminating this time and I'm sure it will again.

GURNEY: Sorry, F. Do you want me to nick Stalin's notes again?

F: Yes. But this time, use the biro cam, not the photocopy engineer.

GURNEY: Okay, F.

F: I've looked into your diminutive doorman, Gurney, and there's more to him than meets the eye. He has been in receipt of diplomatic packages from a sensitive location in Sub-Saharan Africa. I think there's a military connection. Indubitably deniable.

GURNEY: Gosh, F.

F: Quite.

CHAPTER 11

The British police are the best in the world. Not.

How could a militant bureaucrat like Chief Inspector Stalin run an investigation into anything more important than a missed meal break? And his sidekick was no better. What was a duck-loving thug doing with a badge? It was no surprise the pair of plonkers had been humiliated by a merkin-maker.

The National Stealth Service won't be winning any medals either. I'm not unpatriotic, but Gurney was a catastrophe on legs and F wasn't exactly the sharpest of spanners. Why on Earth had it had taken him this long to discern that there might be something martial about Bill's background? The bloke couldn't be more soldierly if he had been the lovechild of Chris Ryan and Andy McNab.

But right now, Bill Tell wasn't on the battlefield, he was at the florists. He hadn't killed anyone recently, but his colleagues almost certainly had. The tell-tale bouquet placed Belladonna's Floral Deliveries firmly in the frame. I wondered how long it would take Bill to wise up to the true nature of the florists:

JOURNAL – EX-SERGEANT BILL TELL

London Borough of Wandsworth

Monday 18 May, 08.03

After spending a weekend lost in La Mancha, my mind was ready to accept whatever challenges reality threw at it, even another letter from Charles. I was surprised to receive it so soon after Friday's update, but I could only assume that things in Outer Ggaga were in a state of flux:

Dear Bill,

The whole place has gone potty and I'm running around like a blue-arsed chicken. The Brotherhood are too busy ramming Zeppelin pods to pay the flower gatherers and even the most Ultra Loyalist Semi-Pygmies are slacking. The roses are wilting unharvested and the whole floral economy is going to rot.

The missionaries are in a right pickle: The Sisters are merciless, The Brotherhood is losing its religion and, when it comes to ruthless skirmishing and violent reprisals, there's no one quite like Grandma Superior.

The Semi-Pygmies have seized their moment and they're on the march. Stanley's Bentley is leading the charge. They've stuffed Esther the crocodile and adopted her as a revolutionary symbol. Apparently, the vast beast was floating in a papyrus swamp, dead as a doornail. Just imagine the size of the predator that did for it! Maybe there's some kind of killer plesiosaur in the depths. Anyway, the little chaps have designed some rather nifty Insurgency flags sporting the stuffed croc's head. I'll send you a photocopy if you like.

The Walloons have imposed a curfew, but the missionaries don't get out much and the Semi-Pygmies live outdoors, so it's been a bit of a damp squib.

The Deniables were rudderless for an hour or two, but Kes has filled your yomping boots. He's thick with the Ambassador, inseparable. What they're up to though, I have no idea.

Wee Jock wanted to challenge the NGOs to a pitch-and-putt tournament, but Kes put the kibosh on it. The lads are looking pretty droopy, to be honest – I think Kes is struggling in the popularity stakes. Still, he is the new boss, so they are all going along with his orders. Not that he's ordering much right now. There's damn all intervention as far as I can see. I am sure you'd have tried to patch things up between the Walloons, The Brotherhood, and the Semi-Pygmies. But not old Kes; he's done nothing. It's almost as if he and The Ambassador are happy to sit back and watch civil war break out.

My career has continued to be side-lined and I've been asked to monitor covert news bulletins. I am frustratingly ahead of the covert headlines. I know what has happened while it's happening, but I can't tell anyone. The Secret Services can be bloody cagey.

To help pass the time, I have been learning the Hidden Journalism Code; it's based on Irish Braille and Lithuanian Morse – bumpy dots and dashes. It takes an age to unscramble.

I am looking for an out, but I am not sure how covert media experience will look on the old CV. How's your job search? Managing to explain away the deniable decades?

Covertly Yours,

Charles

I'm not sure whether to tell Charles that I've got a job as a florist. I have got a feeling that Kes and Wee Jock might think it's a bit poncy for an ex-squaddie, but then again, they haven't met my colleagues.

09.00

I fought my way through Belladonna Floral Deliveries' window display, only to be ambushed by my comrades in petal-pushing.

"Potter wants a word," Leonard said.

"It's about the delivery," Rankin said.

"And how you didn't deliver," Leonard said.

"Thanks," I replied. I knew I was due for a bollocking, but a full-frontal verbal assault held few fears for me. My old Sergeant Major would practice his insults for hours, mining dictionaries and thesauruses for new forms of abuse. Once, I had been carpeted for over-zealous bayonet use and I had consigned his rebuke to memory in case it ever came in useful: "You granny-shagging nonce you rectum-tunnelling tapeworm you weeping sore on Satan's nob you flesh-eating maggot you ugly great mutant you walking emetic you fetid heap of rat carcasses you cretinous vegetable you lobotomised inbred horrible little man!"

The bloke thought grammar was for liberals.

I marched through to Potter's office. Its satinwood walls were crammed with lotus blossoms, Madonna lilies and azalea swags; the carpet was decorated with ivory rose cartouches and a paper-white Narcissus rested on an Edwardian desk. Potter sat behind it, facing away from me, and apparently contemplating an oil painting. It was as wide as Potter was tall and represented an African Queen-style steamboat ploughing its way through what looked like an endless green field.

"Day one and he's looking in when he should be looking out," Potter said. "Next time, he's the one going in."

"With flowers," I added, whilst standing to attention.

"Silence! I'm holding a meeting with myself. You're only here to take the minutes."

I pulled a miniature notebook and pencil out of my shirt pocket.

"He has killed before, that's obvious," Potter continued. "A simple delivery shouldn't be a problem, as long as he's not busy window-shopping." Without turning, Potter handed me a gift card. "Here's the address. Ask Leonard for a nice bunch of dahlias."

"Bunch of dahlias, sir."

"But don't let her have it until she's handed you The Precious."

I've penetrated Scud Boxes, snatched hysterical hostages from blazing aircraft in mid-air and outfoxed Danish narco-masterminds. Now, I had a new mission, even though I didn't really understand what Potter was on about.

CHAPTER 12

So, Kes had supplanted Tell in The Deniables, and civil war was raging in Outer Ggaga. Things were almost as bad in Wandsworth, where Bill was being cajoled into assassinating a woman Potter believed to have the diamond from Mount Heha. Why was he going along with it? Bill was either a spineless numpty, or he was up to something. My money was on the latter.

As a life coach, I have often advised my clients against going along with things. It is much better to be awkward, to go against the flow, and to be your own man. That's probably why I am unemployed.

Next up, was a felt-tip note from Bill reading, "Here are some more of the notes Gurney the retarded intelligence officer nicked from Stalin the copper. Gurney probably forgot to give them to F because there's no mention of them in his transcripts. Either that, or Gurney simply didn't give me all of the Stealth Service transcripts. Two rival cock-up theories with equal merit. If I had access to The Deniables' central computer system at Weston-super-Mare, I could run a full *Moronic Behaviour Analysis*, but I don't so I can't. Good luck mate, I'm counting on you."

Chief Inspector Stalin, Wandsworth CID

Case Notes – Monday 18 May

Time until dinner: Three hours twenty minutes.
Location: My office.
Risk Assessment: One window panel broken – possible danger of hypothermia if temperature drops dramatically (currently quite warm). Printer feeding mechanism unreliable: ink stains and fingertip snags almost inevitable.

I bled all over the post-mortem results. Workplace hazards do have a habit of surprising me. I had been a bit hasty with the envelope and my forefinger paid the price. Luckily, I am Designated First-Aider, so I was able to self-medicate until Donald had finished reading out the pathological waffle about the deceased pawnbroker.

"So, it was the bullet through the temple that killed him rather than the lilies?"

"Yes, Guv."

"Pathologists - what would we do without them?"

"Don't know, Guv."

"Any news from the insurers?"

"Yes. The killers didn't take any diamonds."

"Why would a crummy Wandsworth pawnshop have so much bling on the premises?"

"No idea, Guv, but they found this in his trousers," Donald shook the claret-covered envelope and a business card plonked onto the desk. It read, *Butterworth & Butterworth - Contemporary Ice Sculptures* in a frosty typeface.

"Guv?"

"What is it, Sergeant?"

"I've never seen an ice sculpture before."

"They do sound good, don't they?"

"Can we go, Guv? Please."

"Better wrap up warm."

Time until dinner: One hour fifty-seven minutes.
Location: Police Car.
Risk Assessment: aggressive driver (my sergeant), other motorists, uneven road surfaces.

After the folk music altercation and the bollards, our last car was a write-off, so The Super had downsized us to a Ford Fiesta as punishment.

The roads were snarled up again, so I had plenty of time to examine the scenery. If colour is a language, Wandsworth is only fluent in grey. Its shades don't leap out at you; they loiter in doorways. The shapes are no better - oblong cloud scratchers, flat blocks of concrete and mind-bending roundabouts. The gyratory system was clogged with an infinite cycle of near-stationary cars, destination Purgatory. Humanity had created its own helplessness. Growling engines, pointless honks, and nerve-shredding sound systems. Where did they come from? Where were they going? I certainly didn't know. At least we had a Northumbrian rope-makers' ballad on the stereo to keep our spirits up. Donald had taken to wearing a pair of orange blobs in his ears; he said it was to help him hear better, but they looked more like earplugs to me.

The windows of *Butterworth & Butterworth* were so heavily frosted that Donald and I could not detect a single ice-sculpture when we peered inside. Shame really - we were both quite excited.

When the door finally buzzed open, we stepped into an environment designed for huskies rather than humans. It was a Health and Safety nightmare: the cold bit into our skin, breathing was painful, and Donald began to shiver uncontrollably. Donald was kind enough to point out that at least I had my own blubber supply to fall back on.

Even though the shop-owner was wrapped up like an Eskimo, you could tell that he was an ugly great bruiser. We were too cold to speak, so Donald flashed him his badge.

Two duffel coats, a couple of bobble hats and a brace of mittens later, I was almost satisfied that working conditions were not in breach of any major Health and Safety legislation.

Butterworth's voice was a surprise. He looked like a bouncer but sounded like a ballerina. He gave us a tour of the premises, flouncing and pouting as he gesticulated dramatically. The main display was a suburban garden sculpted out of ice. There was a shed, a lawnmower, and a broken deckchair, all glittering and transparent.

"People assume ice sculpting is all about wedding swans and Christmas fantasies," Butterworth bimbled. "But I prefer realism."

After he had shown us ice-sculptures of a car park, a newsagent, and a bus queue, we got the message – no castles and princesses, just bloody mundane miserabilism.

Donald was deeply disappointed. "Got any ice reindeer?"

Butterworth looked disgusted. "We might have one in storage." He led us towards an industrial-sized freezer on the far side of the premises.

"Where's the other Butterworth?" I asked on the way.

"My sleeping partner?" Butterworth asked.

"Spare us the sordid details," Donald said.

I raised a warning eyebrow at my bigot-brained sergeant.

"The other Butterworth is in Africa," Butterworth said. "He imports roses."

"Your dad?" I ventured.

"No." Butterworth unlocked the freezer door and swung it towards him. "Twin brother." At that, he froze and keeled over in a vertical plunge.

While Donald checked the decked ice sculptor's pulse, I peered into the freezer. Entombed in a block of ice, covered in blood, and clutching a bouquet of roses was a bloke who could only be Butterworth's identical twin.

A testicle-freezing half-hour later, I was stood next to our pathologist, watching my sergeant and a dozen scene-of-crime officers struggle to lug the ice-coffined corpse into an ambulance. They didn't bother with artificial respiration.

"He'll need to thaw before I conduct the post-mortem," the pathologist said.

"Don't suppose they make microwaves big enough," I speculated.

"We can't rush it without compromising the corpse."

"Suicide?" I asked, for a laugh.

The pathologist shook his head. "We can probably rule out natural causes too."

"Time of death?"

"I usually go by body temperature and rigor mortis. But by the look of him, I'd say he's sub-zero and stiff as an Ice Pop."

"So?"

"So, he's probably been dead for a bit."

"Thanks a bunch." I stepped on the pathologist's toes with my full bodyweight.

The SOCOs lost their chalk in the snow and their tape wouldn't stick to the ice. The photographer had no wounds to record, and the Exhibits Officer had no clues to bag. There were no plastic sacks large enough to cover the deceased, and no witnesses. Sometimes, the logistics of death were illogical.

While all this was going on, the surviving Butterworth twin was pacing around his ice shed, shaking his head, and wiping away freezing tears. "I knew they'd kill Buster in the end."

"Who?" I asked.

"The florists. Roses were his license to criss-cross Africa with...other cargoes. His body might be in Wandsworth, but he sold his soul in the Walloon Republic of Outer Ggaga."

I looked at my sergeant. He obviously hadn't got a bloody clue where it was either.

CHAPTER 13

The cops had finally found out about Outer Ggaga. How a country had managed to hide for so long, I had no idea. It wasn't as if it could lie low in a mate's house or grow a moustache.

Buster Butterworth had been well and truly iced, poor sod. Judging by his encounter with Bill in Marie-Thérèse's National Library-Brothel, he was a crashing crime-bore but a mean fighter – no one else had matched Bill fist-for-fist or boot-for-boot. I wondered who'd had the gonads to put him in the deep freezer.

No one has ever accused me of being quick on the uptake, but even I could see that all this floristry malarkey was a cover for an illicit import-export business. When is an import-export business ever fully legit? It is always drugs, guns, or conflict diamonds, never candyfloss or cuddly toys.

Bill had acted on The Ambassador's instructions and infiltrated Belladonna's Floral Deliveries, but surely that didn't mean he had to do whatever that bunch of homicidal gangsters wanted. He was cheerfully skipping off to retrieve their conflict diamond and assassinate the woman who had it, as if this was as much a part of a florist's annual routine as Valentine's Day. Bill was only following orders, but I sincerely wished he wouldn't. I didn't want to have to avenge the death of a murdering moron.

The world can get a bit much sometimes, particularly when it comes to other people. Headphones can help, but they are not always enough to shut everything out. I recommend a life-cancelling helmet. It's easy to knock one up yourself – simply steal a motorbike helmet and wrap the visor in eighteen or nineteen layers of duct tape. Plonk it over your head and you have yourself a mobile sensory deprivation chamber.

Wherever you go, you can be completely oblivious of the world, with all its demands, irritations, and distractions. I took mine for a walk down Marylebone High Street and it was massively liberating, until I got run over by a dustcart.

I don't suppose Bill ever wanted to shut out the world. He seemed much more likely to look the world in the eyes and arm-wrestle it into submission:

JOURNAL – EX-SERGEANT BILL TELL

Monday 18 May, 11.13

While Leonard drove Belladonna's Floral Delivery stretch Bedford down Magdalene Road, I shared the back seat with a bouquet of dahlias and gazed out at Wandsworth Cemetery: a sculpture park of grimy angels, ivy-smothered tombs, and armless cherubs.

No doubt inspired by all that death, Rankin turned back to face me from the passenger seat. "How many people have you killed?"

"About four hundred and eighty," I hazarded.

"Bit of a temper," Leonard observed.

"I don't often miss."

"What were you doing in Africa?" Rankin asked.

"I was a BG."

"Sorry to hear about Maurice and Robin," Leonard said.

"Tragedy," Rankin said.

"I was a bodyguard. How did you know I was in Africa?"

11.31

The sun had broken cover, but it was that time of year when a blue sky was not to be trusted. The stretch Bedford eased past suburban streets of Neo-Georgian terraces, Mock Tudor semis, and executive cul-de-sacs, each boasting sparkling SUVs, lovingly nurtured lawns, and amateur topiary. Every home was whitewashed, apart from the odd rebellious lemon. I thought that security precautions were pitiful; burglar alarms looked poorly maintained, fences lacked barbed wire topping and ample foliage offered easy concealment.

Leonard parked beside a pair of miniature sphinxes. The woman-headed lion-eagle crossbreeds guarded an immaculate front garden in full bloom. It was Wandsworth's answer to an Outer Ggagaan rose field: a riotous profusion of cultivated colour. I wondered why we were delivering cut flowers to an address so rich in live ones.

Leonard stayed at the wheel with the engine running and Rankin patrolled the pavement, while I marched up the path with my dahlias and pressed the doorbell. I could hear bushes murmuring in the wind - a conspiracy of leaves.

When the door finally buzzed open, my jaw dropped, as did the dahlias. Black walls lit by flame-effect torches led to an upright coffin emblazoned with the words *Welcome To Hell*. A tall, worried-looking dominatrix stood in the hallway, resplendent in thigh-high boots, fishnets, and a blood-red leather dress. Her hair was long, straight, and black, and she wore pale foundation, dark eye make-up and fearsome nail extensions.

"This way." The pale woman spoke from the diaphragm; abrupt and precise, ideal for dispensing orders. But it wasn't her voice that floored me: she was ferociously gorgeous. Her eyes were like pools, and I wanted to Nicaraguan-doggie-paddle several widths across them. My heart pumped like a machine-gun. Blood bomb-blasted along my veins, sweat drenched my ops pants and goose bumps prickled my skin like dagger blades. I had been decked by Cupid's Warhead.

I picked up the dahlias, stepped inside and closed the door behind me. The woman's heels echoed as she vamped along the stone-flagged hallway. There was a strong smell of incense, and the flame-effect torches gave off an impressive flicker. As we approached the welcoming coffin, the dominatrix turned to face a heavy oak door. She loosened a chain and the door creaked open. I followed her into the place where most people have a living room and found a dungeon decorated with manacles, whips, racks, stocks, and bridles. Clearly, the Geneva Convention was being given a rather loose interpretation in this lounge. I recalled my prisoner-of-war drill. *Name, rank, and number*, that's what they'd taught me in the regiment. Just give them your *name rank and number* and do your best to endure the first twenty-four hours. After that, you could start drip-feeding the enemy low-grade information, nothing that would compromise operational security. I had survived interrogation by the Taliban, the Chechens and the Outer Ggagaan Walloons, and I was determined to dodge whatever the dominatrix had to throw at me.

The dungeon décor was a tad theatrical. There was a wooden stool, a velvet throne, a metre-high cell built into the wall, and a variety of mysterious accessories covered in black drapes. An object resembling a fluffy pink cue-case lay abandoned in the middle of the flagstones, but everything else had a medieval vibe, including the rusty cage that dangled from the ceiling. Behind its bars, a gigantic bald man cowered in a nappy.

The dominatrix turned to me. "I seem to have mislaid the cage key."

React as the situation dictates, that's the regimental way. I handed her the dahlias. "Can you hold these a minute, please?"

As she received the flowers, her arms shook slightly. Maybe the bouquet was heavier than usual; my mind had been on other things. It was odd though. A weak dominatrix was probably in the wrong job.

I thanked her and tore my blazer open. It rasped; like all regimental jackets, it was held together with Velcro. My hand swooped into an inside pocket. The dominatrix flinched, but I didn't draw a weapon, I drew a tool.

"What's that?" she asked, petrified.

"A Leatherman."

'I've got plenty of leather men on my client list." She handed back the dahlias, strutted over to the wall and turned a metal handle. Each rotation creaked the cage lower by a few inches.

"Will this take long?" the caged nappy-man asked. "I'm due back in court in half-an-hour."

The dominatrix stormed over to a rack of formidable implements, selected a cat o' nine tails and cracked it over the bars of his cage. "Silence, Your Honour."

"Forgive me, mistress." The man cringed in pleasure.

Putting two and two together, the bloke had to be an off-duty judge. I suppose he liked his justice served both ways.

The dominatrix dropped her whip and turned back to me. "Sorry about that. How are you getting on?"

"It's just a little rusty." I worked the lock and, a few seconds later, the cage door sprang open.

The judge freed himself without uttering a sentence.

An elderly maid emerged from a side room and handed him a pinstriped suit on a coat hanger. "There you go dear." She sounded like a favourite aunt indulging a small child. The judge suited himself over his nappy.

The pale young woman turned and thanked me in a far milder voice than she had used on the judge.

I took Potter's gift card out of my jacket, read it, and asked, "Are you Jezebel O'Hell?"

"My real name's Geraldine."

Geraldine! It was a name to launch a thousand Exocets. She fluttered her lashes, and her eyes breached my defences in a pincer movement, blockading my breathing, sabotaging my circulation, and inflicting collateral damage on my concentration. She had precision-bombed my soppy cells.

"Then these are for you." I passed her the dahlias once again.

Geraldine took the weight of the bouquet on both forearms.

"How much do I owe you?" She heaved the dahlias onto a whipping bench.

"All part of the service." I gave her a glinty grin.

The bald judge, now fully dressed, handed the maid a wad of notes and adjusted his tie. She ushered him towards a back door, patted him on the back and said, "See you next Tuesday, dear. Three o'clock sharp." He turned briefly and nodded; his face flushed in exquisite embarrassment.

Geraldine smiled at me. For a dominatrix, it was a surprisingly perky, life-affirming sort of smile. Her eyes twinkled beneath heavy mascara.

My guts turned girly-giddy. It was a mortal love wound; and I was haemorrhaging sentiment. I fancied her something spectacular. Did that make me a pansified ponce? Probably, but it was way too late to de-escalate my desires.

"I'd love to stay and chat," I said, "But it's my first week at the florists."

I didn't leave and Geraldine didn't seem to be in a hurry for me to go. There were no clocks in the dungeon, but substantial seconds passed between us.

My military discipline melted, and my brain turned puppylike, skipping, and smiling for approval. Why had I been killing people all these years when life could have been soppy-sweet? She had got my heart in a Welsh Death-grip.

Eventually, Geraldine said, "Goodbye then," but neither of us moved.

I had been kamikaze-kissed out of the sky. Why had I yomped away half my life? I could have been learning to tango or busking my way around Europe instead of manoeuvring mindlessly on the parade ground. I resolved to ditch the Glock and take up poetry as soon as I got home to my mum.

It was hard to be certain, but I wondered whether Geraldine was blushing under her foundation. A man could but hope. After a bit, I saluted, turned, and tripped over the fluffy pink cue-case.

"Careful," Geraldine said. "That's precious."

"Sorry." I marched to the oak door, my boots clip-clopping on the flagstones.

I closed the door on the dungeon and ambled out into the magnificent front garden. Rankin took this as his cue to charge into the stretch Bedford.

Leonard gunned the engine, while I sauntered down the garden path.

"Oi!" Leonard shouted. "Where did you bleeding train, The Harold Lloyd Centre?"

I upped my pace, opened the van door and was halfway in when Leonard hammered the accelerator.

"Are you hyper-inactive?" Rankin asked, riveting me with a glare.

"Should I be?" I replied, thinking only of Geraldine.

"Did you make the delivery?" Rankin asked.

"Sure. What's the hurry'?'

"What do you think's the bleeding hurry?" Leonard was irate.

"Honestly, mate," Rankin said. "You've got more lie-down-and-stay than get-up-and-go."

I had obviously cocked things up something spectacular.

The stretch Bedford overtook a lorry with lunatic recklessness. I was pretty certain that our van's engine had been swapped for a more powerful unit, and Leonard was making the most of it. Approaching headlights blazed in anger, horns blared. I waved a hand to placate the driver of the oncoming Skoda Fabia.

"Who the fuck do you think you are, the cunting King?" Leonard inquired.

I know exactly who I am. *By example I lead*, as they taught me in the regiment, and I had exactly the same approach as a trainee florist.

"What did you do with the gun?" Rankin asked.

"What gun?"

"The gun you just used to kill the target," Rankin said.

"What target? I didn't kill anyone."

"Where's The Precious?" Leonard asked.

I shrugged. "Mordor?"

Leonard stood on the brakes, and we all lunged forward. Vehicles piled up behind us: horns blared, alarms bleated, voices bawled abuse.

"So, the gun is still in the dahlias," Rankin said.

"They did seem a little heavy."

"Tell me, how are Kermit and rest of The Muppets?" Leonard stamped on the accelerator.

The souped-up stretch Bedford hurtled forwards, leaving the crumpled vehicles and their furious owners behind. I had a feeling that my comrades in floristry weren't too happy with my delivery. But I was determined not to be discouraged. I would persist, train, and master all the necessary skills, even if I had to persuade mum to stay up really late testing me on bouquet arrangement.

12.38

"Wait by the gardenia," Leonard ordered, when we got back to the florists.

While I stood to attention beside the flowering indoor plant, Leonard and Rankin went in to see Potter. Seconds later, they were back.

"The boss wants a word," Rankin said.

"Dickhead," Leonard added.

12.41

Once again, I stood to attention in Potter's office and looked at his odd oil painting. It reminded me of my visual reasoning training in the regiment: *the boat ploughed through a green field*. It had to be a pun or a saying, but before I could think of a solution, Potter swivelled his chair to face me.

'Tell me, Tell. Do you like my picture?"

"Very surreal."

"Only too real. Lake Victoria, Africa's biggest. Fishing built my hometown. Now, the lake is a football pitch."

'How come?"

"A missionary imported some water hyacinths – he thought they'd look *pukka* in his pond. Now, my people have to scrape a living by sculpting animals for tourists." He handed me a soapstone elephant. "This picture, if looked at in ignorance, then yes, it's surreal, but looked at with knowledge, it's simply how things are." Potter's face glowed, a tribute to the regular application of Vaseline. As his fingers moved across his cheeks, I almost expected them to squeak on the shiny surface: a well-polished dinner table. "Do you understand?"

"Not really."

Potter lifted a dozen red roses out of their vase. "A rose is a rose is a gun." A revolver dropped out of the stems. "The postman always rings twice. The florist is more persistent. Finish the job tomorrow. Collect the gun. Leave her dead in the dahlias."

I saluted in horror. He wanted me to pull the plug on the new love of my life. There is a lot more to floristry than most people think.

CHAPTER 14

Floristry certainly was a funny old game. A dominatrix had melted Sergeant Tell's heart, and now he was being ordered to kill her. It was a bit of a pickle, and no mistake.

To be honest, I was starting to feel a little lonely. Bill had found love, and all I had found was an empty strip club. I thought about all the beautiful, nubile young women who weren't there, and decided to take another walk around the place.

I passed through the empty dressing room, with its uninhabited catsuits, legless fishnets, and nipple-less tassels, and imagined all the absent bickering, bitching, and banter. I stepped onto the stage and was instantly overwhelmed by the thought of all the unperformed dance moves: the splits, the swings, the hooks; all lost to posterity. The poles looked bereft.

I looked out onto the empty seats. Where were all the coked-up bankers, the lairy pissheads, the tragic perverts? Post-apocalyptic pangs of sorrow shot through my body, and I was close to despair.

I thought about all the life-coaching advice I had dispensed over my cataclysmic career. There was "self-indifference", the antidote to self-care, where you take a long, hard look in the mirror and say, "I do not give a shit about you". There was the pre-dawn drinking routine, where you set your alarm religiously for 5.05 am and plough through at least eight pints before 9am – that will certainly set you up for the day. There was "cluttering", where you gather useless objects from car boot sales, bins, and skips, and fill your home with them. There was "conversation confrontation", where you make those phone calls you have been delaying for years - contact your estranged brother, build a bridge with your disappointed father, make peace with your ex-partner – but do it in an unrecognisable voice, pretend you are conducting a consumer survey, and wait for them to put the phone down on you. And, of course, there was "destructive construction", where you spend hours building a housing estate out of playing cards, then attack it with a rubber mallet whilst screaming the word, "AAAAAAAAAAAGGGGGGHHHHHHH".

None of these techniques worked, which was why I was unemployed. Maybe my gloom was just down to the hangover. I got over myself and returned to Bill's paper pile. He was relying on me to discover the truth and act on it, and I was not going to let him down.

Bill had left me another felt-tip note reading, "Here are some more transcripts from the retarded intelligence officer. He remembered to give DCI Stalin's scribblings to F this time, but I doubt that will be enough for him to pass his probation."

Bill was right. I felt sorry for Gurney, but not very – he was a useless pillock.

NATIONAL STEALTH SERVICE

Transcription of Recorded Appraisal Meeting

Wed 20 May , 9.32 a.m.

Present: "F" (Head of Operational Discretion, National Stealth Service) and George Gurney (Trainee Junior Watcher, Remedial Unit, National Stealth Service).

Appraisal exercise: Damage limitation of Gurney's internship. Police notes relevant to Tuesday 19 May.

GURNEY: Stalin's solved the case, F.

F: Good God, Gurney. Has he?

GURNEY: April Fool!

F: It's May.

GURNEY: Sorry F. I've got some more of his notes, though.

F: So, the cover story we provided for you proved efficacious.

GURNEY: Not really, F. I couldn't be bothered to put on the overalls.

F: But we'd taken considerable pains to build you a legend as a plumber.

GURNEY: I just waited until Stalin was out and told the Custody Officer I was from the Government.

F: You did what?

GURNEY: Honesty seemed like the best policy, F.

F: Not on His Majesty's Secret Service, it isn't.

GURNEY: I was acting in a spirit of openness. Why did you just hit me, F?

GURNEY: I was acting in a spirit of vengeance.

F: Fair enough. Here are the notes:

Chief Inspector Stalin, Wandsworth CID.

Case Notes – Tuesday 19 May

Time: One hour since breakfast.

Location: Cemetery.

Risk Assessment: Uneven ground, stone trip hazards, working outdoors (waterproof clothing and thermal underwear recommended).

Say what you like about your shopping centres and gyratory systems, there's no doubt in my mind that Wandsworth Cemetery is the most life-affirming sight in the Borough. It almost made me feel glad not to be dead.

As I watched four sombre attendants lower the pawnbroker's body into the ground, I sincerely hoped that they had completed the Manual Handling section of their risk assessment. It was a flashy coffin: polished mahogany with panelled sides and sculpted handles. I was sure the worms would be impressed.

I wondered what they would do with me after I had booted the bucket. I doubted medical science would want my body. Sailors had burial at sea, gullible billionaires had cryonic suspension and vegans had eco-friendly cardboard boxes, but the Police Federation didn't have an official policy on funerals. The wife once offered to shoot my ashes into space, but that was after we'd had a bit of a barney and I think she had wanted to burn me alive first.

There were four mourners in total and we were two of them. DS Donald was sobbing like a pansy. I really do wish he'd keep his emotions in check – he didn't even know the ruddy corpse. There was a young bloke in a beret, mysteriously keeping his distance, and closer by, a middle aged, middle eastern man in a desert suit and a half-and-half scarf: fifty percent Palestinian checkers, fifty percent Israeli stars.

The Arab-Israeli bloke shuffled towards me and whispered, "Flowers didn't seem right in the circumstances."

I looked the man up and down: the tinted glasses disclosed nothing, but the Rolex watch spoke volumes. I nodded in the direction of the young bloke in the beret and asked, "That his son?"

"No. He's from *Médecins Sans Frontières*. They got all his money."

"No widow?"

"Women threw themselves at him, but he was a rotten catch.'

"Did you know him well?"

"Strictly business. I just came to pay my respects and to make sure he was dead. He gave us a bad reputation."

'Who's us?"

"Diamond dealers."

"Glamorous line of work."

"Does that look glamorous?" He indicated the attendants shovelling earth onto the pawnbroker's coffin.

"Not particularly." I offered my hand. "This is DS Donald. I'm DCI Stalin."

"Ratner." The Arab-Israeli man accepted my grip. "Call me Mohammed." He handed me a gold-embossed business card. "If I can be of any assistance, just drop by."

"Likewise," I scrawled my own contact details on the back of the blood-spattered post-mortem envelope.

Time: Nearly lunch.
Location: Police car (Ford Fiesta, unmarked).
Risk Assessment: Aggressive driver (my sergeant), uneven road surfaces, faulty traffic lights (planned engineering works).

I was singing along to one of my favourite folk ballads, an expertly crafted protest ditty by a bunch of disillusioned Mancunian iron-moulders, when we motored past the Point Pleasant sewerage works.

"Close the window, will you, Donald?"

He obliged, taking a hand off the steering wheel and veering towards a pedestrian.

"Bloody hellfire, sergeant."

"Sorry about that, Guv."

I had been meaning to have a heart-to-heart with Donald for some months, but I had been heavily impeded by my Federation duties and this murder inquiry hadn't exactly helped matters. Still, I owed it to him to play a straight bat and appraised him of the full SP.

"I've just gone through the annual complaint figures, Sergeant, and you're top of the league."

"Thanks, Guv."

"You're the only happily married teetotaller in the force."

"Yes, Guv."

"Your main hobby is re-homing rescue ducks in your self-built pond."

"Hence the nickname *Mallard*, Guv."

"So, Donald, why are you a violent, psychotic, trigger-happy thug?"

Donald blasted his horn, scattering schoolchildren. "Don't know, Guv."

"Did you see the shrink?"

"Yes, Guv."

"And?"

"She thinks I'm having a Confident Breakdown. I've got a grip, but I'm gripping too hard, my socks are pulled up higher than they should be, and everything seems to be holding together, only a little too tightly."

"What's the cure?"

"Maybe I should spend more time with the ducks, Guv."

Donald's driving frightened a group of language school students at Piccadilly

Circus, terrified some American pensioners on Shaftsbury Avenue and sent a shop assistant running for her life in New Oxford Street. He took the first exit off the Holborn Circus Roundabout and, a few near misses later, we were in *The Garden*, London's gem quarter, home to hundreds of diamond merchants - some rough, some polished. This was a world of portable fortunes and paperless transactions: a deadly business, built on trust. Health and Safety were entirely alien concepts. The Garden had its own underworld, *The Secret Garden*, where the street's less scrupulous master cutters and polishers would give your money a makeover. Whether you were Russian Mafia, Al-Qaida or a home-grown villain, *The Secret Garden* was Britain's best laundry: it had helped wash the Brinks-Mat gold whiter than white.

The local metres were notoriously ravenous, so parking was a piece of piss. We crossed the road and approached an impressive concrete building. Outside, plain-clothes security guards, identifiable by their bulk and restless eyeballs, conspired through a concealed radio network. Inside, uniformed guards paced a marble foyer, bulletproof vests peeking out from their collars. Security cameras overlooked queuing diamond dealers, muttering impenetrably in Afrikaans, French and Hebrew.

A formidable wall was broken by two electronic bubble gates, which enclosed one diamond dealer at a time. Honestly, if everyone took security this seriously, I would be out of a job.

Donald squared up to a glass cube and spoke into a microphone. "We're here to see Mohammed Ratner."

"Do you have an appointment?" The receptionist was terrifying: her eyes interrogatory, her hair disciplined into a bun. We could do with her down the nick.

Donald waved his sergeant's badge.

'Been frisked?" the receptionist asked.

"You've seen the badge," Donald replied.

The receptionist shrugged contemptuously, pressed a buzzer and a pair of security guards searched us intimately. While some gorilla grappled with my crotch, I shut my eyes and tried to visualize my next Federation booze-up: it didn't help much.

When it was all over, the guards ushered us towards the electronic gates. Glass bubbles swallowed us up, x-rayed us and spat us out the other side.

Mohammed Ratner, resplendent in his half-and-half Arab-Israeli scarf and desert suit, was waiting to meet us. He shook our hands with enthusiasm.

"Mohammed," I said.

"Stalin," Mohammed said.

'Mohammed,' Donald said.

"Gentlemen," Mohammed led the way along a series of identical corridors lit by eye-frying fluorescent beams.

"So, Mohammed," I said. "I hope you don't mind me asking, but that's not a football scarf, is it?"

"My mother was in Mossad; my father was in the PLO. It was love at first sight, a complication in a double honey trap. He was meant to lure her to Lebanon, she was meant to betray him to Begin. In the end, they both buggered off to Bethnal Green. Safe to say, I'm conflicted."

A CCTV camera recorded us as Mohammed opened a series of locks on his office door. Inside, an intelligent light switch illuminated an immaculate, minimalist space with a single desktop computer and a display screen across the back wall.

"Are there many Arab-Israeli diamond dealers in London?" I asked, as Mohammed disabled an alarm and walked over to the computer.

"I'm as rare as the Great Star of Africa." Mohammed moved his mouse and a pear-shaped diamond appeared on the screen-wall.

"Very nice, Mohammed."

"It's cut from the world's largest diamond. Over five hundred carats. Flawless, but not quite colourless."

"Does that matter?"

"Every diamond is lettered. Z-colour is the least valuable. This is D-colour. No one's found a C, B or A-colour yet. Not officially."

"But unofficially?" I asked.

"There are rumours, but Africa, as they say, is swaddled in lies."

"Wandsworth's bad enough."

Mohammed showed us images of famous diamonds: *The Unnamed Brown*, *The Mountain of Light*, *The Idol's Eye*, then explained the four 'C's: Carat, Clarity, Colour and Cut. He talked about rough diamonds: their marking, mapping, and allocation, then outlined the different varieties of cut: *The Round Brilliant*, *The Old European* and *The Rose*. It would have been fascinating if I had been interested in that sort of thing. Mohammed could talk the hind legs off a camel.

"A gemmologist might bend the ears of an engaged couple about the passion of ruby, the harmony of aquamarine, the optimism of opal, the romance of emerald and the sincerity of sapphire, but diamonds are eternal," he said.

"Indestructible?"

"Not quite. Diamond is the hardest mineral on earth, but it isn't tough. There is a difference: a diamond will survive a nuclear explosion but hit it with a hammer and it shatters."

"Hard, not tough," Donald said.

"We've arrested a few of those," I said.

"You need to watch out for simulants," Mohammed said.

"Just like *Blade Runner*," Donald said.

"That's replicants," I said.

"Replicants are probably easier to spot," Mohammed said. "When I authenticate a diamond, I look for blemishes on the outside and inclusions on the inside. I measure crown angle and symmetry, seek out hearts-and-arrow images, assess light leakage, and identify signs of bearding, clouding, and feathering. I have a magnifying glass, a UV light for testing fluorescence and a countertop viewer for measuring brilliance, yet still, there is margin for error."

I had no use for all this gubbins, and I didn't want to end up going into overtime, so I got to the point. "Our friend, the deceased, you mentioned that he gave you a bad reputation. Why?"

"He polished conflict diamonds. They'd start off in machete-torn hellholes like Angola, Sierra Leone or Liberia and end up migrating to Wandsworth, where he'd smooth away all traces of their bloody origins."

"So, he mixed in dangerous circles."

"None deadlier. As he proved."

NATIONAL STEALTH SERVICE

Transcription - Appraisal Meeting

Wed 20 May, 10.06 a.m.

Present: "F" (Head of Operational Discretion, National Stealth Service) and George Gurney (Trainee Junior Watcher, Remedial Unit, National Stealth Service).
Appraisal exercise: damage limitation.

GURNEY: That Stalin's a real piece of leisure, isn't he, F?
F: They say he's in line to head up Wandsworth's Reluctant Response Unit.
GURNEY: Really?
F: No, Gurney.
GURNEY: Oh. What shall we do now?
F: Well, Gurney, I'm going to stay here at my desk."
GURNEY: Yes, F?
F: And you're going to go away.
GURNEY: Thanks, F.

CHAPTER 15

My calves were cramped, so I stood up and did a few stretches, forgetting that I was wearing a sofa cover. I fell over and squashed my groin. It is astonishing how much a carpet can hurt when there is a floor under it. My eyes watered, my head throbbed, my knees ached. I tried standing up, but I had all the agility of a beached whale.

I wriggled along the carpet in my fabric sarcophagus until I had reached the nearest wall, turned, and shuffled myself up to a seated position in a series of caterpillar shrugs. I was no longer flat on my face, which was a plus, but I was still stuck. When I think of humanity's achievements: space flight, the Renaissance, the pyramids of Giza, it is sobering to think that a man's loftiest ambitions can be curtailed by a sofa cover.

I leant back into the wall, reverse-squatted up to a standing position, then fell over again. In many ways, the second fall was more painful than the first, but it came as less of a surprise.

I repeated the wriggle and wall-shrug but resolved to take more time on the reverse squat. I didn't fall over, but I did decide that I would be better off in my pants. I extracted myself from the sofa cover and, in an instant, I was both free and freezing. The shock shuddered through my body and dragged my mind back to last night. Was this what it had been like for Marcel Proust and his madeleines? No idea.

What I did know was that until that moment, my final memory had been of drinking alone on a park bench. Now, a succession of additional events became accessible to my memory. Enlivened by "benching" a six pack of beer, I had hit *The Lion & Lettuce* with a vengeance. It was one of South London's ropiest pubs and I'd fitted in perfectly. After losing a game of darts to a one-eyed pensioner, I got outsmarted by a fruit machine, chatted up a woman until she slapped me, and held a long discussion with the barman about the up-and-coming "influencer" football team Hashtag United. We couldn't agree where Hashtag was - he reckoned it was somewhere near Telford, and I thought it was much further south, maybe in Kent. After that, everything was a blur, but all in all, it had been a typical start to a session, and there was nothing to suggest it would end with me tied up nude in a deserted pole-dancing joint.

I returned to Bill's dossier in the hope that developments in Wandsworth might make more sense.

JOURNAL – EX-SERGEANT BILL TELL

Tuesday 19 May, 07.48

I took my mum tea and toast, then executed two hundred press-ups, one hundred and eighty squat thrusts and ninety-seven Tibetan lunges in the hallway. I showered thoroughly, dressed for the florists, and checked the post. There was a bill from Wandsworth Council and a special delivery package from the Walloon Republic of Outer Ggaga. The parcel contained a pair of letters - the first from Charles:

Dear Bill,

If there is anything barmier than colonialism, it's post-colonialism. The Sons of The Brotherhood have desecrated Land of My Fathers, the Semi-Pygmies have set fire to the rose fields and the Walloons have trashed Marie-Thérèse's library. She is putting a brave face on it, but the poor girl is in bits.

Kes has tripled the guard on The Ambassador, so there is not much time for daft Deniable bets anymore. Basically, The Petal War has kicked off big time.

I am having a constant battle with my paper shredder, but I am determined to beat some sense into it and show it who's boss. It is a bonkers procedure: receive covert news bulletin, précis it pronto, lob it off to security wonks across the globe via encrypted "Shush-Mail", then spend the next twenty minutes wrestling with the aforementioned shredder whilst attempting to destroy all evidence of said bulletin.

Marie-Thérèse has written another note for you. Unforgivable, I know, but I couldn't resist a peek – aren't you a little swat?

Yours,

Charles

Now, don't get me wrong, I'm not unsympathetic to Charles's paper shredder problems. It is just that the civil war seemed a bit more pressing. The Ambassador was in mortal danger and there was f-all I could do about it, close protection being ineffective over long distances. Land of My Fathers meant everything to the Semi-Pygmies and the thought of millions of young, unharvested roses roasting in their fields was a sobbing shame. But worst of all, poor Marie-Thérèse had been rendered bookless by the Walloons. It was an atrocious atrocity. I read her note with a heavy heart:

Dear Bill,

Thanks for your homework. Hope all is well in Wandsworth. It is far from well here, so forgive the brevity. I really enjoyed reading *Don Quixote – knight or nit?* I think the wilderness of La Mancha is fertile ground, so here's another one: *Who is Dulcinea?*

Love,

MT x

I choked back a sob. She had lost everything and barely gave it a mention. How she managed to find the strength to set me an essay, I'll never know. It was one of the bravest dispatches I have ever eyeballed in my military career.

I cursed at the air miles that separated Wandsworth from the Walloon Republic of Outer Ggaga. I wanted to do for the bastards who had wrecked Marie-Thérèse's library, but I didn't have an inter-continental ballistic missile to hand. At least I had an open channel of communication via Charles. I held a Chinese Parliament with myself and resolved on a two-stage strategy: foment revolution and donate books.

Dear Charles,

Sorry to hear about the shredder. I usually make a practice of eating sensitive information. Please can you hand the rest of this package to Marie-Thérèse.

Thanks again,

Bill

Dear Marie-Thérèse,

Please find enclosed my entire book collection: Lawrence of Arabia's *Ten Pillars of Wisdom*, Colonel Brian Fortescue's *Illustrated Guide to Grappling* and Hal Iggulden's *The Dangerous Book for Boys*. Mum will throw in *Advanced Matchstick Modelling* as soon as she has finished Lincoln Cathedral. It is not far off: just a chunk of altar and a few gargoyles to go. Thinking of Lawrence of Arabia, you could always have a crack at reuniting the Semi-Pygmies. It worked with Arabs. Why not initiate a Semi-Pygmy peace process and gang up on the Walloons? I have knocked up a morale-boosting speech in case it comes in handy. Here you go:

"There is a corner of an Outer Ggagaan rose field that is forever Semi-Pygmy. Defy the potpourri bombs, topple the Routemasters and write your will across the sky in burst Zeppelins. Never forget, a man who is afraid of Death is tired of Life. Re-consecrate *Land of My Fathers* and honour your ancestors, as your children will honour you. War is quite simply to die for. I have nothing to offer but nuns, Zeppelins and Walloons, but offence is the new defence. Seize the moment and don't let it go, even if it wriggles. It's time to win the most obscure conflict of the twenty-first century. Pamper your allies, pester your enemies, and stare Death in the eyes until it blinks. United, the Semi-Pygmy people stand tall."

Hope that does the trick. I've got to nip off to the florists now.

Cheers,

Bill.

P.S. You're my Dulcinea.

08.47

Is Marie-Thérèse really my Dulcinea? I would fight for her, but I suppose I would fight for anyone. Battle is not about courtly love; it is about muddy hate. Honour has got nothing on achievable objectives and decent kit. Do I love Marie-Thérèse? Possibly. Do I fancy Geraldine O'Hell? More than all the petals in The Walloon Republic of Outer Ggaga.

09.22

Belladonna's stretch Bedford cut up a motorcyclist on its way through Wandsworth. Leonard drove, Rankin glowered beside him, and I sat in the back.

"I hate returning to the scene of a crime," Rankin said.

"What crime?" I asked.

I hadn't committed one and that was the problem. They both looked ready to kill me, but killing seemed to be my job, worse luck.

The stretch Bedford pulled up outside Geraldine's suburban dungeon. Leonard waited at the wheel, Rankin paced the pavement, and I walked up the garden path, passing burgeoning azaleas and a plastic Venus de Milo. I pressed the bell and, a few seconds later, the old maid welcomed me back into the dungeon.

"Lucky you've come, dear," she said. "The novelty handcuffs have jammed."

I followed her slippers as they flip-flopped along the flagstones. "Been working for Geraldine long?"

"Twenty-six years. I'm her mum."

"You don't mind?"

"Not at all, dear. She's got the safest job in the world. No one comes to the house wishing her any harm. They just want her to harm them." She unchained the door to her daughter's dungeon and opened it. "She doesn't disappoint, does she, Mr Blagrove?"

A suited man cuffed to a Gothic throne gave his muffled assent through a gag.

Geraldine, done up in her full leather finery, was scrabbling through a fistful of key rings and swearing to herself.

"Cage key, is it?" I asked.

"It's the handcuffs this time," she replied.

Geraldine had serious key issues. They were a fundamental part of her trade, and she really ought to have kept them in better order. The regiment taught me that all kit had to be maintained and accounted for, and she simply hadn't developed a sufficiently stringent system for her equipment. The masochist did not look particularly happy about being cuffed permanently to the throne, and I could see that a call to the fire brigade might prove awkward.

Luckily, I had successfully completed *The Mossad Cat Burglary Course* at Tonbridge Wells, so I was quietly optimistic that I would be able to open the novelty handcuffs. I tore open my blazer's concealed Velcro join and pulled out my pick gun.

Geraldine gasped. The maid cowered. Mr Blagrove groaned through his gag.

It was only a tool. Sometimes, the public's grasp of artillery could be shamefully rudimentary.

I held the pick gun against the handcuffs and squeezed its trigger repeatedly. All that remained was to extract a tension wrench from my ops pants and finish the job. The handcuffs flopped open. Mission accomplished.

Mr Blagrove rubbed his wrists and gave the maid a wad of readies with a "harumph".

"See you next Tuesday, dear. 10am." The maid ushered him out the back.

Geraldine turned to me and dropped her dominatrix shtick. "Now he knows what it feels like."

"Does he?"

"He's a prison governor."

Sometimes, I wish the regiment offered courses in small talk. The best I could manage was, "How are the dahlias?"

"Heavy." Geraldine pointed her spectacular nail extensions towards the far corner of the dungeon. The dahlias were in a black vase shaped like the kind of cat no self-respecting witch should be seen without.

The fluffy, pink cue-case I had tripped over on my previous visit still sat mysteriously on the flagstones. I doubted it belonged to the departed prison governor, and it looked completely out of place, what with the dungeon décor and the total absence of a fluffy, pink pool table. It didn't seem to present any kind of threat, so I stepped over it without comment on my way to the flowers. "Mind if I check the stems?"

"Why would I mind?"

I lifted the dahlias out of the vase. A revolver dropped from the dripping stalks, clattered onto the flagstones, and echoed around the dungeon walls.

Geraldine trembled. "That one's not for picking locks, is it?"

I leant down and retrieved the revolver. I shook it, peered down the barrel and dried it on my sleeve. "Sorry."

"Why?" Geraldine's tears muddied her mascara.

"Sorry about this."

"Sorry you're going to kill me or sorry you mislaid your gun in my dahlias?"

"Sorry I mislaid my gun in your dahlias."

"Get you and your gun out."

"I can explain." I couldn't.

The dungeon doorbell chimed a doom-laden Gothic dirge. I hadn't been saved by the bell; I had been damned.

Geraldine ignored it and glared at me. "I don't know what's going on and I don't want to. Just leave."

"I can't. You're in danger."

"Says the man with the gun." Geraldine grabbed a scourge and waved it around her head.

The maid walked back into the dungeon. "Nice to see you two are getting to know each other. You've got a client outside. Office fantasy."

"Not very original." Geraldine lowered the scourge a fraction. "But he's got great timing."

While the maid retreated to a cosier part of the house, Geraldine undraped an office desk and chair. I retreated towards the rear exit and dodged behind a whipping bench. I crouched motionless and silent, waiting for Geraldine to exit the dungeon and greet her guest by the hallway's welcoming coffin. Once she had left, I commando-crawled along the floor, climbed into the three-by-five-foot wall-cage occupied by the judge on my last visit, and barred myself in. It only provided a degree of temporary concealment, but I had a feeling that Geraldine might find her new client a little distracting.

Geraldine strode back, dominating the dungeon in her hastily reassumed role. Rankin followed in feigned submission, his head bowed, shoulders slumped and knees sagging.

"The desk is over there," Geraldine declared, as authoritative as a CEO.

Rankin took a seat, as meek as an intern, and Geraldine chucked him a pad and pen.

I observed proceedings from my cage. I had forced my body against the cage's back wall, the only unlit area. Cupping my left hand, I emptied the revolver's magazine and dried the bullets on my ops pants. This was a seriously soggy weapon; its accuracy would be impossible to predict, but I had to be ready for when Rankin dropped the pretence and made his move.

"A little dictation, if you please," Geraldine bellowed in her testicle-shredding character.

Rankin took up the pad and pen, as placid as a teacher's pet.

Geraldine paced as she spoke, cradling a cat o' nine tails. "Dear Sirs, Regarding your order for…" She paused briefly before speaking at triple speed. "…Epoxy-coated field windings model 954WCHQIN, speed-core thin wall bit core shanks model

428RPFSJNFFR, plunge-based random orbit sanders model 4283614 and rotary hammer depth gauges model 871SSYRGGW..." Rankin's biro snapped, and Geraldine continued with sadistic glee. "Double-sealed carbide tipped bits, variable hex drives for precise plunging and flange kits with orbital action jigsaws."

I scrabbled in the dark, struggling to reinsert the ammo and, like a prize plonker, I dropped a bullet.

I swallowed a "bollocks" as Rankin's head snapped towards my cage. I had lost my place in the regiment; now I had lost my discipline, endangering an innocent young dominatrix. Luckily, Geraldine was oblivious to my monumental cock-up and whipped Rankin. He grabbed the end of her scourge, yanked her towards him and employed it as a garrotte.

I grabbed a cell bar in fury, triggering an automatic lock. Own goal of the century! What a monumental pillock! Poor old Geraldine hadn't done anyone any harm; no one who didn't want harming, anyway. Now, I had compromised her safety. I had almost no room to manoeuvre, but I was just able to inch out my gun and take aim through the bars.

Rankin tightened the leather noose and Geraldine's legs kicked an involuntary, terminal can-can. I pulled the trigger. The whip dropped away from Geraldine's windpipe. Rankin fell to the floor, a dark circle in the middle of his forehead. The maid burst in, screaming. Geraldine hugged her and they sobbed into each other's arms.

I had dropped Rankin, but I knew that Leonard, an equally homicidal florist, was waiting outside and it wouldn't take him long to force his way into the dungeon. I checked that the women were out of range and blew through the cage lock. The bullet ricocheted, shattering Geraldine's cat-vase. The dahlias flopped onto the flagstones and a puddle formed around them. The maid shrieked once again. Geraldine dragged her towards the back door, grabbing the fluffy, pink cue case on her way across the dungeon flagstones.

I was about to launch myself after them, but I held a quick Chinese Parliament with myself and changed direction. Leonard was out the front, so Geraldine and her mother were running away from danger. Clearly, I would be more use as a decoy.

I clambered out of the cage and bounded across the dungeon. I gripped Rankin under the arms, bent his knees and dragged my fellow florist's body across the stone floor. He weighed at least fifty ponds more than me, but he was a lot lighter than Forestière had been, and I had lugged that porky prelate halfway up Mount Heha. I shoved Rankin's corpse into the cage I had just vacated and covered the bars with a black drape: it wasn't quite full military honours, but he was no soldier, and it gave him more dignity than he deserved.

I paused to update my situational awareness. As far as Leonard was concerned, I had just carried out the hit on Geraldine and the longer he believed this, the more time I was buying for the dominatrix and her mother. I slammed the dungeon door behind me, bomb-blasted down the garden path and leapt into the stretch Bedford, roaring, "Step on it!"

"Where's Rankin?" Leonard demanded.

"He ran out the back," I lied. Sometimes, acting skills are an essential part of TTP: Tactics, Techniques and Procedures.

Leonard stared at me.

I returned the compliment. Luckily, I had completed the *Regimental Staring Course* at Watford Junction, so I was pretty damned convincing.

Leonard broke his gaze and slammed his foot down on the accelerator. The florist's van was turbo-charged; its engine would not have disgraced Formula One. As its high-rev shriek pierced my eardrums, I noticed that the wings were armour-plated.

"What kept you?" Leonard's freakishly prominent veins pulsed puce.

"The gun was wet."

"No Precious?"

I shook my head.

Leonard swung the stretch Bedford into a side street. "If the delivery went off okay, why did Rankin run out the back?"

"You'll have to ask him that."

Leonard gave me a death-glare. He should have kept his peepers glued to the road. Brakes screeched, spokes crunched, and a cyclist flew past the windscreen, crashing onto the bonnet inches away from my face.

I swallowed my second "bollocks" of the morning.

The cyclist climbed off the bonnet and leant in through Leonard's window, flushed with self-righteous anger.

"You motorists!" The cyclist jabbed his finger in front of Leonard's face. "You fill the air with petrol fumes and forget you're in charge of a deadly weapon."

Leonard pulled out a pistol.

The cyclist stepped back from the van.

"Good boy," Leonard said. "Now remember, today is the beginning of the rest of your life - however short that turns out to be."

The cyclist ran away, dragging the bike behind him. Friction sparks flew off the tarmac.

As Leonard drove the van down Wandsworth High Street, I pretended to look for Rankin, gawping out the windows and checking the mirrors as if I didn't know he was dead in a dungeon.

"It's not like Rankin to do a runner," Leonard said. "If you're lying, you'll have to answer to Potter."

"Harry Potter," I japed.

"Harold Potter," Leonard corrected. "No wizard jokes. Touchy subject."

The chain of command at the florists was muddier than the regiment's, but there was no doubt that Potter was my commanding officer and that the incomprehensible orders had come directly from him. Disobedience might mean a court martial and a lengthy stay in the glasshouse. Or perhaps the greenhouse.

Traffic, fumes, and litter circulated around the Wandsworth Gyratory System. Roundabouts interlocked and unwound; angular feeder lanes sent vehicles swerving in, out and around, ambushing each other from unexpected directions. Luckily, I had completed the *Confusing Environments Course* at Milton Keynes. Unluckily, Leonard had just spotted Geraldine. She clocked him too, sprinted across a Pelican and marooned herself on a traffic island.

"If you made the delivery, Tell, why's the target jaywalking across the Wandsworth Gyratory System?"

Leonard didn't wait for an answer, but before his knuckles made contact, I broke his arm with a *Takenouchi-Ryu* sword-arm-snap. It's amazing what you can learn off repeats of *Teenage Mutant Ninja Turtles*. Leonard howled and the stretch Bedford veered across three lanes. Horns blared and drivers screamed abuse.

Leonard took his other arm off the steering wheel, pulled his pistol on me, and snarled, "Happy deathday and no returns."

I smashed the pistol out of Leonard's hand and elbowed him between the eyes, sending his head onto the horn and the van through a red. The stretch Bedford was doing forty and, after I'd leapt out, so was I.

As I jumped, my revolver dropped, kissing Leonard's pistol in the footwell. I broke my fall with a gym roll and landed upright and stable, bang in front of a London

Borough of Wandsworth Fly Tipping Rapid Response Vehicle. I flung myself sideways, just in time to watch Leonard smash into a Police Panda, sending both vehicles spinning in a ballet macabre.

Geraldine was now running blindly, playing headless chicken with the traffic. I raced after her until a forty-ton juggernaut touched bumpers with a bulldozer, blocking my path. I was almost short enough to bomb-blast beneath the juggernaut's undercarriage, but I didn't fancy a face-to-face encounter with a moving axle. I half-crawled, half-scuttled until, twenty vehicles ahead, an amber light joined its red comrade and began to flash. Four sets of giant wheels started to turn, and I froze, ready to die like a hedgehog.

The dirty metal engine roared overhead, light reappeared, and sensation returned to my legs. I dived out the way of the bulldozer, just in time to avoid being crushed. I dodged the site of the Panda-Bedford collision and jumped across the bonnets of rubberneckers until I reached a roundabout.

Curved metal strips supported an electronic sign flashing *Welcome to Wandsworth* and a hoarding advertising extra-strength vodka. Eight metres below, triangles of overgrown bush divided a nest of unhygienic walkways. I eyeballed Geraldine on her way down one of them. She stumbled over a sign reading; *This Roundabout is Sponsored by Rentokil*.

My legs are more like a warthog's than a gazelle's, but I had trained Ghurkhas to yomp, and, within seconds, I was right behind her. She span and shouted for help, but the traffic's rumble smothered her words. I placed a hand on her shoulder. She screamed; then froze. I smiled, guided her gently beneath the branches of a cedar and began building a hide out of branches, turf, and dead flowers. I had constructed sand shelters in the Gobi; tree pits in Siberia and snow graves in the Arctic - a cedar hide on Wandsworth Gyratory System was well within my grasp.

"Who the hell are you?" Geraldine asked.

"I'm a florist."

"And I'm a nun."

"No, I really am a florist."

"Are most florists armed?"

"It's a dangerous business."

"So, you're green-fingered?"

"You could write what I know about flowers on the front of a stamp without defacing the King."

"Then how did you end up becoming a florist?"

"I shot a priest and had a fight in a bar."

"Sounds like a rigorous recruiting process."

This wasn't the time to discuss floristry recruitment procedures; this was the time for survival.

Luckily, the roundabout was a defendable area with good concealment and the hide was coming on a treat: it was invisible even at close quarters, there was a choice of camouflaged escape routes and there were no wild animals in the vicinity.

"Why are you building a garden feature?"

"It's a hide."

"Shall I close my eyes and count up to twenty?"

"You're in danger."

"From you?"

"From my boss."

"The head florist."

"He wants you deadheaded."

"And you were supposed to kill me?"

"Yes. And now I'm going to save you.'

"But you gave me flowers...."

"Don't mention it."

"...with a revolver hidden in the stems."

"I didn't know. I came to get it back, and to warn you."

"To warn me - or to kill me?"

"Rankin wanted to kill you."

"I noticed." Geraldine massaged her neck where the scourge had left a dark mark.

"Your surname's not really O'Hell, is it?"

"No."

I knew it! My years spent conducting military investigations were paying dividends.

"*Hell* is meant to provide a tingle of fear and the *O* bit's there because most masochistic Englishmen prefer to be hit by Celts."

An ice-cream van stalled in front of the hide. It sported a revolving cone reading, *Mr Whippy*.

"I'd prefer not to be hit at all."

"Same here, but you're so straight, Bill, it's almost a perversion." Geraldine's eyes flashed with mischief.

"Thanks,' I was fairly certain that this was a compliment.

"Bill?"

"What?"

"Is that a pair of coppers running towards us?"

She was right. It was. I had built a faultless hide but forgotten to hide in it. Bit of a cock-up in technique. In the circumstances, I calculated that the best chance of a successful evasion was flight rather than camouflage. I held out my hand to Geraldine. "Your danger is my danger."

My face could not have been more earnest, but Geraldine's certainly could. I held a Chinese Parliament with myself and concluded that she would not be able to outrun the cozzers unaided; I would have to carry her. But how? There was the *Fireman's Lift* and the *Gone-With-The-Wind Cradle*, but I have always believed that the most efficient method of carrying a load is on your back. I had once lugged my own bodyweight up Ben Nevis without breaking sweat, after all.

I assessed Geraldine as man-portable, but this proved over-optimistic. Lugging her up onto my shoulders was an achievable objective. However, once she was there, she beat me repeatedly over the head with her fluffy pink cue-case and stilettos, yanked my hair and squeezed my ribs with her ankles. I told myself to adopt an endurance mindset: pain is pleasure; discomfort is comfortable. Mind over matter, I told myself, mind over matter, but as Geraldine tore a wedge of scalp from my skull, matter seemed to matter more.

Either way, I had to get my skates on, and dodge the cozzers. Luckily, I had done the *Regimental Evasion Course* on Eel Pie Island, so I knew the drill: *avoid stations and terminals; hijack a private car if possible* and *use public transport only if you are completely confident of how the system works*. I had been away from London for a while, but I was still TFL-confident. I span three-hundred-and-sixty degrees and eyeballed a bendy bus. Its doors were shutting, and its engine was lurching into life, but it represented an achievable yomping target. After a few bounds, I was ready to bomb-burst on board. It would have been a glowing success, had I remembered to duck.

When you are my height, ducking is not often a necessity, but this time I had a dominatrix on my shoulders. Or rather I had had a dominatrix on my shoulders. After a loud "Clunk!" and a "Dickhead!" she was flat on her back, bottom half on the bus deck, top half on the pavement.

"I'm not a rucksack!" Geraldine protested, horizontally and a tad too late.

"Sorry." I helped Geraldine up and handed her the pink, fluffy cue case and stilettos she had dropped after involuntarily headbutting the bus.

The doors closed behind us, I swiped my deniable credit card, and we set off. The bus-yomp had not been the smoothest of evasion manoeuvres, but it had befuddled the cozzers and we were no longer in imminent danger of arrest.

I was pleased, but Geraldine was ambivalent at best. She scrutinized me through a suspicious squint. "You're definitely no florist."

"What makes you think that?"

"You're a spooky kind of squaddie, aren't you?"

"I'm not a deniable operative."

"That's exactly what you'd say if you were."

She was right, of course, but my immediate concern was our poor state of camouflage. Geraldine was in full dominatrix gear; I was in blazer, tie, and hyper-creased trousers. Our appearance was not evasion-grey; it was get-captured neon. I decided to simulate a low state of alertness by initiating a conversation.

"How did you end up working in a dungeon?"

"I was a PA in a power tool company: I kept the MD's diary, and it soon became pretty clear that there were some appointments he didn't want me to write down. He would disappear mysteriously and return bruised but smiling. My flatmate worked in the business - she told me how powerful men often liked to unwind by being tied up and humiliated. With most of the sex trade, you're coping with a cross-section of blokes, but as a dominatrix, you are generally dealing with an elite. Average men are dominated all week: they don't need to pay someone to add to their misery. It is just the bosses who pay to be bossed. They've got the money and most of them deserve all they get. They pay top whack to be whacked and that suits me. Anyway, my flatmate took me to a sex shop up the road and the owner introduced me to a local businessman, who lent me the money for the dungeon-conversion."

"Enjoy it?"

"It's like acting, but with a captive audience."

"And how did you end up here?"

"Boredom makes people kinky and I'm in Wandsworth."

"It is quite dull, isn't it?"

"In Wandsworth no one can hear you yawn."

"What's in the cue-case?"

There was a flicker of hesitation before she replied, "Bullwhip, handcuffs, and a vibrating gimp mask. Want me to get them out?"

I blushed.

"A sensitive soldier! You've got to be married!"

"Not right now. You?"

"I'm concentrating on my career."

"But you work in a dungeon."

Geraldine didn't respond. I was glad she didn't, partly because I had been tactless and partly because all the other passengers were paying increasingly rapt attention to our conversation.

12.47

A torched ambulance fumed outside The Victory estate. Small children pointed at the wreckage and laughed.

"Where are you taking me?" Geraldine asked as I led her along. "I don't like the look of this."

"There's no place like it."

"Like where?"

"Home."

As we approached, the child arsonists scampered.

"What are they afraid of?" Geraldine asked.

"Me, I should think."

"You?"

"I'm an urban myth."

A heavily armed Yardie gang smiled and saluted as we passed each other on the estate staircase.

13.06

Rose Tell answered the door. Her face lit up as soon as she saw me, and it stayed lit when she saw the dominatrix stood beside me. Result!

"Hello, mum. This is my friend, Geraldine."

"It's so lovely to meet a young lady who takes pride in her appearance," mum said.

"Thanks," Geraldine replied.

We sat in the living room nibbling Battenberg while mum poured tea into her best China.

"And what do you do for a living, Geraldine?" mum asked.

Years of armed conflict have taught me never to panic; it clouds thought. There were plenty of near-death scenarios in Mosul, Afghanistan and Outer Ggaga to moisten the y-fronts, empty the bowels and send a man's life story spinning past his eyeballs, but rarely had I experienced such terror: every goose bump prickled like a Commando Dagger.

After what seemed like an eternity, Geraldine replied, "I manage personnel."

Relief flooded my corpuscles.

"A personnel manager. How lovely!" Mum smiled. "Which firm?"

"Very firm."

Ten minutes of genial but nerve-racking small talk later, mum decided to leave us to our own devices: "If you'll excuse me, I'll just nip out to buy some more matches for the cathedral." She winked at me. "It's bound to take a little while."

"Okay mum."

When mum had gone, I showed Geraldine her matchstick modelling. Geraldine was so impressed, she snogged me. *Always expect the unexpected*, that's what my regimental training had taught me, so I took the dominatrix's kiss in my stride.

"Where's your bedroom?" Geraldine asked.

"I've only got a single bed."

"Then we'll have to lie on top of each other." Geraldine really did possess excellent problem-solving abilities.

"Okay. It's behind you."

13.12

I had expected Geraldine's underwear to be leather and frightening, but it was comfy and tent-like.

"I'm more M & S than S & M," she explained.

Geraldine undressed me, revealing an inner layer of military hardware.

"Should I ask?"

"Flameproof long johns, armoured assault vest, bulletproof elbow pads and an abseiling harness."

"I think they look quite sexy."

After I had emptied my ops pants of kit, I made comprehensive preparations for an overt insertion. I attained the objective, and we made love quietly and accurately in the missionary position. The *Coital Alignment Technique* I had learned at the Regiment's boot camp in Rochdale refined the traditional thrusting approach with its hit-and-miss attitude to clitoral stimulation. It also helped compensate for the difference in our heights. I lifted myself up and effected entry at a higher angle, leaning seventeen degrees to the right of Geraldine's torso. I had been preparing myself mentally for a while. *Prior Planning Prevents Poor Performance*, as they say in the regiment.

"Relax," Geraldine whispered. "You're not penetrating enemy lines."

"Sorry."

The dominatrix effected a 180-degree rotation, straddled me, and executed a ferociously undisciplined but fearsomely committed rogering.

Twenty minutes later, all operational targets had been achieved and it was time for a tactical withdrawal. We lay in each other's arms on my single bed. Things were intimate but cramped.

"Was that too boring?" Geraldine asked.

"Course not."

"It's just that, off-duty, I like things as straight as possible."

"Suits me."

"It does suit you. It suits you rather well."

I kissed her.

"You're very affectionate for a military man."

"Ever thought of signing up?"

"I'm a dominatrix. I don't take orders - I give them."

"Fair enough."

"Your mum's nice."

"Thanks. So's yours."

"My mum!" Geraldine leapt up and scrambled for her clothes.

"Something I said?"

"Yes! I've abandoned my mum!"

Geraldine ran out, just as my own mum shuffled in.

"I'll look after this for her, Bill." Mum cradled Geraldine's fluffy, pink cue-case. "You run along, dear."

"Thanks, mum." I bomb-blasted after Geraldine.

14.59

Geraldine was easy to catch, but that didn't mean she was easy to persuade. Her instinct was to sprint back home to her dungeon as quickly as possible, but I was certain that the situation required a covert approach. After an intense bicker, I manage to convince her that, for the urban evader, pavements were perilous, and I led her through Wandsworth's dark underbelly, seeking shelter in shopping centres, multi-storey car parks, and public conveniences. We emerged from cubicles with painstaking care, firing off glances North, South, East and West; we crawled behind parked cars, peeking over bonnets and peering beneath undercarriages; we prized open fire doors, disabling alarms and climbing down escape ladders.

An hour or two later, I calculated that it was safe to make a disguised approach towards the dungeon.

Geraldine's patience was wearing thin. "That wasn't just a paranoid episode, Bill, it was an omnibus edition."

"I don't want you to get dropped."

"You're morbidly obsessed with toilets, car parks and fire escapes. Are you autistic?"

"I'm quite good at drawing."

"Moron," she observed, ruffling my hair with both affection and violence.

"Look, running away isn't just about length, it's about creating angles."

"Like so much in life." Geraldine winked. "You're not armed, are you?"

Information could be a dangerous burden; it should be dispensed on a need-to-know basis. Did she need to know? No. Did I want to show off? Yes. "The holster's covert."

"You mean it's in your pants."

"That's standard operating procedure."

"Why can't you talk like a human?"

"I'm a soldier." There, the cat was well and truly out of the bag.

17.15

Geraldine wanted to go through her front door, but I preferred a secure approach, scaling the fence, tripping over a collapsed tower of gardening equipment, crawling along a muddy alley, and fighting through waist-high weeds.

Once inside, Geraldine made for the dining room, threw open the door and cradled her mum. "You shouldn't have come back here."

"I'd left my knitting behind."

"I don't want you to get hurt."

"There are all your young men to think of." Geraldine's mum nodded at a cheap CCTV screen: a line of fuzzy A-types shuffled in frustration, twitching at dark desires unfulfilled. "Some of them have been queuing an awfully long time. What do you want me to do?"

Geraldine sighed and let go of her mum. "I suppose we'll have to try sensory deprivation again."

"Sensory deprivation it is, dear."

I watched Geraldine and her mum empty an ebony cupboard of inflatable body suits, wigs, blindfolds, chain-mail waistcoats, gas masks, iron jockstraps and eyeless sacks.

"Is that your dressing up box?" I enquired.

"Cowboys and Indians!" Geraldine's mum laughed.

"Cops and robbers!" Geraldine giggled.

"Geraldine used to make a lovely fairy princess," her mum said.

"She still does," I added.

Geraldine lifted a pile of pig masks out of the cupboard and matched each one with a pair of donkey earmuffs.

"Are you sure about this?" I asked.

"How else am I going to get rid of the queue?" Geraldine's finger hovered over the door release button.

I intercepted her digit. "Give me five minutes. The dead florist is still in the dungeon."

Geraldine retreated to restore her vampiric make-up, while I walked across the dungeon with her mum.

"You can put him in the coffin if you like, dear."

"What coffin?"

"The vertical one in the hallway that reads, *Welcome to Hell*."

"Oh. That coffin. Thanks."

"You go ahead, dear. I'm missing *Gardener's Question Time*."

18.42

I opened the concealed cage and held a Chinese Parliament with myself, debating the best method of shifting my fellow florist's body a significant distance across the flagstones. There were several carrying techniques available: the side drag, the piggyback and the webbing stretcher, but there really was no easy way for a five-foot-two-inch bantamweight to lift a six-foot-three-inch, steroid-inflated corpse. I considered lifting the dungeon door off its hinges and using it as a stretcher, but it was solid and covered in chains.

Improvisation isn't just for thespians; it can also be a highly effective approach to corpse disposal, so I decided to make stuff up. I squatted across the departed florist, tied his arms together and looped them around my neck. I then used the immense power in my highly developed thighs to raise myself to a standing position. As Rankin had been over a foot taller than me, this was only achievable by letting his legs protrude between my own. I was now face-to-face with the assassin I had just killed, and we resembled the worst couple in the history of *Strictly Come Dancing*. I walked at a waddle, Rankin's hefty legs dragging along the flagstones behind me, as we made our way out of the dungeon and along the hallway. He was like a slaughtered ox, a mountain of lifeless muscle, and progress was slow.

Once we had reached Geraldine's vertical coffin, I ducked my head out of Rankin's arms, and attempted to shut the lid on him. He flopped forwards and I caught him awkwardly. I shoved him back in and repeated the process, achieving the same result. There was probably a reason why coffins tended towards the horizontal. At my third attempt, I got my timing right and shoved both lid and corpse into place simultaneously. Back of the net!

18.47

When I returned to the dungeon, I found half-a-dozen smartly suited men sat around the dungeon in pig masks and donkey earmuffs. Each of them was cuffed to a different cage, cross or bench and they had all been thoroughly secured. I was impressed - taking prisoners was a craft - but I did worry that Geraldine and her mum might be lacking in the long-term strategy department. "Are you just going to leave them there?"

"They all seem quite happy." Geraldine smiled.

"And each bloke really reckons he is the only client?"

"Oh yes. Privacy's essential. The pig masks are eyeless, and the donkey muffs are impervious." Geraldine wiggled on her heels and looked directly into my eyes. "Want to take a look upstairs?"

I was curious, but a tad worried that we would be testing her clients' patience.

"They'll expect a sensory deprivation session to last at least forty-five minutes," Geraldine explained. "Mum can keep them unhappy."

"Don't you worry, dear," Geraldine's mum said, flourishing a carpet-beater.

18.53

Geraldine's apartment was no dungeon; it was a decidedly cheery cross between an art gallery and a junk shop. An inflatable globe dangled from the ceiling; cheap, churchy objects covered the tabletops and for some reason, she had gone and framed a tube map. The map was probably of pensionable age, just like the retro signs she had pinned to the walls. There was an *Emergency Exit* above the entrance, a *Telephone* over the telephone and a *No Smoking* by the fireplace.

"It's good to make things nice and clear,' I observed. I have always admired comprehensive signage.

"Thanks."

I picked up a *Jesus and Mary Post-It*. "You're religious?"

"Evangelically agnostic."

I trod on something fluffy, triggering a distressed whistle. I flung us both to the floor and braced myself for a blast.

"It's only a *Clanger*," Geraldine complained.

"Oh."

"It won't explode."

"Good," I said, overjoyed that we weren't dead, but gutted at the implications of a cuddly toy. "You've got kids?"

"No." Geraldine laughed at the thought. "I just like Clangers." She pointed at her mantelpiece, where six of the crocheted alien rodents sat in line.

I didn't object to Clangers. I fondly recalled their whistle-based communications, their soup dragon, and their small, blue planet. But I did have a problem making sense of Geraldine. Whilst some of the on-site visual evidence was correct, much of it seemed designed to attract inaccurate conclusions. Thoughts raced through my mind, but they were too fast for me. I had completed the *Understanding Subtlety Course* at Doncaster, but it wasn't my strong point. I rubbed my temple, struggling for clarity. "I don't get it."

"Confusing, people, aren't they?"

I wasn't sure how best to answer, so I just said, "You know where you are with yomps."

Geraldine laughed, but I had meant it. A wet yomp is one of the purest things on Earth. The mental image of boot on mud put my military mindset on full alert and I scanned the room for points of access and egress. The *Emergency Exit* sign indicated a route to the stairs we had ascended and there were windows offering fifteen-foot drops onto the front garden and back passage, but something else caught my eye for the first time – a set of uneven bumps in her rug.

"Stop staring at my trapdoor," Geraldine protested with a giggle.

I lifted the rug, and she was right – it concealed a trapdoor. I opened it and looked directly down into the dungeon. A heavy chain dangled down to the flagstones below.

"Some clients like me to make a dramatic entrance," she explained.

I pictured Geraldine swinging down the chain like a Gothic Tarzan. It was an image to launch a thousand whips.

I replaced the rug and started checking the windows for external threats.

"Sit down and chill out, Bill. I'm sure that florist was heavy. Get some rest."

"I'll sleep when I'm tired." I twitched a front curtain and my diligence paid off big time. "Geraldine?"

"Bill?"

"Are you expecting a large group of heavily armed clients?"

"No."

"You're sure?"

"I'd have remembered."

"Then it's time to get out the worry beads."

CHAPTER 16

Bill had assassinated an assassin, dominated a dominatrix, and successfully introduced her to his mum. I had no doubt that he would deal equally effectively with the heavily armed arrivals.

I tried to imagine a universe in which I was that successful; a world where my actions didn't rebound on me at every turn, and where stuff turned out all right. It was a bit of a stretch.

I decided to stop feeling sorry for myself and took a moment to perform what I call "Bin Fire Therapy". I pictured an industrial skip; one of those roll-on, roll-off numbers popular with construction companies and people traffickers. I then gathered up all my failures: my terminated marriages, my criminal convictions, my addictions, my lost jobs, my eviction notices, my county court judgments, and my bankruptcy orders. Then I plonked all of this unhelpful mental baggage in the imaginary skip, doused it in petrol and set fire to it. The flames engulfed my troubles, sending clouds of noxious fumes into the atmosphere and singeing my eyebrows. I felt lighter, freer, and a bit embarrassed.

Bin Fire Therapy can work wonders, but it can't cure loneliness. Some would say, "What are you complaining about? You've got an entire strip club to yourself, you ungrateful little herbert!" But what use is a strip club without strippers, cheesy music, and dodgy customers? All the world's an empty stage, as Shakespeare would have said if he had been an unemployed life coach in my predicament.

But enough about me. The next page in Bill's dossier was a felt-tip note reading, "Time for some more security transcripts and case notes. The Stealth Service had taken an age to notice me and, given that I am basically working for their interests, this was a bit bloody late in the day. Her Majesty's finest spooks really do leave no trick unmissed. James Bloody Bond oversells their talents so much, he should be done by Advertising Standards."

NATIONAL STEALTH SERVICE

Transcription of Appraisal Meeting

Wednesday 20 May 9.32 a.m.

Present: "F" (Tutor, Head of Operational Discretion, National Stealth Service) and George Gurney (Trainee Junior Watcher, Remedial Unit, National Stealth Service).
Appraisal exercise: Dignity retrieval.

GURNEY: Hello, F.
F: Gurney.
GURNEY: That doorman has turned up again.
F: To which doorman are you referring?
GURNEY: The tiny one. From Bar Achilles.
F: Thought he might.
GURNEY: You know him?
F: His combat skills were somewhat distinctive.
GURNEY: Totally legend, more like.
F: Legendary, Gurney. Do pay some attention to grammar. Where, precisely, has he turned up?
GURNEY: A dungeon.
F: Good God.
GURNEY: In Wandsworth.
F: Oh yes. I know the one.
GURNEY: You do?

F: Jezebel O'Hell. She's meant to be rather good.

GURNEY: Shall I read you Stalin's notes?

F: Please go ahead. My breath is thoroughly bated.

Chief Inspector Stalin, Wandsworth CID

Case Notes – Tuesday 19 May

Time until dinner: One hour sixteen minutes.
Location: Interview room.
Risk Assessment: Potentially unsafe proximity to suspicious-looking member of the public (injured florist).

I glowered across a wobbly desk at Leonard while Donald paced around menacingly. Leonard smelt like a rose garden but looked as battered as Clint Eastwood in the closing stages of *Unforgiven*. I decided to start gently. "How's the arm?"

"Fine," he replied, inaccurately.

According to the doctor, Leonard's arm had been broken in twelve different places. Most people would have screamed the station down, but Leonard just sat there, looking vengeful.

Donald got up from the seat beside me and started pacing. It was sufficiently menacing to end Leonard's silence.

"The doctor asked me to cough, but I'll never cough. I'm no grass."

I had never seen a less likely looking flower-fancier. "Perhaps if I bumped into a bloke like you on the slopes of Mount Doom, I wouldn't bat an eyelid, but surrounded by dahlias, you're a little out of place."

"I'm a legitimate florist."

"But compared to say, Alan Titchmarsh, you look a tad - what's the word?'

"Murderous, Guv," Donald said.

"Looks aren't everything." Leonard scratched his heavily bandaged conk.

Donald grabbed Leonard's nose and squeezed his nostrils. Leonard smashed his fist onto the desk. It collapsed.

"Impressive," Donald said.

"Heavy work, is it, floristry?' I asked.

"Some arrangements can be arduous." Leonard's prominent veins pulsed puce.

I gave him the once-over. He was an ugly specimen, but ferociously strong. He wasn't exactly muscle-bound, but he didn't have an ounce of fat on him. I was intrigued. "Tell me, can you build sinew'?"

"If you live on your nerves," Leonard replied.

It was my nerves he was getting on, so I cut to the chase. "You totalled a police car whilst carrying two firearms, numerous injuries and a cargo of dahlias."

"I was car-jacked," Leonard replied. "A nutter held a gun - no, two guns - to my head. I struggled, he did me and that's all I remember."

"This carjacker," I asked. "What did he look like?"

"A midget in a suit. Said his name was Tell. Bill Tell."

"William Tell?" I pictured a Swiss mountaineer with a crossbow, an apple, and an overture. "You're having a laugh."

"That's what he said."

"A carjacker told you his name?' Donald picked up a shattered desk plank and held it to Leonard's head. "Sociable sort, was he?'

"No," Leonard replied, "Just violent."

Time until dinner: Forty-four minutes.

Location: Reception, Smugglers Way Police Station.

Risk Assessment: angry florist within striking distance.

As fond farewells went, Leonard's parting wasn't exactly up there with Bogart and Bergman's, but Wandsworth has very little in common with Casablanca.

"You may think you know what you're dealing with," Leonard warned as we walked him towards the door. "But believe me, you don't."

"This is Wandsworth, not Chinatown." I wasn't going to miss looking at him. If it was true that you ended up with the face you deserved, Leonard had been a very naughty boy indeed.

Donald gave Leonard's nose a final tweak. "That must really smart,"

Leonard shoved him off. "Only when I breathe."

"Don't feel obliged to," I said.

"If you're ever in need of a wreath, your next of kin are welcome to drop in at the florists." Leonard threw the door open.

I enjoyed watching it rebound on his broken arm.

"So, Guv," Donald said once Leonard had stomped out of earshot. "The sex shop gave us a description; the florist gave us a name…'

"And I'll give us a snout. Get your coat."

Time until dinner: Thirty-two minutes (with any luck).

Location: Wandsworth streets (various).

Risk assessment: Unacceptable levels of pollution, severe weather conditions, uneven pavements.

Wandsworth High Street was looking even grimmer than usual. Something unmentionable was blocking a drain and the rainwater swelled into a litter-crested torrent. Rain bounced off Donald's Burberry and soaked through my trench coat. It may not have been remotely waterproof, but at least it was aptly named: appearing to have spent several months in a trench. The stains were heavy and varied, a colourful collage of beer, ketchup, and fried egg. One day, I'll take it to the dry cleaners, but I like its smell and it seems a shame to spoil it.

"Thirsty?' I asked my sergeant, steering him towards a flat-roofed pub before he could reply. Creaking above the door, a sign depicted a mounted monarch rearing his steed's hooves over the words *The King Billy*. The beer – an Ulster concoction called "Bottle of the Boyne." – was not my favourite, but I had promised Donald a snout, and there was a prime one inside.

The King Billy was stuffed with enough Ulster Unionist bumf to start an argument. Clockwork Orangemen beat drums and blew into flutes; red and white bunting lingered from St George's Day celebrations and a mural depicted a Union Jack-swathed King Charles and Queen Camilla posing with Kalashnikovs. A trivia machine interrogated customers on topics including *Jesuit Plots*, *Glasgow Rangers Victories* and *Catholic Executions*. Where most pubs had signs reading, "You don't have to be mad to work here, but it helps", The King Billy had gold-leafed inscriptions proclaiming,

"God Save Ulster!", "Kill All Taigs!" and "Down with Fenian Scum, Spawn of Rome!". There were no photographs of darts teams or Christmas parties; just framed pictures of Orange Order marches alongside a list of pool fixtures: The Loyalist Volunteer Force versus The Ulster Defence Association; The Orange Volunteers versus The Red Hand Defenders. There was an alcohol-free area selling tea and scones to the Presbyterians: the scariest customers. A notice proclaimed that unruly drinkers weren't just barred; they were given twenty-four hours to leave the country.

As we made our way to the bar, customers sang *God Save The King*, as RUC collection tins were passed around. I did my best to join in but could not remember the lyrics and had to mouth most of them. Shame really, as I like a good singsong. If it had been the *Internationale*, I'd have been laughing.

The landlord was a pumped-up heavy with precision-parted hair and a red, white, and blue t-shirt. He wasn't the friendliest of fellows, but he had proven a useful snout over the years.

"A Bottle of the Boyne," I said.

"And a Virgin Mary," Donald added, before I could stop him.

The national anthem performed an emergency stop and silence filled the pub like an unspoken threat. The landlord shook his head in disgust, jaw jutting, eyes aflame. "What do you mean ordering a Virgin Mary? We'll have no Papists in here!"

"Sorry, Ian,' I said. "It's just a Bloody Mary without the booze."

He stifled a curse, pulled a pint, and prepared a Virgin Mary, plonking a Union Jack cocktail flag into the glass when he had finished.

I handed him a twenty. "Name *Bill Tell* mean anything to you?'

He turned pale and dropped the drinks. Donald's Virgin Mary smashed on the bar and drenched my white shirt in blood-red goo. The landlord didn't apologize, he just said, "The man who infiltrated the UDF and the Real IRA simultaneously and convinced them to kneecap each other's quartermasters?'

"Wouldn't put it past him," I said.

"Little bloke in a blazer," Donald added.

"Lives with his mum," the landlord said. "British Security has him under surveillance."

"How do you know?" I asked.

"We've had British Security under surveillance for the best part of five decades," he replied.

"Don't blame you," I said. "In my experience, they show scant respect for Health and Safety legislation, so they're well worth keeping an eye on."

"Ach, the spooks are getting worse. They've assigned a brainless little twerp of about twelve to Tell's case. I don't think they know who they're dealing with."

"Have you got an address for Tell's mum?"

"Excuse me a moment."

The landlord withdrew up a staff staircase.

While we waited, I used a Boyne beer towel to wipe the Virgin Mary off my shirt. I didn't make much progress. In fact, the more I rubbed the angry red stain, the more it looked like I had been shot, or gut-capped as they probably said in Northern Ireland.

When the landlord returned, he scrawled two addresses on a Boyne bitter mat and handed it across the bar. "Here you go. But he's not at his mum's, he was last seen at the second address with a dominatrix. Be careful, she'll probably be armed with something kinky."

Time until dinner: At least an hour ago.
Location: Pub.
Risk assessment: Danger of starvation.

We probably should have acted on the tip-off immediately, but it would have been criminal to leave a pub without drinking, and the landlord had been good enough to offer replacements for our spilled drinks on the house. Boozing on duty has its opponents within the Force, but I find it helps combat stress and provides officers with a protective haze to keep anxiety at bay.

After I had downed my pint, we stopped off at a bakery. Long experience has taught me that, for Health and Safety reasons, monumental quantities of post-pub pastry should be consumed to balance the liquid intake. Today, I had already munched my way through three sausage rolls, and a cheese and onion pasty. Adding a steak and kidney pudding would complete my five recommended portions of lard a day. Once I had made the purchase, I called the station, summoned an armed response unit to the dominatrix's address, and headed for the car.

Time until dinner: Pie o'clock!
Location: Police vehicle (unmarked).

Risk assessment: Aggressive driver (sergeant).

While Donald drove, I got stuck into my steak and kidney pudding. Ah, the Pie of Life: a magic cauldron lidded in pastry, its hidden ingredients bound together by a mysterious alchemy. A decent pie was like a lover, every bite an intimate encounter, a kiss with tongues.

"Ready for the raid, Guv?" Donald crested a speed bump and landed with such force that hot steak and kidney pudding spilled onto my crotch.

"Bollocks!"

"Sorry, Guv."

"Can you slow down while I finish my pie?"

"Thought we were in a hurry to get to the dungeon?"

"I've got to do the risk assessment first."

"Can't you just make it up afterwards, Guv?"

"Certainly not, Sergeant. I refuse to take a cavalier attitude towards my colleagues. I'll do it when we get there."

"Don't you think the armed officers will get a bit impatient, Guv?"

"We're not rushing in willy-nilly. Just imagine how many trip hazards there are in a dungeon."

"Hardly bears thinking about, Guv."

I necked the pastry and gawped out of the window, watching the roads get posher and less interesting. Suburbia was somewhere to sneer at in youth and inhabit shortly afterwards. Below its soulless surface lay oceanic depths of tedium: concrete griffins stood watch over Mock Tudor mini-mansions, disappointed women nurtured resentments to maturity and surrendered husbands sought sanctuary in their sheds. The silence was only occasionally broken by a cornered cat's scream, the shouts of bored teenagers or a car alarm's electronic hysterics. Fragile peace deceived: a disputed boundary, a neglected garden or a car parked out of place could provoke anonymous threats, inventive vandalism, and poisonous wars of attrition, as my officers knew only too well.

This was a place of quiet envy: the loftless resented the vertically extended and the street-parkers envied the garage-owners. The people most to be envied, the yachting, company-floating, country house-inhabiting elite, didn't live in the suburbs at all; but they did find themselves drawn to suburban dungeons on occasion.

The dominatrix's road was safe, sleepy, and comfortable, but her clients were seekers after discomfort. Their careers had been well rewarded, but they all knew that they deserved to be punished.

Urban raids were usually about small-time drug dealers: three or four burly cozzers and a guard on the drainpipe. Suburban raids were rarer, but often more serious - drug importers, fraudsters, and successful pimps. Murder was another matter; we were mob-handed.

For a surprise raid, this had all the subtlety of a Pro-Celebrity Caber Toss with brass band accompaniment. SO19 officers levelled sub-machine guns over the bonnets of armed response vehicles and snatch squads squatted in the shrubbery.

I sneaked behind a hedge to finish off my risk assessment. DS Donald stood beside me, pointing a torch onto my notepad, and shielding me from the other coppers.

Their Senior Firearms Officer hadn't clocked that I was in hearing range and asked my sergeant, "Are you the SIO?'

"The Senior Investigating Officer?' queried my DS.

"Yes."

"No."

"Well, what's he doing then?"

"Writing a risk assessment."

"It's not that prat Stalin, is it?"

"He's protecting his officers."

"He's covering his arse." The SFO turned to his colleagues. "We could be some time lads. An arse the size of Stalin's will take some covering."

"It's Federation business," Donald said.

"Pie Night at *The Blind Beggar*, more like." The SFO said.

"He may look like a veteran gut-barging champion...' Donald began.

"...But deep down he's thin?" the SFO added.

"He's a lean, mean, nicking machine," an Authorised Firearms Officer said with heavy sarcasm.

"Hungry," another AFO said.

"He's always hungry," the SFO said.

"He's in a hedge," Donald explained.

"What's he doing sat in a hedge?" the SFO asked.

It was high time to make myself known, so I crawled out of the undergrowth.

"I'm taking ruddy responsibility, I'll have you know. I'm writing method descriptions, making safety cases, and categorising accidents. This is just as important as going on the actual raid. It's all very well charging into places with guns, but someone has to take on the burden of identifying hazards, rating them on a scale of one to twelve and outlining steps to minimise risk."

"We've already identified escape routes and observation points through infrared scans," the SFO said. "What else do you want us to do?"

"It's a hostile environment," I replied.

"We're in Wandsworth," the SFO said.

"Exactly."

"The posh bit."

"Even more hazardous."

"This is an Armed Response Unit, SO-bleeding-19."

"The dominatrix might very well be armed too."

"Maybe with something leather," Donald added.

"We're equipped with Glock 17 self-loading pistols and Heckler & Koch MP5 carbines," the SFO said.

"There's a homicidal florist in there," I said.

"What's he going to do, rearrange our petals?"

"Any pollen allergies?"

"We're The Yard's most highly trained marksman, fully accustomed to tackling terrorist units and capable of rescuing hostages from chemical, biological or nuclear environments."

"Have you got a fallback sandwich option?"

"We're all veterans of the Milton Simulation Gallery, abseil-trained and shotgun-ready with immaculate results on National Rapid Intervention Shoots. We don't bother with sarnies."

"Have you scheduled in a tea break?"

"We carry rehydration pellets."

"Are you wearing high visibility jackets?"

"They're under our bullet-proof vests."

"Do you know the quickest route to the local Outpatients Department in case of sprains?"

"We've got GPS systems in our armour-plated vehicles."

"I'm afraid that doesn't quite dice the Dijon. You need photocopied maps - and just look at all these trip hazards. The garden is a potential death trap: the pea shingle is slippery, there's a lot of give in the decking and the ground-effects bark looks treacherous."

"We've got spring-loaded battering rams, anti-ballistic shields, window smashers, hydraulic door opening devices, flashlights, and smoke and concussion pyrotechnics."

"All perfect for causing actionable injuries. We'll have to call it off. It's way too dangerous."

DS Donald nudged me aside for a man-to-man conspire. "It's Friday afternoon. If we don't nab the little florist soon, Guv, the Super will make us do weekend overtime."

"Ok," I said. "Go on then."

"Thanks, Guv."

"Be careful."

"I will." Donald turned to the armed officers and bawled, "Go, go, go!"

Nothing happened, so Donald repeated his shouted, "Go, go, go!"

No one went.

"Have you got a stutter?" the SFO asked.

"No," Donald said.

"Oh," the SFO said.

We waited like a bunch of plonkers until I realised that, as the Senior Investigating Officer, it was down to me to give the go-ahead, so I shouted a weary, "Go ruddy go-go!"

They went. Hefty cozzers emerged from all angles; ran down the garden path and banjoed Geraldine's door with a battering ram. Hinges squealed as SO19 stormed into the dungeon.

I settled down behind a variegated yucca to keep an ear on the radios and to have a bit of a rest. Bottle of the Boyne bitter can carry a bit of a punch, however much you moderate its effects with pastry.

I had only just fallen asleep when Donald's voice broke through the fuzz. "They're already handcuffed, Guv."

"What are you complaining about, then? The job's half done."

"They're nearly all in pig masks and donkey earmuffs, Guv."

"I don't care if they're in hot pants! Snatch the lot of them."

Time since dinner: An eternity.

Location: Suburban Street, Wandsworth (the posh bit).

Risk assessment: Dominatrix and florist (murder suspect), poor lighting conditions, angry masochists.

The pig-masked masochists knew that they were going to be made to squeal. I watched them, huddled in the police van like livestock to the slaughter. I couldn't see their faces, but I could tell by their tailoring that they were Lodge-lice to a man: aficionados of the silken noose, the bared breast and the rolled-up trouser leg. These upstanding pillocks of the community had pledged allegiance to their "craft", sworn to make good men better and promised to support others in times of need. This was their time of need. They had transgressed and, for these crafty fellows and grand masters, transgression could see their tongues packed off to the seaside, their hearts served to ravenous birds and their bowels burned to ashes, the poor little tosspots.

Time since dinner: Epochs.

Time to last orders: 1 hour 59 minutes.

Location: Exterior SO19 Armed Response Vehicle, suburban street.

Risk assessment: Weapons (mislaid). Dangerous florist at large.

SO19 came out unarmed, which was decidedly odd for an armed response unit.

"Where are your guns?" I asked.

"The florist disarmed us," the SFO said. "Lovely bloke. He didn't mind us arresting him if we didn't hurt the dominatrix."

"But he's a murder suspect."

"He's a gent," an AFO said.

"There you go, sir." The tiny florist handed me a heap of artillery. He saluted, about turned, and joined his dominatrix in the back of a Panda.

Time to last orders: 1 hour 44 minutes.

Location: Police vehicle (unmarked).

Risk assessment: Aggressive driver (my sergeant). Streetlights in woefully inadequate state of repair.

The journey back to the nick was bleaker than a crackhead's prospects: disappointing superstores, deadly office blocks and unpopular housing developments overlooked post-human landscapes. Workers in luminous waistcoats annoyed motorists by unloading traffic calming equipment, and engines bled petrol across cracked tarmac. If Wandsworth was a state of mind, it would be depressive psychosis.

Not a single word passed between me and Donald, and I didn't even consider playing any socialist folk music. My brain was occupied by one thing and one thing only: how the devil had the little florist disarmed an entire armed unit single handed?

Time to last orders: 1 hour 22 minutes.
Location: Police station.
Risk assessment: Numerous trip hazards, harsh lighting, poorly positioned desks, shoddily maintained ceilings, inadequate ventilation, hostile colleagues. Shall I go on?

Before we could get our teeth into the dominatrix and the florist, we had to process the masochists. What sort of bloke pays to be handcuffed, pig masked, and donkey muffed? I doubted that they were regular, happily married chaps struggling to make ends meet.

DS Donald followed me through Custody, muttering about his ducks. I generally do my best to be supportive, but on this occasion, I failed to feign interest. I lifted the first cell's viewing flap and found myself peering at a fuming septuagenarian I had encountered a number of times before.

"He's a High Court judge," I said. "I've got to give evidence before him next week."

"Sorry, Guv," Donald said.

I peeked into the second cell, where a bland man was slouching in a grey suit. I didn't know him personally, but he had been on the news. "He's a senior civil servant. Currently chairing a committee fixing police pay."

"That's not good, is it Guv?"

"Not for us, no."

I looked into the third cell, where a coiffured City gent was pacing up and down furiously. Now, I don't make a practise of consorting with capitalists, but this bloke I knew. "He's a banker who was about to donate two-hundred-and-eighty grand to the Police Benevolent Fund. He also plays golf with The Super."

"Bloody hell. What's The Super going to say?"

"Ask him yourself, Sergeant. He's in the next cell."

The Super looked like an anger bomb ready to detonate. Luckily, he could only see our eyes, and we didn't keep his cell-flap open for long.

DS Donald was not easily shocked. He had witnessed some horrendous injuries over the course of his career (he had inflicted most of them), but I had never seen him look so pale. Superintendent Whiteread was our über-Stilton and we had nicked him. As career moves went, it wasn't the shrewdest.

"How about our florist?' Donald asked.

I pointed to a cell on the opposite side of the corridor. Donald trudged over and lifted the flap, revealing Bill Tell, a sarky little snurge saluting in a suit. At least we would have someone to take it all out on once we had freed the Masonic masochists.

Time to last orders: 52 minutes.
Time since discovered vending machine empty: Ten minutes.
Location: Custody.
Risk assessment: Powerful masochists bent on vengeance.

My sergeant and I stood contritely beside each cell, apologising in unison to the eminent masochists as they were released by a custody officer.

"Sorry sir," we said to the septuagenarian judge.

He made an obscene gesture and stormed out.

"Sorry sir," we said to the civil servant.

He elbowed me in the gut as he passed and asked whether we were looking forward to our pay cut.

"Sorry, sir," we said to the investment banker.

He mimed the violent mutilation of an invisible chequebook.

"Sorry sir," we said to The Super.

"One word about this," The Super said. "And you're on lollipop parade."

The Super had risen through conformity; an office politician, bland, unimaginative, and talentless but bursting with deference, a finger ever ready to point blame in any convenient direction. He had stitched up most of his rivals, but I had survived. I had the Federation on my side, after all. But just because I was there for the foreseeable future, that didn't mean The Super liked me; it meant quite the opposite. He treated me like the son he wished he'd never had.

With the masochists out of our hair, we just had the florist and the dominatrix to deal with. As a rule, the sergeant and I relish face-to-face interviews. They give DS Donald the opportunity to threaten people and I enjoy gaining a first-hand, socio-economic insight into the causes of a particular crime. But after the monumental failure of the masochist-snatch, we weren't really in the mood.

"IR1, Guv?"

"Suppose so."

Interview Room 1 was the smelliest, which had the advantage of discomforting the interviewees. However, it also discomforted us, and I wasn't particularly raring to endure its delights.

"Shall we get some kip first?"

"Good thinking, Donald. Sleep deprivation is an avoidable hazard."

CHAPTER 17

I could not have admired Bill Tell more if he had saved all my children from drowning and assassinated all my ex-wives. This geezer was the real deal – he had stood his ground and made prize plonkers of the police. What a hero! I was only too happy to avenge his death.

I had to know how he had pulled it off, and luckily, the bumf's next offerings were a slice of diary, a dollop of case notes, and another slice of diary: a veritable Stalin-sandwich.

JOURNAL - EX-SERGEANT BILL TELL

Wednesday 20 May, 03.24

I had not resigned myself passively to captivity. From the moment I arrived in the Custody Area, I had taken steps to build a prisoner-of-war infrastructure. Firstly, there had been the question of personnel. Unfortunately, the available personnel were all questionable. I was forced to make a chronic alcoholic my adjutant, a burglar my quartermaster and three jabbering crackheads my Heads of Welfare, Education and Entertainment. When the police threw me into my cell, I rolled the bed blanket into a ring, held my face to the hole and tried to talk through the walls. No one answered, so I decided to maintain my morale by pretending to be on parade.

I stood to attention in my cell, motionless and undefeated, and recalled the armed raid on Geraldine's dungeon. I remembered eyeballing SO19 through her upstairs curtains and holding a Chinese parliament with myself. Was the best policy fight or flight? Going down in a blaze of glorified gunfire is super-duper if you've only got yourself to think of, but I was not alone. Flight seemed over-optimistic, given that there were only two available exits. Concealment had worked with Rankin. I was fully aware that a single florist was a different proposition to a heavily armed unit, but I conceived a plan that would allow me to disarm my adversaries, thereby guaranteeing the safety of the dominatrix and her mother. After that, surrender would be a monumental victory.

I heard a hat trick of *Go, go, goes!* from below. In the regiment, we only ever require a single set of *Go, go, goes!* before we go, but this lot clearly lacked our get-up-and-go. Gun magazines clicked home and my training kicked in: *Reject fear, it can kill. Action is all.*

"Don't worry, Geraldine," I had said. "I'm a CP specialist."

"So am I," she had replied.

"CP?"

"Corporal Punishment."

"Close Protection." I was always the closest protector, the man in the line of fire; the only one who didn't look like a bodyguard. The big guys were the window dressing, and I was the window. I had run war games in the Urban Terrain Centre on Orkney and led regimental courses in *Attack Reaction*, *Route Security*, and *Close Quarter Combat* in Bourton-on-the-Water. SO19 did not stand a chance.

I lifted Geraldine's rug, opened her trapdoor, and effected dungeon entry through the descendible cage-chain. Her mum was mid-way through thumping a pig-masked masochist when I swept her off her feet.

"Mind my hip, dear," she had said. "It's not real."

I shouldered her with painstaking care and shimmied back up the metal links to the first floor. Geraldine was delighted to see her mum emerge through the trapdoor, but the celebrations were cut short by the fearsome thunk of the dungeon door below as it yielded to SO19's battering rams.

I secreted Geraldine's mum in the bathroom and plunged back down the trapdoor. As I had suspected, the armed response unit had been temporarily disarmed by the sight of the pig-faced, donkey-eared masochists. Paralysed by incredulity, SO19 were helpless, so I span the cage-chain, whipping away their weapons while they gawped slack-jawed and gobsmacked. I knew their collective double-take wouldn't last long, so I span back up the cage-chain sharpish.

As soon as I rose through the trapdoor, I grabbed Geraldine and did a bomb-burst, hitting the deck and covering her with my body. *In speed lies success*, as the regiment taught me on Ruislip Lido. At least this wasn't an SAS raid: they would have used trip wire booby traps with thunder flash connections, but I knew SO19 would still be working on the principle of *P for Plenty* and *V for Vindictive*.

I heard the armed cozzers put all their aggro into snatching the masochists (daft sods, as if they wanted to do anyone any harm). They should have neutralised the threat - and, as the threat, I should know. But it suited them to block me from their minds and get on with the obvious arrests. It was classic Stockport Syndrome: ignore what you can't explain and crack on with the job in hand.

As soon as I heard the last copper plod out of the dungeon, I nodded to Geraldine, and led us downstairs to surrender in safety.

The coppers seemed pleased to be reunited with their weapons and I was delighted to hand us in unscathed. The situation was defused, and the rest was routine. Result!

Chief Inspector Stalin, Wandsworth CID

Case Notes – Wednesday 20 May

Time until breakfast (early sitting): Won't be long but can't be soon enough.
Location: Police station.
Risk assessment: Unacceptably intimate proximity to dominatrix (unarmed). Poor ventilation. Conditions unacceptably cramped.

I slept badly, haunted by visions of the Masonic masochists, but work didn't exactly lighten the mood. The station's interview rooms were all windowless with poorly concealed cameras and faulty panic buttons, but Interview Room 1 smelled of fear, violence, betrayal, and takeaways.

Cassettes were labelled and inserted; biros were primed for action. I identified the date, time, and scene of our interview with Jezebel O'Hell (née Geraldine Smith) and we were about to begin our interrogation when she interrupted.

"Call this a dungeon? It's a miracle you've got any inmates. There's no character."

"Oh, we're not short of inmates," I said.

"I'm surprised. There's no atmosphere. You need more chains."

I took a moment to assess the dominatrix. Was she an oppressor or a worker? Did she own her own weapons of torment or was she creating excess pain for others to cream off? Her socio-economic status was highly ambiguous, and I couldn't help but get philosophical. "One day, humanity will get around to breaking its mental chains. But you want to chain us all up. Why?"

"Men pay me to get the better of them. Many of those men are boys in blue – usually boys in black and blue, by the time I've finished with them."

Looking at her, I could well believe it. "Is punishment a rewarding line of work?"

"Well, I don't have to stick to a nine-to-five, Monday-to-Friday routine, and there's no need to commute, what with the dungeon being en suite - but I don't like the daily bump and grind. Domination's a bit like administration. Cages break just as often as photocopiers, appointments get forgotten, new clients need nurturing and old ones need reassuring. Names must be remembered, services personalised, and records maintained."

She could go on a bit, but it was better than the usual "no comment" malarkey.

"Are you V.A.T. registered?" I asked.

"The Inland Revenue list me as a *frontal osteopath*."

I was too busy smothering a guffaw, so Donald spoke for me. "How do you find clients?"

"I don't solicit. I've got word of mouth."

"Screams?" I ventured.

"They're usually the best recommendations."

I still couldn't really work her out. "Doesn't it get you down, working in a dungeon?"

"It's a bit bleak at times. I don't want the neighbours to hound me out of Wandsworth, so I can never open the curtains. The dungeon décor's not exactly uplifting either - it's not as if I can bung in a few jaunty beanbags and coloured throws, or stencil cheerful messages on the walls."

"Much as I sympathise with your interior design issues, what the bleeding hell happened with this short-arsed florist?"

"Bill freed a judge in a nappy and gave me a bunch of dahlias. When he came back, he retrieved his revolver from my vase, freed an off-duty prison governor, hid in a cage, and stopped an aggressive masochist from throttling me. I ran away and Bill caught up with me on the Wandsworth Gyratory System. He carried me onto a bendy bus, and we had a nice bit of Battenberg with his mum."

"He still lives with her, doesn't he?"

"Lovely lady, Mrs Tell - builds matchstick cathedrals. Anyway, I would have stayed the night, but I remembered that I'd forgotten about my own mum, and we raced back to make sure she was all right. When we got back to the dungeon, my mum was fine, but there was a long queue of masochists in the garden. We confused them all with pig masks and donkey earmuffs and slipped away for a chat while my mum thumped them. That's when you stormed the dungeon."

"Oh." I was reeling from the nonsense, and Donald's eyes were double-glazed.

"I can't make it clearer than that, can I?"

"Yes, love. But don't. Please." I meant it.

"I don't remember arresting anyone's mum," DS Donald said.

"You didn't," Geraldine said. "She's a harmless old lady."

"That doesn't usually stop DS Donald."

"Bill hid her," the dominatrix explained.

"And he disarmed SO19 single-handed?"

"Yes," she did a gooey gawp into the middle-distance. "He's a very nice man. Can I see him?"

"No," I replied. You can't divide and conquer if you let suspects mingle.

"I don't mind waiting."

"Fair enough," I said. "But he'll be between twenty and twenty-five years."

The dominatrix started laughing. "If you think you can hold onto Bill for longer than he wants to stay, you're even thicker than you look."

She was the most infuriating woman I had ever encountered, apart from my wife. I looked up for divine guidance. None came. Maybe God's got something against atheists.

"Look, love," I said. "I'm going to follow my gut."

"I don't think you've got any choice."

"And why's that then?"

"Well, by the look of it, your gut arrives in a room at least ten seconds before the rest of you."

"Then, with any luck, love, I'll beat the other coppers to the canteen. Come along Sergeant."

Time: Breakfast (early sitting).
Location: Police canteen.
Risk assessment: Hazards include starvation caused by queue length and food (botulism, salmonella, indigestion).

The sergeant and I received a round of applause for joining the breakfast queue, even though we had joined it at the front. No one objected, not because Donald would have hit them if they had (although he would), but because word had got around that we had caged the Super.

"Canteen culture," I murmured to Donald. "I've seen more culture in a petri dish."

"I'm more at home with ducks, Guv."

Management had taken Full English off the menu for health reasons. What remained was about as tempting as a December dip in Skegness Bay: vegan goulash, wheat-free rolls, and soya steak substitute. Whatever happened to toad-in-the-hole and spotted dick? The fridge offered a "Selection of healthy handheld snacks for deskside consumption". Twat-fodder, that's what it was.

"You get a free gym voucher with every sunflower seed snack, Guv," Donald observed in a misguided attempt to entice me.

"Gym? With a job like mine, why on Earth would I need more treadmills?"

We took our places on opposite sides of a battered table. I dipped my breadless roll into some meatless Hungarian goo, took one bite and dropped the bugger.

"Happy with the interview, Guv?"

"She was bloody uncooperative, even for a dominatrix."

"Can we hold on to her for a bit, Guv? She's quite pretty."

"Somehow, I don't think the CPS will let us. The dominatrix's client list read like a Freemasons' convention."

"Nothing wrong with builders, Guv."

"But there's plenty wrong with Lodge-lice and the justice system's riddled with them." I was off on one. "Contempt of court? How could a decent copper have anything else? Twelve bored men and true, a pair of bewigged, prancing prannies and a beetroot-jowled judge, gouty and borderline senile. What chance does a decent copper have of nailing vermin when there are dodgy-handshake merchants all over the shop? It makes the blood in my hardened arteries boil."

"Fair enough, Guv, but what do we do with the dominatrix?"

"Let her go."

"I'll miss her, Guv."

"Not for long, you won't. We'll put a tail on her."

"Won't that make her look ridiculous, Guv?"

"Quite possibly but letting her go will help us wind up the florist no end."

"Is that safe, Guv?"

"Safe? He's a five-foot-two-inch florist!"

"I know. But look at what he's done."

Donald had a point. But I had a plan - and I would rather be pointless than planless any day.

JOURNAL - EX-SERGEANT BILL TELL

Wednesday 20 May

09.26

For reasons best known to Stalin, DS Donald was tackling me alone. He is a foot taller than me and a great deal uglier, but I have never pulled back from a one-on-one. I faced my adversary across a battered desk, looking slightly askance. *Never look your interrogator in the eye - you may give yourself away*, as the regiment taught me at Richmond Upon Thames.

"Let's start at the beginning, shall we?" Donald flexed a bicep.

I'm not intimidated by muscles - I've faced down anti-aircraft missiles, so I simply didn't respond. *Don't cooperate - it will only prolong the interrogation*, as the regiment taught me at Cockermouth.

"Tell me what happened! And stick to the facts."

I could have stayed silent, but *never let a chance go by to get one over on the enemy*, as the regiment taught me at Berwick-upon-Tweed. "I freed a giant in a nappy."

"Bollocks," Donald remarked.

I cursed myself for not devising a pre-arranged cover story with Geraldine. All I could do was make life difficult for my captors, by telling the truth. "I hid in a cage." *Show neither bravado nor humility - fade into the furniture*, as the regiment taught me in Vegas.

Donald looked like a perplexed gibbon. "Explain yourself."

I knew that interrogators would try all available methods to force cooperation: information control, petty rule enforcement and, in the case of the Walloons, beard trimming. I had to fight back. In survival situations, only positive action can save you. "Have you informed the Red Cross?"

"What about?"

"My capture."

"Your arrest."

"I claim my postal privileges."

"What postal privileges?"

I knew I didn't have any, but he was clearly rattled by my counter interrogation strategies. The sheer randomness of my requests, explanations and demands soon reduced Donald to a childish state and he began doodling his duck pond on the interrogation desk.

At that point, Stalin's gut entered the room, not so closely followed by the rest of him.

He thunked his enormous arse down on the chair opposite me and uttered a blatant porky. "The dominatrix told us everything. You topped the pawnbroker, car-jacked Leonard the florist and you were about to kill her."

I wondered how much yomping Stalin would have to do before he could pass a basic fitness test. A couple of global circumnavigations? Quite possibly. But was his brain as flabby as his torso? I kicked my counterattack by misquoting Winston Churchill. "There are a lot of lies in this world. Some of them are true, but that one isn't."

Donald rose to the bait. "I'll wipe that smile off your face, you smarmy little git."

I followed through with another Churchill-bomb. "Success is the ability to go from one failure to another with no loss of enthusiasm."

"Who do you think you are?" Donald asked.

"*Exemplo Ducemis*," I replied, upping the ante.

'What?" Stalin asked.

'By example we lead,' I translated roughly from the Latin. "Military motto."

"*Fray Bentos*," Stalin said.

I shrugged.

"Pies," Stalin explained.

"Tinned?" I queried.

"Confess!" Donald screamed.

I completed my Churchill hat-trick. "When the eagles are silent, the parrots begin to jabber."

Donald smashed a chair to splinters, roaring obscenities.

I waited for him to pause for breath, before saying, "You've got my name, rank, and number. Stick to the Geneva Convention. This is Wandsworth, not Guantanamo."

DS Donald thrust a wooden spike at my face, but the weapon's trajectory was halted by the bleat of his mobile. Stalin and I watched in silence as the hulking DS reached into his jacket and held the receiver to his cauliflower ear. Donald's face crinkled and he began to cry.

"What's wrong, Donald?" Stalin asked.

A soppy smile spread across Donald's tear-stained face. "My ducklings! They can fly!"

The spike clattered to the floor. I unclenched my fists, heaved a sigh of relief, and grinned. Even if Donald was my adversary, good news was still good news, and I was more than happy to share in it.

CHAPTER 18

I have never trusted ducks. There is something about their beady eyes that makes me suspect they are plotting against humanity. Their comic quacks are simply a decoy designed to distract us from their evil intentions. But each to his own. If ducklings took DS Donald's mind off committing acts of police brutality from time to time, then that was fine by me.

Waterfowl aside, the journal and case notes had shown that Bill's training, quick thinking, and all-round swashbuckling skills were more than a match for the cozzers. The boys in blue were getting well and truly stuffed by the boy in green. Bill's success was something people called "humbling" these days. What they usually meant by this was that their achievements had made their egos swell to such humongous dimensions that their skulls were about to explode. How had humbling reversed its meaning without asking anyone's permission? It was so irritating that I decided to get up and gaze out the window for a bit.

Tooting offered little in the way of inspiration, so I looked across at the skyline. London was so big and old that people often thought about it in mythical terms, banging on about its rivers and ancient buildings as if they had human personalities. I wondered whether the same could be done with all the newer bits. Was there a Spirit of The Shard? I pictured a sinister, supercilious supervillain. A God of The Gherkin? I imagined a camp, cheeky chap with a penchant for boy bands. A Witch of Westfield Shopping Centre? Terrifying. A North Circular Road Deity? Couldn't see him picking up many worshippers.

None of this was helping much. I wondered whether Bill's military mindset could offer many techniques relevant to life coaching. I was planning a few new ventures, and I was severely lacking in the content department. I particularly wanted to launch a course for people whose dreams have been broken. Too many courses target young, aspirational people with hopes for the future, and I could see a gap in the market for older codgers whose careers had crashed and whose personal lives had descended into loneliness and misery. No one catered for the desperate and the disappointed, which struck me as an oversight, given how very many there were.

I thought of Gurney. His career was just beginning. He would be full of ambition, hope, and excitement, but anyone could see that he would fail, and end up bitter, sad, and frustrated. That would be the right time to turn to my course. Not now, when he still had dreams, but in a couple of decades when all hope had fled. That was my target audience, and I knew from experience that it was an enormous one. What could I offer them? No idea, but I would figure it out.

I returned to Bill's box. Gurney was next on the menu, and it occurred to me that he had forgotten to discuss the last instalment of Stalin's case notes with F. Maybe he was on the fast track to the scrap heap.

NATIONAL STEALTH SERVICE

Transcription of Recorded Appraisal Meeting

Recorded Wednesday, 20 May, 13.34

Present: "F" (Head of Operational Discretion, National Stealth Service) and George Gurney (Trainee Junior Watcher, Remedial Unit, National Stealth Service).

Appraisal exercise: to support the trainee's surveillance performance on what started as an insignificant snoop into a dubious floristry operation and is rapidly becoming a matter of national security.

F: Any updates?

GURNEY: Yes.

F: Go on then.

GURNEY: I forgot to update you.

F: That's the update?

GURNEY: Yes.

F: What was the update about?

GURNEY: Stalin's last case notes.

F: Why did you forget?

GURNEY: I've got a new girlfriend and she's really distracting.

F: Whilst I'm delighted for you, you do need to do your actual job.

GURNEY: Sorry F.

F: Can you summarise the contents?

GURNEY: Yes.

F: Then please do.

GURNEY: Stalin tapped up an informant in a pub, drank a beer, ate a pie, and tracked the small florist down to a dominatrix's dungeon. He delayed the operation by filling in a risk assessment in a hedge, then the small florist disarmed the entire unit. He let them arrest him, the dominatrix, and a number of pig-masked, donkey muffed masochists. The masochists were all high-placed Masons and included Stalin's own Superintendent. The detectives interviewed the dominatrix, then put a tail on her.

F: I see.

GURNEY: You didn't miss much.

F: So, the small florist remains in custody and the dominatrix has disappeared?

GURNEY: Yes. And no.

F: Which?

GURNEY: Yes, he's in custody. No, she's not disappeared.

F: Where is she?

GURNEY: We put a tail on her tail, but it wasn't really necessary.

F: Not necessary?

GURNEY: Not necessarily necessary, no. Bronze picked her up outside the police station, so all his hidden cameras and microphones covered it all.

F: Bronze knows her?

GURNEY: Yes, F. He runs an extensive dominatrix network.

F: You've surely not conducted some actual research, Gurney?

GURNEY: Yes! I looked him up on my National Stealth Service app. Ernie Bronze, a.k.a. The Maltese Vulture, a.k.a. The Dungeon Master. Saddle-skinned, silver-haired, cruel eyed – and that's just how his friends describe him. He used to own first floor "models", clip joints and video shops across the West End. He has run near-beer joints, strip clubs and orange-box flats. He's been a flat-farmer, a clocker in of circuit girls, and an established member of The Syndicate. But he's a Soho face no longer - not now the Turks and Albanians have moved in. He's adjusted his angles and now has a network of dungeons in Harrow, Kensal Rise, Colindale, Tooting Bec, Parsons Green, Walthamstow, and Wandsworth.

F: Why suburban dungeons, do you think, Gurney?

GURNEY: According to the app, they don't need much protecting. Clients are meek and wealthy. Drugs don't enter the equation. Girls are middle class. Their workload is light: they're sheltered and outwardly respectable. The only issue is the soundproofing.

F: Jolly good, Gurney. Perhaps there's hope for you yet.

GURNEY: Really?

F: No.

GURNEY: Oh. Shall I start?

F: Yes. I'm not getting any younger.

GURNEY: Okay, F:

The dominatrix walks out of the police station. Ernie Bronze follows in his gold XK8 Jaguar, matching her pace. He opens the window and initiates a conversation.

BRONZE: Where are you headed?

GERALDINE: Home.

BRONZE: From one dungeon to another.

GERALDINE: Why not? It's a free country.

BRONZE: There's no such thing.

GERALDINE: You're thinking of lunch.

BRONZE: I'm thinking of you. Get in before the florists try to make another delivery.

She gets in. Recording continues inside the vehicle.

GERALDINE: I thought you ran Wandsworth.

BRONZE: I didn't authorise your delivery.

GERALDINE: Who's trying to kill me?

BRONZE: Potter. Harold Potter.

GERALDINE: How do you know?

BRONZE: South of the river, he's the only florist capable of mounting attacks of such ferocity.

Bronze's Jaguar pulls up outside "Petal's Private Shop". Bronze and the dominatrix enter a purveyor of luxury teasers, pearly panties, and inflatable butt plugs. The proprietor, Petal, emerges from a display of novelty vibrators. All events recorded on the shop's CCTV feed (hacked into by The Stealth Service) and Bronze's personal microphones (worn under his shirt and pants).

PETAL: Hi Babes. You're alive.

GERALDINE: You sound surprised.

PETAL: Don't get your thong in a twist. I wouldn't want you dropped for all the sleaze in Soho.

GERALDINE: But Potter would.

PETAL: Where's The Precious?

GERALDINE: Snug in its cue case.

PETAL: Pink?

GERALDINE: Shocking.

PETAL: Shocking pink?

GERALDINE: Very.

BRONZE: Keep it to hand. Remember. When I financed your dungeon-conversion, you agreed to look after little things for me now and again.

GERALDINE: When can I give it back?

BRONZE: After the Chelsea Flower Show.

PETAL: Then you'll be free of it.

BRONZE: And free of your debt to me.

Petal and Bronze watch Geraldine leave the shop, then continue their conversation.

PETAL: She's minutes from a slab.

BRONZE: If your pawnbroker hadn't blabbed, there'd only have been one delivery.

PETAL: He had a bouquet levelled at his forehead.

BRONZE: I didn't think they'd use it.

PETAL: Looks like you chose the wrong florist, Babes. We've taken a lot of punters to the cleaners, but this time, we're the ones who are going to end up spin-dried.

End of recording.

F: Did you really have to do the voices, Gurney?

GURNEY: Sorry, F. I got carried away.

F: As did the florists.

GURNEY: I believe Petal has extensive underworld contacts.

F: Underwear contacts?

GURNEY: Underworld, F. The pants are a front.

F: It seems that Petal was involved with the deceased pawnbroker?

GURNEY: Until the florists delivered him, yes.

F: And Bronze had a side-scam going with Petal.

GURNEY: Looks like it, F. If there's one thing I really hate, it's dishonesty.

F: Then what are you doing in The National Stealth Service?

GURNEY: My best, F.

F: It's not the boy scouts, Gurney.

GURNEY: I left after the cubs.

F: That aside, it does appear that Bronze has been deceiving both us and Belladonna's Floral Deliveries. We are temporarily at an advantage because we are now aware of this fact and the florists are not.

GURNEY: Yes, F. Belladonna's blamed the pawnbroker for switching his diamonds and paid him a visit with a loaded bouquet. The pawnbroker tried to save his skin by telling Leonard that the dominatrix had the genuine gem. Leonard topped him anyway and Potter recruited Bill Tell to kill the dominatrix and retrieve the original diamond. Unfortunately for them, Tell fancied the dominatrix, and didn't kill her.

F: Presumably, she is still in possession of the diamond.

GURNEY: In a shocking pink cue-case. A fluffy one.

F: Quite.

GURNEY: Bronze wouldn't have wanted the real diamond on his premises because he knows his gaff is comprehensively fitted with Stealth Service cameras. Geraldine was beholden to him for the dungeon conversion loan and her house is one of the most secure in suburbia.

F: Is it though? There is a near-constant flow of clients.

GURNEY: Masochists.

F: An assassin could masquerade as a masochist.

GURNEY: They are big on masks.

F: Most witty, Gurney.

GURNEY: Petal does seem pretty certain that the florists are going to kill the dominatrix, doesn't she?

F: Very observant, Gurney.

GURNEY: Bronze isn't going to protect her, is he?

F: No.

GURNEY: Stalin won't have figured any of this out, will he?

F: What do you think?

GURNEY: He's clearly clueless, F. Can't we save her?

F: Not without giving ourselves away.

GURNEY: Then she's dead, isn't she?

F: She has a protector.

GURNEY: He's in prison. And if he ever escapes, they'll kill him too.

F: Optimistic sort, aren't you, Gurney?

GURNEY: I try to keep cheerful, F. But I've got evidence.

F: More surveillance?

GURNEY: From the florists. We rigged up a load of bouquets with cameras and microphones.

F: Impressive.

GURNEY: Thanks, F. Here you go:

Belladonna's Floral Deliveries, Wandsworth. Potter sits behind desk. Leonard stands before him.

POTTER: Let me sniff. No, that's not the sweet smell of success, it's the fetid fug of failure.

LEONARD: Tell made the wrong delivery.

POTTER: Again.

LEONARD: He delivered Rankin and received the target.

POTTER: Rankin's dead?

LEONARD: And the dominatrix isn't.

Leonard tries to scratch his arm but fails to reach under his plaster cast.

LEONARD: If it's all right with you, I'd like to deadhead him, take some cuttings, and rot him in a compost bin. We need some moisture-retaining organic matter for the sweet peas.

POTTER: Mulch him but recruit a competent executioner. With The Chelsea Flower Show coming up, I don't want to worry about staffing.

Potter swivels his chair to face his picture of Lake Victoria.

End of recording.

F: So, Rankin has already tried to kill the dominatrix?

GURNEY: Seems so.

F: And Bill Tell killed Rankin.

GURNEY: Looks like it.

F: And the police are unaware of this?

GURNEY: They're not very good.

F: Stalin isn't, but there was an entire SO19 unit in the dungeon. One would have thought that the corpse of a large floricultural assassin would not have escaped their attention.

GURNEY: He must have hidden it well.

F: Undoubtedly.

CHAPTER 19

I had never realised that Wandsworth was such a hotbed of devilry. Outer Ggaga was a dodgy enough destination, but Wandsworth made it seem as peaceful as an off-season Alpine resort. I wondered whether my empty strip club was part of the conspiracy. Was it a front for a cartel of multinational gun-launderers? Or a safe house for traffickers running humans? It felt as though the suburbs were no longer to be trusted, particularly this suburb.

I decided to employ a life coaching technique and went for a run in my head. The route was spectacular – a coastal path followed by a forest trek. I was entirely absorbed in the activity, focused on the moment. All my anxieties fell away, the endorphins kicked in and I felt overwhelmingly positive and relaxed. Life didn't have to be complicated – it was there to be enjoyed. Then a dogwalker blocked my path. They had eight untrained and unleashed beasts and every one of them hated humans. They barked, snarled, and yipped, snapping at my shins and threatening to bite my groin. The owner only had eyes for her furry friends and did not acknowledge me. She simply called out their names and was ignored by all eight of them. The dogs had forced me to a complete stop, shattered any sense of calm or positivity, and sent my blood pressure skywards. Frankly, I would have been better of going for an imaginary traffic jam.

I returned to the dossier. The police operation was arresting; they really had shot themselves in the foot with a marksman's accuracy. Rather than taking muggers and drug dealers off the street, they had targeted masochistic Masons, released a vulnerable dominatrix, and taken Bill off the streets. He was Geraldine's best source of protection, and now he couldn't help her.

If I have to avenge her death as well as Bill's, I will be seriously narked. I didn't sign up for that at all.

JOURNAL - EX-SERGEANT BILL TELL

Wednesday 20 May, 11.58

I didn't have a wall-breaching cannon, a hydraulic battering ram or a Harvey Wallbanger to effect a hole-in-the-wall exit from Wandsworth nick, but I did have a positive mental attitude and at the end of the day, that's what mattered most. If you stayed alert and kept up your will to survive, escape was never impossible. During my career, I had confused thermal imaging systems, evaded tunnel searches, and headed escape committees - I was a man who knew how to cause diversions in the enemy rear.

I racked my brain for the ideal technique and landed on a tactic sometimes used to bend spoons. If a soldier can marshal sufficient psychic energy in one spot, even the hardest of barriers can be rendered floppy. I marched over to the cell door, pressed gently on the upper hinge with my index finger, and concentrated intently. The door offered little in the way of psychic resistance. After five seconds, I removed my finger and repeated the action with the lower hinge. The door didn't stand a chance. I had escaped solitary confinement by Mossad, waltzed out of H-Blocks and busted out of Belmarsh - a Wandsworth cell was tissue paper in comparison. I lifted the door off its hinges, stepped around it and hoisted the portal back on again. I executed a quick East-West and locked up behind me, ever mindful of the Country Code. I moved silently, but at a steady pace. I reminded myself that I was not a fugitive; I was just another human being - a grey man.

The Custody Officer was engrossed in a gardening magazine. I clocked a headline about "The Lost Garden of Heligan". Even the cozzers were getting green-fingered.

I proceeded along the police station corridors, past posters glorifying *Operation Eagle Eye* and encouraging neighbours to be watchful. As I approached the reception area, I clocked a huddle of woolly suits. This was a possible contact. If I was recognised, I would have to outrun the lot of them. Cozzers don't yomp, so pace wasn't a problem, but I would have preferred to slope out in a less conspicuous fashion. Luckily, they were all wrapped up in each other's gossip. I eavesdropped as I approached:

"Haven't you heard?" Cozzer Number One asked. "Donald arrested the Super."

"For a bet?" Cozzer Two asked.

"For visiting a brothel," Cozzer One replied.

"In a pig mask," Cozzer Three added.

"And donkey earmuffs," Cozzer One said.

"Have you been smoking crack again?" Cozzer Two asked.

"That was a one-off," Cozzer One replied, sheepishly.

"The Super was in a dungeon, handcuffed to a cage," Cozzer Three said.

'A stag night?" Cozzer Two asked.

"With a judge, a banker and a senior civil servant," Cozzer One said.

"Excuse me," I said.

"Sorry," they said in unison, as they let me pass.

I progressed towards Exit One, only to find egress impeded by an elderly lady clutching a Zimmer frame. I smiled through the glass, eased the door open and stepped aside for her. It was the final, critical stage of my escape, but, in my heart, I was still representing the regiment. I may have been kicked out on my bollocks, but by example I still led.

'Thank you, dear,' the octogenarian said, as she walked in.

"No problem, madam" I marched out into the Wandsworth sunshine.

The first few hours of any evasion were crucial, especially in urban terrain. If I was to survive, I would have to change my appearance whilst remaining unobtrusive. I could survive by becoming a vagrant, I could pretend to be insane, or I could operate as a grey man, dull enough to warrant no attention whatever. My height was against me, and greyness was not in my nature - deep down, I'm stripy. But this was a matter of survival.

I advanced along Wandsworth High Street in a crouching attitude, using counter-surveillance techniques to move unseen through the pedestrians. I zigzagged to create false trails and eyeballed reflective surfaces for pursuers. I caught a glimpse of a National Stealth spook and crash-dived behind a parked Proton. There was no doubt he was a Watcher: his equipment was stuffed under his cagoule - only a National Stealth spook would conceal his surveillance cameras that inadequately.

I hugged the tarmac and glanced up at the Proton's wing-mirror. Once again, a spook's reflection passed. I commando-crawled past some road works and bomb-burst behind a Portaloo. The plastic street convenience didn't provide a lot of cover, but I had to make use of whatever shelter the terrain had to offer. *Fighting in a Built-Up Area* had been one of my favourite courses at Dartmoor.

I did a quick East-West and eyeballed a charity shop. I took a covert approach, then bomb-burst inside past crushed heaps of unwanted garments and bric-a-brac. Jaundiced bestsellers wobbled on a carousel and decapitated mannequins paraded polyester clothing with historical sweat stains on the collars and armpits. This was a final resting place for mouldy jackets, sole-less shoes, piece-less board games, speech-less dolls, and faded watercolours. I rummaged through racks and cardboard boxes, pulling out the scruffiest clothes available.

Operation complete, I commando-crawled to the till with a mound of rags and addressed an elderly volunteer. "Where are the fitting rooms?"

"Sorry, dear. We haven't got any."

"Can I improvise one?"

"If you like, love."

I worked quickly and with survivalist precision, creating a Double Lean-To fitting room out of clothes racks, children's toys, and cardboard boxes. I would have preferred conifers, elephant grass and wattle panels, but a soldier must utilise the materials at hand. I have improvised igloos, constructed sod houses, and raised parachute tepees in my time: a bric-a-brac shelter was a yomp in the park. It wouldn't win any architectural awards, but it provided adequate concealment. *Take pride in small things: morale means medals*, as they taught me at Tring.

I emerged in a torn trilby, oil-stained dungarees, and 1970s-style National Health glasses. Vanity has no place in urban survival.

"That'll be two pounds fifty, dear.' The volunteer smiled for her life.

"Here's a donation." I handed over my suit in lieu of money. I could tell she had never seen such well-pressed trousers.

CHAPTER 20

Bill really was a pint-sized man-and-a-half. His combat skills made John Wick seem like a Crown Green Bowling enthusiast; and his panache made him a veritable Cyrano de Wandsworth. The bloke had literally waltzed out of custody.

I had serious bloke envy. I wished I could go through life making mugs of the cops, but it's always been the other way around, as my lengthy criminal record attests. But what was the point in envying Bill, given that he was dead?

I wondered what elite army unit had taken him down. Had they used a nuclear attack-drone? A bespoke ballistic missile? Or some fiendishly devious trap? Potter could definitely do "fiendishly devious", but Gurney and Stalin would struggle to achieve anything more than "bleeding obvious".

The next pages comprised more transcripts from The National Stealth Service and Stalin's case notes. It was mind-boggling that these had been secured through a pair of Carabao Cup tickets. The price of treachery was low-quality football, it transpired.

NATIONAL STEALTH SERVICE

Transcription of Recorded Appraisal Meeting

Wednesday, 20 May, 16.03

Present: "F" (Head of Operational Discretion, National Stealth Service) and George Gurney (Trainee Junior Watcher, Remedial Unit, National Stealth Service).
Appraisal exercise: to rescue critical situation assigned to novice Watcher.

GURNEY: These appraisals, F?

F: Yes, Gurney.

GURNEY: Well, they're extremely regular.

F: But necessary.

GURNEY: The other trainees have two a week.

F: I doubt they're watching anyone quite as interesting as you are.

GURNEY: Did you choose me specially, F?

F: Not especially.

GURNEY: What then?

F: Regrettably, Gurney.

GURNEY: You chose me regrettably?

F: Unfortunately, yes.

GURNEY: Oh.

F: Gurney?

GURNEY: Yes, F.

F: Stalin's notes?

GURNEY: Yes.

F: Do you have them?

GURNEY: Yes, F. I didn't get caught.

F: Good.

GURNEY: Not by the police, at least.

F: Then by whom?

GURNEY: Bill Tell.

F: Tell caught you?

GURNEY: He caught sight of me.

F: What happened?

GURNEY: He ducked behind a car then disappeared.

F: Disappeared where?

GURNEY: Wandsworth.

F: Which bit?

GURNEY: No idea.

F: Probably for the best. Too early for direct contact. Now, Gurney, Stalin's case notes.

GURNEY: Okay, F:

Chief Inspector Stalin, Wandsworth CID

Case Notes – Wednesday 20 May

Time since breakfast: Ruddy ages.
Location: Own office.
Risk assessment: Environment likely to trigger depressive episodes.

Broken blinds filtered the Wandsworth light, illuminating the bargain-basement beige of CID's carpets, cupboards, and cabinets. Paperwork yellowed, marker pens dried, and I lurked in a walk-in storage cupboard, devouring a veal and ham pie.

My mug proclaimed "I Love My Work" in chunky, red letters. I'd added the words, "To Rule" on a strip of evidence tape. The coffee was real - fair trade and boiled in my own kettle. I took a swig and contemplated my "Hours of Duty" wall chart. Yesterday's read "Nine to Five a.m." Every other entry read either "Nine to Five p.m.", "Dental Appointment", "Doctor's Appointment", or "Mental Health Day".

The Super often said that I had a work-life imbalance. He thought my scales were tilted too firmly in favour of life. The bastard took a hard line on absence management. He would phone my doctor, call me at home and send woolly suits round to "make sure I was all right." The Super had even considered unleashing a private detective on his most suspect detective. He was no fan of what he called my "home-skiving", "flexible resting" and "drinking from home". But what could he do? I was the Federation Rep.

Donald sat at the Murder Desk. Above him, victims shared wall space with suspects. There were glossy colour photographs of Buster Butterworth in his ice block and the pawnbroker prostrate on his diamond deathbed, both corpses clutching bouquets in their stiff little fingers.

I slapped my gut, the only seat of truth, and asked, "Has Butterworth thawed yet?"

"Rock solid, Guv." Donald was still beaming about his birds like the Wright Brothers over Kitty Hawk. I was pleased for him. His fluffy little miracles were airborne; they had mastered the forces of lift and drag, elevation and pitch, and jolly good for them. But, at the end of the day, they were ducks, and we had a murder inquiry to pursue.

"How about the dungeon gun - any news from ballistics?"

"Yes, Guv."

"What?"

"We won't need to bother with DNA. The fingerprints on the revolver match Tell's."

"Christ on a chopper! Let's go and have a gloat."

We sauntered off to the cells, passing Custody Sergeant Seamus "Hawkeye" O'Ryan. Sleepy, pipe-smoking Seamus, his face drooping under the burden of gravity, his eyelids too heavy to lift. Hand Seamus a fishing rod, sit him by a water feature and he would make someone a nice gnome. Seamus had long since tired of receiving, charging, and releasing Wandsworth's pond life and was losing himself in the latest edition of *Gardener's World*. One day, with luck, everyone will be Seamus for fifteen minutes.

Like me, Seamus was both a time-server and a Federation activist, but he was only really bothered about pensions. Seamus didn't care about working conditions, partly because he never did any work. In fact, I had rarely seen him move; it looked as though he had been potted, gathering moss and annual salary increments behind his desk.

"Morning, Seamus,' I said. "How's the allotment?"

"My leeks are springing up. I might be off there tonight if the wife lets me escape."

I turned to Donald. The tiny florist's fingerprint-match was a major result, and we both deserved a slap on the back. "Well done, son. This just goes to show what coppers can achieve without going into overtime or breaching any Health and Safety guidelines."

Donald beamed and opened Tell's cell-flap. The word "Guv" dropped from his gaping gob.

I couldn't bear to look, and when Seamus unlocked Tell's cell, it was as empty as I'd feared. All I could say was "Pinch me."

Donald did. It hurt.

"Sorry, Guv."

"He's gone."

"He's a clever bastard."

"Look, he's not Keyser Söze, he's a very small florist.'

"True, Guv."

"That bastard is seriously wanted. I'll make him more famous than Beyoncé's arse!"

Time to lunch: Negligible.
Location: Station TV room.
Risk Assessment: Square eyes possible.

I munched a lardy cake and watched a TV report. An equine-jawed newsreader with sculpted hair and an over-precise manner sat behind a prop laptop and said, "The suspect is described as immaculately dressed, baby-faced and around five-foot-two inches tall." The programme cut to a photo-fit image of Tell. "He is between thirty-three and thirty-six years old but may look much younger. He is Caucasian and has a keen interest in floristry." The programme cut back to the newsreader in vision. "Members of the public are advised not to approach him, as he may be dangerous. Police are taking the matter extremely seriously." The programme cut to a shot of me devouring a steak and kidney pudding in a stationery cupboard.

"Bollocks!" I exclaimed. I never noticed a camera crew. The bastards must have had a long lens. There was nothing for it, we were going to have to crack on with the investigation and pay a visit to Tell's mum.

Time since lunch: 1 hour 3 minutes.

Location: Council estate (sunk).

Risk assessment: Multiple hazards. Fatalities on the cards.

The landlord of The King Billy had given us two addresses – one for the dominatrix's dungeon and one for Tell's mum. The dungeon had required an armed response unit, and, in all honesty, we would have been better off taking one to his mum's house too.

Me and the sergeant knew all about the Victory Estate, having fingerprinted numerous members of *The Agincourt Crew*, *The Waterloo Posse* and *The El Alamein Soldiers* in person. It was certainly colourful; every one of the council's concrete canvases had been bombed with tribal hieroglyphics, rival crews lining each other out in an artistic turf war to become Kings of The Victory. Their creativity was not restricted to the spray can: one of them had removed an *r* and a *v* from *Drive* in the estate's sign, which now read, *Welcome to The Victory Estate. Please Die Carefully.*

After we had passed teenagers unloading televisions, consoles, and speakers from the back of a lorry, we were welcomed energetically by a gauntlet of small children, all cheerfully shouting abuse, and throwing stones.

"Hanging's too good for them," Donald said.

"Nothing's too good for them," I said. "They're the urban proletariat - alienated, excluded, without a stake to hold."

"But they're throwing rocks at us."

"They're just kids."

"No, rocks. Are you going to stand for this, Guv?"

"Yes." A slice of pavement bounced off my forehead.

If Donald hadn't had the strength of a silverback, he might have struggled to lug me to my feet. It was lucky he did, as moments later, a shopping trolley landed on the area of tarmac I had previously occupied. A dozen storeys up, teenage silhouettes celebrated as we ran for shelter.

The Victory Estate was a Health and Safety nightmare, but we hadn't gone into overtime, and I was quite keen to catch our man. Maybe even more than quite. In fact, I was dead determined to visit the tiny florist's mum. An unfamiliar substance, possibly even adrenalin, made my heart beat a bit.

A resident's sound system filled Agincourt's stairways with crap rap.

"Is that shed?" I asked.

"You mean garage."

"Garage, that's it."

"It's not."

"What the bloody hell is it then?"

"Grime, Guv."

"This place is grimy enough. Bring back folk music."

These days, The Victory was a stinking labyrinth, a stranger's grave ruled by the law of the lawless. Property meant nothing; cars were for wrapping around lampposts, smacking into night buses, and exploding with fireworks. Death came by drive-by or walk-by; sometimes they'd just ambush a passer-by.

"Social deprivation," I said, as we approached Tell's floor. "That's what spawned our murderer. If your home is a fly tip, your heart is a cesspool of resentment. Just look at this - boarded-up windows, graffiti, syringes, rubber johnnies. It's no surprise he plugged a pawnbroker, hijacked a stretch Bedford, and disarmed SO19. What number is it again?"

"Forty-six, Guv."

"It can't be."

"It is, Guv."

"But look at it!"

We were face-to-face with the most immaculate council flat entrance known to Man, with hanging baskets, stained glass windows and a framed watercolour of Bill Tell. I shrugged and rang the bell.

Mrs Tell was laughing to herself as she opened the door. I think she must have been expecting someone else because her face dropped in disappointment. It didn't last long. As soon as we flashed our badges, her eyes lit up and a pair of jolly dimples revealed themselves.

"How lovely!" Mrs Tell exclaimed. "I thought we were a no-go zone."

"There are no no-go zones," I said.

"Just places we choose not to go," Donald explained.

"Don't go there," I said.

"Tea?" Mrs Tell asked.

"Please."

"Cakes?"

"Absolutely."

"Rich fruit or fairy?"

"Both please."

We trod along her freshly vacuumed shagpile and entered a pristine lounge.

"Nice cathedral," Donald observed.

He was right. It was poetry in matchsticks.

I scanned her dustless mantle-piece and fingered Bill Tell's graduation photograph. "You must be very proud."

"Thank you."

Donald admired Tell's Gerrards Cross. "Good shot, is he?"

"Never misses."

"Where is he, Mrs Tell?" I asked.

"He'll be back for his tea."

"Isn't he a lucky lad?"

Mrs Tell blushed with pride.

"Very lucky, Guv," Donald said.

"Given what he's done," I said.

CHAPTER 21

My heart broke for Rose Tell. These clodhopping, duck fancying pie-munching cops were about to blow everything she had ever believed about her beloved son out of the proverbial water.

People don't like heroes much. They serve their purpose, then outstay their welcome. Luckily, I have never been accused of heroism. Competence would have been nice, but I have never been accused of that either.

I looked out of the office window. The skies were darkening over Tooting, but it was only weather. When did strip clubs open? Daytime stripping did occur, but in my experience, it was as dispiriting as daytime television and the clubs smelled of bleach and suicide. This was not that kind of place. Give it some strippers, some punters, and some indecent music and it would make a reasonable nocturnal hangout.

At a guess, someone would arrive to open up at around five, six, or maybe seven. A manager? A bar tender? A cleaner? Probably not a stripper; they wouldn't be given the keys.

I have never been a fan of being locked in. I blame prison. Most of my sojourns at Her Majesty's Pleasure had been anything but pleasurable: grim, pungent, and uneventful, in fact.

I didn't want to dwell on these unwanted memories, so I went for another imaginary pint. I closed my eyes and pictured a country pub: bare beams, wet dogs, wellies. It was the sort of establishment that made a habit of barring me in the real world, but in my head I was welcome. As I drank and opined, locals hung on my every word – parish councillors, Women's Institute stalwarts, thrusting Young Farmers. To them, I was as wise as I was witty, and I felt enveloped in the warmth of adulation. The beer was great too – as bitter-sweet as a life well lived. I had so many illusory pints that I fell off my imaginary bar stool, and found myself back at the strip club office, munching the carpet.

After I had righted my head, I returned to Tell's dossier with renewed appetite:

JOURNAL - EX-SERGEANT BILL TELL

Wednesday 20 May, 15.17

Dorked-up something scruffy in my charity shop threads, I was able to reach the Victory Estate unrecognised. I improvised an observation post from a burned-out Ford Sierra and conducted a discreet recce. There was no obvious evidence of surveillance, so I stole into Agincourt, dodged up the staircase and found myself mouthing a "bollocks".

I recognized the distinguishing features: the gut on the one, the biceps on the other. I was metres away from Stalin and Donald. I could outrun them, or I could outfight them. Either way, I would draw unwanted attention. There was a third option: stare straight ahead, listen carefully and hope for the best, so I went for that.

"Seemed like a nice old biddy," Donald said.

"I didn't enjoy doing that," Stalin said.

"Don't worry, Guv," Donald said. "Tell can run, but he can't hide."

I passed the detectives undetected, gave it a couple of minutes, then called on my mum.

"I don't buy on the doorstep," she said. "Not even *The Big Issue*."

"Hello, mum." I had two reasons to smile: I was pleased to see her, and I had proved the effectiveness of my disguise. It is amazing what a torn trilby, oil-stained dungarees, and National Health glasses can achieve. But I had smiled too soon.

"William," mum said. "I know what you've done. You're not welcome here."

"I'm on an undercover op."

"You're on a killing spree. The police told me everything. I'm so ashamed, William. Pack your things and go."

I went into my childhood bedroom and wondered what to pack. When you're on the run, a Corby Trouser Press and fifteen identical blue blazers were of little use. I took my journal and left the rest.

"You needn't think you're coming back," mum said as I walked back through the hall.

I stepped outside, then turned back to look my mum in the eye. "I'll prove to you that I'm innocent."

"Not today you won't. Take your post, and leave." Mum bunged a covert parcel at my head.

I dodged the parcel with an expert neck-jerk and caught it blind behind my back single-handed. It was a neat trick, but this was no time to celebrate, it was time for desperation. "Please, mum. I can explain." Could I? No. "Well, I could if I hadn't signed the Unofficial Secrets Act."

"Don't make me call the police on my own son."

In my time, I have been rifle-whipped, gut-knifed and head-stomped, but no strike had ever caused me this much pain; I reeled under its force. I had faced every danger a soldier could face, but now I felt scared. Mum was my anchor and I had just been cut adrift.

While mum removed my picture from her door, I turned and shuffled away. My shoulders slumped, my head bowed and there was no hint of a march in my gait. I had disciplined myself to repress the long-term side-effects of my anti-malarial serum, but, at times of stress, they fought their way back to the surface. My nostrils filled with the death-stench of rotting flowers; my head spun, sweat soaked through my shirt and pain shot through my joints. I scratched at my forearms, harvesting blood. Wandsworth faded from my mind and rusted roses loomed large; each petal smeared in powdery mildew, dark fungus marring the leaves.

I moped down the Agincourt stairs, cradling the covert package my mum had flung at me. I passed a poster: my own baby face beamed between the words *Wanted* and *Warning - This Man Will Fight Back*. I turned a corner and found myself nose-to-knife with a hat trick of hoodies, the same trio who had welcomed me a week earlier. There was no way they would clock me in my charity clobber. Good in one way, but bad in many others. The disguise robbed me of my reputation and made me a target.

I looked once more at the poster; *This Man Will Fight Back*. That man might, but this one couldn't. Under normal circumstances, I would have decked them all with a triple roundhouse kick, but they wouldn't stay knocked out forever and it would have been a bit of a giveaway, Wandsworth not being over-endowed with battle-hardened specialists in close protection.

The Agincourt Crew stood in a puddle of piss and demanded respect. They certainly knew how to hold a stare. I conducted a quick Threat Analysis. In their hands, the spiked plank, the shattered slab, and the spent syringe were weapons of honour, and I didn't doubt that they would follow through if provoked. One hoodie removed my glasses and crushed them in his hands, another pulled a hunting knife, a third produced a pickaxe handle.

"Can I write you a cheque?" I inquired, playing for time.

All three advanced until I lost my footing and tumbled down two flights of stone stairs. Luckily, I had studied Kodokan Judo at Wimbledon and mastered *ukemi*, the art of falling safely. I tumbled with confidence and control, landing on my arse (the greater the area of impact, the less damage is inflicted) and hugging my parcel.

Nothing had really been lost. I had made the right decision and survived without sustaining serious injury. Above all, my cover remained unblown. That had to add up to a victory of sorts.

I yomped to the exit, passed under a broken CCTV camera, and found myself surrounded by the Victory Estate's children, all performing BMX bike stunts. They swarmed around me, taking it in turns to buzz my shins, tormenting me with kickflip hang-nothings, brakeless endos, and no-handed bunny hops, forcing me to stumble at every step.

I had done some outrageously fearsome tabs in the Regiment, but this short walk outside my home estate was no less a test of my mettle and resourcefulness. I was surrounded by freewheeling children. *Never forget - only a positive attitude can save you*, as the regiment had taught me in Redditch.

I pointed with purpose at a random spot on the horizon and shouted, "Look! There's a police car!"

The children cycled gleefully towards the imaginary Panda, squealing, "Get them!"

16.31

I sat on a bench in the least popular corner of Wandsworth Common and opened the package my mum had thrown at my head. It had the unmistakeable visage of an

Outer Ggagaan warthog franked across it, confirming that it had been a covert delivery. I hoped the Semi-Pygmies were faring better than I was. There was only one letter this time, which was a bit of a worry, particularly as it was from Charles and not Marie-Thérèse.

Dear Bill,

Bit of a balls up on the admin front. I got monumentally pissed on formaldehyde beer and inadvertently shredded my expenses. The last three months' worth of receipts for Nile Perch suppers, Brotherhood backhanders, and Walloon protection money landed in a thousand spaghetti strips. It was fun at the time, but every V.A.T. number was obliterated, and I might as well submit a sack of confetti to the deniable accountants. Once I had sobered up, I spent five hours on my hands and knees trying to repair them and ended up gluing my fingers together. I told the shredder precisely what I thought of it and gave it a good kicking. Sadly, my room isn't wired too well, and it doesn't take much to short-circuit it. As explosions go, it was relatively minor, and there was no structural damage to speak of.

In other news, the Civil War is booming. The Brotherhood have downed several Walloon Zeppelins, but they are running low on Routemasters. Both sides have been fighting around the clock and are looking ragged. Tartan habits are getting tatty and Walloon beards are going untended - it's edge of the pants stuff.

The Semi-Pygmy Alliance is a real gamechanger, uniting the Insurgents and the Loyalists in a single short-arsed movement. There is really nothing like a nice spot of nation building! They held a Semi-Pygmy powwow on the banks of a papyrus swamp, and it went swimmingly. Marie-Thérèse read out your speech and it got a rousing reception.

The lads send their love, but if you do get a moment to buzz me on the secure mobile, I have more to impart. Sorry to tantalize, but I dare not put this in writing.

Cheers,

Charles.

I improvised a satellite phone out of the contents of an adjacent litterbin. Moments later, I had punched Charles's number into my apparatus, and I was on the net. (Not the Internet, you understand. It's just a Deniable way of saying I'd got through on the phone. Bit silly really.)

"Wotcha mate," I said into the grimy mouthpiece. "Sorry to hear about the expenses.

I usually make a practice of eating sensitive information."

"Thanks for the belated tip, Bill. Look, a bit of bad news, old chap. My shredder didn't just explode; it scrambled the local covert cloud. So, when I headed back to my room for the night and hit the laptop for a bit of Deniable Pornhub, I found myself in the Ambassador's email box. Now, I know this is a matter of national security and I am a fully signed up subscriber to the Unofficial Secrets Act - far more stringent than the Official version, as we're both all too aware - but it was just too interesting to ignore. Anyway, there were twelve messages in her inbox, mostly entitled things like *Deliver Tell* and *Kill Bill*. They were nearly all from *Belladonna's Floral Deliveries* - I think it's that organisation Buster Butterworth got himself hooked up with. You haven't seen him, have you? Scoundrel still owes me a tenner. Anyway, her sent-box made even rummier reading - seems the old girl's been emailing your CV to a variety of international organisations."

"My covert CV?"

"Afraid so."

"With references and contact details?"

"Yep."

"Bollocks."

"I'm not sure she's got your best interests at heart, Bill. I'd find another careers advisor sharpish."

"Thanks for the sit rep, mate. Which international organisations precisely?"

"Well, FARC."

"Surely not the *Fuerzas Armadas Revolucionarias de Colombia*, South America's deadly aficionados of the kidnap-murder combo?"

"The very same."

"But I laced their last five cocaine shipments with permanent laxative."

"They've not forgotten."

"Arses."

"Indeed."

"And you're certain she sent it?"

"It's the Ambassador. She's not trying to get you a job; she's provoking someone to do a job."

"On me?"

"Undoubtedly."

"But I protected her. Intimately."

"I'm afraid it gets worse, Bill."

"How could it possibly get worse?"

"She also sent your Covert CV to ETA."

"Surely not *Euskadi Ta Askatasuna*, the paramilitary Basque mountaineers I sherpad off an Alp?"

"The survivors are pretty pissed off. But not as angry as Hamas."

"She's not gone and sent my Covert CV to the *Harakat al-Muqawama al-Islamiyy*?"

"Sorry."

"But I put their suicide bombers in touch with the Samaritans."

"They're almost as mad with you as Mossad."

"Surely not ?"

"One of the most ruthlessly efficient state security services known to Man."

"The organization I conned into abducting seventeen of their own undercover agents in a bewilderingly effective April Fool's jape?"

"Bingo!"

"Bollocks."

"She also contacted The Chechen Warlords of Doom."

"But I hypnotized their pet tigers and sent them feral."

"Didn't stop her dropping your CV off to them – or, for that matter, to the Real UDA."

"But I pebble-dashed their war murals."

"She even sent your Covert CV to Agnostic Jihad."

"Surely not *The Righteous Doubt Strugglers of Tomsk*, seeking to impose Dither Law, with its split juries, hung parliaments and open prisons?"

"You got it."

"Bollocks."

"Oh. One bit of good news - I've got a new job doing the commentary on BBC 13's covert coverage of The Chelsea Flower Show! It's a classified feed to the Deniable regions of East Africa, so I won't get to leave Outer Ggaga, but it's still a great gig. You know how big the Chelsea Flower Show is out here. The Rose War will grind to a halt while every faction watches the event on massive public screens. There'll be a real buzz."

"Congratulations," I murmured, pleased for the bloke but bothered brittle by his revelations. "Speak soon, mate."

It felt as though the Walloons had dropped me with one of their potpourri pause bombs. Time froze, my blood froze: God it was cold. The Past had caught up with me. A Deniable operative can't operate when everyone knows what he's been up to. I had infiltrated the world's most dangerous organisations. Now they were going to infiltrate me, and it was going to hurt.

I could not accept The Ambassador's deception. I had trusted her, plonking my life on a variety of hazardous lines on her behalf. I thought she liked me. Only the other day, she had pudged my cheeks. Why on Earth would she spam my CV to FARC, ETA, Hamas, Mossad, Agnostic Jihad, an uneasy coalition of Chechen Warlords and the Real UDA? It wasn't the act of a friend.

CHAPTER 22

The Ambassador's deception was disgusting. She had nuked Bill with his own CV. Never before had a Word document been deployed to such destructive effect.

My own CV lacked the implosive power of Bill's. It had more gaps than a smackhead's teeth, what with my breakdowns, blackouts, and benders. For me, the word "career" conjures up memories of spinning steering wheels, car crashes, and drunken staggers into canals, but I have never been conventionally ambitious. If a prospective employer were to ask me, "Where do you see yourself in five years' time?" I would probably answer, "dead". Sadly, that answer applied all-too-accurately to Bill.

Life is short and it feels even shorter when you keep forgetting what's happened to you. I focused on the climax of last night's shenanigans. Traditionally, my serious boozing sessions end in police stations, hospitals, or recycling bins (why do they always seem like the perfect place to crash when I've drunk myself comatose?). Yesterday's session had ended in an empty strip club. Now, the strip club could not have been entirely empty at the time. Someone had tied me up and locked me in. They may have stripped me, or I may have stripped myself – I can be a bit of a show off when I've had a few.

It was like one of those locked room mysteries, except I was the one locked in the room rather than the corpse. The person who had put me there didn't have to be a master criminal – it could be passed off as little more than a stag night stunt – but why had they done it? And how the hell did I get here?

Like all pubs, *The Lion & Lettuce* had eventually closed. I am pretty sure I departed peacefully, and I may even have left with a blurry friend or two. There had been a lock-in somewhere and I think I may have invented a new dance, either to hip hop, or possibly freeform jazz. I looked at lots of women, but they didn't look at me. I may have stolen someone's cocaine and banged on about life coaching, breaking every rule of client confidentiality in the process. But that was all I could remember: the sound of my own voice, then darkness.

My own internal investigation may have hit a brick wall, but I still had another mystery to solve. Who had killed Bill? I returned to the cardboard box where another National Stealth Service transcription awaited me. Gurney may have been bottom of the Remedial Unit, but he certainly was a busy boy.

NATIONAL STEALTH SERVICE

Transcription of Recorded Appraisal Meeting

Wednesday, May 20, 23.01

Present: "F" (Head of Operational Discretion, National Stealth Service) and George Gurney (Trainee Junior Watcher, Remedial Unit, National Stealth Service).

Appraisal exercise: to salvage something from the wreckage constituting Trainee Junior Watcher Gurney's efforts to date.

F: So, Gurney, anything whatsoever to offer?
GURNEY: Yes, F.
F: Glad to hear it.
GURNEY: Someone's landed.
F: Someone's landed?
GURNEY: Yes, F.
F: Who? Where?
GURNEY: Looks significant, F.

F: Why?

GURNEY: Leonard the florist met him on a Chiltern.

F: Met who?

GURNEY: Well. I'm not quite sure, F.

F: Really?

GURNEY: He looked violent though. And highly trained.

F: A new florist?

GURNEY: He arrived by helicopter. I don't think he had bouquets on his mind.

F: And how was this information garnered?

GURNEY: It was recorded by a Stealth Service intern disguised as a birdwatcher.

F: Really? How?

GURNEY: Hidden cameras in the binoculars, massive microphone in the twitcher-hide.

F: Okay, Gurney. Furnish me with the transcripts.

Leonard watches a yellow helicopter land on the summit of the tallest Chiltern. The chopper is tiny and equipped with radar, infrared sensors, and in-flight refuelling probes. A smartly dressed pilot exits the helicopter, and approaches Leonard. The pilot has a big nose.

LEONARD: Good journey?

PILOT: Dreadful. Outer Ggaga to the Home Counties in a chopper the size of a sofa. I wouldn't wish it on cattle.

LEONARD: Potter thinks it's time we made those deliveries.

PILOT: Does he now?

LEONARD: The Chelsea Flower Show's imminent.

PILOT: Fair one. I'll help do the necessary.

End of recording.

F: Some interesting descriptions there.

GURNEY: Thanks, F.

F: There is certainly some useful technical detail about the helicopter, but I don't see the relevance of the pilot's nasal dimensions.

GURNEY: His nose really was very large, F. Like a beak.

F: Understood. Any idea who this beak-nosed pilot might be, F?

F: Based on the information you've supplied, Gurney, none whatsoever.

GURNEY: Sounds a bit iffy, though, doesn't he?

F: Undoubtedly.

GURNEY: I lost him for a bit, but we caught up with him again at the florists.

F: Belladonna's?

GURNEY: Yes, F. Not Interflora.

F: Ah, sarcasm. You really are racing along, aren't you, Gurney?

GURNEY: Thanks, F.

F: You're the pride of the Remedial Unit. What else have you got?

GURNEY: A recording from Belladonna's Floral Deliveries - Harold Potter's office. Pinhole cameras and microphones were concealed in the flower arrangements.

F: Okay, Gurney, read it out.

Leonard and the big-nosed pilot stand next to each other, looking at Harold Potter through a Sunshine Medley bouquet containing a colourful arrangement of Remember-Me Roses, Clear Crystal Violas, and Burpee Zinnia Hybrids.

POTTER: You know why you're here.

PILOT: Bill Tell.

LEONARD: And his bird.

POTTER: We wanted him to take her out.

LEONARD: He took us at our word.

POTTER: Now they're an item.

LEONARD: An itemised kill.

PILOT: You're my kind of florist.

POTTER: Don't worry about the horticulture.

LEONARD: You'll pick that up.

POTTER: After you've picked up The Precious.

LEONARD: Dropped the dominatrix.

POTTER: And buried the midget.

End of recording.

F: Very good, Gurney.

GURNEY: They're going to kill Bill and the dominatrix.

F: That would seem to be their intention.

GURNEY: The pilot seems to be some kind of big-nosed back-up.

F: Indeed. Can you provide a fuller description?

GURNEY: Huge honker, military bearing, likes flowers.

F: When you say military bearing, what precisely do you mean?

GURNEY: Immaculate suit, precision-pressed trousers. Top of the Special Forces League - a celebrity undercover assassin.

F: Indeed. I've just requested that an identification be made from the footage.

GURNEY: Can they do that?

F: Yes, Gurney, computers can be very clever.

GURNEY: Yes, F. There's a bit more.

F: Really? Well, if you have more information to impart, I'm sure I am fully agog.

GURNEY: We had cameras and microphones concealed on their stretch Bedford.

F: Jolly good.

GURNEY: I can't help thinking we'd get steadier pictures with a low-loader.

F: How do you mean?

GURNEY: You know, like in films. You put the actor's car on a massive trailer and film into it with full-sized cameras.

F: Don't you think they'd notice?

GURNEY: Probably.

F: Then better not, eh?

GURNEY: Yes, F. Here you go:

Belladonna's Stretch Bedford van pulls up outside the dominatrix's dungeon. Leonard drives. The big-nosed Pilot sits beside him.

PILOT: Nice garden.

LEONARD: The individual features are acceptable, but the overall design lacks balance.

PILOT: You know your plants, don't you?

LEONARD: I could tame a wild orchid.

PILOT: Where shall we hide?

LEONARD: I'll take the honeysuckle. You take the hedgerow.

The florists alight from the Stretch Bedford and take up covert positions in the dungeon garden.

Across the street, a Surveillance Officer disguised as a vagrant operates a dog-on-a-string-camera. Stealth Service microphones have been concealed in garden pea gravel and prostrate shrubs.

Thirteen minutes later, the dominatrix returns to her dungeon. Leonard leaps out of a honeysuckle bush. Pilot springs out of a hedge. Dominatrix jumps out of her skin.

PILOT: This accident has been waiting to happen for so long, it's getting impatient.

Dominatrix tears at Leonard's face-flesh, leaving three of her nail extensions embedded in his cheeks. Pilot knocks the legs from under her and lifts her into the air. Dominatrix screams threats. Shouting match ensues. The words "Precious", "Tell" and "Chelsea Flower Show" are clearly audible.

End of recording.

F: So, we have an abduction on our hands.

GURNEY: Yes, F. The dominatrix was abducted by the florist and the pilot with the big nose.

F: How is his nose relevant? Did he employ it as a weapon?

GURNEY: Not as far as I know, F.

F: Then feel free to omit further mention of it.

GURNEY: Okay, F. Want to hear the next bit?

F: Depends what it is.

GURNEY: It's in the basement of Belladonna's Floral Deliveries.

F: Didn't know we had that covered.

GURNEY: It's amazing how easy it is to sneak cameras and microphones into the right kind of bouquet, F.

F: Well, go on then.

GURNEY: Yes, F.

Basement, Belladonna's Floral Deliveries. The Pilot ties the dominatrix to a wrought iron trellis with galvanized garden wire. A harsh, fluorescent bar illuminates a sinister array of gardening equipment and a flip chart. Potter addresses the dominatrix.

POTTER: Welcome to Belladonna's Floral Deliveries.

Leonard lifts the flip chart, revealing the word "Induction".

POTTER: We run the rose routes, deliver on demand, and have a controlling interest in numerous garden centres. We don't want to harm the general public, just other big-name florists in the horticultural underworld.

Pilot gags the dominatrix with heavy-duty arboreal tape. Leonard lifts the "Induction" page, revealing the word "Chelsea".

POTTER: The Chelsea Flower Show is an opportunity to see and be seen before we make moves on our rivals' territory. But Chelsea's not just a turf war - it's also about decking, borders and rockeries, big shiny rockeries. Your average Alpine gardener works in gravel - we'll work in conflict diamond. Belladonna's Garden of Death will leave the Floricultural Walloons horticulturally impotent, and we'll be able to claim victory in Outer Ggaga, the richest rose fields in the world.

Leonard flips the chart, revealing the word "Precious".

POTTER: That's where the Great Star of Mount Heha – codenamed The Precious - comes in. I've designed a glistening gem rockery; sprinkled with cuts from the world's first C-colour diamond. We'll earn the respect of every florist in Europe.

Leonard flips the chart, revealing a felt-tip rockery design. Pilot gives it a round of applause.

POTTER: But we have a problem. Buster Butterworth's pawnbroker cut The Precious and substituted simulants. There's no way we can win Best in Show with fake diamonds. Chelsea's judges are far too shrewd for that. We delivered the pawnbroker, but before he sniffed his last bouquet, he told Leonard that you had the original Precious. Tell us where it is, and we'll keep your death as painless as possible.

Dominatrix struggles to speak but is rendered totally inaudible by the florists' heavy gag.

End of recording.

F: And what do we conclude from this, Gurney?"

GURNEY: That Potter's presentation skills are impressive. He knows his material; he is familiar with his topic; his eye contact is engaging and inclusive; and only the audience displayed any signs of stage fright.

F: Anything else?

GURNEY: Leonard certainly knows how to flip a chart.

F: I think a rather more pertinent conclusion might be that the Chelsea Flower Show may prove the setting for a major international incident.

GURNEY: Golly.

F: Golly, indeed.

GURNEY: There's more, F.

F: Really? Where?

GURNEY: The Stretch Bedford again. Here you go:

Leonard drives Belladonna's Floral Delivery van across Chelsea Bridge. Dominatrix in the back, squashed between Pilot and a consignment of poison ivy.

PILOT: It'll be an ecological burial. Are you organic? Probably, underneath all that skin. Anyway, you look fairly biodegradable.

DOMINATRIX: I haven't got the diamond.

PILOT: We've got a specially themed garden. You can be part of the planting scheme.

DOMINATRIX: It's in a fluffy, pink case I bought from Petal's Private Shop. The diamond's in there with one of her sex toys.

PILOT: Where is it?

DOMINATRIX: I must have left it somewhere.

PILOT: Don't worry. We'll help you remember. The prospect of being mulched alive focuses the mind wonderfully.

End of recording.

GURNEY: They're going to mulch the dominatrix! Should I call the police?

F: How effective have the police proved to date?

GURNEY: Hopeless, F.

F: We will step up surveillance on The Chelsea Flower Show considerably.

GURNEY: It's already on the telly.

F: Quite, although I would hazard that the producers of gardening programmes have somewhat different priorities to The National Stealth Service.

GURNEY: Oh. I nicked some more notes from Wandsworth Nick.

F: Cover story?

GURNEY: Didn't have time, F.

F: No cover story?

GURNEY: Yes, none. I just nicked them.

F: Very well.

GURNEY: Not really. I got caught.

F: Oh dear.

GURNEY: It didn't matter really. I just gave them your name.

F: You did what?

GURNEY: I gave them your name, forged your signature, and scarpered.

F: What name?

GURNEY: *F*.

F: Just *F*.

GURNEY: That's your name, isn't it, F? Hope I spelt it right.

F: Good God.

GURNEY: They put it more strongly than that.

F: I'm speechless.

GURNEY: Sorry, F.

F: I do hope the contents of the case notes were sufficiently enlightening to justify the compromise to National Stealth Service security.

GURNEY: Sort of. They did manage to trace the dominatrix's mum. She sleeps next to the dungeon, but no one noticed her during the raid. Bit of an oversight, really.

F: Quite. How did they trace her?

GURNEY: By answering the phone. She rang to report her daughter's kidnap.

Chief Inspector Stalin, Wandsworth CID

Case Notes – Wednesday 20 May

Time since dinner: One hour three minutes.
Location: Dungeon
Risk assessment: Psychological intimidation triggered by the location. Dealing with elderly and vulnerable member of the public.

My sergeant and I returned to the dungeon with a heavy heart. We were knocking for ages before a granny unchained the heavy oak door.

"Mrs O'Hell?" I asked.

"Go away," she replied. "There won't be any more masochists. I'm the one who'll be punished. Forever."

We issued a joint apology and flashed our badges.

"Oh. You've taken an Age. They snatched her hours ago."

"Sorry, love. I'm on work-to-rule and it would have taken me into overtime."

We followed the elderly maid along the flagstones and into her room, which was crammed with bundles of bungled knitting. Broken needles and flustered crochet rested on her recumbent Catherine Cooksons. Clearly, worry had uncoiled her.

The maid held up a photograph of her daughter with a rosy face, a pink t-shirt, and white jeans. She looked sweet, incapable of dominating a single freemason. The maid tried to pass the photograph over to me for a closer look but could not bring herself to let go. "This is all I've got left of her, isn't it?"

"Don't think like that," I said. "She's a dominatrix. She should be able to look after herself."

"They've taken her."

"Who?"

"The florists."

"How could you tell they were florists?"

"I could see it in their eyes."

"Can you describe them?" Donald asked.

"Hired hitters. Cruel. They kept banging on about the Chelsea Flower Show." She started to sob, her shoulders shrugging rhythmically.

I wanted to hug her, but Federation policy cautions against physical contact with members of the public on Health and Safety grounds.

"Come on, Donald. Let's go and suspect the usuals."

Time since dinner: One hour twenty-seven minutes.

Location: Police car

Risk assessment: Aggressive driver (own sergeant).

Thirty Years a Greying by The Dubliners helped the journey fly by, despite the heavy traffic. The beardy folksters wrenched my heartstrings and Donald's nerves with tales of famine, ecological disaster, and mortally wounded squaddies. Marvellous.

"Guv?"

"Sergeant."

"You know you said, "It's time to go and suspect the usuals"?"

"Yes, Sergeant."

"Well, Guv, I haven't got the faintest clue what you mean by that."

"Bar Achilles."

"Of course, Guv. You should have said."

Time since dinner: Two hours ten minutes.

Location: Bar Achilles.

Risk Assessment: Proximity to Prominent Nominal and his associates in dubious dive.

We were both horribly familiar with *Bar Achilles*. I preferred *The Blind Beggar*, which was proudly unpopular and did regular pie nights. Donald preferred the company of his ducks and his wife, but Ernie Bronze was Wandsworth's top crim – or Prominent Nominal in police parlance - and, as proprietor of the postcode's most violent bar, we had him where we wanted him: in the open. Not only could we keep an eye on Bronze, but we could also monitor most of the Brighter Borough's criminal networks, all of which interlocked at *Bar Achilles*.

A barman with an eye-patch and a series of dart-sized holes in his baseball cap stood guard over Bronze's private table in the VIP area. When he tried to bar our way, Donald elbowed him in the stomach. He crumpled and writhed on the lager-soaked carpet.

"Hello, Stalin." Bronze ignored his employee's pain. "How's Health and Safety?"

I stepped over the barman. "With a homicidal florist on the loose, I've felt safer."

"And you're no health freak. How's his drinking, Donald?"

"The past has been bottled and labelled with *Guv*."

"Cheers, Sergeant."

"Sorry, Guv."

"We've come to suspect the usuals."

"Well, you've come to the right place." Bronze gestured towards a pair of chairs. He was not alone. A large companion in an African robe sat in silence beside him. I decided to ignore the bloke, so we sat down. I passed Bronze a mugshot of Tell. He examined it briefly, then passed it to his companion, who simply nodded.

"Fetch the CVs!" Bronze shouted at the barman, who had only just made it back to his feet.

The barman gave Donald a one-eyed glare and disappeared behind the bar.

"What the bloody hell are you drinking?" I didn't like the look of their gloopy grey cocktails. "Some kind of Manhattan?"

"No," Bronze replied. "It's a Wandsworth. Fancy one?"

"I'm a real ale man, myself."

"Bitter?"

"Extremely."

The barman returned with a weighty ring binder and plonked it on the table. Bronze immediately dispatched him for my bitter and Donald's Virgin Mary.

"Work here long, this Tell, did he?" Donald asked.

"One, maybe two hours. Our doormen do tend to have a short life expectancy." Bronze passed me Bill Tell's CV. Roughly summarised, it read: Handyman (East Africa), Social Worker (Chechnya), Nursery Teacher (Angola), Zookeeper (Belfast), Painter and Decorator (Kosovo), Fertilizer Salesman (Guatemala). Education: Sculpture (Saint Martin's College).

I screwed the CV into a ball and booted it at the barman.

"Guv!" Donald protested. "That's evidence."

"It's cast-iron bollocks, that's what it is."

Bronze confirmed my gut instinct with a cackle. "Well spotted, Stalin. Not a lot gets past you. That's just his official cover stories. I've got his real CV. Someone emailed it to me yesterday."

Bronze opened the ring binder's false bottom and removed a thick document headed, "Sergeant Bill Tell, Second Covert Battalion, The Royal Deniables". The document was correctly laid out with ample spacing, a logical structure and bullet points. I have always admired well-presented paperwork.

In essence, the covert CV was a potted history of modern warfare. Name any conflict zone or no-go area and the miniature florist had gone there and covered himself in glory. The bloke had won more medals than I had gobbed puff pastries.

"Bloody Nora!" I exclaimed. "He's like a mini-Rambo. What's he doing in Wandsworth living with his mum?"

"No idea," Bronze replied.

"You've got to admit it's a fascinating career path," Bronze's companion said in a voice that was distinctive, patrician, and maybe a little Kenyan. This wasn't the kind of voice I was used to hearing in *Bar Achilles* and come to think of it, few of its patrons wore traditional African robes.

"Stalin." Bronze gestured at his companion. "This is Mr Potter."

"And what do you do, sir?" I asked.

"Do?" He mimicked the word as if it were some kind of insult. "I don't do. I make."

"Make what?"

"Deliveries."

"You're a delivery boy?"

The African rose in fury, dwarfing even Donald.

At that point, my mobile intoned *The Manchester Rambler*, one of my favourite banjo ballads. I took the call with a stern, "Stalin."

It was the pathologist. He's not much of a conversationalist, so we were done in under eight seconds.

"Good news, Guv?"

"Butterworth's thawed."

The words sent a jolt through Bronze. He jumped, knocking his *Wandsworth* cocktail over my trousers.

Time since dinner: Ages. Ready for bed.
Location: Morgue.
Risk assessment: Deadly.

"The corpse flooded the lab," the pathologist explained, as we sploshed through the morgue in Federation-issue wellies.

Buster Butterworth's corpse was stiffer than the usual morgue-fodder. It stood fully erect, and the right hand still exerted a firm grip on a dripping bouquet.

"It's still too solid to examine properly," the pathologist said. "But I thought I'd let you have a look as soon as the ice had thawed."

"Thanks." I perused the corpse. "Three bullet wounds?"

"Two to the torso, one to the forehead."

"Classic Mozambique Drill – clearly a pro."

"Ex-forces, probably."

"Or a rival florist," I said, mystifying the pathologist.

While I'd been gawping at the corpse, Donald had been busying himself with Butterworth's personal possessions. "His covered in warthogs, Guv."

Sometimes, Donald gives me cause to doubt his sanity, so I was relieved to find that

Butterworth's passport was indeed plastered in Outer Ggagaan visas, each complete with a silver hologram of a smiling warthog. As national symbols went, it was a few rungs below a British bulldog.

"Reckon this place is worth investigating, Guv?"

"What, Outer Ggaga?"

"Yes, Guv."

"Well, it's off the usual commuter routes."

"I've not been away for ages."

"Same. Not since a Federation away-day to Toxteth."

"Shall we make the request?"

"No harm in trying."

Thursday 21 May

Time since breakfast: Ten minutes.
Location: Police station.
Risk assessment: Vindictive superior officer.

My sergeant and I waited dutifully on The Super's rug while he pondered a crossword clue in *Masochism Weekly*.

After he had finally filled in the word *handcuff*, I said, "It's about travel expenses, sir."

The Super didn't bother looking up. "Mileage or ticketed actuality'?"

"Both, sir."

"Inside the borough?"

"Outer..."

"Ggaga, sir," interrupted Donald.

"No problem." The Super filled in another clue: *punish*.

"Really?" I could not believe my ears.

"One way." The Super looked up for the first time and gave us an evil grin.

Time since breakfast: Twenty-five minutes.

Location: Police station.

Risk assessment: Sergeant distracted by ducklings.

I sat at my desk, scrawling the word 'cancelled' through my *Avoiding Trip Hazards in the Workplace* leaflets. I had campaigned on more issues than I had eaten hot pies: mandatory vest wearing; ergonomic desk design and the inseparability of traffic policing from mainstream law enforcement. The Federation mattered, but murder mattered more. I would have to postpone the trip-hazard meeting until we had returned from a warthog-ridden corner of Africa.

Donald seemed unusually thoughtful. "Guv, I'm a bit worried about the tickets."

"Don't be. They'll be fully legit – I'll have the Federation lawyer run his eyes over them."

"But what about the returns?"

"Don't get ahead of yourself."

"Won't we be stuck out there forever?"

"I shouldn't think so, no."

"How would we get back?"

"A plane, I should imagine. It's a ruddy long way to walk."

"Do we even know where it is, Guv?"

"We'll have to investigate."

"But it's officially non-existent."

"Then we'll just have to track it down. Call yourself a detective?"

"You don't think The Super just wants to get rid of us?"

"Possibly." After the masochist raid, we weren't exactly in his good books.

"Do we really have to go?" Donald was started to sound like a whingeing kid.

"It's part of our murder investigation."

"But what about my ducklings, Guv?"

"They can fly now."

"You'll miss Pie Night at *The Blind Beggar*."

The thought of steak-and-kidney pudding stopped me in my tracks. "Fair enough, Donald. Pie Night is too good miss."

NATIONAL STEALTH SERVICE

Transcription - Appraisal Meeting

Wednesday, May 20, 23.58

Present: "F" (Head of Operational Discretion, National Stealth Service) and George Gurney (Trainee Junior Watcher, Remedial Unit, National Stealth Service).
Appraisal exercise: reaction to purloined police notes.

GURNEY: Seems like Stalin prefers pies to travel.

F: There never would have been a return journey. Steak and kidney saved them from a lifetime of exile.

GURNEY: Their Super will be disappointed.

F: But not The Stealth Service. We can't have fat cops and thuggish duck-lovers gallivanting off to Deniable countries. That would never do.

GURNEY: Better off at Pie Night.

F: Quite possibly. Anyway, we now have an identification on the pilot.

GURNEY: The one with the big nose. How?

F: The Stealth Service does have a somewhat formidable image bank, and whilst we have been savouring Chief Inspector Stalin's pastry preoccupations, our own digital detectives have made a match. The helicopter pilot is a Deniable operative currently based in Outer Ggaga.

GURNEY: But he's not in Easy Africa, he's in Wandsworth.

F: Hence the helicopter.

GURNEY: Oh yeah.

F: His full name is Kenneth Loach, widely known as *Kes*.

GURNEY: Kes?

F: Correct.

GURNEY: Unusual name.

F: I suppose it could be a playful reference to his beaky nose and the titular bird in that northern miserabilist work.

GURNEY: Titular, F?

F: I believe the film was entitled *Kes*.

GURNEY: Like *Des* with a K.

F: No. Like kestrel, the bird of prey. A raptor that kills on sight.

CHAPTER 23

Blokes with big noses are just way too in-your-face. Their huge honks intrude into everyone else's privacy, and generally distract the public. I don't suppose it's their fault, but big-nosed blokes strike me as a bunch of attention seekers. Look at me with my enormous great schnoz! Size does matter, but in the nose department, modesty is the colour of virtue, as they say in church.

So, it seems that Bill's old mate Kes is on the side of the florists. I never liked the sound of the bloke, but it's hard to believe that a Deniable would turn on one of his own. Ambassadors are one thing, with their diplomatic double-dealing and supercilious smarminess, but a comrade-in-arms is another matter altogether. Bill and Kes had stood together, facing down the Walloons, the Semi-Pygmy Insurgency, The Sons of The Brotherhood and renegade nuns – surely that had built an unbreakable bond.

Personally, I could understand Stalin's preference for pies over East Africa. I have never enjoyed long-haul flights, as I tend to get cramp and the cabin crew stop me drinking my usual measure. They don't realise that my alcohol tolerance is world-beating. I genuinely can drink like an Olympian, and they simply don't believe me. Four or five drinks are not enough to get me through a cross-Channel flight, and they certainly won't do for inter-continental. But the flights are just the first bit. The trouble really starts when you land. Everything is different, which you might think would be to the advantage of someone who struggles so much with life at home, but it isn't. After my third marriage collapsed, I was wrongly awarded a substantial sum and I blew it on a round-the-world tour. It didn't go well. I was deported from India for insulting a cow, I fell down a Bavarian ski slope and dislocated both eyes, I capsized a camel in Morocco and ended up buried in a sand dune, I tobogganed off the Great Wall of China and landed on a senior communist party official. I went busking in Mexico and was forced to play guitar for eighteen hours non-stop at a cartel boss's wedding, I got into a dispute in a Neapolitan pizzeria and triggered a mafia war, and I offended a Russian oligarch on a bear hunt and got shot in the arse. After all that, I decided to stick to staycations.

I delved into my bankrupt memory bank for any further recollections of the previous night. I was in the lock-in, dancing my new dance, getting ignored by women, and mouthing off about my life-coaching clients. Was anybody listening? It seemed unlikely. But hang on - someone was. For once, somebody was paying attention to me. Normally, it's just yawns, looks over my shoulder, and insults. But not this time. They were hanging on my every word. That never happened. How could I have forgotten? But what did they look like? Male, probably – if it had been a woman, I would have remembered. But that was it. I returned to the dossier, which began with more Gurney, bless him:

NATIONAL STEALTH SERVICE

Transcription - Appraisal Meeting

Thursday 21 May

Present: "F" (Tutor, Remedial Unit, National Stealth Service) and George Gurney (Trainee Junior Watcher, Remedial Unit, National Stealth Service).
Appraisal exercise: to rescue critical situation wrongly assigned to novice Watcher.

F: Tell me, Gurney, are you aware of the Hidden Journalism Code?
GURNEY: No, F. Sorry.
F: Really? It's based on Irish Braille and Lithuanian Morse. Are you really familiar with neither?

GURNEY: They're both Greek to me.

F: Oh dear. It used to be part of the standard induction course, even in the Remedial Unit. It's the language of covert news. I've just intercepted a rather apposite message from a hidden hack in Outer Ggaga.

GURNEY: Golly! Well done, F.

F: Your congratulations are much appreciated, but a little untimely, as I'm sure you will appreciate after I have read you the message I have just deciphered: "The Walloons are crumbling. The Zeppelins are deflated. The Sons, Sisters, and Fathers of the Brotherhood are tearing at each other's cassocks. The Semi-Pygmies are united and poised for liberty. The Chelsea Flower Show is about to start transmitting on Fan Zone screens right across the whooping willow jungles, rose fields and papyrus swamps. If Belladonna's Floral Deliveries' Garden of Death wins Best in Show with its Conflict Diamond Rockery, it will be a disaster. Potter - a Kenyan national based in the London Borough of Wandsworth - will be well-placed to reunite The Brotherhood, divide the Semi-Pygmies and snatch overall control of Outer Ggaga. It is absolutely vital to ensure that The Great Star of Mount Heha does not come into the possession of Belladonna's Floral Deliveries. Good luck to all spooks. Rule Britannia! Charles Brithazard, Covert Correspondent, Outer Ggaga."

GURNEY: Wow! You deciphered all that from Irish Braille and Lithuanian Morse?

F: Correct. Now, if you are in possession of any more surveillance notes, Gurney, it would be much appreciated.

GURNEY: Plenty.

F: Legible?

GURNEY: Not really, F.

F: Then I suppose you'll have to read them to me.

GURNEY: Can I do the voices?

F: If you must, but don't get too excited and do try to remain in your seat.

GURNEY: Okay, F. Promise:

Belladonna Floral Deliveries' Stretch Bedford takes a left along the north bank of the Thames and turns in to The Chelsea Flower Show through the Bull Ring Gate. Members of the public queue for admission. The Stretch Bedford parks up alongside Belladonna's Garden of Death. The florists alight with the dominatrix at gunpoint.

Surveillance continues (officers disguised as gardeners operate compost-cams;

microphones are concealed in assorted shrubberies).

LEONARD (TO DOMINATRIX): I think we'll probably poison you. The only trouble is, we're spoilt for choice.

Leonard names each lethal plant as he makes final border-checks on the Garden of Death.

LEONARD: Dogbane, Snakeroot, Belladonna, Hemlock, Devil's trumpet, Dutchman's breeches, Moonseed, Pokeweed, Black locust, Death Camas, Poison ivy, Panther Cap, Hairy vetch. Any preferences?

Kes wheels a mulching bin across a burial mound feature.

LEONARD (TO DOMINATRIX): Forgive my manners. I never got around to introducing you formally. This is Kes. He's your Life Development Canceller.

KES: Charmed.

LEONARD: He's going to entomb you in a mulching bin. It's full of lots of environmentally friendly organic material. You'll be decomposed alive.

Kes lifts the dominatrix into the mulching bin. Leonard shuts her in. Kes leans on the lid.

End of recording.

F: Lucky we stepped up the surveillance at Chelsea.

GURNEY: I think she needs more than surveillance.

F: If we intervene to protect one individual, our operation is over.

GURNEY: But she seems lovely.

F: Does she really?

GURNEY: Well, for someone who hits people for a living, yes.

F: No one deserves to be mulched to death, I agree. But gardening is a ruthless game.

GURNEY: There's some more surveillance material from Bar Achilles. It's about the pawnbroker's death.

F: Jolly good. Fire away.

Bronze and Potter are at a Bar Achilles' Private Table. The word 'Reserved' has been carved into the wood. A barmaid serves them grey, gloopy Wandsworth cocktails. Bronze squeezes her left buttock. The barmaid seeks sanctuary in the kitchen.

BRONZE: A perfect English rose.

POTTER: There's nothing English about a rose. They grow in African fields;

they're tended by Africans, and they're gathered by African hands.

BRONZE: Should I be taking notes?

POTTER: You should be taking care. Your fence is permanently broken.

BRONZE: He had never failed me before, but you were within your rights to deliver him.

POTTER: So, we delivered the pawnbroker. What does it matter? The Father's dead.

BRONZE: Whose father?

POTTER: Forestière. The Father of The Brotherhood. Our link to the Walloons. The African rose routes are our arteries, and he was a major corpuscle.

BRONZE: So, you're out of circulation.

POTTER: The Chelsea Flower Show is about to get our hearts pounding again.

BRONZE: Good. Look, the pawnbroker had a partner.

POTTER: Petal.

BRONZE: The pawnbroker's pornographer.

POTTER: Due a delivery?

BRONZE: Long ago.

End of recording.

F: Good Lord, Gurney, that is both a confession to the pawnbroker's murder and evidence of conspiracy to murder the merkin-maker.

GURNEY: Golly, F. How exciting.

F: I wouldn't have said *exciting* is the correct word. For Petal, I would say *terrifying* might be more accurate.

GURNEY: So you do care!

F: Naturally.

GURNEY: Is Bronze supposed to kill people?

F: Not if he can help it, no, but we recruited him because of his underworld connections. He's no choirboy.

GURNEY: Shall I recruit a choirboy?

F: No. Did they proceed with their plan?

GURNEY: Yes.

F: How do we know?

GURNEY: We hid some covert cameras and microphones in Petal's merkins.

F: When?

GURNEY: We had a work trip to her sex shop. It was quite popular.

F: Jolly good, Gurney. Do go ahead:

Petal's Private Shop. Bronze and Potter pretend to admire her merchandise. Neither man exhibits any acting talent, but they give it their best.

BRONZE: What craftsmanship!

Bronze brandishes a "Dancing Dolphin" vibrator.

POTTER: What technology!

Potter examines a Self-Lubricating Cyber-skin Dildo.

POTTER: Back home, these are sculpted out of soapstone.

Petal emerges from behind a rack of assorted PVC uniforms.

PETAL: Listening to you two is like The Vagina Dialogues. You're a right pair of...

Potter pulls out a revolver.

POTTER: Swivel.

Petal turns her back on them. Potter hands the gun to Bronze and winks. Bronze hesitates then aims the barrel at Petal.

POTTER: When a sex shop owner and a small-time pawnbroker take on Belladonna's Floral Deliveries, that's when good neighbours become dead friends. Where is it?

PETAL: I never hated a man enough to give him a diamond back.

Potter walks behind Bronze and pulls a second gun. The metal kisses the base of Bronze's skull. Potter leans forward and whispers into his ear.

POTTER: Fire.

Bronze squeezes his trigger. So does Potter. Bronze and Petal drop dead simultaneously, setting off every battery-powered sex toy in the shop.

End of recording.

F: Oh dear.

GURNEY: Shouldn't we have stopped it, F?

F: Bronze was no longer on our side, and Petal had conspired with Buster Butterworth and the pawnbroker to steal a conflict diamond from one of the world's most deadly Deniable countries.

GURNEY: So, they had it coming?

F: Not for me to judge, Gurney, but I do need someone to act on our behalf.

GURNEY: A solicitor?

F: No. You need to find Tell.

GURNEY: Isn't he in jail?

F: Shouldn't think so. Not by now.

GURNEY: You think Stalin's released him?

F: I think he's probably released himself.

GURNEY: Won't Tell kill me?

F: I shouldn't think so. He's not really a florist.

GURNEY: He's never one of ours?

F: Through and through.

GURNEY: Oh. I suppose I'll probably be all right then.

F: Good luck with your first mission, Gurney.

CHAPTER 24

Events were moving on apace, what with diamond dildos, double fatalities in sex shops, and ornamental gardens of death.

I did worry about the wisdom of sending Gurney on a mission. Posting a letter would stretch the limits of his abilities, never mind locating a highly skilled undercover operative.

It was all a bit of a concern, so I decided to practise one of my life coaching techniques. Reverse Yoga, or Agoy for short. Agoy comprises a series of exercises designed to make you feel tense, anxious, and uncomfortable. It twists the spine, represses your energy, and compresses the muscles. There are some wonderful positions: The Broken Spanner, The Distracted Pensioner, The Injured Pilchard, The Upward Badger, The Stiff Gibbon, The Fitting Piranha and The Hyperactive Nutjob. I began by rotating my torso one-hundred-and-eighty degrees and looking at my arse. I repositioned, then touched my nose with my toes and fell over. I righted myself, leant backwards and touched the floor with the back of my head, arching my spine to breaking point. Once the pain had passed, I reset, stood on one leg, leant forward, and placed my forehead on my left knee. I repositioned and completed the sequence by standing on my elbows and performing a backflip whilst chanting the mantra, "Call an ambulance."

I felt much worse, so I gave up and returned to the dossier:

JOURNAL - EX-SERGEANT BILL TELL

Wednesday 20 May

17.10

I ambled around Wandsworth Common wondering whether I had met my Waterloo. Just as Napoleon's imperial power had shrivelled in the face of inglorious defeat, my regimental get-up-and-go had got-up-and-gone after The Ambassador's deception. For a moment, I was so riddled with doubt that I was sorely tempted to join Agnostic Jihad.

But a true combatant recovers from even the bitterest blow, and I decided to prepare for my adversaries. I ran the most fearful recipients of my covert CV through my head and began to strategize. FARC, South America's deadly aficionados of the kidnap-murder combo, were out to get me because I had laced their last five cocaine shipments with permanent laxative and left them in the shit. Colombians had a lively, party-loving culture, so I was probably best-off decoying them to the most tedious battle-ground possible – Hillingdon should lower their morale nicely. ETA were paramilitary Basque mountaineers and, on reflection I probably should not have sherpad so many of them off that Alp. If I was to take them on, I would be best off working at low altitude, perhaps at the bottom of the Thames Valley. Hamas were an Islamic Resistance Movement and I had put their suicide bombers in touch with the Samaritans – it had been a humane gesture, but it had rendered them redundant. I would be at an advantage somewhere life-affirming – Alton Towers might make a suitably cheerful field of conflict. The Real UDA were some of Northern Island's most passionate art loving killers and I probably should have thought twice before pebble-dashing their war murals. If I could lure them to Shoreditch, the hipster hangout's abundant street art would remind them sorely of their lost murals and I would have them at a serious disadvantage. Agnostic Jihad were the real worry. These Tomsk-based aficionados of Dither Law, with its split juries, hung parliaments and open prisons, were some of the most feared procrastinators on the planet, and I had sprayed their HQ with a decisiveness drug. If I could source some more supplies of that, it should irritate the pants off them.

I formulated a plan for every enemy. There was no guarantee that I could pull them all off, but at least I was no longer completely unprepared, and my morale shifted up a notch to around two out of eight hundred.

My warlike wool-gatherings were interrupted by an "Oi!" shouted from across the common. A pair of uniformed policemen were running towards me across the bowling green and pointing wildly. Neither of them seemed to be particularly fit and they were only armed with batons, tasers and boots. I could have let them catch me, selected one of the seventy-eight or so martial arts I mastered in the regiment, and kicked their heads in. But instead, I decided to go along with their game and play chase. I outpaced them with a gentle jog, dodged past a couple of fishermen, disappeared behind the café, and sped off into an affluent area dubbed *The Toast Rack* on account of its evenly sliced streets. I heard a few distant whistles and wheezes, but essentially my evasion was complete.

"Turned out nice again," a high-pitched male voice remarked.

I swivelled, ready to attack its owner with some serious self-defence.

A young bloke smiled back soppily. His suit didn't fit, his tie was covered in brown sauce, and he hadn't bothered to tuck his shirt in. I assessed the threat level as Negligible-to-None.

"I've been sent by the authorities," he explained.

"On whose authority?"

"Intelligence."

"Clever."

"Not really. I'm in the Remedial Unit."

"Congratulations."

"We're an elite group of morons."

"Entry requirements stringent?"

"Social Security passed them my details." He offered me his hand.

I shook it, possibly a little too firmly. I hadn't meant to make him cry.

"My name's Bill."

"I know."

"How?"

"I'm not meant to let on."

"Oh."

"Sorry."

"That's okay."

"I'm Gurney, Gerald Gurney."

"Nice name." If this Muppet really was from The National Stealth Service, then national security was as flimsy as tissue paper.

"Look, Mr Tell, can we do a deal?"

"I don't know. Can we?"

"You know you've triggered a full-scale police investigation."

"It did cross my mind during the armed raid."

"Can we go somewhere quiet?"

I looked around at Baskerville Road's five-million-quid houses, sedate bushes, and empty pavements, and said, "How quiet do you want?"

Gurney just said, "I have some documents and some information."

"What? Your tax return? Liberal Democrat Manifesto? Subbuteo statistics?" The Ambassador's deception had mainlined my sarcasm channels. I could see how disappointed the lad looked, and he was right - I wasn't behaving with the dignity expected. I about-turned my attitude and started being a decent bloke again. "All right. Let me check that you've not been followed."

I led us a merry dance, casting confusion trails, checking reflective surfaces, and dodging behind lampposts until I was satisfied that no one had put a tail on either of us. After that, I followed him to his vehicle and got in beside him. It was the sort of car you might learn to drive in – small, smelly, and a few months off the scrapheap. It even had probationary P-plates. Gurney took his time to check his mirrors, indicate, miss several opportunities to turn out into the road, and stall. He apologised and repeated the process, this time successfully. Progress was slow, and Gurney rarely dared to venture above second gear. Traffic lights provided further opportunities to stall, and no roundabout was conquered without triggering a chorus of horn blasts. Luckily, I was able to direct him away from the perils of Wandsworth Gyratory System in time.

18.58

Gurney trundled his unimpressive car down one of those narrow, nameless streets often found beneath railway embankments and behind shabby suburban shops. It was lined with rotten pallets, industrial bins, and white vans, and generously decorated with barbed wire and weeds. This was our destination – a row of lockups. London's full of the things, and I don't think a single garage is ever used for parking. They're all stuffed to bloating point with contraband baccy, knocked-off antiques, and dirty money, and on the rare occasions that the garage owners do bump into each other, they never ask each other questions or meet each other's glances.

I calculated that the chances of ambush by FARC, ETA, Mossad, Hamas, The Chechen Warlords of Doom, or Agnostic Jihad were low to middling at worst. The canopy door was battered, but solid, and once Gurney had entered a code, it tilted itself up to reveal a festival of misshapen cardboard boxes lit by naked bulbs. I double-checked the street behind us, and followed Gurney in. The door shut behind us, and we were alone.

"It's certainly quiet," I said.

"I was told to find you."

"Who by?"

"F."

"Do you know why?"

"Why they're called F?"

"No. Why were you told to find me."

Gurney sank into thought. With agents of his calibre on front-line duty, it was no surprise that we were losing the War Against Error.

After a while, he said, "Quite a lot's been going on."

"Tell me about it."

"I keep everything here."

"The information?"

"Yes."

"And you want to share it all with me?"

Gurney shrugged.

"Is that what F said to do?"

"No."

"Did he have any orders for me?"

"F wasn't very clear, but you're a highly decorated Deniable and I think your fighting's brilliant."

"Cheers."

"I'm sure you can figure out what's best to do from the documents."

"Can I offer you anything in return for all your information?"

Gurney looked perplexed. "What have you got?"

I thought of the most worthless object in my possession. "Do you follow football?"

"Rather."

I handed him the Cup tickets Normal had given me in Outer Ggaga. Gurney was so delighted that he didn't notice they were out of date.

In exchange, Gurney yanked open one of the newer looking boxes and explained that they contained all the relevant Stealth Service's surveillance transcriptions and the police case notes.

I thanked him, but he still didn't go away.

"It's okay, Gurney. I'll take it from here."

"Oh. Are you sure?"

I could have been honest and told Gurney that he was about as much use as an inflatable dartboard, but I decided to be kind and just told him to go away. Once the door had closed behind him and I'd heard him stall a few times, and drive away in second gear, I got stuck in.

I completed the regimental speed-reading course at Reading, so I was able to make short work of Gurney's bumf. The documents were shocking, both as an indictment of contemporary policing standards and of The National Stealth Service's Remedial Unit. They begged plenty of questions: the spooks seemed to know everything but do nothing, and the police had the opposite problem. Passive intelligence on one side and brainless action on the other – what a rubbish combo!

As I sped-read, I inserted relevant sections from my journal, scrawled an introduction and the odd additional note, and checked that everything was in a reasonably logical order. I then boxed up the whole bunch and parked my secrets, ready for The Stealth Service to discover in the event of my death.

Action was required and there was no question in my mind what that would be – I was going to have to attend The Chelsea Flower Show.

I knew that it meant near-certain death; there was no question about that. I would be a sitting target for everyone The Ambassador had emailed - Hamas, ETA, FARC, Mossad, Agnostic Jihad, the Real UDA, and an uneasy coalition of Chechen Warlords. Now, I could add Belladonna's Floral Deliveries to the list.

Maybe I was going to join the spectral ranks of *The Old and Bold*, but Geraldine was about to be mulched. I loved her with every fibre of my ops pants, and I could not allow her to become compost! Love is not just for wusses; it is literally all you need. Shame my life was coming to an end when I was just starting to get the hang of it, but I had to free my dominatrix from the florists.

CHAPTER 25

Never had I read the words *Chelsea Flower Show* with such trepidation. Death lurked behind every petal. The horticultural extravaganza spelled doom for Bill, and I truly feared for him and Geraldine. Planet Earth has really got it in for us, hasn't it? We think we've got the measure of the place, but it's the other way around. Life is just a twisted joke at humanity's expense; a joke that falls flat in an indifferent universe. Still, mustn't grumble.

I went to pick up the next page, but there wasn't one. Had I reached the end? Who out of Hamas, ETA, FARC, Mossad, Agnostic Jihad, the Real UDA, an uneasy coalition of Chechen Warlords, Kes the big-nosed Deniable, and the surviving members of Belladonna's Floral Deliveries had killed Bill? Had I missed the clues? Were they all guilty, like Murder on The Orient Express? I didn't rate my chances of killing any of them, let alone them all.

Even more inconveniently, I was still locked in a strip club. What to do next? Teach myself to pole dance? Try on all the stripping accessories? Jump out the window? It was all beyond frustrating, so I used one of my life coaching techniques: "throwing something against a wall". It can be expensive, but I have often found that it provides temporary relief. I picked up the empty box, chucked it, and didn't feel any better. So, I resorted to a second technique: "booting an object repeatedly around a room". On my twelfth kick of the box, a small wad flopped onto the carpet. Result! The box must have had a false bottom. I grabbed the wad. More journal. Result! I was about to start reading when I heard the pensive blips of a pre-alarm. Either someone was breaking in, and it was about to launch into full scream mode, or someone with a set of keys and a code had arrived for work. It was possibly nothing to worry about, but it probably was.

How to prepare? Take up a defensive position behind a dancing pole? Hide in Bill's box? Disguise myself with a pair of nipple tassels? The questions were endless, and I only had one answer: finish the journal.

The pre-alarm went silent. The new arrival was legit, or at least knew the code, but that didn't mean they weren't about to kill me. I decided to take cover as a sofa. I purloined some cushions from the dressing room, stuffed them and myself into the sofa cover, and crouched on all-fours, aiming to make myself as furniture shaped as possible. I placed the remaining pages of the journal on the floor, and hoped I could reach the end before my disguise was discovered.

JOURNAL - EX-SERGEANT BILL TELL

THE THAMES

Wednesday 20 May

21.52

Chelsea Suspension Bridge was illuminated. Its golden galleons shined from lamp stands, the galvanized steel wires glistened, and the pseudo-Egyptian pylon gleamed.

Thirty metres away, I shared a gravel bank with a gull, a rusty chain, and several sacks of ballast. I took out my wallet and eyeballed a photo of my mum: the dimply smile, the optimistic eyes, and the matchstick-modelling glue on her forehead. I dropped a tear onto her cheek, stood up and started to remove my outer clothes. I placed my jacket, shirt, and trilby in an orderly pile, but I kept a firm grip on my trousers: I had other plans for them.

The moon lit the river septic green. Scum floated on the murk, but I am not afraid of scum. I yomped into the Thames. It didn't take long for the water to reach my ops pants. As soon as the water margin was within gulping distance, I knotted the empty trouser legs, swung them around my head until they inflated; and utilised them as a floatation device. With my spare hand, I rolled the tear-stained photograph into a tube, dunked my head underwater and employed my mum's picture as a breathing pipe.

It wouldn't be an easy crossing, but I had swum the Euphrates under hostile fire, survived a crocodile attack in a papyrus swamp and fended off hippos single-handed on Lake Victoria. In theory, the Thames should have been a doddle. Or so I had thought. An undercurrent snatched away my legs and my complacency. I switched to backstroke, but weeds wound themselves around my ankles. I turned to breast and a drifting bait hook snagged my palm. Only the trousers kept me afloat. Cramp competed with cold shock, numbing my limbs.

My life was hanging by a trouser leg. Had I travelled the world only to drown in the shadow of Battersea Power Station? I breathed through my mum's photograph and held a Chinese Parliament with myself: advance or retreat? Bravery demanded the former, wisdom the latter – but I am far more brave than wise, so I forced myself onward through the murk, sporting my inflated trouser legs like a pair of honour badges. After ingesting a gallon of stinking water, I reached solid concrete.

The moment I had climbed up onto the pavement, a homeless man asked, "Spare us some change?"

I deflated my trousers, reached inside my ops pants, and handed him two-pounds-fifty.

21.58

I have penetrated enemy positions in five continents. I have breached borders, burgled compounds, and cracked fortresses, but no covert insertion is precisely like any other.

I took my time to observe my latest target, The Chelsea Flower Show. Royal Horticultural Guards patrolled the perimeter fence with torches and Alsatians. Animals held no fear for me: I can lure caribou on all-fours, ambush ptarmigans with a catapult and catch seals by their breathing holes. I moved silently, scaling the walls like a spider, then dropped to the ground and crawled on my belly. I paused to stripe my face with soil and disguise my silhouette with spiky vegetation.

I infiltrated the hostile horticultural terrain, crawling through thorn thickets, scaling a mountain of high-grade sod, and diving down an acrylic waterfall. I made low, deliberate movements, willing myself not to blunder into anything. A searchlight illuminated show gardens, greenhouses, and nursery pavilions. I could dodge the beam, but I hoped to God the RHS guards didn't have night viewing aids.

At least the climatic conditions were favourable. The wind-chill factor was unthreatening, this being West London in May. I created a covert observation post by scooping compost out of the ground, then climbed into my man-made hole and roofed it with branches.

I spent a dark, damp hour worrying about Geraldine. The thought of the florists delivering her was almost too much to bear. My jaw tightened as an RHS guard approached my lying-up position. The horticultural enthusiast was a pensioner; quite possibly a grandfather, but I couldn't allow myself to be sentimental – I had been compromised.

I flattened myself against the soil and held my breath, but the old codger clocked me. I weighed up the options: I could top him, tie him up or let him carry on patrolling the planting schemes. An eye-to-eye encounter was an outrageous risk, but I didn't want a civilian death on my conscience. I returned his gawp.

After what seemed like a lifetime, the old boy flung me a "Lovely Day," in a Norfolk accent, which I mimicked in reply. *Always try to blend in. Be the grey man,* that's what the regiment taught me at Blackpool Pleasure Beach.

As soon as the pensioner turned away, I did a dummy run to a pergola then switched back west to a refreshments tent, tracing an anti-clockwise loop. From a tactical point of view, high ground was advantageous. I boxed around some cottage borders and hollyhock spires, circumnavigated a greenhouse, and took up position behind a Miniature Matterhorn. It was made of Perspex, but it provided tactical cover.

The sunrise allowed me to conduct a quick appreciation, but caution was still necessary. High ground offered perspective, but I couldn't let myself be skylined. Equally, I didn't want the visitors to get slotted. They had paid to see designer gardens, not World War Three.

I made a quick audio-assessment. My ears buzzed with elderly ladies chattering. There was no operationally relevant communication in their overlapping monologues, just a torrent of unfiltered trivia about grandchildren, dogs, and funerals.

Having completed the audio assessment, I moved on to a visual analysis of the target. The Chelsea Flower Show was a vast location. There were formal gardens with symmetrical patterns and informal designs with unexpected features. *Belladonna's Garden of Death* would be a well-protected objective. I could not just rush in; I needed to blend in as much as operational security allowed. I weighed up a variety of scenarios and decided I would be more plausible as a worker than a visitor.

I scanned the horizon and eyeballed genteel volunteers queuing for uniforms outside a marquee. Their colleagues exited the tent in colourful jumpsuits with the words *Can I Help You?* printed across the chests. I needed that kit! With it, I could pass muster as an RHS volunteer.

I conducted a thorough recce – this was no time for inaccuracy, it was time for facts. Loads of them. The marquee's alloy frames were covered in translucent PVC fabric. It was around three-point-six metres at the eave, eight metres at the centre and it was partitioned into reception and dining areas. The floor was suspended to give a level solid surface. This was an assailable objective.

I belly-crawled out of my hide and sprinted at a hunch, darting into the tent through a gap in the canvas. Moments later, I emerged triumphant in a *Can I Help You?* jumpsuit, looking a right prat. But now was not the moment for fashion, it was the moment for action. Do or die, no less. I did a sharp three-sixty: there were thousands of petal pushers in plastic pavilions. Landscape gardeners jostled with sweat-pea salesmen, sculptors hawked novelty gnomes and hundreds of local hobby clubs bumbled cheerfully from exhibit to exhibit.

The terrain was bewilderingly varied, and my training should have seen me through, but the horticultural enthusiasts were an embuggerance. Collateral damage was unthinkable - if a single Middle England pensioner tasted lead, I would never be able to forgive myself.

Slap bang in the middle of Belladonna's Garden of Death; a bloke was leaning on a compost bin. He had a stonking great conk. Frankly, his schnoz was unmistakeable. It was my old comrade, Kes. Now, the National Stealth Service had drawn the most negative conclusions possible from their surveillance, but when it comes to a fellow Deniable, I will always give them the benefit of the doubt. I made a covert approach to the allotment and whispered, "Wotcha, mate."

"Nice jumpsuit, Big Man." Kes shook my hand, but didn't ease his weight off the bin-lid. A disconcerting thump banged from inside the depository, but it could just have been a trapped badger.

"Thanks, mate. How's Outer Ggaga?"

"Noisy," Kes replied. The bin resounded oddly, but he didn't acknowledge it.

"Really?"

"That's Civil War for you."

"Fair one. Lads okay?"

"It's not been the same without you, Big Man."

"Ambassador?"

"She won't let on, but she feels the same."

After what she had done, I knew this couldn't be true, but there was someone more important on my mind. "Marie-Thérèse?"

"Sorry, Big Man. No one's seen her since the Walloons totalled her library."

I had spent many months with Kes on patrol, on stag, and on parade, but I never expected to encounter him at The Chelsea Flower Show. "Didn't know you gardened."

"Helps pass the time."

"So, you're not in Outer Ggaga".

"Not a lot gets past you, does it, Big Man?"

"Thanks, Kes." I had topped my year in the regiment's *Noticing Things* Course at Oldham. "Are you on leave?"

"Looks like it, Big Man."

"Compost bin's noisy?"

"That'll be the fertilizer vibrating."

"Vibrating fertilizer?"

"Accelerates the mulching process."

The compost bin issued a muffled yell.

"Kes?"

"Big Man."

"The mulch just screamed."

Kes's body convulsed with laughter. I reciprocated. Then he decked me. It was a bloody good thing that he did, because a bullet zinged through the space I had just involuntarily vacated and hit a tomato plant. Things were kicking off and Kes had almost punched my lights out.

From the far corner of consciousness, I eyeballed the compost bin upending itself. Was it a hallucination triggered by Kes's thump? No, it was a heavily soiled humanoid clambering out, shaking an armful of fertilizer out of its hair, and running for dear life. I couldn't believe my irises. It was Geraldine, still stunning, even when heavily mulched.

Kes sprinted after the muddy dominatrix. I was gobsmacked by my comrade's betrayal. He was in the regiment – we had always stood together. My world had performed a sharp one-eighty and I was staring into Oblivion.

I would have bomb-blasted after the two of them, but a sharp burst of gunfire sent me diving for a herbaceous border. I rolled sideways and eyeballed the shooter. It was Leonard the florist, sneering as he let loose a Heckler & Koch.

I needed to make a series of mental readjustments, a tricky feat to pull off whilst being pursued by a heavily armed florist. I yomped through Oriental mountainscapes, crouched behind a faux temple, and sprinted up a raked gravel stream. Garden features blocked, snagged, and scratched from all directions.

Leonard let loose a couple of zinging rounds. I dived behind a low-growing hedge and eyeballed Geraldine zigzagging along an avenue of silver birch. Kes pursued her, opening fire. Bullets bounced off the bark, and she tripped on some decorative pebbling. Kes bore down on her, unleashing a steady crack-crack of shots.

Geraldine was out in the open, coverless. I willed her to get well clear of the area. *Make yourself a hard target; use the lie of the ground*, as the regiment had taught me at Royal Tunbridge Wells.

There was nothing I could do but draw fire. I ran across a series of ornamental lawns, shouting and waving my arms. Bullets zinged past my ears as I yomped up a pea gravel path, keeping up a fearsome tab. A burst of heavy machine gun fire zipped past me, decapitating a row of Elgar Peonies. I belly-flopped into some Japanese blood grass.

Twenty metres ahead, Geraldine froze, stranded on a semi-circular patio. Leonard pounded along a succession of dressed-stone planks, searched a stuccoed grotto, and trampled some semi-erect cilicicum. I ran at right angles and came into Leonard's line of sight. He let loose a burst from his barrel, decking an evergreen myrtle flag. I ducked north, past some Can-Can Begonias.

I kept going with my head down and sheltered behind some formal topiary. For a moment, I thought I had lost sight of her, but Geraldine's shadow played across a nearby wall. Bullets riddled the brightly coloured bricks behind her. She sought natural cover in some structural plants. Kes followed through with a deafening roar. Geraldine sprinted to a pergola, gaining temporary sanctuary.

I paralleled a lemon tree avenue. Leonard clocked me. My heart skipped a beat. The florist took aim. I leapt behind a slatted trellis. Bullets bounced off a bubble fountain. I tabbed as fast as I could, beating a retreat down sinuous pathways of circular paving.

In mixed terrain, navigation is always paramount, so I searched for a suitable marker and my gaze settled on a banner. It read *Puddletown Farmers Club*, but there was nothing agricultural about their ringleader. Even though he was disguised in a cloth-cap, battered Barbour and smelly wellies, I clocked him for one of the Mossad assassins I had honey-trapped on that unforgettable April Fool's Day a few years back. I had only meant it as a friendly jape, but the Israeli Intelligence Organisation had suffered a serious sense of humour failure.

Realising he had been pinged, the fake farmer let fly a Hassidic Coma-kick. He had fearsome knee-joints and blood-curdling thighs, but I couldn't allow myself to be intimidated. I disoriented him with a Sicilian Armpit Taunt, hobbled the bastard with a Danish Shin Jibe then did him with an Armenian Wedgie. As he gurgled his last, I felt sorry for the bloke, but there's a time for pity and The Chelsea Flower Show was not it.

A hand grabbed my shoulder. I turned and found myself confronted by a stuffy suit enquiring, "What the hell do you think you're doing?"

"Who are you?" I asked back.

"I'm a member."

"A member of what?"

"The RHS."

"ETA, more like." I recognised the Basque Separatist by his unmistakeable eyebrow scar. I don't think he had forgiven me for posing as a Swiss nomad and sherpa-ing his comrades off that Alp. He tried to do me with a Basque Bollock-twist, but I gave him the good news with a Polish Knee Knobble, a Gallic Bear Hug, and a Guernsey Spine Snap. He was one mountaineer who wouldn't be bagging any more Wainwrights.

An imperious voice made me swivel.

"What the devil's going on here?" The badge read, *Judge: Decking Section*, but his face read *Agnostic Jihad*. It was their chief ditherer, Timor The Vague. While he procrastinated about the best way to launch his attack, I did him with a Rhodesian Roundhouse, tormented him with a Thai Toe Job and finished him off with a Parisian Pillow-bite.

A noise made me perform a sharp one-eighty. It was a bloody good thing I did. An irate caterer had dropped his Pimm's jug and was about to rush me. But this was no ordinary refreshment vendor - he had Real UDA written all over him. As he launched a Loyalist Lung Lunge, I executed a Shetland Elbow Ping, administered a Swedish Nipple Twist, and paralysed him with a Tibetan Slap. He hadn't seen that one coming.

"Spare us some change?" a voice pleaded from behind me. I about turned to face a collector for the *Bamchester Bridge Bereavement Group*. He was way too cheerful. It had to be Hamas. I fought back with a Viking Gizzard Yank, a Uruguayan Throat Squeeze, and a Galway Tickle.

I looked up at the nearest display. *The Wormington Trump Orchid Society* was exhibiting an array of Love-Lies-Bleeding. The specimens were outstanding, pink-flushed with pendulous panicles. A peaceful scene? Not really. This was not an Orchid Society, it was FARC, a bunch of Columbian guerrillas. Three Andean desperados prepared to launch a Bogotá Bumming, but I countered with a Triple Ninja Prance and gave them the good news with a hat trick of Glasgow Kisses.

I was approached by a delegation of RHS Guards. Or so they wanted me to think. They seemed slightly uncomfortable with each other, so I could tell they were an uneasy coalition of Chechen Warlords. I did them with a Mancunian Fondle, a Scouse Bonk, and a Northampton Knee-Trembler.

I commando-crawled behind a box bush and watched a television presenter perform a piece-to-camera in Belladonna's Garden of Death.

"This year," the posh woman enthused into the lens, "Chelsea's designers have come up with everything from romantic cascades to floral clocks, but nothing is quite as intriguing as *Belladonna's Garden of Death*. Just look at the exploding poison capsules on this sandbox tree."

The presenter smiled as she fondled a sinister plant with her protective gloves. "These toxic locoweeds cause frenzied behaviour, loss of muscle control, blindness, and painful death. Shame the diamond rockery's lacking a single diamond."

Gunfire blocked out the rest of her lines. I span, expecting Leonard, but it was his boss, Harold Potter. I had not forgotten that he had served in the Happy Valley Super Duper Troopers, the Kenyan equivalent of the SAS. Potter's artillery felled a *Michael Fish Chrysanthemum*. Tragic really, it's an awesomely gorgeous flower.

I swerved behind some upright perennials with terminal spikes, then belly-crawled through perimeter planting and made a bolt for it past some impressive box parterres. I told myself: *Don't slack - it's not over yet.*

The florists were giving it some seriously good bursts. Their firepower was fearsome - they were putting in round after round, firing in a frenzy. Confusion was total. It was outrageous. Geraldine was safe below the line of fire, but not safe enough. I had to change that. I dived under a ferocious barrage of bullets, and crawled on my belly through a patch of *Dark Warrior Orchids*.

I eyeballed Chelsea's *Garden of Love*. Cascading water surged past romantically textured foliage. Leonard appeared in a rose-shrouded archway. Geraldine ran for shelter in a honeysuckle smothered boathouse. Bullets struck a bronze cherub, knocking its bow-and-arrow to the ground.

But with Potter in pursuit, I had problems of my own. I dived into a raised pond, hid beneath a lily pad and breathed through a hollow reed. Potter passed oblivious. I waited before resurfacing then spat out a goldfish. *Better to risk all and fight another day than die in a water feature*, as the regiment taught me at Welwyn Garden City.

I reappraised the situation, rejecting a route across a minimalist garden; it lacked cover. I entered the *Spirit of Essex Garden* and yomped across a stretch of leopardskin decking and crazy paving. It was possibly an even more tasteless environment than Forestière's hacienda, but I braced myself.

Potter leapt out from behind a shocking-pink gazebo and opened fire. I ducked behind a fountain of topless, surgically enhanced mermaids and ran at a crouch. *Get through it. Don't let Fear get the better of you. At the end of the day, why worry? It's only Death*, as they taught me at Peterborough. I fought for oxygen, crawling on my hands and knees. My lungs heaved, but I had to battle on. I bomb-blasted through a yucca plant forest feature and entered Chelsea's Gladiator Garden. Leonard opened fire from the shelter of a miniature Temple of Apollo. I dodged behind an Etruscan porch and checked out Geraldine's progress. She was sprinting past a row of neo-classical busts. Potter pounded after her across a mosaic patio. Geraldine toppled Julius Caesar's head and shoulders. Potter tripped over the felled emperor, Leonard tripped over Potter and they both landed in a bed of *Rip van Winkle Daffodils*.

While the homicidal florists floundered, I yomped into the Tropical Seacoast Garden. There were mangrove trees, pong-pong plants and a canopy of monkey-pod trees, all resonating to the recorded calls of a spangled drongo. I looked up at a Bendy Tree, its heart-shaped leaves punctuated with yellow and purple flowers. I held a Chinese parliament with myself and decided to scale the trunk. When I reached the end of a long branch, it bent beneath my weight. I wasn't heavy, but that was the thing about Bendy Trees; they were sensitive flowers. I reached inside my *Can I Help You?* jumpsuit, undid my charity shop belt and tied myself to a crooked branch.

As I had anticipated, Geraldine ran into the adjacent Pagan Rock Garden and hid between two miniature megaliths. Leonard blocked her left-hand exit. Potter blocked her right-hand exit. They pulled guns simultaneously and took aim at the love of my life.

"Diamonds are forever," Potter said. "But you girl, are not."

Leonard and Potter exchanged nods.

Timing is paramount in tree-based hostage rescue scenarios, and this was my microsecond of opportunity. I released the Bendy branch.

The florists pressed their triggers. I twanged Geraldine six feet in the air. The bullets passed through the gap she had vacated and entered Leonard and Potter. The florists shared a moment of bewilderment before dropping stone dead.

"If it worked in the jungles of Guatemala, I knew it would work at The Chelsea Flower Show," I told Geraldine as The Bendy branch flung me and Geraldine through the air.

She just said, "Good catch."

"You are."

"Thanks."

I landed on a mossy hillock. Geraldine landed on me. I was glad to be of service, but she was quite heavy.

"What did they do to you?"

"They gave me a presentation."

"Bastards."

"Who the hell is the florist with the beaky nose?"

"Kes. He's a regimental renegade and an underworld florist and you don't get much more lethal than that."

"Bill?"

"Geraldine."

"You saved my life."

"Thanks, but you're not safe yet. If we're going to survive this, I need you answer one question: where's the pink, fluffy case?"

Geraldine looked blank, then blanched. "Your mum's."

"My mum's!"

"She said she'd look after it. Remember, when I panicked and scarpered after my own mum?"

How could I forget? I grabbed Geraldine's hand, and we made a run for it. We dodged behind the Grand Pavilion, tabbed past the display gardens and bomb-blasted out of The Chelsea Flower Show.

"Did you really kill all those gardeners, Bill?" Geraldine asked, once we had made it out of shooting range.

"I didn't kill any gardeners."

"Thank God for that."

"They were agents of ETA, FARC, Hamas, an uneasy coalition of Chechen Warlords, Mossad, the Real UDA, and Agnostic Jihad."

"How about the pawnbroker?"

"That was the florists."

"The bastards who kidnapped me?"

"Belladonna's Floral Deliveries. Two of them shot each other in the Tropical Seacoast Garden, another is dead in your dungeon, and there's one left – he's deadly. he's highly trained, and he's got a big nose."

Geraldine yanked on my hand. "I can't live like this, Bill."

"You can't live without this. If we don't drop Kes, we're history, and so is my mum."

"One more delivery, Bill and you promise me you'll forget about floristry forever." By the look of Geraldine's face, it was ultimatum o'clock.

"I'll never arrange another bouquet. I swear on the blood of my fallen comrades."

"Good. There's a bendy bus over there."

It wasn't as good as a Bendy Tree, but it would do the job. We bomb-blasted aboard, paid our fares, and pounded along the deck to the pushchair area.

"Why don't you sit down, Bill?" Geraldine asked. "There are plenty of seats."

"Thanks, but I need to hold a Chinese Parliament with myself, and, for that, I need to stand."

"Suit yourself, Bill."

Adrenalin pumped. Sweat poured. The bus indicated. A million thoughts raged through my brain. Kes was a traitor: my own second-in-command had turned florist. The thought of his betrayal churned my guts up something nauseous. Course for course, battle for battle, Kes was my closest match in the entire Covert Battalion. A one-on-one would be too close to call.

12.01

The Victory Estate's children blocked the entrance to Agincourt, but not for long. I wiped off my camouflage, threw away my *Can I Help You?* jumpsuit and stood there in my ops pants. It was embarrassing and chilly, but my identity was unmistakeable. They scattered.

12.04

We tabbed along the external corridor, past graffiti-covered doorways. The Agincourt Crew recognised me immediately.

"Where have you been, Mr Tell?" a revolver-sporting gangster asked.

"The Chelsea Flower Show," I replied.

"Win any medals?" a blood with a blade enquired.

"Not this time."

"Well, better luck next year," a Yardie with a sawn-off shotgun said.

"Thanks." I meant it.

Ideally, I would have been able to observe my mum's flat through a shared wall with a fibre optic probe, eavesdropped through covert mics and rehearsed the raid with my comrades in a mock-up of the estate at the Regimental Practice Pit at Chipping Barnet. We would simply cut the power, effect simultaneous roof-and window-entry and disorientate Kes with Confusion Bombs. Unfortunately, given that there was just me and a distressed dominatrix, I had to use her nail file. Seconds later, we were in. We flattened ourselves against the hall wall and took in the conflict arena: Kes and mum were sharing a Battenberg in the lounge.

I itched for an opportunity to free my mum from the threat. Armed florists were one thing, but a renegade regimentalist was quite another. She was in mortal danger from one of my own. He may have been sipping tea and nibbling multi-coloured cake, but he could turn in an instant. I prepared my assault, but Kes spotted me first.

"Big Man!" Kes boomed with fake jollity. "Don't be shy!"

I traversed my mum's shagpile in a series of carefully measured bounds, then did Kes with a classic Peruvian Leg Swivel. He fell, crunching my mum's Cathedral. I followed through with a Glaswegian Gut Wrench, a Bermondsey Bum Blessing, and a Henley Fisting. I turned to apologise to my mum for the damage we had inflicted on her matchstick model. It was a fatal mistake. Kes leapt to his feet and got me in a Welsh Death Grip. It is the ultimate hold, killing with the stealth of invisible music, silent painting, or unwritten poetry. I held a Chinese Parliament with myself and decided that

I was history.

But Kes didn't kill me. He just loosened his grip and said, "I'm on your side, Big Man."

"Then why did you just try to kill me?"

"Self-defence, Big Man. But no hard feelings, eh?"

"I need some answers."

"Ask away."

"Why did you defect to the florists?"

"Operational imperative. I infiltrated Belladonna's Floral Deliveries in case you needed some help."

"And you thought it would help if you kidnapped me?" Geraldine looked close to inflicting the sort of violence even her regular clients would not have enjoyed.

"I kept you alive." Kes said. "Potter wanted you potted. I pierced breathing holes in your mulching bin."

"Then why did you chase me across the display gardens firing a gun?" Geraldine asked, not unreasonably.

"I had to keep up appearances. The bullets never went near you."

I wasn't convinced. "Why did you deck me by the mulching bin?"

"I saved you from a bullet. There was no time to tell you to duck."

"What really happened to the priest."

"Sorry, Big Man, but we helped frame you for his death."

"Who's we?" I asked, gobsmacked.

"It was a pyramid of geezers."

"Bastards, more like."

"And The Ambassador."

"I don't understand."

"The Ambassador heard about Stanley the Semi-Pygmy's diamond discovery from the manager of The Stamford Bridge Hotel. He keeps his ear to the ground and the Ambassador was grateful. She whisked him out of the country for his own safety, and the hotel went to pot. That might have annoyed old Charlie Boy, but so what?"

I thought about Charles Brithazard's rants about skinks in the kitchen and hippos in the pool – it all seemed like a distant nightmare.

"Anyway," Kes continued. "The Ambassador consulted The National Stealth Service, and they were seriously worried about the diamond. When a Deniable country becomes rose-rich, that's bad enough. But when it gets diamond-rich, the spooks start worrying that it won't be Deniable for much longer. So, horny old Father Forestière tells Marie-Thérèse about his deal with Stanley The Semi-Pygmy, and says he wants to arrange an intimate celebration with her. Now, you may not know this, but Marie-Thérèse's has been on a retainer for yonks, so she's duty bound to report anything unusual to The Embassy. Things don't get much more unusual than this, so Marie-Thérèse told The Ambassador, who instructs her to agree on condition that he bring along the diamond to show her after the deed was done. It turned out that The Stealth Service didn't just want the diamond, they also wanted rid of Forestière. He was getting too big for his boots, and as the main go-between for the Walloons, The Brotherhood, and the Semi-Pygmies, they wanted to control his succession."

Kes took a nibble of my mum's Battenberg and continued. "The Ambassador asked me to arrange a last-minute kickboxing bout to distract the Walloons and, while you were practising your combat skills in the compound, they organised a demonically devious scheme. A mud path, a rose field and a personalised warthog homing device were wrangled. Scally and I were briefed and ordered to remain sober after your victory."

"How did you know I'd win?"

"You always do."

"Cheers."

"Anyway, as expected, you won, and you celebrated - quite rightly. Scally escorted you sozzled to the designated point on our mud path, triggering the horizontal warthog homing device at the field's apex. The bushpig rammed Charles as it scarpered towards the siren – the frequency is only audible to swine. Just as you were cocking your gun at the sky, the warthog whomped you in the ribs, and knocked you horizontal. Your shot traversed an empty rose field, killing no one, but frightening a hippo into the hotel swimming pool."

So, I hadn't killed anyone. I had been comprehensively conned into thinking I had killed the priest. Hippo scaring alone would never have got me thrown out of the regiment. I had been played for a mug.

Kes accepted a second slice of Battenberg from my mum and continued. "Scally then led you lot back to the compound to get even more comprehensively rat-arsed. As soon as you were comatose, he cued Marie-Thérèse to lead Forestière across the rose field to the place marked by the horizontal warthog-homing device. She switched it off and got down to business, cueing the next stage. I used a Night Vision Finder and a rifle to locate and pierce the frontal mid-point of the priest's skull and hastened his charter to Paradise with the trigger. As soon as he was a posthumous priest, Marie-Thérèse was briefed to frisk his cassock for gems, but we wouldn't know the result of her diamond-delve until later."

Kes had killed the priest and Marie-Thérèse was in on the whole shebang. Slap me on the arse and call me Susan! It was so cunning it could have been an Outer Ggagaan episode of *Midsomer Murders*.

Kes, the conky great conspirator, continued unapologetically. "The Semi-Pygmies are adept at track-covering, so The Ambassador ordered a cadre of Insurgents to rotate the copulating couple so that the angle of entry matched up with your barrel's point of descent immediately after your warthog encounter. We provided the Insurgency with a precision compass and a set of dividers. Nigel and Derek worked efficiently and accurately. We were impressed. All we had to do was wait for you to collect the body and the diamond. What we didn't know was that Forestière had not brought along the diamond. Buster Butterworth had made him an offer he couldn't refuse earlier in the evening. Priests, eh?"

I knew it! Belladonna's Floral Deliveries were at the conspiracy's bottom.

Kes gobbed another square of Battenberg. "No one knew that the Walloons and The Brotherhood had got wind of the diamond-find. I do hope the Walloons' tweezers didn't cause you any permanent injuries."

I recalled my fall from the Zeppelin. It had been the tweezers that had saved me.

"How about the tartan nuns?"

"Oh, The Sisters of The Brotherhood were out to avenge Forestière's death and to recoup the diamond. They had Marie-Thérèse fingered – they weren't after you in the papyrus swamp, if that's any comfort."

Comfort! As if Kes cared about my comfort. "Why frame me?"

"The National Stealth Service wanted you out of the country and back in Wandsworth. They were desperate to nail Belladonna's Floral Deliveries – and you were their sharpest weapon."

It was so obvious! I had been a fool. But there was no time for regret. I thought of Gurney's transcriptions and one massive mystery remained. "Fair one, mate, but I'm still well below speed. There's this high-level Stealth Service spook behind everything, manipulating the world like a spherical Rubik's Cube. Where the hell is *F*?"

"I'm here, love," mum said.

"You're F?"

"Yes, dear."

"But you're my mum."

"Yes, love."

"You make matchstick models, not international conspiracies."

"Not conspiracies, dear. Covert operations."

"I've read the transcriptions and you don't sound anything like you."

"They sent me on a course."

"Not the *Sounding Pompous Simulation* at Sonning Common?"

"That's the one, dear."

"Wow! I never managed to get on that."

"It was arduous, dear. But I wouldn't have reached the thirty-eighth floor without it."

"You're thirty-eighth floor, mum? The National Stealth Service doesn't get any loftier than that."

"Yes, dear, but don't worry, they put a nice comfy chair in my lift."

"The National Stealth Service gave you your own lift?"

"They're very good to me and they've helped me look after you. I was able to assign Gurney to your case. He's our least effective operative and I knew he wouldn't get in your way. It was the same with the police. I had a tea and Battenberg with the local Superintendent and made sure that Stalin and Donald were on murder duty in the build-up to Chelsea. That way, there was no danger of you being convicted of anything. They're not exactly Holmes and Watson."

"But if you're thirty-eighth floor in The National Stealth Service, mum, why are you still living here in a council flat?"

"I'm deeply embedded in Wandsworth."

"Of course."

"Look, Bill, you're a good boy. I know you're too nice to mention it, but your danger money's safe. You've been a very generous lad, sending all that cash to your mum every month for the past couple of decades. I've been saving it for you – there's more than enough for a place of your own."

"I'm not leaving you here on your own."

"I've got a house in Knightsbridge."

"How come I've never seen it?"

"You're hardly ever here, Bill."

"Sorry, mum."

"Don't be sorry, son."

"Why did you make me think you'd rejected me forever?"

"I needed to fire you up a bit. Make sure you didn't get hurt."

So, mum had been cruel to be kind. The darkest of thoughts crossed my mind, and there was only one way to deal with it. "Mum?"

"Bill?"

"Why did you persuade The Ambassador to email my Covert CV to all those international terror groups and state security organisations?"

"Sorry, love, but I wanted to lure all their Wandsworth agents to The Chelsea Flower Show so you could eliminate them in one go."

"Hamas have a Wandsworth agent?"

"Tea shop by the Gyratory System."

"Agnostic Jihad?"

"Newsagent by the Arndale Centre."

"Chechen Warlords?"

"Dry cleaners near the station."

"I had no idea."

"Wandsworth's a dangerous place." Mum seemed to remember something. She checked her watch, scrabbled inside her cardigan, and retrieved a remote control. It was not her usual one; I did a double take as I clocked it for a covert model. She aimed it at the telly and switched from *Gay and Haunted* to *Planet Makeover* to BBC13.

Charles Brithazard stood beside the hippo-smashed swimming pool, addressing the camera with a beer stein in his right hand and a stick microphone in the other.

"Earlier today, The Chelsea Flower Show broke ratings records as almost the entire population of Outer Ggaga watched live coverage of the event on giant Fan Zone screens across the country."

The broadcast cut to crowds of expectant Semi-Pygmies glued to covert coverage of The Chelsea Flower Show on IMax-sized screens in whooping willow jungles, rose fields, and mountain slopes.

"Thanks to the heroic efforts of former Outer Ggaga resident Bill Tell, Belladonna's Floral Deliveries' gem rockery was devoid of diamonds and, consequently, their Garden of Death failed to win Best in Show."

The broadcast cut to mass Semi-Pygmy ecstasy.

"This was enough to trigger a coup. The Walloons and The Brotherhood had been so busy belting seventeen shades of beige out of each other, that their reserves were severely depleted. All it took was a determined uprising and that is precisely what happened."

The broadcast cut to footage of departing dirigibles and reversing Routemasters.

"The Walloons have zipped off in their Zeppelins and The Brotherhood have buggered off in their buses. Now, the Semi-Pygmy Alliance have found a new leader and we can go over live to the investiture."

The broadcast cut to The Stamford Bridge Hotel's Mayan Pilates Hall. The Outer Ggagaan national anthem was in full swing, and the entire place had been decorated with whooping willow branches. Semi-Pygmy troops lined the walls. They all wore flat caps and held ceremonial whippets on leads. An audience of Semi-Pygmies and NGOs sat in rows. Wee Jock, Normal, Ginger and Scally accompanied The Ambassador along a central aisle to a makeshift altar constructed out of a stuffed crocodile. The expired reptile's dimensions were so gargantuan that it could only have been Esther. Semi-Pygmy trumpets blew as Marie-Thérèse entered through the hippo-shaped hole in the wall. She was resplendent in a ceremonial smock sewn together from praying mantis skins.

Once she had reached the stuffed crocodile altar, Marie-Thérèse turned and addressed the Hall in fluent Semi-Pygmy: "We are an ancient people with ancient pride, dominated for too long by Zeppelin-wielding beard-barbers, tartan clerics, and Wandsworth florists. I'd like to thank you all, with a special mention to the Royal Deniables and Bill's mum. Cheers."

The Semi-Pygmy soldiers delivered a celebratory "Eh-Up!" in broad Yorkshire accents.

Everyone applauded their new leader with wild enthusiasm.

The broadcast cut back to Charles at the broken swimming pool. "So, welcome to the Autonomous Semi-Pygmy Republic of Outer Ggaga. The Semi-Pygmy Insurgents Nigel and Derek have been made Covert Secretaries of Deniable State for Finance and Education respectively. Stanley is Covert Minister for Transport, largely because, with his Bentley, he's the only bloke who's got any. And Yours Truly is Covert Minister for Deniable Information, bless me. The main thing is, there'll be no more Walloons, Brotherhoods, and homicidal florists to rip everyone off. Thank you, and good night."

Charles was replaced by some clunky graphics and a continuity announcer said, "Press your red button now to enter our topical phone quiz? Is the Chelsea Flower Show?

1. A football team

2. A pensioner

3. A flower show

Remember to ask your social worker for permission to use the phone, as calls cost £11.99 per second."

Mum pressed the off switch on her covert remote and shoved it back in her cardigan pocket. "Well, that's all lovely, isn't it."

"Just one thing, mum. Where's the diamond now?"

"Ah. Give me a minute." Mum shuffled over to a cabinet and took out Geraldine's fluffy, pink cue case. "I kept it safe for you, dear." She prised it open, and The Great Star of Mount Heha glittered from the end of a dildo.

"Petal hid it in a sex toy," Geraldine said. "I just did Bronze a favour. He lent me the money for the dungeon conversion on condition that I helped him out from time to time. He needed someone to look after the genuine article. Petal hid it in this, and the pawnbroker swapped the genuine diamond for counterfeits."

I mulled over the diamond dildo for a few moments. "It's okay, Geraldine. I don't blame you."

"Thanks, Bill."

"Glad we can talk at last, Big Man," Kes said.

"Same here, mate."

"I've brought a message from The Ambassador."

"Where is it?"

"It's too bloody short to write down. Welcome back into the regiment."

I thought of the regiment with its medals, camaraderie, and high adventure. I thought of Wandsworth with its Gyratory System, knackered estates, and soul-crushing shopping centres. Then I thought of Geraldine, and my mum. There was no contest.

"Thanks, Kes, but I'm staying in Wandsworth."

"You what?"

"I've got Geraldine."

"And he's got me," mum said.

"How are you going to survive without the Deniable salary?" Kes asked.

"Well, he can help out in the dungeon from time to time," Geraldine said. "There's often the odd masochist to unlock."

"Course he can, dear," mum said. "But you've got to appreciate that he will also be working for me. Or should I say, F. He may have delivered the florists, the terrorist groups and all those state security enforcers, but Wandsworth is still riddled with international conspiracies."

"Together we'll beat them, mum."

"That's my boy."

Everything had gone tits up. Now, the tits were down again. Why the tits mattered so much, I'm not sure. But they mattered to me.

I had dared. I had won. Now I was home, and my mum was much happier.

CHAPTER 26

Bill had survived! I would have celebrated on both counts had I not been disguised as a sofa. Now I had finished, I could focus on the strip club's mysterious new arrival. I crawled around in my upholstery, scanning the place through the cover. Once I had found the bloke, I followed them as discreetly as I could, whilst remaining as sofa shaped as possible. It was tough on the knees and elbows, and when we reached the strip club stage, a shot of cramp wracked my body, and I had no choice but to leap to my feet.

The man shrieked. How threatening could a sofa really be? He held his hands up in surrender, as if I were pointing a Beretta at his chest rather than posing as an item of soft furnishing.

"Help!" The man said in a barely broken voice.

I uncovered myself, dropped the upholstery and cushions on the floor, and stood there in my pants. I recognised him immediately. It was the bloke from the lock-in. He was young, soppy looking, and wore an ill-fitting, stained suit and an untucked shirt. Come to think of it, this had to be Gurney.

"Cuthbert! I thought you ..."

"What?"

"I don't know really. I wasn't expecting a sofa to come to life."

"You're real, aren't you?"

Gurney pinched himself to make sure. "I think so."

"So, is everything else real?"

"Yes. What did you make of it?"

"I thought I'd have to avenge Bill."

"Sorry about that. He didn't think he'd live."

"He doesn't need avenging, does he?"

"Not now that no one has killed him."

"Great."

"Do you think you'd have been good at avenging?"

"Not really, no."

"Same here."

"I think Bill's probably much better at avenging things."

"Did you get to the end?"

"Yes."

"The very end, I mean."

"It was hidden in the box's false bottom."

"Yes. Sorry. Bill gave me that to add after he unexpectedly survived. It was his mum's idea."

"Why am I here?"

"Thought you might ask that."

"Well, it had crossed my mind a couple of times over the past twelve hours or so."

"How much do you remember about last night?"

I told him about the incident with my three ex-wives, the Rottweiler, and the gambling addict's e-scooter, my pre-drinks on a bench. I recalled losing darts to the one-eyed pensioner in *The Lion & Lettuce*, getting outsmarted by its fruit machine, being slapped by the woman, and debating the geographical location of the town of Hashtag with the barman. Then I moved on to the lock-in with my invented dance, stealing the cocaine, and banging on about life coaching and my failed career. Finally, I told him about the face I remembered just before becoming unconscious and how that face had, I now realised, belonged to him.

"You don't remember telling me that you wanted to become a spy?"

"No."

"Surely you remember me telling you about The Remedial Unit?"

"Definitely not."

"Nothing about how we were looking for people no one would believe."

"Really?"

"And how I was fed up with being bottom of The Remedial Unit and wanted someone who would put me in a good light?"

"No."

"They just needed to be unemployed and able to complete a simple task alone in an unfamiliar environment."

"A simple task?"

"Yes. Like reading a dossier to the end."

"What exactly are you saying?"

"Well, if you want the job, it's yours."

I signed up to The National Stealth Service's Remedial Unit and have never looked back.

The End

***

If you're looking for a complete life do-over, a thirty-day loser programme, or a galaxy of dangerously ineffective life hacks, Cuthbert's your man.

The entire Legend of Cuthbert Huntsman is available now. Get *Blurred Visionary* and enjoy all three novels in one volume by scanning here:

HELP CUTHBERT - HE NEEDS IT

I f you enjoyed *Trigger Warning*, please leave a review.

It'll cheer up Cuthbert no end.

If you enjoyed *Blurred Visionary*, even better! Please leave a review for that too.

Thanks! It would mean a lot.

FREE BOOK

When the world's worst life coach falls out with his AI assistant, it cuts off his oxygen supply, and the race is on to record his final advice for humanity.

Get Cuthbert's novella *Artificial Stupidity* for free by scanning this:

FOLLOW CUTHBERT

For more terrible life coaching advice, why not follow Cuthbert? After all, he's one of Britain's top bad influencers, or "Binfluencers".

Cuthbert is on TikTok, YouTube, Twitter/X, Instagram and Facebook. He's not hard to find – there's only one Cuthbert Huntsman (probably).

His website is cuthberthuntsman.com.

Do please email richnash@cuthberthuntsman.com if he's bothering you.

***

When the world's worst life coach falls out with his AI assistant, it cuts off his oxygen supply, and the race is on to record his final advice for humanity.

Get Cuthbert's novella *Artificial Stupidity* for free by scanning this:

SAS FLOWER ARRANGING - GLOSSARY

AR *assault rifle*
   CPM *cut plant materials*
   CTR *close target recce*
   FBWL *foliage below the water line*
   GPMG *general- purpose machine gun*
   HHLF *heavy-headed lotus flower*
   IA *intelligence assessment*
   LEP *leafy external portion*
   LSP *light strike vehicle*
   LSPM *long-stem plant material*
   LUP *lying up position*
   NPH *needlepoint holder*
   NTR *nothing to report*
   PV *porcelain vase*
   QRF *quick reaction force*
   SBWF *small bunch of wired flowers*
   S60 *anti-aircraft gun*
   SWPH *solid-walled pin holders*
   VCP *vehicle control points*
   WAPF *water-absorbing plastic foam*
   WBC *wall-breaching cannon*

ABOUT THE AUTHOR

Rich Nash was senior producer of Warner Bros' and HBO's Harry Potter Reunion, which wasn't intentionally funny but was Emmy-nominated (it lost to Adele). His TV shows have featured Meg Ryan, Hugh Grant, Vic Reeves, Jimmy Carr, Joe Wilkinson, Josh Widdicombe, Ross Noble, Sean Lock, Felix Dexter, Katherine Ryan, Bill Bailey, Jonathan Ross, Seann Walsh, Susan Calman, David Haye and even John Noakes. He lives in London, read English at King's College, Cambridge, and once had dreams of literary greatness before Cuthbert Huntsman ruined everything.

This is the first full-length novel in the Cuthbert Huntsman trilogy. The next books, *Cop Lives Probably Matter* and *Trigger Warning*, complete the loosely conjoined threesome. The novella, Artificial Stupidity, is packed with Cuthbert's useless wisdom, and can be read at any time without spoilers.

All the books reflect the language, standards, and attitudes of Cuthbert Huntsman, a gratuitously offensive and misguided individual. An insensitivity reader was employed to ensure that everything is as triggering as possible. If you are affected by any of the issues raised, there's no helpline - just pull yourself together.

Do not under any circumstances follow Cuthbert's advice, unless under the direct supervision of a psychiatrist and an ambulance crew. There is a reason he is an unemployed life coach.

***

When the world's worst life coach falls out with his AI assistant, it cuts off his oxygen supply, and the race is on to record his final advice for humanity.

Get Cuthbert's novella *Artificial Stupidity* for free by scanning here:

Alternatively, visit www.cuthberthuntsman.com or https://dl.bookfunnel.com/liyp9cmdat

ALSO BY RICH NASH

Artificial Stupidity – A Cuthbert Huntsman Novella

FILM ADAPTATIONS & OPTIONS

How Not To Live Your Life exists in other dimensions:

The screenplay of *What Goes Around Comes Around, But Some People Duck* has been optioned under the title *The Moons of Martin*.

Work Hard, Die Hard was produced as *Edible Snow Beasts*, starring Susan Sheridan, Brian Bowles, Wayne Forester and Kate Lock.

Filmed monologues of many of the other stories were performed as part of the *Semitasking* comedy project by a professional cast, including Ronald Top, Tony Marrese, Nigel Pilkington, Harriet Carmichael, Jane Collingwood, Suzy Ioannides, and Brian Bowles.

***

When the world's worst life coach falls out with his AI assistant, it cuts off his oxygen supply, and the race is on to record his final advice for humanity.

Get Cuthbert's novella *Artificial Stupidity* for free by scanning here:

Or visit: www.cuthberthuntsman.com

And: https://dl.bookfunnel.com/liyp9cmdat

Printed in Great Britain
by Amazon